Essential C# 5.0

Essential
C# 5.0

■ **Mark Michaelis**
with Eric Lippert

♦♦Addison-Wesley

Upper Saddle River, NJ • Boston • Indianapolis • San Francisco
New York • Toronto • Montreal • London • Munich • Paris • Madrid
Capetown • Sydney • Tokyo • Singapore • Mexico City

The publisher offers excellent discounts on this book when ordered in quantity for bulk purchases or special sales, which may include electronic versions and/or custom covers and content particular to your business, training goals, marketing focus, and branding interests. For more information, please contact:

U.S. Corporate and Government Sales
(800) 382-3419
corpsales@pearsontechgroup.com

For sales outside the United States, please contact:

International Sales
international@pearson.com

Visit us on the Web: informit.com/aw

Library of Congress Cataloging-in-Publication Data

Michaelis, Mark.
  Essential C# 5.0 / Mark Michaelis with Eric Lippert.
    pages cm
  Includes index.
  ISBN 0-321-87758-6 (pbk. : alk. paper)
  1. C# (Computer program language) 2. Microsoft .NET Framework. I. Lippert, Eric. II. Title.
  QA76.73.C154M5238 2013
  006.7'882—dc23   2012036148

ISBN-13: 978-0-321-87758-1
ISBN-10:   0-321-87758-6
Text printed in the United States on recycled paper at Edwards Brothers Malloy in Ann Arbor, Michigan.
First printing, November 2012

To my family: Elisabeth, Benjamin, Hanna, and Abigail,

You have sacrificed a husband and daddy for countless hours of writing, frequently at times when he was needed most.

Thanks!

■

Contents at a Glance

Contents

Figures

Tables

Foreword

WELCOME TO ONE of the greatest collaborations you could dream of in the world of C# books—and probably far beyond! Mark Michaelis' Essential C# series is already a classic, and teaming up with famous C# blogger Eric Lippert on the new edition is another masterstroke!

You may think of Eric as writing blogs and Mark as writing books, but that is not how I first got to know them.

In 2005 when LINQ (Language Integrated Query) was disclosed, I had only just joined Microsoft, and I got to tag along to the PDC conference for the big reveal. Despite my almost total lack of contribution to the technology, I thoroughly enjoyed the hype. The talks were overflowing, the printed leaflets were flying like hotcakes: It was a big day for C# and .NET, and I was having a great time.

It was pretty quiet in the hands-on labs area, though, where people could try out the technology preview themselves with nice scripted walkthroughs. That's where I ran into Mark. Needless to say, he wasn't following the script. He was doing his own experiments, combing through the docs, talking to other folks, busily pulling together his own picture.

As a newcomer to the C# community, I think I may have met a lot of people for the first time at that conference—people that I have since formed great relationships with. But to be honest, I don't remember it. The only one I remember is Mark. Here is why: When I asked him if he was liking the new stuff, he didn't just join the rave. He was totally level-headed: *"I don't know yet. I haven't made up my mind about it."* He wanted to absorb and understand the full package, and until then he wasn't going to let anyone tell him what to think.

So instead of the quick sugar rush of affirmation I might have expected, I got to have a frank and wholesome conversation, the first of many over the years, about details, consequences, and concerns with this new technology. And so it remains: Mark is an incredibly valuable community member for us language designers to have, because he is super smart, insists on understanding everything to the core, and has phenomenal insight into how things affect real developers. But perhaps most of all because he is forthright and never afraid to speak his mind. If something passes the Mark Test then we know we can start feeling pretty good about it!

These are the same qualities that make Mark such a great writer. He goes right to the essence and communicates with great integrity, no sugarcoating, and a keen eye for practical value and real-world problems.

Eric is, of course, my colleague of seven years on the C# team. He's been here much longer than I have, and the first I recall of him, he was explaining to the team how to untangle a bowl of spaghetti. More precisely, our C# compiler code base at the time was in need of some serious architectural TLC, and was exceedingly hard to add new features to—something we desperately needed to be able to do with LINQ. Eric had been investigating what kind of architecture we ought to have (Phases! We didn't even really have those!), and more importantly, how to get from here to there, step by step. The remarkable thing was that as complex as this was, and as new as I was to the team and the code base, I immediately understood what he was saying!

You may recognize from his blogs the super-clear and well-structured untangling of the problem, the convincing clarity of enumerated solutions, and the occasional unmitigated hilarity. Well, you don't know the half of it! Every time Eric is grappling with a complex issue and is sharing his thoughts about it with the team, his emails about it are just as meticulous and every bit as hilarious. You fundamentally can't ignore an issue raised by Eric because you can't wait to read his prose about it. They're even purple, too! So I essentially get to enjoy a continuous supply of what amounts to unpublished installments of his blog, as well as, of course, his pleasant and insightful presence as a member of the C# compiler team and language design team.

In summary, I am truly grateful to get to work with these two amazing people on a regular basis: Eric to help keep my thinking straight and Mark to help keep me honest. They share a great gift of providing clarity and elucidation, and by combining their "inside" and "outside" perspective on C#, this book reaches a new level of completeness. No one will help you get C# 5.0 like these two gentlemen do.

Enjoy!

—Mads Torgersen,
C# Program Manager,
Microsoft

Preface

THROUGHOUT THE HISTORY of software engineering, the methodology used to write computer programs has undergone several paradigm shifts, each building on the foundation of the former by increasing code organization and decreasing complexity. This book takes you through these same paradigm shifts.

The beginning chapters take you through **sequential programming structure** in which statements are executed in the order in which they are written. The problem with this model is that complexity increases exponentially as the requirements increase. To reduce this complexity, code blocks are moved into methods, creating a **structured programming model.** This allows you to call the same code block from multiple locations within a program, without duplicating code. Even with this construct, however, programs quickly become unwieldy and require further abstraction. Object-oriented programming, discussed in Chapter 5, was the response. In subsequent chapters, you will learn about additional methodologies, such as interface-based programming, LINQ (and the transformation it makes to the collection API), and eventually rudimentary forms of declarative programming (in Chapter 17) via attributes.

This book has three main functions.

- It provides comprehensive coverage of the C# language, going beyond a tutorial and offering a foundation upon which you can begin effective software development projects.

- For readers already familiar with C#, this book provides insight into some of the more complex programming paradigms and provides in-depth coverage of the features introduced in the latest version of the language, C# 5.0 and .NET Framework 4.5.

• It serves as a timeless reference, even after you gain proficiency with the language.

The key to successfully learning C# is to start coding as soon as possible. Don't wait until you are an "expert" in theory; start writing software immediately. As a believer in iterative development, I hope this book enables even a novice programmer to begin writing basic C# code by the end of Chapter 2.

A number of topics are not covered in this book. You won't find coverage of topics such as ASP.NET, ADO.NET, smart client development, distributed programming, and so on. Although these topics are relevant to the .NET Framework, to do them justice requires books of their own. Fortunately, Addison-Wesley's Microsoft Windows Development Series provides a wealth of writing on these topics. *Essential C# 5.0* focuses on C# and the types within the Base Class Library. Reading this book will prepare you to focus on and develop expertise in any of the areas covered by the rest of the series.

Target Audience for This Book

My challenge with this book was to keep advanced developers awake while not abandoning beginners by using words such as *assembly, link, chain, thread,* and *fusion,* as though the topic was more appropriate for blacksmiths than for programmers. This book's primary audience is experienced developers looking to add another language to their quiver. However, I have carefully assembled this book to provide significant value to developers at all levels.

• *Beginners:* If you are new to programming, this book serves as a resource to help transition you from an entry-level programmer to a C# developer, comfortable with any C# programming task that's thrown your way. This book not only teaches you syntax, but also trains you in good programming practices that will serve you throughout your programming career.

- *Structured programmers:* Just as it's best to learn a foreign language through immersion, learning a computer language is most effective when you begin using it before you know all the intricacies. In this vein, this book begins with a tutorial that will be comfortable for those familiar with structured programming, and by the end of Chapter 4, developers in this category should feel at home writing basic control flow programs. However, the key to excellence for C# developers is not memorizing syntax. To transition from simple programs to enterprise development, the C# developer must think natively in terms of objects and their relationships. To this end, Chapter 5's Beginner Topics introduce classes and object-oriented development. The role of historically structured programming languages such as C, COBOL, and FORTRAN is still significant but shrinking, so it behooves software engineers to become familiar with object-oriented development. C# is an ideal language for making this transition because it was designed with object-oriented development as one of its core tenets.

- *Object-based and object-oriented developers:* C++ and Java programmers, and many experienced Visual Basic programmers, fall into this category. Many of you are already completely comfortable with semicolons and curly braces. A brief glance at the code in Chapter 1 reveals that, at its core, C# is similar to the C and C++ style languages that you already know.

- *C# professionals:* For those already versed in C#, this book provides a convenient reference for less frequently encountered syntax. Furthermore, it provides answers to language details and subtleties that are seldom addressed. Most importantly, it presents the guidelines and patterns for programming robust and maintainable code. This book also aids in the task of teaching C# to others. With the emergence of C# 3.0, 4.0, and 5.0, some of the most prominent enhancements are

    - Implicitly typed variables (see Chapter 2)
    - Extension methods (see Chapter 5)
    - Partial methods (see Chapter 5)
    - Anonymous types (see Chapter 11)
    - Generics (see Chapter 11)
    - Lambda statements and expressions (see Chapter 12)
    - Expression trees (see Chapter 12)

- Standard query operators (see Chapter 14)
- Query expressions (see Chapter 15)
- Dynamic programming (Chapter 17)
- Multithreaded programming with the Task Programming Library and `async` (Chapter 18)
- Parallel query processing with PLINQ (Chapter 18)
- Concurrent collections (Chapter 19)

These topics are covered in detail for those not already familiar with them. Also pertinent to advanced C# development is the subject of pointers, in Chapter 21. Even experienced C# developers often do not understand this topic well.

Features of This Book

Essential C# 5.0 is a language book that adheres to the core C# Language 5.0 Specification. To help you understand the various C# constructs, it provides numerous examples demonstrating each feature. Accompanying each concept are guidelines and best practices, ensuring that code compiles, avoids likely pitfalls, and achieves maximum maintainability.

To improve readability, code is specially formatted and chapters are outlined using mind maps.

C# Coding Guidelines

One of the more significant enhancements added to *Essential C# 5.0*, and not explicitly called out in previous editions, was the addition of C# coding guidelines, as shown in the following example taken from Chapter 16:

Guidelines

DO ensure that equal objects have equal hash codes.

DO ensure that the hash code of an object never changes while it is in a hash table.

DO ensure that the hashing algorithm quickly produces a well-distributed hash.

DO ensure that the hashing algorithm is robust in any possible object state.

These guidelines are the key to differentiating a programmer who knows the syntax from an expert who is able to discern the most effective code to write based on the circumstances. Such an expert not only gets the code to compile, but does so while following best practices that minimize bugs and enable maintenance well into the future. The coding guidelines highlight some of the key principles that readers will want to be sure to incorporate into their development.

Code Samples

The code snippets in most of this text can run on any implementation of the Common Language Infrastructure (CLI), including the Mono, Rotor, and Microsoft .NET platforms. Platform- or vendor-specific libraries are seldom used, except when communicating important concepts relevant only to those platforms (appropriately handling the single-threaded user interface of Windows, for example). Any code that specifically requires C# 3.0, 4.0, or 5.0 compliance is called out in the C# version indexes at the end of the book.

Here is a sample code listing.

LISTING 1.9: Declaring and Assigning a Variable

```
class MiracleMax
{
  static void Main()
  {
          data type
          ⌒⌒⌒⌒
          string max;
                  variable
      max = "Have fun storming the castle!";

      System.Console.WriteLine(max);
  }
}
```

The formatting is as follows.

- Comments are shown in italics.

  ```
  /* Display a greeting to the console
     using composite formatting. */
  ```

- Keywords are shown in bold.

```
static void Main()
```

- Highlighted code calls out specific code snippets that may have changed from an earlier listing, or demonstrates the concept described in the text.

```
System.Console.Write /* No new Line */ (
```

Highlighting can appear on an entire line or on just a few characters within a line.

```
System.Console.WriteLine(
    "Your full name is {0} {1}.",
```

- Incomplete listings contain an ellipsis to denote irrelevant code that has been omitted.

```
// ...
```

- Console output is the output from a particular listing that appears following the listing.

OUTPUT 1.4

```
>HeyYou.exe
Hey you!
Enter your first name: Inigo
Enter your last name: Montoya
```

User input for the program appears in boldface.

Although it might have been convenient to provide full code samples that you could copy into your own programs, doing so would detract you from learning a particular topic. Therefore, you need to modify the code samples before you can incorporate them into your programs. The core omission is error checking, such as exception handling. Also, code samples do not explicitly include using System statements. You need to assume the statement throughout all samples.

You can find sample code at intellitect.com/essentialcsharp and at informit.com/mswinseries.

Mind Maps

Each chapter's introduction includes a **mind map,** which serves as an outline that provides at-a-glance reference to each chapter's content. Here is an example (taken from Chapter 5).

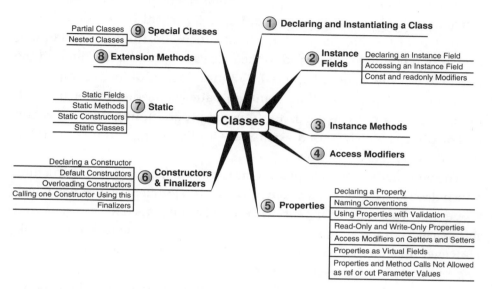

The theme of each chapter appears in the mind map's center. High-level topics spread out from the core. Mind maps allow you to absorb the flow from high-level to more detailed concepts easily, with less chance of encountering very specific knowledge that you might not be looking for.

Helpful Notes

Depending on your level of experience, special code blocks will help you navigate through the text.

- Beginner Topics provide definitions or explanations targeted specifically toward entry-level programmers.
- Advanced Topics enable experienced developers to focus on the material that is most relevant to them.
- Callout notes highlight key principles in callout boxes so that readers easily recognize their significance.
- Language Contrast sidebars identify key differences between C# and its predecessors to aid those familiar with other languages.

How This Book Is Organized

At a high level, software engineering is about managing complexity, and it is toward this end that I have organized *Essential C# 5.0*. Chapters 1–4 introduce structured programming, which enable you to start writing simple functioning code immediately. Chapters 5–9 present the object-oriented constructs of C#. Novice readers should focus on fully understanding this section before they proceed to the more advanced topics found in the remainder of this book. Chapters 11–13 introduce additional complexity-reducing constructs, handling common patterns needed by virtually all modern programs. This leads to dynamic programming with reflection and attributes, which is used extensively for threading and interoperability in the chapters that follow.

The book ends with a chapter on the Common Language Infrastructure, which describes C# within the context of the development platform in which it operates. This chapter appears at the end because it is not C# specific and it departs from the syntax and programming style in the rest of the book. However, this chapter is suitable for reading at any time, perhaps most appropriately immediately following Chapter 1.

Here is a description of each chapter (in this list, chapter numbers shown in **bold** indicate the presence of C# 3.0–5.0 material).

- *Chapter 1—Introducing C#:* After presenting the C# HelloWorld program, this chapter proceeds to dissect it. This should familiarize readers with the look and feel of a C# program and provide details on how to compile and debug their own programs. It also touches on the context of a C# program's execution and its intermediate language.
- ***Chapter 2**—Data Types:* Functioning programs manipulate data, and this chapter introduces the primitive data types of C#. This includes coverage of two type categories, value types and reference types, along with conversion between types and support for arrays.
- *Chapter 3—Operators and Control Flow:* To take advantage of the iterative capabilities in a computer, you need to know how to include loops and conditional logic within your program. This chapter also covers the C# operators, data conversion, and preprocessor directives.
- ***Chapter 4**—Methods and Parameters:* This chapter investigates the details of methods and their parameters. It includes passing by value,

passing by reference, and returning data via an out parameter. In C# 4.0 default parameter support was added and this chapter explains how to use them.

- **Chapter 5**—*Classes:* Given the basic building blocks of a class, this chapter combines these constructs together to form fully functional types. Classes form the core of object-oriented technology by defining the template for an object.

- *Chapter 6*—*Inheritance:* Although inheritance is a programming fundamental to many developers, C# provides some unique constructs, such as the new modifier. This chapter discusses the details of the inheritance syntax, including overriding.

- **Chapter 7**—*Interfaces:* This chapter demonstrates how interfaces are used to define the "versionable" interaction contract between classes. C# includes both explicit and implicit interface member implementation, enabling an additional encapsulation level not supported by most other languages.

- *Chapter 8*—*Value Types:* Although not as prevalent as defining reference types, it is sometimes necessary to define value types that behave in a fashion similar to the primitive types built into C#. This chapter describes how to define structures, while exposing the idiosyncrasies they may introduce.

- *Chapter 9*—*Well-Formed Types:* This chapter discusses more advanced type definition. It explains how to implement operators, such as + and casts, and describes how to encapsulate multiple classes into a single library. In addition, the chapter demonstrates defining namespaces and XML comments, and discusses how to design classes for garbage collection.

- *Chapter 10*—*Exception Handling:* This chapter expands on the exception-handling introduction from Chapter 4 and describes how exceptions follow a hierarchy that enables creating custom exceptions. It also includes some best practices on exception handling.

- **Chapter 11**—*Generics:* Generics is perhaps the core feature missing from C# 1.0. This chapter fully covers this 2.0 feature. In addition, C# 4.0 added support for covariance and contravariance—something covered in the context of generics in this chapter.

- *Chapter 12—Delegates and Lambda Expressions:* Delegates begin clearly distinguishing C# from its predecessors by defining patterns for handling events within code. This virtually eliminates the need for writing routines that poll. Lambda expressions are the key concept that make C# 3.0's LINQ possible. This chapter explains how lambda expressions build on the delegate construct by providing a more elegant and succinct syntax. This chapter forms the foundation for the new collection API discussed next.

- *Chapter 13—Events:* Encapsulated delegates, known as events, are a core construct of the Common Language Runtime. Anonymous methods, another C# 2.0 feature, are also presented here.

- *Chapter 14—Collection Interfaces with Standard Query Operators:* The simple and yet elegantly powerful changes introduced in C# 3.0 begin to shine in this chapter as we take a look at the extension methods of the new Enumerable class. This class makes available an entirely new collection API known as the standard query operators and discussed in detail here.

- *Chapter 15—LINQ with Query Expressions:* Using standard query operators alone results in some long statements that are hard to decipher. However, query expressions provide an alternative syntax that matches closely with SQL, as described in this chapter.

- *Chapter 16—Building Custom Collections:* In building custom APIs that work against business objects, it is sometimes necessary to create custom collections. This chapter details how to do this, and in the process introduces contextual keywords that make custom collection building easier.

- *Chapter 17—Reflection, Attributes, and Dynamic Programming:* Object-oriented programming formed the basis for a paradigm shift in program structure in the late 1980s. In a similar way, attributes facilitate declarative programming and embedded metadata, ushering in a new paradigm. This chapter looks at attributes and discusses how to retrieve them via reflection. It also covers file input and output via the serialization framework within the Base Class Library. In C# 4.0 a new keyword, dynamic, was added to the language. This removed all type checking until runtime, a significant expansion of what can be done with C#.

- *Chapter 18—Multithreading:* Most modern programs require the use of threads to execute long-running tasks while ensuring active response to simultaneous events. As programs become more sophisticated, they must take additional precautions to protect data in these advanced environments. Programming multithreaded applications is complex. This chapter discusses how to work with threads and provides best practices to avoid the problems that plague multithreaded applications.

- *Chapter 19—Thread Synchronization:* Building on the preceding chapter, this one demonstrates some of the built-in threading pattern support that can simplify the explicit control of multithreaded code.

- *Chapter 20—Platform Interoperability and Unsafe Code:* Given that C# is a relatively young language, far more code is written in other languages than in C#. To take advantage of this preexisting code, C# supports interoperability—the calling of unmanaged code—through P/Invoke. In addition, C# provides for the use of pointers and direct memory manipulation. Although code with pointers requires special privileges to run, it provides the power to interoperate fully with traditional C-based application programming interfaces.

- *Chapter 21—The Common Language Infrastructure:* Fundamentally, C# is the syntax that was designed as the most effective programming language on top of the underlying Common Language Infrastructure. This chapter delves into how C# programs relate to the underlying runtime and its specifications.

- *Appendix A—Downloading and Installing the C# Compiler and CLI Platform:* This appendix provides instructions for setting up a C# compiler and the platform on which to run the code, Microsoft .NET or Mono.

- *Appendix B—Tic-Tac-Toe Source Code Listing:* This appendix provides a full listing of the source code displayed in parts within Chapter 3 and Chapter 4.

- *Appendix C—Interfacing with Mulithreading Patterns prior to the TPL and C# 5.0:* This appendix provides details on multithreading patterns for development prior to C# 5.0 and/or the Task Parallel Library.

- *Appendix D—Timers prior to the Async/Await Pattern of C# 5.0:* This appendix describes three different types of timers for use when .NET 4.5/C# 5.0 is not available.

- *C# 3.0, 4.0, 5.0 Index:* These indexes provide a quick reference for the features added in C# 3.0–5.0. They are specifically designed to help programmers quickly update their language skills to a more recent version.

I hope you find this book to be a great resource in establishing your C# expertise and that you continue to reference it for those areas that you use less frequently well after you are proficient in C#.

—*Mark Michaelis*
IntelliTect.com/mark
Twitter: @Intellitect, @MarkMichaelis

Acknowledgments

NO BOOK CAN be published by the author alone, and I am extremely grateful for the multitude of people who helped me with this one. The order in which I thank people is not significant, except for those that come first. By far, my family has made the biggest sacrifice to allow me to complete this. Benjamin, Hanna, and Abigail often had a Daddy distracted by this book, but Elisabeth suffered even more so. She was often left to take care of things, holding the family's world together on her own. I would like to say it got easier with each edition but, alas, no; as the kids got older, life became more hectic, and without me Elisabeth was stretched to the breaking point virtually all the time. A huge sorry and ginormous "Thank You!"

Many technical editors reviewed each chapter in minute detail to ensure technical accuracy. I was often amazed by the subtle errors these folks still managed to catch: Paul Bramsman, Kody Brown, Ian Davis, Doug Dechow, Gerard Frantz, Thomas Heavey, Anson Horton, Brian Jones, Shane Kercheval, Angelika Langer, Eric Lippert, John Michaelis, Jason Morse, Nicholas Paldino, Jon Skeet, Michael Stokesbary, Robert Stokesbary, John Timney, and Stephen Toub. Thanks also to Mandy Frei who diligently kept notes of changes needed for reprints.

Eric is no less than amazing. His grasp of the C# vocabulary is truly astounding and I am very appreciative of his edits, especially when he pushed for perfection in terminology. His improvements to the C# 3.0 chapters were incredibly significant, and in the second edition my only regret was that I didn't have him review all the chapters. However, that regret is no longer. Eric painstakingly reviewed every *Essential C# 5.0* chapter with amazing detail and precision. I am extremely grateful for his contribution to making this book even better than the earlier editions. Thanks, Eric! I can't imagine anyone better for the job. You deserve all the credit for raising the bar from good to great.

Like Eric and C#, there are fewer than a handful of people who know .NET multithreading as well as Stephen Toub. Accordingly, Stephen focused on the two rewritten (for a third time) multithreading chapters and their new focus on asynchronous support in C# 5.0. Thanks, Stephen!

Thanks to everyone at Addison-Wesley for their patience in working with me in spite of my frequent focus on everything else except the manuscript. Thanks to Elizabeth Ryan, Audrey Doyle, Vicki Rowland, Curt Johnson, and Joan Murray. Joan deserves a special medal of patience for the number of times I delayed not only with deliverables but even responding to emails.

About the Authors

Mark Michaelis is the founder of IntelliTect and serves as the Chief Technical Architect and Trainer. Since 1996, he has been a Microsoft MVP for C#, Visual Studio Team System, and the Windows SDK, and in 2007 he was recognized as a Microsoft Regional Director. He also serves on several Microsoft software design review teams, including C#, the Connected Systems, Office/SharePoint, and Visual Studio. He speaks at developer conferences and has written numerous articles and other books. He holds a bachelor of arts degree in philosophy from the University of Illinois and a master's degree in computer science from the Illinois Institute of Technology. When not bonding with his computer, he is busy with his family or training for another triathlon (having completed his first Ironman in 2008). He lives in Spokane, Washington, with his wife Elisabeth and three children, Benjamin, Hanna, and Abigail.

Eric Lippert is a principal developer on the C# compiler team at Microsoft. He has worked on the design and implementation of the Visual Basic, VB-Script, Jscript, and C# languages and on Visual Studio Tools For Office, and is a member of the C# language design team. When not writing or editing books about C#, he does his best to keep his tiny sailboat upright. He lives in Seattle with his wife, Leah.

■1■

Introducing C#

C# IS NOW A WELL-ESTABLISHED LANGUAGE that builds on features found in its predecessor C-style languages (C, C++, and Java), making it immediately familiar to many experienced programmers.[1] Part of a larger, more complex execution platform called the Common Language Infrastructure (CLI), C# is a programming language for building software components and applications.

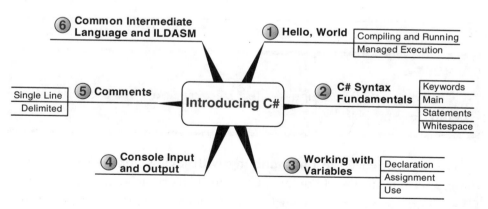

This chapter introduces C# using the traditional HelloWorld program. The chapter focuses on C# syntax fundamentals, including defining an entry point into the C# program executable. This will familiarize you with the C#

---

1. The first C# design meeting took place in 1998.

syntax style and structure, and it will enable you to produce the simplest of C# programs. Prior to the discussion of C# syntax fundamentals is a summary of managed execution context, which explains how a C# program executes at runtime. This chapter ends with a discussion of variable declaration, writing and retrieving data from the console, and the basics of commenting code in C#.

Hello, World

The best way to learn a new programming language is to write code. The first example is the classic HelloWorld program. In this program, you will display some text to the screen.

Listing 1.1 shows the complete HelloWorld program; in the following sections, you will compile the code.

LISTING 1.1: HelloWorld in C#[2]

```
class HelloWorld
{
  static void Main()
  {
    System.Console.WriteLine("Hello. My name is Inigo Montoya.");
  }
}
```

■ NOTE

C# is a case-sensitive language: Incorrect case prevents the code from compiling successfully.

Those experienced in programming with Java, C, or C++ will immediately see similarities. Like Java, C# inherits its basic syntax from C and C++.[3] Syntactic punctuation (such as semicolons and curly braces), features (such as case sensitivity), and keywords (such as class, public, and void)

---

2. Refer to the movie *The Princess Bride* if you're confused about the Inigo Montoya references.
3. When creating C#, the language creators sat down with the specifications for C/C++, literally crossing out the features they didn't like and creating a list of the ones they did like. The group also included designers with strong backgrounds in other languages.

are familiar to programmers experienced in these languages. Beginners and programmers from other languages will quickly find these constructs intuitive.

Compiling and Running the Application

The C# compiler allows any file extension for files containing C# source code, but .cs is typically used. After saving the source code to a file, developers must compile it. (Appendix A provides instructions for installing the compiler.) Because the mechanics of the command are not part of the C# standard, the compilation command varies depending on the C# compiler implementation.

If you place Listing 1.1 into a file called HelloWorld.cs, the compilation command in Output 1.1 will work with the Microsoft .NET compiler (assuming appropriate paths to the compiler are set up).[4]

OUTPUT 1.1

```
>csc.exe HelloWorld.cs
Microsoft (R) Visual C# Compiler version 4.0.30319.17626
for Microsoft (R) .NET Framework 4.5
Copyright (C) Microsoft Corporation. All rights reserved.
```

The exact output will vary depending on what version of the compiler you use.

Running the resultant program, HelloWorld.exe, displays the message shown in Output 1.2.

OUTPUT 1.2

```
>HelloWorld.exe
Hello. My name is Inigo Montoya.
```

The program created by the C# compiler, HelloWorld.exe, is an **assembly.** Instead of creating an entire program that can be executed independently,

---

4. Compilation using the Mono compiler, an open source compiler now available from www. mono-project.com, is virtually identical, except that the compiler name is mcs.exe rather than csc.exe. Although I would very much have liked to place instructions for each platform here, doing so detracts from the topic of introducing C#. See Appendix A for details on Mono.

developers can create a library of code that can be referenced by another, larger program. Libraries (or class libraries) use the filename extension .dll, which stands for Dynamic Link Library (DLL). A library is also an assembly. In other words, the output from a successful C# compile is an assembly regardless of whether it is a program or a library.

Language Contrast: Java—Filename Must Match Class Name

In Java, the filename must follow the name of the class. In C#, this convention is frequently followed but is not required. In C#, it is possible to have two classes in one file, and starting with C# 2.0, it's possible to have a single class span multiple files.

C# Syntax Fundamentals

Once you successfully compile and run the HelloWorld program, you are ready to start dissecting the code to learn its individual parts. First, consider the C# keywords along with the identifiers that the developer chooses.

■ BEGINNER TOPIC

Keywords

In order for the compiler to interpret the code, certain words within C# have special status and meaning. Known as **keywords,** they provide the concrete syntax that the compiler uses to interpret the expressions the programmer writes. In the HelloWorld program, class, static, and void are examples of keywords.

The compiler uses the keywords to identify the structure and organization of the code. Because the compiler interprets these words with elevated significance, C# requires that developers place keywords only in certain locations. When programmers violate these rules, the compiler will issue errors.

C# Keywords

Table 1.1 shows the C# keywords.

TABLE 1.1: C# Keywords

abstract	else	let* (3)	sizeof
add*	enum	lock	stackalloc
alias* (2)	equals* (3)	long	static
as	event	namespace	string
ascending* (3)	explicit	new	struct
async* (5)	extern	null	switch
await* (5)	false	object	this
base	finally	on* (3)	throw
bool	fixed	operator	true
break	float	orderby* (3)	try
by* (3)	for	out	typeof
byte	foreach	override	uint
case	from* (3)	params	ulong
catch	get* (1)	partial* (2)	unchecked
char	global* (2)	private	unsafe
checked	goto	protected	ushort
class	group* (3)	public	using
const	if	readonly	value* (1)
continue	implicit	ref	var* (3)
decimal	in	remove*	virtual
default	int	return	void
delegate	interface	sbyte	volatile
descending* (3)	internal	sealed	where* (3)
do	into* (3)	select* (3)	while
double	is	set* (1)	yield* (2)
dynamic* (4)	join* (3)	short	

* Contextual keyword

Numbers in parentheses (*n*) identify in which version the contextual keyword was added.

After C# 1.0, no new **reserved keywords** were introduced to C#. However, some constructs in later versions use **contextual keywords,** which are significant only in specific locations. Outside these designated locations, contextual keywords have no special significance.[5] By this method, most C# 1.0 code is compatible with the later standards.[6]

Identifiers

Like other languages, C# includes **identifiers** to identify constructs that the programmer codes. In Listing 1.1, `HelloWorld` and `Main` are examples of identifiers. The identifiers assigned to a construct are used to refer back to the construct later, so it is important that the names the developer assigns are meaningful rather than arbitrary.

A keen ability to select succinct and indicative names is an important characteristic of a strong programmer because it means the resultant code will be easier to understand and reuse. Clarity coupled with consistency is important enough that the .NET Framework Guidelines advise against the use of abbreviations or contractions in identifier names and even recommend avoiding acronyms that are not widely accepted. If an acronym is sufficiently well established (HTML, for example) use it consistently: Avoid spelling out the accepted acronym at some times but not others. Generally, adding the constraint that all acronyms be included in a glossary of terms places enough overhead on the use of acronyms such that they are not used flippantly. Ultimately, select clear, possibly even verbose names—especially when working on a team or when developing a library against which others will program.

There are two basic casing formats for an identifier. **Pascal case** (henceforth PascalCase), as the CLI creators refer to it because of its popularity in

---

5. For example, early in the design of C# 2.0, the language designers designated `yield` as a keyword, and Microsoft released alpha versions of the C# 2.0 compiler, with `yield` as a designated keyword, to thousands of developers. However, the language designers eventually determined that by using `yield return` rather than `yield`, they could ultimately avoid adding `yield` as a keyword because it would have no special significance outside its proximity to `return`.
6. There are some rare and unfortunate incompatibilities, such as the following:
   - C# 2.0 requiring implementation of `IDisposable` with the `using` statement, rather than simply a `Dispose()` method
   - Some rare generic expressions such as `F(G<A,B>(7));` in C# 1.0, that means `F( (G<A) , (B>7) )` and in C# 2.0, that means to call generic method `G<A,B>` with argument `7` and pass the result to `F`

the Pascal programming language, capitalizes the first letter of each word in an identifier name; examples include `ComponentModel`, `Configuration`, and `HttpFileCollection`. As `HttpFileCollection` demonstrates with HTTP, when using acronyms that are more than two letters long only the first letter is capitalized. The second format, camel case (henceforth camelCase), follows the same convention, except that the first letter is lowercase; examples include `quotient`, `firstName`, `httpFileCollection`, `ioStream`, and `theDreadPirateRoberts`.

Guidelines

DO favor clarity over brevity when naming identifiers.

DO NOT use abbreviations or contractions within identifier names.

DO NOT use any acronyms unless they are widely accepted, and even then, only when necessary.

Notice that although underscores are legal, generally there are no underscores, hyphens, or other nonalphanumeric characters in identifier names. Furthermore, C# doesn't follow its predecessors in that Hungarian notation (prefixing a name with a data type abbreviation) is not used. This avoids the variable rename that is necessary when data types change, and the inconsistency in the data type prefix that is frequently encountered when using Hungarian notation.

In some rare cases, some identifiers, such as `Main`, can have a special meaning in the C# language.

Guidelines

DO capitalize both characters in two-character acronyms, except for the first word of a camelCased identifier.

DO capitalize only the first character in acronyms with three or more characters, except for the first word of a camelCased identifier.

DO NOT capitalize any of the characters in acronyms at the beginning of a camelCased identifier.

DO NOT use Hungarian notation (that is, do not encode the type of a variable in its name).

■ ADVANCED TOPIC

Keywords

Although it is rare, keywords may be used as identifiers if they include "@" as a prefix. For example, you could name a local variable @return. Similarly (although it doesn't conform to the casing standards of C# coding standards), it is possible to name a method @throw().

There are also four undocumented reserved keywords in the Microsoft implementation: __arglist, __makeref, __reftype, and __refvalue. These are required only in rare interop scenarios and you can ignore them for all practical purposes. Note that these four special keywords begin with two underscores. The designers of C# reserve the right to make any identifier that begins with two underscores into a keyword in a future version; for safety, avoid ever creating such an identifier yourself.

Type Definition

All executable code in C# appears within a type definition, and the most common type definition begins with the keyword class. A **class definition** is the section of code that generally begins with class identifier { ... }, as shown in Listing 1.2.

LISTING 1.2: **Basic Class Declaration**

```csharp
class HelloWorld
{
  //...
}
```

The name used for the type (in this case, HelloWorld) can vary, but by convention, it must be PascalCased. For this particular example, therefore, other possible names are Greetings, HelloInigoMontoya, Hello, or simply Program. (Program is a good convention to follow when the class contains the Main() method, described next.)

Guidelines

DO name classes with nouns or noun phrases.

DO use PascalCasing for all class names.

Generally, programs contain multiple types, each containing multiple methods.

Main

What Is a Method?

Syntactically, a **method** in C# is a named block of code introduced by a method declaration (for example, `static void Main()`) and (usually) followed by zero or more statements within curly braces. Methods perform computations and/or actions. Similar to paragraphs in written languages, methods provide a means of structuring and organizing code so that it is more readable. More importantly, methods can be reused and called from multiple places, and so avoid the need to duplicate code. The method declaration introduces the method and defines the method name along with the data passed to and from the method. In Listing 1.3, `Main()` followed by { ... } is an example of a C# method.

The location where C# programs begin execution is the **Main method,** which begins with `static void Main()`. When you execute the program by typing `HelloWorld.exe` at the command console, the program starts up, resolves the location of `Main`, and begins executing the first statement within Listing 1.3.

LISTING 1.3: **Breaking Apart** HelloWorld

```
class HelloWorld
{
  static void Main()          } Method Declaration                          Main
  {
    System.Console.WriteLine("Hello, My name is Inigo Montoya");
  }                                          Statement
}
```

Class Definition

Although the Main method declaration can vary to some degree, `static` and the method name, `Main`, are always required for a program.

■ADVANCED TOPIC

Declaration of the Main Method

C# requires that the Main method return either void or int, and that it take either no parameters, or a single array of strings. Listing 1.4 shows the full declaration of the Main method.

LISTING 1.4: The Main Method, with Parameters and a Return

```
static int Main(string[] args)
{
    //...
}
```

The args parameter is an array of strings corresponding to the command-line arguments. However, the first element of the array is not the program name but the first command-line parameter to appear after the executable name, unlike in C and C++. To retrieve the full command used to execute the program use System.Environment.CommandLine.

The int returned from Main is the status code and it indicates the success of the program's execution. A return of a nonzero value generally indicates an error.

Language Contrast: C++/Java—main() Is All Lowercase

Unlike its C-style predecessors, C# uses an uppercase *M* for the Main method in order to be consistent with the PascalCased naming conventions of C#.

The designation of the Main method as static indicates that other methods may call it directly off the class definition. Without the static designation, the command console that started the program would need to perform additional work (known as **instantiation**) before calling the method. (Chapter 5 contains an entire section devoted to the topic of static members.)

Placing void prior to Main() indicates that this method does not return any data. (This is explained further in Chapter 2.)

One distinctive C/C++ style characteristic followed by C# is the use of curly braces for the body of a construct, such as the class or the method. For example, the Main method contains curly braces that surround its implementation; in this case, only one statement appears in the method.

Statements and Statement Delimiters

The Main method includes a single statement, System.Console.WriteLine(), which is used to write a line of text to the console. C# generally uses a semicolon to indicate the end of a **statement,** where a statement comprises one or more actions that the code will perform. Declaring a variable, controlling the program flow, and calling a method are typical uses of statements.

Language Contrast: Visual Basic—Line-Based Statements

Some languages are line-based, meaning that without a special annotation, statements cannot span a line. Until Visual Basic 2010, Visual Basic was an example of a line-based language. It required an underscore at the end of a line to indicate that a statement spans multiple lines. Starting with Visual Basic 2010, many cases were introduced where the line continuation character was optional.

■ ADVANCED TOPIC

Statements without Semicolons

Many programming elements in C# end with a semicolon. One example that does not include the semicolon is a switch statement. Because curly braces are always included in a switch statement, C# does not require a semicolon following the statement. In fact, code blocks themselves are considered statements (they are also composed of statements) and they don't require closure using a semicolon. Similarly, there are cases, such as the using declarative, in which a semicolon occurs at the end but it is not a statement.

Since creation of a newline does not separate statements, you can place multiple statements on the same line and the C# compiler will interpret the line to have multiple instructions. For example, Listing 1.5 contains two statements on a single line that, in combination, display Up and Down on two separate lines.

LISTING 1.5: **Multiple Statements on One Line**

```
System.Console.WriteLine("Up");System.Console.WriteLine("Down");
```

C# also allows the splitting of a statement across multiple lines. Again, the C# compiler looks for a semicolon to indicate the end of a statement (see Listing 1.6).

LISTING 1.6: **Splitting a Single Statement across Multiple Lines**

```
System.Console.WriteLine(
   "Hello. My name is Inigo Montoya.");
```

In Listing 1.6, the original `WriteLine()` statement from the `HelloWorld` program is split across multiple lines.

■ BEGINNER TOPIC

What Is Whitespace?
Whitespace is the combination of one or more consecutive formatting characters such as tab, space, and newline characters. Eliminating all whitespace between words is obviously significant, as is whitespace within a quoted string.

Whitespace
The semicolon makes it possible for the C# compiler to ignore whitespace in code. Apart from a few exceptions, C# allows developers to insert whitespace throughout the code without altering its semantic meaning. In Listing 1.5 and Listing 1.6, it didn't matter whether a newline was inserted within a statement or between statements, and doing so had no effect on the resultant executable created by the compiler.

Frequently, programmers use whitespace to indent code for greater readability. Consider the two variations on `HelloWorld` shown in Listing 1.7 and Listing 1.8.

LISTING 1.7: **No Indentation Formatting**

```
class HelloWorld
{
static void Main()
{
System.Console.WriteLine("Hello Inigo Montoya");
}
}
```

LISTING 1.8: Removing Whitespace

```
class HelloWorld{static void Main()
{System.Console.WriteLine("Hello Inigo Montoya");}}
```

Although these two examples look significantly different from the original program, the C# compiler sees them as identical.

■ BEGINNER TOPIC

Formatting Code with Whitespace

Indenting the code using whitespace is important for greater readability. As you begin writing code, you need to follow established coding standards and conventions in order to enhance code readability.

The convention used in this book is to place curly braces on their own line and to indent the code contained between the curly brace pair. If another curly brace pair appears within the first pair, all the code within the second set of braces is also indented.

This is not a uniform C# standard, but a stylistic preference.

Working with Variables

Now that you've been introduced to the most basic C# program, it's time to declare a local variable. Once a variable is declared, you can assign it a value, replace that value with a new value, and use it in calculations, output, and so on. However, you cannot change the data type of the variable. In Listing 1.9, `string max` is a variable declaration.

LISTING 1.9: Declaring and Assigning a Variable

```
class MiracleMax
{
    static void Main()
    {
              data type
            ⌒⌒⌒⌒
        string max;
              ⌣⌣
            variable
        max = "Have fun storming the castle!";

        System.Console.WriteLine(max);
    }
}
```

■ **BEGINNER TOPIC**

Local Variables

A **variable** refers to a storage location by a name that the program can later assign and modify. *Local* indicates that the programmer **declared** the variable within a method.

To declare a variable is to define it, which you do by

1. Specifying the type of data which the variable will contain
2. Assigning it an identifier (name)

Data Types

Listing 1.9 declares a variable with the data type `string`. Other common data types used in this chapter are `int` and `char`.

- `int` is the C# designation of an integer type that is 32 bits in size.
- `char` is used for a character type. It is 16 bits, large enough for (nonsurrogate) Unicode characters.

The next chapter looks at these and other common data types in more detail.

■ **BEGINNER TOPIC**

What Is a Data Type?

The type of data that a variable declaration specifies is called a **data type** (or object type). A data type, or simply **type,** is a classification of things that share similar characteristics and behavior. For example, *animal* is a type. It classifies all things (monkeys, warthogs, and platypuses) that have animal characteristics (multicellular, capacity for locomotion, and so on). Similarly, in programming languages, a type is a definition for several items endowed with similar qualities.

Declaring a Variable

In Listing 1.9, `string max` is a variable declaration of a string type whose name is `max`. It is possible to declare multiple variables within the same statement by specifying the data type once and separating each identifier with a comma. Listing 1.10 demonstrates this.

LISTING 1.10: Declaring Two Variables within One Statement

```
string message1, message2;
```

Because a multivariable declaration statement allows developers to provide the data type only once within a declaration, all variables will be of the same type.

In C#, the name of the variable may begin with any letter or an underscore (_), followed by any number of letters, numbers, and/or underscores. By convention, however, local variable names are camelCased (the first letter in each word is capitalized, except for the first word) and do not include underscores.

Guidelines

DO use camelCasing for local variables.

Assigning a Variable

After declaring a local variable, you must assign it a value before reading from it. One way to do this is to use the = **operator,** also known as the **simple assignment operator.** Operators are symbols used to identify the function the code is to perform. Listing 1.11 demonstrates how to use the assignment operator to designate the string values to which the variables max[7] and valerie will point.

LISTING 1.11: Changing the Value of a Variable

```
class MiracleMax
{
  static void Main()
  {
      string valerie;
      string max = "Have fun storming the castle!";

      valerie = "Think it will work?";

      System.Console.WriteLine(max);
      System.Console.WriteLine(valerie);
```

---

7. max does not mean the math function here, but rather is used as a variable name.

```
      max = "It would take a miracle.";
    System.Console.WriteLine(max);
  }
}
```

From this listing, observe that it is possible to assign a variable as part of the variable declaration (as it was for max), or afterward in a separate statement (as with the variable valerie). The value assigned must always be on the right side.

Running the compiled MiracleMax.exe program produces the code shown in Output 1.3.

OUTPUT 1.3

```
>MiracleMax.exe
Have fun storming the castle!
Think it will work?
It would take a miracle.
```

C# requires that local variables be determined by the compiler to be "definitely assigned" before they are read. Additionally, an assignment returns a value. Therefore, C# allows two assignments within the same statement, as demonstrated in Listing 1.12.

LISTING 1.12: Assignment Returning a Value That Can Be Assigned Again

```
class MiracleMax
{
  static void Main()
  {
    // ...
    string requirements, max;
    requirements = max = "It would take a miracle.";
    // ...
  }
}
```

Using a Variable

The result of the assignment, of course, is that you can then refer to the value using the variable identifier. Therefore, when you use the variable max within the System.Console.WriteLine(max) statement, the program displays Have fun storming the castle!, the value of max, on the console. Changing the value of max and executing the same System.Console.WriteLine(max) statement causes the new max value, It would take a miracle., to be displayed.

■ ADVANCED TOPIC

Strings Are Immutable

All data of type string, whether string literals or otherwise, is immutable (or unmodifiable). For example, it is not possible to change the string "Come As You Are" to "Come As You Age." A change such as this requires that you reassign the variable to point to a new location in memory, instead of modifying the data to which the variable originally referred.

Console Input and Output

This chapter already used System.Console.WriteLine repeatedly for writing out text to the command console. In addition to being able to write out data, a program needs to be able to accept data that a user may enter.

Getting Input from the Console

One way to retrieve text that is entered at the console is to use System.Console.ReadLine(). This method stops the program execution so that the user can enter characters. When the user presses the Enter key, creating a newline, the program continues. The output, also known as the **return,** from the System.Console.ReadLine() method is the string of text that was entered. Consider Listing 1.13 and the corresponding output shown in Output 1.4.

LISTING 1.13: **Using** System.Console.ReadLine()

```
class HeyYou
{
  static void Main()
  {
      string firstName;
      string lastName;

      System.Console.WriteLine("Hey you!");

      System.Console.Write("Enter your first name: ");
      firstName = System.Console.ReadLine();
```

```
        System.Console.Write("Enter your last name: ");
        lastName = System.Console.ReadLine();

        ...

    }
}
```

OUTPUT 1.4

```
>HeyYou.exe
Hey you!
Enter your first name: Inigo
Enter your last name: Montoya
```

After each prompt, this program uses the System.Console.ReadLine() method to retrieve the text the user entered and assign it to an appropriate variable. By the time the second System.Console.ReadLine() assignment completes, firstName contains the value Inigo and lastName refers to the value Montoya.

■ ADVANCED TOPIC

System.Console.Read()

In addition to the System.Console.ReadLine() method, there is also a System.Console.Read() method. However, the data type returned by the System.Console.Read() method is an integer corresponding to the character value read, or –1 if no more characters are available. To retrieve the actual character, it is necessary to first cast the integer to a character, as shown in Listing 1.14.

LISTING 1.14: Using System.Console.Read()

```
int readValue;
char character;
readValue = System.Console.Read();
character = (char) readValue;
System.Console.Write(character);
```

The System.Console.Read() method does not return the input until the user presses the Enter key; no processing of characters will begin, even if the user types multiple characters before pressing the Enter key.

In C# 2.0, there appears a new method called `System.Console.ReadKey()` which, in contrast to `System.Console.Read()`, returns the input after a single keystroke. It allows the developer to intercept the keystroke and perform actions such as key validation, restricting the characters to numerics.

Writing Output to the Console

In Listing 1.13, you prompt the user for his first and last names using the method `System.Console.Write()` rather than `System.Console.WriteLine()`. Instead of placing a newline character after displaying the text, the `System.Console.Write()` method leaves the current position on the same line. In this way, any text the user enters will be on the same line as the prompt for input. The output from Listing 1.13 demonstrates the effect of `System.Console.Write()`.

The next step is to write the values retrieved using `System.Console.ReadLine()` back to the console. In the case of Listing 1.15, the program writes out the user's full name. However, instead of using `System.Console.WriteLine()` as before, this code will use a slight variation. Output 1.5 shows the corresponding output.

LISTING 1.15: **Formatting Using** `System.Console.WriteLine()`

```
class HeyYou
{
  static void Main()
  {
      string firstName;
      string lastName;

      System.Console.WriteLine("Hey you!");

      System.Console.Write("Enter your first name: ");
      firstName = System.Console.ReadLine();

      System.Console.Write("Enter your last name: ");
      lastName = System.Console.ReadLine();

      System.Console.WriteLine(
        "Your full name is {0} {1}.", firstName, lastName);
  }
}
```

OUTPUT 1.5

```
Hey you!
Enter your first name: Inigo
Enter your last name: Montoya
Your full name is Inigo Montoya.
```

Instead of writing out Your full name is followed by another Write statement for firstName, a third Write statement for the space, and finally a WriteLine statement for lastName, Listing 1.15 writes out the entire output using **composite formatting.** With composite formatting, the code first supplies a **format string** to define the output format. In this example, the format string is "Your full name is {0} {1}.". It identifies two indexed placeholders for data insertion in the string.

Note that the index value begins at zero. Each inserted parameter (known as a **format item**) appears after the format string in the order corresponding to the index value. In this example, since firstName is the first parameter to follow immediately after the format string, it corresponds to index value 0. Similarly, lastName corresponds to index value 1.

Note that the placeholders within the format string need not appear in order. For example, Listing 1.16 switches the order of the indexed placeholders and adds a comma, which changes the way the name is displayed (see Output 1.6).

LISTING 1.16: **Swapping the Indexed Placeholders and Corresponding Variables**

```
System.Console.WriteLine("Your full name is {1}, {0}",
    firstName, lastName);
```

OUTPUT 1.6

```
Hey you!
Enter your first name: Inigo
Enter your last name: Montoya
Your full name is Montoya, Inigo
```

In addition to not having the placeholders appear consecutively within the format string, it is possible to use the same placeholder multiple times within a format string. Furthermore, it is possible to omit a placeholder. It is not possible, however, to have placeholders that do not have a corresponding parameter.

Comments

In this section, we modify the program in Listing 1.15 by adding comments. In no way does this vary the execution of the program; rather, providing comments within the code makes the code more understandable. Listing 1.17 shows the new code, and Output 1.7 shows the corresponding output.

LISTING 1.17: **Commenting Your Code**

```
class CommentSamples
{
  static void Main()
  {
                              single-line comment
    string firstName; // Variable for storing the first name
    string lastName;  // Variable for storing the last name

    System.Console.WriteLine("Hey you!");

                    delimited comment inside statement
    System.Console.Write /* No new line */ (
        "Enter your first name: ");
    firstName = System.Console.ReadLine();

    System.Console.Write /* No new line */ (
        "Enter your last name: ");
    lastName = System.Console.ReadLine();

    /* Display a greeting to the console
       using composite formatting. */        } delimited comment
    System.Console.WriteLine("Your full name is {0} {1}.",
        firstName, lastName);
    // This is the end
    // of the program listing
  }
}
```

OUTPUT 1.7

```
Hey you!
Enter your first name: Inigo
Enter your last name: Montoya
Your full name is Inigo Montoya.
```

In spite of the inserted comments, compiling and executing the new program produces the same output as before.

Programmers use comments to describe and explain the code they are writing, especially where the syntax itself is difficult to understand, or perhaps a particular algorithm implementation is surprising. Since comments are pertinent only to the programmer reviewing the code, the compiler ignores comments and generates an assembly that is devoid of any trace that comments were part of the original source code.

Table 1.2 shows four different C# comment types. The program in Listing 1.17 includes two of these.

TABLE 1.2: C# Comment Types

Comment Type	Description	Example
Delimited comments	A forward slash followed by an asterisk, /*, identifies the beginning of a delimited comment. To end the comment use an asterisk followed by a forward slash: */. Comments of this form may span multiple lines in the code file or appear embedded within a line of code. The asterisks that appear at the beginning of the lines but within the delimiters are simply for formatting.	`/*comment*/`
Single-line comments	Comments may also be declared with a delimiter comprising two consecutive forward slash characters: //. The compiler treats all text from the delimiter to the end of the line as a comment. Comments of this form comprise a single line. It is possible, however, to place sequential single-line comments one after another, as is the case with the last comment in Listing 1.17.	`//comment`
XML delimited comments	Comments that begin with /** and end with **/ are called XML delimited comments. They have the same characteristics as regular delimited comments, except that instead of ignoring XML comments entirely, the compiler can place them into a separate text file. XML delimited comments were only explicitly added in C# 2.0, but the syntax is compatible with C# 1.0.	`/**comment**/`
XML single-line comments	XML single-line comments begin with /// and continue to the end of the line. In addition, the compiler can save single-line comments into a separate file with the XML delimited comments.	`///comment`

A more comprehensive discussion of the XML comments appears in Chapter 9, where we further discuss the various XML tags.

There was a period in programming history where a prolific set of comments implied a disciplined and experienced programmer. This is no longer the case. Instead, the code that is readable without comments is more valuable than that which requires comments in order to clarify what it does. If developers find it necessary to enter comments in order to clarify what a particular code block is doing, they should favor rewriting the code more clearly over commenting it. Writing comments that are simply a repeat of what the code clearly shows serves only to clutter, decrease readability, and increase the likelihood of the comments going out of date because the code changes without the comments getting updated.

Guidelines

DO NOT use comments unless they describe something that is not obvious to someone other than the developer who wrote the code.

DO favor writing clearer code over entering comments to clarify a complicated algorithm.

■ BEGINNER TOPIC

Extensible Markup Language (XML)

The Extensible Markup Language (XML) is a simple and flexible text format frequently used within Web applications and for exchanging data between applications. XML is extensible because included within an XML document is information that describes the data, known as **metadata.** Here is a sample XML file.

```xml
<?xml version="1.0" encoding="utf-8" ?>
<body>
  <book title="Essential C# 5.0">
    <chapters>
        <chapter title="Introducing C#"/>
        <chapter title="Operators and Control Flow"/>
        ...
    </chapters>
  </book>
</body>
```

The file starts with a header indicating the version and character encoding of the XML file. After that appears one main "book" element. Elements begin with a word in angle brackets, such as `<body>`. To end an element, place the same word in angle brackets and add a forward slash to prefix the word, as in `</body>`. In addition to elements, XML supports attributes. `title="Essential C# 5.0"` is an example of an XML attribute. Note that the metadata (book title, chapter, and so on) describing the data ("Essential C# 5.0", "Operators and Control Flow") is included in the XML file. This can result in rather bloated files, but it offers the advantage that the data includes a description to aid in interpreting the data.

Managed Execution and the Common Language Infrastructure

The processor cannot directly interpret an assembly. Assemblies consist mainly of a second language known as the **Common Intermediate Language** (**CIL**), or **IL** for short.[8] The C# compiler transforms the C# source file into this intermediate language. An additional step, usually performed at execution time, is required to change the CIL code into **machine code** that the processor can understand. This involves an important element in the execution of a C# program: the **Virtual Execution System** (**VES**). The VES, also casually referred to as the **runtime,** compiles CIL code as needed (this process is known as **just-in-time** compilation or **jitting**). The code that executes under the context of an agent such as the runtime is **managed code,** and the process of executing under control of the runtime is **managed execution.** The code is "managed" because the runtime controls significant portions of the program's behavior by managing aspects such as memory allocation, security, and just-in-time compilation. Code that does not require the runtime in order to execute is **native code** (or **unmanaged code**).

The specification for a VES is included in a broader specification known as the **Common Language Infrastructure** (**CLI**) specification.[9] An international standard, the CLI includes specifications for the following:

- The VES or runtime
- The CIL

---

8. A third term for CIL is Microsoft IL (MSIL). This book uses the term *CIL* because it is the term adopted by the CLI standard. IL is prevalent in conversation among people writing C# code because they assume that IL refers to CIL rather than other types of intermediate languages.
9. Miller, J., and S. Ragsdale. 2004. *The Common Language Infrastructure Annotated Standard.* Boston: Addison-Wesley.

- A type system that supports language interoperability, known as the **Common Type System (CTS)**
- Guidance on how to write libraries that are accessible from CLI-compatible languages (available in the **Common Language Specification [CLS]**)
- Metadata that enables many of the services identified by the CLI (including specifications for the layout or file format of assemblies)
- A common programming framework, the Base Class Library (BCL), which developers in all languages can utilize

---

■ NOTE

The term *runtime* can refer to either execution time or the Virtual Execution System. To help clarify, this book uses the term *execution time* to indicate when the program is executing, and it uses the term *runtime* when discussing the agent responsible for managing the execution of a C# program while it executes.

Running within the context of a CLI implementation enables support for a number of services and features that programmers do not need to code for directly, including the following.

- *Language interoperability:* interoperability between different source languages. This is possible because the language compilers translate each source language to the same intermediate language (CIL).
- *Type safety:* checks for conversion between types, ensuring that only conversions between compatible types will occur. This helps prevent the occurrence of buffer overruns, a leading cause of security vulnerabilities.
- *Code access security:* certification that the assembly developer's code has permission to execute on the computer.
- *Garbage collection:* memory management that automatically de-allocates memory previously allocated by the runtime.
- *Platform portability:* support for potentially running the same assembly on a variety of operating systems. One obvious restriction is that no platform-dependent libraries are used; therefore, as with Java, there

are potentially some platform dependencies idiosyncrasies that need to be worked out.

- *BCL:* provides a large foundation of code that developers can depend on (in all CLI implementations) so that they do not have to develop the code themselves.

▪ NOTE

This section gives a brief synopsis of the CLI to familiarize you with the context in which a C# program executes. It also provides a summary of some of the terms that appear throughout this book. Chapter 21 is devoted to the topic of the CLI and its relevance to C# developers. Although the chapter appears last in the book, it does not depend on any earlier chapters, so if you want to become more familiar with the CLI, you can jump to it at any time.

C# and .NET Versioning

Readers will notice that Output 1.1 refers to the ".NET Framework version 4.5." At the time of this writing, Microsoft had six major releases to the .NET Framework and only five C# compiler releases. .NET Framework version 3.0 was an additional set of API libraries released in between C# compiler releases (and Visual Studio 2005 and 2008 versions). As a result, the .NET Framework version that corresponded with C# 3.0 was 3.5. With the release of C# 4.0 and the .NET Framework 4.0, the version numbers were synchronized. However, the .NET version for C# 5.0 is .NET Framework 4.5, so version numbers in the current generation are no longer aligned. Table 1.3 is a brief overview of the C# and .NET releases.

The majority of all code within this text will work with platforms other than Microsoft's as long as the compiler version corresponds to the version of code required. Although providing full details on each C# platform would be helpful for some, it proved to detract from the focus of learning C#, so the main body of the text is restricted to information on Microsoft's platform, .NET. This is simply because Microsoft has the predominant (by far) implementation. Furthermore, translation to another platform is fairly trivial.

TABLE 1.3: C# and .NET Versions

Comment Type	Description
C# 1.0 with .NET Framework 1.0/1.1 (Visual Studio 2002 and 2003)	The initial release of C#. A language built from the ground up to support .NET programming.
C# 2.0 with .NET Framework 2.0 (Visual Studio 2005)	Added generics to the C# language and libraries that supported generics to the .NET Framework 2.0.
.NET Framework 3.0	An additional set of APIs for distributed communications (Windows Communication Foundation—WCF), rich client presentation (Windows Presentation Foundation—WPF), workflow (Windows Workflow—WF), and Web authentication (Cardspaces).
C# 3.0 with .NET Framework 3.5 (Visual Studio 2008)	Added support for LINQ, a significant improvement to the APIs used for programming collections. The .NET Framework 3.5 provided libraries that extended existing APIs to make LINQ possible.
C# 4.0 with .NET Framework 4 (Visual Studio 2010)	Added support for dynamic typing along with significant improvements in the API for writing multithreaded programs that capitalized on multiple processors and cores within those processors.
C# 5.0 with .NET Framework 4.5 (Visual Studio 11) and WinRT integration	Added support for asynchronous method invocation without the explicit registration of a delegate callback. An additional change in the framework was support for interoperability with the Windows Runtime (WinRT).

Perhaps the biggest feature added to .NET 4.5 was support for calling into components within the Windows Runtime (WinRT). Internally, WinRT is native code that provides an entirely new platform in which .NET can execute. However, in both the style of its API and the behavior of its runtime, it resembles .NET. For practical purposes, components in WinRT are a new set of APIs—with significant functionality overlap with the .NET Framework. The difference is that this new API is only available on Windows 8 and it has been designed from the ground up to provide a .NET-like programming experience for functionality that was previously only available in "Win32"

APIs with .NET wrappers. Although significant, the addition of WinRT as a platform is mostly orthogonal to the learning of .NET and C#. Therefore, this book does not provide in-depth coverage of WinRT.

Common Intermediate Language and ILDASM

As mentioned in the preceding section, the C# compiler converts C# code to CIL code and not to machine code. The processor can directly understand machine code, but CIL code needs to be converted before the processor can execute it. Given an assembly (either a DLL or an executable), it is possible to view the CIL code using a CIL disassembler utility to deconstruct the assembly into its CIL representation. (The CIL disassembler is commonly referred to by its Microsoft-specific filename, ILDASM, which stands for IL Disassembler.) This program will disassemble a program or its class libraries, displaying the CIL generated by the C# compiler.

The exact command used for the CIL disassembler depends on which implementation of the CLI is used. You can execute the .NET CIL disassembler from the command line as shown in Output 1.8.

OUTPUT 1.8

```
>ildasm /text HelloWorld.exe
```

The /text portion is used so that the output appears on the command console rather than in a new window. The stream of output that results by executing these commands is a dump of CIL code included in the HelloWorld.exe program. Note that CIL code is significantly easier to understand than machine code. For many developers, this may raise a concern because it is easier for programs to be decompiled and algorithms understood without explicitly redistributing the source code.

As with any program, CLI-based or not, the only foolproof way of preventing disassembly is to disallow access to the compiled program altogether (for example, only hosting a program on a web site instead of distributing it out to a user's machine). However, if decreased accessibility to the source code is all that is required, there are several obfuscators available. These obfuscators open up the IL code and munge the code so that it does the same thing but in a way that is much more difficult to understand.

This prevents the casual developer from accessing the code and instead creates assemblies that are much more difficult and tedious to decompile into comprehensible code. Unless a program requires a high degree of algorithm security, these obfuscators are generally sufficient.

▪ ADVANCED TOPIC

CIL Output for `HelloWorld.exe`
Listing 1.18 shows the CIL code created by ILDASM.

LISTING 1.18: Sample CIL Output

```
// Microsoft (R) .NET Framework IL Disassembler.  Version 4.0.30319.17369
// Copyright (c) Microsoft Corporation.  All rights reserved.



// Metadata version: v4.0.30319
.assembly extern mscorlib
{
  .publickeytoken = (B7 7A 5C 56 19 34 E0 89 )                        //
➥ .z\V.4..
  .ver 4:0:0:0
}
.assembly HelloWorld
{
  .custom instance void [mscorlib]System.Runtime.CompilerServices.Compilat
➥ ionRelaxationsAttribute::.ctor(int32) = ( 01 00 08 00 00 00 00 00 )
  .custom instance void [mscorlib]System.Runtime.CompilerServices.Runtime
➥ CompatibilityAttribute::.ctor() = ( 01 00 01 00 54 02 16 57 72 61 70 4E 6F
➥ 6E 45 78    // ....T..WrapNonEx

➥ 63 65 70 74 69 6F 6E 54 68 72 6F 77 73 01 )       // ceptionThrows.
  .hash algorithm 0x00008004
  .ver 0:0:0:0
}
.module HelloWorld.exe
// MVID: {D229AC10-1DEC-47A1-AA62-3BA19389E37E}
.imagebase 0x00400000
.file alignment 0x00000200
.stackreserve 0x00100000
.subsystem 0x0003       // WINDOWS_CUI
.corflags 0x00000001    // ILONLY
// Image base: 0x00490000


// =============== CLASS MEMBERS DECLARATION ===================
```

```
.class private auto ansi beforefieldinit HelloWorld
       extends [mscorlib]System.Object
{
  .method private hidebysig static void  Main() cil managed
  {
    .entrypoint
    // Code size       13 (0xd)
    .maxstack  8
    IL_0000:  nop
    IL_0001:  ldstr       "Hello. My name is Inigo Montoya."
    IL_0006:  call        void [mscorlib]System.Console::WriteLine(string)
    IL_000b:  nop
    IL_000c:  ret
  } // end of method HelloWorld::Main

  .method public hidebysig specialname rtspecialname
         instance void  .ctor() cil managed
  {
    // Code size       7 (0x7)
    .maxstack  8
    IL_0000:  ldarg.0
    IL_0001:  call        instance void [mscorlib]System.Object::.ctor()
    IL_0006:  ret
  } // end of method HelloWorld::.ctor

} // end of class HelloWorld


// ================================================================

// *********** DISASSEMBLY COMPLETE ***********************
```

The beginning of the listing is the manifest information. It includes not only the full name of the disassembled module (HelloWorld.exe), but also all the modules and assemblies it depends on, along with their version information.

Perhaps the most interesting thing that you can glean from such a listing is how relatively easy it is to follow what the program is doing compared to trying to read and understand machine code (assembler). In the listing, an explicit reference to System.Console.WriteLine() appears. There is a lot of peripheral information to the CIL code listing, but if a developer wanted to understand the inner workings of a C# module (or any CLI-based program) without having access to the original source code, it would be relatively easy unless an obfuscator is used. In fact, several free tools are available (such as Red Gate's Reflector, ILSpy, JustDecompile, dotPeek, and CodeReflect) that can decompile from CIL to C# automatically.

SUMMARY

This chapter served as a rudimentary introduction to C#. It provided a means of familiarizing you with basic C# syntax. Because of C#'s similarity to C++ style languages, much of this might not have been new material to you. However, C# and managed code do have some distinct characteristics, such as compilation down to CIL. Although it is not unique, another key characteristic is that C# includes full support for object-oriented programming. Even tasks such as reading and writing data to the console are object-oriented. Object orientation is foundational to C#, and you will see this throughout this book.

The next chapter examines the fundamental data types that are part of the C# language, and discusses how you can use these data types with operands to form expressions.

■2■
Data Types

F ROM CHAPTER 1's `HelloWorld` program, you got a feel for the C# language, its structure, basic syntax characteristics, and how to write the simplest of programs. This chapter continues to discuss the C# basics by investigating the fundamental C# types.

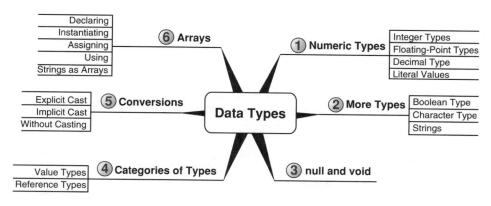

Until now, you have worked with only a few primitive data types, with little explanation. In C# thousands of types exist, and you can combine types to create new types. A few types in C#, however, are relatively simple and are considered the building blocks of all other types. These types are **predefined types** or **primitives.** The C# language's primitive types include eight integer types, two binary floating-point types for scientific calculations and one decimal float for financial calculations, one Boolean type, and a character type. This chapter investigates these primitives, looks more closely at the `string` type, and introduces arrays.

Fundamental Numeric Types

The basic numeric types in C# have keywords associated with them. These types include integer types, floating-point types, and a special floating-point type called `decimal` to store large numbers with no representation error.

Integer Types

There are eight C# integer types. This variety allows you to select a data type large enough to hold its intended range of values without wasting resources. Table 2.1 lists each integer type.

TABLE 2.1: Integer Types

Type	Size	Range (Inclusive)	BCL Name	Signed	Literal Suffix
sbyte	8 bits	−128 to 127	System.SByte	Yes	
byte	8 bits	0 to 255	System.Byte	No	
short	16 bits	−32,768 to 32,767	System.Int16	Yes	
ushort	16 bits	0 to 65,535	System.UInt16	No	
int	32 bits	−2,147,483,648 to 2,147,483,647	System.Int32	Yes	
uint	32 bits	0 to 4,294,967,295	System.UInt32	No	U or u
long	64 bits	−9,223,372,036,854,775,808 to 9,223,372,036,854,775,807	System.Int64	Yes	L or l
ulong	64 bits	0 to 18,446,744,073,709,551,615	System.UInt64	No	UL or ul

Included in Table 2.1 (and in Tables 2.2 and 2.3) is a column for the full name of each type; we discuss the literal suffix later in the chapter. All the fundamental types in C# have a short name and a full name. The full name corresponds to the type as it is named in the Base Class Library (BCL). This name is the same across all languages and it uniquely identifies the type within an assembly. Because of the fundamental nature of primitive types C# also supplies keywords as short names or abbreviations to the full names of fundamental types. From the compiler's perspective, both names are exactly the same, producing exactly the same code. In fact, an examination of the resultant CIL code would provide no indication of which name was used.

Although C# supports using both the full BCL name and the keyword, as developers we are left with the choice of which to use when. Rather than switching back and forth, it is better to use one or the other consistently. For this reason, C# developers generally go with using the C# keyword form—choosing, for example, int rather than System.Int32 and string rather than System.String (or a possible shortcut of String).

> ### Guidelines
>
> **DO** use the C# keyword rather than the BCL name when specifying a data type (for example, string rather than String).
>
> **DO** favor consistency rather than variety within your code.

The choice for consistency frequently may be at odds with other guidelines. For example, given the guideline to use the C# keyword in place of the BCL name, there may be occasions when you find yourself maintaining a file (or library of files) with the opposite style. In these cases it would better to stay consistent with the previous style than to inject a new style and inconsistencies in the conventions. Even so, if the "style" was in fact a bad coding practice that was likely to introduce bugs and obstruct successful maintenance, by all means correct the issue throughout.

> ### Language Contrast: C++—short Data Type
>
> In C/C++, the short data type is an abbreviation for short int. In C#, short on its own is the actual data type.

Floating-Point Types (float, double)

Floating-point numbers have varying degrees of precision, and binary floating-point types can only represent numbers exactly if they are a fraction with a power of two as the denominator. If you were to set the value of a floating-point variable to be 0.1, it could very easily be represented as

0.0999999999999999 or 0.10000000000000001 or some other number very close to 0.1. Similarly, setting a variable to a large number such as Avogadro's number, 6.02×10^{23}, could lead to a representation error of around 10^8, which after all is a tiny fraction of that number. The accuracy of a floating-point number is in proportion to the magnitude of the number it represents. A floating-point number is precise to a certain number of significant digits, not by a fixed value such as ±0.01.

C# supports the two binary floating-point number types listed in Table 2.2.

TABLE 2.2: Floating-Point Types

Type	Size	Range (Inclusive)	BCL Name	Significant Digits	Literal Suffix
float	32 bits	$\pm 1.5 \times 10^{-45}$ to $\pm 3.4 \times 10^{38}$	System.Single	7	F or f
double	64 bits	$\pm 5.0 \times 10^{-324}$ to $\pm 1.7 \times 10^{308}$	System.Double	15–16	⸏

Binary numbers appear as base 10 (denary) numbers for human readability. The number of bits (binary digits) converts to 15 decimal digits, with a remainder that contributes to a sixteenth decimal digit as expressed in Table 2.2. Specifically, numbers between $1.7 * 10^{307}$ and less than $1 * 10^{308}$ have only 15 significant digits. However, numbers ranging from $1 * 10^{308}$ to $1.7 * 10^{308}$ will have 16 significant digits. A similar range of significant digits occurs with the decimal type as well.

Decimal Type

C# also provides a decimal floating-point type with 128-bit precision (see Table 2.3). This type is suitable for financial calculations.

TABLE 2.3: decimal Type

Type	Size	Range (Inclusive)	BCL Name	Significant Digits	Literal Suffix
decimal	128 bits	1.0×10^{-28} to approximately 7.9×10^{28}	System .Decimal	28–29	M or m

Unlike binary floating-point numbers, the decimal type maintains exact accuracy for all denary numbers within its range. With the decimal type, therefore, a value of 0.1 is exactly 0.1. However, while the decimal type has greater precision than the floating-point types, it has a smaller range. Thus, conversions from floating-point types to the decimal type may result in overflow errors. Also, calculations with decimal are slightly (generally imperceptibly) slower.

■ ADVANCED TOPIC

Floating-Point Types Dissected

Denary numbers within the range and precision limits of the decimal type are represented exactly. In contrast, the binary floating-point representation of many denary numbers introduces a rounding error. Just as ⅓ cannot be represented exactly in any finite number of decimal digits, so too ¹¹⁄₁₀ cannot be represented exactly in any finite number of binary digits. In both cases, we end up with a rounding error of some kind.

A decimal is represented by ±N * 10^k where the following is true.

- N, the mantissa, is a positive 96-bit integer.
- k, the exponent, is given by -28 <= k <= 0.

In contrast, a binary float is any number ±N * 2^k where the following is true.

- N is a positive 24-bit (for float) or 53-bit (for double) integer.
- k is an integer ranging from -149 to +104 for float and -1075 to +970 for double.

Literal Values

A **literal value** is a representation of a constant value within source code. For example, if you want to have System.Console.WriteLine() print out the integer value 42 and the double value 1.618034, you could use the code shown in Listing 2.1.

LISTING 2.1: Specifying Literal Values

```
System.Console.WriteLine(42);
System.Console.WriteLine(1.618034);
```

Output 2.1 shows the results of Listing 2.1.

OUTPUT 2.1

```
42
1.618034
```

■ BEGINNER TOPIC

Use Caution When Hardcoding Values

The practice of placing a value directly into source code is called **hardcoding,** because changing the values means recompiling the code. Developers must carefully consider the choice between hardcoding values within their code and retrieving them from an external source, such as a configuration file, so that the values are modifiable without recompiling.

By default, when you specify a literal number with a decimal point, the compiler interprets it as a double type. Conversely, a literal value with no decimal point generally defaults to an int, assuming the value is not too large to be stored in an integer. If the value is too large, the compiler will interpret it as a long. Furthermore, the C# compiler allows assignment to a numeric type other than an int, assuming the literal value is appropriate for the target data type. short s = 42 and byte b = 77 are allowed, for example. However, this is appropriate only for constant values; b = s is not allowed without additional syntax, as discussed in the section Conversions between Data Types, later in this chapter.

As previously discussed in the section Fundamental Numeric Types, there are many different numeric types in C#. In Listing 2.2, a literal value is placed within C# code. Since numbers with a decimal point will default to the double data type, the output, shown in Output 2.2, is 1.61803398874989 (the last digit, 5, is missing), corresponding to the expected accuracy of a double.

LISTING 2.2: **Specifying a Literal** double

```
System.Console.WriteLine(1.618033988749895);
```

OUTPUT 2.2

```
1.61803398874989
```

To view the intended number with its full accuracy, you must declare explicitly the literal value as a decimal type by appending an M (or m) (see Listing 2.3 and Output 2.3).

LISTING 2.3: **Specifying a Literal** decimal

```
System.Console.WriteLine(1.618033988749895M);
```

OUTPUT 2.3

```
1.618033988749895
```

Now the output of Listing 2.3 is as expected: 1.618033988749895. Note that d is for double. To remember that m should be used to identify a decimal, remember that "m is for monetary calculations."

You can also add a suffix to a value to explicitly declare a literal as float or double by using the F and D suffixes, respectively. For integer data types, the suffixes are U, L, LU, and UL. The type of an integer literal can be determined as follows.

- Numeric literals with no suffix resolve to the first data type that can store the value in this order: int, uint, long, and ulong.
- Numeric literals with the suffix U resolve to the first data type that can store the value in the order uint and then ulong.
- Numeric literals with the suffix L resolve to the first data type that can store the value in the order long and then ulong.
- If the numeric literal has the suffix UL or LU, it is of type ulong.

Note that suffixes for literals are case-insensitive. However, uppercase is generally preferred to avoid any ambiguity between the lowercase letter *l* and the digit 1.

In some situations, you may wish to use exponential notation instead of writing out several zeroes before or after the decimal point. To use exponential notation, supply the e or E infix, follow the infix character with a positive or negative integer number, and complete the literal with the appropriate data type suffix. For example, you could print out Avogadro's number as a float, as shown in Listing 2.4 and Output 2.4.

LISTING 2.4: Exponential Notation

```
System.Console.WriteLine(6.023E23F);
```

OUTPUT 2.4

```
6.023E+23
```

Guidelines

DO use uppercase literal suffixes (for example, 1.618033988749895M).

■ **BEGINNER TOPIC**

Hexadecimal Notation

Usually you work with numbers that are represented with a base of 10, meaning there are ten symbols (0–9) for each digit in the number. If a number is displayed with hexadecimal notation, it is displayed with a base of 16 numbers, meaning 16 symbols are used: 0–9, A–F (lowercase can also be used). Therefore, 0x000A corresponds to the decimal value 10 and 0x002A corresponds to the decimal value 42, being 2 x 16 + 10. The actual number is the same. Switching from hexadecimal to decimal or vice versa does not change the number itself, just the representation of the number.

Each hex digit is four bits, so a byte can represent two hex digits.

In all discussions of literal numeric values so far, we have covered only base 10 type values. C# also supports the ability to specify hexadecimal values. To specify a hexadecimal value, prefix the value with 0x and then use any hexadecimal digit, as shown in Listing 2.5.

LISTING 2.5: Hexadecimal Literal Value

```
// Display the value 42 using a hexadecimal literal.
System.Console.WriteLine(0x002A);
```

Output 2.5 shows the results of Listing 2.5.

OUTPUT 2.5

```
42
```

Note that this code still displays 42, not 0x002A.

■ ADVANCED TOPIC

Formatting Numbers As Hexadecimal

To display a numeric value in its hexadecimal format, it is necessary to use the x or X numeric formatting specifier. The casing determines whether the hexadecimal letters appear in lowercase or uppercase. Listing 2.6 shows an example of how to do this.

LISTING 2.6: Example of a Hexadecimal Format Specifier

```
// Displays "0x2A"
System.Console.WriteLine("0x{0:X}", 42);
```

Output 2.6 shows the results.

OUTPUT 2.6

```
0x2A
```

Note that the numeric literal (42) can be in decimal or hexadecimal form. The result will be the same.

■ **ADVANCED TOPIC**

Round-Trip Formatting

By default, `System.Console.WriteLine(1.618033988749895);` displays `1.61803398874989`, with the last digit missing. To more accurately identify the string representation of the double value it is possible to convert it using a format string and the round-trip format specifier, `R` (or `r`). `string.Format("{0:R}", 1.618033988749895)`, for example, will return the result `1.6180339887498949`.

The round-trip format specifier returns a string that, if converted back into a numeric value, will always result in the original value. Listing 2.7, therefore, will show the numbers are not equal without the round-trip format.

LISTING 2.7: Formatting Using the R Format Specifier

```
// ...
const double number = 1.618033988749895;
double result;
string text;

text = string.Format("{0}", number);
result = double.Parse(text);
System.Console.WriteLine("{0}: result != number",
  result != number);

text = string.Format("{0:R}", number);
result = double.Parse(text);
System.Console.WriteLine("{0}: result == number",
  result == number);
// ...
```

Output 2.7 shows the resultant output.

OUTPUT 2.7

```
True: result != number
True: result == number
```

When assigning `text` the first time, there is no round-trip format specifier and, as a result, the value returned by `double.Parse(text)` is not the same as the original `number` value. In contrast, when the round-trip format specifier is used, `double.Parse(text)` returns the original value.

For those unfamiliar with the == syntax from C-based languages, result == number returns true if result is equal to number, while result != number does the opposite. Both assignment and equality operators are discussed in the next chapter.

More Fundamental Types

The fundamental types discussed so far are numeric types. C# includes some additional types as well: bool, char, and string.

Boolean Type (bool)

Another C# primitive is a Boolean or conditional type, bool, which represents true or false in conditional statements and expressions. Allowable values are the keywords true and false. The BCL name for bool is System.Boolean. For example, in order to compare two strings in a case-insensitive manner, you call the string.Compare() method and pass a bool literal true (see Listing 2.8).

LISTING 2.8: A Case-Insensitive Comparison of Two Strings

```
string option;
...
int comparison = string.Compare(option, "/Help", true);
```

In this case, you make a case-insensitive comparison of the contents of the variable option with the literal text /Help and assign the result to comparison.

Although theoretically a single bit could hold the value of a Boolean, the size of bool is 1 byte.

Character Type (char)

A char type represents 16-bit characters whose set of possible values are drawn from the Unicode character set's UTF-16 encoding. A char is the same size as a 16-bit unsigned integer (ushort), which represents values between 0 and 65,535. However, char is a unique type in C# and code should treat it as such.

The BCL name for char is System.Char.

■ **BEGINNER TOPIC**

The Unicode Standard

Unicode is an international standard for representing characters found in the majority of human languages. It provides computer systems with functionality for building **localized** applications, applications that display the appropriate language and culture characteristics for different cultures.

■ **ADVANCED TOPIC**

16 Bits Is Too Small for All Unicode Characters

Unfortunately, not all Unicode characters can be represented by just one 16-bit char. The original Unicode designers believed that 16 bits would be enough, but as more languages were supported, it was realized that this assumption was incorrect. As a result, some (rarely used) Unicode characters are composed of "surrogate pairs" of two char values.

To construct a literal char, place the character within single quotes, as in 'A'. Allowable characters comprise the full range of keyboard characters, including letters, numbers, and special symbols.

Some characters cannot be placed directly into the source code and instead require special handling. These characters are prefixed with a backslash (\) followed by a special character code. In combination, the backslash and special character code are an **escape sequence.** For example, \n represents a newline, and \t represents a tab. Since a backslash indicates the beginning of an escape sequence, it can no longer identify a simple backslash; instead, you need to use \\ to represent a single backslash character.

Listing 2.9 writes out one single quote because the character represented by \' corresponds to a single quote.

LISTING 2.9: **Displaying a Single Quote Using an Escape Sequence**

```
class SingleQuote
{
  static void Main()
  {
      System.Console.WriteLine('\'');
  }
}
```

In addition to showing the escape sequence, Table 2.4 includes the Unicode representation of characters.

TABLE 2.4: Escape Characters

Escape Sequence	Character Name	Unicode Encoding
\'	Single quote	\u0027
\"	Double quote	\u0022
\\	Backslash	\u005C
\0	Null	\u0000
\a	Alert (system beep)	\u0007
\b	Backspace	\u0008
\f	Form feed	\u000C
\n	Line feed (sometimes referred to as a newline)	\u000A
\r	Carriage return	\u000D
\t	Horizontal tab	\u0009
\v	Vertical tab	\u000B
\uxxxx	Unicode character in hex	\u0029
\x[n][n][n]n	Unicode character in hex (first three placeholders are options); variable length version of \uxxxx	\u3A
\Uxxxxxxxx	Unicode escape sequence for creating surrogate pairs	\UD840DC01 (𠀁)

You can represent any character using Unicode encoding. To do so, prefix the Unicode value with \u. You represent Unicode characters in hexadecimal notation. The letter *A*, for example, is the hexadecimal value 0x41. Listing 2.10 uses Unicode characters to display a smiley face (:)), and Output 2.8 shows the results.

LISTING 2.10: Using Unicode Encoding to Display a Smiley Face

```
System.Console.Write('\u003A');
System.Console.WriteLine('\u0029');
```

OUTPUT 2.8

```
:)
```

Strings

A finite sequence of zero or more characters is called a **string.** The string type in C# is string, whose BCL name is System.String. The string type includes some special characteristics that may be unexpected to developers familiar with other programming languages. The characteristics include a "verbatim string" prefix character, @, and the fact that strings are immutable.

Literals

You can enter a literal string into code by placing the text in double quotes ("), as you saw in the HelloWorld program. Strings are composed of characters, and because of this, character escape sequences can be embedded within a string.

In Listing 2.11, for example, two lines of text are displayed. However, instead of using System.Console.WriteLine(), the code listing shows System.Console.Write() with the newline character, \n. Output 2.9 shows the results.

LISTING 2.11: Using the \n Character to Insert a Newline

```csharp
class DuelOfWits
{
  static void Main()
  {
      System.Console.Write(
          "\"Truly, you have a dizzying intellect.\"");
      System.Console.Write("\n\"Wait 'til I get going!\"\n");
  }
}
```

OUTPUT 2.9

```
"Truly, you have a dizzying intellect."
"Wait 'til I get going!"
```

The escape sequence for double quotes differentiates the printed double quotes from the double quotes that define the beginning and end of the string.

In C#, you can use the @ symbol in front of a string to signify that a backslash should not be interpreted as the beginning of an escape sequence. The resultant **verbatim string literal** does not reinterpret just the backslash character. Whitespace is also taken verbatim when using the @ string syntax. The triangle in Listing 2.12, for example, appears in the console exactly as typed, including the backslashes, newlines, and indentation. Output 2.10 shows the results.

LISTING 2.12: **Displaying a Triangle Using a Verbatim String Literal**

```
class Triangle
{
  static void Main()
  {
      System.Console.Write(@"begin
                /\
               /  \
              /    \
             /      \
            /_____\
  end");
  }
}
```

OUTPUT 2.10

Without the @ character, this code would not even compile. In fact, even if you changed the shape to a square, eliminating the backslashes, the code still would not compile because a newline cannot be placed directly within a string that is not prefaced with the @ symbol.

The only escape sequence the verbatim string does support is "", which signifies double quotes and does not terminate the string.

Language Contrast: C++—String Concatenation at Compile Time

Unlike C++, C# does not automatically concatenate literal strings. You cannot, for example, specify a string literal as follows:

```
"Major Strasser has been shot. "
"Round up the usual suspects."
```

Rather, concatenation requires the use of the addition operator. (If the compiler can calculate the result at compile time, however, the resultant CIL code will be a single string.)

If the same literal string appears within an assembly multiple times, the compiler will define the string only once within the assembly and all variables will refer to the same string. That way, if the same string literal containing thousands of characters was placed multiple times into the code, the resultant assembly would reflect the size of only one of them.

String Methods

The string type, like the `System.Console` type, includes several methods. There are methods, for example, for formatting, concatenating, and comparing strings.

The `Format()` method in Table 2.5 behaves exactly like the `Console.Write()` and `Console.WriteLine()` methods, except that instead of displaying the result in the console window, `string.Format()` returns the result to the caller.

All of the methods in Table 2.5 are **static.** This means that, to call the method, it is necessary to prefix the method name (for example, `Concat`) with the type that contains the method (for example, `string`). As illustrated below, however, some of the methods in the string class are **instance** methods. Instead of prefixing the method with the type, instance methods use the variable name (or some other reference to an instance). Table 2.6 shows a few of these methods, along with an example.

Table 2.5: **string Static Methods**

Statement	Example

static string string.Format(
    string format,
    ...)
	string text, firstName, lastName;
	//...
	text = string.Format("Your full name is {0} {1}.",
	  firstName, lastName);
	// Display
	// "Your full name is <firstName> <lastName>."
	System.Console.WriteLine(text);

static string string.Concat(
    string str0,
    string str1)
	string text, firstName, lastName;
	//...
	text = string.Concat(firstName, lastName);
	// Display "<firstName><lastName>", notice
	// that there is no space between names.
	System.Console.WriteLine(text);

static int string.Compare(
    string str0,
    string str1)
	string option;
	//...
	// String comparison in which case matters.
	int result = string.Compare(option, "/help");
	
	// Display:
	// 0 if equal
	// negative if option < /help
	// positive if option > /help
	System.Console.WriteLine(result);

	string option;
	//...
	// Case-insensitive string comparison
	int result = string.Compare(
	    option, "/Help", true);
	
	// Display:
	// 0 if equal
	// < 0 if option < /help
	// > 0 if option > /help
	System.Console.WriteLine(result);

TABLE 2.6: **string Methods**

Statement	Example

bool StartsWith(
    string value)
bool EndsWith(
    string value)
	string lastName
	//...
	bool isPhd = lastName.EndsWith("Ph.D.");
	bool isDr = lastName.StartsWith("Dr.");

string ToLower()
string ToUpper()
	string severity = "warning";
	// Display the severity in uppercase
	System.Console.WriteLine(severity.ToUpper());

string Trim()
string Trim(...)
string TrimEnd()
string TrimStart()
	// Remove any whitespace at the start or end.
	username = username.Trim();

string Replace(
    string oldValue,
    string newValue)
	string filename;
	//...
	// Remove ?'s from the string
	filename = filename.Replace("?", "");;

New Line

When writing out a new line, the exact characters for the new line will depend on the operating system on which you are executing. On Microsoft Windows platforms, the new line is the combination of both the \r and \n characters, while a single \n is used on Unix. One way to overcome the discrepancy between platforms is simply to use System.Console.WriteLine () in order to output a blank line. Another approach, virtually essential when you are not outputting to the console yet still require execution on multiple platforms, is to use System.Environment.NewLine. In other words, System.Console.WriteLine("Hello World") and System.Console.Write("Hello World" + System.Environment.NewLine) are equivalent.

▪ ADVANCED TOPIC

C# Properties

Technically, the Length member referred to in the following section is not actually a method, as indicated by the fact that there are no parentheses following its call. Length is a property of string, and C# syntax allows access to a property as though it were a member variable (known in C#

as a **field**). In other words, a property has the behavior of special methods called setters and getters, but the syntax for accessing that behavior is that of a field.

Examining the underlying CIL implementation of a property reveals that it compiles into two methods: `set_<PropertyName>` and `get_<PropertyName>`. Neither of these, however, is directly accessible from C# code, except through the C# property constructs. See Chapter 5 for more detail on properties.

String Length

To determine the length of a string you use a string member called `Length`. This particular member is called a **read-only property.** As such, it can't be set, nor does calling it require any parameters. Listing 2.13 demonstrates how to use the `Length` property, and Output 2.11 shows the results.

LISTING 2.13: **Using** `string`'s `Length` **Member**

```
class PalindromeLength
{
  static void Main()
  {
    string palindrome;

    System.Console.Write("Enter a palindrome: ");
    palindrome = System.Console.ReadLine();

    System.Console.WriteLine(
        "The palindrome, \"{0}\" is {1} characters.",
        palindrome, palindrome.Length);
  }
}
```

OUTPUT 2.11

```
Enter a palindrome: Never odd or even
The palindrome, "Never odd or even" is 17 characters.
```

The length for a string cannot be set directly; it is calculated from the number of characters in the string. Furthermore, the length of a string cannot change because a string is **immutable.**

Strings Are Immutable

A key characteristic of the string type is that it is immutable. A string variable can be assigned an entirely new value but there is no facility for modifying the contents of a string. It is not possible, therefore, to convert a string to all uppercase letters. It is trivial to create a new string that is composed of an uppercase version of the old string, but the old string is not modified in the process. Consider Listing 2.14 as an example.

LISTING 2.14: **Error;** string **Is Immutable**

```
class Uppercase
{
  static void Main()
  {
      string text;

      System.Console.Write("Enter text: ");
      text = System.Console.ReadLine();

      // UNEXPECTED:  Does not convert text to uppercase
      text.ToUpper();

      System.Console.WriteLine(text);
  }
}
```

Output 2.12 shows the results of Listing 2.14.

OUTPUT 2.12

```
Enter text: This is a test of the emergency broadcast system.
This is a test of the emergency broadcast system.
```

At a glance, it would appear that text.ToUpper() should convert the characters within text to uppercase. However, strings are immutable and, therefore, text.ToUpper() will make no such modification. Instead, text.ToUpper() returns a new string that needs to be saved into a variable or passed to System.Console.WriteLine() directly. The corrected code is shown in Listing 2.15, and its output is shown in Output 2.13.

LISTING 2.15: **Working with Strings**

```
class Uppercase
{
```

```
static void Main()
{
    string text, uppercase;

    System.Console.Write("Enter text: ");
    text = System.Console.ReadLine();

    // Return a new string in uppercase
    uppercase = text.ToUpper();

    System.Console.WriteLine(uppercase);
}
}
```

OUTPUT 2.13

```
Enter text: This is a test of the emergency broadcast system.
THIS IS A TEST OF THE EMERGENCY BROADCAST SYSTEM.
```

If the immutability of a string is ignored, mistakes similar to those shown in Listing 2.14 can occur with other string methods as well.

To actually change the value in text, assign the value from ToUpper() back into text, as in the following:

```
text = text.ToUpper();
```

System.Text.StringBuilder

If considerable string modification is needed, such as when constructing a long string in multiple steps, you should use the data type System.Text.StringBuilder rather than string. The StringBuilder type includes methods such as Append(), AppendFormat(), Insert(), Remove(), and Replace(), some of which also appear on string. The key difference, however, is that on StringBuilder these methods will modify the data in the StringBuilder itself, and will not simply return a new string.

null and void

Two additional keywords relating to types are null and void. null is a value which indicates that the variable does not refer to any valid object. void is used to indicate the absence of a type or the absence of any value altogether.

null

null can also be used as a type of string "literal." null indicates that a variable is set to nothing. Reference types, pointer types, and nullable value types can be assigned the value null. The only reference type covered so far in this book is string; Chapter 5 covers the topic of creating classes (which are reference types) in detail. For now, suffice it to say that a variable of reference type contains a reference to a location in memory that is different from that of the variable. Code that sets a variable to null explicitly assigns the reference to refer to no valid value. In fact, it is even possible to check whether a reference refers to nothing. Listing 2.16 demonstrates assigning null to a string variable.

LISTING 2.16: **Assigning** null **to a String**

```csharp
static void Main()
{
    string faxNumber;
    // ...

    // Clear the value of faxNumber.
    faxNumber = null;

    // ...
}
```

It is important to note that assigning the value null to a reference type is distinct from not assigning it at all. In other words, a variable that has been assigned null has still been set, and a variable with no assignment has not been set and, therefore, will often cause a compile error if used prior to assignment.

Assigning the value null to a string is distinctly different from assigning an empty string, "". null indicates that the variable has no value. "" indicates that there is a value: an empty string. This type of distinction can be quite useful. For example, the programming logic could interpret a faxNumber of null to mean that the fax number is unknown, while a faxNumber value of "" could indicate that there is no fax number.

The void "Type"

Sometimes the C# syntax requires a data type to be specified but no data is actually passed. For example, if no return from a method is needed, C# allows the use of void to be specified as the data type instead. The declaration of Main within the HelloWorld program is an example. The use of void as the return type indicates that the method is not returning any data and tells the compiler not to expect a value. void is not a data type per se, but rather an indication that there is no data being returned.

Language Contrast: C++

In both C++ and C#, void has two meanings: as a marker that a method does not return any data, and to represent a pointer to a storage location of unknown type. In C++ programs it is quite common to see pointer types like void**. C# can also represent pointers to storage locations of unknown type using the same syntax, but this usage is comparatively rare in C# and typically only encountered when writing programs that interoperate with unmanaged code libraries.

Language Contrast: Visual Basic—Returning void Is Like Defining a Subroutine

The Visual Basic equivalent of returning a void in C# is to define a subroutine (Sub/End Sub) rather than a function that returns a value.

ADVANCED TOPIC

Implicitly Typed Local Variables

C# 3.0 added a contextual keyword, var, for declaring an **implicitly typed local variable.** As long as the code initializes a variable at declaration time with an expression of unambiguous type, C# 3.0 and later allow for the variable data type to be implied rather than stated, as shown in Listing 2.17.

LISTING 2.17: **Working with Strings**

```
class Uppercase
{
  static void Main()
  {
```

```
        System.Console.Write("Enter text: ");
        var text = System.Console.ReadLine();

        // Return a new string in uppercase
        var uppercase = text.ToUpper();

        System.Console.WriteLine(uppercase);
    }
}
```

This listing is different from Listing 2.15 in two ways. First, rather than using the explicit data type string for the declaration, Listing 2.17 uses var. The resultant CIL code is identical to using string explicitly. However, var indicates to the compiler that it should determine the data type from the value (System.Console.ReadLine()) that is assigned within the declaration.

Second, the variables text and uppercase are not declared without assignment at declaration time. To do so would result in an error at compile time. As mentioned earlier, via assignment the compiler retrieves the data type of the right-hand side expression and declares the variable accordingly, just as it would if the programmer specified the type explicitly.

Although using var rather than the explicit data type is allowed, consider avoiding such use when the data type is known—for example, use string for the declaration of text and uppercase. Not only does this make the code more understandable, but it also verifies that the data type returned by the right-hand side expression is the type expected. When using a var declared variable, the right-hand side data type should be obvious; if it isn't, using the var declaration should be avoided.

var support was added to the language in C# 3.0 to support anonymous types. Anonymous types are data types that are declared "on the fly" within a method, rather than through explicit class definitions, as shown in Listing 2.18. (See Chapter 14 for more details on anonymous types.)

LISTING 2.18: Implicit Local Variables with Anonymous Types

```
class Program
{
    static void Main()
    {
        var patent1 =
            new { Title = "Bifocals",
            YearOfPublication = "1784" };
        var patent2 =
            new { Title = "Phonograph",
            YearOfPublication = "1877" };
```

```
        System.Console.WriteLine("{0} ({1})",
            patent1.Title, patent1.YearOfPublication);
        System.Console.WriteLine("{0} ({1})",
            patent2.Title, patent1.YearOfPublication);
    }
}
```

The corresponding output is shown in Output 2.14.

OUTPUT 2.14

```
Bifocals (1784)
Phonograph (1784)
```

Listing 2.18 demonstrates the anonymous type assignment to an implicitly typed (var) local variable. This type of operation provides critical functionality with C# 3.0 support for joining (associating) data types or reducing the size of a particular type down to fewer data elements.

Categories of Types

All types fall into two categories: **value types** and **reference types.** The differences between the types in each category stem from how they are copied: Value type data is always copied by value, while reference type data is always copied by reference.

Value Types

With the exception of string, all the predefined types in the book so far have been value types. Variables of value types contain the value directly. In other words, the variable refers to the same location in memory where the value is stored. Because of this, when a different variable is assigned the same value, a copy of the original variable's value is made to the location of the new variable. A second variable of the same value type cannot refer to the same location in memory as the first variable. So changing the value of the first variable will not affect the value in the second. Figure 2.1 demonstrates this. number1 refers to a particular location in memory that contains the value 42. After assigning number1 to number2, both variables will contain the value 42. However, modifying either variable's value will not affect the other.

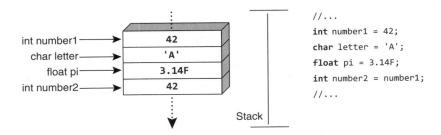

FIGURE 2.1: Value Types Contain the Data Directly

Similarly, passing a value type to a method such as `Console.WriteLine()` will also result in a memory copy, and any changes to the parameter inside the method will not affect the original value within the calling function. Since value types require a memory copy, they generally should be defined to consume a small amount of memory; value types should almost always be less than 16 bytes in size.

Reference Types

By contrast, the value of a variable of reference type is a reference to a storage location that contains data. Reference types store the reference where the data is located instead of storing the data directly, as value types do. Therefore, to access the data, the runtime will read the memory location out of the variable and then "jump" to the location in memory that contains the data. The memory area of the data a reference type points to is called the **heap** (see Figure 2.2).

A reference type does not require the same memory copy of the data that a value type does, which makes copying reference types far more efficient than copying large value types. When assigning the value of one reference type variable to another reference type variable, only the reference is copied, not the data referred to. In practice, a reference is always the same size as the "native size" of the processor: A 32-bit processor will copy a 32-bit reference and a 64-bit processor will copy a 64-bit reference, and so on. Obviously, copying the small reference to a large block of data is faster than copying the entire block, as a value type would.

Since reference types copy a reference to data, two different variables can refer to the same data. If two variables refer to the same object, changing

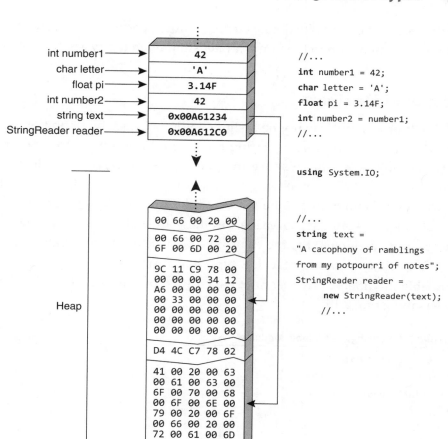

```
int number1 ─────────► ┌─────────────────┐   //...
                       │       42        │   int number1 = 42;
char letter ─────────► │      'A'        │   char letter = 'A';
float pi ────────────► │     3.14F       │   float pi = 3.14F;
int number2 ─────────► │       42        │   int number2 = number1;
string text ─────────► │   0x00A61234    │   //...
StringReader reader ─► │   0x00A612C0    │
                       └─────────────────┘
                                              using System.IO;


                       ┌─────────────────┐   //...
                       │  00 66 00 20 00 │   string text =
                       │                 │   "A cacophony of ramblings
                       │  00 66 00 72 00 │   from my potpourri of notes";
                       │  6F 00 6D 00 20 │   StringReader reader =
Heap                   │                 │        new StringReader(text);
                       │  9C 11 C9 78 00 │      //...
                       │  00 00 00 34 12 │
                       │  A6 00 00 00 00 │
                       │  00 33 00 00 00 │
                       │  00 00 00 00 00 │
                       │  00 00 00 00 00 │
                       │  00 00 00 00 00 │
                       │                 │
                       │  D4 4C C7 78 02 │
                       │                 │
                       │  41 00 20 00 63 │
                       │  00 61 00 63 00 │
                       │  6F 00 70 00 68 │
                       │  00 6F 00 6E 00 │
                       │  79 00 20 00 6F │
                       │  00 66 00 20 00 │
                       │  72 00 61 00 6D │
                       └─────────────────┘
```

FIGURE 2.2: Reference Types Point to the Heap

a field of the object through one variable causes the effect to be seen when accessing the field via another variable. This happens both for assignment and for method calls. Therefore, a method can affect the data of a reference type, and that change can be observed when control returns to the caller. For this reason, a key factor when choosing between defining a reference type or a value type is whether the object is logically like an immutable value of fixed size (and therefore possibly a value type), or logically a mutable thing that can be referred to (and therefore likely to be a reference type).

Besides `string` and any custom classes such as `Program`, all types discussed so far are value types. However, most types are reference types.

Although it is possible to define custom value types, it is relatively rare to do so in comparison to the number of custom reference types.

Nullable Modifier

Value types cannot usually be assigned null because, by definition, they can't contain references, including references to nothing. However, this presents a problem because we frequently wish to represent values that are "missing." When specifying a count, for example, what do you enter if the count is unknown? One possible solution is to designate a "magic" value, such as -1 or int.MaxValue, but these are valid integers. Rather, it is desirable to assign null to the value type because this is not a valid integer.

To declare variables of value type that can store null you use the nullable modifier, ?. This feature, which was introduced with C# 2.0, appears in Listing 2.19.

LISTING 2.19: Using the Nullable Modifier

```
static void Main()
{
  int? count = null;
  do
  {
     // ...
  }
  while(count == null);
}
```

Assigning null to value types is especially attractive in database programming. Frequently, value type columns in database tables allow nulls. Retrieving such columns and assigning them to corresponding fields within C# code is problematic, unless the fields can contain null as well. Fortunately, the nullable modifier is designed to handle such a scenario specifically.

Conversions between Data Types

Given the thousands of types predefined in the various CLI implementations and the unlimited number of types that code can define, it is important that types support conversion from one to another where it makes sense. The most common operation that results in a conversion is **casting.**

Consider the conversion between two numerical types: converting from a variable of type `long` to a variable of type `int`. A `long` type can contain values as large as 9,223,372,036,854,775,808; however, the maximum size of an `int` is 2,147,483,647. As such, that conversion could result in a loss of data—for example, if the variable of type `long` contains a value greater than the maximum size of an `int`. Any conversion that could result in a loss of magnitude or an exception because the conversion failed requires an **explicit cast.** Conversely, a conversion operation that will not lose magnitude and will not throw an exception regardless of the operand types is an **implicit conversion.**

Explicit Cast

In C#, you cast using the **cast operator.** By specifying the type you would like the variable converted to within parentheses, you acknowledge that if an explicit cast is occurring, there may be a loss of precision and data, or an exception may result. The code in Listing 2.20 converts a `long` to an `int` and explicitly tells the system to attempt the operation.

LISTING 2.20: **Explicit Cast Example**

```
long longNumber = 50918309109;
int intNumber = (int) longNumber;
                  ‿‿‿
                 cast operator
```

With the cast operator, the programmer essentially says to the compiler, "Trust me, I know what I am doing. I know that the value will fit into the target type." Making such a choice will cause the compiler to allow the conversion. However, with an explicit conversion, there is still a chance that an error, in the form of an exception, might occur while executing if the data does not convert successfully. It is, therefore, the programmer's responsibility to ensure the data will successfully convert, or else to provide the necessary error-handling code when it doesn't.

■ ADVANCED TOPIC

Checked and Unchecked Conversions

C# provides special keywords for marking a code block to indicate what should happen if the target data type is too small to contain the assigned data. By default, if the target data type cannot contain the assigned data, the data will truncate during assignment. For an example, see Listing 2.21.

LISTING 2.21: **Overflowing an Integer Value**

```
public class Program
{
  public static void Main()
  {
      // int.MaxValue equals 2147483647
      int n = int.MaxValue;
      n = n + 1 ;
      System.Console.WriteLine(n);
  }
}
```

Output 2.15 shows the results.

OUTPUT 2.15

```
-2147483648
```

Listing 2.21 writes the value -2147483648 to the console. However, placing the code within a checked block, or using the checked option when running the compiler, will cause the runtime to throw an exception of type System.OverflowException. The syntax for a checked block uses the checked keyword, as shown in Listing 2.22.

LISTING 2.22: **A Checked Block Example**

```
public class Program
{
  public static void Main()
  {
      checked
      {
          // int.MaxValue equals 2147483647
          int n = int.MaxValue;
          n = n + 1 ;
          System.Console.WriteLine(n);
```

```
        }
      }
    }
```

Output 2.16 shows the results.

OUTPUT 2.16

```
Unhandled Exception: System.OverflowException: Arithmetic operation
resulted in an overflow at Program.Main() in ...Program.cs:line 12
```

The result is that an exception is thrown if, within the checked block, an overflow assignment occurs at runtime.

The C# compiler provides a command-line option for changing the default checked behavior from unchecked to checked. C# also supports an unchecked block that overflows the data instead of throwing an exception for assignments within the block (see Listing 2.23).

LISTING 2.23: An Unchecked Block Example

```csharp
using System;

public class Program
{
  public static void Main()
  {
      unchecked
      {
          // int.MaxValue equals 2147483647
          int n = int.MaxValue;
          n = n + 1 ;
          System.Console.WriteLine(n);
      }
  }
}
```

Output 2.17 shows the results.

OUTPUT 2.17

```
-2147483648
```

Even if the checked option is on during compilation, the unchecked keyword in the preceding code will prevent the runtime from throwing an exception during execution.

You cannot convert any type to any other type simply because you designate the conversion explicitly using the cast operator. The compiler will still check that the operation is valid. For example, you cannot convert a `long` to a `bool`. No such conversion is defined, and therefore, the compiler does not allow such a cast.

Language Contrast: Converting Numbers to Booleans

It may be surprising that there is no valid cast from a numeric type to a Boolean type, since this is common in many other languages. The reason no such conversion exists in C# is to avoid any ambiguity, such as whether −1 corresponds to true or false. More importantly, as you will see in the next chapter, this also reduces the chance of using the assignment operator in place of the equality operator (avoiding `if(x=42){...}` when `if(x==42){...}` was intended, for example).

Implicit Conversion

In other instances, such as going from an `int` type to a `long` type, there is no loss of precision and there will be no fundamental change in the value of the type. In these cases, code needs only to specify the assignment operator and the conversion is **implicit.** In other words, the compiler is able to determine that such a conversion will work correctly. The code in Listing 2.24 converts from an `int` to a `long` by simply using the assignment operator.

LISTING 2.24: Not Using the Cast Operator for an Implicit Cast

```
int intNumber = 31416;
long longNumber = intNumber;
```

Even when no explicit cast operator is required (because an implicit conversion is allowed), it is still possible to include the cast operator (see Listing 2.25).

LISTING 2.25: Using the Cast Operator for an Implicit Cast

```
int intNumber = 31416;
long longNumber = (long) intNumber;
```

Type Conversion without Casting

No conversion is defined from a string to a numeric type, so methods such as `Parse()` are required. Each numeric data type includes a `Parse()` function that enables conversion from a string to the corresponding numeric type. Listing 2.26 demonstrates this call.

LISTING 2.26: Using `int.Parse()` to Convert a `string` to a Numeric Data Type

```
string text = "9.11E-31";
float kgElectronMass = float.Parse(text);
```

Another special type is available for converting one type to the next. The type is `System.Convert` and an example of its use appears in Listing 2.27.

LISTING 2.27: Type Conversion Using `System.Convert`

```
string middleCText = "261.626";
double middleC = System.Convert.ToDouble(middleCText);
bool boolean = System.Convert.ToBoolean(middleC);
```

`System.Convert` supports only a predefined number of types and it is not extensible. It allows conversion from any primitive type (`bool`, `char`, `sbyte`, `short`, `int`, `long`, `ushort`, `uint`, `ulong`, `float`, `double`, `decimal`, `DateTime`, and `string`) to any other primitive type.

Furthermore, all types support a `ToString()` method that can be used to provide a string representation of a type. Listing 2.28 demonstrates how to use this method. The resultant output is shown in Output 2.18.

LISTING 2.28: Using `ToString()` to Convert to a `string`

```
bool boolean = true;
string text = boolean.ToString();
// Display "True"
System.Console.WriteLine(text);
```

OUTPUT 2.18

```
True
```

For the majority of types, the `ToString()` method will return the name of the data type rather than a string representation of the data. The string representation is returned only if the type has an explicit implementation of

ToString(). One last point to make is that it is possible to code custom conversion methods, and many such methods are available for classes in the runtime.

■ ADVANCED TOPIC

TryParse()

Starting with C# 2.0 (.NET 2.0), all the numeric primitive types include a static TryParse() method. This method is very similar to the Parse() method, except that instead of throwing an exception if the conversion fails, the TryParse() method returns false, as demonstrated in Listing 2.29.

LISTING 2.29: Using TryParse() in Place of an Invalid Cast Exception

```csharp
double number;
string input;

System.Console.Write("Enter a number: ");
input = System.Console.ReadLine();
if (double.TryParse(input, out number))
{
    // Converted correctly, now use number
    // ...
}
else
{
    System.Console.WriteLine(
        "The text entered was not a valid number.");
}
```

Output 2.19 shows the results of Listing 2.27.

OUTPUT 2.19

```
Enter a number: forty-two
The text entered was not a valid number.
```

The resultant value the code parses from the input string is returned via an out parameter—in this case, number.

The key difference between Parse() and TryParse() is the fact that TryParse() won't throw an exception if it fails. Frequently, the conversion from a string to a numeric type depends on a user entering the text. It is expected, in such scenarios, that the user will enter invalid data that will not parse successfully. By using `TryParse()` rather than `Parse()`, you can avoid throwing exceptions in expected situations. (The expected situation in this case is that the user will enter invalid data and we try to avoid throwing exceptions for expected scenarios.)

Arrays

One particular aspect of variable declaration that Chapter 1 didn't cover is array declaration. With array declaration, you can store multiple items of the same type using a single variable and still access them individually using the index when required. In C#, the array index starts at zero. Therefore, arrays in C# are zero-based.

■ BEGINNER TOPIC

Arrays

Arrays provide a means of declaring a collection of data items that are of the same type using a single variable. Each item within the array is uniquely designated using an integer value called the **index.** The first item in a C# array is accessed using index 0. Programmers should be careful to specify an index value that is less than the array size. Since C# arrays are zero-based, the index for the last element in an array is one less than the total number of items in the array.

For beginners, it is helpful sometimes to think of the index as an offset. The first item is zero away from the start of the array. The second item is one away from the start of the array—and so on.

Arrays are a fundamental part of nearly every programming language, so they are required learning for virtually all developers. Though arrays are frequently used in C# programming, and necessary for the beginner to understand, most programs now use generic collection types rather than arrays when storing collections of data. Therefore, readers should skim over the following section, Declaring an Array, simply to become familiar with their instantiation and assignment rather. Table 2.7 provides the highlights of what to note. Generic collections will be covered in detail in Chapter 14.

TABLE 2.7 **Array Highlights**

Description	Example
Declaration Note that the brackets appear with the data type. Multidimensional arrays are declared using commas where the comma+1 specifies the number of dimensions.	```csharp\nstring[] languages; // one dimensional\nint[,] cells; // two dimensional\n```
Assignment The new keyword and the corresponding data type are optional at declaration time. Following declaration, the new keyword is required when instantiating an array. Arrays can be assigned without literal values. As a result, the value of each item in the array is initialized to its default. If no literal values are provided, the size of the array must be specified. (The size does not have to be a constant; it can be a variable calculated at runtime.) Starting with C# 3.0, specifying the data type is optional.	```csharp\nstring[] languages = { "C#", "COBOL", "Java",\n "C++", "Visual Basic", "Pascal",\n "Fortran", "Lisp", "J#"};\nlanguages = new string[9];\nlanguages = new string[]{"C#", "COBOL", "Java",\n "C++", "Visual Basic", "Pascal",\n "Fortran", "Lisp", "J#" };\n\n// Multidimensional array assignment\n// and initialization.\nint[,] cells = int[3,3];\ncells = {\n {1, 0, 2},\n {1, 2, 0},\n {1, 2, 1}\n};\n```
default *Keyword* The explicit default of any data type is available using the default operator.	```csharp\nint count = default(int);\n```
Accessing an Array Arrays are 0-based, so the first element in an array is at index 0. The square brackets are used to store and retrieve data from an array.	```csharp\nstring[] languages = new string[9]{\n "C#", "COBOL", "Java",\n "C++", "Visual Basic", "Pascal",\n "Fortran", "Lisp", "J#"};\n// Save "C++" to variable called Language.\nstring language = languages[3];\n// Assign "Java" to the C++ position.\nlanguages[3] = languages[2];\n// Assign language to location of "Java".\nlanguages[2] = language;\n```

In addition, the final section of the chapter, Common Array Errors, provides a review of some of the array idiosyncrasies.

Declaring an Array

In C#, you declare arrays using square brackets. First, you specify the element type of the array, followed by open and closed square brackets; then you enter the name of the variable. Listing 2.30 declares a variable called `languages` to be an array of strings.

LISTING 2.30: Declaring an Array

```
string[] languages;
```

Obviously, the first part of the array identifies the data type of the elements within the array. The square brackets that are part of the declaration identify the **rank,** or the number of dimensions, for the array; in this case, it is an array of rank one. These two pieces form the data type for the variable `languages`.

Language Contrast: C++ and Java—Array Declaration

The square brackets for an array in C# appear immediately following the data type instead of after the variable declaration. This keeps all the type information together instead of splitting it up both before and after the identifier, as occurs in C++ and Java.

Listing 2.30 defines an array with a rank of one. Commas within the square brackets define additional dimensions. Listing 2.31, for example, defines a two-dimensional array of cells for a game of chess or tic-tac-toe.

LISTING 2.31: Declaring a Two-Dimensional Array

```
//    |   |
// ---+---+---
//    |   |
// ---+---+---
//    |   |
int[,] cells;
```

In Listing 2.31, the array has a rank of two. The first dimension could correspond to cells going across and the second dimension represents cells going down. Additional dimensions are added, with additional commas, and the total rank is one more than the number of commas. Note that the number of items that occur for a particular dimension is not part of the variable declaration. This is specified when creating (instantiating) the array and allocating space for each element.

Instantiating and Assigning Arrays

Once an array is declared, you can immediately fill its values using a comma-delimited list of items enclosed within a pair of curly braces. Listing 2.32 declares an array of strings and then assigns the names of nine languages within curly braces.

LISTING 2.32: Array Declaration with Assignment

```
string[] languages = { "C#", "COBOL", "Java",
    "C++", "Visual Basic", "Pascal",
    "Fortran", "Lisp", "J#"};
```

The first item in the comma-delimited list becomes the first item in the array; the second item in the list becomes the second item in the array, and so on. The curly brackets are the notation for defining an array literal.

The assignment syntax shown in Listing 2.32 is available only if you declare and assign the value within one statement. To assign the value after declaration requires the use of the keyword new as shown in Listing 2.33.

LISTING 2.33: Array Assignment Following Declaration

```
string[] languages;
languages = new string[]{"C#", "COBOL", "Java",
    "C++", "Visual Basic", "Pascal",
    "Fortran", "Lisp", "J#" };
```

Starting in C# 3.0, specifying the data type of the array (string) following new is optional as long as the compiler is able to deduce the element type of the array from the types of the elements in the array initializer. The square brackets are still required.

C# also allows use of the new keyword as part of the declaration statement, so it allows the assignment and the declaration shown in Listing 2.34.

LISTING 2.34: Array Assignment with new during Declaration

```
string[] languages = new string[]{
    "C#", "COBOL", "Java",
    "C++", "Visual Basic", "Pascal",
    "Fortran", "Lisp", "J#"};
```

The use of the new keyword tells the runtime to allocate memory for the data type. It instructs the runtime to instantiate the data type—in this case, an array.

Whenever you use the new keyword as part of an array assignment, you may also specify the size of the array within the square brackets. Listing 2.35 demonstrates this syntax.

LISTING 2.35: Declaration and Assignment with the new Keyword

```
string[] languages = new string[9]{
    "C#", "COBOL", "Java",
    "C++", "Visual Basic", "Pascal",
    "Fortran", "Lisp", "J#"};
```

The array size in the initialization statement and the number of elements contained within the curly braces must match. Furthermore, it is possible to assign an array but not specify the initial values of the array, as demonstrated in Listing 2.36.

LISTING 2.36: Assigning without Literal Values

```
string[] languages = new string[9];
```

Assigning an array but not initializing the initial values will still initialize each element. The runtime initializes elements to their default values, as follows.

- Reference types (such as string) are initialized to null.
- Numeric types are initialized to zero.
- bool is initialized to false.
- char is initialized to \0.

Nonprimitive value types are recursively initialized by initializing each of their fields to their default values. As a result, it is not necessary to individually assign each element of an array before using it.

In C# 2.0, it is possible to use the default() operator to produce the default value of a data type. default() takes a data type as a parameter. default(int), for example, produces 0 and default(bool) produces false.

Because the array size is not included as part of the variable declaration, it is possible to specify the size at runtime. For example, Listing 2.37 creates an array based on the size specified in the `Console.ReadLine()` call.

LISTING 2.37: **Defining the Array Size at Runtime**

```
string[] groceryList;
System.Console.Write("How many items on the list? ");
int size = int.Parse(System.Console.ReadLine());
groceryList = new string[size];
// ...
```

C# initializes multidimensional arrays similarly. A comma separates the size of each rank. Listing 2.38 initializes a tic-tac-toe board with no moves.

LISTING 2.38: **Declaring a Two-Dimensional Array**

```
int[,] cells = int[3,3];
```

Initializing a tic-tac-toe board with a specific position instead could be done as shown in Listing 2.39.

LISTING 2.39: **Initializing a Two-Dimensional Array of Integers**

```
int[,] cells = {
        {1, 0, 2},
        {1, 2, 0},
        {1, 2, 1}
    };
```

The initialization follows the pattern in which there is an array of three elements of type `int[]`, and each element has the same size; in this example, the size is 3. Note that the sizes of each `int[]` element must all be identical. The declaration shown in Listing 2.40, therefore, is not valid.

LISTING 2.40: **A Multidimensional Array with Inconsistent Size, Causing an Error**

```
// ERROR:  Each dimension must be consistently sized.
int[,] cells = {
        {1, 0, 2, 0},
        {1, 2, 0},
        {1, 2}
        {1}
    };
```

Representing tic-tac-toe does not require an integer in each position. One alternative is a separate virtual board for each player, and with each board containing a `bool` that indicates which positions the players selected. Listing 2.41 corresponds to a three-dimensional board.

LISTING 2.41: Initializing a Three-Dimensional Array

```
bool[,,] cells;
cells = new bool[2,3,3]
  {
      // Player 1 moves              // X |   |
      {   {true, false, false},      // ---+---+---
          {true, false, false},      // X |   |
          {true, false, true} },     // ---+---+---
                                      // X |   | X

      // Player 2 moves              //   |   | O
      {   {false, false, true},      // ---+---+---
          {false, true, false},      //   | O |
          {false, true, true} }      // ---+---+---
                                      //   | O |
  };
```

In this example, the board is initialized and the size of each rank is explicitly identified. In addition to identifying the size as part of the new expression, the literal values for the array are provided. The literal values of type `bool[,,]` are broken into two arrays of type `bool[,]`, size 3x3. Each two-dimensional array is composed of three `bool` arrays, size 3.

As already mentioned, each dimension in a multidimensional array must be consistently sized. However, it is also possible to define a **jagged array,** which is an array of arrays. Jagged array syntax is slightly different from that of a multidimensional array, and furthermore, jagged arrays do not need to be consistently sized. Therefore, it is possible to initialize a jagged array as shown in Listing 2.42.

LISTING 2.42: Initializing a Jagged Array

```
int[][] cells = {
    new int[]{1, 0, 2, 0},
    new int[]{1, 2, 0},
    new int[]{1, 2},
    new int[]{1}
};
```

A jagged array doesn't use a comma to identify a new dimension. Rather, a jagged array defines an array of arrays. In Listing 2.42, `[]` is placed after the data type `int[]`, thereby declaring an array of type `int[]`.

Notice that a jagged array requires an array instance (or null) for each internal array. In this example, you use new to instantiate the internal element of the jagged arrays. Leaving out the instantiation would cause a compile error.

Using an Array

You access a specific item in an array using the square bracket notation, known as the **array accessor.** To retrieve the first item from an array, you specify zero as the index. In Listing 2.43, the value of the fifth item (using the index 4 because the first item is index 0) in the languages variable is stored in the variable language.

LISTING 2.43: **Declaring and Accessing an Array**

```
string[] languages = new string[9]{
    "C#", "COBOL", "Java",
    "C++", "Visual Basic", "Pascal",
    "Fortran", "Lisp", "J#"};
// Retrieve 3rd item in languages array (Java)
string language = languages[4];
```

The square bracket notation is also used to store data into an array. Listing 2.44 switches the order of "C++" and "Java".

LISTING 2.44: **Swapping Data between Positions in an Array**

```
string[] languages = new string[9]{
    "C#", "COBOL", "Java",
    "C++", "Visual Basic", "Pascal",
    "Fortran", "Lisp", "J#"};
// Save "C++" to variable called language.
string language = languages[3];
// Assign "Java" to the C++ position.
languages[3] = languages[2];
// Assign language to location of "Java".
languages[2] = language;
```

For multidimensional arrays, an element is identified with an index for each dimension, as shown in Listing 2.45.

LISTING 2.45: **Initializing a Two-Dimensional Array of Integers**

```
int[,] cells = {
        {1, 0, 2},
        {0, 2, 0},
```

```
        {1, 2, 1}
    };
    // Set the winning tic-tac-toe move to be player 1.
    cells[1,0] = 1;
```

Jagged array element assignment is slightly different because it is consistent with the jagged array declaration. The first element is an array within the array of arrays. The second index specifies the item within the selected array element (see Listing 2.46).

LISTING 2.46: Declaring a Jagged Array

```
int[][] cells = {
    new int[]{1, 0, 2},
  new int[]{0, 2, 0},
  new int[]{1, 2, 1}
};

cells[1][0] = 1;
// ...
```

Length

You can obtain the length of an array, as shown in Listing 2.47.

LISTING 2.47: Retrieving the Length of an Array

```
Console.WriteLine("There are {0} languages in the array.",
    languages.Length);
```

Arrays have a fixed length; they are bound such that the length cannot be changed without re-creating the array. Furthermore, overstepping the **bounds** (or length) of the array will cause the runtime to report an error. This can occur by accessing (either retrieving or assigning) the array with an index for which no element exists in the array. Such an error frequently occurs when you use the array length as an index into the array, as shown in Listing 2.48.

LISTING 2.48: Accessing Outside the Bounds of an Array, Throwing an Exception

```
string languages = new string[9];
...
// RUNTIME ERROR: index out of bounds - should
// be 8 for the last element
languages[4] = languages[9];
```

■ **NOTE**

The Length member returns the number of items in the array, not the highest index. The Length member for the languages variable is 9, but the highest index for the languages variable is 8, because that is how far it is from the start.

Language Contrast: C++—Buffer Overflow Bugs

Unmanaged C++ does not always check whether you overstep the bounds on an array. Not only can this be difficult to debug, but making this mistake can also result in a potential security error called a **buffer overrun.** In contrast, the Common Language Runtime protects all C# (and Managed C++) code from overstepping array bounds, virtually eliminating the possibility of a buffer overrun issue in managed code.

It is a good practice to use Length in place of the hardcoded array size. To use Length as an index, for example, it is necessary to subtract 1 to avoid an out-of-bounds error (see Listing 2.49).

LISTING 2.49: Using Length - 1 in the Array Index

```
string languages = new string[9];
...
languages[4] = languages[languages.Length - 1];
```

To avoid overstepping the bounds on an array use a length check to verify it has a length greater than 0 as well as using Length – 1 in place of a hardcoded value when accessing the last item in the array (see Listing 2.49).

Length returns the total number of elements in an array. Therefore, if you had a multidimensional array such as bool cells[,,] of size 2·3·3, Length would return the total number of elements, 18.

For a jagged array, Length returns the number of elements in the first array—a jagged array is an array of arrays, so Length evaluates only the outside, containing array and returns its element count, regardless of what is inside the internal arrays.

More Array Methods

Arrays include additional methods for manipulating the elements within the array. These include Sort(), BinarySearch(), Reverse(), and Clear() (see Listing 2.50).

LISTING 2.50: Additional Array Methods

```csharp
class ProgrammingLanguages
{
  static void Main()
  {
      string[] languages = new string[]{
          "C#", "COBOL", "Java",
          "C++", "Visual Basic", "Pascal",
          "Fortran", "Lisp", "J#"};

      System.Array.Sort(languages);

      string searchString = "COBOL";
      int index = System.Array.BinarySearch(
          languages, searchString);
      System.Console.WriteLine(
          "The wave of the future, {0}, is at index {1}.",
          searchString, index);

      System.Console.WriteLine();
      System.Console.WriteLine("{0,-20}\t{1,-20}",
          "First Element", "Last Element");
      System.Console.WriteLine("{0,-20}\t{1,-20}",
          "-------------", "------------");
      System.Console.WriteLine("{0,-20}\t{1,-20}",
          languages[0], languages[languages.Length-1]);

      System.Array.Reverse(languages);
      System.Console.WriteLine("{0,-20}\t{1,-20}",
          languages[0], languages[languages.Length-1]);

      // Note this does not remove all items from the array.
      // Rather it sets each item to the type's default value.
      System.Array.Clear(languages, 0, languages.Length);
      System.Console.WriteLine("{0,-20}\t{1,-20}",
          languages[0], languages[languages.Length-1]);
      System.Console.WriteLine(
          "After clearing, the array size is: {0}",
          languages.Length);
  }
}
```

The results of Listing 2.50 are shown in Output 2.20.

OUTPUT 2.20

```
The wave of the future, COBOL, is at index 1.

First Element           Last Element
-------------           ------------
C#                      Visual Basic
Visual Basic            C#

After clearing, the array size is: 9
```

Access to these methods is on the `System.Array` class. For the most part, using these methods is self-explanatory, except for two noteworthy items.

- Before using the `BinarySearch()` method, it is important to sort the array. If values are not sorted in increasing order, the incorrect index may be returned. If the search element does not exist, the value returned is negative. (Using the complement operator, `~index`, returns the first index, if any, that is larger than the searched value.)

- The `Clear()` method does not remove elements of the array and does not set the length to zero. The array size is fixed and cannot be modified. Therefore, the `Clear()` method sets each element in the array to its default value (`false`, `0`, or `null`). This explains why `Console.WriteLine()` creates a blank line when writing out the array after `Clear()` is called.

Language Contrast: Visual Basic—Redimensioning Arrays

Visual Basic includes a `Redim` statement for changing the number of items in an array. Although there is no equivalent C# specific keyword, there is a method available in .NET 2.0 that will re-create the array and then copy all the elements over to the new array. The method is called `System.Array.Resize`.

Array Instance Methods

Like strings, arrays have instance members that are accessed not from the data type, but directly from the variable. `Length` is an example of an instance member because access to Length is through the array variable, not the class. Other significant instance members are GetLength(), Rank, and Clone().

Retrieving the length of a particular dimension does not require the Length property. To retrieve the size of a particular rank, an array includes a GetLength() instance method. When calling this method, it is necessary to specify the rank whose length will be returned (see Listing 2.51).

LISTING 2.51: Retrieving a Particular Dimension's Size

```
bool[,,] cells;
cells = new bool[2,3,3];
System.Console.WriteLine(cells.GetLength(0));    // Displays 2
```

The results of Listing 2.51 appear in Output 2.21.

OUTPUT 2.21

```
2
```

Listing 2.51 displays 2 because this is the number of elements in the first dimension.

It is also possible to retrieve the entire array's rank by accessing the array's Rank member. cells.Rank, for example, will return 3.

By default, assigning one array variable to another copies only the array reference, not the individual elements of the array. To make an entirely new copy of the array, use the array's Clone() method. The Clone() method will return a copy of the array; changing any of the members of this new array will not affect the members of the original array.

Strings As Arrays

Variables of type string are accessible like an array of characters. For example, to retrieve the fourth character of a string called palindrome you can call palindrome[3]. Note, however, that because strings are immutable, it is not possible to assign particular characters within a string. C#, therefore, would not allow palindrome[3]='a', where palindrome is declared as a string. Listing 2.52 uses the array accessor to determine whether an argument on the command line is an option, where an option is identified by a dash as the first character.

LISTING 2.52: **Looking for Command-Line Options**

```
string[] args;
...
if(args[0][0]=='-')
{
    //This parameter is an option
}
```

This snippet uses the `if` statement, which is covered in Chapter 3. In addition, it presents an interesting example because you use the array accessor to retrieve the first element in the array of strings, `args`. Following the first array accessor is a second one, this time to retrieve the first character of the string. The code, therefore, is equivalent to that shown in Listing 2.53.

LISTING 2.53: **Looking for Command-Line Options (Simplified)**

```
string[] args;
...
string arg = args[0];
if(arg[0] == '-')
{
    //This parameter is an option
}
```

Not only can string characters be accessed individually using the array accessor, but it is also possible to retrieve the entire string as an array of characters using the string's `ToCharArray()` method. Using this method, you could reverse the string using the `System.Array.Reverse()` method, as demonstrated in Listing 2.54, which determines whether a string is a palindrome.

LISTING 2.54: **Reversing a String**

```
class Palindrome
{
  static void Main()
  {
      string reverse, palindrome;
      char[] temp;

      System.Console.Write("Enter a palindrome: ");
      palindrome = System.Console.ReadLine();

      // Remove spaces and convert to lowercase
      reverse = palindrome.Replace(" ", "");
```

```
        reverse = reverse.ToLower();

        // Convert to an array
        temp = reverse.ToCharArray();

        // Reverse the array
        System.Array.Reverse(temp);

        // Convert the array back to a string and
        // check if reverse string is the same.
        if(reverse == new string(temp))
        {
            System.Console.WriteLine("\"{0}\" is a palindrome.",
                palindrome);
        }
        else
        {
            System.Console.WriteLine(
                "\"{0}\" is NOT a palindrome.",
                palindrome);
        }
    }
}
```

The results of Listing 2.54 appear in Output 2.22.

OUTPUT 2.22

```
Enter a palindrome: NeverOddOrEven
"NeverOddOrEven" is a palindrome.
```

This example uses the new keyword; this time, it creates a new string from the reversed array of characters.

Common Array Errors

This section introduced the three different types of arrays: single-dimension, multidimensional, and jagged arrays. Several rules and idiosyncrasies govern array declaration and use. Table 2.8 points out some of the most common errors and helps solidify the rules. Readers should consider reviewing the code in the Common Mistake column first (without looking at the Error Description and Corrected Code columns) as a way of verifying their understanding of arrays and their syntax.

TABLE 2.8: Common Array Coding Errors

Common Mistake	Error Description	Corrected Code
`int numbers[];`	The square braces for declaring an array appear after the data type, not after the variable identifier.	`int[] numbers;`
`int[] numbers; numbers = {42, 84, 168 };`	When assigning an array after declaration, it is necessary to use the new keyword and then specify the data type.	`int[] numbers; numbers = new int[]{ 42, 84, 168 }`
`int[3] numbers = { 42, 84, 168 };`	It is not possible to specify the array size as part of the variable declaration.	`int[] numbers = { 42, 84, 168 };`
`int[] numbers = new int[];`	The array size is required at initialization time unless an array literal is provided.	`int[] numbers = new int[3];`
`int[] numbers = new int[3]{}`	The array size is specified as 3, but there are no elements in the array literal. The array size must match the number of elements in the array literal.	`int[] numbers = new int[3]{ 42, 84, 168 };`
`int[] numbers = new int[3]; Console.WriteLine( numbers[3]);`	Array indexes start at zero. Therefore, the last item is one less than the array size. (Note that this is a runtime error, not a compile-time error.)	`int[] numbers = new int[3]; Console.WriteLine( numbers[2]);`
`int[] numbers = new int[3]; numbers[numbers.Length] = 42;`	Same as previous error: 1 needs to be subtracted from the Length to access the last element. (Note that this is a runtime error, not a compile-time error.)	`int[] numbers = new int[3]; numbers[numbers.Length-1] = 42;`
`int[] numbers; Console.WriteLine( numbers[0]);`	numbers has not yet been assigned an instantiated array, and therefore, it cannot be accessed.	`int[] numbers = {42, 84}; Console.WriteLine( numbers[0]);`
`int[,] numbers = { {42}, {84, 42} };`	Multidimensional arrays must be structured consistently.	`int[,] numbers = { {42, 168}, {84, 42} };`
`int[][] numbers = { {42, 84}, {84, 42} };`	Jagged arrays require instantiated arrays to be specified for the arrays within the array.	`int[][] numbers = { new int[]{42, 84}, new int[]{84, 42} };`

SUMMARY

Even for experienced programmers, C# introduces several new programming constructs. For example, as part of the section on data types, this chapter covered the type `decimal` that can be used accurately for financial calculations. In addition, the chapter introduced the fact that the Boolean type, `bool`, does not convert implicitly to or from an integer, thereby preventing the mistaken use of the assignment operator in a conditional expression. Other unique characteristics of C# from many of its predecessors are the @ verbatim string qualifier that forces a string to ignore the escape character and the fact that the `string` data type is immutable.

C# permits both implicit and explicit conversions (that is, conversions that require a cast operation) to convert expressions to a given data type. In the following chapters, you will learn how to define customized conversion operators on your own types.

This chapter closed with coverage of C# syntax for arrays, along with the various means of manipulating arrays. For many developers, the syntax can become rather daunting at first, so the section included a list of the common errors associated with coding arrays.

The next chapter looks at expressions and control flow statements. The `if` statement, which appeared a few times toward the end of this chapter, is discussed as well.

3

Operators and Control Flow

IN THIS CHAPTER, YOU WILL learn about operators, control flow statements, and the C# preprocessor. **Operators** provide syntax for performing different calculations or actions appropriate for the operands within the calculation. **Control flow statements** provide the means for conditional logic within a program or looping over a section of code multiple times. After introducing the `if` control flow statement, the chapter looks at the concept of Boolean expressions, which are embedded within many control flow statements. Included is mention of how integers will not cast (even

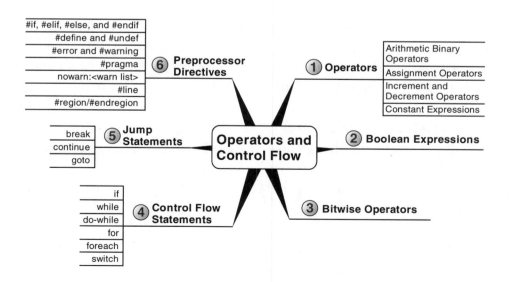

explicitly) to bool and the advantages of this restriction. The chapter ends with a discussion of the C# preprocessor directives.

Operators

Now that you have been introduced to the predefined data types (refer to Chapter 2), you can begin to learn more about how to use these data types in combination with operators in order to perform calculations. For example, you can make calculations on variables that you have declared.

■ BEGINNER TOPIC

Operators

Operators are used to perform mathematical or logical operations on values (or variables) called **operands** to produce a new value, called the **result.** For example, in Listing 3.1 the subtraction operator, -, is used to subtract two operands, the numbers 4 and 2. The result of the subtraction is stored in the variable `difference`.

LISTING 3.1: A Simple Operator Example

```
int difference = 4 - 2;
```

Operators are generally broken down into three categories: unary, binary, and ternary, corresponding to the number of operands 1, 2, and 3, respectively. This section covers some of the most basic unary and binary operators. Introduction to the ternary operator appears later in the chapter.

Plus and Minus Unary Operators (+, -)

Sometimes you may want to change the sign of a numerical value. In these cases, the unary minus operator (-) comes in handy. For example, Listing 3.2 changes the total current U.S. debt to a negative value to indicate that it is an amount owed.

LISTING 3.2: Specifying Negative Values[1]

```
//National Debt to the Penny
decimal debt = -15236332233848.35M;
```

Using the minus operator *is equivalent to subtracting the operand from zero.*

The unary plus operator (+) rarely[2] has any effect on a value. It is a superfluous addition to the C# language and was included for the sake of symmetry.

Arithmetic Binary Operators (+, -, *, /, %)

Binary operators require two operands. C# uses infix notation for binary operators: The operator appears between the left and right operands. The result of every binary operator other than assignment must be used somehow: for example, by using it as an operand in another expression such as an assignment.

Language Contrast: C++—Operator-Only Statements

In contrast to the rule mentioned above, C++ will allow a single binary expression to form the entirety of a statement, such as 4+5;, to compile. In C#, only call, increment, decrement, and object creation expressions are allowed to be the entirety of a statement.

The subtraction example in Listing 3.3 is an example of a binary operator—more specifically, an arithmetic binary operator. The operands appear on each side of the arithmetic operator and then the calculated value is assigned. The other arithmetic binary operators are addition (+), division (/), multiplication (*), and remainder (%)—sometimes called the mod operator.

LISTING 3.3: Using Binary Operators

```
class Division
{
  static void Main()
```

---

1. As of January 12, 2012, according to www.treasurydirect.gov.
2. The unary + operator is defined to take operands of type int, uint, long, ulong, float, double, and decimal (and nullable versions of those types). Using it on other numeric types such as short will convert its operand to one of these types as appropriate.

```
{
    int numerator;
    int denominator;
    int quotient;
    int remainder;

    System.Console.Write("Enter the numerator: ");
    numerator = int.Parse(System.Console.ReadLine());

    System.Console.Write("Enter the denominator: ");
    denominator = int.Parse(System.Console.ReadLine());

    quotient = numerator / denominator;
    remainder = numerator % denominator;

    System.Console.WriteLine(
        "{0} / {1} = {2} with remainder {3}",
        numerator, denominator, quotient, remainder);
}
}
```

Output 3.1 shows the results of Listing 3.3.

OUTPUT 3.1

```
Enter the numerator: 23
Enter the denominator: 3
23 / 3 = 7 with remainder 2
```

In the highlighted assignment statements above, the division and re-mainder operations are executed before the assignments. The order in which operators are executed is determined by their **precedence** and **associativity.** The precedence for the operators used so far is as follows.

1. *, /, and % have highest precedence.
2. + and - have lower precedence.
3. = has the lowest precedence of these six operators.

Therefore, you can assume that the statement behaves as expected, with the division and remainder operators executing before the assignment.

If you forget to assign the result of one of these binary operators, you will receive the compile error shown in Output 3.2.

OUTPUT 3.2

```
... error CS0201: Only assignment, call, increment, decrement,
and new object expressions can be used as a statement
```

■ **BEGINNER TOPIC**

Parentheses, Associativity, Precedence, and Evaluation

When an expression contains multiple operators it can be unclear what precisely the operands of each operator are. For example, in the expression x+y*z clearly the expression x is an operand of the addition and z is an operand of the multiplication. But is y an operand of the addition or the multiplication?

Parentheses allow you to unambiguously associate an operand with its operator. If you wish y to be a summand, you can write the expression as (x+y)*z; if you want it to be a multiplicand, you can write x+(y*z).

However, C# does not require you to parenthesize every expression containing more than one operator; instead, the compiler can use associativity and precedence to figure out from the context what parentheses you have omitted. **Associativity** determines how similar operators are parenthesized; **precedence** determines how dissimilar operators are parenthesized.

A binary operator may be "left-associative" or "right-associative," depending on whether the expression "in the middle" belongs to the operator on the left or the right. For example, a-b-c is assumed to mean (a-b)-c, and not a-(b-c); subtraction is therefore said to be "left-associative." Most operators in C# are left-associative; the assignment operators are right-associative.

When the operators are dissimilar, the **precedence** for those operators is used to determine which side the operand in the middle belongs to. For example, multiplication has higher precedence than addition, and therefore, the expression x+y*z is evaluated as x+(y*z) rather than (x+y)*z.

It is often still a good practice to use parentheses to make the code more readable even when use of parentheses does not change the meaning of the expression. For example, when performing a Celsius-to-Fahrenheit temperature conversion, (c*9.0/5.0)+32.0 is easier to read than c*9.0/5.0+32.0, even though the parentheses are completely unnecessary.

Guidelines

DO use parentheses to make code more readable, particularly if the operator precedence is not clear to the casual reader.

Clearly, operators of higher precedence must execute before adjoining operators of lower precedence: in x+y*z the multiplication must be executed before the addition because the result of the multiplication is the left-hand operand of the addition. However, it is important to realize that precedence and associativity affect only the order in which the *operators* themselves are executed; they do not in any way affect the order in which the *operands* are evaluated.

Operands are always evaluated left-to-right in C#. In an expression with three method calls such as A()+B()*C(), first A() is evaluated, then B(), then C(), then the multiplication operator determines the product, and then the addition operator determines the sum. Just because C() is involved in a multiplication and A() is involved in a lower-precedence addition does not imply that method invocation C() happens before method invocation A().

Language Contrast: C++: Evaluation Order of Operands

In contrast to the rule mentioned above, the C++ specification allows an implementation broad latitude to decide the evaluation order of operands. When given an expression such as A()+B()*C(), a C++ compiler can choose to evaluate the function calls in any order, just so long as the product is one of the summands. For example, a legal compiler could evaluate B(), then A(), then C(), then the product, and then the sum.

Using the Addition Operator with Strings

Operators can also work with non-numeric operands. For example, it is possible to use the addition operator to concatenate two or more strings, as shown in Listing 3.4.

LISTING 3.4: **Using Binary Operators with Non-Numeric Types**

```
class FortyTwo
{
  static void Main()
  {
    short windSpeed = 42;
    System.Console.WriteLine(
        "The original Tacoma Bridge in Washington\nwas "
        + "brought down by a "
        + windSpeed + " mile/hour wind.");
  }
}
```

Output 3.3 shows the results of Listing 3.4.

OUTPUT 3.3

```
The original Tacoma Bridge in Washington
was brought down by a 42 mile/hour wind.
```

Because sentence structure varies among languages in different cultures, developers should be careful not to use the addition operator with strings that require localization. Composite formatting is preferred (refer to Chapter 1).

Guidelines

DO favor composite formatting over the addition operator for concatenating strings.

Using Characters in Arithmetic Operations

When introducing the char type in the preceding chapter, we mentioned that even though it stores characters and not numbers, the char type is an **integral** type ("integral" means it is based on an integer). It can participate in arithmetic operations with other integer types. However, interpretation of the value of the char type is not based on the character stored within it, but rather on its underlying value. The digit 3, for example, contains a Unicode value of 0x33 (hexadecimal), which in base 10 is 51. The digit 4, on the other hand, contains a Unicode value of 0x34, or 52 in base 10. Adding 3 and 4 in Listing 3.5 results in a hexadecimal value of 0x167, or 103 in base 10, which is equivalent to the letter g.

LISTING 3.5: Using the Plus Operator with the char Data Type

```
int n = '3' + '4';
char c = (char)n;
System.Console.WriteLine(c);   // Writes out g.
```

Output 3.4 shows the results of Listing 3.5.

OUTPUT 3.4

```
g
```

You can use this trait of character types to determine how far two characters are from each other. For example, the letter f is three characters away from the letter c. You can determine this value by subtracting the letter c from the letter f, as Listing 3.6 demonstrates.

LISTING 3.6: Determining the Character Difference between Two Characters

```
int distance = 'f' - 'c';
System.Console.WriteLine(distance);
```

Output 3.5 shows the results of Listing 3.6.

OUTPUT 3.5

```
3
```

Special Floating-Point Characteristics

The binary floating-point types, float and double, have some special characteristics, such as the way they handle precision. This section looks at some specific examples, as well as some unique floating-point type characteristics.

A float, with seven decimal digits of precision, can hold the value 1,234,567 and the value 0.1234567. However, if you add these two floats together, the result will be rounded to 1234567, because the exact result requires more precision than the seven significant digits that a `float` can hold. The error introduced by rounding off to seven digits can become large compared to the value computed, especially with repeated calculations. (See also the upcoming Advanced Topic, Unexpected Inequality with Floating-Point Types.)

Note that internally the binary floating-point types actually store a binary fraction, not a decimal fraction. This means that "representation error" inaccuracies can occur with a simple assignment, such as `double number = 140.6F`. The exact value of 140.6 is the fraction 703/5, but the denominator of that fraction is not a power of two, and therefore, it cannot be represented exactly by a binary floating-point number. The value actually represented is the closest fraction with a power of two in the denominator that will fit into the 16 bits of a `float`.

Since the `double` can hold a more accurate value than the `float` can store, the C# compiler will actually evaluate this expression to `double number = 140.600006103516` because `140.600006103516` is the closest binary fraction to 140.6 as a `float`. This fraction is slightly larger than 140.6 when represented as a `double`.

Guidelines

AVOID binary floating-point types when exact decimal arithmetic is required; use the `decimal` floating-point type instead.

■ ADVANCED TOPIC

Unexpected Inequality with Floating-Point Types

Because floating-point numbers can be unexpectedly rounded off to non-decimal fractions, comparing floating-point values for equality can be quite confusing. Consider Listing 3.7.

LISTING 3.7: Unexpected Inequality Due to Floating-Point Inaccuracies

```
decimal decimalNumber = 4.2M;
double doubleNumber1 = 0.1F * 42F;
double doubleNumber2 = 0.1D * 42D;
float floatNumber = 0.1F * 42F;

Trace.Assert(decimalNumber != (decimal)doubleNumber1);
// Displays: 4.2 != 4.20000006258488
System.Console.WriteLine(
    "{0} != {1}", decimalNumber, (decimal)doubleNumber1);

Trace.Assert((double)decimalNumber != doubleNumber1);
// Displays: 4.2 != 4.20000006258488
System.Console.WriteLine(
    "{0} != {1}", (double)decimalNumber, doubleNumber1);

Trace.Assert((float)decimalNumber != floatNumber);
// Displays: (float)4.2M != 4.2F
System.Console.WriteLine(
    "(float){0}M != {1}F",
    (float)decimalNumber, floatNumber);

Trace.Assert(doubleNumber1 != (double)floatNumber);
// Displays: 4.20000006258488 != 4.20000028610229
System.Console.WriteLine(
    "{0} != {1}", doubleNumber1, (double)floatNumber);

Trace.Assert(doubleNumber1 != doubleNumber2);
// Displays: 4.20000006258488 != 4.2
System.Console.WriteLine(
    "{0} != {1}", doubleNumber1, doubleNumber2);

Trace.Assert(floatNumber != doubleNumber2);
// Displays: 4.2F != 4.2D
System.Console.WriteLine(
    "{0}F != {1}D", floatNumber, doubleNumber2);

Trace.Assert((double)4.2F != 4.2D);
// Display: 4.19999980926514 != 4.2
System.Console.WriteLine(
    "{0} != {1}", (double)4.2F, 4.2D);

Trace.Assert(4.2F != 4.2D);
// Display: 4.2F != 4.2D
System.Console.WriteLine(
    "{0}F != {1}D", 4.2F, 4.2D);
```

Output 3.6 shows the results of Listing 3.7.

OUTPUT 3.6

```
4.2 != 4.20000006258488
4.2 != 4.20000006258488
(float)4.2M != 4.2F
4.20000006258488 != 4.20000028610229
4.20000006258488 != 4.2
4.2F != 4.2D
4.19999980926514 != 4.2
4.2F != 4.2D
```

The `Assert()` methods alert the developer whenever their argument evaluates to `false`. However, of all the `Assert()` calls in this code listing, only half have arguments that evaluate to `true`. In spite of the apparent equality of the values in the code listing, they are in fact not equivalent due to the inaccuracies of a `float`.

Guidelines

AVOID using equality conditionals with binary floating-point types. Either subtract the two values and see if their difference is less than a tolerance, or use the `decimal` type.

You should be aware of some additional unique floating-point characteristics as well. For instance, you would expect that dividing an integer by zero would result in an error, and it does with data types such as `int` and `decimal`. The `float` and `double` types instead allow for certain special values. Consider Listing 3.8, and its resultant output, Output 3.7.

LISTING 3.8: Dividing a Float by Zero, Displaying NaN

```
float n=0f;
// Displays: NaN
System.Console.WriteLine(n / 0);
```

OUTPUT 3.7

```
NaN
```

In mathematics, certain mathematical operations are undefined, including dividing zero by itself. In C#, the result of dividing the float zero by zero results in a special "Not a Number" value; all attempts to print the output of such a number will result in NaN. Similarly, taking the square root of a negative number with System.Math.Sqrt(-1) will result in NaN.

A floating-point number could overflow its bounds as well. For example, the upper bound of the float type is approximately 3.4×10^{38}. Should the number overflow that bound, the result would be stored as "positive infinity" and the output of printing the number would be Infinity. Similarly, the lower bound of a float type is -3.4×10^{38}, and computing a value below that bound would result in "negative infinity," which would be represented by the string -Infinity. Listing 3.9 produces negative and positive infinity, respectively, and Output 3.8 shows the results.

LISTING 3.9: **Overflowing the Bounds of a** float

```
// Displays: -Infinity
System.Console.WriteLine(-1f / 0);
// Displays: Infinity
System.Console.WriteLine(3.402823E+38f * 2f);
```

OUTPUT 3.8

```
-Infinity
Infinity
```

Further examination of the floating-point number reveals that it can contain a value very close to zero, without actually containing zero. If the value exceeds the lower threshold for the float or double type, the value of the number can be represented as "negative zero" or "positive zero," depending on whether the number is negative or positive, and is represented in output as -0 or 0.

Compound Assignment Operators (+=, -=, *=, /=, %=)

Chapter 1 discussed the simple assignment operator, which places the value of the right-hand side of the operator into the variable on the left-hand side. Compound assignment operators combine common binary operator calculations with the assignment operator. Take Listing 3.10, for example.

LISTING 3.10: Common Increment Calculation

```
int x = 123;
x = x + 2;
```

In this assignment, first you calculate the value of x + 2 and then you assign the calculated value back to x. Since this type of operation is relatively frequent, an assignment operator exists to handle both the calculation and the assignment with one operator. The += operator increments the variable on the left-hand side of the operator with the value on the right-hand side of the operator, as shown in Listing 3.11.

LISTING 3.11: Using the += Operator

```
int x = 123;
x += 2;
```

This code, therefore, is equivalent to Listing 3.10.

Numerous other combination assignment operators exist to provide similar functionality. You can also use the assignment operator with subtraction, multiplication, division and the remainder operators (Listing 3.12 demonstrates).

LISTING 3.12: Other Assignment Operator Examples

```
x -= 2;
x /= 2;
x *= 2;
x %= 2;
```

Increment and Decrement Operators (++, --)

C# includes special unary operators for incrementing and decrementing counters. The **increment operator,** ++, increments a variable by one each time it is used. In other words, all of the code lines shown in Listing 3.13 are equivalent.

LISTING 3.13: Increment Operator

```
spaceCount = spaceCount + 1;
spaceCount += 1;
spaceCount++;
```

Similarly, you can also decrement a variable by one using the **decrement operator,** --. Therefore, all of the code lines shown in Listing 3.14 are also equivalent.

LISTING 3.14: Decrement Operator

```
lines = lines - 1;
lines -= 1;
lines--;
```

■ BEGINNER TOPIC

A Decrement Example in a Loop

The increment and decrement operators are especially prevalent in loops, such as the `while` loop described later in the chapter. For example, Listing 3.15 uses the decrement operator in order to iterate backward through each letter in the alphabet.

LISTING 3.15: Displaying Each Character's Unicode Value in Descending Order

```
char current;
int unicodeValue;

// Set the initial value of current.
current='z';

do
{
  // Retrieve the Unicode value of current.
  unicodeValue = current;
  System.Console.Write("{0}={1}\t", current, unicodeValue);

  // Proceed to the previous letter in the alphabet;
  current--;
}
while(current>='a');
```

Output 3.9 shows the results of Listing 3.15.

OUTPUT 3.9

```
z=122    y=121    x=120    w=119    v=118    u=117    t=116    s=115    r=114
q=113    p=112    o=111    n=110    m=109    l=108    k=107    j=106    i=105
h=104    g=103    f=102    e=101    d=100    c=99     b=98     a=97
```

The increment and decrement operators are used to control how many times a particular operation is performed. Notice also that in this example, the increment operator is used on a character (char) data type. You can use increment and decrement operators on various data types as long as some meaning is assigned to the concept of the "next" or "previous" value for that data type.

We saw that the assignment operator first computes the value to be assigned, and then causes the assignment. The result of the assignment operator is the value that was assigned. The increment and decrement operators are similar: They compute the value to be assigned, perform the assignment, and result in a value. It is therefore possible to use the assignment operator with the increment or decrement operator, though doing so carelessly can be extremely confusing. See Listing 3.16 and Output 3.10 for an example.

LISTING 3.16: Using the Post-Increment Operator

```
int count = 123;
int result;
result = count++;
System.Console.WriteLine(
    "result = {0} and count = {1}", result, count);
```

OUTPUT 3.10

```
result = 123 and count = 124
```

You might be surprised that result was assigned the value that was count *before* count was incremented. Where you place the increment or decrement operator determines whether the assigned value should be the value of the operand before or after the calculation. If you want the value of result to be the value assigned to count, you need to place the operator before the variable being incremented, as shown in Listing 3.17.

LISTING 3.17: Using the Pre-Increment Operator

```
int count = 123;
int result;
result = ++count;
System.Console.WriteLine(
    "result = {0} and count = {1}", result, count);
```

Output 3.11 shows the results of Listing 3.17.

OUTPUT 3.11

```
result = 124 and count = 124
```

In this example, the increment operator appears before the operand, so the result of the expression is the value assigned to the variable after the increment. If count is 123, ++count will assign 124 to count and produce the result 124. By contrast, the postfix increment operator count++ assigns 124 to count and produces the value that count held before the increment: 123. Regardless of whether the operator is postfix or prefix, the variable count will be incremented before the value is produced; the only difference is which value is produced. The difference between prefix and postfix behavior appears in Listing 3.18. The resultant output is shown in Output 3.12.

LISTING 3.18: Comparing the Prefix and Postfix Increment Operators

```csharp
class IncrementExample
{
  public static void Main()
  {
      int x = 123;
      // Displays 123, 124, 125.
      System.Console.WriteLine("{0}, {1}, {2}", x++, x++, x);
      // x now contains the value 125.
      // Displays 126, 127, 128
      System.Console.WriteLine("{0}, {1}, {2}", ++x, ++x, x);
      // x now contains the value 128.
  }
}
```

OUTPUT 3.12

```
123, 124, 125
126, 127, 128
```

As Listing 3.18 demonstrates, where the increment and decrement operators appear relative to the operand can affect the result produced by the expression. The result of the prefix operators is the value that the variable had before it was incremented or decremented. The result of the postfix operators is the value that the variable had after it was incremented or decremented. Use caution when embedding these operators in the middle of a statement. When in doubt as to what will happen, use these operators independently, placing them within their own statements. This way, the code is also more readable and there is no mistaking the intention.

Language Contrast: C++—Implementation-Defined Behavior

Earlier we discussed how in C++, the operands in an expression can be evaluated in any order, whereas in C# they are always evaluated left to right. Similarly, in C++ an implementation may legally perform the side effects of increments and decrements in any order. For example, in C++ a call of the form M(x++, x++) where x begins as 1 can legally call M(1,2) or M(2,1) at the whim of the compiler; C# will always call M(1,2) because C# makes two guarantees: first, that the arguments to a call are always computed left to right, and second, that the assignment of the incremented value to the variable always happens before the value of the expression is used. C++ makes neither guarantee.

Guidelines

AVOID confusing usages of the increment and decrement operators.

DO be cautious when porting code between C, C++, and C# that uses increment and decrement operators; C and C++ implementations need not follow the same rules as C#.

■ ADVANCED TOPIC

Thread-Safe Incrementing and Decrementing

In spite of the brevity of the increment and decrement operators, these operators are not atomic. A thread context switch can occur during the execution of the operator and can cause a race condition. You could use a lock statement to prevent the race condition. However, for simple increments and decrements, a less expensive alternative is to use the thread-safe Increment()

and `Decrement()` methods from the `System.Threading.Interlocked` class. These methods rely on processor functions for performing fast thread-safe increments and decrements. See Chapter 19 for more details.

Constant Expressions and Constant Locals

The preceding chapter discussed literal values, or values embedded directly into the code. It is possible to combine multiple literal values in a **constant expression** using operators. By definition, a constant expression is one that the C# compiler can evaluate at compile time (instead of calculating it when the program runs) because it is composed entirely of constant operands. Constant expressions can then be used to initialize constant locals, which allow you to give a name to a constant value (similar to the way local variables allow you to give a name to a storage location). For example, the computation of the number of seconds in a day can be a constant expression that is then used in other expressions by name.

The `const` keyword in Listing 3.19 declares a constant local. Since a constant local is by definition the opposite of a **variable**—"constant" means "not able to vary"—any attempt to modify the value later in the code would result in a compile-time error.

Guidelines

DO NOT use a constant for any value that can possibly change over time. The value of pi and the number of protons in an atom of gold are constants; the price of gold, the name of your company, and the version number of your program can change.

Note that the expression assigned to `secondsPerWeek` is a constant expression because all the operands in the expression are also constants.

LISTING 3.19: **Declaring a Constant**

```
// ...
public long Main()
{                                   Constant Expression
    const int secondsPerDay = 60 * 60 * 24;
    const int secondsPerWeek = secondsPerDay * 7;

                    Constant
    // ...
}
```

Introducing Flow Control

Later in this chapter is a code listing (Listing 3.43) that shows a simple way to view a number in its binary form. Even such a simple program, however, cannot be written without using control flow statements. Such statements control the execution path of the program. This section discusses how to change the order of statement execution based on conditional checks. Later on, you will learn how to execute statement groups repeatedly through loop constructs.

A summary of the control flow statements appears in Table 3.1. Note that the General Syntax Structure column indicates common statement use, not the complete lexical structure.

An embedded-statement in Table 3.1 may be any statement other than a labeled statement or a declaration, but it is typically a block statement.

Each C# control flow statement in Table 3.1 appears in the tic-tac-toe[3] program and is available in Appendix B and for download with the rest of the source code listings from the book. The program displays the tic-tac-toe board, prompts each player, and updates with each move.

The remainder of this chapter looks at each statement in more detail. After covering the if statement, it introduces code blocks, scope, Boolean expressions, and bitwise operators before continuing with the remaining control flow statements. Readers who find the table familiar because of C#'s similarities to other languages can jump ahead to the section titled C# Preprocessor Directives or skip to the Summary section at the end of the chapter.

---

3. Known as noughts and crosses to readers outside the United States.

TABLE 3.1: Control Flow Statements

Statement	General Syntax Structure	Example
if statement	if(*boolean-expression*) *embedded-statement*	```if (input == "quit")
{
System.Console.WriteLine(
"Game end");
return;
}```

	if(*boolean-expression*)
	  embedded-statement
	else
	  embedded-statement
		``if (input == "quit")

{
System.Console.WriteLine(
"Game end");
return;
}
else
GetNextMove();```
while statement	while(*boolean-expression*) *embedded-statement*	```while(count < total)
{
System.Console.WriteLine(
"count = {0}", count);
count++;
}```
do while statement	do *embedded-statement* while(*boolean-expression*);	```do
{
System.Console.WriteLine(
"Enter name:");
input =
System.Console.ReadLine();
}
while(input != "exit");```

TABLE 3.1: Control Flow Statements, *Continued*

Statement	General Syntax Structure	Example

for statement	for(*for-initializer;*
	    boolean-expression;
	    for-iterator)
	    embedded-statement
		``for (int count = 1;

count <= 10;
count++)
{
System.Console.WriteLine(
"count = {0}", count);
}```

foreach statement	foreach(*type identifier* in
	    expression)
	    embedded-statement
		``foreach (char letter in email)

{
if(!insideDomain)
{
if (letter == '@')
{
insideDomain = true;
}
continue;
}
System.Console.Write(
letter);
}```
continue statement	continue;	

Continues

TABLE 3.1: Control Flow Statements, *Continued*

Statement	General Syntax Structure	Example

`switch statement`	`switch(governing-type-expression)`
	`{`
	  `...`
	  `case const-expression:`
	    `statement-list`
	    `jump-statement`
	  `default:`
	    `statement-list`
	    `jump-statement`
	`}`
		`switch(input)`
		`{`
		  `case "exit":`
		  `case "quit":`
		    `System.Console.WriteLine(`
		      `"Exiting app....");`
		    `break;`
		  `case "restart":`
		    `Reset();`
		    `goto case "start";`
		  `case "start":`
		    `GetMove();`
		    `break;`
		  `default:`
		    `System.Console.WriteLine(`
		      `input);`
		    `break;`
		`}`

`break statement`	`break;`	
`goto statement`	`goto identifier;`	
	`goto case const-expression;`	
	`goto default;`	

The remainder of this chapter looks at each statement in more detail. After covering the if statement, it introduces code blocks, scope, Boolean expressions, and bitwise operators before continuing with the remaining control flow statements. Readers who find the table familiar because of C#'s similarities to other languages can jump ahead to the section titled C# Preprocessor Directives or skip to the Summary section at the end of the chapter.

if **Statement**

The if statement is one of the most common statements in C#. It evaluates a **Boolean expression** (an expression that results in either true or false) called the **condition.** If the condition is true, the **consequence statement** is executed. An if statement may optionally have an else clause that contains an **alternative statement** to be executed if the condition is false. The general form is as follows:

```
if (condition)
    consequence-statement
else
    alternative-statement
```

LISTING 3.20: if/else **Statement Example**

```csharp
class TicTacToe        // Declares the TicTacToe class.
{
  static void Main() // Declares the entry point of the program.
  {
      string input;

      // Prompt the user to select a 1- or 2-player game.
      System.Console.Write (
          "1 - Play against the computer\n" +
          "2 - Play against another player.\n" +
          "Choose:"
      );
      input = System.Console.ReadLine();

      if(input=="1")
          // The user selected to play the computer.
          System.Console.WriteLine(
              "Play against computer selected.");
      else
          // Default to 2 players (even if user didn't enter 2).
          System.Console.WriteLine(
              "Play against another player.");
  }
}
```

In Listing 3.20, if the user enters 1, the program displays "Play against computer selected.". Otherwise, it displays "Play against another player.".

Nested if

Sometimes code requires multiple if statements. The code in Listing 3.21 first determines whether the user has chosen to exit by entering a number less than or equal to 0; if not, it checks whether the user knows the maximum number of turns in tic-tac-toe.

LISTING 3.21: **Nested** if **Statements**

```
1.   class TicTacToeTrivia
2.   {
3.     static void Main()
4.     {
5.         int input;     // Declare a variable to store the input.
6.
7.         System.Console.Write(
8.             "What is the maximum number " +
9.             "of turns in tic-tac-toe?" +
10.            "(Enter 0 to exit.): ");
11.
12.        // int.Parse() converts the ReadLine()
13.        // return to an int data type.
14.        input = int.Parse(System.Console.ReadLine());
15.
16.        if (input <= 0)
17.                // Input is less than or equal to 0.
18.            System.Console.WriteLine("Exiting...");
19.        else
20.            if (input < 9)
21.                // Input is less than 9.
22.                System.Console.WriteLine(
23.                    "Tic-tac-toe has more than {0}" +
24.                    " maximum turns.", input);
25.            else
26.                if(input>9)
27.                    // Input is greater than 9.
28.                    System.Console.WriteLine(
29.                        "Tic-tac-toe has fewer than {0}" +
30.                        " maximum turns.", input);
31.                else
32.                    // Input equals 9.
33.                    System.Console.WriteLine(
34.                        "Correct, tic-tac-toe " +
35.                        "has a max. of 9 turns.");
36.    }
37. }
```

Output 3.13 shows the results of Listing 3.21.

OUTPUT 3.13

```
What is the maximum number of turns in tic-tac-toe? (Enter 0 to exit.): 9
Correct, tic-tac-toe has a max. of 9 turns.
```

Assume the user enters 9 when prompted at line 14. Here is the execution path.

1. *Line 16:* Check if input is less than 0. Since it is not, jump to line 20.
2. *Line 20:* Check if input is less than 9. Since it is not, jump to line 26.
3. *Line 26:* Check if input is greater than 9. Since it is not, jump to line 33.
4. *Line 33:* Display that the answer was correct.

Listing 3.21 contains nested `if` statements. To clarify the nesting, the lines are indented. However, as you learned in Chapter 1, whitespace does not affect the execution path. Without indenting and without newlines, the execution would be the same. The code that appears in the nested `if` statement in Listing 3.22 is equivalent to Listing 3.21.

LISTING 3.22: `if/else` **Formatted Sequentially**

```
if (input < 0)
  System.Console.WriteLine("Exiting...");
else if (input < 9)
  System.Console.WriteLine(
      "Tic-tac-toe has more than {0}" +
      " maximum turns.", input);
else if(input < 9)
  System.Console.WriteLine(
      "Tic-tac-toe has less than {0}" +
      " maximum turns.", input);
else
  System.Console.WriteLine(
      "Correct, tic-tac-toe has a maximum " +
      " of 9 turns.");
```

Although the latter format is more common, in each situation use the format that results in the clearest code.

Each `if` statement listing above omits the use of braces. However, as discussed next, this is not in accordance with the guidelines, which advocate the use of code blocks except, perhaps, in the simplest of single-line scenarios.

Code Blocks ({ })

In the previous if statement examples, only one statement follows if and else: a single System.Console.WriteLine(), similar to Listing 3.23.

LISTING 3.23: if **Statement with No Code Block**

```
if(input < 9)
   System.Console.WriteLine("Exiting");
```

With curly braces, however, we can combine statements into a single statement called a **block statement** or **code block,** allowing the grouping of multiple statements into a single statement that is the consequence. Take, for example, the highlighted code block in the radius calculation in Listing 3.24.

LISTING 3.24: if **Statement Followed by a Code Block**

```
class CircleAreaCalculator
{
  static void Main()
  {
     double radius;  // Declare a variable to store the radius.
     double area;    // Declare a variable to store the area.

     System.Console.Write("Enter the radius of the circle: ");

     // double.Parse converts the ReadLine()
     // return to a double.
     radius = double.Parse(System.Console.ReadLine());

     if(radius>=0)
     {
        // Calculate the area of the circle.
        area = 3.14*radius*radius;
        System.Console.WriteLine(
           "The area of the circle is: {0}", area);
     }
     else
     {
        System.Console.WriteLine(
           "{0} is not a valid radius.", radius);
     }
  }
}
```

Output 3.14 shows the results of Listing 3.24.

OUTPUT 3.14

```
Enter the radius of the circle: 3
The area of the circle is: 28.26
```

In this example, the `if` statement checks whether the `radius` is positive. If so, the area of the circle is calculated and displayed; otherwise, an invalid radius message is displayed.

Notice that in this example, two statements follow the first `if`. However, these two statements appear within curly braces. The curly braces combine the statements into a **code block, which is itself a single statement.**

If you omit the curly braces that create a code block in Listing 3.24, only the statement immediately following the Boolean expression executes conditionally. Subsequent statements will execute regardless of the `if` statement's Boolean expression. The invalid code is shown in Listing 3.25.

LISTING 3.25: Relying on Indentation, Resulting in Invalid Code

```
if(radius>=0)
  area = 3.14 * radius *radius;
  System.Console.WriteLine(
      "The area of the circle is: {0}", area);
```

In C#, indentation is for code readability only. The compiler ignores it, and therefore, the previous code is semantically equivalent to Listing 3.26.

LISTING 3.26: Semantically Equivalent to Listing 3.25

```
if(radius>=0)
{
  area = 3.14*radius*radius;
}
System.Console.WriteLine(
  "The area of the circle is: {0}", area);
```

Programmers should take great care to avoid subtle bugs such as this, perhaps even going so far as to always include a code block after a control flow statement, even if there is only one statement. In fact, the guideline is to avoid omitting braces, except possibly for the simplest of single-line if statements.

Although unusual, it is possible to have a code block that is not lexically a direct part of a control flow statement. In other words, placing curly braces on their own (without a conditional or loop, for example) is legal syntax.

Guidelines

AVOID omitting braces, except for the simplest of single-line if statements.

■ **ADVANCED TOPIC**

Math Constants

In Listing 3.25 and Listing 3.26, the value of pi as 3.14 was hardcoded—a crude approximation at best. There are much more accurate definitions for pi and E in the System.Math class. Instead of hardcoding a value, code should use System.Math.PI and System.Math.E.

Code Blocks, Scopes, and Declaration Spaces

Code blocks are often referred to as "scopes," but the two terms are not exactly interchangeable. The scope of a named thing is the region of source code in which it is legal to refer to the thing by its unqualified name. The scope of a local variable is exactly the text of the code block that encloses it, which explains why it is common to refer to code blocks as "scopes."

Scopes are often confused with declaration spaces. A **declaration space** is a logical container of named things in which two things may not have the same name. A code block not only defines a scope, it also defines a local variable declaration space; it is illegal for two local variable declarations with the same name to appear in the same declaration space. Similarly, it is not possible to declare two methods with the signature of Main() within the same class. (Though the rule is relaxed somewhat for methods; two methods may have the same name in a declaration space provided that they have different signatures.) A code block not only defines a scope, it also defines a local variable declaration space. That is to say, within a block a local can be mentioned by name and must be the unique thing that is declared with that name in the block. Outside the declaring block there is no way to refer to a local by its name; the local is said to be "out of scope" outside the block.

In short: A scope is used to determine what thing a name refers to; a declaration space determines when two things declared with the same name conflict with each other. In Listing 3.27, declaring the local variable `message` inside the block statement embedded in the `if` statement restricts its scope to the block statement only; the local is "out of scope" when its name is used later on in the method. To avoid the error, you must declare the variable outside the `if` statement.

LISTING 3.27: **Variables Inaccessible outside Their Scope**

```
class Program
{
    static void Main(string[] args)
    {
        int playerCount;
        System.Console.Write(
            "Enter the number of players (1 or 2):");
        playerCount = int.Parse(System.Console.ReadLine());
        if (playerCount != 1 && playerCount != 2)
        {
            string message =
                "You entered an invalid number of players.";
        }
        else
        {
            // ...
        }
        // Error:  message is not in scope.
        System.Console.WriteLine(message);
    }
}
```

Output 3.15 shows the results of Listing 3.27.

OUTPUT 3.15

```
...

...\Program.cs(18,26): error CS0103: The name 'message' does not exist
in the current context
```

The declaration space throughout which a local's name must be unique includes all the child code blocks textually enclosed within the block that originally declared the local. The C# compiler prevents the name of a local variable declared immediately within a method code block (or as a parameter) from being reused within a child code block. In Listing 3.27, because `args` and `playerCount` are declared within the method code block, they cannot be declared again anywhere within the method.

The name `message` refers to this local variable throughout the scope of the local variable: that is, the block immediately enclosing the declaration. Similarly, `playerCount` refers to the same variable throughout the block containing the declaration, including within both of the child blocks that are the consequence and alternative of the `if` statement.

Language Contrast: C++—Local Variable Scope

In C++, a local variable declared in a block is in scope from the point of the declaration statement through the end of the block; an attempt to refer to the local variable before its declaration will fail to find the local because the local is not in scope. If there is another thing with that name "in scope," the C++ language will resolve the name to that thing, which might not be what you intended. In C#, the rule is subtly different; a local is in scope throughout the entire block in which it is declared, but it is illegal to refer to the local before its declaration. That is, the attempt to find the local succeeds and the usage is then treated as an error. This is just one of C#'s many rules that attempt to prevent errors common in C++ programs.

Boolean Expressions

The parenthesized condition of the `if` statement is a **Boolean expression.** In Listing 3.28, the condition is highlighted.

LISTING 3.28: Boolean Expression

```
if(input < 9)
{
    // Input is less than 9.
```

```
System.Console.WriteLine(
    "Tic-tac-toe has more than {0}" +
    " maximum turns.", input);
}
// ...
```

Boolean expressions appear within many control flow statements. Their key characteristic is that they always evaluate to `true` or `false`. For `input<9` to be allowed as a Boolean expression, it must result in a `bool`. The compiler disallows `x=42`, for example, because it assigns `x` and results in the value that was assigned, instead of checking whether the value of the variable is 42.

> ## Language Contrast: C++—Mistakenly Using = in Place of ==
>
> C# eliminates a coding error common in C and C++. In C++, Listing 3.29 is allowed.
>
> **LISTING 3.29: C++, But Not C#, Allows Assignment As a Condition**
>
> ```
> if(input=9)     // Allowed in C++, not in C#.
>     System.Console.WriteLine(
>         "Correct, tic-tac-toe has a maximum of 9 turns.");
> ```
>
> Although at a glance this appears to check whether `input` equals 9, Chapter 1 showed that = represents the assignment operator, not a check for equality. The return from the assignment operator is the value assigned to the variable—in this case, 9. However, 9 is an `int`, and as such it does not qualify as a Boolean expression and is not allowed by the C# compiler. The C and C++ languages treat integers that are nonzero as true, and integers that are zero as false. C#, by contrast, requires that the condition actually be of a Boolean type; integers are not allowed.

Relational and Equality Operators

Relational and **equality** operators determine whether a value is greater than, less than, or equal to another value. Table 3.2 lists all the relational and equality operators. All are binary operators.

TABLE 3.2: Relational and Equality Operators

Operator	Description	Example
<	Less than	`input<9;`
>	Greater than	`input>9;`
<=	Less than or equal to	`input<=9;`
>=	Greater than or equal to	`input>=9;`
==	Equality operator	`input==9;`
!=	Inequality operator	`input!=9;`

The C# syntax for equality uses ==, just as many other programming languages do. For example, to determine whether input equals 9 you use input==9. The equality operator uses two equal signs to distinguish it from the assignment operator, =. The exclamation point signifies NOT in C#, so to test for inequality you use the inequality operator, !=.

Relational and equality operators always produce a bool value, as shown in Listing 3.30.

LISTING 3.30: Assigning the Result of a Relational Operator to a bool Variable

```
bool result = 70 > 7;
```

In the tic-tac-toe program (see Appendix B), you use the equality operator to determine whether a user has quit. The Boolean expression of Listing 3.31 includes an OR (||) logical operator, which the next section discusses in detail.

LISTING 3.31: Using the Equality Operator in a Boolean Expression

```
if (input == "" || input == "quit")
{
  System.Console.WriteLine("Player {0} quit!!", currentPlayer);
  break;
}
```

Logical Boolean Operators

The logical operators have Boolean operands and produce a Boolean result. Logical operators allow you to combine multiple Boolean expressions to form more complex Boolean expressions. The logical operators are |, ||, &, &&, and ^, corresponding to OR, AND, and exclusive OR. The | and & versions of OR and AND are only rarely used for Boolean logic, for reasons which we discuss below.

OR Operator (||)

In Listing 3.31, if the user enters quit or presses the Enter key without typing in a value, it is assumed that she wants to exit the program. To enable two ways for the user to resign, you use the logical OR operator, ||.

The || operator evaluates Boolean expressions and results in a true value if *either* operand is true (see Listing 3.32).

LISTING 3.32: **Using the OR Operator**

```
if((hourOfTheDay > 23) || (hourOfTheDay < 0))
    System.Console.WriteLine("The time you entered is invalid.");
```

It is not necessary to evaluate both sides of an OR expression because if either operand is true, the result is known to be true regardless of the value of the other operand. Like all operators in C#, the left operand is evaluated before the right one, so if the left portion of the expression evaluates to true, the right portion is ignored. In the example above, if hourOfTheDay has the value 33, (hourOfTheDay > 23) will evaluate to true and the OR operator will ignore the second half of the expression, **short-circuiting** it. Short-circuiting an expression also occurs with the Boolean AND operator. (Note that the parentheses are not necessary here; the logical operators are of higher precedence than the relational operators. However, it is clearer to the novice reader to parenthesize the subexpressions for clarity.)

AND Operator (&&)

The Boolean AND operator, &&, evaluates to true only if both operands evaluate to true. If either operand is false, the result will be false. Listing 3.33 writes a message if the given variable is both greater than 10 and less than 24.[4] Similarly to the OR operator, the AND operator will not always evaluate the right side of the expression. If the left operand is determined to be false, the overall result will be false regardless of the value of the right operand, so the runtime skips evaluating the right operand.

---

4. The typical hours that programmers work.

LISTING 3.33: Using the AND Operator

```
if ((10 < hourOfTheDay) && (hourOfTheDay < 24))
  System.Console.WriteLine(
  "Hi-Ho, Hi-Ho, it's off to work we go.");
```

Exclusive OR Operator (^)

The caret symbol, ^, is the "exclusive OR" (XOR) operator. When applied to two Boolean operands, the XOR operator returns true only if exactly one of the operands is true, as shown in Table 3.3.

TABLE 3.3: Conditional Values for the XOR Operator

Left Operand	Right Operand	Result
True	True	False
True	False	True
False	True	True
False	False	False

Unlike the Boolean AND and Boolean OR operators, the Boolean XOR operator does not short-circuit: It always checks both operands, because the result cannot be determined unless the values of both operands are known. Note that the XOR operator is exactly the same as the Boolean inequality operator.

Logical Negation Operator (!)

The **logical negation operator, or NOT operator,** !, inverts a bool value. This operator is a unary operator, meaning it requires only one operand. Listing 3.34 demonstrates how it works, and Output 3.16 shows the results.

LISTING 3.34: Using the Logical Negation Operator

```
bool valid = false;
bool result = !valid;
// Displays "result = True".
System.Console.WriteLine("result = {0}", result);
```

OUTPUT 3.16

```
result = True
```

To begin, valid is set to false. You then use the negation operator on valid and assign the value to result.

Conditional Operator (?:)

In place of an if-else statement used to select one of two values, you can use the **conditional** operator. The conditional operator uses both a question mark and a colon; the general format is as follows:

```
condition ? consequence : alternative
```

The conditional operator is a "ternary" operator because it has three operands: condition, consequence, and alternative. (As it is the only ternary operator in C#, it is often called "the ternary operator," but it is clearer to refer to it by its name than by the number of operands it takes.) Like the logical operators, the conditional operator uses a form of short-circuiting. If the condition evaluates to true, the conditional operator evaluates only consequence. If the conditional evaluates to false, it evaluates only alternative. The result of the operator is the evaluated expression.

Listing 3.35 is an example of how to use the conditional operator. The full listing of this program appears in Appendix B.

LISTING 3.35: Conditional Operator

```
public class TicTacToe
{
  public static string Main()
  {
      // Initially set the currentPlayer to Player 1;
      int currentPlayer = 1;

      // ...

      for (int turn = 1; turn <= 10; turn++)
      {
        // ...

        // Switch players
        currentPlayer = (currentPlayer == 2) ? 1 : 2;
      }
  }
}
```

The program swaps the current player. To do this, it checks whether the current value is 2. This is the conditional portion of the conditional expression. If the result of the condition is `true`, the conditional operator results in the "consequence" value 1. Otherwise, it results in the "alternative" value 2. Unlike an `if` statement, the result of the conditional operator must be assigned (or passed as a parameter). It cannot appear as an entire statement on its own.

Guidelines

CONSIDER using an `if`/`else` statement instead of an overly complicated conditional expression.

The C# language requires that the consequence and alternative expressions in a conditional operator be consistently typed, and that the consistent type be determined without examination of the surrounding context of the expression. For example, `f ? "abc" : 123` is not a legal conditional expression because the consequence and alternative are a string and a number, neither of which is convertible to the other. Even if you say `object result = f ? "abc" : 123;` the C# compiler will still flag this expression as illegal because the type that is consistent with both expressions (that is, `object`) is found outside the conditional expression.

Null Coalescing Operator (??)

The **null coalescing operator** is a concise way to express "if this value is null then use this other value." Its form is:

expression1 ?? *expression2;*

The null coalescing operator also uses a form of short-circuiting. If `expression1` is not null, its value is the result of the operation and the other expression is not evaluated. If `expression1` does evaluate to null, the value of `expression2` is the result of the operator. Unlike the conditional operator, the null coalescing operator is a binary operator.

Listing 3.36 is an example of how to use the null coalescing operator.

LISTING 3.36: **Null Coalescing Operator**

```
string fileName = GetFileName();
// ...
string fullName = fileName ?? "default.txt";
// ...
```

In this listing, we use the null coalescing operator to set `fullName` to `"default.txt"` if `fileName` is null. If `fileName` is not null, `fullName` is simply assigned the value of `fileName`.

The coalescing operator "chains" nicely; an expression of the form x ?? y ?? z results in x if x is not null; otherwise, it results in y if y is not null; otherwise, it results in z. That is, it goes from left to right and picks out the first non-null expression, or uses the last expression if all the previous expressions were null.

The null coalescing operator was added to C# in version 2.0 along with nullable value types; the null coalescing operator works on both operands of nullable value types and reference types.

Bitwise Operators (<<, >>, |, &, ^, ~)

An additional set of operators that is common to virtually all programming languages is the set of operators for manipulating values in their binary formats: the bit operators.

▪ **BEGINNER TOPIC**

Bits and Bytes

All values within a computer are represented in a binary format of 1s and 0s, called **binary digits (bits)**. Bits are grouped together in sets of eight, called **bytes.** In a byte, each successive bit corresponds to a value of 2 raised to a power, starting from 2^0 on the right, to 2^7 on the left, as shown in Figure 3.1.

0	0	0	0	0	0	0	0
2^7	2^6	2^5	2^4	2^3	2^2	2^1	2^0

FIGURE 3.1: Corresponding Placeholder Values

In many scenarios, particularly when dealing with low-level or system services, information is retrieved as binary data. In order to manipulate these devices and services, you need to perform manipulations of binary data.

As shown in Figure 3.2, each box corresponds to a value of 2 raised to the power shown. The value of the byte (8-bit number) is the sum of the powers of 2 of all of the eight bits that are set to 1.

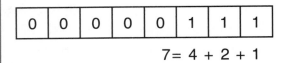

$$7 = 4 + 2 + 1$$

FIGURE 3.2: Calculating the Value of an Unsigned Byte

The binary translation just described is significantly different for signed numbers. Signed numbers (long, short, int) are represented using a "twos complement" notation. This is so that addition continues to work when adding a negative number to a positive number as though both were positive operands. With this notation, negative numbers behave differently than positive numbers. Negative numbers are identified by a 1 in the leftmost location. If the leftmost location contains a 1, you add the locations with 0s rather than the locations with 1s. Each location corresponds to the negative power of 2 value. Furthermore, from the result, it is also necessary to subtract 1. This is demonstrated in Figure 3.3.

1	1	1	1	1	0	0	1

$$-7 = -4 \ -2 \ +0$$

FIGURE 3.3: Calculating the Value of a Signed Byte

Therefore, 1111 1111 1111 1111 corresponds to −1 and 1111 1111 1111 1001 holds the value −7. 1000 0000 0000 0000 corresponds to the lowest negative value that a 16-bit integer can hold.

Shift Operators (<<, >>, <<=, >>=)

Sometimes you want to shift the binary value of a number to the right or left. In executing a left shift, all bits in a number's binary representation are shifted to the left by the number of locations specified by the operand on the right of the shift operator. Zeroes are then used to backfill the locations on the right side of the binary number. A right-shift operator does almost the same thing in the opposite direction. However, if the number is a negative value of a signed type, the values used to backfill the left side of the binary number are ones and not zeroes. The shift operators are `>>` and `<<`, the right-shift and left-shift operators, respectively. In addition, there are combined shift and assignment operators, `<<=` and `>>=`.

Consider the following example. Suppose you had the `int` value `-7`, which would have a binary representation of `1111 1111 1111 1111 1111 1111 1111 1001`. In Listing 3.37, you right-shift the binary representation of the number –7 by two locations.

LISTING 3.37: **Using the Right-Shift Operator**

```
int x;
x = (-7 >> 2); // 11111111111111111111111111111001 becomes
               // 11111111111111111111111111111110
// Write out "x is -2."
System.Console.WriteLine("x = {0}.", x);
```

Output 3.17 shows the results of Listing 3.37.

OUTPUT 3.17

```
x = -2.
```

Because of the right shift, the value of the bit in the rightmost location has "dropped off" the edge and the negative bit indicator on the left shifts by two locations to be replaced with 1s. The result is `-2`.

Although legend has it that `x << 2` is faster than `x * 4`, do not use bit shift operators for multiplication or division. This might have been true in certain C compilers in the 1970s, but modern compilers and modern microprocessors are perfectly capable of optimizing arithmetic. Using shifting for multiplication or division is confusing and frequently leads to errors when code maintainers forget that the shift operators are lower precedence than the arithmetic operators.

Bitwise Operators (&, |, ^)

In some instances, you might need to perform logical operations, such as AND, OR, and XOR, on a bit-by-bit basis for two operands. You do this via the `&`, `|`, and `^` operators, respectively.

■ **BEGINNER TOPIC**

Logical Operators Explained

If you have two numbers, as shown in Figure 3.4, the bitwise operations will compare the values of the locations beginning at the leftmost significant value and continuing right until the end. The value of "1" in a location is treated as "true," and the value of "0" in a location is treated as "false."

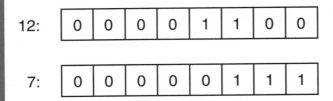

FIGURE 3.4: The Numbers 12 and 7 Represented in Binary

Therefore, the bitwise AND of the two values in Figure 3.4 would be the bit-by-bit comparison of bits in the first operand (12) with the bits in the second operand (7), resulting in the binary value 000000100, which is 4. Alternatively, a bitwise OR of the two values would produce 00001111, the binary equivalent of 15. The XOR result would be 00001011, or decimal 11.

Listing 3.38 demonstrates how to use these bitwise operators. The results of Listing 3.38 appear in Output 3.18.

LISTING 3.38: Using Bitwise Operators

```
byte and, or, xor;
and = 12 & 7;    // and = 4
or = 12 | 7;     // or = 15
xor = 12 ^ 7;    // xor = 11
System.Console.WriteLine(
    "and = {0} \nor = {1}\nxor = {2}",
    and, or, xor);
```

OUTPUT 3.18

```
and = 4
or = 15
xor = 11
```

In Listing 3.38, the value 7 is the **mask;** it is used to expose or eliminate specific bits within the first operand using the particular operator expression. Note that, unlike the AND (&&) operator, the & operator always evaluates *both* sides even if the left portion is false. Similarly, the | version of the OR operator is *not* "short-circuiting." It always evaluates both operands even if the left operand is true. The bit versions of the AND and OR operators, therefore, are not short-circuiting.

In order to convert a number to its binary representation, you need to iterate across each bit in a number. Listing 3.39 is an example of a program that converts an integer to a string of its binary representation. The results of Listing 3.39 appear in Output 3.19.

LISTING 3.39: **Getting a String Representation of a Binary Display**

```
public class BinaryConverter
{
  public static void Main()
  {
      const int size = 64;
      ulong value;
      char bit;

      System.Console.Write ("Enter an integer: ");
      // Use Long.Parse() so as to support negative numbers
      // Assumes unchecked assignment to ulong.
      value = (ulong)long.Parse(System.Console.ReadLine());

      // Set initial mask to 100....
      ulong mask = 1UL << size - 1;
      for (int count = 0; count < size; count++)
      {
          bit = ((mask & value) != 0) ? '1': '0';
          System.Console.Write(bit);
          // Shift mask one location over to the right
          mask >>= 1;
      }
      System.Console.WriteLine();
  }
}
```

OUTPUT 3.19

```
Enter an integer: 42
0000000000000000000000000000000000000000000000000000000000101010
```

Notice that within each iteration of the `for` loop (discussed later in this chapter), you use the right-shift assignment operator to create a mask corresponding to each bit position in `value`. By using the `&` bit operator to mask a particular bit, you can determine whether the bit is set. If the mask test produces a nonzero result, you write `1` to the console; otherwise, `0` is written. In this way, you create output describing the binary value of an unsigned long.

Note also that the parentheses in `(mask & value) != 0` are necessary because inequality is higher precedence than the AND operator; without the explicit parentheses this would be equivalent to `mask & (value != 0)`, which does not make any sense; the left side of the `&` is a `ulong` and the right side is a `bool`.

Bitwise Compound Assignment Operators (&=, |=, ^=)

Not surprisingly, you can combine these bitwise operators with assignment operators as follows: `&=`, `|=`, and `^=`. As a result, you could take a variable, OR it with a number, and assign the result back to the original variable, which Listing 3.40 demonstrates.

LISTING 3.40: **Using Logical Assignment Operators**

```
byte and = 12, or = 12, xor = 12;
and &= 7;    // and = 4
or  |= 7;    // or = 15
xor ^= 7;    // xor = 11
System.Console.WriteLine(
    "and = {0} \nor = {1}\nxor = {2}",
    and, or, xor);
```

The results of Listing 3.40 appear in Output 3.20.

OUTPUT 3.20

```
and = 4
or = 15
xor = 11
```

Combining a bitmap with a mask using something like `fields &= mask` clears the bits in `fields` that are not set in the `mask`. The opposite, `fields &= ~mask`, clears out the bits in `fields` that are set in `mask`.

Bitwise Complement Operator (~)

The **bitwise complement operator** takes the complement of each bit in the operand, where the operand can be an `int`, `uint`, `long`, or `ulong`. `~1`, therefore, returns the value with binary notation 1111 1111 1111 1111 1111 1111 1111 1110, and `~(1<<31)` returns the number with binary notation 0111 1111 1111 1111 1111 1111 1111 1111.

Control Flow Statements, Continued

Now that we've described Boolean expressions in more detail we can more clearly describe the control flow statements supported by C#. Many of these statements will be familiar to experienced programmers, so you can skim this section looking for details specific to C#. Note in particular the `foreach` loop, as this may be new to many programmers.

The `while` and `do/while` Loops

Thus far you have learned how to write programs that do something only once. However, computers can easily perform similar operations multiple times. In order to do this, you need to create an instruction loop. The first instruction loop we will discuss is the `while` loop, because it is the simplest conditional loop. The general form of the `while` statement is as follows:

```
while (condition)
    statement
```

The computer will repeatedly execute the statement that is the "body" of the loop as long as the condition (which must be a Boolean expression) evaluates to `true`. If the condition evaluates to `false`, code execution skips the body and executes the code following the loop statement. Note that `statement` will continue to execute even if it causes the condition to become `false`. It isn't until the condition is reevaluated "at the top of the loop" that the loop exits. The Fibonacci calculator shown in Listing 3.41 demonstrates the `while` loop.

LISTING 3.41: `while` Loop Example

```csharp
class FibonacciCalculator
{
  static void Main()
  {
```

```csharp
decimal current;
decimal previous;
decimal temp;
decimal input;

System.Console.Write("Enter a positive integer:");

// decimal.Parse convert the ReadLine to a decimal.
input = decimal.Parse(System.Console.ReadLine());

// Initialize current and previous to 1, the first
// two numbers in the Fibonacci series.
current = previous = 1;

// While the current Fibonacci number in the series is
// less than the value input by the user.
while(current <= input)
{
    temp = current;
    current = previous + current;
    previous = temp; // Executes even if previous
    // statement caused current to exceed input
}

System.Console.WriteLine(
    "The Fibonacci number following this is {0}",
    current);
}
}
```

A **Fibonacci number** is a member of the **Fibonacci series,** which includes all numbers that are the sum of the previous two numbers in the series, beginning with 1 and 1. In Listing 3.41, you prompt the user for an integer. Then you use a `while` loop to find the first Fibonacci number that is greater than the number the user entered.

■ BEGINNER TOPIC

When to Use a `while` Loop

The remainder of this chapter considers other statements that cause a block of code to execute repeatedly. The term *loop body* refers to the statement (frequently a code block) that is to be executed within the `while` statement, since the code is executed in a "loop" until the exit condition is achieved. It is important to understand which loop construct to select. You use a `while` construct to iterate while the condition evaluates to `true`. A `for` loop is used most appropriately whenever the number of repetitions is known, such as counting from 0 to *n*. A do/while is similar to a while loop, except that it will always execute the loop body at least once.

The do/while loop is very similar to the while loop except that a do/while loop is preferred when the number of repetitions is from 1 to *n* and *n* is not known when iterating begins. This pattern frequently occurs when prompting a user for input. Listing 3.42 is taken from the tic-tac-toe program.

LISTING 3.42: do/while **Loop Example**

```
// Repeatedly request player to move until he
// enter a valid position on the board.
bool valid;
do
{
  valid = false;

  // Request a move from the current player.
  System.Console.Write(
    "\nPlayer {0}: Enter move:", currentPlayer);
  input = System.Console.ReadLine();

  // Check the current player's input.
  // ...

} while (!valid);
```

In Listing 3.42, you always initialize valid to false at the beginning of each **iteration,** or loop repetition. Next, you prompt and retrieve the number the user input. Although not shown here, you then check whether the input was correct, and if it was, you assign valid equal to true. Since the code uses a do/while statement rather than a while statement, the user will be prompted for input at least once.

The general form of the do/while loop is as follows:

```
do
  statement
while (condition);
```

As with all the control flow statements, a code block is generally used as the single statement in order to allow multiple statements to be executed as the loop body. However, any single statement except for a labeled statement or a local variable declaration can be used.

The for Loop

The for loop iterates a code block until a specified condition is reached. In that way, it is very similar to the while loop. The difference is that the for loop has built-in syntax for initializing, incrementing, and testing the value of a counter, known as the **loop variable.** Because there is a specific location in the loop syntax for an increment operation, the increment and decrement operators are frequently used as part of a for loop.

Listing 3.43 shows the for loop used to display an integer in binary form. The results of this listing appear in Output 3.21.

LISTING 3.43: Using the for Loop

```
public class BinaryConverter
{
  public static void Main()
  {
      const int size = 64;
      ulong value;
      char bit;

      System.Console.Write ("Enter an integer: ");
      // Use Long.Parse() so as to support negative numbers
      // Assumes unchecked assignment to ulong.
      value = (ulong)long.Parse(System.Console.ReadLine());

      // Set initial mask to 100....
      ulong mask = 1UL << size - 1;
      for (int count = 0; count < size; count++)
      {
          bit = ((mask & value) > 0) ? '1': '0';
          System.Console.Write(bit);
          // Shift mask one location over to the right
          mask >>= 1;
      }
  }
}
```

OUTPUT 3.21

```
Enter an integer: -42
1111111111111111111111111111111111111111111111111111111111010110
```

Listing 3.43 performs a bit mask 64 times, once for each bit in the number. The three parts of the for loop header first declare and initialize the variable count, then describe the condition that must be met for the loop body to be executed, and finally describe the operation that updates the loop variable. The general form of the `for` loop is as follows:

```
for (initial ; condition ; loop)
    statement
```

Here is a breakdown of the `for` loop.

- The `initial` section performs operations that precede the first iteration. In Listing 3.43, it declares and initializes the variable `count`. The `initial` expression does not have to be a declaration of a new variable (though it frequently is). It is possible, for example, to declare the variable beforehand and simply initialize it in the `for` loop, or to skip the initialization section entirely by leaving it blank. Variables declared here are in scope throughout the header and body of the `for` statement.
- The `condition` portion of the `for` loop specifies an end condition. The loop exits when this condition is `false` exactly like the `while` loop does. The `for` loop will execute the body only as long as the condition evaluates to `true`. In the preceding example, the loop exits when `count` is greater than or equal to 64.
- The `loop` expression executes after each iteration. In the preceding example, `count++` executes after the right shift of the mask (`mask >>= 1`), but before the condition is evaluated. During the sixty-fourth iteration, `count` is incremented to 64, causing the condition to become `false`, and therefore terminating the loop.
- The `statement` portion of the `for` loop is the "loop body" code that executes while the conditional expression remains `true`.

If you wrote out each `for` loop execution step in pseudocode without using a `for` loop expression, it would look like this.

1. Declare and initialize `count` to 0.
2. If `count` is less than 64, continue to step 3; otherwise, go to step 7.
3. Calculate `bit` and display it.
4. Shift the mask.
5. Increment `count` by one.
6. Jump back to line 2.
7. Continue the execution of the program after the loop.

The `for` statement doesn't require any of the elements in its header. `for(;;){ ... }` is perfectly valid; although there still needs to be a means to escape from the loop to avoid executing infinitely. (If the condition is missing, it is assumed to be the constant `true`.)

The initial and loop expressions have an unusual syntax to support loops that require multiple loop variables, as shown in Listing 3.44.

LISTING 3.44: `for` **Loop Using Multiple Expressions**

```
for(int x=0, y=5; ((x<=5) && (y>=0)); y--, x++)
{
  System.Console.Write("{0}{1}{2}\t",
     x, (x>y? '>' : '<'), y);
}
```

The results of Listing 3.44 appear in Output 3.22.

OUTPUT 3.22

```
0<5     1<4     2<3     3>2     4>1     5>0
```

Here the initialization clause contains a complex declaration that declares and initializes two loop variables, but this is at least similar to a declaration statement that declares multiple local variables. The loop clause is quite unusual, as it can consist of a comma-separated list of expressions, not just a single expression.

> **Guidelines**
>
> **CONSIDER** refactoring the method to make the control flow easier to understand if you find yourself writing `for` loops with complex conditionals and multiple loop variables.

The `for` loop is little more than a more convenient way to write a `while` loop; you can always rewrite a `for` loop like this:

```
{
  initial;
  while(condition)
  {
```

```
    statement;
    loop;
  }
}
```

The `foreach` Loop

The last loop statement in the C# language is `foreach`. The `foreach` loop iterates through a collection of items, setting a loop variable to represent each item in turn. In the body of the loop, operations may be performed on the item. A nice property of the `foreach` loop is that every item is iterated over exactly once; it is not possible to accidentally miscount and iterate past the end of the collection as can happen with other loops.

The general form of the `foreach` statement is as follows:

```
foreach(type variable in collection)
    statement
```

Here is a breakdown of the `foreach` statement.

- `type` is used to declare the data type of the variable for each item within the collection. It may be var, in which case the compiler infers the type of the item from the type of the collection.

- `variable` is a read-only variable into which the `foreach` loop will automatically assign the next item within the collection. The scope of the variable is limited to the body of the loop.

- `collection` is an expression, such as an array, representing any number of items.

- `statement` is the loop body that executes for each iteration of the loop.

Consider the foreach loop in the context of the simple example shown in Listing 3.45.

LISTING 3.45: **Determining Remaining Moves Using the** foreach **Loop**

```
class TicTacToe      // Declares the TicTacToe class.
{
  static void Main() // Declares the entry point of the program.
  {
    // Hardcode initial board as follows
    // ---+---+---
    //  1 | 2 | 3
    // ---+---+---
    //  4 | 5 | 6
    // ---+---+---
    //  7 | 8 | 9
    // ---+---+---
    char[] cells = {
      '1', '2', '3', '4', '5', '6', '7', '8', '9'
    };

    System.Console.Write(
        "The available moves are as follows: ");

    // Write out the initial available moves
    foreach (char cell in cells)
    {
      if (cell != 'O' && cell != 'X')
      {
          System.Console.Write("{0} ", cell);
      }
    }
  }
}
```

Output 3.23 shows the results of Listing 3.45.

OUTPUT 3.23

```
The available moves are as follows: 1 2 3 4 5 6 7 8 9
```

When the execution engine reaches the foreach statement, it assigns to the variable cell the first item in the cells array—in this case, the value '1'. It then executes the code within the block that makes up the foreach loop body. The if statement determines whether the value of cell is 'O' or 'X'.

If it is neither, the value of `cell` is written out to the console. The next iteration then assigns the next array value to `cell`, and so on.

It is important to note that the compiler prevents modification of the variable (`cell`) during the execution of a `foreach` loop. Also, the loop variable has a subtly different behavior in C# 5 than it did in previous versions; the difference is only apparent when the loop body contains a lambda expression or anonymous method that uses the loop variable. See Chapter 12 for details.

■ **BEGINNER TOPIC**

Where the `switch` Statement Is More Appropriate

Sometimes you might compare the same value in several continuous `if` statements, as shown with the `input` variable in Listing 3.46.

LISTING 3.46: Checking the Player's Input with an `if` Statement

```
// ...

bool valid = false;

// Check the current player's input.
if( (input == "1") ||
  (input == "2") ||
  (input == "3") ||
  (input == "4") ||
  (input == "5") ||
  (input == "6") ||
  (input == "7") ||
  (input == "8") ||
  (input == "9") )
{
    // Save/move as the player directed.
    // ...

    valid = true;
}
else if( (input == "") || (input == "quit") )
{
    valid = true;
}
else
{
    System.Console.WriteLine(
      "\nERROR:  Enter a value from 1-9. "
      + "Push ENTER to quit");
```

```
    }
    // ...
```

This code validates the text entered to ensure that it is a valid tic-tac-toe move. If the value of `input` were 9, for example, the program would have to perform nine different evaluations. It would be preferable to jump to the correct code after only one evaluation. To enable this, you use a `switch` statement.

The `switch` **Statement**

A `switch` statement is simpler to understand than a complex `if` statement when you have a value that must be compared against may different constant values. The `switch` statement looks like this:

```
switch(expression)
{
    case constant:
        statements
    default:
        statements
}
```

Here is a breakdown of the `switch` statement.

- `expression` is the value that is being compared against the different constants. The type of this expression determines the "governing type" of the switch. Allowable governing data types are `bool`, `sbyte`, `byte`, `short`, `ushort`, `int`, `uint`, `long`, `ulong`, `char`, any `enum` type (covered in Chapter 8), the corresponding nullable types of each of those value types, and `string`.
- `constant` is any constant expression compatible with the governing type.
- A group of one or more case labels (or the default label) followed by a group of one or more statements is called a **switch section.** The pattern above has two switch sections; Listing 3.47 shows a `switch` statement with three switch sections.
- `statements` is one or more statements to be executed when the expression equals one of the constant values mentioned in a label in the

switch section. The end point of the group of statements must not be reachable. Typically the last statement is a jump statement such as a break, return, or goto statement.

A switch statement should have at least one switch section; switch(x){} is legal but will generate a warning. Also, earlier the guideline was to avoid omitting braces in general. One exception is to omit braces for case and break statements because they serve to indicate the beginning and end of a block.

Listing 3.47, with a switch statement, is semantically equivalent to the series of if statements in Listing 3.46.

LISTING 3.47: Replacing the if Statement with a switch Statement

```
static bool ValidateAndMove(
  int[] playerPositions, int currentPlayer, string input)
{
  bool valid = false;

  // Check the current player's input.
  switch (input)
  {
    case "1" :
    case "2" :
    case "3" :
    case "4" :
    case "5" :
    case "6" :
    case "7" :
    case "8" :
    case "9" :
      // Save/move as the player directed.
      ...
      valid = true;
      break;

    case "" :
    case "quit" :
      valid = true;
```

```
      break;
    default :
      // If none of the other case statements
      // is encountered then the text is invalid.
      System.Console.WriteLine(
        "\nERROR:  Enter a value from 1-9. "
        + "Push ENTER to quit");
      break;
  }

  return valid;
}
```

In Listing 3.47, input is the test expression. Since input is a string, the governing type is string. If the value of input is one of the strings 1, 2, 3, 4, 5, 6, 7, 8, or 9, the move is valid and you change the appropriate cell to match that of the current user's token (X or O). Once execution encounters a break statement, control leaves the switch statement.

The next switch section describes how to handle the empty string or the string quit; it sets valid to true if input equals either value. The default switch section is executed if no other switch section had a case label that matched the test expression.

Language Contrast: C++—switch Statement Fall-Through

In C++, if a switch section does not end with a jump statement, control "falls through" to the next switch section, executing its code. Because unintended fall-through is a common error in C++, C# does not allow control to accidentally fall through from one switch section to the next. The C# designers believed it was better to prevent this common source of bugs and encourage better code readability than to match the potentially confusing C++ behavior. If you do want one switch section to execute the statements of another switch section, you may do so explicitly with a goto statement, as demonstrated later in this chapter.

There are several things to note about the switch statement.

• A switch statement with no switch sections will generate a compiler warning, but the statement will still compile.

- Switch sections can appear in any order; the default section does not have to appear last. In fact, the default switch section does not have to appear at all; it is optional.

- The C# language requires that the end point of every switch section, including the last section, be unreachable. This means that switch sections usually end with a break, return, or goto.

Jump Statements

It is possible to alter the execution path of a loop. In fact, with jump statements, it is possible to escape out of the loop or to skip the remaining portion of an iteration and begin with the next iteration, even when the loop condition remains true. This section considers some of the ways to jump the execution path from one location to another.

The break Statement

To escape out of a loop or a switch statement, C# uses a break statement. Whenever the break statement is encountered, control immediately leaves the loop or switch. Listing 3.48 examines the foreach loop from the tic-tac-toe program.

LISTING 3.48: Using break to Escape Once a Winner Is Found

```
class TicTacToe        // Declares the TicTacToe class.
{
  static void Main() // Declares the entry point of the program.
  {
      int winner=0;
      // Stores locations each player has moved.
      int[] playerPositions = {0,0};

      // Hardcoded board position
      // X | 2 | O
      // ---+---+---
      // O | O | 6
      // ---+---+---
      // X | X | X
      playerPositions[0] = 449;
      playerPositions[1] = 28;

      // Determine if there is a winner
      int[] winningMasks = {
            7, 56, 448, 73, 146, 292, 84, 273 };
```

```
      // Iterate through each winning mask to determine
      // if there is a winner.
      foreach (int mask in winningMasks)
      {
          if ((mask & playerPositions[0]) == mask)
          {
              winner = 1;
              break;
          }
          else if ((mask & playerPositions[1]) == mask)
          {
              winner = 2;
              break;
          }
      }

      System.Console.WriteLine(
          "Player {0} was the winner", winner);
  }
}
```

Output 3.24 shows the results of Listing 3.48.

OUTPUT 3.24

```
Player 1 was the winner
```

Listing 3.48 uses a break statement when a player holds a winning position. The break statement forces its enclosing loop (or a switch statement) to cease execution, and control moves to the next line outside the loop. For this listing, if the bit comparison returns true (if the board holds a winning position), the break statement causes control to jump and display the winner.

▪ BEGINNER TOPIC

Bitwise Operators for Positions

The tic-tac-toe example (the full listing is available in Appendix B) uses the bitwise operators to determine which player wins the game. First, the code saves the positions of each player into a bitmap called playerPositions. (It uses an array so that the positions for both players can be saved.)

To begin, both playerPositions are 0. As each player moves, the bit corresponding to the move is set. If, for example, the player selects cell

3, shifter is set to 3 – 1. The code subtracts 1 because C# is zero-based and you need to adjust for 0 as the first position instead of 1. Next, the code sets position, the bit corresponding to cell 3, using the shift operator 000000000000001 << shifter, where shifter now has a value of 2. Lastly, it sets playerPositions for the current player (subtracting 1 again to shift to zero-based) to 0000000000000100. Listing 3.49 uses |= so that previous moves are combined with the current move.

LISTING 3.49: **Setting the Bit That Corresponds to Each Player's Move**

```
int shifter;  // The number of places to shift
              // over in order to set a bit.
int position;  // The bit which is to be set.

// int.Parse() converts "input" to an integer.
// "int.Parse(input) - 1" because arrays
// are zero-based.
shifter = int.Parse(input) - 1;

// Shift mask of 00000000000000000000000000000001
// over by cellLocations.
position = 1 << shifter;

// Take the current player cells and OR them to set the
// new position as well.
// Since currentPlayer is either 1 or 2,
// subtract one to use currentPlayer as an
// index in a 0-based array.
playerPositions[currentPlayer-1] |= position;
```

Later in the program, you can iterate over each mask corresponding to winning positions on the board to determine whether the current player has a winning position, as shown in Listing 3.48.

The continue **Statement**

You might have a block containing a series of statements within a loop. If you determine that some conditions warrant executing only a portion of these statements for some iterations, you can use the continue statement to jump to the end of the current iteration and begin the next iteration. The continue statement exits the current iteration (regardless of whether additional statements remain) and jumps to the loop condition. At that point, if the loop conditional is still true, the loop will continue execution.

Listing 3.50 uses the continue statement so that only the letters of the domain portion of an email are displayed. Output 3.25 shows the results of Listing 3.50.

LISTING 3.50: Determining the Domain of an Email Address

```csharp
class EmailDomain
{
  static void Main()
  {
      string email;
      bool insideDomain = false;
      System.Console.WriteLine("Enter an email address: ");

      email = System.Console.ReadLine();

      System.Console.Write("The email domain is: ");

      // Iterate through each letter in the email address.
      foreach (char letter in email)
      {
          if (!insideDomain)
          {
              if (letter == '@')
              {
                  insideDomain = true;
              }
              continue;
          }

          System.Console.Write(letter);
      }
  }
}
```

OUTPUT 3.25

```
Enter an email address:
mark@dotnetprogramming.com
The email domain is: dotnetprogramming.com
```

In Listing 3.50, if you are not yet inside the domain portion of the email address, you can use a continue statement to move control to the end of the loop, and process the next character in the email address.

You can almost always use an if statement in place of a continue statement, and this is usually more readable. The problem with the continue statement is that it provides multiple flows of control within a single iteration, and this compromises readability. In Listing 3.51, the sample has been rewritten, replacing the continue statement with the if/else construct to demonstrate a more readable version that does not use the continue statement.

LISTING 3.51: Replacing a continue with an if Statement

```
foreach (char letter in email)
{
  if (insideDomain)
  {
      System.Console.Write(letter);
  }
  else
  {
      if (letter == '@')
      {
          insideDomain = true;
      }
  }
}
```

The goto Statement

Early programming languages lacked the relatively sophisticated "structured" control flows that modern languages such as C# have as a matter of course, and instead relied upon simple conditional branching (if) and unconditional branching (goto) statements for most of their control flow needs. The resultant programs were often hard to understand. The continued existence of a goto statement within C# seems like an anachronism to many experienced programmers. However, C# supports goto, and it is the only method for supporting fall-through within a switch statement. In Listing 3.52, if the /out option is set, code execution jumps to the default case using the goto statement; similarly for /f.

LISTING 3.52: Demonstrating a switch with goto Statements

```
// ...
static void Main(string[] args)
{
  bool isOutputSet = false;
  bool isFiltered = false;

  foreach (string option in args)
  {
```

```
switch (option)
{
    case "/out":
        isOutputSet = true;
        isFiltered = false;
        goto default;
    case "/f":
        isFiltered = true;
        isRecursive = false;
        goto default;
    default:
        if (isRecursive)
        {
            // Recurse down the hierarchy
            // ...

        }
        else if (isFiltered)
        {
            // Add option to list of filters.
            // ...
        }
        break;
    }

}

// ...

}
```

Output 3.26 shows how to execute the code shown in Listing 3.52.

OUTPUT 3.26

```
C:\SAMPLES>Generate /out fizbottle.bin /f "*.xml" "*.wsdl"
```

To branch to a switch section label other than the default label, you can use the syntax goto case constant; where constant is the constant associated with the case label you wish to branch to. To branch to a statement that is not associated with a switch section, precede the target statement with any identifier followed by a colon; you can then use that identifier with the goto statement. For example, you could have a labeled statement myLabel : Console.WriteLine(); and then the statement goto myLabel; would branch to the labeled statement. Fortunately, C# prevents using goto to branch *into* a code block; it may only be used to branch within a code block or to an enclosing code block. By making these restrictions, C# avoids most of the serious goto abuses possible in other languages.

In spite of the improvements, using goto is generally considered to be inelegant, difficult to understand, and symptomatic of poorly structured code. If you need to execute a section of code multiple times or under different circumstances, either use a loop or extract code to a method of its own.

> ### Guidelines
>
> **AVOID** using *goto*.

C# Preprocessor Directives

Control flow statements evaluate expressions at runtime. In contrast, the C# preprocessor is invoked during compilation. The preprocessor commands are directives to the C# compiler, specifying the sections of code to compile or identifying how to handle specific errors and warnings within the code. C# preprocessor commands can also provide directives to C# editors regarding the organization of code.

> ### Language Contrast: C++—Preprocessing
>
> Languages such as C and C++ use a **preprocessor** to perform actions on the code based on special tokens. Preprocessor directives generally tell the compiler how to compile the code in a file and do not participate in the compilation process itself. In contrast, the C# compiler handles "preprocessor" directives as part of the regular lexical analysis of the source code. As a result, C# does not support preprocessor macros beyond defining a constant. In fact, the term *preprocessor* is generally a misnomer for C#.

Each preprocessor directive begins with a hash symbol (#), and all preprocessor directives must appear on one line. A newline rather than a semicolon indicates the end of the directive.

A list of each preprocessor directive appears in Table 3.4.

TABLE 3.4: Preprocessor Directives

Statement or Expression	General Syntax Structure	Example

#if directive	**#if** preprocessor-expression
	    code
	#endif
		#if CSHARP2
		    Console.Clear();
		#endif

#elif directive	**#if** preprocessor-expression1
	    code
	#elif preprocessor-expression2
	    code
	#endif
		#if LINUX
		    ...
		#elif WINDOWS
		    ...
		#endif

#else directive	**#if**
	    code
	#else
	    code
	#endif
		#if CSHARP1
		    ...
		#else
		    ...
		#endif

#define directive	**#define** conditional-symbol	**#define** CSHARP2
#undef directive	**#undef** conditional-symbol	**#undef** CSHARP2
#error directive	**#error** proc-message	**#error** Buggy implementation
#warning directive	**#warning** preproc-message	**#warning** Needs code review
#pragma directive	**#pragma** warning	**#pragma** warning disable 1030
#line directive	**#line** org-line new-line **#line default**	**#line** 467 "TicTacToe.cs" ... #line default

#region directive	**#region** pre-proc-message
	    code
	#endregion
		#region Methods
		    ...
		#endregion

Excluding and Including Code (#if, #elif, #else, #endif)

Perhaps the most common use of preprocessor directives is in controlling when and how code is included. For example, to write code that could be compiled by both C# 2.0 and later compilers and the prior version 1.2 compilers, you use a preprocessor directive to exclude C# 2.0-specific code when compiling with a 1.2 compiler. You can see this in the tic-tac-toe example and in Listing 3.53.

LISTING 3.53: **Excluding C# 2.0 Code from a C# 1.x Compiler**

```
#if CSHARP2
System.Console.Clear();
#endif
```

In this case, you call the `System.Console.Clear()` method, which is available only in 2.0 CLI and later versions. Using the `#if` and `#endif` preprocessor directives, this line of code will be compiled only if the preprocessor symbol `CSHARP2` is defined.

Another use of the preprocessor directive would be to handle differences among platforms, such as surrounding Windows- and Linux-specific APIs with `WINDOWS` and `LINUX` `#if` directives. Developers often use these directives in place of multiline comments (`/*...*/`) because they are easier to remove by defining the appropriate symbol or via a search and replace. A final common use of the directives is for debugging. If you surround code with an `#if DEBUG`, you will remove the code from a release build on most IDEs. The IDEs define the `DEBUG` symbol by default in a debug compile and `RELEASE` by default for release builds.

To handle an else-if condition, you can use the `#elif` directive within the `#if` directive, instead of creating two entirely separate `#if` blocks, as shown in Listing 3.54.

LISTING 3.54: **Using** `#if`, `#elif`, **and** `#endif` **Directives**

```
#if LINUX
...
#elif WINDOWS
...
#endif
```

Defining Preprocessor Symbols (#define, #undef)

You can define a preprocessor symbol in two ways. The first is with the `#define` directive, as shown in Listing 3.55.

LISTING 3.55: **A** `#define` **Example**

```
#define CSHARP2
```

The second method uses the `define` option when compiling for .NET, as shown in Output 3.27.

OUTPUT 3.27

```
>csc.exe /define:CSHARP2 TicTacToe.cs
```

Output 3.28 shows the same functionality using the Mono compiler.

OUTPUT 3.28

```
>mcs.exe -define:CSHARP2 TicTacToe.cs
```

To add multiple definitions, separate them with a semicolon. The advantage of the `define` complier option is that no source code changes are required, so you may use the same source files to produce two different binaries.

To undefine a symbol you use the `#undef` directive in the same way you use `#define`.

Emitting Errors and Warnings (#error, #warning)

Sometimes you may want to flag a potential problem with your code. You do this by inserting `#error` and `#warning` directives to emit an error or warning, respectively. Listing 3.56 uses the tic-tac-toe sample to warn that the code does not yet prevent players from entering the same move multiple times. The results of Listing 3.56 appear in Output 3.29.

LISTING 3.56: Defining a Warning with #warning

```
#warning     "Same move allowed multiple times."
```

OUTPUT 3.29

```
Performing main compilation...
...\tictactoe.cs(471,16): warning CS1030: #warning: '"Same move allowed
multiple times."'

Build complete -- 0 errors, 1 warnings
```

By including the #warning directive, you ensure that the compiler will re-port a warning, as shown in Output 3.29. This particular warning is a way of flagging the fact that there is a potential enhancement or bug within the code. It could be a simple way of reminding the developer of a pending task.

Turning Off Warning Messages (#pragma)

Warnings are helpful because they point to code that could potentially be troublesome. However, sometimes it is preferred to turn off particular warnings explicitly because they can be ignored legitimately. C# 2.0 and later compilers provide the preprocessor #pragma directive for just this purpose (see Listing 3.57).

LISTING 3.57: Using the Preprocessor #pragma Directive to Disable the #warning Directive

```
#pragma warning disable  1030
```

Note that warning numbers are prefixed with the letters *CS* in the com-piler output. However, this prefix is not used in the #pragma warning di-rective. The number corresponds to the warning error number emitted by the compiler when there is no preprocessor command.

To reenable the warning, #pragma supports the restore option following the warning, as shown in Listing 3.58.

LISTING 3.58: Using the Preprocessor #pragma Directive to Restore a Warning

```
#pragma warning restore  1030
```

In combination, these two directives can surround a particular block of code where the warning is explicitly determined to be irrelevant.

Perhaps one of the most common warnings to disable is CS1591, as this appears when you elect to generate XML documentation using the /doc compiler option, but you neglect to document all of the public items within your program.

nowarn:<warn list> Option

In addition to the #pragma directive, C# compilers generally support the nowarn:<warn list> option. This achieves the same result as #pragma, except that instead of adding it to the source code, you can insert the com-mand as a compiler option. In addition, the nowarn option affects the entire

as the one in the Microsoft Visual Studio .NET IDE, can search through source code and find these directives to provide editor features when writing code. C# allows you to declare a region of code using the #region directive. You must pair the #region directive with a matching #endregion directive, both of which may optionally include a descriptive string following the directive. In addition, you may nest regions within one another.

Again, Listing 3.60 shows the tic-tac-toe program as an example.

LISTING 3.60: A #region **and** #endregion **Preprocessor Directive**

```
...
#region Display Tic-tac-toe Board

#if CSHARP2
  System.Console.Clear();
#endif

// Display the current board;
border = 0;   // set the first border (border[0] = "|")

// Display the top line of dashes.
// ("\n---+---+---\n")
System.Console.Write(borders[2]);
foreach (char cell in cells)
{
  // Write out a cell value and the border that comes after it.
  System.Console.Write(" {0} {1}", cell, borders[border]);

  // Increment to the next border;
  border++;

  // Reset border to 0 if it is 3.
  if (border == 3)
  {
    border = 0;
  }
}
#endregion Display Tic-tac-toe Board
...
```

One example of how these preprocessor directives are used is with Microsoft Visual Studio .NET. Visual Studio .NET examines the code and provides a tree control to open and collapse the code (on the left-hand side of the code editor window) that matches the region demarcated by the #region directives (see Figure 3.5).

FIGURE 3.5: Collapsed Region in Microsoft Visual Studio .NET

SUMMARY

This chapter began with an introduction to the C# operators related to assignment and arithmetic. Next, you used the operators along with the `const` keyword to declare constants. Coverage of all the C# operators was not sequential, however. Before discussing the relational and logical comparison operators, the chapter introduced the `if` statement and the important concepts of code blocks and scope. To close out the coverage of operators we discussed the bitwise operators, especially regarding masks. We also discussed other control flow statements such as loops, `switch`, and `goto`, and ended the chapter with a discussion of the C# preprocessor directives.

Operator precedence was discussed earlier in the chapter; Table 3.5 summarizes the order of precedence across all operators, including several that are not yet covered.

TABLE 3.5: Operator Order of Precedence*

Category	Operators

Primary	`x.y  f(x)  a[x]  x++  x--  new`
	 `typeof(T)  checked(x)  unchecked(x) default(T)`
	 `delegate{}   ()`

Unary	`+  -  !  ~  ++x  --x  (T)x`
Multiplicative	`*  /  %`
Additive	`+  -`
Shift	`<<  >>`
Relational and type testing	`<  >  <=  >=  is  as`
Equality	`==  !=`
Logical AND	`&`
Logical XOR	`^`
Logical OR	`|`
Conditional AND	`&&`
Conditional OR	`||`
Null coalescing	`??`
Conditional	`?:`
Assignment and lambda	`=  *=  /=  %=  +=  -=  <<=  >>=  &=  ^=  |=  =>`

* Rows appear in order of precedence from highest to lowest.

Perhaps one of the best ways to review all of the content covered in Chapters 1–3 is to look at the tic-tac-toe program found in Appendix B. By reviewing the program, you can see one way in which you can combine all that you have learned into a complete program.

■ 4 ■
Methods and Parameters

ROM WHAT YOU HAVE LEARNED about C# programming so far you should be able to write straightforward programs consisting of a list of statements, similar to the way programs were created in the 1970s. Programming has come a long way since the 1970s; as programs became more complex, new paradigms were needed to manage that complexity. "Procedural" or "structured" programming provides constructs by which statements are grouped together to form units. Furthermore, with structured programming, it is possible to pass data to a group of statements and then have data returned once the statements have executed.

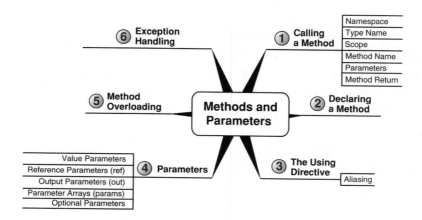

Besides the basics of calling and defining methods, this chapter also covers some slightly more advanced concepts—namely, recursion, method overloading, optional parameters, and named arguments. All method calls discussed so far and through the end of this chapter are static (a concept which Chapter 5 explores in detail).

Even as early as the `HelloWorld` program in Chapter 1, you learned how to define a method. In that example, you defined the `Main()` method. In this chapter, you will learn about method creation in more detail, including the special C# syntaxes (`ref` and `out`) for parameters that pass variables rather than values to methods. Lastly, we will touch on some rudimentary error handling.

Calling a Method

■ BEGINNER TOPIC

What Is a Method?

Up to this point, all of the statements in the programs you have written have appeared together in one grouping called a `Main()` method. When programs become any more complex than those we have seen thus far, a single method implementation quickly becomes difficult to maintain and complex to read through and understand.

A **method** is a means of grouping together a sequence of statements to perform a particular action or compute a particular result. This provides greater structure and organization for the statements that comprise a program. Consider, for example, a `Main()` method that counts the lines of source code in a directory. Instead of having one large `Main()` method, you can provide a shorter version that allows you to hone in on the details of each method implementation as necessary. Listing 4.1 shows an example.

LISTING 4.1: Grouping Statements into Methods

```csharp
class LineCount
{
  static void Main()
  {
      int lineCount;
      string files;
```

```
        DisplayHelpText();
        files = GetFiles();
        lineCount = CountLines(files);
        DisplayLineCount(lineCount);
    }
    // ...
    }
```

Instead of placing all of the statements into `Main()`, the listing breaks them into groups called methods. The `System.Console.WriteLine()` statements that display the help text have been moved to the `DisplayHelpText()` method. All of the statements used to determine which files to count appear in the `GetFiles()` method. To actually count the files, the code calls the `CountLines()` method before displaying the results using the `DisplayLineCount()` method. With a quick glance, it is easy to review the code and gain an overview, because the method name describes the purpose of the method.

Guidelines

DO give methods names that are verbs or verb phrases.

A method is always associated with a type—usually a **class**—that provides a means of grouping related methods together.

Methods can receive data via **arguments** that are supplied for by their **parameters.** Parameters are variables used for passing data from the **caller** (the code containing the method call) to the invoked method (`Write()`, `WriteLine()`, `GetFiles()`, `CountLines()`, and so on). In Listing 4.1, `files` and `lineCount` are examples of arguments passed to the `CountLines()` and `DisplayLineCount()` methods via their parameters. Methods can also return data back to the caller via a **return value** (in Listing 4.1, the `GetFiles()` method call has a return value that is assigned to `files`).

To begin, we will reexamine `System.Console.Write()`, `System.Console.WriteLine()`, and `System.Console.ReadLine()` from Chapter 1. This time we will look at them as examples of method calls in general, instead of looking at the specifics of printing and retrieving data from the console. Listing 4.2 shows each of the three methods in use.

LISTING 4.2: A Simple Method Call

```
class HeyYou
{
  static void Main()
  {
      string firstName;
      string lastName;

      System.Console.WriteLine("Hey you!");

      System.Console.Write("Enter your first name: ");

      firstName = System.Console.ReadLine();
      System.Console.Write("Enter your last name: ");
      lastName = System.Console.ReadLine();
      System.Console.WriteLine("Your full name is {0} {1}.",
          firstName, lastName);
  }
}
```

(annotations on the `System.Console.Write("Enter your first name: ");` line: **Namespace** over `System`, **Type Name** under `Console`, **Method Name** over `Write`, **Parameters** over `"Enter your first name: "`)

The parts of the method call include the method name, argument list, and returned value. A fully qualified method name includes a namespace, type name, and method name; a period separates each part of a fully qualified method name. As we will see, methods are often called with only a part of their fully qualified name.

Namespaces

Namespaces are a categorization mechanism for grouping all types related to a particular area of functionality. Namespaces are hierarchical, and can have arbitrarily many levels in the hierarchy, though namespaces with more than half a dozen levels are rare. Typically the hierarchy begins with a company name, and then a product name, and then the functional area. For example, in `Microsoft.Win32.Networking`, the outermost namespace is `Microsoft`, which contains an inner namespace `Win32`, which in turn contains an even more deeply nested `Networking` namespace.

Namespaces are primarily used to organize types by area of functionality so that they can be more easily found and understood, but namespaces can also be used to avoid type name collisions. For example, the compiler can distinguish between two types with the name `Button` as long as each type has a different namespace. Thus you can disambiguate types `System.Web.UI.WebControls.Button` and `System.Windows.Controls.Button`.

In Listing 4.2, the `Console` type is found within the `System` namespace. The `System` namespace contains the types that enable the programmer to perform many fundamental programming activities. Virtually all C# programs use types within the `System` namespace. Table 4.1 provides a listing of other common namespaces.

TABLE 4.1: Common Namespaces

Namespace	Description
System	Contains the fundamental types, and types for conversion between types, mathematics, program invocation, and environment management.
System.Collections	Contains types for working with collections of objects such as lists and dictionaries.
System.Collections.Generics	Contains strongly typed collections that use generics.
System.Data	Contains types used for working with databases.
System.Drawing	Contains types for drawing to the display device and working with images.
System.IO	Contains types for working with directories and manipulating, loading, and saving files.
System.Linq	Contains classes and interfaces for querying data in collections using a Language Integrated Query.
System.Text	Contains types for working with strings and various text encodings, and for converting between those encodings.
System.Text.RegularExpressions	Contains types for working with regular expressions.
System.Threading	Contains types for multithreaded programming.
System.Threading.Tasks	Contains types for task-based asynchrony.
System.Web	Contains types that enable browser-to-server communication, generally over HTTP. The functionality within this namespace is used to support ASP.NET.

Continues

TABLE 4.1: Common Namespaces, *Continued*

Namespace	Description
System.ServiceModel	The Windows Communication Foundation (WCF) that contains types for sending and retrieving data between service and client applications, enabling the distributed communication between both .NET and non-.NET technologies.
System.Windows	Contains types for creating rich user interfaces starting with .NET 3.0 using a UI technology called Windows Presentation Framework (WPF) that leverages Extensible Application Markup Language (XAML) for declarative design of the UI.
System.Windows.Forms	Contains types for creating rich user interfaces and the components within them.
System.Xml	Contains standards-based support for XML processing.

It is not always necessary to provide the namespace when calling a method. For example, if the call expression appears in a type in the same namespace as the called method, the compiler can infer the namespace to be the namespace which contains the type. Later in this chapter, you will see how the using directive eliminates the need for a namespace qualifier as well.

Guidelines

DO use PascalCasing for namespace names.

CONSIDER organizing the directory hierarchy for source code files to match the namespace hierarchy.

Type Name

Calls to static methods require the type name qualifier as long as the target method is not within the same type.[1] For example, a call expression found in method HelloWorld.Main() to Console.WriteLine() requires the type, Console, to be stated. However, just as with the namespace, C# allows the omission of the type name from a method call whenever the method is a

---

1. Or base class.

member of the type containing the call expression. (Examples of method calls such as this appear in Listing 4.4.) The type name is unnecessary in such cases because the compiler infers the type from the location of the call. If the compiler can make no such inference, the name must be provided as part of the method call.

At their core, types are a means of grouping together methods and their associated data. For example, Console is the type that contains the Write(), WriteLine(), and ReadLine() methods (among others). All of these methods are in the same "group" because they belong to the Console type.

Scope

In the previous chapter you learned that the "scope" of a program element is the region of text in which it can be referred to by its unqualified name. A call that appears inside a type declaration to a method declared in that type does not require the type qualifier because the method is "in scope" throughout its containing type. Similarly, a type is "in scope" throughout the namespace that declares it; therefore, a method call that appears in a type in a particular namespace need not specify that namespace in the method call name.

Method Name

Every method call contains a method name, which might or might not be qualified with a namespace and type name, as we have discussed. After the method name comes the argument list; the argument list is a parenthesized, comma-separated list of the values that correspond to the parameters of the method.

Parameters and Arguments

A method can take any number of parameters, and each parameter is of a specific data type. The values that the caller supplies for parameters are called the **arguments;** every argument must correspond to a particular parameter. For example, the following method call, used in Listing 4.2, has three arguments:

```
System.Console.WriteLine(
    "Your full name is {1} {0}", lastName, firstName)
```

This method is declared to have three parameters, the first being of type string and the second and third being of type object. (Note that here the arguments are all strings; the compiler allows this because all strings are compatible with the data type object.)

Method Return Values

In contrast to System.Console.WriteLine(), the method call System.Console.ReadLine() in Listing 4.2 does not have any arguments because the method is declared to take no parameters. However, this method happens to have a **method return value.** The method return value is a means of transferring results from a called method back to the caller. Because System.Console.ReadLine() has a return value, it is possible to assign the return value to the variable firstName. In addition, it is possible to pass this method return value itself as an argument to another method call, as shown in Listing 4.3.

LISTING 4.3: **Passing a Method Return Value As an Argument to Another Method Call**

```
class Program
{
  static void Main()
  {
      System.Console.Write("Enter your first name: ");
      System.Console.WriteLine("Hello {0}!",
          System.Console.ReadLine());
  }
}
```

Instead of assigning the returned value to a variable and then using that variable as an argument to the call to System.Console.WriteLine(), Listing 4.3 calls the System.Console.ReadLine() method within the call to System.Console.WriteLine(). At execution time, the System.Console.ReadLine() method executes first and its return value is passed directly into the System.Console.WriteLine() method, rather than into a variable.

Not all methods return data. Both versions of System.Console.Write() and System.Console.WriteLine() are examples of such methods. As you will see shortly, these methods specify a return type of void just as the HelloWorld declaration of Main returned void.

Statement versus Method Call

Listing 4.3 provides a demonstration of the difference between a state-ment and a method call. Although `System.Console.WriteLine("Hello {0}!", System.Console.ReadLine());` is a single statement, it contains two method calls. A statement often contains one or more expressions, and in this example, two of those expressions are method calls. Therefore, method calls form parts of statements.

Although coding multiple method calls in a single statement often re-duces the amount of code, it does not necessarily increase the readability and seldom offers a significant performance advantage. Developers should favor readability over brevity.

> **■ NOTE**
>
> In general, developers should favor readability over brevity. Readabil-ity is critical to writing code that is self-documenting and, therefore, more maintainable over time.

Declaring a Method

This section expands on the explanation of declaring a method to include parameters or a return type. Listing 4.4 contains examples of these con-cepts, and Output 4.1 shows the results.

LISTING 4.4: Declaring a Method

```csharp
class IntroducingMethods
{
  static void Main()
  {
    string firstName;
    string lastName;
    string fullName;

    System.Console.WriteLine("Hey you!");

    firstName = GetUserInput("Enter your first name: ");
    lastName = GetUserInput("Enter your last name: ");

    fullName = GetFullName(firstName, lastName);

    DisplayGreeting(fullName);
```

```
    }

    static string GetUserInput(string prompt)
    {
        System.Console.Write(prompt);
        return System.Console.ReadLine();
    }

    static string GetFullName(string firstName, string lastName)
    {
        return firstName + " " + lastName;
    }

    static void DisplayGreeting(string name)
    {
        System.Console.WriteLine("Your full name is {0}.", name);
        return;
    }
}
```

OUTPUT 4.1

```
Hey you!
Enter your first name: Inigo
Enter your last name: Montoya
Your full name is Inigo Montoya.
```

Four methods are declared in Listing 4.4. From `Main()` the code calls `GetUserInput()`, followed by a call to `GetFullName()`. Both of these methods return a value and take arguments. In addition, the listing calls `DisplayGreeting()`, which doesn't return any data. No method in C# can exist outside the confines of an enclosing type; in this case, the enclosing type is the `IntroducingMethods` class. Even the `Main` method examined in Chapter 1 must be within a type.

Language Contrast: C++/Visual Basic—Global Methods

C# provides no global method support; everything must appear within a type declaration. This is why the `Main()` method was marked as `static`—the C# equivalent of a C++ global and Visual Basic "shared" method.

■ BEGINNER TOPIC

Refactoring into Methods

Moving a set of statements into a method instead of leaving them inline within a larger method is a form of **refactoring.** Refactoring reduces code duplication, because you can call the method from multiple places instead of duplicating the code. Refactoring also increases code readability. As part of the coding process, it is a best practice to continually review your code and look for opportunities to refactor. This involves looking for blocks of code that are difficult to understand at a glance and moving them into a method with a name that clearly defines the code's behavior. This practice is often preferred over commenting a block of code, because the method name serves to describe what the implementation does.

For example, the `Main()` method that is shown in Listing 4.4 results in the same behavior as does the `Main()` method that is shown in Listing 1.15 in Chapter 1. Perhaps even more noteworthy is that although both listings are trivial to follow, Listing 4.4 is easier to grasp at a glance by just viewing the `Main()` method and not worrying about the details of each called method's implementation.

In Visual Studio you can select a group of statements, right-click on it, and then select the Extract Method refactoring from the Refactoring section of the context menu to automatically move a group of statements to a new method.

Formal Parameter Declaration

Consider the declaration of the `DisplayGreeting()` and `GetFullName()` methods. The text that appears between the parentheses of a method declaration is the **formal parameter list.** (As we will see when we discuss generics, methods may also have a **type parameter list.** When it is clear from context which kind of parameter we are discussing, we will simply refer to them as "parameters" in a "parameter list.") Each parameter in the parameter list includes the type of the parameter along with the parameter name. A comma separates each parameter in the list.

Behaviorally, most parameters are virtually identical to local variables, and the naming convention of parameters follows accordingly. Therefore, parameter names are camelCase. Also, it is not possible to declare a local variable (a variable declared inside a method) with the same name as a parameter of the containing method, because this would create two "local variables" of the same name.

Guidelines

DO use "camelCasing" for parameter names.

Method Return Type Declaration

In addition to `GetUserInput()` and `GetFullName()` requiring parameters to be specified, both of these methods also include a **method return type.** You can tell that this method returns a value because a data type appears immediately before the method name of the method declaration. For both `GetUserInput()` and `GetFullName()`, the return type is `string`. Unlike parameters, of which there can be any number, only one method return type is allowable.

A method with a return type almost always contains one or more "return statements" that return control to the caller. A `return` statement consists of the `return` keyword followed by an expression that computes the value the method is returning. For example, the `GetFullName()` method's return statement is `return firstName + " " + lastName;`. The expression following the `return` keyword must be compatible with the stated return type of the method.

If a method has a return type, the block of statements that makes up the body of the method must have an "unreachable endpoint." That is, there must be no way for control to "fall off the end" of a method without it returning a value. Often the easiest way to ensure that this condition is met is to make the last statement of the method a `return` statement. However, `return` statements can appear in locations other than at the end of a method implementation. For example, an `if` or `switch` statement in a method implementation could include a `return` statement within it; see Listing 4.5 for an example.

LISTING 4.5: **A** return **Statement before the End of a Method**

```
class Program
{
  static bool MyMethod()
  {
      string command = ObtainCommand();
      switch(command)
      {
          case "quit":
              return false;
          // ... omitted, other cases
          default:
              return true;
      }
  }
}
```

(Note that a `return` statement transfers control out of the `switch`, so no break statement is required to prevent illegal fall-through in a switch section that ends with a return statement.)

In Listing 4.5, the last statement in the method is not a `return` statement; it is a `switch` statement. However, the compiler can deduce that every possible code path through the method results in a `return`, and that therefore the end point of the method is not reachable. Thus this method is legal, even though it does not end with a `return` statement.

If particular code paths include unreachable statements following the `return`, the compiler will issue a warning that indicates that the additional statements will never execute.

In spite of the C# allowance for early returns, code is generally more readable and easier to maintain if there is a single exit location rather than multiple returns sprinkled through various code paths of the method.

Specifying `void` as a return type indicates that there is no return value from the method. As a result, the method does not support assignment to a variable or use as a parameter type at the call site. A void method may only be used as a statement. Furthermore, within the body of the method the `return` statement becomes optional, and when it is specified, there is no value following the `return` keyword. For example, the return of `Main()` in Listing 4.4 is `void` and there is no `return` statement within the method. However, `DisplayGreeting()` includes a `return` statement that is not followed by any returned result.

Language Contrast: C++—Header Files

Unlike C++, C# classes never separate the implementation from the declaration. In C# there is no header (.h) file or implementation (.cpp) file. Instead, declaration and implementation appear together in the same file. (C# does support an advanced feature called "partial methods" in which the method's defining declaration is separate from its implementation, but for the purposes of this chapter we will consider only nonpartial methods.) The lack of separate declaration and implementation in C# removes the requirement to maintain redundant declaration information in two places found in languages such as C++ which have separate header and implementation files.

■ BEGINNER TOPIC

Namespaces

As we described above, **namespaces** are an organizational mechanism for categorizing and grouping together related types. Developers can discover related types by examining other types within the same namespace as a familiar type. Additionally, through namespaces, two or more types may have the same name as long as they are disambiguated by different namespaces.

The using Directive

As we've seen, fully qualified namespace names can become quite long and unwieldy. It is possible to "import" all the types from one or more namespaces into a file so that they can be used without full qualification. To achieve this, the C# programmer includes a using directive, generally at the top of the file. For example, in Listing 4.6, Console is not prefixed with System. The namespace may be omitted because of the using System; directive at the top of the listing.

LISTING 4.6: using **Directive Example**

```
// The using directive imports all types from the
// specified namespace into the entire file.
using System;

class HelloWorld
{
  static void Main()
  {
      // No need to qualify Console with System
      // because of the using directive above.
      Console.WriteLine("Hello, my name is Inigo Montoya");
  }
}
```

The results of Listing 4.6 appear in Output 4.2.

OUTPUT 4.2

```
Hello, my name is Inigo Montoya
```

A using directive such as using System does not enable the omission of System from a type declared within a child namespace of System. For example, if your code accessed the StringBuilder type from the System.Text namespace, you would have to either include an additional using System.Text; directive, or fully qualify the type as System.Text.StringBuilder, not just Text.StringBuilder. In short, a using directive does not "import" types from any **nested namespaces.** Nested namespaces, identified by the period in the namespace, always need to be imported explicitly.

Language Contrast: Java—Wildcards in import **Directive**

Java allows for importing namespaces using a wildcard such as the following:

```
import javax.swing.*;
```

In contrast, C# does not support a wildcard using directive, and instead requires each namespace to be imported explicitly.

Language Contrast: Visual Basic .NET—Project Scope Imports Directive

Unlike C#, Visual Basic .NET supports the ability to specify the `using` directive equivalent, `Imports`, for an entire project, rather than just for a specific file. In other words, Visual Basic .NET provides a command-line means of the `using` directive that will span an entire compilation.

Frequent use of types within a particular namespace typically results in the addition of a `using` directive for that namespace, instead of fully qualifying all types within the namespace. Following this tendency, virtually all files include the `using System` directive at the top. Throughout the remainder of this book, code listings will often omit the `using System` directive. Other namespace directives will be included explicitly, however.

One interesting effect of the `using System` directive is that the string data type can be identified with varying case: `String` or `string`. The former version relies on the `using System` directive and the latter uses the `string` keyword. Both are valid C# references to the `System.String` data type, and the resultant CIL code is unaffected by which version is chosen.[2]

■ ADVANCED TOPIC

Nested `using` Directives

Not only can you have `using` directives at the top of a file, but you also can include them at the top of a namespace declaration. For example, if a new namespace, `EssentialCSharp`, were declared, it would be possible to add a `using` declarative at the top of the namespace declaration (see Listing 4.7).

LISTING 4.7: Specifying the `using` Directive inside a Namespace Declaration

```
namespace EssentialCSharp
{
    using System;

    class HelloWorld
```

---

2. I prefer the `string` keyword, but whichever representation a programmer selects, the code within a project ideally should be consistent.

```
{
    static void Main()
    {
        // No need to qualify Console with System
        // because of the using directive above.
        Console.WriteLine("Hello, my name is Inigo Montoya");
    }
  }
}
```

The results of Listing 4.7 appear in Output 4.3.

OUTPUT 4.3

```
Hello, my name is Inigo Montoya
```

The difference between placing the using directive at the top of a file rather than at the top of a namespace declaration is that the directive is active only within the namespace declaration. If the code includes a new namespace declaration above or below the EssentialCSharp declaration, the using System directive within a different namespace would not be active. Code seldom is written this way, especially given the standard practice of a single type declaration per file.

Aliasing

The using directive also allows **aliasing** a namespace or type. An alias is an alternative name that you can use within the text to which the using directive applies. The two most common reasons for aliasing are to disambiguate two types that have the same name and to abbreviate a long name. In Listing 4.8, for example, the CountDownTimer alias is declared as a means of referring to the type System.Timers.Timer. Simply adding a using System.Timers directive will not sufficiently enable the code to avoid fully qualifying the Timer type. The reason is that System.Threading also includes a type called Timer, and therefore, just using Timer within the code will be ambiguous.

LISTING 4.8: Declaring a Type Alias

```
using System;
using System.Threading;
```

```
using CountDownTimer = System.Timers.Timer;

class HelloWorld
{
  static void Main()
  {
    CountDownTimer timer;

    // ...
  }
}
```

Listing 4.8 uses an entirely new name, CountDownTimer, as the alias. It is possible, however, to specify the alias as Timer, as shown in Listing 4.9.

LISTING 4.9: Declaring a Type Alias with the Same Name

```
using System;
using System.Threading;

// Declare alias Timer to refer to System.Timers.Timer to
// avoid code ambiguity with System.Threading.Timer
using Timer = System.Timers.Timer;

class HelloWorld
{
  static void Main()
  {
    Timer timer;

    // ...
  }
}
```

Because of the alias directive, "Timer" is not an ambiguous reference. Furthermore, to refer to the System.Threading.Timer type, you will have to either qualify the type or define a different alias.

Returns and Parameters on Main()

So far, declaration of an executable's Main() method has been the simplest declaration possible. You have not included any parameters or nonvoid return type in your Main() method declarations. However, C# supports the ability to retrieve the command-line arguments when executing a program, and it is possible to return a status indicator from the Main() method.

The runtime passes the command-line arguments to Main() using a single string array parameter. All you need to do to retrieve the parameters is to access the array, as demonstrated in Listing 4.10. The purpose of this program is to download a file whose location is given by a URL. The first command-line argument identifies the URL, and the optional second argument is the filename to which to save the file. The listing begins with a switch statement that evaluates the number of parameters (args.Length) as follows.

1. If there are not two parameters, display an error indicating that it is necessary to provide the URL and filename.
2. The presence of two arguments indicates the user has provided both the URL of the resource and the download target filename.

LISTING 4.10: **Passing Command-Line Arguments to** Main

```csharp
using System;
using System.IO;
using System.Net;

class Program
{
    static int Main(string[] args)
    {
        int result;
        string targetFileName;
        string url;
        switch (args.Length)
        {
            default:
                // Exactly two arguments must be specified; give an error.
                Console.WriteLine(
                    "ERROR:  You must specify the "
                    + "URL and the file name");
                targetFileName = null;
                url = null;
                break;
            case 2:
                url = args[0];
                targetFileName = args[1];
                break;
        }

        if (targetFileName != null && url != null)
        {
            WebClient webClient = new WebClient();
```

```
            webClient.DownloadFile(url, targetFileName);
        result = 0;
    }
    else
    {
        Console.WriteLine(
            "Usage: Downloader.exe <URL> <TargetFileName>");
        result = 1;
    }
    return result;
    }


}
```

The results of Listing 4.10 appear in Output 4.4.

OUTPUT 4.4

```
>Downloader.exe
ERROR:  You must specify the URL to be downloaded
Downloader.exe <URL> <TargetFileName>
```

If you were successful in calculating the target filename, you would use
it to save the downloaded file. Otherwise, you would display the help text.
The Main() method also returns an int rather than a void. This is optional
for a Main() declaration, but if it is used, the program can return a status
code to a caller, such as a script or a batch file. By convention, a return other
than zero indicates an error.

Although all command-line arguments can be passed to Main() via an array of strings, sometimes it is convenient to access the arguments from inside a
method other than Main(). The System.Environment.GetCommandLineArgs()
method returns the command-line arguments array in the same form that
Main(string[] args) passes the arguments into Main().

■ ADVANCED TOPIC

Disambiguate Multiple Main() Methods

If a program includes two classes with Main() methods, it is possible to
specify on the command line which class to use for the Main() declaration.
csc.exe includes an /m option to specify the fully qualified class name of
Main().

Call Stack and Call Site

As code executes, methods call more methods that in turn call additional methods, and so on. In the simple case of Listing 4.4, `Main()` calls `GetUserInput()`, which in turn calls `System.Console.ReadLine()`, which in turn calls even more methods internally. Every time a new method is invoked, the runtime creates an "activation frame" that contains information about the arguments passed to the new call, the local variables of the new call, and information about where control should resume when the new method returns. The set of calls within calls within calls, and so on, produces a series of activation frames that is termed the **call stack.** As program complexity increases, the call stack generally gets larger and larger as each method calls another method. As calls complete, however, the call stack shrinks until another method is invoked. The term for describing the process of removing activation frames from the call stack is **stack unwinding.** Stack unwinding always occurs in the reverse order of the method calls. The result of method completion is that execution will return to the **call site,** which is the location from which the method was invoked.

Advanced Method Parameters

So far this chapter's examples have returned data via the method return value. This section demonstrates how methods can return data via their method parameters and also shows how a method may take a variable number of arguments.

Value Parameters

Arguments to method calls are usually **passed by value,** which means the value of the argument expression is copied into the target parameter. For example, in Listing 4.11, the value of each variable that `Main()` uses when calling `Combine()` will be copied into the parameters of the `Combine()` method. Output 4.5 shows the results of this listing.

LISTING 4.11: Passing Variables by Value

```
class Program
{
  static void Main()
```

```
    {
        // ...
        string fullName;
        string driveLetter = "C:";
        string folderPath  = "Data";
        string fileName     = "index.html";

        fullName = Combine(driveLetter, folderPath, fileName);

        Console.WriteLine(fullName);
        // ...
    }

    static string Combine(
        string driveLetter, string folderPath, string fileName)
    {
        string path;
        path = string.Format("{1}{0}{2}{0}{3}",
            System.IO.Path.DirectorySeparatorChar,
            driveLetter, folderPath, fileName);
        return path;
    }
}
```

OUTPUT 4.5

```
C:\Data\index.html
```

Even if the `Combine()` method assigns `null` to `driveLetter`, `folderPath`, and `fileName` before returning, the corresponding variables within `Main()` will maintain their original values because the variables are copied when calling a method. When the call stack unwinds at the end of a call, the copied data is thrown away.

■ **BEGINNER TOPIC**

Matching Caller Variables with Parameter Names

In Listing 4.11, the variable names in the caller exactly matched the parameter names in the called method. This matching is simply for readability; whether names match or not is entirely irrelevant to the behavior of the method call. The parameters of the called method and the local variables of the calling method are in different declaration spaces and have nothing to do with each other.

■ADVANCED TOPIC

Reference Types versus Value Types

For the purposes of this section, it is inconsequential whether the parameter passed is a value type or a reference type. The issue is whether the called method can write a value into the caller's original variable. Since a copy of the caller variable's value is made, the caller's variable cannot be reassigned. Nevertheless, it is helpful to understand the difference between a variable that contains a value type and a variable that contains a reference type.

The value of a reference type variable is, as the name implies, a reference to the location where the data associated with the object is stored. How the runtime chooses to represent the value of a reference type variable is an implementation detail of the runtime; typically it is represented as the address of the memory location in which the object's data is stored, but it need not be.

If a reference type variable is passed by value, the reference itself is copied from the caller to the method parameter. As a result, the target method cannot update the caller variable's value but it may update the data referred to by the reference.

Alternatively, if the method parameter is a value type, the value itself is copied into the parameter, and changing the parameter in the called method will not affect the original caller's variable.

Reference Parameters (ref)

Consider Listing 4.12, which calls a function to swap two values, and Output 4.6, which shows the results.

LISTING 4.12: Passing Variables by Reference

```
class Program
{
  static void Main()
  {
      // ...
      string first = "hello";
      string second = "goodbye";
      Swap(ref first, ref second);

      System.Console.WriteLine(
```

```
        @"first = ""{0}""", second = ""{1}""",
        first, second);
    // ...
}
```

```
static void Swap(ref string x, ref string y)
{
    string temp = x;
    x = y;
    y = temp;
}
}
```

OUTPUT 4.6

```
first = "goodbye", second = "hello"
```

The values assigned to first and second are successfully switched. To do this, the variables are **passed by reference.** The obvious difference between the call to Swap() and Listing 4.11's call to Combine() is the use of the keyword ref in front of the parameter's data type. This keyword changes the call such that the variables used as arguments are passed by reference, so the called method can update the original caller's variables with new values.

When the called method specifies a parameter as ref, the caller is required to supply a variable, not a value, as an argument, and to place ref in front of the variables passed. In so doing, the caller explicitly recognizes that the target method could reassign the values of the variables associated with any ref parameters it receives. Furthermore, it is necessary to initialize any local variables passed as ref because target methods could read data from ref parameters without first assigning them. In Listing 4.12, for example, temp is assigned the value of first, assuming that the variable passed in first was initialized by the caller. Effectively, a ref parameter is an alias for the variable passed. In other words, it is essentially giving a parameter name to an existing variable, rather than creating a new variable and copying the value of the argument into it.

Output Parameters (out)

As mentioned above, a variable used as a ref parameter must be assigned before it is passed to the called method, because the called method might read from the variable. The "swap" example given above must read and write from both variables passed to it. However, it is often the case that a method that takes a reference to a variable intends to write to the variable, but not to read from it. In such cases, clearly it could be safe to pass an uninitialized local variable by reference.

To achieve this, code needs to decorate parameter types with the keyword out, as shown in the TryGetPhoneButton() method in Listing 4.13 that returns the phone button corresponding to a character.

LISTING 4.13: Passing Variables Out Only

```csharp
class ConvertToPhoneNumber
{
    static int Main(string[] args)
    {
        char button;

        if(args.Length == 0)
        {
            Console.WriteLine(
                "ConvertToPhoneNumber.exe <phrase>");
            Console.WriteLine(
                "'_' indicates no standard phone button");
            return 1;
        }
        foreach(string word in args)
        {
            foreach(char character in word)
            {
                if(TryGetPhoneButton(character, out button))
                {
                    Console.Write(button);
                }
                else
                {
                    Console.Write('_');
                }
            }
        }
        Console.WriteLine();
        return 0;
    }

    static bool TryGetPhoneButton(char character, out char button)
    {
        bool success = true;
        switch( char.ToLower(character) )
        {
            case '1':
                button = '1';
                break;
```

```
        case '2': case 'a': case 'b': case 'c':
            button = '2';
            break;

        // ...

        case '-':
            button = '-';
            break;
        default:
            // Set the button to indicate an invalid value
            button = '_';
            success = false;
            break;
    }
    return success;
  }
}
```

Output 4.7 shows the results of Listing 4.13.

OUTPUT 4.7

```
>ConvertToPhoneNumber.exe CSharpIsGood
274277474663
```

In this example, the `TryGetPhoneButton()` method returns `true` if it can successfully determine the `character`'s corresponding phone button. The function also returns the corresponding button by using the `button` parameter which is decorated with `out`.

An out parameter is functionally identical to a `ref` parameter; the only difference is what requirements the language enforces regarding how the aliased variable is read from and written to. Whenever a parameter is marked with `out`, the compiler will check that the parameter is set for all code paths within the method that return normally. If, for example, the code does not assign `button` a value in some code path, the compiler will issue an error indicating that the code didn't initialize `button`. Listing 4.13 assigns `button` to the underscore character because even though it cannot determine the correct phone button, it is still necessary to assign a value.

The developer of a method may declare one or more out parameters in order to get around the restriction that a method may only have one return type; a method which needs to return two values can do so by returning one value normally, as the return value of the method, and a second value by writing it into an aliased variable passed as an out parameter. Though this pattern is both common and legal, there are usually better ways to achieve that aim. First off, if you are considering returning two or more values from a method, you might actually be better off writing two methods, one for each value. If the method must return two values, use of tuple types (to represent multiple values) or nullable value types (to represent a value that might not be "valid," as in the example above) can eliminate the need to pass variables by reference.

Parameter Arrays (params)

In all the examples so far, the number of arguments that must be passed is fixed by the number of parameters declared in the target method declaration. However, sometimes it is convenient if the number of arguments may vary. Consider the Combine() method from Listing 4.11. In that method, you passed the drive letter, folder path, and filename. What if the path had more than one folder, and the caller wanted the method to join additional folders to form the full path? Perhaps the best option would be to pass an array of strings for the folders. However, this would make the calling code a little more complex, because it would be necessary to construct an array to pass as an argument.

To make it easier on the callers of such a method, C# provides a keyword that enables the number of arguments to vary in the calling code instead of being set by the target method. Before we discuss the method declaration, observe the calling code declared within Main(), as shown in Listing 4.14.

LISTING 4.14: **Passing a Variable Parameter List**

```
using System.IO;

class PathEx
{
  static void Main()
  {
      string fullName;

      // ...

      // Call Combine() with four arguments
      fullName = Combine(
          Directory.GetCurrentDirectory(),
          "bin", "config", "index.html");
```

```
        Console.WriteLine(fullName);

        // ...

        // Call Combine() with only three arguments
        fullName = Combine(
            Environment.SystemDirectory,
            "Temp", "index.html");
        Console.WriteLine(fullName);

        // ...

        // Call Combine() with an array
        fullName = Combine(
            new string[] {
                "C:\\", "Data",
                "HomeDir", "index.html"} );
        Console.WriteLine(fullName);
        // ...
    }

    static string Combine(params string[] paths)
    {
        string result = string.Empty;
        foreach (string path in paths)
        {
            result = System.IO.Path.Combine(result, path);
        }
        return result;
    }
}
```

Output 4.8 shows the results of Listing 4.14.

OUTPUT 4.8

```
C:\Data\mark\bin\config\index.html
C:\WINDOWS\system32\Temp\index.html
C:\Data\HomeDir\index.html
```

In the first call to Combine(), four arguments are specified. The second call contains only three arguments. In the final call, a single argument is passed using an array. In other words, the Combine() method takes a variable number of arguments; either any number of string arguments separated by commas or as a single array of strings. The former syntax is called the "expanded" form of the method call, and the second form is called the "normal" form.

To allow this, the `Combine()` method does the following:

1. Places `params` immediately before the last parameter in the method declaration
2. Declares the last parameter as an array

With a **parameter array** declaration, it is possible to access each corresponding argument as a member of the `params` array. In the `Combine()` method implementation, you iterate over the elements of the `paths` array and call `System.IO.Path.Combine()`. This method automatically combines the parts of the path, appropriately using the platform-specific directory-separator-character. (`PathEx.Combine()` is identical to `Path.Combine()`, except that `PathEx.Combine()` handles a variable number of parameters rather than simply two.)

There are a few notable characteristics of the parameter array.

- The parameter array is not necessarily the only parameter on a method. However, the parameter array must be the last parameter in the method declaration. Since only the last parameter may be a parameter array, a method cannot have more than one parameter array.
- The caller can specify zero arguments that correspond to the parameter array parameter, which will result in an array of zero items being passed as the parameter array.
- Parameter arrays are type-safe—the arguments given must be compatible with the element type of the parameter array.
- The caller can use an explicit array rather than a comma-separated list of parameters. The resultant code is identical.
- If the target method implementation requires a minimum number of parameters, those parameters should appear explicitly within the method declaration, forcing a compile error instead of relying on run-time error handling if required parameters are missing. For example, if you have a method that requires one or more integer arguments, declare the method as `int Max(int first, params int[] operands)` rather than `int Max(params int[] operands)` so that at least one value is passed to `Max()`.

Using a parameter array, you can pass a variable number of arguments of the same type into a method. The section Method Overloading, later in this chapter, discusses a means of supporting a variable number of arguments that are not necessarily of the same type.

Recursion

Calling a method **recursively** or implementing the method using **recursion** refers to a method that calls itself. Recursion is sometimes the simplest way to implement a particular algorithm. Listing 4.15 counts the lines of all the C# source files (*.cs) in a directory and its subdirectory.

LISTING 4.15: Counting the Lines within *.cs Files, Given a Directory

```csharp
using System.IO;

public static class LineCounter
{
    // Use the first argument as the directory
    // to search, or default to the current directory.
    public static void Main(string[] args)
    {
        int totalLineCount = 0;
        string directory;
        if (args.Length > 0)
        {
            directory = args[0];
        }
        else
        {
            directory = Directory.GetCurrentDirectory();
        }
        totalLineCount = DirectoryCountLines(directory);
        System.Console.WriteLine(totalLineCount);
    }

    static int DirectoryCountLines(string directory)
    {
        int lineCount = 0;
        foreach (string file in
            Directory.GetFiles(directory, "*.cs"))
        {
            lineCount += CountLines(file);
        }

        foreach (string subdirectory in
            Directory.GetDirectories(directory))
```

```
        {
            lineCount += DirectoryCountLines(subdirectory);
        }

        return lineCount;
    }

    private static int CountLines(string file)
    {
        string line;
        int lineCount = 0;
        FileStream stream =
            new FileStream(file, FileMode.Open);³
        StreamReader reader = new StreamReader(stream);
        line = reader.ReadLine();

        while(line != null)
        {
            if (line.Trim() != "")
            {
                lineCount++;
            }
            line = reader.ReadLine();
        }

        reader.Close();  // Automatically closes the stream
        return lineCount;
    }
}
```

Output 4.9 shows the results of Listing 4.15.

OUTPUT 4.9

```
104
```

The program begins by passing the first command-line argument to
`DirectoryCountLines()`, or by using the current directory if no argument
was provided. This method first iterates through all the files in the current
directory and totals the source code lines for each file. After each file in the
directory, the code processes each subdirectory by passing the subdirectory
back into the `DirectoryCountLines()` method, rerunning the method using

---

3. This code could be improved with a using statement, a construct that we have avoided
   because it has not yet been introduced.

the subdirectory. The same process is repeated recursively through each subdirectory until no more directories remain to process.

Readers unfamiliar with recursion may find it confusing at first. Regardless, it is often the simplest pattern to code, especially with hierarchical type data such as the filesystem. However, although it may be the most readable, it is generally not the fastest implementation. If performance becomes an issue, developers should seek an alternative solution in place of a recursive implementation. The choice generally hinges on balancing readability with performance.

■ BEGINNER TOPIC

Infinite Recursion Error

A common programming error in recursive method implementations appears in the form of a stack overflow during program execution. This usually happens because of **infinite recursion,** in which the method continually calls back on itself, never reaching a point that indicates the end of the recursion. It is a good practice for programmers to review any method that uses recursion and to verify that the recursion calls are finite.

A common pattern for recursion using pseudocode is as follows:

```
M(x)
{
  if x is trivial
    Return the result
  else
      a. Do some work to make the problem smaller
      b. Recursively call M to solve the smaller problem
      c. Compute the result based on a. and b.
      return the result
}
```

Things go wrong when this pattern is not followed. For example, if you don't make the problem smaller or if you don't handle all possible "smallest" cases, the recursion never terminates.

Method Overloading

Listing 4.15 called `DirectoryCountLines()`, which counted the lines of `*.cs` files. However, if you want to count code in `*.h`/`*.cpp` files or in `*.vb` files, DirectoryCountLines() will not work. Instead, you need a method that takes the file extension, but still keeps the existing method definition so that it handles *.cs files by default.

All methods within a class must have a unique signature, and C# defines uniqueness by variation in the method name, parameter data types, or number of parameters. This does not include method return data types; defining two methods that differ only in their return data types will cause a compile error. **Method overloading** occurs when a class has two or more methods with the same name and the parameter count and/or data types vary between the overloaded methods.

Method overloading is a type of **operational polymorphism.** Polymorphism occurs when the same logical operation takes on many ("poly") forms ("morphs") because the data varies. Calling WriteLine() and passing a format string along with some parameters is implemented differently than calling WriteLine() and specifying an integer. However, logically, to the caller, the method takes care of writing the data and it is somewhat irrelevant how the internal implementation occurs. Listing 4.16 provides an example, and Output 4.10 shows the results.

LISTING 4.16: **Counting the Lines within** *.cs **Files Using Overloading**

```csharp
using System.IO;

public static class LineCounter
{
  public static void Main(string[] args)
  {
      int totalLineCount;

      if (args.Length > 1)
      {
          totalLineCount =
              DirectoryCountLines(args[0], args[1]);
      }
      if (args.Length > 0)
      {
          totalLineCount = DirectoryCountLines(args[0]);
      }
      else
      {
          totalLineCount = DirectoryCountLines();
      }

      System.Console.WriteLine(totalLineCount);
  }
```

```
static int DirectoryCountLines()
{
    return DirectoryCountLines(
        Directory.GetCurrentDirectory());
}


static int DirectoryCountLines(string directory)
{
    return DirectoryCountLines(directory, "*.cs");
}

static int DirectoryCountLines(
    string directory, string extension)
{
    int lineCount = 0;
    foreach (string file in
        Directory.GetFiles(directory, extension))
    {
        lineCount += CountLines(file);
    }

    foreach (string subdirectory in
        Directory.GetDirectories(directory))
    {
        lineCount += DirectoryCountLines(subdirectory);
    }

    return lineCount;
}

private static int CountLines(string file)
{
    int lineCount = 0;
    string line;
    FileStream stream =
        new FileStream(file, FileMode.Open);[4]
    StreamReader reader = new StreamReader(stream);
    line = reader.ReadLine();
    while(line != null)
    {
        if (line.Trim() != "")
        {
            lineCount++;
        }
        line = reader.ReadLine();
    }

    reader.Close();  // Automatically closes the stream
    return lineCount;
```

4. This code could be improved with a using statement, a construct that we have avoided because it has not yet been introduced.

```
    }
  }
```

OUTPUT 4.10

```
>LineCounter.exe .\ *.cs
28
```

The effect of method overloading is to provide optional ways to call the method. As demonstrated inside `Main()`, you can call the `DirectoryCountLines()` method with or without passing the directory to search and the file extension.

Notice that the parameterless implementation of `DirectoryCountLines()` was changed to call the single-parameter version (`int DirectoryCountLines(string directory)`). This is a common pattern when implementing overloaded methods. The idea is that developers implement only the core logic in one method and all the other overloaded methods will call that single method. If the core implementation changes, it needs to be modified in only one location rather than within each implementation. This pattern is especially prevalent when using method overloading to enable optional parameters that do not have compile-time determined values and so they cannot be specified using optional parameters.

Optional Parameters

Starting with C# 4.0, the language designers added support for **optional parameters.** By allowing the association of a parameter with a constant value as part of the method declaration, it is possible to call a method without passing an argument for every parameter of the method (see Listing 4.17).

LISTING 4.17: Methods with Optional Parameters

```
using System.IO;

public static class LineCounter
{
  public static void Main(string[] args)
  {
    int totalLineCount;
```

```csharp
    if (args.Length > 1)
    {
        totalLineCount =
            DirectoryCountLines(args[0], args[1]);
    }
    if (args.Length > 0)
    {
        totalLineCount = DirectoryCountLines(args[0]);
    }
    else
    {
        totalLineCount  = DirectoryCountLines();
    }

    System.Console.WriteLine(totalLineCount);
}

static int DirectoryCountLines()
{
    // ...
}


/*
static int DirectoryCountLines(string directory)
{ ... }
*/

static int DirectoryCountLines(
    string directory, string extension = "*.cs")
{
    int lineCount = 0;
    foreach (string file in
        Directory.GetFiles(directory, extension))
    {
        lineCount += CountLines(file);
    }

    foreach (string subdirectory in
        Directory.GetDirectories(directory))
    {
        lineCount += DirectoryCountLines(subdirectory);
    }

    return lineCount;
}

private static int CountLines(string file)
{
    // ...
}
}
```

In Listing 4.17, for example, the `DirectoryCountLines()` method declaration with a single parameter has been removed (commented out), but the call from `Main()` (specifying one parameter) remains. When no `extension` parameter is specified in the call, the value assigned to `extension` within the declaration (`*.cs` in this case) is used. This allows the calling code to not specify a value if desired, and eliminates the additional overload that would be required in C# 3.0 and earlier. Note that optional parameters must appear after all required parameters (those that don't have default values). Also, the fact that the default value needs to be a constant, compile-time-resolved value is fairly restrictive. You can't, for example, declare a method like this:

```
DirectoryCountLines(
    string directory = Environment.CurrentDirectory,
    string extension = "*.cs")
```

because `Environment.CurrentDirectory` is not a constant. In contrast, since `"*.cs"` is a constant, C# does allow it for the default value of an optional parameter.

Guidelines

DO provide good defaults for all parameters where possible.

DO provide simple method overloads that have a small number of required parameters.

CONSIDER organizing overloads from the simplest to the most complex.

A second method call feature made available in C# 4.0 was the use of **named arguments**. With named arguments it is possible for the caller to explicitly identify the name of the parameter to be assigned a value, rather than relying only on parameter and argument order to correlate (see Listing 4.18).

LISTING 4.18: **Specifying Parameters by Name**

```
class Program
{
    static void Main()
    {
        DisplayGreeting(
            firstName: "Inigo", lastName: "Montoya");
    }
```

```
public void DisplayGreeting(
    string firstName,
    string middleName = default(string),
    string lastName = default(string))
{
    // ...
}
}
```

In Listing 4.18 the call to `DisplayGreeting()` from within `Main()` assigns a value to a parameter by name. Of the two optional parameters (`middleName` and `lastName`), only `lastName` is given as an argument. For cases where a method has lots of parameters and many of them are optional (a common occurrence when accessing Microsoft COM libraries), using the named argument syntax is certainly a convenience. However, notice that along with the convenience comes an impact on the flexibility of the method interface. In the past, parameter names could be changed without causing other calling C# code to no longer compile. With the addition of named parameters, the parameter name becomes part of the interface because changing the name would cause code that uses the named parameter to no longer compile.

Guidelines

DO treat parameter names as part of the API, and avoid changing the names if version compatibility between APIs is important.

For many experienced C# developers, this is a surprising restriction. However, the restriction has been imposed as part of the Common Language Specification ever since .NET 1.0. Moreover, Visual Basic has always supported calling methods with named arguments. Therefore, library developers should already be following the practice of not changing parameter names to successfully interoperate with other .NET languages from version to version. C# 4.0 now imposes the same restriction on changing parameter names that many other .NET languages already require.

Given the combination of method overloading, optional parameters, and named parameters, resolving which method to call becomes less obvious. A call is **applicable** (compatible) with a method if all parameters have exactly one corresponding argument (either by name or by position) that is type-compatible, unless the parameter is optional (or is a parameter array). Although this restricts the possible number of methods that will be called, it doesn't identify a unique method. To further distinguish which method specifically will be called, the compiler uses only explicitly identified parameters in the caller, ignoring all optional parameters that were not specified at the caller. Therefore, if two methods are applicable because one of them has an optional parameter, the compiler will resolve to the method without the optional parameter.

■ ADVANCED TOPIC

Method Resolution

When the compiler must choose which of several applicable methods is the best one for a particular call, the one with the "most specific" parameter types is chosen. Assuming there are two applicable methods, each requiring an implicit conversion from an argument to a parameter type, the method whose parameter type is the more derived type will be used.

For example, a method that takes a `double` parameter will be chosen over a method that takes an `object` parameter if the caller passes an argument of type `int`. This is because `double` is more specific than `object`. There are objects that are not doubles, but there are no doubles that are not objects, so `double` must be more specific.

If more than one method is applicable and no unique best method can be determined, the compiler will issue an error indicating that the call is ambiguous.

For example, given the following methods:

```
static void Method(object thing){}
static void Method(double thing){}
static void Method(long thing){}
static void Method(int thing){}
```

a call of the form `Method(42)` will resolve as `Method(int thing)` because that is an exact match from the argument type to the parameter type. Were that method to be removed, overload resolution would choose the `long` version because `long` is more specific than either `double` or `object`.

The C# specification includes additional rules governing implicit conversion between `byte`, `ushort`, `uint`, `ulong`, and the other numeric types, but in general it is better to use a cast to make the intended target method more recognizable.

Basic Error Handling with Exceptions

This section examines how to handle error reporting via a mechanism known as **exception handling.**

With exception handling, a method is able to pass information about an error to a calling method without using a return value or explicitly providing any parameters to do so. Listing 4.19 contains a slight modification to the HeyYou program from Chapter 1. Instead of requesting the last name of the user, it prompts for the user's age.

LISTING 4.19: **Converting a** string **to an** int

```csharp
using System;

class ExceptionHandling
{
  static void Main()
  {
      string firstName;
      string ageText;
      int age;

      Console.WriteLine("Hey you!");

      Console.Write("Enter your first name: ");
      firstName = System.Console.ReadLine();

      Console.Write("Enter your age: ");
      ageText = Console.ReadLine();
      age = int.Parse(ageText);

      Console.WriteLine(
          "Hi {0}!  You are {1} months old.",
          firstName, age*12);
  }
}
```

Output 4.11 shows the results of Listing 4.19.

OUTPUT 4.11

```
Hey you!
Enter your first name: Inigo
Enter your age: 42
Hi Inigo!  You are 504 months old.
```

The return value from System.Console.ReadLine() is stored in a variable called ageText and is then passed to a method on the int data type, called Parse(). This method is responsible for taking a string value that represents a number and converting it to an int type.

■ BEGINNER TOPIC

42 As a String versus 42 As an Integer

C# requires that every non-null value has a well-defined type associated with it. Therefore, not only is the data value important, but the type associated with the data is important as well. A string value of 42, therefore, is distinctly different from an integer value of 42. The string is composed of the two characters 4 and 2, whereas the int is the number 42.

Given the converted string, the final System.Console.WriteLine() statement will print the age in months by multiplying the age value by 12.

However, what happens if the user does not enter a valid integer string? For example, what happens if the user enters "forty-two"? The Parse() method cannot handle such a conversion. It expects the user to enter a string that contains only digits. If the Parse() method is sent an invalid value, it needs some way to report this fact back to the caller.

Trapping Errors

To indicate to the calling method that the parameter is invalid, int.Parse() will **throw an exception.** Throwing an exception will halt further execution in the current control flow and instead will jump into the first code block within the call stack that handles the exception.

Since you have not yet provided any such handling, the program reports the exception to the user as an **unhandled exception.** Assuming there is no registered debugger on the system, the error will appear on the console with a message such as that shown in Output 4.12.

OUTPUT 4.12

```
Hey you!
Enter your first name: Inigo
Enter your age: forty-two

Unhandled Exception: System.FormatException: Input string was
    not in a correct format.
  at System.Number.ParseInt32(String s, NumberStyles style,
    NumberFormatInfo info)
  at ExceptionHandling.Main()
```

Obviously, such an error is not particularly helpful. To fix this, it is necessary to provide a mechanism that handles the error, perhaps reporting a more meaningful error message back to the user.

This is known as **catching an exception.** The syntax is demonstrated in Listing 4.20, and the output appears in Output 4.13.

LISTING 4.20: Catching an Exception

```csharp
using System;

class ExceptionHandling
{
  static int Main()
  {
      string firstName;
      string ageText;
      int age;
      int result = 0;

      Console.Write("Enter your first name: ");
      firstName = Console.ReadLine();

      Console.Write("Enter your age: ");
      ageText = Console.ReadLine();

      try
      {
          age = int.Parse(ageText);
          Console.WriteLine(
              "Hi {0}!  You are {1} months old.",
              firstName, age*12);
      }
      catch (FormatException )
      {
          Console.WriteLine(
              "The age entered, {0}, is not valid.",
              ageText);
          result = 1;
```

```
        }
        catch(Exception exception)
        {
            Console.WriteLine(
                "Unexpected error:  {0}", exception.Message);
            result = 1;
        }
        finally
        {
            Console.WriteLine("Goodbye {0}",
                firstName);
        }

        return result;
    }
}
```

OUTPUT 4.13

```
Enter your first name: Inigo
Enter your age: forty-two
The age entered, forty-two, is not valid.
Goodbye Inigo
```

To begin, surround the code that could potentially throw an exception (age = int.Parse()) with a **try block.** This block begins with the try key-word. It is an indication to the compiler that the developer is aware of the possibility that the code within the block could potentially throw an exception, and if it does, one of the **catch blocks** will attempt to handle the exception.

One or more catch blocks (or the finally block) must appear immediately following a try block. The catch block header (see the Advanced Topic titled General catch, later in this chapter) optionally allows you to specify the data type of the exception, and as long as the data type matches the exception type, the catch block will execute. If, however, there is no appropriate catch block, the exception will fall through and go unhandled as though there were no exception handling.

The resultant control flow appears in Figure 4.1.

For example, assume the user enters "forty-two" for the age. In this case, int.Parse() will throw an exception of type System.FormatException, and control will jump to the set of catch blocks. (System.FormatException indicates that the string was not of the correct format to be parsed appropriately.) Since the first catch block matches the type of exception that int.Parse() threw, the code inside this block will execute. If a statement within the try block throws a different exception, the second catch block would execute because all exceptions are of type System.Exception.

If there were no System.FormatException catch block, the System .Exception catch block would execute even though int.Parse throws a

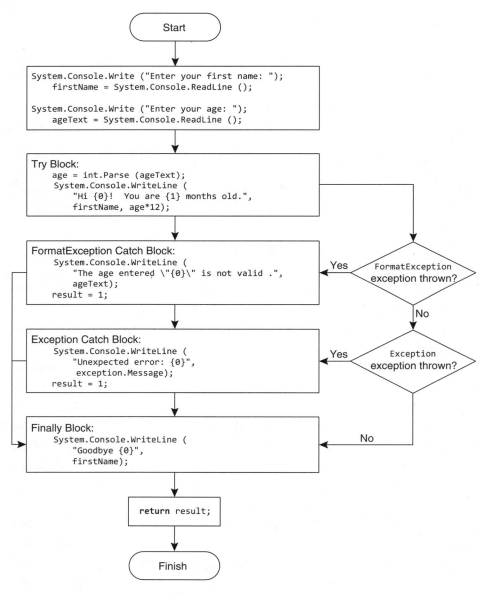

FIGURE 4.1: Exception-Handling Control Flow

System.FormatException. This is because a System.FormatException is also of type System.Exception. (System.FormatException is a more specific implementation of the generic exception, System.Exception.)

The order in which you handle exceptions is significant. Catch blocks must appear from most specific to least specific. The System.Exception data type is least specific, and therefore, it appears last. System.FormatException appears first because it is the most specific exception that Listing 4.20 handles.

Regardless of whether control leaves the try block normally or because the code in the try block throws an exception, the **finally block** of code will execute after control leaves the try-protected region. The purpose of the finally block is to provide a location to place code that will execute regardless of how the try/catch blocks exit—with or without an exception. Finally blocks are useful for cleaning up resources regardless of whether an exception is thrown. In fact, it is possible to have a try block with a finally block and no catch block. The finally block executes regardless of whether the try block throws an exception or whether a catch block is even written to handle the exception. Listing 4.21 demonstrates the try/finally block and Output 4.14 shows the results.

LISTING 4.21: Finally Block without a Catch Block

```
using System;

class ExceptionHandling
{
  static int Main()
  {
      string firstName;
      string ageText;
      int age;
      int result = 0;

      Console.Write("Enter your first name: ");
      firstName = Console.ReadLine();

      Console.Write("Enter your age: ");
      ageText = Console.ReadLine();

      try
      {
          age = int.Parse(ageText);
          Console.WriteLine(
              "Hi {0}!  You are {1} months old.",
              firstName, age*12);
```

```
        }
        finally
        {
            Console.WriteLine("Goodbye {0}",
                firstName);
        }

        return result;
    }
}
```

OUTPUT 4.14

```
Enter your first name: Inigo
Enter your age: forty-two

Unhandled Exception: System.FormatException: Input string was not in a
correct format.
    at System.Number.StringToNumber(String str, NumberStyles options,
NumberBuffer& number, NumberFormatInfo info, Boolean parseDecimal)
    at System.Number.ParseInt32(String s, NumberStyles style,
NumberFormatInfo info)
    at ExceptionHandling.Main()
Goodbye Inigo
```

The attentive reader will have noticed something interesting here: The runtime first reported the unhandled exception, and then ran the finally block. What explains this unusual behavior?

First off, the behavior is legal because when an exception is unhandled, the behavior of the runtime is implementation-defined; any behavior is legal! The runtime chooses this particular behavior because it knows before it chooses to run the finally block that the exception is going to be unhandled; the runtime has already examined all of the activation frames on the call stack and determined that none of them are associated with a catch block that matches the thrown exception.

As soon as the runtime determines that the exception is going to be unhandled, it checks to see if there is a debugger installed on the machine, because you might be the software developer who is analyzing this failure. If there is, it offers the user the chance to attach the debugger to the process *before* the finally block runs. If there is no debugger installed, or if the user declines to debug the problem, the default behavior is to print the unhandled exception to the console, and then see if there are any finally blocks that could run. Note that due to the "implementation-defined" nature of the situation, the runtime is not required to run finally blocks in this situation; an implementation may choose to do so or not.

Guidelines

AVOID explicitly throwing exceptions from finally blocks. (Implicitly thrown exceptions resulting from method calls are acceptable.)

DO favor try/finally and avoid using try/catch for cleanup code.

DO throw exceptions that describe what exceptional circumstance occurred, and if possible, how to prevent it.

■ ADVANCED TOPIC

Exception Class Inheritance

Starting in C# 2.0, all objects thrown as exceptions derive from `System.Exception`. (Objects thrown from other languages which do not derive from `System.Exception` are automatically "wrapped" by an object which does.) Therefore, they can be handled by the `catch(System.Exception exception)` block. It is preferable, however, to include a catch block that is specific to the most derived type (`System.FormatException`, for example), because then it is possible to get the most information about an exception and handle it less generically. In so doing, the `catch` statement that uses the most derived type is able to handle the exception type specifically, accessing data related to the exception thrown, and avoiding conditional logic to determine what type of exception occurred.

This is why C# enforces that catch blocks appear from most derived to least derived. For example, a `catch` statement that catches `System.Exception` cannot appear before a statement that catches `System.FormatException` because `System.FormatException` derives from `System.Exception`.

A method could throw many exception types. Table 4.2 lists some of the more common ones within the framework.

TABLE 4.2: Common Exception Types

Exception Type	Description
System.Exception	The "base" exception from which all other exceptions derive.
System.ArgumentException	Indicates that one of the arguments passed into the method is invalid.
System.ArgumentNullException	Indicates that a particular argument is null and that this is not a valid value for that parameter.
System.ApplicationException	To be avoided. Originally the idea that you might want to have one kind of handling for "system" exceptions and another for "application" exceptions, although plausible, doesn't actually work well in the real world.
System.FormatException	Indicates that the string format is not valid for conversion.
System.IndexOutOfRangeException	Indicates that an attempt was made to access an array or other collection element that does not exist.
System.InvalidCastException	Indicates that an attempt to convert from one data type to another was not a valid conversion.
System.NotImplementedException	Indicates that although the method signature exists, it has not been fully implemented.
System.NullReferenceException	Throws when code tries to find the object referred to by a reference which is null.
System.ArithmeticException	Indicates an invalid math operation, not including divide by zero.
System.ArrayTypeMismatchException	Occurs when attempting to store an element of the wrong type into an array.
System.StackOverflowException	Indicates an unexpectedly deep recursion.

■ ADVANCED TOPIC

General catch

It is possible to specify a catch block that takes no parameters, as shown in Listing 4.22.

LISTING 4.22: General Catch Blocks

```
...
try
{
    age = int.Parse(ageText);
    System.Console.WriteLine(
        "Hi {0}!  You are {1} months old.",
        firstName, age*12);
}
catch (System.FormatException exception)
{
    System.Console.WriteLine(
        "The age entered ,{0}, is not valid.",
        ageText);
    result = 1;
}
catch(System.Exception exception)
{
    System.Console.WriteLine(
        "Unexpected error:  {0}", exception.Message);
    result = 1;
}
catch
{
    System.Console.WriteLine(
        "Unexpected error!");
    result = 1;
}
finally
{
    System.Console.WriteLine("Goodbye {0}",
        firstName);
}
...
```

A catch block with no data type, called a **general catch block,** is equivalent to specifying a catch block that takes an object data type: for instance, catch(object exception){...}. And since all classes ultimately derive from object, a catch block with no data type must appear last.

General catch blocks are rarely used because there is no way to capture any information about the exception. In addition, C# doesn't support the ability to throw an exception of type object. (Only libraries written in languages such as C++ allow exceptions of any type.)

The behavior starting in C# 2.0 varies slightly from the earlier C# behavior. In C# 2.0, if a language allows throwing non-System.Exceptions, the object of the thrown exception will be wrapped in a System .Runtime.CompilerServices.RuntimeWrappedException which does derive from System.Exception. Therefore, all exceptions, whether deriving from System.Exception or not, will propagate into C# assemblies as derived from System.Exception.

The result is that System.Exception catch blocks will catch all exceptions not caught by earlier blocks, and a general catch block, following a System.Exception catch block, will never be invoked. Because of this, following a System.Exception catch block with a general catch block in C# 2.0 or later will result in a compiler warning indicating that the general catch block will never execute.

Guidelines

AVOID general catch blocks and replace them with a catch of System.Exception.

AVOID catching exceptions for which the appropriate action is unknown. It is better to let an exception go unhandled than to handle it incorrectly.

AVOID catching and logging an exception before rethrowing. Rather allow the exception to escape until it can be handled appropriately.

Reporting Errors Using a throw Statement

C# allows developers to throw exceptions from their code, as demonstrated in Listing 4.23 and Output 4.15.

LISTING 4.23: Throwing an Exception

```csharp
using System;
class ThrowingExceptions
{
  static void Main()
  {
      try
      {
```

```
            Console.WriteLine("Begin executing");
            Console.WriteLine("Throw exception...");
            throw new Exception("Arbitrary exception");
            Console.WriteLine("End executing");
        }
        catch (FormatException exception)
        {
            Console.WriteLine(
                "A FormateException was thrown");
        }
        catch(Exception exception)
        {
            Console.WriteLine(
                "Unexpected error:  {0}", exception.Message);
        }
        catch
        {
            Console.WriteLine("Unexpected error!");
        }

        Console.WriteLine(
            "Shutting down...");
    }
}
```

OUTPUT 4.15

```
Begin executing
Throw exception...
Unexpected error:  Arbitrary exception
Shutting down...
```

As the arrows in Listing 4.23 depict, throwing an exception jumps execution from where the exception is thrown into the first catch block within the stack that is compatible with the thrown exception type.[5] In this case, the second catch block handles the exception and writes out an error message. In Listing 4.23, there is no finally block, so execution falls through to the System.Console.WriteLine() statement following the try/catch block.

In order to throw an exception, it is necessary to have an instance of an exception. Listing 4.23 creates an instance using the keyword new followed by the type of the exception. Most exception types allow a message as part of throwing the exception so that when the exception occurs, the message can be retrieved.

---

5. Technically it could be caught by a compatible catch filter as well.

Sometimes a catch block will trap an exception but be unable to handle it appropriately or fully. In these circumstances, a catch block can rethrow the exception using the `throw` statement without specifying any exception, as shown in Listing 4.24.

LISTING 4.24: **Rethrowing an Exception**

```
...
      catch(Exception exception)
      {
          Console.WriteLine(
              "Rethrowing unexpected error:  {0}",
              exception.Message);
          throw;
      }
...
```

Notice that in Listing 4.24 the `throw` statement is "empty" rather than specifying that the exception referred to by the `exception` variable is to be thrown. This illustrates a subtle difference: `throw;` preserves the "call stack" information in the exception whereas `throw exception;` replaces that information with the current call stack information. For debugging purposes it is usually better to know the original call stack.

Guidelines

DO prefer using an empty throw when catching and rethrowing an exception so as to preserve the call stack.

DO report execution failures by throwing exceptions rather than returning error codes.

DO NOT have public members that return exceptions as return values or an out parameter. Throw exceptions to indicate errors; do not use them as return values to indicate errors.

Avoid Using Exception Handling to Deal with Expected Situations

Developers should make an effort to avoid throwing exceptions for expected conditions or normal control flow. For example, developers should not expect users to enter valid text when specifying their age.[6] Therefore,

---

6. In general, developers should expect their users to perform unexpected actions, and therefore they should code defensively to handle "stupid user tricks."

instead of relying on an exception to validate data entered by the user, developers should provide a means of checking the data before attempting the conversion. (Better yet, you should prevent the user from entering invalid data in the first place.) Exceptions are designed specifically for tracking exceptional, unexpected, and potentially fatal situations. Using them for an unintended purpose such as expected situations will cause your code to be hard to read, understand, and maintain.

Additionally, (as with most languages) C# incurs a slight performance hit when throwing an exception—taking microseconds compared to the nanoseconds most operations take. This delay is generally not noticeable in human time—except when the exception goes unhandled. For example, when executing Listing 4.19 and entering an invalid age the exception is unhandled and there is a noticeable delay while the runtime searches the environment to see whether there is a debugger to load. Fortunately, slow performance when a program is shutting down isn't generally a factor to be concerned with.

Guidelines

DO NOT use exceptions for handling normal, expected conditions; use them for exceptional, unexpected conditions.

■ ADVANCED TOPIC

Numeric Conversion with `TryParse()`

One of the problems with the `Parse()` method is that the only way to determine whether the conversion will be successful is to attempt the cast and then catch the exception if it doesn't work. Because throwing an exception is a relatively expensive operation, it is better to attempt the conversion without exception handling. In the first release of C#, the only data type that enabled this was a `double` method called `double.TryParse()`. However, the CLI added this method to all numeric primitive types in the CLI 2.0 version. It requires the use of the `out` keyword because the return from the `TryParse()` function is a `bool` rather than the converted value. Here is a code snippet that demonstrates the conversion using `int.TryParse()`.

```
...
if (int.TryParse(ageText, out age))
{
    System.Console.WriteLine(
        "Hi {0}!  You are {1} months old.", firstName,
        age * 12);
}
else
{
    System.Console.WriteLine(
        "The age entered ,{0}, is not valid.", ageText);
}
...
```

With the .NET Framework 4, a `TryParse()` method was also added to enum types.

With the `TryParse()` method, it is no longer necessary to include a try/catch block simply for the purpose of handling the string-to-numeric conversion.

SUMMARY

This chapter discussed the details of declaring and calling methods, including the use of the keywords out and ref to pass variables rather than their values. In addition to method declaration, this chapter introduced exception handling.

Methods are a fundamental construct that is a key to writing readable code. Instead of writing large methods with lots of statements, you should use methods for "paragraphs" within your code, whose lengths target roughly ten lines or less. The process of breaking large functions into smaller pieces is one of the ways you can refactor your code to make it more readable and maintainable.

The next chapter considers the class construct and how it encapsulates methods (behavior) and fields (data) into a single unit.

■ 5 ■
Classes

YOU BRIEFLY SAW IN CHAPTER 1 how to declare a new class called HelloWorld. In Chapter 2, you learned about the built-in primitive types included with C#. Since you have now also learned about control flow and how to declare methods, it is time to discuss defining your own types. This is the core construct of any C# program; this support for classes and the objects created from them is what makes C# an object-oriented language.

This chapter introduces you to the basics of object-oriented programming using C#. A key focus is on how to define **classes,** which are the templates for objects themselves.

All of the constructs of structured programming from the previous chapters still apply within object-oriented programming. However, by wrapping those constructs within classes, you can create larger, more organized programs that are more maintainable. The transition from structured, control-flow-based programs to object-oriented programs revolutionized programming because it provided an extra level of organization. The result was that smaller programs were simplified somewhat; but more importantly, it was easier to create much larger programs because the code within those programs was better organized.

One of the key advantages of object-oriented programming is that instead of creating new programs entirely from scratch, you can assemble a collection of existing objects from prior work, extending the classes with new features, adding more classes, and thereby providing new functionality.

Readers unfamiliar with object-oriented programming should read the Beginner Topic blocks for an introduction. The general text outside the Beginner Topics focuses on using C# for object-oriented programming with the assumption that readers are already familiar with object-oriented concepts.

This chapter delves into how C# supports encapsulation through its support of constructs such as classes, properties, and access modifiers; we covered methods in the preceding chapter. The next chapter builds on this foundation with the introduction of inheritance and the polymorphism that object-oriented programming enables.

■■ BEGINNER TOPIC

Object-Oriented Programming

The key to programming successfully today is in the ability to provide organization and structure to the implementation of the complex requirements of large applications. Object-oriented programming provides one of the key methodologies in accomplishing this, to the point that it is difficult for object-oriented programmers to envision transitioning back to structured programming, except for the most trivial programs.

The most fundamental construct to object-oriented programming is the class. A group of classes form a programming abstraction, model, or template of what is often a real-world concept. The class `OpticalStorageMedia`, for example, may have an `Eject()` method on it that causes a disk to eject from the player. The `OpticalStorageMedia` class is the programming abstraction of the real-world object of a CD or DVD player.

Classes exhibit the three principal characteristics of object-oriented programming: encapsulation, inheritance, and polymorphism.

Encapsulation

Encapsulation allows you to hide details. The details can still be accessed when necessary, but by intelligently encapsulating the details, large programs are made easier to understand, data is protected from inadvertent modification, and code becomes easier to maintain because the effects of a code change are limited to the scope of the encapsulation. Methods are examples of encapsulation. Although it is possible to take the code from a method and embed it directly inline with the caller's code, refactoring of code into a method provides encapsulation benefits.

Inheritance

Consider the following example: A DVD drive is a type of optical media device. It has a specific storage capacity along with the ability to hold a digital movie. A CD drive is also a type of optical media device, but it has different characteristics. The copy protection on CDs is different from DVD copy protection, and the storage capacity is different as well. Both CD drives and DVD drives are different from hard drives, USB drives, and floppy drives (remember those?). All fit into the category of storage devices, but each has special characteristics, even for fundamental functions such as the supported filesystems and whether instances of the media are read-only or read/write.

Inheritance in object-oriented programming allows you to form "is a kind of" relationships between these similar but different items. It is reasonable to say that a DVD drive "is a kind of" storage media and that a CD drive "is a kind of" storage media, and as such, that each has storage capacity. We could also reasonably say that both have an "is a kind of" relationship with "optical storage media," which in turn "is a kind of" storage media.

If you define classes corresponding to each type of storage device mentioned, you will have defined a **class hierarchy,** which is a series of "is a kind of" relationships. The base class, from which all storage devices derive, could be the class StorageMedia. As such, classes to represent CD drives, DVD drives, hard drives, USB drives, and floppy drives are derived from the class StorageMedia. However, the classes for CD and DVD drives don't need to derive from StorageMedia directly. Instead, they can derive from an intermediate class, OpticalStorageMedia. You can view the class hierarchy graphically using a Unified Modeling Language (UML)-like class diagram, as shown in Figure 5.1.

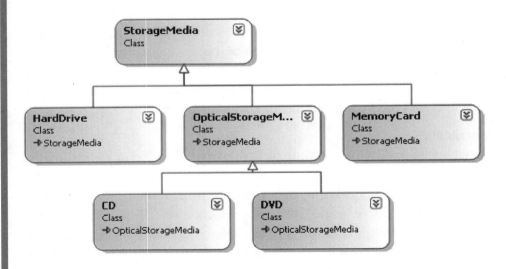

FIGURE 5.1: Class Hierarchy

The inheritance relationship involves a minimum of two classes such that one class is a more specific kind of the other; in Figure 5.1, HardDrive is a more specific kind of StorageMedia. Although the more specialized type, HardDrive, is a kind of StorageMedia, the reverse is not true; an instance of StorageMedia is not necessarily a HardDrive. As Figure 5.1 shows, inheritance can involve more than two classes.

The more specialized type is called the **derived type** or the **subtype.** The more general type is called the **base type** or the **super type.** The base type is also often called the "parent" type and its derived types are often called its "child" types. Though this usage is common, it can be confusing; after all, a child is not a kind of parent! In this book we will stick to "derived type" and "base type."

To **derive** or **inherit** from another type is to **specialize** that type, which means to customize the base type so that it is more suitable for a specific purpose. The base type may contain those implementation details that are common to all of the derived types.

The key feature of inheritance is that all derived types inherit the members of the base type. Often, the implementation of the base members can be modified, but regardless, the derived type contains the base type's members in addition to any other members that the derived type contains explicitly.

Derived types allow you to organize your classes into a coherent hierarchy where the derived types have greater specificity than their base types.

Polymorphism

Polymorphism is formed from "poly" meaning "many" and "morph" meaning "form." In the context of objects, polymorphism means that a single method or type can have many forms of implementation. Suppose you have a media player that can play both CD music discs and DVDs containing MP3s. However, the exact implementation of the `Play()` method will vary depending on the media type. Calling `Play()` on an object representing a music CD or on an object representing a music DVD will play music in both cases, because each object's type understands the intricacies of playing. All that the media player knows about is the common base type, `OpticalStorageMedia`, and the fact that it defines the `Play()` method. Polymorphism is the principle that a type can take care of the exact details of a method's implementation because the method appears on multiple derived types that each share a common base type (or interface) that also contains the same method signature.

Declaring and Instantiating a Class

Defining a class involves first specifying the keyword `class`, followed by an identifier, as shown in Listing 5.1.

LISTING 5.1: Defining a Class

```
class Employee
{
}
```

All code that belongs to the class will appear between the curly braces following the class declaration. Although not a requirement, generally you place each class into its own file. This makes it easier to find the code that defines a particular class, because the convention is to name the file using the class name.

> ### Guidelines
>
> **DO NOT** place more than one class in a single source file.
> **DO** name the source file with the name of the public type it contains.

Once you have defined a new class, you can use that class as though it were built into the framework. In other words, you can declare a variable of that type or define a method that takes a parameter of the new class type. Listing 5.2 demonstrates.

LISTING 5.2: **Declaring Variables of the Class Type**

```csharp
class Program
{
  static void Main()
  {
      Employee employee1, employee2;
      // ...
  }

  static void IncreaseSalary(Employee employee)
  {
      // ...
  }
}
```

■ BEGINNER TOPIC

Objects and Classes Defined

In casual conversation, the terms *class* and *object* appear interchangeably. However, object and class have distinct meanings. A **class** is a template for what an object will look like at instantiation time. An **object,** therefore, is an instance of a class. Classes are like the mold for what a widget will look like. Objects correspond to widgets created by the mold. The process of creating an object from a class is **instantiation** because an object is an instance of a class.

Now that you have defined a new class type, it is time to instantiate an object of that type. Mimicking its predecessors, C# uses the new keyword to instantiate an object (see Listing 5.3).

LISTING 5.3: **Instantiating a Class**

```
class Program
{
  static void Main()
  {
      Employee employee1 = new Employee();
      Employee employee2;
      employee2 = new Employee();

      IncreaseSalary(employee1);
  }
}
```

Not surprisingly, the assignment can occur in the same statement as the declaration, or in a separate statement.

Unlike the primitive types you have worked with so far, there is no literal way to specify an Employee. Instead, the new operator provides an instruction to the runtime to allocate memory for an Employee object, instantiate the object, and return a reference to the instance.

Though there is an explicit operator for allocating memory, there is no such operator for de-allocating the memory. Instead, the runtime automatically reclaims the memory sometime after the object becomes inaccessible. The **garbage collector** is responsible for the automatic de-allocation. It determines which objects are no longer referenced by other active objects and then de-allocates the memory for those objects. The result is that there is no compile-time-determined program location where the memory will be collected and restored to the system.

In this trivial example, no explicit data or methods are associated with an Employee, and this renders the object essentially useless. The next section focuses on adding data to an object.

■ **BEGINNER TOPIC**

Encapsulation Part 1: Objects Group Data with Methods

If you received a stack of index cards with employees' first names, a stack of index cards with their last names, and a stack of index cards with their salaries, the cards would be of little value unless you knew that the cards were in the same order in each stack. Even so, the data would be difficult to work with because determining a person's full name would require searching through two stacks. Worse, if you dropped one of the stacks, there would be no way to reassociate the first name with the last name and the salary. Instead, you would need one stack of employee cards in which all the data was grouped on one card. In this way, first names, last names, and salaries would be encapsulated together.

Outside the object-oriented programming context, to **encapsulate** a set of items is to enclose those items within a capsule. Similarly, object-oriented programming encapsulates methods and data together into an object. This provides a grouping of all of the class **members** (the data and methods within a class) so that they no longer need to be handled individually. Instead of passing first name, last name, and salary as three separate parameters to a method, objects enable a call to pass a reference to an employee object. Once the called method receives the object reference, it can send a message (it can call a method such as `AdjustSalary()`, for example) on the object to perform a particular operation.

Language Contrast: C++—delete Operator

C# programmers should view the new operator as a call to instantiate an object, not as a call to allocate memory. Both objects allocated on the heap and objects allocated on the stack support the new operator, emphasizing the point that new is not about memory allocation and whether de-allocation is necessary.

Thus C# does not need the delete operator found in C++. Memory allocation and de-allocation is a detail that the runtime manages, allowing the developer to focus more on domain logic. However, though memory is managed by the runtime, the runtime does not manage other resources such as database connections, network ports, and so on. Unlike C++, C# does not support **implicit deterministic resource cleanup** (the occurrence of implicit object destruction at a compile-time-defined location in the code). Fortunately, C# does support **explicit deterministic resource cleanup** via a using statement, and **implicit nondeterministic resource cleanup** using finalizers.

Instance Fields

One of the key aspects of object-oriented design is the grouping of data to provide structure. This section discusses how to add data to the Employee class. The general object-oriented term for a variable that stores data within a class is **member variable.** This term is well understood in C#, but the more standard term and the one used in the specification is **field,** which is a named unit of storage associated with the containing type. **Instance fields** are variables declared at the class level to store data associated with an object. Hence, **association** is the relationship between the field data type and the containing field.

Declaring an Instance Field

In Listing 5.4, the class Employee has been modified to include three fields: FirstName, LastName, and Salary.

LISTING 5.4: Declaring Fields

```
class Employee
{
  public string FirstName;
  public string LastName;
  public string Salary;
}
```

With these fields added, it is possible to store some fundamental data with every Employee instance. In this case, you prefix the fields with an access modifier of public. public on a field indicates that the data within the field is accessible from classes other than Employee (see the section Access Modifiers, later in this chapter).

As with local variable declarations, a field declaration includes the data type to which the field refers. Furthermore, it is possible to assign fields an initial value at declaration time, as demonstrated with the Salary field in Listing 5.5.

LISTING 5.5: Setting Initial Values of Fields at Declaration Time

```
class Employee
{
  public string FirstName;
  public string LastName;
  public string Salary = "Not enough";
}
```

We delay the guidelines of naming and coding fields until later in the chapter, after the C# properties topic has been introduced. Suffice it to say, Listing 5.5 does *not* follow the general convention.

Accessing an Instance Field

You can set and retrieve the data within fields. However, the fact that the field does not include a `static` modifier indicates that it is an instance field. You can access an instance field only from an instance of the containing class (an object). You cannot access it from the class directly (without first creating an instance, in other words).

Listing 5.6 shows an updated look at the `Program` class and its utilization of the `Employee` class, and Output 5.1 shows the results.

LISTING 5.6: Accessing Fields

```
class Program
{
  static void Main()
  {
      Employee employee1 = new Employee();
      Employee employee2;
      employee2 = new Employee();

      employee1.FirstName = "Inigo";
      employee1.LastName = "Montoya";
      employee1.Salary = "Too Little";
      IncreaseSalary(employee1);
      Console.WriteLine(
          "{0} {1}: {2}",
          employee1.FirstName,
          employee1.LastName,
          employee1.Salary);
      // ...
  }

  static void IncreaseSalary(Employee employee)
  {
      employee.Salary = "Enough to survive on";
  }
}
```

OUTPUT 5.1

```
Inigo Montoya: Enough to survive on
```

Listing 5.6 instantiates two `Employee` objects, as you saw before. Next, it sets each field, calls `IncreaseSalary()` to change the salary, and then displays each field associated with the object referenced by `employee1`.

Notice that you first have to specify which `Employee` instance you are working with. Therefore, the `employee1` variable appears as a prefix to the field name when assigning and accessing the field.

Instance Methods

One alternative to formatting the names in the `WriteLine()` method call within `Main()` is to provide a method in the `Employee` class that takes care of the formatting. Changing the functionality to be within the `Employee` class rather than a member of `Program` is consistent with the encapsulation of a class. Why not group the methods relating to the employee's full name with the class that contains the data that forms the name?

Listing 5.7 demonstrates the creation of such a method.

LISTING 5.7: Accessing Fields from within the Containing Class

```csharp
class Employee
{
  public string FirstName;
  public string LastName;
  public string Salary;

    public string GetName()
    {
        return FirstName + " " + LastName;
    }
}
```

There is nothing particularly special about this method compared to what you learned in Chapter 4, except that now the `GetName()` method accesses fields on the object instead of just local variables. In addition, the method declaration is not marked with `static`. As you will see later in this chapter, static methods cannot directly access instance fields within a class. Instead, it is necessary to obtain an instance of the class in order to call any instance member, whether a method or a field.

Given the addition of the `GetName()` method, you can update `Program.Main()` to use the method, as shown in Listing 5.8 and Output 5.2.

LISTING 5.8: **Accessing Fields from outside the Containing Class**

```csharp
class Program
{
  static void Main()
  {
      Employee employee1 = new Employee();
      Employee employee2;
      employee2 = new Employee();

      employee1.FirstName = "Inigo";
      employee1.LastName = "Montoya";
      employee1.Salary = "Too Little";
      IncreaseSalary(employee1);
      Console.WriteLine(
          "{0}: {1}",
          employee1.GetName(),
          employee1.Salary);
      // ...
  }
  // ...
}
```

OUTPUT 5.2

```
Inigo Montoya: Enough to survive on
```

Using the this **Keyword**

You can obtain the reference to a class from within instance members that belong to the class. To indicate explicitly that the field or method accessed is an instance member of the containing class in C#, you use the keyword this. this is implicit when calling any instance member and it returns an instance of the object itself.

For example, consider the SetName() method shown in Listing 5.9.

LISTING 5.9: **Using** this **to Identify the Field's Owner Explicitly**

```csharp
class Employee
{
  public string FirstName;
  public string LastName;
  public string Salary;

  public string GetName()
  {
      return FirstName + " " + LastName;
  }
```

```
public void SetName(
    string newFirstName, string newLastName)
{
    this.FirstName = newFirstName;
    this.LastName = newLastName;
}
}
```

This example uses the keyword this to indicate that the fields FirstName and LastName are instance members of the class.

Although the this keyword can prefix any and all references to local class members, the general guideline is not to clutter code when there is no additional value. Therefore, avoid using the this keyword unless it is required. Listing 5.12 is an example of one of the few circumstances when such a requirement exists. Listings 5.9 and 5.10, however, are not good examples. In Listing 5.9, this can be dropped entirely without changing the meaning of the code. And in Listing 5.10, by changing the naming convention for fields, we can avoid any ambiguity between local variables and fields.

■ BEGINNER TOPIC

Relying on Coding Style to Avoid Ambiguity

In the SetName() method, you did not have to use the this keyword because FirstName is obviously different from newFirstName. Consider, however, if instead of calling the parameter "newFirstName" you called it "FirstName" (using Pascal case), as shown in Listing 5.10.

LISTING 5.10: Using this to Avoid Ambiguity

```
class Employee
{
  public string FirstName;
  public string LastName;
  public string Salary;

  public string GetName()
  {
      return FirstName + " " + LastName;
  }

  // Caution:  Parameter names use Pascal case
  public void SetName(string FirstName, string LastName)
  {
```

```
        this.FirstName = FirstName;
        this.LastName = LastName;
    }
}
```

In this example, it is not possible to refer to the `FirstName` field without explicitly indicating that the `Employee` object owns the variable. `this` acts just like the `employee1` variable prefix used in the `Program.Main()` method (see Listing 5.8); it identifies the reference as the one on which `SetName()` was called.

Listing 5.10 does not follow the C# naming convention in which parameters are declared like local variables, using camel case. This can lead to subtle bugs because assigning `FirstName` (intending to refer to the field) to `FirstName` (the parameter) will still compile and even run. To avoid this problem it is a good practice to have a different naming convention for parameters and local variables than the naming convention for fields. We demonstrate one such convention later in this chapter.

Language Contrast: Visual Basic—Accessing a Class Instance with Me

The C# keyword `this` is identical to the Visual Basic keyword `Me`.

In Listing 5.9 and Listing 5.10, the `this` keyword is not used in the `GetName()` method—it is optional. However, if local variables or parameters exist with the same name as the field (see the `SetName()` method in Listing 5.10), leaving off `this` would result in accessing the local variable/parameter when the intention was the field , so `this` is required.

You also can use the keyword `this` to access a class's methods explicitly. `this.GetName()` is allowed within the `SetName()` method, for example, permitting you to print out the newly assigned name (see Listing 5.11 and Output 5.3).

LISTING 5.11: Using `this` with a Method

```
class Employee
{
    // ...
```

```csharp
    public string GetName()
    {
        return FirstName + " " + LastName;
    }

    public void SetName(string newFirstName, string newLastName)
    {
        this.FirstName = newFirstName;
        this.LastName = newLastName;
        Console.WriteLine("Name changed to '{0}'",
            this.GetName());
    }
}

class Program
{
  static void Main()
  {
      Employee employee = new Employee();

      employee.SetName("Inigo", "Montoya");
      // ...
  }
  // ...
}
```

OUTPUT 5.3

```
Name changed to 'Inigo Montoya'
```

Sometimes it may be necessary to use this in order to pass a reference to the currently executing object. Consider the Save() method in Listing 5.12.

LISTING 5.12: Passing this in a Method Call

```csharp
class Employee
{
  public string FirstName;
  public string LastName;
  public string Salary;

  public void Save()
  {
      DataStorage.Store(this);
  }
}
class DataStorage
{
```

```
    // Save an employee object to a file
    // named with the Employee name.
    public static void Store(Employee employee)
    {
        // ...
    }
}
```

The Save() method calls a method on the DataStorage class, called Store().
The Store() method, however, needs to be passed the Employee object that
needs to be persisted. This is done using the keyword this, which passes
the instance of the Employee object on which Save() was called.

■ ADVANCED TOPIC

Storing and Loading with Files

The actual implementation of the Store() method inside DataStorage
involves classes within the System.IO namespace, as shown in Listing 5.13. Inside Store(), you begin by instantiating a FileStream object
that you associate with a file corresponding to the employee's full name.
The FileMode.Create parameter indicates that you want a new file to be
created if there isn't already one with the <firstname><lastname>.dat
name; if the file exists already, it will be overwritten. Next, you create a
StreamWriter class. The StreamWriter class is responsible for writing text
into the FileStream. You write the data using WriteLine() methods, just
as though writing to the console.

LISTING 5.13: Data Persistence to a File

```
using System;
// IO namespace
using System.IO;

class DataStorage
{
    // Save an employee object to a file
    // named with the Employee name.
    // Error handling not shown.
    public static void Store(Employee employee)
    {
        // Instantiate a FileStream using FirstNameLastName.dat
        // for the filename. FileMode.Create will force
        // a new file to be created or override an
        // existing file.
```

```
        FileStream stream = new FileStream(
            employee.FirstName + employee.LastName + ".dat",
            FileMode.Create);¹

        // Create a StreamWriter object for writing text
        // into the FileStream
        StreamWriter writer = new StreamWriter(stream);

        // Write all the data associated with the employee.
        writer.WriteLine(employee.FirstName);
        writer.WriteLine(employee.LastName);
        writer.WriteLine(employee.Salary);

        // Close the StreamWriter and its Stream.
        writer.Close();  // Automatically closes the stream
    }
    // ...
}
```

Once the write operations are completed, both the FileStream and the
StreamWriter need to be closed so that they are not left open indefinitely
while waiting for the garbage collector to run. This listing does not include
any error handling, so if an exception is thrown, neither Close() method
will be called.

The load process is similar (see Listing 5.14).

LISTING 5.14: Data Retrieval from a File

```
class Employee
{
  // ...
}
```

```
// IO namespace
using System;
using System.IO;

class DataStorage
{
  // ...

  public static Employee Load(string firstName, string lastName)
  {
      Employee employee = new Employee();

      // Instantiate a FileStream using FirstNameLastName.dat
```

---

1. This code could be improved with a using statement, a construct that we have avoided
    because it has not yet been introduced.

```
        // for the filename. FileMode.Open will open
        // an existing file or else report an error.
        FileStream stream = new FileStream(

            firstName + lastName + ".dat", FileMode.Open);²

        // Create a SteamReader for reading text from the file.
        StreamReader reader = new StreamReader(stream);

        // Read each line from the file and place it into
        // the associated property.
        employee.FirstName = reader.ReadLine();
        employee.LastName = reader.ReadLine();
        employee.Salary = reader.ReadLine();

        // Close the StreamReader and its Stream.
        reader.Close();  // Automatically closes the stream

        return employee;

    }
}
```

```
class Program
{
  static void Main()
  {
        Employee employee1;

        Employee employee2 = new Employee();
        employee2.SetName("Inigo", "Montoya");
        employee2.Save();

        // Modify employee2 after saving.
        IncreaseSalary(employee2);

        // Load employee1 from the saved version of employee2
        employee1 = DataStorage.Load("Inigo", "Montoya");

        Console.WriteLine(
            "{0}: {1}",
            employee1.GetName(),
            employee1.Salary);

        // ...
    }
    // ...
}
```

Output 5.4 shows the results.

---

2. This code could be improved with a using statement, a construct that we have avoided because it has not yet been introduced.

OUTPUT 5.4

```
Name changed to 'Inigo Montoya'
Inigo Montoya:
```

The reverse of the save process appears in Listing 5.14, which uses a `StreamReader` rather than a `StreamWriter`. Again, `Close()` needs to be called on both `FileStream` and `StreamReader` once the data has been read.

Output 5.4 does not show any salary after `Inigo Montoya:` because `Salary` was not set to `Enough to survive on` by a call to `IncreaseSalary()` until after the call to `Save()`.

Notice in `Main()` that we can call `Save()` from an instance of an employee, but to load a new employee we call `DataStorage.Load()`. To load an employee, we generally don't already have an employee instance to load into, so an instance method on `Employee` would be less than ideal. An alternative to calling `Load` on `DataStorage` would be to add a static `Load()` method (see the section Static Members, later in this chapter) to `Employee` so that it would be possible to call `Employee.Load()` (using the `Employee` class, not an instance of `Employee`).

Observe the inclusion of the `using System.IO` directive at the top of the listing. This makes each `IO` class accessible without prefixing it with the full namespace.

Access Modifiers

When declaring a field earlier in the chapter, you prefixed the field declaration with the keyword `public`. `public` is an **access modifier** that identifies the level of encapsulation associated with the member it decorates. Five access modifiers are available: `public`, `private`, `protected`, `internal`, and `protected internal`. This section considers the first two.

■ **BEGINNER TOPIC**

Encapsulation Part 2: Information Hiding

Besides wrapping data and methods together into a single unit, encapsulation is also about hiding the internal details of an object's data and behavior. To some degree, methods do this; from outside a method, all that is visible to a caller is the method declaration. None of the internal implementation is visible. Object-oriented programming enables this further, however, by providing facilities for controlling the extent to which members are visible from outside the class. Members that are not visible outside the class are **private members.**

In object-oriented programming, *encapsulation* is the term for not only grouping data and behavior, but also hiding data and behavior implementation details within a class (the capsule) so that the inner workings of a class are not exposed. This reduces the chances that callers will modify the data inappropriately or program according to the implementation, only to have it change in the future.

The purpose of an access modifier is to provide encapsulation. By using `public`, you explicitly indicated that it is acceptable that the modified fields are accessible from outside the `Employee` class—in other words, that they are accessible from the `Program` class, for example.

Consider an `Employee` class that includes a `Password` field, however. It should be possible to call an `Employee` object and verify the password using a `Logon()` method. It should not be possible, however, to access the `Password` field on an `Employee` object from outside the class.

To define a `Password` field as hidden and inaccessible from outside the containing class, you use the keyword `private` for the access modifier, in place of `public` (see Listing 5.15). As a result, the `Password` field is not intended for access from inside the `Program` class, for example.

LISTING 5.15: **Using the** private **Access Modifier**

```
class Employee
{
    public string FirstName;
    public string LastName;
    public string Salary;
    private string Password;
    private bool IsAuthenticated;

    public bool Logon(string password)
    {
        if(Password == password)
        {
            IsAuthenticated = true;
        }
        return IsAuthenticated;
    }
```

```
    public bool GetIsAuthenticated()
    {
        return IsAuthenticated;
    }
    // ...
}
```

```
class Program
{
    static void Main()
    {
        Employee employee = new Employee();

        employee.FirstName = "Inigo";
        employee.LastName = "Montoya";

        // ...

        // Password is private, so it cannot be
        // accessed from outside the class.
        // Console.WriteLine(
        //     ("Password = {0}", employee.Password);
    }
    // ...
}
```

Although not shown in Listing 5.15, it is possible to decorate a method with an access modifier of `private` as well.

Note that if no access modifier is placed on a class member, the declaration will default to `private`. In other words, members are private by default and programmers need to specify explicitly that a member is to be public.

Properties

The preceding section, Access Modifiers, demonstrated how you can use the `private` keyword to encapsulate a password, preventing access from outside the class. This type of encapsulation is often too thorough, however. For example, sometimes you might need to define fields that external classes can only read but whose values you can change internally. Alternatively, perhaps you want to allow access to write some data in a class but you need to be able to validate changes made to the data. Still one more example is the need to construct the data on the fly. Traditionally, languages enabled the features found in these examples by marking fields as private and then providing getter and setter methods for accessing and modifying the data. The code in Listing 5.16 changes both `FirstName` and `LastName` to private fields. Public getter and setter methods for each field allow their values to be accessed and changed.

LISTING 5.16: Declaring Getter and Setter Methods

```csharp
class Employee
{

   private string FirstName;
   // FirstName getter
   public string GetFirstName()
   {
      return FirstName;
   }
   // FirstName setter
   public void SetFirstName(string newFirstName)
   {
      if(newFirstName != null && newFirstName != "")
      {
         FirstName = newFirstName;
      }
   }

   private string LastName;
   // LastName getter
   public string GetLastName()
   {
      return LastName;
   }
   // LastName setter
   public void SetLastName(string newLastName)
   {
      if(newLastName != null && newLastName != "")
      {
         LastName = newLastName;
      }
   }
   // ...
}
```

Unfortunately, this change affects the programmability of the `Employee` class. No longer can you use the assignment operator to set data within the class, nor access data without calling a method.

Declaring a Property

Considering the frequency of this type of pattern, the C# designers decided to provide explicit syntax for it. This syntax is called a **property** (see Listing 5.17 and Output 5.5).

LISTING 5.17: **Defining Properties**

```csharp
class Program
{
  static void Main()
  {
      Employee employee = new Employee();

      // Call the FirstName property's setter.
      employee.FirstName = "Inigo";

      // Call the FirstName property's getter.
      System.Console.WriteLine(employee.FirstName);
  }
}
```

```csharp
class Employee
{
  // FirstName property
  public string FirstName
  {
      get
      {
          return _FirstName;
      }
      set
      {
          _FirstName = value;
      }
  }
  private string _FirstName;

  // LastName property
  public string LastName
  {
      get
      {
          return _LastName;
      }
      set
      {
          _LastName = value;
      }
  }
  private string _LastName;
  // ...
}
```

OUTPUT 5.5

```
Inigo
```

The first thing to notice in Listing 5.17 is not the property code itself, but the code within the `Program` class. Although you no longer have the fields with the `FirstName` and `LastName` identifiers, you cannot see this by looking at the `Program` class. The API for accessing an employee's first and last names has not changed at all. It is still possible to assign the parts of the name using a simple assignment operator, for example (`employee.FirstName = "Inigo"`).

The key feature is that properties provide an API that looks programmatically like a field. In actuality, however, no such fields exist. A property declaration looks exactly like a field declaration, but following it are curly braces in which to place the property implementation. Two optional parts make up the property implementation. The `get` part defines the getter portion of the property. It corresponds directly to the `GetFirstName()` and `GetLastName()` functions defined in Listing 5.16. To access the `FirstName` property you call `employee.FirstName`. Similarly, setters (the `set` portion of the implementation) enable the calling syntax of the field assignment:

```
employee.FirstName = "Inigo";
```

Property definition syntax uses three contextual keywords. You use the `get` and `set` keywords to identify either the retrieval or the assignment portion of the property, respectively. In addition, the setter uses the `value` keyword to refer to the right side of the assignment operation. When `Program.Main()` calls `employee.FirstName = "Inigo"`, therefore, `value` is set to "Inigo" inside the setter and can be used to assign `_FirstName`. Listing 5.17's property implementations are the most common. When the getter is called (such as in `Console.WriteLine(employee.FirstName)`), the value from the field (`_FirstName`) is obtained and written to the console.

Automatically Implemented Properties

In C# 3.0, property syntax includes a shorthand version. Since a property with a single backing field that is assigned and retrieved by the get and set accessors is so trivial and common (see the implementations of `FirstName` and `LastName`), the C# 3.0 compiler (and higher) allows the declaration of a property without any accessor implementation or backing field declaration. Listing 5.18 demonstrates the syntax, and Output 5.6 shows the results.

LISTING 5.18: **Automatically Implemented Properties**

```
class Program
{
```

```csharp
    static void Main()
    {
        Employee employee1 =
            new Employee();
        Employee employee2 =
            new Employee();

        // Call the FirstName property's setter.
        employee1.FirstName = "Inigo";

        // Call the FirstName property's getter.
        System.Console.WriteLine(employee1.FirstName);

        // Assign an auto-implemented property
        employee2.Title = "Computer Nerd";
        employee1.Manager = employee2;

        // Print employee1's manager's title.
        System.Console.WriteLine(employee1.Manager.Title);
    }
}
```

```csharp
class Employee
{
  // FirstName property
  public string FirstName
  {
      get
      {
          return _FirstName;
      }
      set
      {
          _FirstName = value;
      }
  }
  private string _FirstName;

  // LastName property
  public string LastName
  {
      get
      {
          return _LastName;
      }
      set
      {
          _LastName = value;
      }
  }
  private string _LastName;
  // ...
```

```
// Title property
public string Title { get; set; }
```

```
// Manager property
public Employee Manager { get; set; }
```

```
}
```

OUTPUT 5.6

```
Inigo
Computer Nerd
```

Auto-implemented properties provide for a simpler way of writing properties in addition to reading them. Furthermore, when it comes time to add something such as validation to the setter, any existing code that calls the property will not have to change even though the property declaration will have changed to include an implementation.

Throughout the remainder of the book, we will frequently use this C# 3.0 or later syntax without indicating that it is a C# 3.0 introduced feature.

Property and Field Guidelines

Given that it is possible to write explicit setter and getter methods rather than properties, on occasion a question may arise as to whether to use a property or a method. The general guideline is that methods should represent actions and properties should represent data. Properties are for simple access to simple data with a simple computation. The expectation is that invoking a property is not significantly more expensive than accessing a field.

With regard to naming, notice that in Listing 5.18 the property name is FirstName, and the field name changed from earlier listings to _FirstName—PascalCase with an underscore suffix. Other common naming conventions for the private field that backs a property are _firstName and m_FirstName (a holdover from C++ where the *m* stands for member variable), and on occasion the camelCase convention just like local variables.[3] The camelCase convention should be avoided, however. Using camelCase for property names

---

3. We prefer _FirstName because the *m* in front of the name is unnecessary when compared with simply _, and by using the same casing as the property, it is possible to have only one string within the Visual Studio code template expansion tools, instead of having one for both the property name and the field name.

is the same as the naming convention for local variables and parameters, causing overlap to be highly probable. Also, to keep with the principles of encapsulation, fields should not be declared as public or protected.

> ## Guidelines
>
> **DO** use properties for simple access to simple data with simple computations.
>
> **AVOID** throwing exceptions from property getters.
>
> **DO** preserve the original property value if the property throws an exception.

Regardless of which naming pattern you use for private fields, the coding standard for properties is PascalCase. Therefore, properties should use the `LastName` and `FirstName` pattern with names that represent nouns, noun phrases, or adjectives. It is not uncommon, in fact, that the property name is the same as the type name. Consider an `Address` property of type `Address` on a `Person` object, for example.

> ## Guidelines
>
> **CONSIDER** using the same casing on a property's backing field as what is used in the property, distinguishing the backing field with an "_" prefix. Do not, however, use two underscores; identifiers beginning with two underscores are reserved for the use of the C# compiler itself.
>
> **DO** name properties using a noun, noun phrase, or adjective.
>
> **CONSIDER** giving a property the same name as its type.
>
> **AVOID** naming fields with camelCase.
>
> **DO** favor prefixing Boolean properties with "Is," "Can," or "Has," when it adds value.
>
> **DO NOT** declare instance fields that are public or protected. (Instead, expose via a property.)
>
> **DO** name properties with PascalCase.
>
> **DO** favor automatically implemented properties over fields.
>
> **DO** favor automatically implemented properties over using fully expanded ones if there is no additional implementation logic.

Using Properties with Validation

Notice in Listing 5.19 that the `Initialize()` method of `Employee` uses the property rather than the field for assignment as well. Although this is not required, the result is that any validation within the property setter will be invoked both inside and outside the class. Consider, for example, what would happen if you changed the `LastName` property so that it checked value for `null` or an empty string, before assigning it to `_LastName`.

LISTING 5.19: Providing Property Validation

```
class Employee
{
  // ...
  public void Initialize(
      string newFirstName, string newLastName)
  {
      // Use property inside the Employee
      // class as well.
      FirstName = newFirstName;
      LastName = newLastName;
  }


  // LastName property
  public string LastName
  {
      get
      {
          return _LastName;
      }
      set
      {
          // Validate LastName assignment
          if(value == null)
          {
              // Report error
              throw new ArgumentNullException("value");
          }
          else
          {
              // Remove any whitespace around
              // the new last name.
              value = value.Trim();
              if(value == "")
              {
                  throw new ArgumentException(
                      "LastName cannot be blank.", "value");[4]
              }
```

4. Apologies to Teller, Cher, Sting, Madonna, Bono, Prince, Liberace, et al.

```
                else
                    _LastName = value;
            }
        }
    }
    private string _LastName;
    // ...
}
```

With this new implementation, the code throws an exception if `LastName` is assigned an invalid value, either from another member of the same class or via a direct assignment to `LastName` from inside `Program.Main()`. The ability to intercept an assignment and validate the parameters by providing a field-like API is one of the advantages of properties.

It is a good practice to only access a property-backing field from inside the property implementation. In other words, always use the property, rather than calling the field directly. In many cases, this is true even from code within the same class as the property. If following this practice, when code such as validation code is added, the entire class immediately takes advantage of it. (As described later in the chapter, one exception to this occurs when the field is marked as read-only because then the value cannot be set once class instantiation completes, even in a property setter.)

Although rare, it is possible to assign a value inside the setter, as Listing 5.19 does. In this case, the call to `value.Trim()` removes any whitespace surrounding the new last name value.

Guidelines

AVOID accessing the backing field of a property outside the property, even from within the containing class.

DO use "value" for the paramName argument when calling the `ArgumentException()` or `ArgumentNullException()` constructor ("value" is the implicit name of the parameter on property setters).

Read-Only and Write-Only Properties

By removing either the getter or the setter portion of a property, you can change a property's accessibility. Properties with only a setter are write-only, which is a relatively rare occurrence. Similarly, providing only a getter will cause the property to be read-only; any attempts to assign a value will cause a compile error. To make `Id` read-only, for example, you would code it as shown in Listing 5.20.

LISTING 5.20: Defining a Read-Only Property

```csharp
class Program
{
  static void Main()
  {
      Employee employee1 = new Employee();
      employee1.Initialize(42);

      // ERROR:  Property or indexer 'Employee.Id'
      // cannot be assigned to -- it is read-only
      employee1.Id = "490";
  }
}

class Employee
{
  public void Initialize(int id)
  {
      // Use field because Id property has no setter,
      // it is read-only.
      _Id = id.ToString();
  }

  // ...
  // Id property declaration
  public string Id
  {
      get
      {
          return _Id;
      }
      // No setter provided.
  }
  private string _Id;

}
```

Listing 5.20 assigns the field from within the `Employee` constructor rather than the property (`_Id = id`). Assigning via the property causes a compile error, as it does in `Program.Main()`.

> ### Guidelines
>
> **DO** create get-only properties if the caller should not be able to change the value of the property.

Access Modifiers on Getters and Setters

As previously mentioned, it is a good practice not to access fields from outside their properties because doing so circumvents any validation or additional logic that may be inserted. Unfortunately, C# 1.0 did not allow different levels of encapsulation between the getter and setter portions of a property. It was not possible, therefore, to create a public getter and a private setter so that external classes would have read-only access to the property while code within the class could write to the property.

In C# 2.0, support was added for placing an access modifier on either the get or the set portion of the property implementation (not on both), thereby overriding the access modifier specified on the property declaration. Listing 5.21 demonstrates how to do this.

LISTING 5.21: **Placing Access Modifiers on the Setter**

```csharp
class Program
{
  static void Main()
  {
      Employee employee1 = new Employee();
      employee1.Initialize(42);
      // ERROR: The property or indexer 'Employee.Id'
      // cannot be used in this context because the set
      // accessor is inaccessible
      employee1.Id = "490";
  }
}
```

```csharp
class Employee
{
  public void Initialize(int id)
  {
      // Set Id property
      Id = id.ToString();
  }

  // ...
  // Id property declaration
  public string Id
```

```
    {
        get
        {
            return _Id;
        }
        // Providing an access modifier is in C# 2.0
        // and higher only
        private set
        {
            _Id = value;
        }
    }
    private string _Id;

}
```

By using `private` on the setter, the property appears as read-only to classes other than `Employee`. From within `Employee`, the property appears as read/write, so you can assign the property within the constructor. When specifying an access modifier on the getter or setter, take care that the access modifier is more restrictive than the access modifier on the property as a whole. It is a compile error, for example, to declare the property as `private` and the setter as `public`.

> ### Guidelines
>
> **DO** apply appropriate accessibility modifiers on implementations of getters and setters on all properties.
>
> **DO NOT** provide set-only properties or properties with the setter having broader accessibility than the getter.

Properties As Virtual Fields

As you have seen, properties behave like virtual fields. In some instances, you do not need a backing field at all. Instead, the property getter returns a calculated value while the setter parses the value and persists it to some other member fields (if it even exists). Consider, for example, the `Name` property implementation shown in Listing 5.22. Output 5.7 shows the results.

LISTING 5.22: Defining Properties

```
class Program
{
```

```csharp
   static void Main()
   {
       Employee employee1 = new Employee();

       employee1.Name = "Inigo Montoya";
       System.Console.WriteLine(employee1.Name);

       // ...
   }
}
```

```csharp
class Employee
{
  // ...

  // FirstName property
  public string FirstName
  {
      get
      {
          return _FirstName;
      }
      set
      {
          _FirstName = value;
      }
  }
  private string _FirstName;

  // LastName property
  public string LastName
  {
      get
      {
          return _LastName;
      }
      set
      {
          _LastName = value;
      }
  }
  private string _LastName;
  // ...

    // Name property
    public string Name
    {
        get
        {
            return FirstName + " " + LastName;
        }
        set
        {
```

```
                // Split the assigned value into
                // first and last names.
                string[] names;
                names = value.Split(new char[]{' '});
                if(names.Length == 2)
                {
                    FirstName = names[0];
                    LastName = names[1];
                }
                else
                {
                    // Throw an exception if the full
                    // name was not assigned.
                    throw new System. ArgumentException (
                        string.Format(
                        "Assigned value '{0}' is invalid", value));
                }
            }
        }

    // ...
    }
```

OUTPUT 5.7

```
Inigo Montoya
```

The getter for the Name property concatenates the values returned from the FirstName and LastName properties. In fact, the name value assigned is not actually stored. When the Name property is assigned, the value on the right side is parsed into its first and last name parts.

Properties and Method Calls Not Allowed As ref or out Parameter Values

C# allows properties to be used identically to fields, except when they are passed as ref or out parameter values. ref and out parameter values are internally implemented by passing the memory address to the target method. However, because properties can be virtual fields that have no backing field, or can be read-only or write-only, it is not possible to pass the address for the underlying storage. As a result, you cannot pass properties as ref or out parameter values. The same is true for method calls. Instead, when code needs to pass a property or method call as a ref or out parameter value, the code must first copy the value into a variable and then pass the variable. Once the method call has completed, the code must assign the variable back into the property.

■ ADVANCED TOPIC

Property Internals

Listing 5.23 shows that getters and setters are exposed as get_FirstName() and set_FirstName() in the CIL.

LISTING 5.23: CIL Code Resulting from Properties

```
// ...

.field private string _FirstName
.method public hidebysig specialname instance string
       get_FirstName() cil managed
{
  // Code size       12 (0xc)
  .maxstack  1
  .locals init (string V_0)
  IL_0000:  nop
  IL_0001:  ldarg.0
  IL_0002:  ldfld        string Employee::_FirstName
  IL_0007:  stloc.0
  IL_0008:  br.s         IL_000a

  IL_000a:  ldloc.0
  IL_000b:  ret
} // end of method Employee::get_FirstName

.method public hidebysig specialname instance void
       set_FirstName(string 'value') cil managed
{
  // Code size       9 (0x9)
  .maxstack  8
  IL_0000:  nop
  IL_0001:  ldarg.0
  IL_0002:  ldarg.1
  IL_0003:  stfld        string Employee::_FirstName
  IL_0008:  ret
} // end of method Employee::set_FirstName

.property instance string FirstName()
{
  .get instance string Employee::get_FirstName()
  .set instance void Employee::set_FirstName(string)
} // end of property Employee::FirstName
```

```
// ...
```

Just as important to their appearance as regular methods is the fact that properties are an explicit construct within the CIL, too. As Listing 5.24 shows, the getters and setters are called by CIL properties, which are an explicit construct within the CIL code. Because of this, languages and compilers are not restricted to always interpreting properties based on a naming convention. Instead, CIL properties provide a means for compilers and code editors to provide special syntax.

LISTING 5.24: Properties Are an Explicit Construct in CIL

```
.property instance string FirstName()
{
  .get instance string Program::get_FirstName()
  .set instance void Program::set_FirstName(string)
} // end of property Program::FirstName
```

Notice in Listing 5.23 that the getters and setters that are part of the property include the `specialname` metadata. This modifier is what IDEs, such as Visual Studio, use as a flag to hide the members from IntelliSense.

An automatically implemented property is virtually identical to one for which you define the backing field explicitly. In place of the manually defined backing field the C# compiler generates a field with the name `<PropertyName>k_BackingField` in IL. This generated field includes an attribute (see Chapter 17) called `System.Runtime.CompilerServices` `.CompilerGeneratedAttribute`. Both the getters and the setters are decorated with the same attribute because they too are generated—with the same implementation as in Listings 5.23 and 5.24.

Constructors

Now that you have added fields to a class and can store data, you need to consider the validity of that data. As you saw in Listing 5.3, it is possible to instantiate an object using the `new` operator. The result, however, is the ability to create an employee with invalid data. Immediately following the assignment of `employee`, you have an `Employee` object whose name and salary are not initialized. In this particular listing, you assigned the uninitialized fields immediately following the instantiation of an employee, but if you failed to do the initialization, you would not receive a warning from the compiler. As a result, you could end up with an `Employee` object with an invalid name.

Declaring a Constructor

To correct this, you need to provide a means of specifying the required data when the object is created. You do this using a constructor as demonstrated in Listing 5.25.

LISTING 5.25: Defining a Constructor

```
class Employee
{
    // Employee constructor
    public Employee(string firstName, string lastName)
    {
        FirstName = firstName;
        LastName = lastName;
    }

    public string FirstName{ get; set; }
    public string LastName{ get; set; }
    public string Salary{ get; set; }

    // ...
}
```

To define a constructor you create a method with no return type, whose method name is identical to the class name.

The constructor is the method that the runtime calls to initialize an instance of the object. In this case, the constructor takes the first name and the last name as parameters, allowing the programmer to specify these names when instantiating the `Employee` object. Listing 5.26 is an example of how to call a constructor.

LISTING 5.26: Calling a Constructor

```
class Program
{
    static void Main()
    {
        Employee employee;
        employee = new Employee("Inigo", "Montoya");
        employee.Salary = "Too Little";
```

```
System.Console.WriteLine(
    "{0} {1}: {2}",
    employee.FirstName,
    employee.LastName,
    employee.Salary);
  }
  // ...
}
```

Notice that the new operator returns the type of the object being instantiated (even though no return type or return statement was specified explicitly in the constructor's declaration or implementation). In addition, you
have removed the initialization code for the first and last names because that
occurs within the constructor. In this example, you don't initialize Salary
within the constructor, so the code assigning the salary still appears.

Developers should take care when using both assignment at declaration
time and assignment within constructors. Assignments within the constructor will occur after any assignments are made when a field is declared (such
as string Salary = "Not enough" in Listing 5.5). Therefore, assignment
within a constructor will override any value assigned at declaration time.
This subtlety can lead to a misinterpretation of the code by a casual reader
who assumes the value after instantiation is the one assigned in the field
declaration. Therefore, it is worth considering a coding style that does not
mix both declaration assignment and constructor assignment within the
same class.

■ ADVANCED TOPIC

Implementation Details of the new Operator

Internally, the interaction between the new operator and the constructor is
as follows. The new operator retrieves "empty" memory from the memory
manager and then calls the specified constructor, passing a reference to the
empty memory to the constructor as the implicit this parameter. Next, the
remainder of the constructor chain executes, passing around the reference
between constructors. None of the constructors have a return type; behaviorally they all return void. When execution completes on the constructor
chain, the new operator returns the memory reference, now referring to the
memory in its initialized form.

Default Constructors

It is important to note that by adding a constructor explicitly, you can no longer instantiate an `Employee` from within `Main()` without specifying the first and last names. The code shown in Listing 5.27, therefore, will not compile.

LISTING 5.27: Default Constructor No Longer Available

```
class Program
{
  static void Main()
  {
      Employee employee;
      // ERROR:       No overload for method 'Employee'
      // takes '0' arguments.
      employee = new Employee();

      // ...
  }
}
```

If a class has no explicitly defined constructor, the C# compiler adds one during compilation. This constructor takes no parameters and is, therefore, the **default constructor** by definition. As soon as you add an explicit constructor to a class, the C# compiler no longer provides a default constructor. Therefore, with `Employee(string firstName, string lastName)` defined, the default constructor, `Employee()`, is not added by the compiler. You could manually add such a constructor, but then you would again be allowing construction of an `Employee` without specifying the employee name.

It is not necessary to rely on the default constructor defined by the compiler. It is also possible for programmers to define a default constructor explicitly, perhaps one that initializes some fields to particular values. Defining the default constructor simply involves declaring a constructor that takes no parameters.

Object Initializers

Starting with C# 3.0, the C# language team added functionality to initialize an object's accessible fields and properties using an **object initializer.** The object initializer consists of a set of member initializers enclosed in curly braces following the constructor call to create the object. Each member initializer is the assignment of an accessible field or property name with a value (see Listing 5.28).

LISTING 5.28: Calling an Object Initializer

```
class Program
{
  static void Main()
  {
      Employee employee1 = new Employee("Inigo", "Montoya")
          { Title = "Computer Nerd", Salary = "Not enough"};
      // ...
  }
}
```

Notice that the same constructor rules apply even when using an object initializer. In fact, the resultant CIL is exactly the same as it would be if the fields or properties were assigned within separate statements immediately following the constructor call. The order of member initializers in C# provides the sequence for property and field assignment in the statements following the constructor call within CIL.

In general, all properties should be initialized to reasonable default values by the time the constructor exits. And by using validation logic on the setter, it is possible to restrict the assignment of invalid data to a property. However, on occasion, the values on one or more properties may cause other properties on the same object to contain invalid values. When this occurs, exceptions from the invalid state should be postponed until the invalid interrelated property values become relevant.

Guidelines

DO provide sensible defaults for all properties, ensuring that defaults do not result in a security hole or significantly inefficient code. For automatically implemented properties, set the default via the constructor.

DO allow properties to be set in any order even if this results in a temporarily invalid object state.

■ ADVANCED TOPIC

Collection Initializers

Using a similar syntax to that of object initializers, collection initializers were added in C# 3.0. Collection initializers support a similar feature set as object initializers, only with collections. Specifically, a collection initializer allows the assignment of items within the collection at the time of the collection's instantiation. Borrowing on the same syntax used for arrays, the collection initializer initializes each item within the collection as part of collection creation. Initializing a list of Employees, for example, involves specifying each item within curly braces following the constructor call, as Listing 5.29 shows.

LISTING 5.29: Calling an Object Initializer

```csharp
class Program
{
  static void Main()
  {
      List<Employee> employees = new List<Employee>()
        {
            new Employee("Inigo", "Montoya"),
            new Employee("Chuck", "McAtee")
        };
      // ...
  }
}
```

After the assignment of a new collection instance, the compiler-generated code instantiates each object in sequence and adds them to the collection via the Add() method.

■ ADVANCED TOPIC

Finalizers

Constructors define what happens during the instantiation process of a class. To define what happens when an object is destroyed, C# provides the finalizer construct. Unlike destructors in C++, finalizers do not run immediately after an object goes out of scope. Rather, the finalizer executes at some unspecified time after an object is determined to be "unreachable." Specifically, the garbage collector identifies objects with finalizers during a garbage collection cycle, and instead of immediately de-allocating those objects, it adds them to a finalization queue. A separate thread runs through each object in the finalization queue and calls the object's finalizer before removing it from the queue and making it available for the garbage collector again. Chapter 9 discusses this process, along with resource cleanup, in depth.

Overloading Constructors

Constructors can be overloaded—you can have more than one constructor as long as the number or types of the parameters vary. For example, as Listing 5.30 shows, you could provide a constructor that has an employee ID with first and last names, or even just the employee ID.

LISTING 5.30: **Overloading a Constructor**

```csharp
class Employee
{
  public Employee(string firstName, string lastName)
  {
      FirstName = firstName;
      LastName = lastName;
  }

  public Employee(
      int id, string firstName, string lastName )
  {
      Id = id;
      FirstName = firstName;
      LastName = lastName;
  }

  public Employee(int id)
  {
      Id = id;

      // Look up employee name...
      // ...
  }

  public int Id { get; set; }
  public string FirstName { get; set; }
  public string LastName { get; set; }
  public string Salary { get; set; }

  // ...
}
```

This enables `Program.Main()` to instantiate an employee from the first and last names either by passing in the employee ID only, or by passing both the names and the IDs. You would use the constructor with both the names and the IDs when creating a new employee in the system. You would use the constructor with only the ID to load up the employee from a file or a database.

As is the case with method overloading, multiple constructors are used to support simple scenarios using a small number of parameters and complex scenarios with additional parameters. Consider using optional parameters in favor of overloading so that the default values for "defaulted" properties are visible in the API. For example, a constructor signature of `Person(string firstName, string lastName, int? age = null)` provides signature documentation that if the `Age` of a `Person` is not specified it will default to `null`.

> ### Guidelines
>
> **DO** use the same name for constructor parameters (camelCase) and properties (PascalCase) if the constructor parameters are used to simply set the property.
>
> **DO** provide constructor optional parameters and/or convenience constructor overloads that initialize properties with good defaults.
>
> **DO** allow properties to be set in any order even if this results in a temporarily invalid object state.

Constructor Chaining: Calling Another Constructor Using `this`

Notice in Listing 5.30 that the initialization code for the `Employee` object is now duplicated in multiple places and, therefore, has to be maintained in multiple places. The amount of code is small, but there are ways to eliminate the duplication by calling one constructor from another—**constructor chaining**—using **constructor initializers.** Constructor initializers determine which constructor to call before executing the implementation of the current constructor (see Listing 5.31).

LISTING 5.31: Calling One Constructor from Another

```csharp
class Employee
{
  public Employee(string firstName, string lastName)
  {
      FirstName = firstName;
      LastName = lastName;
  }
```

```csharp
public Employee(
    int id, string firstName, string lastName )
    : this(firstName, lastName)
{
    Id = id;
}

public Employee(int id)
{
    Id = id;

    // Look up employee name...
    // ...

        // NOTE:  Member constructors cannot be
        // called explicitly inline
        // this(id, firstName, lastName);
}

public int Id { get; set; }
public string FirstName { get; set; }
public string LastName { get; set; }
public string Salary { get; set; }

// ...
}
```

To call one constructor from another within the same class (for the same object instance) C# uses a colon followed by the `this` keyword followed by the parameter list on the callee constructor's declaration. In this case, the constructor that takes all three parameters calls the constructor that takes two. Often, the calling pattern is reversed; the constructor with the fewest parameters calls the constructor with the most parameters, passing defaults for the parameters that are not known.

■ BEGINNER TOPIC

Centralizing Initialization

Notice that in the `Employee(int id)` constructor implementation from Listing 5.31, you cannot call `this(firstName, LastName)` because no such parameters exist on this constructor. To enable such a pattern in which all initialization code happens through one method you must create a separate method, as shown in Listing 5.32.

LISTING 5.32: **Providing an Initialization Method**

```csharp
class Employee
{
  public Employee(string firstName, string lastName)
  {
    int id;
    // Generate an employee ID...
    // ...
    Initialize(id, firstName, lastName);
  }

  public Employee(int id, string firstName, string lastName )
  {
    Initialize(id, firstName, lastName);
  }

  public Employee(int id)
  {
    string firstName;
    string lastName;
    Id = id;

    // Look up employee data
    // ...

    Initialize(id, firstName, lastName);
  }

  private void Initialize(
    int id, string firstName, string lastName)
  {
    Id = id;
    FirstName = firstName;
    LastName = lastName;
  }
  // ...
}
```

In this case, the method is called `Initialize()` and it takes both the names and the employee IDs. Note that you can continue to call one constructor from another, as shown in Listing 5.31.

ADVANCED TOPIC

Anonymous Types

C# 3.0 introduced support for anonymous types. These are data types that are generated by the compiler "on the fly" rather than through explicit class definitions. Listing 5.33 shows such a declaration.

LISTING 5.33: Implicit Local Variables with Anonymous Types

```csharp
using System;

class Program
{
  static void Main()
  {
      var patent1 =
          new
          {
              Title = "Bifocals",
              YearOfPublication = "1784"
          };
      var patent2 =
          new
          {
              Title = "Phonograph",
              YearOfPublication = "1877"
          };
      var patent3 =
          new
          {
              patent1.Title,
              Year = patent1.YearOfPublication
          };

      System.Console.WriteLine("{0} ({1})",
          patent1.Title, patent1.YearOfPublication);
      System.Console.WriteLine("{0} ({1})",
          patent2.Title, patent1.YearOfPublication);

      Console.WriteLine();
      Console.WriteLine(patent1);
      Console.WriteLine(patent2);

      Console.WriteLine();
      Console.WriteLine(patent3);
  }
}
```

The corresponding output is shown in Output 5.8.

OUTPUT 5.8

```
Bifocals (1784)
Phonograph (1877)

{ Title = Bifocals, YearOfPublication = 1784 }
{ Title = Phonograph, YearOfPublication = 1877 }

{ Title = Bifocals, Year = 1784 }
```

Listing 5.33 demonstrates the assignment of an anonymous type to an implicitly typed (`var`) local variable.

When the compiler encounters the anonymous type syntax, it generates a class with properties corresponding to the named values and data types in the anonymous type declaration. Although there is no available name in C# for the generated type, it is still statically typed. For example, the properties of the type are fully accessible. In Listing 5.33, `patent1.Title` and `patent2.YearOfPublication` are called within the `Console.WriteLine()` statement. Any attempts to call nonexistent members will result in compile errors. Even IntelliSense in IDEs such as Visual Studio 2008 works with the anonymous type.

In Listing 5.33, member names on the anonymous types are explicitly identified using the assignment of the value to the name (see `Title` and `YearOfPublication` in `patent1` and `patent2` assignments). However, if the value assigned is a property or field, the name will default to the name of the field or property if not specified explicitly. `patent3`, for example, is defined using a property name "Title" rather than an assignment to an implicit name. As Output 5.8 shows, the resultant property name is determined by the compiler to match the property from where the value was retrieved.

Although the compiler allows anonymous type declarations such as the ones shown in Listing 5.33, you should generally avoid anonymous type declarations and even the associated implicit typing with `var` until you are working with lambda and query expressions that associate data from different types or you are horizontally projecting the data so that for a particular type, there is less data overall. Until frequent querying of data out of collections makes explicit type declaration burdensome, it is preferable to explicitly declare types as outlined in this chapter.

Static Members

The `HelloWorld` example in Chapter 1 briefly touched on the keyword `static`. This section defines the `static` keyword more fully.

To begin, consider an example. Assume that the employee `Id` value needs to be unique for each employee. One way to accomplish this is to store a counter to track each employee ID. If the value is stored as an instance field, however, every time you instantiate an object, a new `NextId` field will be created such that every instance of the `Employee` object would consume memory for that field. The biggest problem is that each time an `Employee` object instantiated, the `NextId` value on all of the previously instantiated `Employee` objects would need to be updated with the next ID value. What you need is a single field that all `Employee` object instances share.

Language Contrast: C++/Visual Basic—Global Variables and Functions

Unlike many of the languages that came before it, C# does not have global variables or global functions. All fields and methods in C# appear within the context of a class. The equivalent of a global field or function within the realm of C# is a static field or function. There is no functional difference between global variables/functions and C# static fields/methods, except that static fields/methods can include access modifiers, such as `private`, that can limit the access and provide better encapsulation.

Static Fields

To define data that is available across multiple instances, you use the `static` keyword, as demonstrated in Listing 5.34.

LISTING 5.34: Declaring a Static Field

```csharp
class Employee
{
  public Employee(string firstName, string lastName)
  {
      FirstName = firstName;
      LastName = lastName;
      Id = NextId;
      NextId++;
  }

  // ...

  public static int NextId;
  public int Id { get; set; }
  public string FirstName { get; set; }
  public string LastName { get; set; }
  public string Salary { get; set; }
```

```
    // ...
  }
```

In this example, the `NextId` field declaration includes the `static` modifier, and therefore is called a **static field.** Unlike `Id`, a single storage location for `NextId` is shared across all instances of `Employee`. Inside the `Employee` constructor, you assign the new `Employee` object's `Id` the value of `NextId` immediately before incrementing it. When another `Employee` class is created, `NextId` will be incremented and the new `Employee` object's `Id` field will hold a different value.

Just as **instance fields** (nonstatic fields) can be initialized at declaration time, so can static fields, as demonstrated in Listing 5.35.

LISTING 5.35: **Assigning a Static Field at Declaration**

```
class Employee
{
  // ...
    public static int NextId = 42;
  // ...
}
```

Unlike with instance fields, if no initialization for a static field is provided, the static field will automatically be assigned its default value (`0`, `null`, `false`, and so on)—the equivalent of `default(T)` where `T` is the name of the type. As a result, it will be possible to access the static field even if it has never been explicitly assigned in the C# code.

Nonstatic fields, or instance fields, have a new storage location for each object to which they belong. In contrast, static fields don't belong to the instance, but rather to the class itself. As a result, you access a static field from outside a class via the class name. Consider the new `Program` class shown in Listing 5.36 (using the `Employee` class from Listing 5.34).

LISTING 5.36: **Accessing a Static Field**

```
using System;

class Program
{
  static void Main()
  {
      Employee.NextId = 1000000;
```

```
Employee employee1 = new Employee(
    "Inigo", "Montoya");
Employee employee2 = new Employee(
    "Princess", "Buttercup");

Console.WriteLine(
    "{0} {1} ({2})",
    employee1.FirstName,
    employee1.LastName,
    employee1.Id);
Console.WriteLine(
    "{0} {1} ({2})",
    employee2.FirstName,
    employee2.LastName,
    employee2.Id);

    Console.WriteLine("NextId = {0}", Employee.NextId);
  }

  // ...
}
```

Output 5.9 shows the results of Listing 5.36.

OUTPUT 5.9

```
Inigo Montoya (1000000)
Princess Buttercup (1000001)
NextId = 1000002
```

To set and retrieve the initial value of the `NextId` static field, you use the class name, `Employee`, rather than a reference to an instance of the type. The only place you can omit the class name is within the class itself (or a derived class). In other words, the `Employee(...)` constructor did not need to use `Employee.NextId` because the code appeared within the context of the `Employee` class itself, and therefore, the context was already understood. The scope of a variable is the program text in which the variable can be referred to by its unqualified name; the scope of a static field is the text of the class (and any derived classes).

Even though you refer to static fields slightly differently than instance fields, it is not possible to define a static and an instance field with the same name in the same class. The possibility of mistakenly referring to the wrong field is high, and therefore, the C# designers decided to prevent such code. As such, overlap in names will introduce conflict within the declaration space.

Data Can Be Associated with Both a Class and an Object

Both classes and objects can have associated data, just as can the molds and the widgets created from them.

For example, a mold could have data corresponding to the number of widgets it created, the serial number of the next widget, the current color of the plastic injected into the mold, and the number of widgets it produces per hour. Similarly, a widget has its own serial number, its own color, and perhaps the date and time when the widget was created. Although the color of the widget corresponds to the color of the plastic within the mold at the time the widget was created, it obviously does not contain data corresponding to the color of the plastic currently in the mold, or the serial number of the next widget to be produced.

In designing objects, programmers should take care to declare both fields and methods appropriately as static- or instance-based. In general, you should declare methods that don't access any instance data as static methods, and methods that access instance data (where the instance is not passed in as a parameter) as instance methods. Static fields store data corresponding to the class, such as defaults for new instances or the number of instances that have been created. Instance fields store data associated with the object.

Static Methods

Just like static fields, you access static methods directly off the class name (`Console.ReadLine()`, for example). Furthermore, it is not necessary to have an instance in order to access the method.

Listing 5.37 provides another example of both declaring and calling a static method.

LISTING 5.37: **Defining a Static Method on** DirectoryInfo

```
public static class DirectoryInfoExtension
{
    public static void CopyTo(
        DirectoryInfo sourceDirectory, string target,
        SearchOption option, string searchPattern)
    {
        if (target[target.Length - 1] !=
            Path.DirectorySeparatorChar)
```

```
        {
            target += Path.DirectorySeparatorChar;
        }
        if (!Directory.Exists(target))
        {
            Directory.CreateDirectory(target);
        }

        for (int i = 0; i < searchPattern.Length; i++)
        {
            foreach (string file in
                Directory.GetFiles(
                    sourceDirectory.FullName, searchPattern))
            {
                File.Copy(file,
                    target + Path.GetFileName(file), true);
            }
        }

        //Copy SubDirectories (recursively)
        if (option == SearchOption.AllDirectories)
        {
            foreach(string element in
                Directory.GetDirectories(
                    sourceDirectory.FullName))
            {
                Copy(element,
                    target + Path.GetFileName(element),
                    searchPattern);
            }
        }
    }
}
```

```
// ...
DirectoryInfo directory = new DirectoryInfo(".\\Source");
directory.MoveTo(".\\Root");
DirectoryInfoExtension.CopyTo(
    directory, ".\\Target",
    SearchOption.AllDirectories, "*");
// ...
```

The `DirectoryInfoExtension.Copy()` method takes a `DirectoryInfo` object and copies the underlying directory structure to a new location.

Because static methods are not referenced through a particular instance, the `this` keyword is invalid inside a static method. In addition, it is not possible to access either an instance field or an instance method directly from within a static method without a reference to the particular instance to which the field or method belongs. (Note that `Main()` is another example of a static method.)

One might have expected this method on the `System.IO.Directory` class or as an instance method on `System.IO.DirectoryInfo`. Since neither exists, Listing 5.37 defines such a method on an entirely new class. In the section Extension Methods, later in this chapter, we show how to make it appear as an instance method on `DirectoryInfo`.

Static Constructors

In addition to static fields and methods C# also supports **static constructors.** Static constructors are provided as a means to initialize the class itself, rather than the instances of a class. Static constructors are not called explicitly; instead, the runtime calls static constructors automatically upon first access to the class, whether via calling a regular constructor or accessing a static method or field on the class. Since the static constructor cannot be called explicitly, no parameters are allowed on static constructors.

You use static constructors to initialize the static data within the class to a particular value, mainly when the initial value involves more complexity than a simple assignment at declaration time. Consider Listing 5.38.

LISTING 5.38: Declaring a Static Constructor

```
class Employee
{
  static Employee()
  {
      Random randomGenerator = new Random();
      NextId = randomGenerator.Next(101, 999);
  }

  // ...
  public static int NextId = 42;
  // ...
}
```

Listing 5.38 assigns the initial value of `NextId` to be a random integer between 100 and 1,000. Because the initial value involves a method call, the `NextId` initialization code appears within a static constructor and not as part of the declaration.

If assignment of `NextId` occurs within both the static constructor and the declaration, it is not obvious what the value will be when initialization concludes. The C# compiler generates CIL in which the declaration assignment is moved to be the first statement within the static constructor. Therefore, NextId will contain the value returned by randomGenerator.Next(101, 999) instead of a value assigned during NextId's declaration. Assignments within the static constructor, therefore, will take precedence over assignments that occur as part of the field declaration, as was the case with instance fields. Note that there is no support for defining a static finalizer.

Be careful not to throw an exception from a static constructor, as this will render the type unusable for the remainder of the application's lifetime.[5]

■ ADVANCED TOPIC

Favor Static Initialization during Declaration

Static constructors execute before the first access to any member of a class, whether it is a static field, another static member, or an instance constructor. In order to support this, the compiler injects a check into all type static members and constructors to ensure that the static constructor runs first.

Without the static constructor, the compiler instead initializes all static members to their default value and avoids adding the static constructor check. The result is for static assignment initialization to be called before accessing any static fields but not necessarily before all static methods or any instance constructor is invoked. This might provide a performance improvement if initialization of static members is expensive and is not needed before accessing a static field. As a result, consider initializing static fields inline rather than using a static constructor, or initializing them at declaration time.

Guidelines

CONSIDER initializing static fields inline rather than explicitly using static constructors or declaration assigned values.

---

5. Technically the application domain lifetime; the CLR's virtual equivalent of an operating system process.

Static Properties

You also can declare properties as static. For example, Listing 5.39 wraps the data for the next ID into a property.

LISTING 5.39: Declaring a Static Property

```
class Employee
{
  // ...
  public static int NextId
  {
    get
    {
      return _NextId;
    }
    private set
    {
      _NextId = value;
    }
  }
  public static int _NextId = 42;
  // ...
}
```

It is almost always better to use a static property rather than a public static field, because public static fields are callable from anywhere whereas a static property offers at least some level of encapsulation.

Static Classes

Some classes do not contain any instance fields. Consider, for example, a Math class that has functions corresponding to the mathematical operations Max() and Min(), as shown in Listing 5.40.

LISTING 5.40: Declaring a Static Class

```
// Static class introduced in C# 2.0
public static class SimpleMath
{
  // params allows the number of parameters to vary.
  static int Max(params int[] numbers)
  {
    // Check that there is a Least one item in numbers.
    if(numbers.Length == 0)
    {
      throw new ArgumentException(
        "numbers cannot be empty");
    }
```

```
        int result;
        result = numbers[0];
        foreach (int number in numbers)
        {
            if(number > result)
            {
                result = number;
            }
        }
        return result;
    }

    // params allows the number of parameters to vary.
    static int Min(params int[] numbers)
    {
        // Check that there is a least one item in numbers.
        if(numbers.Length == 0)
        {
            throw new ArgumentException(
                "numbers cannot be empty");
        }

        int result;
        result = numbers[0];
        foreach (int number in numbers)
        {
            if(number < result)
            {
                result = number;
            }
        }
        return result;
    }
}
```

This class does not have any instance fields (or methods), and therefore, creation of such a class would be pointless. Because of this, the class is decorated with the static keyword. The static keyword on a class provides two facilities. First, it prevents a programmer from writing code that instantiates the SimpleMath class. Second, it prevents the declaration of any instance fields or methods within the class. Since the class cannot be instantiated, instance members would be pointless. The Program class in prior listings is another good candidate for a static class since it only contains static members.

One more distinguishing characteristic of the static class is that the C# compiler automatically marks it as abstract and sealed within the CIL.

This designates the class as **inextensible;** in other words, no class can be derived from it or instantiate it.

Extension Methods

Consider the `System.IO.DirectoryInfo` class that is used to manipulate filesystem directories. The class supports functionality to list the files and subdirectories (`DirectoryInfo.GetFiles()`) as well as the capability to move the directory (`DirectoryInfo.Move()`). One feature it doesn't support directly is the copy feature. If you needed such a method you would have to implement it, as shown earlier in Listing 5.37.

The `DirectoryInfoExtension.Copy()` method is a standard static method declaration. However, notice that calling this `Copy()` method is different from calling the `DirectoryInfo.Move()` method. This is unfortunate. Ideally, we want to add a method to `DirectoryInfo` so that, given an instance, we could call `Copy()` as an instance method—`directory.Copy()`.

C# 3.0 simulates the creation of an instance method on a different class via **extension methods.** To do this we simply change the signature of our static method so that the first parameter, the data type we are extending, is prefixed with the `this` keyword (see Listing 5.41).

LISTING 5.41: **Static Copy Method for** `DirectoryInfo`

```csharp
public static class DirectoryInfoExtension
{
  public static void CopyTo(
    this DirectoryInfo sourceDirectory, string target,
    SearchOption option, string searchPattern)
  {
    // ...
  }
}
```

```csharp
// ...
    DirectoryInfo directory = new DirectoryInfo(".\\Source");
    directory.CopyTo(".\\Target",
        SearchOption.AllDirectories, "*");
    // ...
```

Via this simple addition to C# 3.0, it is now possible to add "instance methods" to any class, even classes that are not within the same assembly.

The resultant CIL code, however, is identical to what the compiler creates when calling the extension method as a normal static method.

Extension method requirements are as follows.

- The first parameter corresponds to the type on which the method extends or operates.
- To designate the extension method, prefix the extended type with the `this` modifier.
- To access the method as an extension method, import the extending type's namespace via a `using` directive (or place the extending class in the same namespace as the calling code).

If the extension method signature matches a signature on the extended type already (that is, if `CopyTo()` already existed on `DirectoryInfo`), the extension method will never be called except as a normal static method.

Note that specializing a type via inheritance (covered in detail in Chapter 6) is preferable to using an extension method. Extension methods do not provide a clean versioning mechanism since the addition of a matching signature to the extended type will take precedence over the extension method without warning of the change. The subtlety of this is more pronounced for extended classes whose source code you don't control. Another minor point is that, although development IDEs support IntelliSense for extension methods, it is not obvious that a method is an extension method by simply reading through the calling code.

In general, use extension methods sparingly. Do not, for example, define them on type `object`. Chapter 6 discusses how to use extension methods in association with an interface. Without such an association, defining extension methods is rare.

Guidelines

AVOID frivolously defining extension methods, especially on types you don't own.

Encapsulating the Data

In addition to properties and the access modifiers we looked at earlier in the chapter, there are several other specialized ways of encapsulating the data within a class. For instance, there are two more field modifiers. The first is the `const` modifier, which you already encountered when declaring local variables. The second is the capability of fields to be defined as read-only.

const

Just as with `const` values, a `const` field contains a compile-time-determined value that cannot be changed at runtime. Values such as pi make good candidates for constant field declarations. Listing 5.42 shows an example of declaring a `const` field.

LISTING 5.42: **Declaring a Constant Field**

```csharp
class ConvertUnits
{
    public const float CentimetersPerInch = 2.54F;
    public const int CupsPerGallon = 16;
    // ...
}
```

Constant fields are static automatically, since no new field instance is required for each object instance. Declaring a constant field as `static` explicitly will cause a compile error. Also, constant fields are usually only declared for types that have literal values (`string`, `int`, and `double`, for example). Types such as `Program` or `System.Guid` cannot be used for constant fields.

It is important that the types of values used in `public` constant expressions are permanent in time. Values such as pi, Avogadro's number, and the circumference of the Earth are good examples. However, values that could potentially change over time are not. Build numbers, population counts, and exchange rates would be poor choices for constants.

Guidelines

DO use constant field for values that will never change.
DO NOT use constant field for values that will change over time.

■ **ADVANCED TOPIC**

Public Constants Should Be Permanent Values

Publicly accessible constants should be permanent, because changing the value of a constant will not necessarily take effect in the assemblies that use it. If an assembly references a constant from a different assembly, the value of the constant is compiled directly into the referencing assembly. Therefore, if the value in the referenced assembly is changed but the referencing assembly is not recompiled, the referencing assembly will still use the original value, not the new value. Values that could potentially change in the future should be specified as readonly instead.

readonly

Unlike const, the readonly modifier is available only for fields (not for local variables) and it declares that the field value is modifiable only from inside the constructor or directly during declaration. Listing 5.43 demonstrates how to declare a readonly field.

LISTING 5.43: **Declaring a Field As** readonly

```
class Employee
{
  public Employee(int id)
  {
    Id = id;
  }

  // ...
  public readonly int Id;
  public void SetId(int newId)
  {
    // ERROR:  read-only fields cannot be set
    //         outside the constructor.
    // Id = newId;
  }

  // ...
}
```

Unlike constant fields, readonly fields can vary from one instance to the next. In fact, a readonly field's value can change within the constructor. Furthermore, readonly fields occur as either instance or static fields. Another key distinction is that you can assign the value of a readonly field at execution time rather than just at compile time. Given that readonly fields must be set in the constructor, such fields are the one case where the compiler requires the fields be accessed from code outside their corresponding property. Besides this one exception, avoid accessing a backing field from anywhere other than its wrapping property.

Another important feature of readonly fields over const fields is that readonly fields are not limited to types with literal values. It is possible, for example, to declare a readonly System.Guid instance field but not a similar constant field, as shown in Listing 5.44.

LISTING 5.44: Declaring a readonly Field of a Type with no Literal Values

```csharp
class CommonGuid
{
  public static readonly Guid ComIUnknownGuid =
      new Guid("00000000-0000-0000-C000-000000000046");
  public static readonly Guid ComIClassFactoryGuid =
      new Guid("00000001-0000-0000-C000-000000000046");
  public static readonly Guid ComIDispatchGuid =
      new Guid("00020400-0000-0000-C000-000000000046");
  public static readonly Guid ComITypeInfoGuid =
      new Guid("00020401-0000-0000-C000-000000000046");
  // ...
}
```

Using readonly with an array does not freeze the contents of the array. It freezes the number of elements in the array because it is not possible to reassign the readonly field to a new instance. However, the elements of the array are still writeable.

Guidelines

DO use public static readonly fields for predefined object instances.

Nested Classes

In addition to defining methods and fields within a class, it is also possible to define a class within a class. Such classes are **nested classes.** You use a nested class when the class makes little sense outside the context of its containing class.

Consider a class that handles the command-line options of a program. Such a class is generally unique to each program and there is no reason to make a CommandLine class accessible from outside the class that contains Main(). Listing 5.45 demonstrates such a nested class.

LISTING 5.45: Defining a Nested Class

```csharp
// CommandLine is nested within Program
class Program
{
   // Define a nested class for processing the command line.
   private class CommandLine
   {
       public CommandLine(string[] arguments)
       {
           for(int argumentCounter=0;
               argumentCounter<arguments.Length;
               argumentCounter++)
           {
               switch (argumentCounter)
               {
                   case 0:
                       Action = arguments[0].ToLower();
                       break;
                   case 1:
                       Id = arguments[1];
                       break;
                   case 2:
                       FirstName = arguments[2];
                       break;
                   case 3:
                       LastName = arguments[3];
                       break;
               }
           }
       }
       public string Action;
       public string Id;
       public string FirstName;
       public string LastName;
   }

   static void Main(string[] args)
   {
       CommandLine commandLine = new CommandLine(args);

       switch (commandLine.Action)
       {
           case "new":
               // Create a new employee
               // ...
```

```
            break;
    case "update":
        // Update an existing employee's data
        // ...
        break;
    case "delete":
        // Remove an existing employee's file.
        // ...
        break;
    default:
        Console.WriteLine(
            "Employee.exe " +
    "new|update|delete <id> [firstname] [lastname]");
        break;
    }
  }
}
```

The nested class in this example is `Program.CommandLine`. As with all class members, no containing class identifier is needed from inside the containing class, so you can simply refer to it as `CommandLine`.

One unique characteristic of nested classes is the ability to specify `private` as an access modifier for the class itself. Because the purpose of this class is to parse the command line and place each argument into a separate field, `Program.CommandLine` is relevant only to the `Program` class in this application. The use of the `private` access modifier defines the intended accessibility of the class and prevents access from outside the class. You can do this only if the class is nested.

The `this` member within a nested class refers to an instance of the nested class, not the containing class. One way for a nested class to access an instance of the containing class is if the containing class instance is explicitly passed, such as via a constructor or method parameter.

Another interesting characteristic of nested classes is that they can access any member on the containing class, including private members. The converse is not true, however: It is not possible for the containing class to access a private member of the nested class.

Nested classes are rare. They should not be defined if they are likely to be referenced outside the containing type. Furthermore, treat `public` nested classes suspiciously; they indicate potentially poor code that is likely to be confusing and hard to discover.

Guidelines

AVOID publicly exposed nested types. The only exception is if the declaration of such a type is unlikely or pertains to an advanced customization scenario.

Language Contrast: Java—Inner Classes

Java includes not only the concept of a nested class, but also the concept of an inner class. Inner classes correspond to objects that are associated with the containing class instance rather than just a syntactic relationship. In C#, you can achieve the same structure by including an instance field of a nested type within the outer class. A factory method or constructor can ensure a reference to the corresponding instance of the outer class is set within the inner class instance as well.

Partial Classes

Another language feature added in C# 2.0 is **partial classes.** Partial classes are portions of a class that the compiler can combine to form a complete class. Although you could define two or more partial classes within the same file, the general purpose of a partial class is to allow the splitting of a class definition across multiple files. Primarily this is useful for tools that are generating or modifying code. With partial classes, the tools can work on a file separate from the one the developer is manually coding.

Defining a Partial Class

C# 2.0 (and later) allows declaration of a partial class by prepending a contextual keyword, `partial`, immediately before `class`, as Listing 5.46 shows.

LISTING 5.46: Defining a Partial Class

```
// File: Program1.cs
partial class Program
{
}
```

```
// File: Program2.cs
partial class Program
{
}
```

In this case, each portion of `Program` is placed into a separate file, as identified by the comment.

Besides their use with code generators, another common use of partial classes is to place any nested classes into their own files. This is in accordance with the coding convention that places each class definition within its own file. For example, Listing 5.47 places the `Program.CommandLine` class into a file separate from the core `Program` members.

LISTING 5.47: Defining a Nested Class in a Separate Partial Class

```
// File: Program.cs
partial class Program
{
  static void Main(string[] args)
  {
    CommandLine commandLine = new CommandLine(args);

    switch (commandLine.Action)
    {
      // ...
    }
  }
}
```

```
// File: Program+CommandLine.cs
partial class Program
{
  // Define a nested class for processing the command line.
  private class CommandLine
  {
    // ...
  }
}
```

Partial classes do not allow extending compiled classes, or classes in other assemblies. They are only a means of splitting a class implementation across multiple files within the same assembly.

Partial Methods

Beginning with C# 3.0, the language designers added the concept of partial methods, extending the partial class concept of C# 2.0. Partial methods are allowed only within partial classes, and like partial classes, the primary purpose is to accommodate code generation.

Consider a code generation tool that generates the `Person.Designer.cs` file for the `Person` class based on a `Person` table within a database. The tool will examine the table and create properties for each column in the table. The problem, however, is that frequently the tool cannot generate any validation logic that may be required because this logic is based on business rules that are not embedded into the database table definition. Instead, the developer of the `Person` class needs to add the validation logic. It is undesirable to modify `Person.Designer.cs` directly because if the file is regenerated (to accommodate an additional column in the database, for example), the changes would be lost. Instead, the structure of the code for `Person` needs to be separated out so that the generated code appears in one file and the custom code (with business rules) is placed into a separate file unaffected by any regeneration. As we saw in the preceding section, partial classes are well suited for the task of splitting a class across multiple files. However, they are not sufficient. Frequently, we also need **partial methods.**

Partial methods allow for a declaration of a method without requiring an implementation. However, when the optional implementation is included, it can be located in one of the sister partial class definitions, likely in a separate file. Listing 5.48 shows the partial method declaration and the implementation for the `Person` class.

LISTING 5.48: Defining a Nested Class in a Separate Partial Class

```csharp
// File: Person.Designer.cs
public partial class Person
{
    #region Extensibility Method Definitions
    partial void OnLastNameChanging(string value);
    partial void OnFirstNameChanging(string value);
    #endregion

    // ...
    public System.Guid PersonId
    {
        // ...
    }
    private System.Guid _PersonId;

    // ...
    public string LastName
    {
```

```csharp
        get
        {
            return _LastName;
        }
        set
        {
            if ((_LastName != value))
            {
                OnLastNameChanging(value);
                _LastName = value;
            }
        }
    }
    private string _LastName;

    // ...
    public string FirstName
    {
        get
        {
            return _FirstName;
        }
        set
        {
            if ((_FirstName != value))
            {
                OnFirstNameChanging(value);
                _FirstName = value;
            }
        }
    }
    private string _FirstName;

}
```

```csharp
// File: Person.cs
partial class Person
{
  partial void OnLastNameChanging(string value)
  {
      if (value == null)
      {
          throw new ArgumentNullException("LastName");
      }
      if(value.Trim().Length == 0)
      {
          throw new ArgumentException(
              "LastName cannot be empty.");
      }
  }
}
```

In the listing of `Person.Designer.cs` are declarations for the `OnLast NameChanging()` and `OnFirstNameChanging()` methods. Furthermore, the properties for the last and first names make calls to their corresponding changing methods. Even though the declarations of the changing methods contain no implementation, this code will successfully compile. The key is that the method declarations are prefixed with the contextual keyword `partial` in addition to the class that contains such methods.

In Listing 5.48, only the `OnLastNameChanging()` method is implemented. In this case, the implementation checks the suggested new `LastName` value and throws an exception if it is not valid. Notice that the signatures for `OnLastNameChanging()` between the two locations match.

It is important to note that a partial method must return `void`. If the method didn't return `void` and the implementation was not provided, what would the expected return be from a call to a nonimplemented method? To avoid any invalid assumptions about the return, the C# designers decided to prohibit methods with returns other than `void`. Similarly, out parameters are not allowed on partial methods. If a return value is required, `ref` parameters may be used.

In summary, partial methods allow generated code to call methods that have not necessarily been implemented. Furthermore, if there is no implementation provided for a partial method, no trace of the partial method appears in the CIL. This helps keep code size small while keeping flexibility high.

SUMMARY

This chapter explained C# constructs for classes and object orientation in C#. This included a discussion of fields, and a discussion of how to access them on a class instance.

This chapter also discussed the key concept of whether to store data on a per-instance basis or across all instances of a type. Static data is associated with the class and instance data is stored on each object.

In addition, the chapter explored encapsulation in the context of access modifiers for methods and data. The C# construct of properties was introduced, and you saw how to use it to encapsulate private fields.

The next chapter focuses on how to associate classes with each other via inheritance, and the benefits derived from this object-oriented construct.

■ 6 ■

Inheritance

THE PRECEDING CHAPTER DISCUSSED HOW one class can reference other classes via fields and properties. This chapter discusses how to use the inheritance relationship between classes to build class hierarchies that form an "is a" relationship.

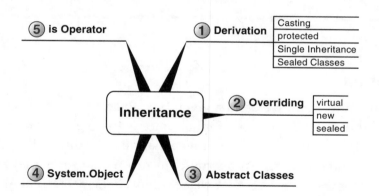

Inheritance Definitions
The preceding chapter provided an overview of inheritance. Here's a review of the defined terms.

- *Derive/inherit:* Specialize a base class to include additional members or customization of the base class members.
- *Derived/sub/child type:* The specialized type that inherits the members of the more general type.
- *Base/super/parent type:* The general type whose members a derived type inherits.

Inheritance forms an "is a kind of" relationship. The derived type is always implicitly also of the base type. Just as a hard drive is a kind of storage device, any other type derived from the storage device type is a kind of storage device. Notice that the converse is not necessarily true. A storage device is not necessarily a hard drive.

> **■■ NOTE**
>
> Inheritance within code is used to define an "is a kind of" relationship between two classes where the derived class is a specialization of the base class.

Derivation

It is common to want to extend a given type to add features, such as behavior and data. The purpose of inheritance is to do exactly that. Given a `Person` class, you create an `Employee` class that additionally contains `EmployeeId` and `Department` properties. The reverse approach may also occur. Given, for example, a `Contact` class within a Personal Digital Assistant (PDA), you decide you also can add calendaring support. Toward this effort, you create an `Appointment` class. However, instead of redefining the methods and properties that are common to both classes, you **refactor** the `Contact` class. Specifically, you move the common methods and properties on `Contact` into a base class called `PdaItem` from which both `Contact` and `Appointment` derive, as shown in Figure 6.1.

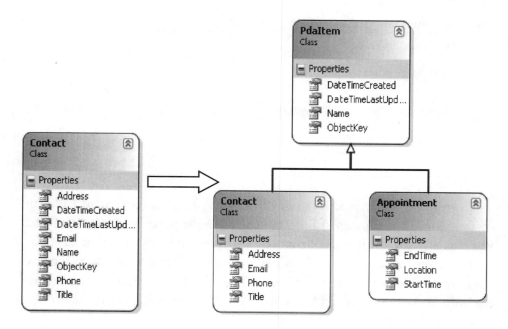

FIGURE 6.1: Refactoring into a Base Class

The common items in this case are `Created`, `LastUpdated`, `Name`, `ObjectKey`, and the like. Through derivation, the methods defined on the base class, `PdaItem`, are accessible from all classes derived from `PdaItem`.

When declaring a derived class, follow the class identifier with a colon and then the base class, as Listing 6.1 demonstrates.

LISTING 6.1: Deriving One Class from Another

```csharp
public class PdaItem
{
  public string Name { get; set; }

  public DateTime LastUpdated { get; set; }
}
```

```csharp
// Define the Contact class as inheriting the PdaItem class
public class Contact : PdaItem
{
  public string Address { get; set; }
  public string Phone { get; set; }
}
```

Listing 6.2 shows how to access the properties defined in `Contact`.

LISTING 6.2: **Using Inherited Methods**

```
public class Program
{
  public static void Main()
  {
      Contact contact = new Contact();
      contact.Name = "Inigo Montoya";

      // ...
  }
}
```

Even though `Contact` does not directly have a property called `Name`, all instances of `Contact` can still access the `Name` property from `PdaItem` and use it as though it was part of `Contact`. Furthermore, any additional classes that derive from `Contact` will also inherit the members of `PdaItem`, or any class from which `PdaItem` was derived. The inheritance chain has no practical limit and each derived class will have all the members of its base class inheritance chain combined (see Listing 6.3).

> ▪ **NOTE**
>
> Via inheritance, each member of a base class will also appear within the chain of derived classes.

LISTING 6.3: **Classes Deriving from Each Other to Form an Inheritance Chain**

```
public class PdaItem : object
{
  // ...
}
```

```
public class Appointment : PdaItem
{
  // ...
}
```

```
public class Contact : PdaItem
{
  // ...
}
```

```
public class Customer : Contact
{
  // ...
}
```

In other words, although `Customer` doesn't derive from `PdaItem` directly, it still inherits the members of `PdaItem`.

In Listing 6.3, `PdaItem` is shown explicitly to derive from `object`. Although C# allows such syntax, it is unnecessary because all classes that don't have some other derivation will derive from `object`, regardless of whether it is specified.

> **NOTE**
>
> Unless an alternate base class is specified, all classes will derive from `object` by default.

Casting between Base and Derived Types

As Listing 6.4 shows, because derivation forms an "is a" relationship, a derived type value can always be directly assigned to a base type variable.

LISTING 6.4: Implicit Base Type Casting

```
public class Program
{
  public static void Main()
  {
    // Derived types can be implicitly converted to
    // base types
    Contact contact = new Contact();
    PdaItem item = contact;
    // ...

    // Base types must be cast explicitly to derived types
    contact = (Contact)item;
    // ...
  }
}
```

The derived type, `Contact`, is a `PdaItem` and can be assigned directly to a variable of type `PdaItem`. This is known as an **implicit conversion** because no cast operator is required and the conversion will, on principle, always succeed; it will not throw an exception.

The reverse, however, is not true. A PdaItem is not necessarily a Contact; it could be an Appointment or some other derived type. Therefore, casting from the base type to the derived type requires an **explicit cast,** which at runtime could fail. To perform an explicit cast, identify the target type within parentheses prior to the original reference, as Listing 6.4 demonstrates.

With the explicit cast, the programmer essentially communicates to the compiler to trust her—she knows what she is doing—and the C# compiler allows the conversion as long as the target type is derived from the originating type. Although the C# compiler allows an explicit conversion at compile time between potentially compatible types, the CLR will still verify the explicit cast at execution time, throwing an exception if in fact the object instance is not of the targeted type.

The C# compiler allows the cast operator even when the type hierarchy allows an implicit cast. For example, the assignment from contact to item could use a cast operator as follows:

```
item = (PdaItem)contact;
```

or even when no cast is necessary:

```
contact = (Contact)contact;
```

> **▪ NOTE**
>
> A derived object can be implicitly converted to its base class. In contrast, converting from the base class to the derived class requires an explicit cast operator, as the conversion could fail. Although the compiler will allow an explicit cast if it is potentially valid, the runtime will still prevent an invalid cast at execution time by throwing an exception.

BEGINNER TOPIC

Casting within the Inheritance Chain

An implicit conversion to a base class does not instantiate a new instance. Instead, the same instance is simply referred to as the base type and the capabilities (the accessible members) are those of the base type. It is just like referring to a CD-ROM drive as a "storage device." Since not all storage devices support an eject operation, a CD-ROM drive that is viewed as a storage device cannot be ejected either, and a call to `storageDevice.Eject()` would not compile even though the instantiated object may have been a `CDROM` object that supported the `Eject()` method.

Similarly, casting down from the base class to the derived class simply begins referring to the type more specifically, expanding the available operations. The restriction is that the actual instantiated type must be an instance of the targeted type (or something derived from it).

■ ADVANCED TOPIC

Defining Custom Conversions

Conversion between types is not limited to types within a single inheritance chain. It is possible to convert between entirely unrelated types as well. The key is the provision of a conversion operator between the two types. C# allows types to include either explicit or implicit conversion operators. If the operation could possibly fail, such as in a cast from `long` to `int`, developers should choose to define an explicit conversion operator. This warns developers performing the conversion to do so only when they are certain the conversion will succeed, or else to be prepared to catch the exception if it doesn't. They should also use an explicit conversion over an implicit conversion when the conversion is lossy. Converting from a `float` to an `int`, for example, truncates the decimal, which a return cast (from `int` back to `float`) would not recover.

Listing 6.5 shows implicit and explicit conversion operators for `Address` to `string` and vice versa.

LISTING 6.5: Defining Cast Operators

```
class GPSCoordinates
{
  // ...

  public static implicit operator UTMCoordinates(
      GPSCoordinates coordinates)
  {
    // ...
  }
}
```

In this case, you have an implicit conversion from GPSCoordinates to UTMCoordinates. A similar conversion could be written to reverse the process. Note that an explicit conversion could also be written by replacing implicit with explicit.

private **Access Modifier**

All members of a base class, except for constructors and destructors, are inherited by the derived class. However, just because a member is inherited does not mean it is accessible. For example, in Listing 6.6, the private field, _Name, is not available on Contact because private members are only accessible at code locations inside the type that declares them.

LISTING 6.6: **Private Members Are Inherited But Not Accessible**

```csharp
public class PdaItem
{
  private string _Name;
  // ...
}
```

```csharp
public class Contact : PdaItem
{
  // ...
}
```

```csharp
public class Program
{
  public static void Main()
  {
    Contact contact = new Contact();

    // ERROR:  'PdaItem. _Name' is inaccessible
    // due to its protection level
    //contact._Name = "Inigo Montoya";
  }
}
```

As part of keeping with the principle of encapsulation, derived classes cannot access members declared as private.[1] This forces the base class developer to make an explicit choice as to whether a derived class gains access to a member. In this case, the base class is defining an API in which _Name can be changed only via the Name property. That way, if validation is added,

---

1. Except for the corner case when the derived class is also a nested class of the base class.

the derived class will gain the validation benefit automatically because it was unable to access _Name directly from the start.

> **■ NOTE**
>
> Non-nested derived classes cannot access members declared as private in a base class.

protected **Access Modifier**

Encapsulation is finer-grained than just public or private, however. It is possible to define members in base classes that only derived classes can access. Consider the ObjectKey property shown in Listing 6.7, for example.

LISTING 6.7: protected **Members Are Accessible Only from Derived Classes**

```csharp
public class Program
{
  public static void Main()
  {
      Contact contact = new Contact();
      contact.Name = "Inigo Montoya";

      // ERROR:  'PdaItem.ObjectKey' is inaccessible
      // due to its protection level
      // contact.ObjectKey = Guid.NewGuid();
  }
}

public class PdaItem
{
  protected Guid ObjectKey
  {
      get { return _ObjectKey; }
      set { _ObjectKey = value; }
  }
  private Guid _ObjectKey;

  // ...
}

public class Contact : PdaItem
{
  void Save()
  {
      // Instantiate a FileStream using <ObjectKey>.dat
      // for the filename.
      FileStream stream = System.IO.File.OpenWrite(
```

```
            ObjectKey + ".dat");
    }

    void Load(PdaItem pdaItem)
    {
        // ERROR:  'pdaItem.ObjectKey' is inaccessible
        // due to its protection level
        // pdaItem.ObjectKey = ...;

        Contact contact = pdaItem as Contact;
        if(contact != null)
        {
            contact.ObjectKey = ...;
        }

        // ...
    }
}
```

ObjectKey is defined using the protected access modifier. The result is that
it is accessible outside of PdaItem only from classes that derive from PdaItem.
Contact derives from PdaItem, and, therefore all members of Contact have
access to ObjectKey. Since Program does not derive from PdaItem, using the
ObjectKey property within Program results in a compile error.

> **▪ NOTE**
>
> Protected members in the base class are only accessible from the base
> class and other classes within the derivation chain.

A subtlety shown in the Contact.Load() method is worth noting. Developers are often surprised that from code within Contact it is not possible to
access the protected ObjectKey of an explicit PdaItem, even though Contact
derives from PdaItem. The reason is that a PdaItem could potentially be an
Address, and Contact should not be able to access protected members of
Address. Therefore, encapsulation prevents Contact from potentially modifying the ObjectKey of an Address. A successful cast to Contact will bypass
the restriction as shown. The governing rule is that accessing a protected
member from a derived class requires compile-time determination that the
protected member is an instance of the derived class (or a class further
derived from it).

Extension Methods

Extension methods are technically not members of a type, and therefore are not inherited. But because every derived class may be used as an instance of any of its base classes, an extension method on one type also extends every derived type. If we extend a base class such as `PdaItem`, all the extension methods will also be available in the derived classes. However, as with all extension methods, priority is given to instance methods. If a compatible signature appears anywhere within the inheritance chain, this will take precedence over an extension method.

Requiring extension methods on base types is rare. As with extension methods in general, if the base type's code is available, it is preferable to modify the base type directly. Even in cases where the base type's code is unavailable, programmers should consider whether to add extension methods to an interface that the base type or individual derived types implement. We cover interfaces and how to use them with extension methods in the next chapter.

Single Inheritance

In theory, you can place an unlimited number of classes in an inheritance tree. For example, `Customer` derives from `Contact`, which derives from `PdaItem`, which derives from `object`. However, C# is a **single-inheritance** programming language (as is the CIL language to which C# compiles). This means that a class cannot derive from two classes directly. It is not possible, for example, to have `Contact` derive from both `PdaItem` and `Person`.

Language Contrast: C++—Multiple Inheritance

C#'s single inheritance is one of its major differences from C++. It makes for a significant migration path from programming libraries such as Active Template Library (ATL), whose entire approach relies on multiple inheritance.

For the rare cases that require a multiple-inheritance class structure, one solution is to use **aggregation;** instead of one class inheriting from another, one class contains an instance of the other. Figure 6.2 shows an example of this class structure. Aggregation occurs when the association relationship defines a core part of the containing object. For multiple inheritance, this involves picking one class as the primary base class (PdaItem) and deriving a new class (Contact) from that. The second desired base class (Person) is added as a field in the derived class (Contact). Next, all the nonprivate members on the field (Person) are redefined on the derived class (Contact) which then delegates the calls out to the field (Person). Some code duplication occurs because methods are redeclared; however, this is minimal, since the real method body is implemented only within the aggregated class (Person).

In Figure 6.2, Contact contains a private property called InternalPerson that is drawn as an association to the Person class. Contact also contains the FirstName and LastName properties but with no corresponding fields. Instead, the FirstName and LastName properties simply delegate their calls out to InternalPerson.FirstName and InternalPerson.LastName, respectively. Listing 6.8 shows the resultant code.

LISTING 6.8: **Working around Single Inheritance Using Aggregation**

```
public class PdaItem
{
  // ...
}

public class Person
{
  // ...
}

public class Contact : PdaItem
{
  private Person InternalPerson { get; set; }

  public string FirstName
  {
      get { return InternalPerson.FirstName; }
      set { InternalPerson.FirstName = value; }
  }

  public string LastName
  {
      get { return InternalPerson.LastName; }
      set { InternalPerson.LastName = value; }
  }

  // ...
}
```

Besides the added complexity of delegation, another drawback is that any methods added to the field class (Person) will require manual addition to the derived class (Contact); otherwise, Contact will not expose the added functionality.

FIGURE 6.2: Simulating Multiple Inheritance Using Aggregation

Sealed Classes

To design a class correctly that others can extend via derivation can be a tricky task that requires testing with examples to verify the derivation will work successfully. Listing 6.9 shows how to avoid unexpected derivation scenarios and problems by marking classes as **sealed.**

LISTING 6.9: Preventing Derivation with Sealed Classes

```
public sealed class CommandLineParser
{
  // ...
}
```

```
// ERROR:  Sealed classes cannot be derived from
public sealed class DerivedCommandLineParser :
  CommandLineParser
{
  // ...
}
```

Sealed classes include the `sealed` modifier, and the result is that they cannot be derived from. The `string` type is an example of a type that uses the `sealed` modifier to prevent derivation.

Overriding the Base Class

All members of a base class are inherited in the derived class, except for constructors and destructors. However, sometimes the base class does not have the optimal implementation of a particular member. Consider the `Name` property on `PdaItem`, for example. The implementation is probably acceptable when inherited by the `Appointment` class. For the `Contact` class, however, the `Name` property should return the `FirstName` and `LastName` properties combined. Similarly, when `Name` is assigned, it should be split across `FirstName` and `LastName`. In other words, the base class property declaration is appropriate for the derived class, but the implementation is not always valid. There needs to be a mechanism for **overriding** the base class implementation with a custom implementation in the derived class.

virtual **Modifier**

C# supports overriding on instance methods and properties, but not on fields or on any static members. It requires an explicit action within both the base class and the derived class. The base class must mark each member for which it allows overriding as `virtual`. If public or protected members do not include the `virtual` modifier, subclasses will not be able to override those members.

Language Contrast: Java—Virtual Methods by Default

By default, methods in Java are virtual, and they must be explicitly sealed if nonvirtual behavior is preferred. In contrast, C# defaults to nonvirtual.

Listing 6.10 shows an example of property overriding.

LISTING 6.10: **Overriding a Property**

```
public class PdaItem
{
    public virtual string Name { get; set; }
    // ...
}

public class Contact : PdaItem
{
    public override string Name
    {
        get
        {
            return FirstName + " " + LastName;
        }

        set
        {
            string[] names = value.Split(' ');
            // Error handling not shown.
            FirstName = names[0];
            LastName = names[1];
        }
    }

    public string FirstName { get; set; }
    public string LastName { get; set; }

    // ...
}
```

Not only does `PdaItem` include the `virtual` modifier on the `Name` property, but also, `Contact`'s `Name` property is decorated with the keyword `override`.

Eliminating virtual would result in an error and omitting override would cause a warning, as you will see shortly. C# requires the overriding methods to use the override keyword explicitly.

In other words, virtual identifies a method or property as available for replacement (overriding) in the derived type.

Language Contrast: Java and C++—Implicit Overriding

Unlike with Java and C++, the override keyword is required on the derived class. C# does not allow implicit overriding. In order to override a method, both the base class and the derived class members must match and have corresponding virtual and override keywords. Furthermore, if specifying the override keyword, the derived implementation is assumed to replace the base class implementation.

Overloading a member causes the runtime to call the most derived implementation (see Listing 6.11).

LISTING 6.11: Runtime Calling the Most Derived Implementation of a Virtual Method

```csharp
public class Program
{
  public static void Main()
  {
      Contact contact;
      PdaItem item;

      contact = new Contact();
      item = contact;

      // Set the name via PdaItem variable
      item.Name = "Inigo Montoya";

      // Display that FirstName & LastName
      // properties were set.
      Console.WriteLine("{0} {1}",
          contact.FirstName, contact.LastName);
  }
}
```

Output 6.1 shows the results of Listing 6.11.

```
Inigo Montoya
```

In Listing 6.11, `item.Name` is called, where `item` is declared as a `PdaItem`. However, the `contact`'s `FirstName` and `LastName` are still set. The rule is that whenever the runtime encounters a virtual method, it calls the most derived and overriding implementation of the virtual member. In this case, the code instantiates a `Contact` and calls `Contact.Name` because `Contact` contains the most derived implementation of `Name`.

In creating a class, programmers should be careful when choosing to allow overriding a method, since they cannot control the derived implementation. Virtual methods should not include critical code because such methods may never be called if the derived class overrides them. Furthermore, converting a method from a virtual method to a nonvirtual method could break derived classes that override the method. This is a code-breaking change and you should avoid it, especially for assemblies intended for use by third parties.

Listing 6.12 includes a virtual `Run()` method. If the `Controller` programmer calls `Run()` with the expectation that the critical `Start()` and `Stop()` methods will be called, he will run into a problem.

LISTING 6.12: **Carelessly Relying on a Virtual Method Implementation**

```csharp
public class Controller
{
  public void Start()
  {
     // Critical code
  }
  public virtual void Run()
  {
     Start();
     Stop();
  }
  public void Stop()
  {
     // Critical code
  }
}
```

In overriding Run(), a developer could perhaps not call the critical Start() and Stop() methods. To force the Start()/Stop() expectation, the Controller programmer should define the class, as shown in Listing 6.13.

LISTING 6.13: Forcing the Desirable Run() Semantics

```csharp
public class Controller
{
    public void Start()
    {
        // Critical code
    }

    private void Run()
    {
        Start();
        InternalRun();
        Stop();
    }

    protected virtual void InternalRun()
    {
        // Default implementation
    }

    public void Stop()
    {
        // Critical code
    }
}
```

With this new listing, the Controller programmer prevents users from mistakenly calling InternalRun(), because it is protected. On the other hand, declaring Run() as public ensures that Start() and Stop() are invoked appropriately. It is still possible for users to modify the default implementation of how the Controller executes by overriding the protected InternalRun() member from within the derived class.

Virtual methods provide default implementations only, implementations that derived classes could override entirely. However, because of the complexities of inheritance design, it is important to consider (and preferably to implement) a specific scenario that requires the virtual method definition rather than declaring members as virtual by default.

Language Contrast: C++—Dispatch Method Calls during Construction

In C++, methods called during construction will not dispatch the virtual method. Instead, during construction, the type is associated with the base type rather than the derived type, and virtual methods call the base implementation. In contrast, C# dispatches virtual method calls to the most derived type. This is consistent with the principle of calling the most derived virtual member, even if the derived constructor has not completely executed. Regardless, in C# the situation should be avoided.

Finally, only instance members can be `virtual`. The CLR uses the concrete type, specified at instantiation time, to determine where to dispatch a `virtual` method call, so `static virtual` methods are meaningless and the compiler prohibits them.

new **Modifier**

When an overriding method does not use `override`, the compiler issues a warning similar to that shown in Output 6.2 or Output 6.3.

OUTPUT 6.2

```
warning CS0114: '<derived method name>' hides inherited member
'<base method name>'. To make the current member override that
implementation, add the override keyword. Otherwise add the new
keyword.
```

OUTPUT 6.3

```
warning CS0108: The keyword new is required on '<derived property
name>' because it hides inherited member '<base property name>'
```

The obvious solution is to add the `override` modifier (assuming the base member is virtual). However, as the warnings point out, the `new` modifier is also an option. Consider the scenario shown in Table 6.1—a specific example of the more general problem known as the **brittle base class** or **fragile base class** problem.

TABLE 6.1: Why the New Modifier?

Activity	Code
| Programmer A defines class Person that includes properties FirstName and LastName. | ```csharp
public class Person
{
    public string FirstName { get; set; }
    public string LastName { get; set; }
}
``` |
| Programmer B derives from Person and defines Contact with the additional property, Name. In addition, he defines the Program class whose Main() method instantiates Contact, assigns Name, and then prints out the name. | ```csharp
public class Contact : Person
{
    public string Name
    {
        get
        {
            return FirstName + " " + LastName;
        }

        set
        {
            string[] names = value.Split(' ');
            // Error handling not shown.
            FirstName = names[0];
            LastName = names[1];
        }
    }
}
``` |
| Later, Programmer A adds the Name property, but instead of implementing the getter as FirstName + " " + LastName, she implements it as LastName + ", " + FirstName. Furthermore, she doesn't define the property as virtual, and she uses the property in a DisplayName() method. | ```csharp
// ...
public class Person
{
    public string Name
    {
        get
        {
            return LastName + ", " + FirstName;
        }

        set
        {
            string[] names = value.Split(", ");
            // Error handling not shown.
            LastName = names[0];
            FirstName = names[1];
        }
    }
    public static void Display(Person person)
    {
        // Display <LastName>, <FirstName>
        Console.WriteLine( person.Name );
    }
}
``` |
```

Because `Person.Name` is not virtual, Programmer A will expect `Display()` to use the `Person` implementation, even if a `Person`-derived data type, `Contact`, is passed in. However, Programmer B would expect `Contact.Name` to be used in all cases where the variable data type is a `Contact`. (Programmer B would have no code where `Person.Name` was used, since no `Person.Name` property existed initially.) To allow the addition of `Person.Name` without breaking either programmer's expected behavior, you cannot assume `virtual` was intended. Furthermore, since C# requires an override member to explicitly use the `override` modifier, some other semantic must be assumed, instead of allowing the addition of a member in the base class to cause the derived class to no longer compile.

The semantic is the `new` modifier, and it hides a redeclared member of the derived class from the base class. Instead of calling the most derived member, a member of the base class calls the most derived member in the inheritance chain prior to the member with the `new` modifier. If the inheritance chain contains only two classes, a member in the base class will behave as though no method was declared on the derived class (if the derived implementation overrides the base class member). Although the compiler will report the warning shown in either Output 6.2 or Output 6.3, if neither `override` nor `new` is specified, `new` will be assumed, thereby maintaining the desired version safety.

Consider Listing 6.14, for example. Its output appears in Output 6.4.

LISTING 6.14: `override` **versus** `new` **Modifier**

```
public class Program
{
  public class BaseClass
  {
     public void DisplayName()
     {
        Console.WriteLine("BaseClass");
     }
  }

    public class DerivedClass : BaseClass
    {
       // Compiler WARNING: DisplayName() hides inherited
       // member. Use the new keyword if hiding was intended.
       public virtual void DisplayName()
       {
          Console.WriteLine("DerivedClass");
       }
```

```
        }

    public class SubDerivedClass : DerivedClass
    {
        public override void DisplayName()
        {
            Console.WriteLine("SubDerivedClass");
        }
    }

    public class SuperSubDerivedClass : SubDerivedClass
    {
        public new void DisplayName()
        {
            Console.WriteLine("SuperSubDerivedClass");
        }
    }

    public static void Main()
    {
        SuperSubDerivedClass superSubDerivedClass
            = new SuperSubDerivedClass();

        SubDerivedClass subDerivedClass = superSubDerivedClass;
        DerivedClass derivedClass = superSubDerivedClass;
        BaseClass baseClass = superSubDerivedClass;

        superSubDerivedClass.DisplayName();
        subDerivedClass.DisplayName();
        derivedClass.DisplayName();
        baseClass.DisplayName();
    }
}
```

OUTPUT 6.4

```
SuperSubDerivedClass
SubDerivedClass
SubDerivedClass
BaseClass
```

These results occur for the following reasons.

- SuperSubDerivedClass: SuperSubDerivedClass.DisplayName() displays SuperSubDerivedClass because there is no derived class and hence, no overload.
- SubDerivedClass: SubDerivedClass.DisplayName() is the most derived member to override a base class's virtual member. SuperSubDerivedClass.DisplayName() is hidden because of its new modifier.

- SubDerivedClass: DerivedClass.DisplayName() is virtual and SubDerivedClass.DisplayName() is the most derived member to override it. As before, SuperSubDerivedClass.DisplayName() is hidden because of the new modifier.

- BaseClass: BaseClass.DisplayName() does not redeclare any base class member and it is not virtual; therefore, it is called directly.

When it comes to the CIL, the new modifier has no effect on what statements the compiler generates. However, a "new" method results in the generation of the newslot metadata attribute on the method. From the C# perspective, its only effect is to remove the compiler warning that would appear otherwise.

sealed **Modifier**

Just as you can prevent inheritance using the sealed modifier on a class, virtual members may be sealed, too (see Listing 6.15). This prevents a subclass from overriding a base class member that was originally declared as virtual higher in the inheritance chain. The situation arises when a subclass B overrides a base class A's member and then needs to prevent any further overriding below subclass B.

LISTING 6.15: **Sealing Members**

```csharp
class A
{
  public virtual void Method()
  {
  }
}
class B : A
{
  public override sealed void Method()
  {
  }
}

class C : B
{
  // ERROR:  Cannot override sealed members
  // public override void Method()
  // {
  // }
}
```

In this example, the use of the `sealed` modifier on class B's `Method()` declaration prevents C's overriding of `Method()`.

In general, marking a class as `sealed` is rare and should be reserved only if there are strong reasons in favor of such a restriction. In fact, leaving types unsealed is increasingly desirable, as unit testing has become prominent because of the need to support mock (test double) object creation in place of real implementations. One possible scenario is when the cost of sealing individual virtual members outweighs the benefits of leaving the class unsealed. However, a more targeted sealing of individual members—perhaps because there are dependencies in the base implementation for correct behavior—is likely to be preferable.

base **Member**

In choosing to override a member, developers often want to invoke the member on the base class (see Listing 6.16).

LISTING 6.16: **Accessing a Base Member**

```
public class Address
{
    public string StreetAddress;
    public string City;
    public string State;
    public string Zip;

    public override string ToString()
    {
        return string.Format("{0}" + Environment.NewLine +
            "{1}, {2}  {3}",
            StreetAddress, City, State, Zip);
    }
}

public class InternationalAddress : Address
{
    public string Country;

    public override string ToString()
    {
        return base.ToString() + Environment.NewLine +
            Country;
    }
}
```

In Listing 6.16, `InternationalAddress` inherits from `Address` and implements `ToString()`. To call the parent class's implementation you use the `base` keyword. The syntax is virtually identical to `this`, including support for using `base` as part of the constructor (discussed shortly).

Parenthetically, in the `Address.ToString()` implementation, you are required to `override` because `ToString()` is also a member of `object`. Any members that are decorated with `override` are automatically designated as virtual, so additional child classes may further specialize the implementation.

> **■ NOTE**
>
> Any methods decorated with `override` are automatically virtual. A base class method can only be overridden if it is virtual, and the overriding method is therefore virtual as well.

Constructors

When instantiating a derived class, the runtime first invokes the base class's constructor so that the base class initialization is not circumvented. However, if there is no accessible (nonprivate) default constructor on the base class, it is not clear how to construct the base class and the C# compiler reports an error.

To avoid the error caused by no accessible default constructor, programmers need to designate explicitly, in the derived class constructor header, which base constructor to run (see Listing 6.17).

LISTING 6.17: **Specifying Which Base Constructor to Invoke**

```csharp
public class PdaItem
{
  public PdaItem(string name)
  {
    Name = name;
  }

  // ...
}
```

```csharp
public class Contact : PdaItem
{
  public Contact(string name) :
    base(name)
```

```
    {
        Name = name;
    }

    public string Name { get; set; }
    // ...
    }
```

By identifying the base constructor in the code, you let the runtime know which base constructor to invoke before invoking the derived class constructor.

Abstract Classes

Many of the inheritance examples so far have defined a class called `PdaItem` that defines the methods and properties common to `Contact`, `Appointment`, and so on, which are type objects that derive from `PdaItem`. `PdaItem` is not intended to be instantiated itself, however. A `PdaItem` instance has no meaning by itself; it has meaning only when it is used as a base class—to share default method implementations across the set of data types that derive from it. These characteristics are indicative of the need for `PdaItem` to be an **abstract** class rather than a **concrete** class. Abstract classes are designed for derivation only. It is not possible to instantiate an abstract class, except in the context of instantiating a class that derives from it. Classes that are not abstract and can instead be instantiated directly are concrete classes.

■ **BEGINNER TOPIC**

Abstract Classes

Abstract classes represent abstract entities. Their **abstract members** define what an object derived from an abstract entity should contain, but they don't include the implementation. Often, much of the functionality within an abstract class is unimplemented, and before a class can successfully derive from an abstract class, it needs to provide the implementation for the abstract methods in its abstract base class.

To define an abstract class, C# requires the abstract modifier to the class definition, as shown in Listing 6.18.

LISTING 6.18: Defining an Abstract Class

```csharp
// Define an abstract class
public abstract class PdaItem
{
  public PdaItem(string name)
  {
      Name = name;
  }

  public virtual string Name { get; set; }
}

public class Program
{
  public static void Main()
  {
      PdaItem item;
      // ERROR:  Cannot create an instance of the abstract class
      // item = new PdaItem("Inigo Montoya");
  }
}
```

Although abstract classes cannot be instantiated, this restriction is a minor characteristic of an abstract class. Their primary significance is achieved when abstract classes include **abstract members.** An abstract member is a method or property that has no implementation. Its purpose is to force all derived classes to provide the implementation.

Consider Listing 6.19.

LISTING 6.19: Defining Abstract Members

```csharp
// Define an abstract class
public abstract class PdaItem
{
  public PdaItem(string name)
  {
      Name = name;
  }

  public virtual string Name { get; set; }
  public abstract string GetSummary();
}

public class Contact : PdaItem
{
    public override string Name
    {
        get
        {
```

```csharp
            return FirstName + " " + LastName;
        }

        set
        {
            string[] names = value.Split(' ');
            // Error handling not shown.
            FirstName = names[0];
            LastName = names[1];
        }
    }

    public string FirstName { get; set; }
    public string LastName { get; set; }
    public string Address { get; set; }

    public override string GetSummary()
    {
        return string.Format(
            "FirstName: {0}\n"
            + "LastName: {1}\n"
            + "Address: {2}", FirstName, LastName, Address);
    }

    // ...
}

public class Appointment : PdaItem
{
    public Appointment(string name) :
        base(name)
    {
        Name = name;
    }

    public DateTime StartDateTime  { get; set; }
    public DateTime EndDateTime  { get; set; }
    public string Location  { get; set; }

    // ...

    public override string GetSummary()
    {
        return string.Format(
            "Subject: {0}" + Environment.NewLine
            + "Start: {1}"  + Environment.NewLine
            + "End: {2}" + Environment.NewLine
            + "Location: {3}",
            Name, StartDateTime, EndDateTime, Location);
    }
}
```

Listing 6.19 defines the GetSummary() member as abstract, and therefore, it doesn't include any implementation. Then, the code overrides it within Contact and provides the implementation. Because abstract members are supposed to be overridden, such members are automatically virtual and cannot be declared so explicitly. In addition, abstract members cannot be private because derived classes would not be able to see them.

It is surprisingly difficult to develop a well-designed object hierarchy. For this reason, when programming abstract types, be sure to implement at least one (preferably more) concrete type that derives from the abstract type in order to validate the design.

■ NOTE

Abstract members must be overridden, and therefore are automatically virtual and cannot be declared so explicitly.

Language Contrast: C++—Pure Virtual Functions

C++ allows for the definition of abstract functions using the cryptic notation =0. These functions are called pure virtual functions in C++. In contrast with C#, however, C++ does not require the class itself to have any special declaration. Unlike C#'s abstract class modifier, C++ has no class declaration change when the class includes pure virtual functions.

If you provide no GetSummary() implementation in Contact, the compiler will report an error.

■ NOTE

By declaring an abstract member, the abstract class programmer states that in order to form an "is a" relationship between a concrete class and an abstract base class (that is, a PdaItem), it is necessary to implement the abstract members, the members for which the abstract class could not provide an appropriate default implementation.

■ BEGINNER TOPIC

Polymorphism

When the implementation for the same member signature varies between two or more classes, you have a key object-oriented principle: **polymorphism.** "Poly" meaning "many" and "morph" meaning "form," polymorphism refers to the fact that there are multiple implementations of the same signature. And since the same signature cannot be used multiple times within a single class, each implementation of the member signature occurs on a different class.

The idea behind polymorphism is that the object itself knows best how to perform a particular operation, and by enforcing common ways to invoke those operations, polymorphism is also a technique for encouraging code reuse when taking advantage of the commonalities. Given multiple types of documents, each document type class knows best how to perform a `Print()` method for its corresponding document type. Therefore, instead of defining a single print method that includes a `switch` statement with the special logic to print each document type, with polymorphism you call the `Print()` method corresponding to the specific type of document you wish to print. For example, calling `Print()` on a word processing document class behaves according to word processing specifics, and calling the same method on a graphics document class will result in print behavior specific to the graphic. Given the document types, however, all you have to do to print a document is to call `Print()`, regardless of the type.

Moving the custom print implementation out of a `switch` statement offers a number of maintenance advantages. First, the implementation appears in the context of each document type's class rather than in a location far removed; this is in keeping with encapsulation. Second, adding a new document type doesn't require a change to the `switch` statement. Instead, all that is necessary is for the new document type class to implement the `Print()` signature.

Abstract members are intended to be a way to enable polymorphism. The base class specifies the signature of the method and the derived class provides implementation (see Listing 6.20).

LISTING 6.20: Using Polymorphism to List the `PdaItems`

```csharp
public class Program
{
  public static void Main()
```

```
        {
            PdaItem[] pda = new PdaItem[3];

            Contact contact = new Contact("Sherlock Holmes");
            contact.Address = "221B Baker Street, London, England";
            pda[0] = contact;

            Appointment appointment =
                new Appointment("Soccer tournament");
            appointment.StartDateTime = new DateTime(2008, 7, 18);
            appointment.EndDateTime = new DateTime(2008, 7, 19);
            appointment.Location = "Estádio da Machava";
            pda[1] = appointment;

            contact = new Contact("Hercule Poirot");
            contact.Address =
                "Apt 56B, Whitehaven Mansions, Sandhurst Sq, London";
            pda[2] = contact;

            List(pda);
        }

        public static void List(PdaItem[] items)
        {
            // Implemented using polymorphism. The derived
            // type knows the specifics of implementing
            // GetSummary().
            foreach (PdaItem item in items)
            {
                Console.WriteLine("_____");
                Console.WriteLine(item.GetSummary());
            }
        }
    }
}
```

The results of Listing 6.20 appear in Output 6.5.

OUTPUT 6.5

```
FirstName: Sherlock
LastName: Holmes
Address: 221B Baker Street, London, England

Subject: Soccer tournament
Start: 7/18/2008 12:00:00 AM
End: 7/19/2008 12:00:00 AM
Location: Estádio da Machava

FirstName: Hercule
LastName: Poirot
Address: Apt 56B, Whitehaven Mansions, Sandhurst Sq, London
```

In this way, you can call the method on the base class but the implementation is specific to the derived class.

All Classes Derive from `System.Object`

Given any class, whether a custom class or one built into the system, the methods shown in Table 6.2 will be defined.

TABLE 6.2: Members of `System.Object`

Method Name	Description
`public virtual bool Equals(object o)`	Returns `true` if the object supplied as a parameter is equal in *value*, not necessarily in reference, to the instance.
`public virtual int GetHashCode()`	Returns an integer corresponding to an evenly spread hash code. This is useful for collections such as `HashTable` collections.
`public Type GetType()`	Returns an object of type `System.Type` corresponding to the type of the object instance.
`public static bool ReferenceEquals(` `    object a, object b)`	Returns `true` if the two supplied parameters refer to the same object.
`public virtual string ToString()`	Returns a string representation of the object instance.
`public virtual void Finalize()`	An alias for the destructor; informs the object to prepare for termination. C# prevents calling this method directly.
`protected object MemberwiseClone()`	Clones the object in question by performing a shallow copy; references are copied, but not the data within a referenced type.

All of these methods appear on all objects through inheritance; all classes derive (either directly or via an inheritance chain) from `object`. Even literals include these methods, enabling somewhat peculiar-looking code such as this:

```
Console.WriteLine( 42.ToString() );
```

Even class definitions that don't have any explicit derivation from `object` derive from `object` anyway. The two declarations for `PdaItem` in Listing 6.21, therefore, result in identical CIL.

LISTING 6.21: `System.Object` **Derivation Implied When No Derivation Is Specified Explicitly**

```
public class PdaItem
{
  // ...
}
```

```
public class PdaItem : object
{
  // ...
}
```

When the `object`'s default implementation isn't sufficient, programmers can override one or more of the three virtual methods. Chapter 9 describes the details for doing this.

Verifying the Underlying Type with the is Operator

Because C# allows casting down the inheritance chain, it is sometimes desirable to determine what the underlying type is before attempting a conversion. Also, checking the type may be necessary for type-specific actions where polymorphism was not implemented. To determine the underlying type, C# provides the is operator (see Listing 6.22).

LISTING 6.22: is **Operator Determining the Underlying Type**

```
public static void Save(object data)
{
    if (data is string)
    {
        data = Encrypt((string) data);
    }

    // ...
}
```

Listing 6.22 encrypts the data if the underlying type is a `string`. This is significantly different from encrypting, simply because it successfully casts to a `string` since many types support casting to a `string`, and yet their underlying type is not a `string`.

Although this capability is important, you should consider polymorphism prior to using the is operator. Polymorphism enables support for expanding a behavior to other data types without modifying the implementation that defines the behavior. For example, deriving from a common base type and then using that type as the parameter to the Save() method avoids having to check for string explicitly and enables other data types to support encryption during the save by deriving from the same base type.

Conversion Using the as Operator

The advantage of the is operator is that it enables verification that a data item is of a particular type. The as operator goes one step further: It attempts a conversion to a particular data type and assigns null if the source type is not inherently (within the inheritance chain) of the target type. This is significant because it avoids the exception that could result from casting. Listing 6.23 demonstrates using the as operator.

LISTING 6.23: Data Conversion Using the as Operator

```
object Print(IDocument document)
{
  if(thing != null)
  {
      // Print document...
  }
  else
  {
  }
}

static void Main()
{
  object data;

  // ...

  Print(data as Document);
}
```

By using the as operator, you are able to avoid additional try/catch handling code if the conversion is invalid, because the as operator provides a way to attempt a cast without throwing an exception if the cast fails.

One advantage of the `is` operator over the `as` operator is that the latter cannot successfully determine the underlying type. The latter potentially casts up or down an inheritance chain, as well as across to types supporting the cast operator. Therefore, unlike the `as` operator, the `is` operator can determine the underlying type.

SUMMARY

This chapter discussed how to specialize a class by deriving from it and adding additional methods and properties. This included a discussion of the `private` and `protected` access modifiers that control the level of encapsulation.

This chapter also investigated the details of overriding the base class implementation, and alternatively hiding it using the new modifier. To control overriding, C# provides the `virtual` modifier, which identifies to the deriving class developer which members she intends for derivation. For preventing any derivation altogether you learned about the `sealed` modifier on the class. Similarly, the `sealed` modifier on a member prevents further overriding from subclasses.

This chapter ended with a brief discussion of how all types derive from `object`. Chapter 9 discusses this derivation further, with a look at how `object` includes three virtual methods with specific rules and guidelines that govern overloading. Before you get there, however, you need to consider another programming paradigm that builds on object-oriented programming: interfaces. This is the subject of Chapter 7.

■ 7 ■
Interfaces

POLYMORPHISM IS AVAILABLE NOT ONLY via inheritance (as discussed in the preceding chapter), but also via interfaces. Unlike abstract classes, interfaces cannot include any implementation. Like abstract classes, however, interfaces define a set of members that callers can rely on being implemented.

By implementing an interface, a type defines its capabilities. The interface implementation relationship is a "can do" relationship: The type can do what the interface requires an implementing type to do. The interface defines the contract between the types that implement the interface and the code that uses the interface. Types that implement interfaces must declare methods with the same signatures as the methods declared by the implemented interfaces. This chapter discusses implementing and using interfaces.

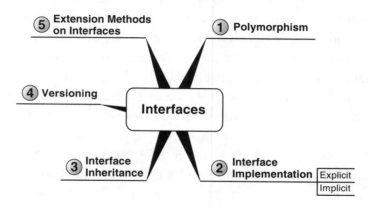

Introducing Interfaces

■ BEGINNER TOPIC

Why Interfaces?

Interfaces are useful because—unlike abstract classes—they enable the complete separation of implementation details from services provided. For a real-world example, consider the "interface" that is an electrical wall socket. How the electrical power gets to the socket is an implementation detail: It might be generated by chemical, nuclear, or solar energy, the generator might be in the next room or far away, and so on. The socket provides a "contract": It will supply a particular voltage at a specific frequency, and requires that the appliance using that interface provide a compatible plug. The appliance need not care anything about the implementation details that get power to the socket; all it needs to worry about is that it provides a compatible plug.

Consider the following example: A huge number of file compression formats are available (`.zip`, `.7-zip`, `.cab`, `.lha`, `.tar`, `.tar.gz`, `.tar.bz2`, `.bh`, `.rar`, `.arj`, `.arc`, `.ace`, `.zoo`, `.gz`, `.bzip2`, `.xxe`, `.mime`, `.uue`, and `.yenc`, just to name a few). If you created classes for each compression format, you could end up with different method signatures for each compression implementation and no ability for a standard calling convention across them. The desired method could be declared as abstract in the base class. However, deriving from a common base class uses up a class's one and only opportunity for inheritance. It is unlikely that there is any code common to various compression implementations that can be put in the base class, thereby making the potential of a base class implementation useless. The key point is that base classes let you share implementation along with the member signatures, whereas interfaces allow you to share the member signatures without the implementation.

Instead of sharing a common base class, each compression class needs to implement a common interface. Interfaces define the contract that a class supports in order to interact with the other classes that expect the interface. If all the classes implemented the `IFileCompression` interface and its `Compress()` and `Uncompress()` methods, the code for calling the algorithm on any particular compression class would simply involve a conversion to the `IFileCompression` interface and a call to the members. The result is polymorphism because each compression class has the same method signature but individual implementations of that signature.

The `IFileCompression` interface shown in Listing 7.1 is an example of an interface implementation.

LISTING 7.1: Defining an Interface

```
interface IFileCompression
{
  void Compress(string targetFileName, string[] fileList);
  void Uncompress(
      string compressedFileName, string expandDirectoryName);
}
```

`IFileCompression` defines the methods a type must implement to be used in the same manner as other compression-related classes. The power of interfaces is that they grant the ability to callers to switch among implementations without modifying the calling code.

One key characteristic of an interface is that it has no implementation and no data. Method declarations in an interface have a single semicolon in place of curly braces after the header. Fields (data) cannot appear in an interface declaration. When an interface requires the derived class to have certain data, it declares a property rather than a field. Since the property does not contain any implementation as part of the interface declaration, it doesn't reference a backing field.

The declared members of an interface describe the members that must be accessible on an implementing type. The purpose of nonpublic members is to make those members inaccessible to other code. Therefore, C# does not allow access modifiers on interface members; instead, it automatically defines them as public.

Guidelines

DO use Pascal casing for interface names, with an "I" prefix.

Polymorphism through Interfaces

Consider another example (see Listing 7.2): `IListable` defines the members a class needs to support in order for the `ConsoleListControl` class to display it. As such, any class that implements `IListable` can use the

ConsoleListControl to display itself. The IListable interface requires a read-only property, ColumnValues.

LISTING 7.2: **Implementing and Using Interfaces**

```csharp
interface IListable
{
  // Return the value of each column in the row.
  string[] ColumnValues
  {
    get;
  }
}
```

```csharp
public abstract class PdaItem
{
  public PdaItem(string name)
  {
    Name = name;
  }

  public virtual string Name{get;set;}
}
```

```csharp
class Contact : PdaItem, IListable
{
    public Contact(string firstName, string lastName,
        string address, string phone) : base(null)
    {
        FirstName = firstName;
        LastName = lastName;
        Address = address;
        Phone = phone;
    }

    public string FirstName { get; set; }
    public string LastName { get; set; }
    public string Address { get; set; }
    public string Phone { get; set; }

    public string[] ColumnValues
    {
        get
        {
            return new string[]
            {
                FirstName,
                LastName,
                Phone,
                Address
            };
```

```csharp
        }
    }

    public static string[] Headers
    {
        get
        {
            return new string[] {
                "First Name", "Last Name    ",
                "Phone        ",
                "Address                        " };
        }
    }

    // ...
}
```

```csharp
class Publication : IListable
{
    public Publication(string title, string author, int year)
    {
        Title = title;
        Author = author;
        Year = year;
    }

    public string Title { get; set; }
    public string Author { get; set; }
    public int Year { get; set; }

    public string[] ColumnValues
    {
        get
        {
            return new string[]
            {
                Title,
                Author,
                Year.ToString()
            };
        }
    }

    public static string[] Headers
    {
        get
        {
            return new string[] {
                "Title                         ",
                "Author          ",
                "Year" };
        }
```

```
    }

    // ...
}
```

```csharp
class Program
{
  public static void Main()
  {
      Contact[] contacts = new Contact[6];
      contacts[0] = new Contact(
          "Dick", "Traci",
          "123 Main St., Spokane, WA   99037",
          "123-123-1234");
      contacts[1] = new Contact(
          "Andrew", "Littman",
          "1417 Palmary St., Dallas, TX 55555",
          "555-123-4567");
      contacts[2] = new Contact(
          "Mary", "Hartfelt",
          "1520 Thunder Way, Elizabethton, PA 44444",
          "444-123-4567");
      contacts[3] = new Contact(
          "John", "Lindherst",
          "1 Aerial Way Dr., Monteray, NH 88888",
          "222-987-6543");
      contacts[4] = new Contact(
          "Pat", "Wilson",
          "565 Irving Dr., Parksdale, FL 22222",
          "123-456-7890");
      contacts[5] = new Contact(
          "Jane", "Doe",
          "123 Main St., Aurora, IL 66666",
          "333-345-6789");

      // Classes are cast implicitly to
      // their supported interfaces
      ConsoleListControl.List(Contact.Headers, contacts);

      Console.WriteLine();

      Publication[] publications = new Publication[3] {
          new Publication("Celebration of Discipline",
              "Richard Foster", 1978),
          new Publication("Orthodoxy",
              "G.K. Chesterton", 1908),
          new Publication(
              "The Hitchhiker's Guide to the Galaxy",
              "Douglas Adams", 1979)
          };
      ConsoleListControl.List(
          Publication.Headers, publications);
```

```
        }
    }

class ConsoleListControl
{
    public static void List(string[] headers, IListable[] items)
    {
        int[] columnWidths = DisplayHeaders(headers);

        for (int count = 0; count < items.Length; count++)
        {
            string[] values = items[count].ColumnValues;
            DisplayItemRow(columnWidths, values);
        }
    }

    /// <summary>Displays the column headers</summary>
    /// <returns>Returns an array of column widths</returns>
    private static int[] DisplayHeaders(string[] headers)
    {
        // ...
    }

    private static void DisplayItemRow(
        int[] columnWidths, string[] values)
    {
        // ...
    }
}
```

The results of Listing 7.2 appear in Output 7.1.

OUTPUT 7.1

```
First Name  Last Name    Phone          Address
Dick        Traci        123-123-1234   123 Main St., Spokane, WA
99037
Andrew      Littman      555-123-4567   1417 Palmary St., Dallas, TX
55555
Mary        Hartfelt     444-123-4567   1520 Thunder Way,
Elizabethton, PA 44444
John        Lindherst    222-987-6543   1 Aerial Way Dr., Monteray,
NH 88888
Pat         Wilson       123-456-7890   565 Irving Dr., Parksdale, FL
22222
Jane        Doe          333-345-6789   123 Main St., Aurora, IL 66666

Title                                   Author          Year
Celebration of Discipline               Richard Foster  1978
Orthodoxy                               G.K. Chesterton 1908
The Hitchhiker's Guide to the Galaxy    Douglas Adams   1979
```

In Listing 7.2, the ConsoleListControl can display seemingly unrelated classes (Contact and Publication). Any class can be displayed provided that it implements the required interface. As a result, the ConsoleListControl.List() method relies on polymorphism to appropriately display whichever set of objects it is passed. Each class has its own implementation of ColumnValues, and converting a class to IListable still allows the particular class's implementation to be invoked.

Interface Implementation

Declaring a class to implement an interface is similar to deriving from a base class: The implemented interfaces appear in a comma-separated list along with the base class. The base class specifier (if there is one) must come first, but otherwise order is not significant. Classes can implement multiple interfaces, but may only derive directly from one base class. An example appears in Listing 7.3.

LISTING 7.3: **Implementing an Interface**

```csharp
public class Contact : PdaItem, IListable, IComparable
{
  // ...

  #region IComparable Members
  /// <summary>
  ///
  /// </summary>
  /// <param name="obj"></param>
  /// <returns>
  /// Less than zero:     This instance is less than obj.
  /// Zero                This instance is equal to obj.
  /// Greater than zero   This instance is greater than obj.
  /// </returns>
  public int CompareTo(object obj)
  {
      int result;
      Contact contact = obj as Contact;

      if (obj == null)
      {
          // This instance is greater than obj.
          result = 1;
      }
      else if (obj != typeof(Contact))
      {
          throw new ArgumentException("obj is not a Contact");
      }
```

```csharp
        else if( Contact.ReferenceEquals(this, obj) )
        {
            result = 0;
        }
        else
        {
            result = LastName.CompareTo(contact.LastName);
            if (result == 0)
            {
                result = FirstName.CompareTo(contact.FirstName);
            }
        }
        return result;
    }
    #endregion

    #region IListable Members
    string[] IListable.ColumnValues
    {
        get
        {
            return new string[]
            {
                FirstName,
                LastName,
                Phone,
                Address
            };
        }
    }
    #endregion
}
```

Once a class declares that it implements an interface, all members of the interface must be implemented. An abstract class is permitted to supply an abstract implementation of an interface member. A nonabstract implementation may throw a NotImplementedException type exception in the method body, but somehow, an implementation of the member must be supplied.

One important characteristic of interfaces is that they can never be instantiated; you cannot use new to create an interface, and therefore, interfaces do not have constructors or finalizers. Interface instances are available only by instantiating a type that implements the interface. Furthermore, interfaces cannot include static members. One key interface purpose is polymorphism, and polymorphism without an instance of the implementing type is of little value.

Each interface member behaves like an abstract method, forcing the derived class to implement the member. Therefore, it is not possible to use the abstract modifier on interface members explicitly.

When implementing an interface member in a type there are two ways to do so: **explicitly** or **implicitly.** So far we've seen only implicit implementations, where the type member that implements the interface member is a public member of the implementing type.

Explicit Member Implementation

Explicitly implemented methods are available only by calling through the interface itself; this is typically achieved by casting an object to the interface. For example, to call `IListable.ColumnValues` in Listing 7.4, you must first cast the contact to `IListable` because of `ColumnValues`' explicit implementation.

LISTING 7.4: Calling Explicit Interface Member Implementations

```
string[] values;
Contact contact1, contact2;

// ...

// ERROR:  Unable to call ColumnValues() directly
//         on a contact.
// values = contact1.ColumnValues;

// First cast to IListable.
values = ((IListable)contact2).ColumnValues;
// ...
```

The cast and the call to `ColumnValues` occur within the same statement in this case. Alternatively, you could assign `contact2` to an `IListable` variable before calling `ColumnValues`.

To declare an explicit interface member implementation, prefix the member name with the interface name (see Listing 7.5).

LISTING 7.5: Explicit Interface Implementation

```
public class Contact : PdaItem, IListable, IComparable
{
  // ...

  public int CompareTo(object obj)
  {
```

```
    // ...
}

#region IListable Members
string[] IListable.ColumnValues
{
    get
    {
        return new string[]
        {
            FirstName,
            LastName,
            Phone,
            Address
        };
    }
}
#endregion
}
```

Listing 7.5 implements `ColumnValues` explicitly by prefixing the property name with `IListable`. Furthermore, since explicit interface implementations are directly associated with the interface, there is no need to modify them with `virtual`, `override`, or `public`, and, in fact, these modifiers are not allowed. The method is not treated as a public member of the class, so marking it as `public` would be misleading.

Implicit Member Implementation

Notice that `CompareTo()` in Listing 7.5 does not include the `IComparable` prefix; it is implemented implicitly. With implicit member implementation, it is only necessary for the member to be public and for the member's signature to match the interface member's signature. Interface member implementation does not require the `override` keyword or any indication that this member is tied to the interface. Furthermore, since the member is declared just as any other class member, code that calls implicitly implemented members can do so directly, just as it would any other class member:

```
result = contact1.CompareTo(contact2);
```

In other words, implicit member implementation does not require a cast because the member is not hidden from direct invocation on the implementing class.

Many of the modifiers disallowed on an explicit member implementation are required or are optional on an implicit implementation. For example, implicit member implementations must be `public`. Furthermore, `virtual` is optional depending on whether derived classes may override the implementation. Eliminating `virtual` will cause the member to behave as though it is `sealed`.

Explicit versus Implicit Interface Implementation

The key difference between implicit and explicit member interface implementation is not in the syntax of the method declaration, but in the ability to access the method by name through an instance of the type rather than via the interface.

When building a class hierarchy, it's desirable to model real-world "is a" relationships—a giraffe is a mammal, for example. These are "semantic" relationships. Interfaces are often used to model "mechanism" relationships. A `PdaItem` "is not a" "comparable," but it might well be `IComparable`. This interface has nothing to do with the semantic model; it's a detail of the implementation mechanism. Explicit interface implementation is a technique for enabling the separation of mechanism concerns from model concerns. Forcing the caller to convert the object to an interface such as `IComparable` before treating the object as "comparable" explicitly separates out in the code when you are talking to the model and when you are dealing with its implementation mechanisms.

In general, it is preferable to limit the public surface area of a class to be "all model" with as little extraneous mechanism as possible. (Unfortunately, some mechanisms are unavoidable in .NET. You cannot get a giraffe's hash code or convert a giraffe to a string. However, you can get a `Giraffe`'s hash code [`GetHashCode()`] and convert it to a `string` [`ToString()`]. By using `object` as a common base class, .NET mixes model code with mechanism code even if only to a limited extent.)

Here are several guidelines that will help you choose between an explicit and an implicit implementation.

- Is the member a core part of the class functionality?

  Consider the `ColumnValues` property implementation on the

Contact class. This member is not an integral part of a Contact type but a peripheral member probably accessed only by the ConsoleListControl class. As such, it doesn't make sense for the member to be immediately visible on a Contact object, cluttering up what could potentially already be a large list of members.

Alternatively, consider the IFileCompression.Compress() member. Including an implicit Compress() implementation on a ZipCompression class is a perfectly reasonable choice, since Compress() is a core part of the ZipCompression class's behavior, so it should be directly accessible from the ZipCompression class.

- Is the interface member name appropriate as a class member?

  Consider an ITrace interface with a member called Dump() that writes out a class's data to a trace log. Implementing Dump() implicitly on a Person or Truck class would result in confusion as to what operation the method performs. Instead, it is preferable to implement the member explicitly so that only from a data type of ITrace, where the meaning is clearer, can the Dump() method be called. Consider using an explicit implementation if a member's purpose is unclear on the implementing class.

- Is there already a class member with the same signature?

  Explicit interface member implementation does not add a named element to the type's declaration space. Therefore, if there is already a potentially conflicting member of a type, a second one can be provided with the same name or signature as long as it is an explicit interface member.

Much of the decision regarding implicit versus explicit interface member implementation comes down to intuition. However, these questions provide suggestions about what to consider when making your choice. Since changing an implementation from implicit to explicit results in a version-breaking change, it is better to err on the side of defining interfaces explicitly, allowing them to be changed to implicit later on. Furthermore, since the decision between implicit and explicit does not have to be consistent across all interface members, defining some methods as explicit and others as implicit is fully supported.

> ### Guidelines
>
> **AVOID** implementing interface members explicitly without a good reason. However, if you're unsure, favor explicit implementation.

Converting between the Implementing Class and Its Interfaces

Just as with a derived type and a base class, a conversion from an implementing type to its implemented interface is an implicit conversion. No cast operator is required because an instance of the implementing type will always provide all the members in the interface, and therefore, the object can always be converted successfully to the interface type.

Although the conversion will always be successful from the implementing type to the implemented interface, many different types could implement a particular interface, so you can never be certain that a "downward" cast from an interface to one of its implementing types will be successful. Therefore, converting from an interface to one of its implementing types requires an explicit cast.

Interface Inheritance

Interfaces can derive from each other, resulting in an interface that inherits all the members in its base interfaces. As shown in Listing 7.6, the interfaces directly derived from `IReadableSettingsProvider` are the explicit base interfaces.

LISTING 7.6: Deriving One Interface from Another

```csharp
interface IReadableSettingsProvider
{
    string GetSetting(string name, string defaultValue);
}

interface ISettingsProvider : IReadableSettingsProvider
{
    void SetSetting(string name, string value);
}

class FileSettingsProvider : ISettingsProvider
{
```

```
    #region ISettingsProvider Members
    public void SetSetting(string name, string value)
    {
        // ...
    }
    #endregion

    #region IReadableSettingsProvider Members
    public string GetSetting(string name, string defaultValue)
    {
        // ...
    }
    #endregion
}
```

In this case, ISettingsProvider derives from IReadableSettingsProvider, and therefore inherits its members. If IReadableSettingsProvider also had an explicit base interface, ISettingsProvider would inherit those members too, and the full set of interfaces in the derivation hierarchy would simply be the accumulation of base interfaces.

It is interesting to note that if GetSetting() is implemented explicitly, it must be done using IReadableSettingsProvider. The declaration with ISettingsProvider in Listing 7.7 will not compile.

LISTING 7.7: Explicit Member Declaration without the Containing Interface (Failure)

```
// ERROR:  GetSetting() not available on ISettingsProvider
string ISettingsProvider.GetSetting(
    string name, string defaultValue)
{
    // ...
}
```

The results of Listing 7.7 appear in Output 7.2.

OUTPUT 7.2

```
'ISettingsProvider.GetSetting' in explicit interface declaration
is not a member of interface.
```

This output appears in addition to an error indicating that IReadable SettingsProvider.GetSetting() is not implemented. The fully qualified interface member name used for explicit interface member implementation must reference the interface name in which it was originally declared.

Even though a class implements an interface (`ISettingsProvider`) which is derived from a base interface (`IReadableSettingsProvider`), the class can still declare an implementation of both interfaces overtly, as Listing 7.8 demonstrates.

LISTING 7.8: **Using a Base Interface in the Class Declaration**

```
class FileSettingsProvider : ISettingsProvider,
    IReadableSettingsProvider
{
    #region ISettingsProvider Members
    public void SetSetting(string name, string value)
    {
        // ...
    }
    #endregion

    #region IReadableSettingsProvider Members
    public string GetSetting(string name, string defaultValue)
    {
        // ...
    }
    #endregion
}
```

In this listing, there is no change to the interface's implementations on the class, and although the additional interface implementation declaration on the class header is superfluous, it can provide better readability.

The decision to provide multiple interfaces rather than just one combined interface depends largely on what the interface designer wants to require of the implementing class. By providing an `IReadableSettingsProvider` interface, the designer communicates that implementers are required only to implement a settings provider that retrieves settings. They do not have to be able to write to those settings. This reduces the implementation burden by not imposing the complexities of writing settings as well.

In contrast, implementing `ISettingsProvider` assumes that there is never a reason to have a class that can write settings without reading them. The inheritance relationship between `ISettingsProvider` and `IReadable SettingsProvider`, therefore, forces the combined total of both interfaces on the `ISettingsProvider` class.

One final but important note: Although *inheritance* is the correct term, conceptually it is more accurate to realize that an interface represents a contract; and one contract is allowed to specify that the provisions of another contract must also be followed. So, the code `ISettingsProvider : IReadable SettingsProvider` conceptually states that the `ISettingsProvider` contract requires also respecting the `IReadableSettingsProvider` contract rather than that the `ISettingsProvider` "is a kind of" `IReadableSettings Provider`. That being said, the remainder of the chapter will continue using the inheritance relationship terminology in accordance with the standard C# terminology.

Multiple Interface Inheritance

Just as classes can implement multiple interfaces, interfaces can inherit from multiple interfaces; the syntax is consistent with class derivation and implementation, as shown in Listing 7.9.

LISTING 7.9: **Multiple Interface Inheritance**

```
interface IReadableSettingsProvider
{
  string GetSetting(string name, string defaultValue);
}

interface IWriteableSettingsProvider
{
  void SetSetting(string name, string value);
}

interface ISettingsProvider : IReadableSettingsProvider,
    IWriteableSettingsProvider
{
}
```

It is unusual to have an interface with no members, but if implementing both interfaces together is predominant, it is a reasonable choice for this case. The difference between Listing 7.9 and Listing 7.6 is that it is now possible to implement `IWriteableSettingsProvider` without supplying any read capability. Listing 7.6's `FileSettingsProvider` is unaffected, but if it used explicit member implementation, specifying which interface a member belongs to changes slightly.

Extension Methods on Interfaces

Perhaps one of the most important features of extension methods is the fact that they work with interfaces in addition to classes. The syntax is identical to that of extension methods for classes. The extended type (the first parameter and the parameter prefixed with `this`) is the interface that we extend. Listing 7.10 shows an extension method for `IListable()`. It is declared on `Listable`.

LISTING 7.10: **Interface Extension Methods**

```
class Program
{
  public static void Main()
  {
      Contact[] contacts = new Contact[6];
      contacts[0] = new Contact(
          "Dick", "Traci",
          "123 Main St., Spokane, WA  99037",
          "123-123-1234");
      // ...

      // Classes are implicitly converted to
      // their supported interfaces
      contacts.List(Contact.Headers);

      Console.WriteLine();

      Publication[] publications = new Publication[3] {
          new Publication("Celebration of Discipline",
              "Richard Foster", 1978),
          new Publication("Orthodoxy",
              "G.K. Chesterton", 1908),
          new Publication(
              "The Hitchhiker's Guide to the Galaxy",
              "Douglas Adams", 1979)
          };
      publications.List(Publication.Headers);
  }
}

static class Listable
{
  public static void List(
      this IListable[] items, string[] headers)
```

```
    {
        int[] columnWidths = DisplayHeaders(headers);

        for (int itemCount = 0; itemCount < items.Length; itemCount++)
        {
            string[] values = items[itemCount].ColumnValues;

            DisplayItemRow(columnWidths, values);
        }
    }
    // ...
}
```

Notice that in this example, the extension method is not on for an `IListable` parameter (although it could have been), but rather an `IListable[]` parameter. This demonstrates that C# allows extension methods not only on an instance of a particular type, but also on a collection of those objects. Support for extension methods is the foundation on which LINQ is implemented. `IEnumerable` is the fundamental interface that all collections implement. By defining extension methods for `IEnumerable`, LINQ support was added to all collections. This radically changed programming with collections; we will explore this topic in detail in Chapter 14.

Implementing Multiple Inheritance via Interfaces

As Listing 7.3 demonstrated, a single class can implement any number of interfaces in addition to deriving from a single class. This feature provides a possible workaround for the lack of multiple inheritance support in C# classes. The process uses aggregation as described in the preceding chapter, but you can vary the structure slightly by adding an interface to the mix, as shown in Listing 7.11.

LISTING 7.11: **Working around Single Inheritance Using Aggregation with Interfaces**

```
public class PdaItem
{
    // ...
}
```

```csharp
interface IPerson
{
    string FirstName
    {
        get;
        set;
    }

    string LastName
    {
        get;
        set;
    }
}
```

```csharp
public class Person : IPerson
{
  // ...
}
```

```csharp
public class Contact : PdaItem, IPerson
{
  private Person Person
  {
      get { return _Person; }
      set { _Person = value; }
  }
  private Person _Person;

  public string FirstName
  {
      get { return _Person.FirstName; }
      set { _Person.FirstName = value; }
  }

  public string LastName
  {
      get { return _Person.LastName; }
      set { _Person.LastName = value; }
  }

  // ...
}
```

IPerson ensures that the signatures between the Person members and the same members duplicated onto Contact are consistent. The implementation is still not synonymous with multiple inheritance, however, because new members added to Person will not be added to Contact.

One possible improvement that works if the implemented members are methods (not properties) is to define interface extension methods for the additional functionality "derived" from the second base class. An extension method on `IPerson` could provide a method called `VerifyCredentials()`, for example, and all classes that implement `IPerson`, even an `IPerson` interface that had no members but just extension methods, would have a default implementation of `VerifyCredentials()`. What makes this a viable approach is that polymorphism is still available, as is overriding. Overriding is supported because any instance implementation of a method will take priority over an extension method with the equivalent static signature.

> ## Guidelines
>
> **CONSIDER** defining interfaces to achieve a similar effect to that of multiple inheritance.

■ BEGINNER TOPIC

Interface Diagramming

Interfaces in a UML-like[1] figure take two possible forms. First, you can show the interface as though it is an inheritance relationship similar to a class inheritance, as demonstrated in Figure 7.1 between `IPerson` and `IContact`. Alternatively, you can show the interface using a small circle, often referred to as a lollipop, exemplified by `IPerson` and `IContact` in Figure 7.1.

In Figure 7.1, `Contact` derives from `PdaItem` and implements `IContact`. In addition, it aggregates the `Person` class, which implements `IPerson`. Although the Visual Studio 2005 Class Designer does not support this, interfaces are sometimes shown as using a derivation-type arrow to a class. For example, `Person` could have an arrow to `IPerson` instead of a lollipop.

---

1. Unified Modeling Language (UML), a standard specification for modeling object design using graphical notation.

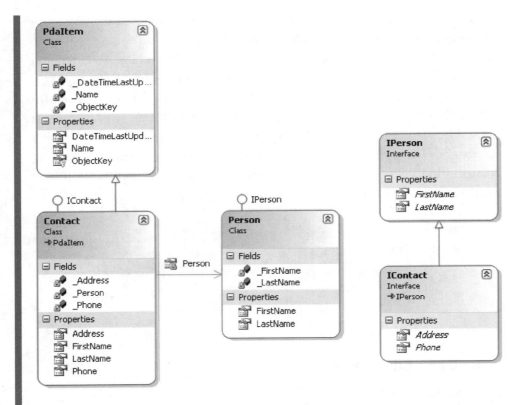

FIGURE 7.1: **Working around Single Inheritances with Aggregation and Interfaces**

Versioning

When creating a new version of a component or application that other developers have programmed against, you should not change interfaces. Because interfaces define a contract between the implementing class and the class using the interface, changing the interface is changing the contract, which will possibly break any code written against the interface.

Changing or removing a particular interface member signature is obviously a code-breaking change, as any call to that member will no longer compile without modification. The same is true when changing public or protected member signatures on a class. However, unlike with classes, adding members to an interface could also prevent code from compiling without additional changes. The problem is that any class implementing the interface must do so entirely, and implementations for all members must be provided.

With new interface members, the compiler will require that developers add new interface members to the class implementing the interface.

> ### Guidelines
>
> **DO NOT** add members to an interface that has already shipped.

The creation of `IDistributedSettingsProvider` in Listing 7.12 serves as a good example of extending an interface in a version-compatible way. Imagine that at first, only the `ISettingsProvider` interface is defined (as it was in Listing 7.6). In the next version, however, it is determined that per-machine settings are required. To enable this, the `IDistributedSettingsProvider` interface is created, and it derives from `ISettingsProvider`.

LISTING 7.12: **Deriving One Interface from Another**

```csharp
interface IDistributedSettingsProvider : ISettingsProvider
{
  /// <summary>
  /// Get the settings for a particular machine.
  /// </summary>
  /// <param name="machineName">
  /// The machine name the setting is related to</param>
  /// <param name="name">The name of the setting</param>
  /// <param name="defaultValue">
  /// The value returned if the setting is not found.</param>
  /// <returns>The specified setting</returns>
  string GetSetting(
      string machineName, string name, string defaultValue);

  /// <summary>
  /// Set the settings for a particular machine.
  /// </summary>
  /// <param name="machineName">
  /// The machine name the setting is related to.</param>
  /// <param name="name">The name of the setting.</param>
  /// <param name="value">The value to be persisted.</param>
  /// <returns>The specified setting</returns>
  void SetSetting(
      string machineName, string name, string value);
}
```

The important factor is that programmers with classes that implement `ISettingsProvider` can choose to upgrade the implementation to include `IDistributedSettingsProvider`, or they can ignore it.

If instead of creating a new interface, the machine-related methods are added to `ISettingsProvider`, classes implementing this interface will no longer successfully compile with the new interface definition, and instead a version-breaking change will occur.

Changing interfaces during the development phase is obviously acceptable, although perhaps laborious if implemented extensively. However, once an interface is released, it should not be changed. Instead, a second interface should be created, possibly deriving from the original interface.

(Listing 7.12 includes XML comments describing the interface members, as discussed further in Chapter 9.)

Interfaces Compared with Classes

Interfaces introduce another category of data types. (They are one of the few categories of types that don't extend `System.Object`.[2]) Unlike classes, however, interfaces can never be instantiated. An interface instance is accessible only via a reference to an object that implements the interface. It is not possible to use the `new` operator with an interface; therefore, interfaces cannot contain any constructors or finalizers. Furthermore, static members are not allowed on interfaces.

Interfaces are closer to abstract classes, sharing such features as the lack of instantiation capability. Table 7.1 lists additional comparisons.

Given that abstract classes and interfaces have their own sets of advantages and disadvantages, you must make a cost-benefit decision based on the comparisons in Table 7.1 and the guidelines below in order to make the right choice.

Guidelines

DO generally favor classes over interfaces. Use abstract classes to decouple contracts (what the type does) from implementation details (how the type does it.)

CONSIDER defining an interface if you need to support its functionality on types that already inherit from some other type.

---

2. The others being pointer types and type parameter types. However, every interface type is convertible to `System.Object`, and it is permissible to call the methods of `System.Object` on any instance of an interface, so this is perhaps a hairsplitting distinction.

TABLE 7.1: Comparing Abstract Classes and Interfaces

Abstract Classes	Interfaces
Cannot be instantiated directly, only by instantiating a derived class.	Cannot be instantiated directly, only by instantiating an implementing type.
Derived classes must either be abstract themselves, or must implement all abstract members.	Implementing types must implement all interface members.
Can add additional nonabstract members that all derived classes can inherit without breaking cross-version compatibility.	Adding additional members to interfaces breaks the version compatibility.
Can declare both properties and fields.	Can declare properties but not fields.
Members may be instance, virtual, abstract, or static and may provide implementations for nonabstract members that can be used by derived classes.	All members are automatically treated as though they were abstract, and therefore cannot include any implementation.
A derived class may derive from only a single base class.	An implementing type may arbitrarily implement many interfaces.

Interfaces Compared with Attributes

Interfaces with no members at all, inherited or otherwise, are sometimes used to represent information about a type. For example, you might create a marker IObsolete interface to indicate that a particular type has been replaced by another type. This is generally considered to be an abuse of the interface mechanism; interfaces should be used to represent what functions a type can perform, not to indicate facts about particular types. Instead of marker interfaces, use attributes. See Chapter 17 for more details.

> ### Guidelines
>
> **AVOID** using "marker" interfaces with no members; use attributes instead.

SUMMARY

Interfaces are a key element of object-oriented programming in C#. They provide functionality similar to abstract classes but without using up the single-inheritance option, and also support implementation of multiple interfaces.

In C#, the implementation of interfaces can be either explicit or implicit, depending on whether the implementing class is to expose an interface member directly or only via a conversion to the interface. Furthermore, the granularity of whether the implementation is explicit or implicit is at the member level: One member may be implicitly implemented while another member of the same interface is explicitly implemented.

The next chapter looks at value types and discusses the importance of defining custom value types; at the same time, the chapter points out the subtle problems that they can introduce.

■8■
Value Types

Y OU HAVE USED VALUE TYPES throughout this book; for example, int is
a value type. This chapter discusses not only using value types, but
also defining custom value types. There are two categories of custom value
types. The first category is structs. This chapter discusses how structs enable programmers to define new value types that behave very similarly to
most of the predefined types discussed in Chapter 2. The key is that any
newly defined value types have their own custom data and methods. The
second category of value types is enums. This chapter discusses how to
use enums to define sets of constant values.

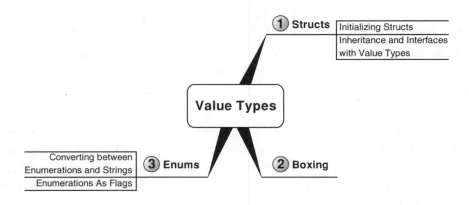

Structs

■ **BEGINNER TOPIC**

Categories of Types

All types discussed so far fall into two categories: reference types and value types. The differences between the types in each category stem from differences in copying strategies, which, in turn, results in each type being stored differently in memory. To review, this Beginner Topic reintroduces the value type/reference type discussion to familiarize those who are unfamiliar with it.

Value Types

Variables of **value types** directly contain their values, as shown in Figure 8.1. The variable name is associated directly with the storage location in memory where the value is stored. Because of this, when a second variable is assigned the value of an original variable, a copy of the original variable's value is made to the storage location associated with the second variable. Two variables never refer to the same storage location (unless one or both are an `out` or `ref` parameter, which are, by definition, aliases for another variable). So, changing the value of the original variable will not affect the value in the second variable, since each variable is associated with a different storage location. Consequently, changing the value of one value type variable cannot affect the value of any other value type variable.

A value type variable is like a piece of paper that has a number written on it. If you want to change the number, you can erase it and replace it with a different number. If you have a second piece of paper, you can copy the number from the first piece of paper, but the two pieces of paper are then independent; erasing and replacing the number on one of them does not change the other.

Similarly, passing an instance of a value type to a method such as `Console.WriteLine()` will also result in a memory copy from the storage location associated with the argument to the storage location associated with the parameter, and any changes to the parameter variable inside the method will not affect the original value within the caller. Since value types require a memory copy, they generally should be defined to consume a small amount of memory (typically 16 bytes or less).

FIGURE 8.1: Value Types Contain the Data Directly

Guidelines

DO NOT create value types that consume more than 16 bytes of memory.

Values of value types are often short-lived; often a value is only needed for a portion of an expression or for the activation of a method. In these cases, variables and temporary values of value types can often be stored on the **temporary storage pool,** often called "the stack." (Though this is a misnomer; there is no requirement that the temporary pool allocates its storage off the stack, and in fact, as an implementation detail, it frequently chooses to allocate storage out of available registers instead.)

The temporary pool is less costly to clean up than the garbage-collected heap; however, value types tend to be copied more than reference types, and that copying can impose a performance cost of its own. Do not fall into the trap of believing that "value types are faster because they can be allocated on the stack."

Reference Types

In contrast, the value of a reference type variable is a reference to an instance of an object (see Figure 8.2). Variables of reference type store the reference (typically implemented as the memory address) where the data for the object instance is located, instead of storing the data directly, as a variable of value type does. Therefore, to access the data, the runtime will read the reference out of the variable and then dereference it to reach the location in memory that actually contains the data for the instance.

A reference type variable, therefore, has two storage locations associated with it: the storage location directly associated with the variable, and the storage location referred to by the reference that is the value stored in the variable.

A reference type variable is, again, like a piece of paper that always has something written on it. Imagine, for example, a piece of paper that has a house address written on it: say, "123 Sesame Street, New York City". The piece of paper is a variable; the address is a reference to a building. Neither the paper nor the address written on it is the building, and the location of the paper need not have anything whatsoever to do with the location of the building its contents refer to. If you make a copy of that reference on another piece of paper, the contents of both pieces of paper refer to the same building. If you then paint that building green, the building referred to by both pieces of paper can be observed to be green, because the references refer to the same thing.

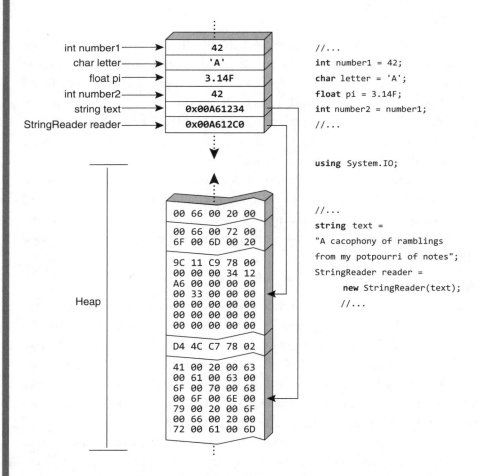

FIGURE 8.2: Reference Types Point to the Heap

The storage location directly associated with the variable (or temporary value) is treated no differently than the storage location associated with a value type variable: If the variable is known to be short-lived it is allocated on the short-term storage pool. The value of a reference type variable is always a reference to a storage location in the garbage-collected heap, or null.

Compared to a variable of value type, which stores the data of the instance directly, accessing the data associated with a reference involves an extra "hop": First the reference must be dereferenced to find the storage location of the actual data, and then the data can be read or written. Copying a reference type value only copies the reference, which is small. (A reference is guaranteed to be no larger than the "bit size" of the processor; a 32-bit machine has 4-byte references, a 64-bit machine has 8-byte references, and so on.) Copying the value of a value type copies all the data, which could be large. Therefore, there are circumstances in which reference types are more efficient to copy. This is why the guideline for value types is to ensure that they are never more than 16 bytes or thereabouts; if a value type is more than four times as expensive to copy as a reference, it probably should simply be a reference type.

Since reference types copy only a reference to the data, two different variables can refer to the same data. Thus, changing the data through one variable will be observed to change the data for the other variable as well. This happens both for assignment and for method calls.

To continue our previous analogy, if you pass the address of a building to a method, you make a copy of the paper containing the reference and hand the copy to the method. The method cannot change the contents of the original paper to refer to a different building. But if the method paints the referred-to building, when the method returns the caller can observe that the building the caller is still referring to is now a different color.

All of the C# "built-in" types, such as `bool` and `decimal`, are value types, with the exception of `string` and `object`, which are reference types. Numerous additional value types are provided within the framework. It also is possible for developers to define their own value types.

To define a custom value type, you use a similar syntax as you would to define class and interface types. The key difference in syntax is that value types use the keyword `struct`, as shown in Listing 8.1. Here we have a value type that describes a high-precision angle in terms of its degrees, minutes, and seconds. (A "minute" is one-sixtieth of a degree, and a second is one-sixtieth of a minute. This system is used in navigation because it has the nice property that an arc of one minute over the surface of the ocean at the equator is exactly one nautical mile.)

LISTING 8.1: **Declaring a** struct

```
// Use keyword struct to declare a value type.
struct Angle
{
    public Angle(int degrees, int minutes, int seconds)
    {
        _Degrees = degrees;
        _Minutes = minutes;
        _Seconds = seconds;
    }

    public int Degrees
    {
        get { return _Degrees; }
    }
    private int _Degrees;

    public int Minutes
    {
        get { return _Minutes; }
    }
    private int _Minutes;

    public int Seconds
    {
        get { return _Seconds; }
    }
    private int _Seconds;

    public Angle Move(int degrees, int minutes, int seconds)
    {
        return new Angle(
            Degrees + degrees,
            Minutes + minutes,
            Seconds + seconds)
    }

}

// Declaring a class - a reference type
// (declaring it as a struct would create a value type
// larger than 16 bytes.)
class Coordinate
{
    public Angle Longitude
```

```
{
    get { return _Longitude; }
    set { _Longitude = value; }
}
private Angle _Longitude;

public Angle Latitude
{
    get { return _Latitude; }
    set { _Latitude = value; }
}
private Angle _Latitude;
}
```

This listing defines `Angle` as a value type that stores the degrees, minutes, and seconds of an angle, either longitude or latitude. The resultant C# type is a **struct.**

NOTE

Although nothing in the language requires it, a good guideline is for value types to be immutable: Once you have instantiated a value type, you should not be able to modify the same instance. In scenarios where modification is desirable, you should create a new instance. Listing 8.1 supplies a `Move()` method that doesn't modify the instance of `Angle`, but instead returns an entirely new instance.

There are two good reasons for this guideline. First, value types should represent values. One does not think of adding two integers together as mutating either of them; rather, the two addends are immutable and a third value is produced as the result.

Second, because value types are copied by value, not by reference, it is very easy to get confused and incorrectly believe that a mutation to one value type variable can be observed to cause a mutation in another, as it would with a reference type.

Guidelines

DO create value types that are immutable.

Initializing Structs

In addition to properties and fields, structs may contain methods and constructors. However, user-defined default (parameterless) constructors are not allowed. Instead, every struct automatically gets a parameterless constructor that initializes all the fields of the struct to their default values. Automatically initialized struct variables, such as the elements of an array of struct type, automatically initialize the variable as though this default constructor had been called. Because the compiler's implementation of an instance field assignment at declaration time is to place the assignment into the type's default constructor, C# prevents instance field assignment at declaration time as well (see Listing 8.2).

LISTING 8.2: Initializing a `struct` Field within a Declaration, Resulting in an Error

```
struct Angle
{
  // ...
  // ERROR:  Fields cannot be initialized at declaration time
  // int _Degrees = 42;
  // ...
}
```

This does not eliminate the need to initialize the field. A local variable of struct type cannot be used until it is known that all the fields of that struct are initialized.

Fortunately, C# supports constructors with parameters and they come with an interesting initialization requirement. To ensure that a local variable of value type can be fully initialized by a constructor, every constructor must initialize all fields within the struct. Failure to do so causes a compile error. The constructor in Listing 8.3 that initializes the property rather than the field, for example, produces a compile error.

LISTING 8.3: Accessing Properties before Initializing All Fields

```
// ERROR:  The 'this' object cannot be used before
//         all of its fields are assigned to
// public Angle(int degrees, int minutes, int seconds)
// {
//     Degrees = degrees;    // Shorthand for this.Hours = hours;
//     Minutes = minutes;    // Shorthand for this.Minutes = ...;
//     Seconds = seconds;    // Shorthand for this.Seconds = ...;
// }
```

The error reports that methods and properties (Hours implies this.Hours) are accessed prior to the initialization of all fields. To resolve the issue, you need to initialize the fields directly, as demonstrated in Listing 8.1.

Guidelines

DO ensure that the default value of a struct is valid; it is always possible to obtain the default "all zero" value of a struct.

■ ADVANCED TOPIC

Using new with Value Types

Invoking the new operator with a reference type causes the runtime to create a new instance of the object on the garbage-collected heap, initialize all of its fields to their default values, and call the constructor, passing a reference to the instance as this. The result is the reference to the instance, which can then be copied to its final destination. In contrast, invoking the new operator with a value type causes the runtime to create a new instance of the object on the temporary storage pool, initialize all of its fields to their default values, call the constructor (passing the temporary storage location as a ref variable as this), and results in the value stored in the temporary storage location, which can then be copied to its final destination.

Unlike classes, structs do not support finalizers. Structs are copied by value; they do not have "referential identity" as reference types do. Therefore, it is hard to know when it would be safe to execute the finalizer and free an unmanaged resource owned by the struct. The garbage collector knows when there are no "live" references to an instance of reference type and can choose to run the finalizer for an instance of reference type at any time after there are no more live references. But no part of the runtime tracks how many copies of a given value type exist at any moment.

Language Contrast: C++—struct Defines Type with Public Members

In C++, the difference between a type declared with `struct` and one declared with `class` is whether the default accessibility is public or private. The contrast is far greater in C#, where the difference is whether instances of the type are copied by value or by reference.

Using the `default` Operator

As described earlier, all value types have an automatically defined parameterless constructor that initializes the storage of a value of value type to its default state. Therefore, it is always legal to use the syntax `new S()` for any value type. As an alternative syntax, you can also use the `default` operator to produce the default value for a struct. In Listing 8.4 we add a second constructor to the `Angle` struct that uses the `default` operator on `int` as an argument to the previously declared three-argument constructor. The expressions `default(int)`, `new int()`, and `0` all produce the same value.

LISTING 8.4: Using the `default` Operator to Obtain the Default Value of a Type

```csharp
// Use keyword struct to declare a value type.
struct Angle
{
  public Angle(int degrees, int minutes)
      : this( degrees, minutes, default(int) )
  {
  }

  // ...
}
```

Inheritance and Interfaces with Value Types

All value types are implicitly sealed. In addition, all non-enum value types derive from `System.ValueType`. This means that the inheritance chain for structs is always from `object` to `System.ValueType` to the struct.

Value types can implement interfaces, too. Many of those built into the framework implement interfaces such as `IComparable` and `IFormattable`.

`System.ValueType` brings with it the behavior of value types, but it does not include any additional members. The `System.ValueType` customizations are in the overriding of all of `object`'s virtual members. The rules for overriding base class methods in a struct are almost the same as those for classes (see Chapter 9). However, one difference is that with value types, the default implementation for `GetHashCode()` is to forward the call to the first non-null field within the struct. Also, `Equals()` makes significant use of reflection. Therefore, if a value type is frequently used inside collections, especially dictionary-type collections that use hash codes, the value type should include overrides for both `Equals()` and `GetHashCode()` to ensure good performance. See Chapter 9 for more details.

> ### Guidelines
>
> **DO** overload the equality operators (`Equals()`, `==`, and `!=`) on value types, if equality is meaningful. (Also consider implementing the `IEquatable<T>` interface.)

Boxing

We know that variables of value type directly contain their data, but variables of reference type contain a reference to another storage location. What happens when a value type is converted to one of its implemented interfaces or to its root base class, `object`? The result of the conversion has to be a reference to a storage location that contains something that looks like an instance of a reference type, but the variable contains a value of value type. Such a conversion is known as a **boxing** conversion and it has special behavior. Converting a variable of value type that directly refers to its data to a reference type that refers to a location on the garbage-collected heap involves several steps.

1. First, memory is allocated on the heap that will contain the value type's data and the other overhead necessary to make the object look like every other instance of a managed object of reference type (namely, a `SyncBlockIndex` and method table pointer).

2. Next, the value of the value type is copied from its current storage location into the newly allocated location on the heap.

3. Finally, the result of the conversion is a reference to the new storage location on the heap.

The reverse operation is **unboxing.** The unboxing conversion checks to ensure that the type of the boxed value is compatible with the type to which the value is being unboxed, and then results in a copy of the value stored in the heap location.

Boxing and unboxing are important to consider because boxing has some performance and behavioral implications. Besides learning how to recognize them within C# code, a developer can count the box/unbox instructions in a particular snippet of code by looking through the CIL. Each operation has specific instructions, as shown in Table 8.1.

TABLE 8.1: Boxing Code in CIL

C# Code	CIL Code
| ```
static void Main()


{



    int number;
    object thing;


    number = 42;



    // Boxing
    thing = number;



    // Unboxing
    number = (int)thing;






    return;
}
``` | ```
.method private hidebysig
        static void  Main() cil managed
{
    .entrypoint
    // Code size        21 (0x15)
    .maxstack  1
    .locals init ([0] int32 number,
              [1] object thing)
    IL_0000:  nop
    IL_0001:  ldc.i4.s    42
    IL_0003:  stloc.0
    IL_0004:  ldloc.0
    IL_0005:  box         [mscorlib]System.Int32
    IL_000a:  stloc.1
    IL_000b:  ldloc.1
    IL_000c:  unbox.any   [mscorlib]System.Int32
    IL_0011:  stloc.0
    IL_0012:  br.s        IL_0014
    IL_0014:  ret
} // end of method Program::Main
``` |

When boxing and unboxing occurs infrequently the performance concerns are irrelevant. However, boxing can occur in some unexpected situations, and frequent occurrences can have a significant impact on performance. Consider Listing 8.5 and Output 8.1. The ArrayList type maintains a list of references to objects, and therefore, adding an integer or floating-point number to the list will box the value so that a reference can be obtained.

LISTING 8.5: Subtle Box and Unbox Instructions

```csharp
class DisplayFibonacci
{
  static void Main()
  {

      int totalCount;
      System.Collections.ArrayList list =
          new System.Collections.ArrayList();

      Console.Write("Enter a number between 2 and 1000:");
      totalCount = int.Parse(Console.ReadLine());

      // Execution-time error:
      // list.Add(0);   // Cast to double or 'D' suffix required
      //                 // Whether cast or using 'D' suffix,
      //                 // CIL is identical.
      list.Add((double)0);
      list.Add((double)1);
      for (int count = 2; count < totalCount; count++)
      {
          list.Add(
              ((double)list[count - 1] +
              (double)list[count - 2]) );
      }

      foreach (double count in list)
      {
          Console.Write("{0}, ", count);
      }
  }
}
```

OUTPUT 8.1

```
Enter a number between 2 and 1000:42
0, 1, 1, 2, 3, 5, 8, 13, 21, 34, 55, 89, 144, 233, 377, 610, 987, 1597,
2584, 4181, 6765, 10946, 17711, 28657, 46368, 75025, 121393, 196418,
317811, 514229, 832040, 1346269, 2178309, 3524578, 5702887, 9227465,
14930352, 24157817, 39088169, 63245986, 102334155, 165580141,
```

The code shown in Listing 8.5, when compiled, produces five box and three unbox instructions in the resultant CIL.

1. The first two box instructions occur in the initial calls to `list.Add()`. The signature for the `ArrayList` method is `int Add(object value)`. As such, any value type passed to this method is boxed.

2. Next are two unbox instructions in the call to `Add()` within the `for` loop. The return from an `ArrayList`'s index operator is always `object` because that is what `ArrayList` contains. In order to add the two values, however, you need to cast them back to `doubles`. This cast from a reference to an object to a value type is implemented as an unbox call.

3. Now you take the result of the addition and place it into the `ArrayList` instance, which again results in a box operation. Note that the first two unbox instructions and this box instruction occur within a loop.

4. In the `foreach` loop, you iterate through each item in `ArrayList` and assign them to `count`. However, as you already saw, the items within `ArrayList` are references to `objects`, so assigning them to a `double` is unboxing each of them.

5. The signature for `Console.WriteLine()` that is called within the `foreach` loop is `void Console.Write(string format, object arg)`. As a result, each call to it boxes the `double` to `object`.

Every boxing operation involves both an allocation and a copy; every unboxing operation involves a type check and a copy. Doing the equivalent work using the unboxed type would eliminate the allocation and type check. Obviously, you can easily improve this code's performance by eliminating many of the boxing operations. Using an `object` rather than `double` in the last `foreach` loop is one improvement you can make. Another would be to change the `ArrayList` data type to a generic collection (see Chapter 11). The point, however, is that boxing can be rather subtle, so developers need to pay special attention and notice situations where it could potentially occur repeatedly and affect performance.

There is another unfortunate runtime-boxing-related problem. If you wanted to change the initial two `Add()` calls so that they did not use a cast (or a double literal), you would have to insert integers into the array list. Since `ints` will implicitly be converted to `doubles`, this would appear to be an innocuous modification. However, the casts to `double` from within the `for` loop, and again in the assignment to `count` in the `foreach` loops, would fail. The problem is that immediately following the unbox operation is an attempt to perform a memory copy of the value of the boxed int into a double. You cannot do this without first casting to an int, because the code will throw an `InvalidCastException` at execution time. Listing 8.6 shows a similar error commented out and followed by the correct cast.

LISTING 8.6: Unboxing Must Be to the Underlying Type

```
// ...
int number;
object thing;
double bigNumber;

number = 42;
thing = number;
// ERROR: InvalidCastException
// bigNumber = (double)thing;
bigNumber = (double)(int)thing;
// ...
```

■ ADVANCED TOPIC

Value Types in the lock Statement

C# supports a `lock` statement for synchronizing code. The statement compiles down to `System.Threading.Monitor`'s `Enter()` and `Exit()` methods. These two methods must be called in pairs. `Enter()` records the unique reference argument passed so that when `Exit()` is called with the same reference, the lock can be released. The trouble with using value types is the boxing. Therefore, each time `Enter()` or `Exit()` is called, a new value is created on the heap. Comparing the reference of one copy to the reference of a different copy will always return `false`, so you cannot hook up `Enter()` with the corresponding `Exit()`. Therefore, value types in the `lock()` statement are not allowed.

Listing 8.7 points out a few more runtime boxing idiosyncrasies and Output 8.2 shows the results.

LISTING 8.7: Subtle Boxing Idiosyncrasies

```
interface IAngle
{
    void MoveTo(int degrees, int minutes, int seconds);
}
```

```csharp
struct Angle : IAngle
{
  // ...

  // NOTE:  This makes Angle mutable, against the general
  //        guideline
  public void MoveTo(int degrees, int minutes, int seconds)
  {
          _Degrees = degrees;
          _Minutes = minutes;
          _Seconds = seconds;
  }
}
```

```csharp
class Program
{
  static void Main()
  {
      // ...

      Angle angle = new Angle(25, 58, 23);
      object objectAngle = angle;  // Box
      Console.Write( ((Angle)objectAngle).Degrees);

      // Unbox, modify unboxed value, and discard value
      ((Angle)objectAngle).MoveTo(26, 58, 23);
      Console.Write(", " +  ((Angle)objectAngle).Degrees);

      // Box, modify boxed value, and discard reference to box
      ((IAngle)angle).MoveTo(26, 58, 23);
      Console.Write(", " + ((Angle)angle).Degrees);

      // Modify boxed value directly
      ((IAngle)objectAngle).MoveTo(26, 58, 23);
      Console.WriteLine(", " + ((Angle)objectAngle).Degrees);

      // ...
  }
}
```

OUTPUT 8.2

```
25, 25, 25, 26
```

Listing 8.7 uses the Angle struct and IAngle interface from Listing 8.1. Note also that the IAngle.MoveTo() interface changes Angle to be mutable. This brings out some of the idiosyncrasies of mutable value types and, in so doing, demonstrates the importance of the guideline to make structs immutable.

In the first two lines, you initialize `angle` and then box it into a variable called `objectAngle`. Next, you call `move` in order to change `Hours` to 26. However, as the output demonstrates, no change actually occurs the first time. The problem is that in order to call `MoveTo()`, the compiler unboxes `objectAngle` and (by definition) makes a copy of the value. Value types are copied by value; that is why they are called value types. Although the resultant value is successfully modified at execution time, this copy of the value is discarded and no change occurs on the heap location referenced by `objectAngle`.

Again, remember our analogy about variables of value type as being like pieces of paper with the value written on them. When you box a value, you make a photocopy of the paper and put the copy in a box. When you unbox the value, you make a photocopy of the paper in the box. Making an edit to this second copy does not change the copy that is in the box.

In the next example, labeled "box, modify boxed value and discard reference to box", a similar problem occurs in reverse. Instead of calling `MoveTo()` directly, the value is cast to `IAngle`. The conversion to interface type boxes the value, so the runtime copies the data in `angle` to the heap and provides a reference to that box. Next, the method call modifies the value in the referenced box. The value stored in variable `angle` remains unmodified.

In the last case, the cast to `IAngle` is a reference conversion, not a boxing conversion; the value has already been boxed by the conversion to `object`. Therefore, no copy of the value occurs on this conversion. The call to `MoveTo()` updates the `_Hours` value stored in the box and the code behaves as desired.

As you can see from this example, mutable value types are quite confusing because it is often unclear when you are mutating a copy of the value, rather than the storage location you actually intend to be mutating. By avoiding mutable value types in the first place, these sorts of confusion can be eliminated.

Guidelines

AVOID mutable value types.

■ ADVANCED TOPIC

How Boxing Can Be Avoided during Method Calls

Anytime a method is called with a receiver of value type, the receiver (represented by this in the body of the method) must be a variable, not a value, because the method might be trying to mutate the receiver. Clearly, it must be mutating the receiver's storage location, rather than mutating a copy of the receiver's value and then discarding it. The second and fourth cases in Listing 8.7 above illustrate how this fact impacts the performance of a method invocation on a boxed value type.

In the second case, the unboxing conversion logically produces the boxed value, not a reference to the storage location on the heap that contains the boxed copy. What storage location, then, is passed as the this to the mutating method call? It cannot be the storage location from the box on the heap, because the unboxing conversion produces a copy of that value, not a reference to that storage location.

When this situation arises—a variable of value type is required but only a value is available—one of two things happens. Either the C# compiler generates code that makes a new, temporary storage location and copies the value from the box into the new location, resulting in the temporary storage location becoming the needed variable, or the compiler produces an error and disallows the operation. In this case, the former strategy is used. The new temporary storage location is then the receiver of the call; after it is mutated, the temporary storage location is discarded.

This process—performing a type check of the boxed value, unboxing to produce the storage location of the boxed value, allocating a temporary variable, copying the value from the box to the temporary variable, and then calling the method with the location of the temporary storage—happens every time you use the unbox-and-then-call pattern, regardless of whether the method actually mutates the variable. Clearly, if it does not mutate the variable, some of this work could be avoided, but the C# compiler does not know whether any particular method you call will try to mutate the receiver, so it must err on the side of caution.

These expenses are all eliminated when calling an interface method on a boxed value type. When calling the interface method, the expectation is that the receiver will be the storage location in the box; if the interface method mutates the storage location, it is the boxed location that should be mutated. Therefore, the expense of performing a type check, allocating new temporary storage, and making a copy is avoided. Rather, the runtime simply uses the storage location in the box as the receiver of the call to the struct's method.

In Listing 8.8 we call the two-argument version of ToString() that is found on the IFormattable interface, which is implemented by the int value type. In this example, the receiver of the call is a boxed value type, but it is not unboxed to make the call to the interface method.

LISTING 8.8: **Avoiding Unboxing and Copying**

```
int number;
object thing;
number = 42;
// Boxing
thing = number;
// No unboxing conversion.
string text = ((IFormattable)thing).ToString(
    "X", null);
Console.WriteLine(text);
```

You might now wonder: Suppose that instead we had called the virtual ToString() method declared by object with an instance of a value type as the receiver. What happens then? Is the instance boxed, unboxed, or what? There are a number of different scenarios here depending on the details:

- If the receiver is unboxed and the struct overrides ToString(), the overridden method is called directly. There is no need for a virtual call because the method cannot be overridden further by a more derived class; all value types are automatically sealed.
- If the receiver is unboxed and the struct does not override ToString(), the base class implementation must be called, and it expects a reference to an object as its receiver. Therefore, the receiver is boxed.
- If the receiver is boxed and the struct overrides ToString(), the storage location in the box is passed to the overriding method without unboxing it.
- If the receiver is boxed and the struct does not override ToString(), the reference to the box is passed to the base class's implementation of the method, which is expecting a reference.

Enums

Compare the two code snippets shown in Listing 8.9.

LISTING 8.9: **Comparing an Integer Switch to an Enum Switch**

```
int connectionState;
// ...
switch (connectionState)
{
    case 0:
        // ...
        break;
    case 1:
        // ...
        break;
    case 2:
        // ...
        break;
    case 3:
        // ...
        break;
}
```

```
ConnectionState connectionState;
// ...
switch (connectionState)
{
    case ConnectionState.Connected:
        // ...
        break;
    case ConnectionState.Connecting:
        // ...
        break;
    case ConnectionState.Disconnected:
        // ...
        break;
    case ConnectionState.Disconnecting:
        // ...
        break;
}
```

Obviously, the difference in terms of readability is tremendous because in the second snippet, the cases are self-documenting. However, the performance at runtime is identical. To achieve this, the second snippet uses **enum values** in each case.

An enum is a value type that the developer can declare. The key characteristic of an enum is that it declares at compile time a set of possible constant values that can be referred to by name, thereby making the code easier to read. The syntax for a typical enum declaration is show in Listing 8.10.

LISTING 8.10: Defining an Enum

```
enum ConnectionState
{
  Disconnected,
  Connecting,
  Connected,
  Disconnecting
}
```

▪ NOTE

An enum can be used as a more readable replacement for Boolean values as well. For example, a method call such as `SetState(true)` is less readable than `SetState(DeviceState.On)`.

You use an enum value by prefixing it with the enum name; to use the `Connected` value, for example, use the syntax `ConnectionState .Connected`. Do not make the enum type name a part of the value's name so as to avoid the redundancy of something such as `ConnectionState.ConnectionStateConnected`. By convention, the enum name itself should be singular (unless the enums are bit flags, as discussed shortly). That is, it should be `ConnectionState`, not `ConnectionStates`.

Enum values are actually implemented as nothing more than integer constants. By default, the first enum value is given the value 0, and each subsequent entry increases by one. However, you can assign explicit values to enums, as shown in Listing 8.11.

LISTING 8.11: Defining an Enum Type

```
enum ConnectionState : short
{
  Disconnected,
  Connecting = 10,
  Connected,
  Joined = Connected,
  Disconnecting
}
```

`Disconnected` has a default value of `0`, `Connecting` has been explicitly assigned `10`, and consequently, `Connected` will be assigned `11`. `Joined` is assigned `11`, the value assigned to `Connected`. (In this case, you do not need to prefix `Connected` with the enum name, since it appears within its scope.) `Disconnecting` is `12`.

An enum always has an underlying type, which may be any integral type other than `char`. In fact, the enum type's performance is identical to that of the underlying type. By default, the underlying value type is `int`, but you can specify a different type using inheritance type syntax. Instead of `int`, for example, Listing 8.11 uses a `short`. For consistency, the syntax emulates that of inheritance, but this doesn't actually make an inheritance relationship. The base class for all enums is `System.Enum`, which, in turn, is derived from `System.ValueType`. Furthermore, these classes are sealed; you can't derive from an existing enum type to add additional members.

> **Guidelines**
>
> **CONSIDER** using the default 32-bit integer type as the underlying type of an enum. Only use a smaller type if you must do so for interoperability or performance reasons; only use a larger type if you are creating a flags enum (see below) with more than 32 flags.

An enum is really nothing more than a set of names thinly layered on top of the underlying type; there is no mechanism that restricts the value of a variable of enumerated type to just the values named in the declaration. For example, because it is possible to cast the integer `42` to `short`, it is also possible to cast the integer `42` to the `ConnectionState` type, even though there is no corresponding `ConnectionState` enum value. If the value can be converted to the underlying type, the conversion to the enum type will also be successful.

The advantage of this odd feature is that enums can have new values added in later API releases, without breaking earlier versions. Additionally, the enum values provide names for the known values while still allowing unknown values to be assigned at runtime. The burden is that developers must code defensively for the possibility of unnamed values. It would be unwise, for example, to replace `case ConnectionState.Disconnecting` with default and expect that the only possible value for the default case was ConnectionState.Disconnecting. Instead, you should handle the Disconnecting case explicitly and the default case should report an error or behave innocuously. As indicated before, however, conversion between the enum and the underlying type, and vice versa, requires an explicit cast; it is not an implicit conversion. For example, code cannot call ReportState(10) if the method's signature is void ReportState(ConnectionState state). The only exception is passing 0 because there is an implicit conversion from 0 to any enum.

Although you can add additional values to an enum in a later version of your code, you should do this with care. Inserting an enum value in the middle of an enum will bump the values of all later enums (adding Flooded or Locked before Connected will change the Connected value, for example). This will affect the versions of all code that is recompiled against the new version. However, any code compiled against the old version will continue to use the old values, making the intended values entirely different. Besides inserting an enum value at the end of the list, one way to avoid changing enum values is to assign values explicitly.

Guidelines

CONSIDER adding new members to existing enums, but keep in mind the compatibility risk.

AVOID creating enums that represent an "incomplete" set of values, such as product version numbers.

AVOID creating "reserved for future use" values in an enum.

AVOID enums that contain a single value. **DO** provide a value of 0 (none) on simple enums, knowing that 0 will be the default value when no explicit initialization is provided.

Enums are slightly different from other value types because enums derive from System.Enum before deriving from System.ValueType.

Type Compatibility between Enums

C# also does not support a direct cast between arrays of two different enums. However, the CLR does, provided that both enums share the same underlying type. To work around this restriction of C#, the trick is to cast first to System.Array, as shown at the end of Listing 8.12.

LISTING 8.12: **Casting between Arrays of Enums**

```
enum ConnectionState1
{
  Disconnected,
  Connecting,
  Connected,
  Disconnecting
}
```

```
enum ConnectionState2
{
  Disconnected,
  Connecting,
  Connected,
  Disconnecting
}
```

```
class Program
{
  static void Main()
  {
      ConnectionState1[] states =
          (ConnectionState1[])(Array)new ConnectionState2[42];
  }
}
```

This exploits the fact that the CLR's notion of assignment compatibility is more lenient than C#'s. (The same trick is possible for other illegal conversions, such as int[] to uint[].) However, use this approach cautiously because there is no C# specification detailing that this should work across different CLR implementations.

Converting between Enums and Strings

One of the conveniences associated with enums is that the ToString() method, which is called by methods such as System.Console.WriteLine(), writes out the enum value identifier:

```
System.Diagnostics.Trace.WriteLine(string.Format(
    "The connection is currently {0}.",
    ConnectionState.Disconnecting));
```

The preceding code will write the text in Output 8.3 to the trace buffer.

OUTPUT 8.3

```
The connection is currently Disconnecting.
```

Conversion from a string to an enum is a little harder to find because it involves a static method on the System.Enum base class. Listing 8.13 provides an example of how to do it without generics (see Chapter 11), and Output 8.4 shows the results.

LISTING 8.13: **Converting a String to an Enum Using** Enum.Parse()

```
ThreadPriorityLevel priority = (ThreadPriorityLevel)Enum.Parse(
  typeof(ThreadPriorityLevel), "Idle");
Console.WriteLine(priority);
```

OUTPUT 8.4

```
Idle
```

The first parameter to Enum.Parse() is the type, which you specify using the keyword typeof(). This is a compile-time way of identifying the type, like a literal for the type value (see Chapter 17).

Until .NET Framework 4, there was no TryParse() method, so code written to target prior versions should include appropriate exception handling if there is a chance the string will not correspond to an enum value identifier. .NET Framework 4's TryParse<T>() method uses generics, but the type parameters can be inferred, resulting in the to-enum conversion example shown in Listing 8.14.

LISTING 8.14: **Converting a String to an Enum Using** Enum.TryParse<T>()

```
System.Diagnostics.ThreadPriorityLevel priority;
if(Enum.TryParse("Idle", out priority))
{
  Console.WriteLine(priority);
}
```

This technique eliminates the need to use exception handling if the string might not convert successfully. Instead, code can check the Boolean result returned from the call to TryParse<T>().

Regardless of whether code uses the "Parse" or "TryParse" approach, the key caution about converting from a string to an enum is that such a cast is not localizable. Therefore, developers should use this type of cast only for messages that are not exposed to users (assuming localization is a requirement).

> **Guidelines**
>
> **AVOID** direct enum/string conversions where the string must be localized into the user's language.

Enums As Flags

Many times, developers not only want enum values to be unique, they also want to be able to represent a combination of values. For example, consider `System.IO.FileAttributes`. This enum, shown in Listing 8.15, indicates various attributes on a file: read-only, hidden, archive, and so on. Unlike the `ConnectionState` attribute, where each enum value was mutually exclusive, the `FileAttributes` enum values can and are intended for combination: A file can be both read-only and hidden. To support this, each enum value is a unique bit.

LISTING 8.15: Using Enums As Flags

```
[Flags] public enum FileAttributes
{
  None =               0,      // 000000000000000
  ReadOnly =           1<<0,   // 000000000000001
  Hidden =             1<<1,   // 000000000000010
  System =             1<<2,   // 000000000000100
  Directory =          1<<4,   // 000000000010000
  Archive =            1<<5,   // 000000000100000
  Device =             1<<6,   // 000000001000000
  Normal =             1<<7,   // 000000010000000
  Temporary =          1<<8,   // 000000100000000
  SparseFile =         1<<9,   // 000001000000000
  ReparsePoint =       1<<10,  // 000010000000000
  Compressed =         1<<11,  // 000100000000000
  Offline =            1<<12,  // 001000000000000
  NotContentIndexed =  1<<13,  // 010000000000000
  Encrypted =          1<<14,  // 100000000000000
}
```

Note that the name of a bit flags enum is usually pluralized, indicating that a value of the type represents a set of flags.

To join enum values you use a bitwise OR operator, and to test for the existence of a particular bit you use the bitwise AND operator, as shown in Listing 8.16.

LISTING 8.16: Using Bitwise OR and AND with Flag Enums

```csharp
using System;
using System.IO;

public class Program
{
  public static void Main()
  {
      // ...

      string fileName = @"enumtest.txt";

      System.IO.FileInfo file =
          new System.IO.FileInfo(fileName);

      file.Attributes = FileAttributes.Hidden |
          FileAttributes.ReadOnly;

      Console.WriteLine("{0} | {1} = {2}",
          FileAttributes.Hidden, FileAttributes.ReadOnly,
          (int)file.Attributes);

      if ( (file.Attributes & FileAttributes.Hidden) !=
          FileAttributes.Hidden)
      {
          throw new Exception("File is not hidden.");
      }

      if (( file.Attributes & FileAttributes.ReadOnly) !=
          FileAttributes.ReadOnly)
      {
          throw new Exception("File is not read-only.");
      }

      // ...
  }
}
```

The results of Listing 8.16 appear in Output 8.5.

OUTPUT 8.5

```
Hidden | ReadOnly = 3
```

Using the bitwise OR operator allows you to set the file to both read-only and hidden. In addition, you can check for specific settings using the bitwise AND operator.

Each value within the enum does not need to correspond to only one flag. It is perfectly reasonable to define additional flags that correspond to frequent combinations of values. Listing 8.17 shows an example.

LISTING 8.17: **Defining Enum Values for Frequent Combinations**

```
[Flags] enum DistributedChannel
{
  None = 0,
  Transacted = 1,
  Queued = 2,
  Encrypted = 4,
  Persisted = 16,
  FaultTolerant =
      Transacted | Queued | Persisted
}
```

It is a good practice to have a zero None member in a flags enum because the initial default value of a field of enum type or an element of an array of enum type is 0. Avoid enum values corresponding to things such as Maximum as the last enum, because Maximum could be interpreted as a valid enum value. To check whether a value is included within an enum use the System.Enum.IsDefined() method.

Guidelines

DO use the FlagsAttribute to mark enums that contain flags.

DO provide a None value equal to 0 for all flag enums.

AVOID creating flag enums where the zero value has a meaning other than "no flags are set".

CONSIDER providing special values for commonly used combinations of flags.

DO NOT include "sentinel" values (such as a value called Maximum); such values can be confusing to the user.

DO use powers of two to ensure that all flag combinations are represented uniquely.

■ ADVANCED TOPIC

FlagsAttribute

If you decide to use bit flag enums, the declaration of the enum should be marked with FlagsAttribute. The attribute appears in square brackets (see Chapter 17), just prior to the enum declaration, as shown in Listing 8.18.

LISTING 8.18: **Using** FlagsAttribute

```csharp
// FileAttributes defined in System.IO.

[Flags] // Decorating an enum with FlagsAttribute.
public enum FileAttributes
{
  ReadOnly =        1<<0,     // 000000000000001
  Hidden =          1<<1,     // 000000000000010
  // ...
}
```

```csharp
using System;
using System.Diagnostics;
using System.IO;

class Program
{
  public static void Main()
  {
      string fileName = @"enumtest.txt";
      FileInfo file = new FileInfo(fileName);
      file.Open(FileMode.Create).Close();

      FileAttributes startingAttributes =
          file.Attributes;

      file.Attributes = FileAttributes.Hidden |
          FileAttributes.ReadOnly;

      Console.WriteLine("\"{0}\" outputs as \"{1}\"",
          file.Attributes.ToString().Replace(",", " |"),
          file.Attributes);

      FileAttributes attributes =
          (FileAttributes) Enum.Parse(typeof(FileAttributes),
          file.Attributes.ToString());

      Console.WriteLine(attributes);

      File.SetAttributes(fileName,
          startingAttributes);
      file.Delete();
```

```
        }
    }
```

The results of Listing 8.18 appear in Output 8.6.

OUTPUT 8.6

```
"ReadOnly | Hidden" outputs as "ReadOnly, Hidden"
ReadOnly, Hidden
```

The attribute documents that the enum values can be combined. Furthermore, it changes the behavior of the `ToString()` and `Parse()` methods. For example, calling `ToString()` on an enum that is decorated with `FlagsAttribute` writes out the strings for each enum flag that is set. In Listing 8.18, `file.Attributes.ToString()` returns `ReadOnly, Hidden` rather than the `3` it would have returned without the `FileAttributes` flag. If two enum values are the same, the `ToString()` call would return the first value. As mentioned earlier, however, you should use this with caution because it is not localizable.

Parsing a value from a string to the enum also works. Each enum value identifier is separated by a comma.

It is important to note that `FlagsAttribute` does not automatically assign unique flag values or check that they have unique values. Doing this wouldn't make sense, since duplicates and combinations are often desirable. Instead, you must assign the values of each enum item explicitly.

SUMMARY

This chapter began with a discussion of how to define custom value types. Because it is easy to write confusing or buggy code when mutating value types, and because value types are usually used to model immutable values, it is a good idea to make value types immutable. We also described how value types are "boxed" when they must be treated polymorphically as reference types.

The idiosyncrasies introduced by boxing are subtle, and the vast majority of them lead to issues at execution time rather than at compile time. Although it is important to know about these in order to try to avoid them, in many ways, focused attention on the potential pitfalls overshadows the usefulness and performance advantages of value types. Programmers should not be overly concerned about using value types. Value types permeate virtually every chapter of this book, and yet the idiosyncrasies do not. We have staged the code surrounding each issue to demonstrate the concern, but in reality, these types of patterns rarely occur. The key to avoiding most of them is to follow the guideline of not creating mutable value types; this is why you don't encounter them within the built-in value types.

Perhaps the only issue to occur with some frequency is repetitive boxing operations within loops. However, generics greatly reduce boxing, and even without them, performance is rarely affected enough to warrant avoidance until a particular algorithm with boxing is identified as a bottleneck.

Furthermore, custom-built structs are relatively rare. They obviously play an important role within C# development, but the number of custom-built structs declared by typical developers is usually tiny compared to the number of custom-built classes. Heavy use of custom-built structs is most common in code targeted at interoperating with unmanaged code.

Guidelines

DO NOT define a struct unless it logically represents a single value, consumes 16 bytes or less of storage, is immutable, and is infrequently boxed.

This chapter also introduced enums. Enumerated types are a standard construct available in many programming languages. They help improve API usability and code readability.

The next chapter presents more guidelines for creating well-formed types, both value types and reference types. It begins by looking at overriding the virtual members of objects and defining operator-overloading methods. These two topics apply to both structs and classes, but they are somewhat more important when completing a struct definition and making it well formed.

9

Well-Formed Types

THE PREVIOUS CHAPTERS COVERED most of the constructs for defining classes and structs. However, several details remain concerning rounding out the type definition with fit-and-finish-type functionality. This chapter introduces how to put the final touches on a type declaration.

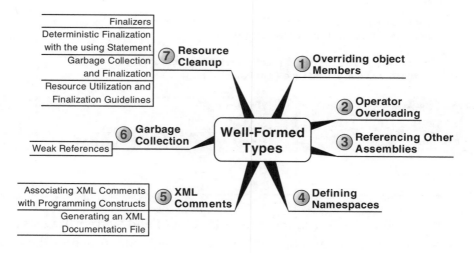

Overriding object Members

Chapter 6 discussed how all classes and structs derive from object. In addition, it reviewed each method available on object and discussed how some of them are virtual. This section discusses the details concerning overriding the virtual methods.

Overriding ToString()

By default, calling ToString() on any object will return the fully qualified name of the class. Calling ToString() on a System.IO.FileStream object will return the string System.IO.FileStream, for example. For some classes, however, ToString() can be more meaningful. On string, for example, ToString() returns the string value itself. Similarly, returning a Contact's name would make more sense. Listing 9.1 overrides ToString() to return a string representation of Coordinate.

LISTING 9.1: Overriding ToString()

```csharp
public struct Coordinate
{
  public Coordinate(Longitude longitude, Latitude latitude)
  {
      _Longitude = longitude;
      _Latitude = latitude;
  }

  public Longitude Longitude { get { return _Longitude; } }
  private readonly Longitude _Longitude;

  public Latitude Latitude { get { return _Latitude; } }
  private readonly Latitude _Latitude;

  public override string ToString()
  {
      return string.Format("{0} {1}", Longitude, Latitude);
  }

  // ...
}
```

Write methods such as Console.WriteLine() and System.Diagnostics .Trace.Write() call an object's ToString() method, so overloading the method often outputs more meaningful information than the default implementation. Therefore, consider overloading the ToString() method whenever relevant diagnostic information can be provided from the output—specifically, when the target audience is developers, since the default object.ToString() output is a type name and is not end-user-friendly. ToString() is useful for debugging from within a developer IDE or writing to a log file. For this reason, keep the strings relatively short (one screen length) so that they are not cut off. However, the lack of localization and other advanced formatting features makes it less suitable for general end-user text display.

Guidelines

DO override ToString() whenever useful developer-oriented diagnostic strings can be returned.

DO try to keep the string returned from ToString() short.

DO NOT return an empty string for null from ToString().

AVOID throwing exceptions or making observable side effects (changing the object state) from ToString().

DO provide an overloaded ToString(string format) or implement IFormattable if the return value is culture-sensitive or requires formatting for example, DateTime).

CONSIDER returning a unique string from ToString() so as to identify the object instance.

Overriding GetHashCode()

Overriding GetHashCode() is more complex than overriding ToString(). Regardless, you should override GetHashCode() when you are overriding Equals(), and there is a compiler warning to indicate this if you don't. Overriding GetHashCode() is also a good practice when you are using it as a key into a hash table collection (System.Collections.Hashtable and System.Collections.Generic.Dictionary, for example).

The purpose of the hash code is to *efficiently balance a hash table* by generating a number that corresponds to the value of an object. Here are some implementation principles for a good GetHashCode() implementation.

- *Required:* Equal objects must have equal hash codes (if a.Equals(b), then a.GetHashCode() == b.GetHashCode()).

- *Required:* GetHashCode()'s returns over the life of a particular object should be constant (the same value), even if the object's data changes. In many cases, you should cache the method return to enforce this.

- *Required:* `GetHashCode()` should not throw any exceptions; `GetHash Code()` must always successfully return a value.

- *Performance:* Hash codes should be unique whenever possible. However, since hash codes return only an `int`, there has to be an overlap in hash codes for objects that have potentially more values than an `int` can hold, which is virtually all types. (An obvious example is `long`, since there are more possible `long` values than an `int` could uniquely identify.)

- *Performance:* The possible hash code values should be distributed evenly over the range of an `int`. For example, creating a hash that doesn't consider the fact that distribution of a string in Latin-based languages primarily centers on the initial 128 ASCII characters would result in a very uneven distribution of string values and would not be a strong `GetHashCode()` algorithm.

- *Performance:* `GetHashCode()` should be optimized for performance. `GetHashCode()` is generally used in `Equals()` implementations to short-circuit a full equals comparison if the hash codes are different. As a result, it is frequently called when the type is used as a key type in dictionary collections.

- *Performance:* Small differences between two objects should result in large differences between hash code values—ideally, a 1-bit difference in the object results in around 16 bits of the hash code changing, on average. This helps ensure that the hash table remains balanced no matter how it is "bucketing" the hash values.

- *Security:* It should be difficult for an attacker to craft an object that has a particular hash code. The attack is to flood a hash table with large amounts of data that all hash to the same value. The hash table implementation can become inefficient, resulting in a possible denial-of-service attack.

These guidelines and rules are, of course, contradictory: It is very difficult to come up with a hash algorithm that is fast and meets all of these guidelines. Like any design problem, you'll have to use a combination of good judgment and realistic performance measurements to come up with a good solution.

Consider the `GetHashCode()` implementation for the `Coordinate` type shown in Listing 9.2.

LISTING 9.2: **Implementing** GetHashCode()

```csharp
public struct Coordinate
{
  public Coordinate(Longitude longitude, Latitude latitude)
  {
      _Longitude = longitude;
      _Latitude = latitude;
  }

  public Longitude Longitude { get { return _Longitude; } }
  private readonly Longitude _Longitude;

  public Latitude Latitude { get { return _Latitude; } }
  private readonly Latitude _Latitude;

  public override int GetHashCode()
  {
      int hashCode = Longitude.GetHashCode();
      // As long as the hash codes are not equal
      if(Longitude.GetHashCode() != Latitude.GetHashCode())
      {
          hashCode ^= Latitude.GetHashCode();   // eXclusive OR
      }
      return hashCode;
  }

  // ...
}
```

Generally, the key is to use the XOR operator over the hash codes from the relevant types, and to make sure the XOR operands are not likely to be close or equal—or else the result will be all zeroes. (In those cases where the operands are close or equal, consider using bitshifts and adds instead.) The alternative operands, AND and OR, have similar restrictions, but the restrictions occur more frequently. Applying AND multiple times tends toward all 0 bits, and applying OR tends toward all 1 bits.

For finer-grained control, split larger-than-int types using the shift operator. For example, GetHashCode() for a long called value is implemented as follows:

```csharp
int GetHashCode() { return ((int)value ^ (int)(value >> 32)) };
```

Also, note that if the base class is not object, base.GetHashCode() should be included in the XOR assignment.

Finally, Coordinate does not cache the value of the hash code. Since each field in the hash code calculation is readonly, the value can't change.

However, implementations should cache the hash code if calculated values could change or if a cached value could offer a significant performance advantage.

Overriding `Equals()`

Overriding `Equals()` without overriding `GetHashCode()` results in a warning such as that shown in Output 9.1.

OUTPUT 9.1

```
warning CS0659: '<Class Name>' overrides Object.Equals(object o) but
does not override Object.GetHashCode()
```

Generally, developers expect overriding `Equals()` to be trivial, but it includes a surprising number of subtleties that require careful thought and testing.

Object Identity versus Equal Object Values

Two references are identical if both refer to the same instance. `object` (and by inheritance, all derived types) includes a static method called `ReferenceEquals()` that explicitly checks for this object identity (see Figure 9.1).

However, reference equality is not the only type of equality. Two object instances can also be called equal if the values of some or all of their members are equal. Consider the comparison of two `ProductSerialNumbers` shown in Listing 9.3.

LISTING 9.3: Overriding the Equality Operator

```csharp
public sealed class ProductSerialNumber
{
    public ProductSerialNumber(
        string productSeries, int model, long id)
    {
        ProductSeries = productSeries;
        Model = model;
        Id = id;
    }

    public readonly string ProductSeries;
    public readonly int Model;
    public readonly long Id;
```

FIGURE 9.1: Identity

```csharp
public override int GetHashCode()
{
    int hashCode = ProductSeries.GetHashCode();
    hashCode ^= Model; // Xor (eXclusive OR)
    hashCode ^= Id.GetHashCode(); // Xor (eXclusive OR)
    return hashCode;
}

public override bool Equals(object obj)
{
    if (obj == null)
    {
        return false;
```

```csharp
        }
        if (ReferenceEquals(this, obj))
        {
            return true;
        }
        if (this.GetType() != obj.GetType())
        {
            return false;
        }
        return Equals((ProductSerialNumber)obj);
    }

    public bool Equals(ProductSerialNumber obj)
    {
        // STEP 3: Possibly check for equivalent hash codes
        // if (this.GetHashCode() != obj.GetHashCode())
        // {
        //     return false;
        // }

        // STEP 4: Check base.Equals if base overrides Equals()
        // System.Diagnostics.Debug.Assert(
        //     base.GetType() != typeof(object));
        // if ( base.Equals(obj) )
        // {
        //     return false;
        // }

        // STEP 1: Check for null
        return ((obj != null)
            // STEP 5: Compare identifying fields for equality.
            && (ProductSeries == obj.ProductSeries) &&
            (Model == obj.Model) &&
            (Id == obj.Id));
    }

    public static bool operator ==(
        ProductSerialNumber leftHandSide,
        ProductSerialNumber rightHandSide)
    {

        // Check if leftHandSide is null.
        // (operator== would be recursive)
        if (ReferenceEquals(leftHandSide, null))
        {
            // Return true if rightHandSide is also null
            // but false otherwise.
            return ReferenceEquals(rightHandSide, null);
        }

        return (leftHandSide.Equals(rightHandSide));
    }
```

```csharp
        public static bool operator !=(
            ProductSerialNumber leftHandSide,
            ProductSerialNumber rightHandSide)
    {
        return !(leftHandSide == rightHandSide);
    }
}
```

```csharp
class Program
{
    static void Main()
    {
        ProductSerialNumber serialNumber1 =
            new ProductSerialNumber("PV", 1000, 09187234);
        ProductSerialNumber serialNumber2 = serialNumber1;
        ProductSerialNumber serialNumber3 =
            new ProductSerialNumber("PV", 1000, 09187234);

        // These serial numbers ARE the same object identity.
        if(!ProductSerialNumber.ReferenceEquals(serialNumber1,
            serialNumber2))
        {
            throw new Exception(
                "serialNumber1 does NOT " +
                "reference equal serialNumber2");
        }
        // and, therefore, they are equal
        else if(!serialNumber1.Equals(serialNumber2))
        {
            throw new Exception(
                "serialNumber1 does NOT equal serialNumber2");
        }
        else
        {
            Console.WriteLine(
                "serialNumber1 reference equals serialNumber2");
            Console.WriteLine(
                "serialNumber1 equals serialNumber2");
        }


        // These serial numbers are NOT the same object identity.
        if (ProductSerialNumber.ReferenceEquals(serialNumber1,
                serialNumber3))
        {
            throw new Exception(
                "serialNumber1 DOES reference " +
                "equal serialNumber3");
        }
        // but they are equal (assuming Equals is overloaded).
        else if(!serialNumber1.Equals(serialNumber3) ||
            serialNumber1 != serialNumber3)
        {
```

```
        throw new Exception(
            "serialNumber1 does NOT equal serialNumber3");
    }

    Console.WriteLine( "serialNumber1 equals serialNumber3" );
  }
}
```

The results of Listing 9.3 appear in Output 9.2.

OUTPUT 9.2

```
serialNumber1 reference equals serialNumber2
serialNumber1 equals serialNumber3
```

As the last assertion demonstrates with `ReferenceEquals()`, `serialNumber1` and `serialNumber3` are not the same reference. However, the code constructs them with the same values and both logically associate with the same physical product. If one instance was created from data in the database and another was created from manually entered data, you would expect the instances would be equal, and therefore that the product would not be duplicated (reentered) in the database. Two identical references are obviously equal; however, two different objects could be equal but not reference equal. Such objects will not have identical object identities, but they may have key data that identifies them as being equal objects.

Only reference types can be reference equal, thereby supporting the concept of identity. Calling `ReferenceEquals()` on value types will always return `false` because value types are boxed when they are converted to `object` for the call. Even when `ReferenceEquals()` passes the same variable in both (value type) parameters to `ReferenceEquals()`, the result will still be `false` because the values are boxed independently. Listing 9.4 demonstrates this behavior. Since each argument is put into a "different box," they are never reference equal.

> ■ **NOTE**
>
> `ReferenceEquals()` on value types will always return `false`.

LISTING 9.4: Value Types Never Reference Equal Themselves

```csharp
public struct Coordinate
{
  public Coordinate(Longitude longitude, Latitude latitude)
  {
      _Longitude = longitude;
      _Latitude = latitude;
  }

  public Longitude Longitude { get { return _Longitude; } }
  private readonly Longitude _Longitude;

  public Latitude Latitude { get { return _Latitude; } }
  private readonly Latitude _Latitude;

  // ...
}
```

```csharp
class Program
{
  public void Main()
  {
      //...

      Coordinate coordinate1 =
          new Coordinate( new Longitude(48, 52),
                          new Latitude(-2, -20));

      // Value types will never be reference equal.
      if ( Coordinate.ReferenceEquals(coordinate1,
          coordinate1) )
      {
          throw new Exception(
              "coordinate1 reference equals coordinate1");
      }

      Console.WriteLine(
          "coordinate1 does NOT reference equal itself" );
  }
}
```

In contrast to the definition of Coordinate as a reference type in Chapter 8, the definition going forward is that of a value type (struct) because the combination of Longitude and Latitude data is logically thought of as a value and the size is less than 16 bytes. (In Chapter 8, Coordinate aggregated Angle rather than Longitude and Latitude.) A contributing factor to declaring Coordinate as a value type is that it is a (complex) numeric value that has particular operations on it. In contrast, a reference type such as `Employee` is not a value that you manipulate numerically, but rather refers to an object in real life.

Implementing *Equals()*

To determine whether two objects are equal (they have the same identifying data), you use an object's `Equals()` method. The implementation of this virtual method on `object` uses `ReferenceEquals()` to evaluate equality. Since this implementation is often inadequate, it is necessary to sometimes override `Equals()` with a more appropriate implementation.

> ■ **NOTE**
>
> The implementation of `object.Equals()`, the default implementation on all objects before overloading, relies on `ReferenceEquals()` alone.

For objects to *equal* one another, the expectation is that the identifying data within them is equal. For `ProductSerialNumbers`, for example, the `ProductSeries`, `Model`, and `Id` must be the same; however, for an `Employee` object, perhaps comparing `EmployeeIds` would be sufficient for equality. To correct `object.Equals()` implementation, it is necessary to override it. Value types, for example, override the `Equals()` implementation to instead use the fields that the type includes.

The steps for overriding `Equals()` are as follows.

1. Check for `null`.
2. Check for reference equality if the type is a reference type.
3. Check for equivalent types.
4. Invoke a typed helper method that can treat the operand as the compared type rather than an object (see the `Equals(Coordinate obj)` method in Listing 9.5).
5. Possibly check for equivalent hash codes to short-circuit an extensive, field-by-field comparison. (Two objects that are equal cannot have different hash codes.)
6. Check `base.Equals()` if the base class overrides `Equals()`.
7. Compare each identifying field for equality.

8. Override `GetHashCode()`.

9. Override the `==` and `!=` operators (see the next section).

Listing 9.5 shows a sample `Equals()` implementation.

LISTING 9.5: Overriding `Equals()`

```csharp
public struct Longitude
{
  // ...
}
```

```csharp
public struct Latitude
{
  // ...
}
```

```csharp
public struct Coordinate
{
    public Coordinate(Longitude longitude, Latitude latitude)
    {
        _Longitude = longitude;
        _Latitude = latitude;
    }

    public Longitude Longitude { get { return _Longitude; } }
    private readonly Longitude _Longitude;

    public Latitude Latitude { get { return _Latitude; } }
    private readonly Latitude _Latitude;

    public override bool Equals(object obj)
    {
        // STEP 1: Check for null
        if (obj == null)
        {
            return false;
        }
        // STEP 3: equivalent data types
        // Can be avoided if type is sealed.
        if (this.GetType() != obj.GetType())
        {
            return false;
        }
        return Equals((Coordinate)obj);
    }
    public bool Equals(Coordinate obj)
    {
        // STEP 1: Check for null if a reference type
        // (e.g., a reference type)
        // if (obj == null)
        // {
```

```
//      return false;
// }

// STEP 2: Check for ReferenceEquals if this
// is a reference type
// if ( ReferenceEquals(this, obj))
// {
//   return true;
// }

// STEP 4: Possibly check for equivalent hash codes
// if (this.GetHashCode() != obj.GetHashCode())
// {
//     return false;
// }

// STEP 5: Check base.Equals if base overrides Equals()
// System.Diagnostics.Debug.Assert(
//     base.GetType() != typeof(object) );
// if ( !base.Equals(obj) )
// {
//     return false;
// }

// STEP 6: Compare identifying fields for equality
//         using an overload of Equals on Longitude.
return ( (Longitude.Equals(obj.Longitude)) &&
    (Latitude.Equals(obj.Latitude)) );
}

// STEP 7: Override GetHashCode.
public override int GetHashCode()
{
    int hashCode = Longitude.GetHashCode();
    hashCode ^= Latitude.GetHashCode(); // Xor (eXclusive OR)
    return hashCode;
}

}
```

In this implementation, the first two checks are relatively obvious. However, it is interesting to point out that step 3 can be avoided if the type is sealed.

Steps 4–6 occur in an overload of Equals() that takes the Coordinate data type specifically. This way, a comparison of two Coordinates will avoid Equals(object obj) and its GetType() check altogether.

Since GetHashCode() is not cached and is no more efficient than step 5, the GetHashCode() comparison is commented out. Similarly, base.Equals()

is not used since the base class is not overriding Equals(). (The assertion checks that base is not of type object, however it does not check that the base class overrides Equals(), which is required to appropriately call base.Equals().) Regardless, since GetHashCode() does not necessarily return a unique value (it only identifies when operands are different), on its own it does not conclusively identify equal objects.

Like GetHashCode(), Equals() should also never throw any exceptions. It is valid to compare any object with any other object, and doing so should never result in an exception.

Guidelines

DO implement GetHashCode(), Equals(), the == operator, and the != operator together, not one without the other three.

DO use the same algorithm when implementing Equals(), ==, and !=.

AVOID throwing exceptions from implementations of GetHashCode(), Equals(), ==, and !=.

AVOID overloading equality operators on mutable reference types or if the implementation would be significantly slower.

DO implement all the equality-related methods when implementing IComparable.

Operator Overloading

The preceding section looked at overriding Equals() and provided the guideline that the class should also implement == and !=. The term for implementing any operator is *operator overloading,* and this section describes how to do this, not only for == and !=, but also for other supported operators.

For example, string provides a + operator that concatenates two strings. This is perhaps not surprising, because string is a predefined type, so it could possibly have special compiler support. However, C# provides for adding + operator support to a class or struct. In fact, all operators are supported except x.y, f(x), new, typeof, default, checked, unchecked, delegate, is, as, =, and =>. One particularly noteworthy operator that cannot be implemented is the assignment operator; there is no way to change the behavior of the = operator.

Before going through the exercise of implementing an operator overload, consider the fact that such operators are not discoverable through IntelliSense. Unless the intent is for a type to act like a primitive type (a numeric type, for example), avoid overloading an operator.

Comparison Operators (==, !=, <, >, <=, >=)

Once `Equals()` is overridden, there is a possible inconsistency. Two objects could return `true` for `Equals()` but `false` for the == operator because == performs a reference equality check by default as well. To correct this it is important to overload the equals (==) and not equals (!=) operators as well.

For the most part, the implementation for these operators can delegate the logic to `Equals()`, or vice versa. However, some initial null checks are required first (see Listing 9.6).

LISTING 9.6: Implementing the == and != Operators

```csharp
public sealed class Coordinate
{

  // ...

  public static bool operator ==(
      Coordinate leftHandSide,
      Coordinate rightHandSide)
  {

      // Check if leftHandSide is null.
      // (operator== would be recursive)
      if (ReferenceEquals(leftHandSide, null))
      {
          // Return true if rightHandSide is also null
          // but false otherwise.
          return ReferenceEquals(rightHandSide, null);
      }

      return (leftHandSide.Equals(rightHandSide));
  }

  public static bool operator !=(
      Coordinate leftHandSide,
      Coordinate rightHandSide)
  {
      return !(leftHandSide == rightHandSide);
  }

}
```

Note that in this example, `Coordinate` is a class, not a struct. Also note that to perform the null checks, you cannot use an equality check for null (`leftHandSide == null`). Doing so would recursively call back into the method, resulting in a loop until the stack overflows. To avoid this you call `ReferenceEquals()` to check for null.

Binary Operators (+, -, *, /, %, &, |, ^, <<, >>)

You can add an `Arc` to a `Coordinate`. However, the code so far provides no support for the addition operator. Instead, you need to define such a method, as Listing 9.7 shows.

LISTING 9.7: Adding an Operator

```csharp
struct Arc
{
  public Arc(
      Longitude longitudeDifference,
      Latitude latitudeDifference)
  {
      _LongitudeDifference = longitudeDifference;
      _LatitudeDifference = latitudeDifference;
  }

  public Longitude LongitudeDifference
  {
      get
      {
          return _LongitudeDifference;
      }
  }
  private readonly Longitude _LongitudeDifference;

  public Latitude LatitudeDifference
  {
      get
      {
          return _LatitudeDifference;
      }
  }
  private readonly Latitude _LatitudeDifference;
}

struct Coordinate
{
  // ...
  public static Coordinate operator +(
      Coordinate source, Arc arc)
  {
```

```
            Coordinate result = new Coordinate(
                new Longitude(
                    source.Longitude + arc.LongitudeDifference),
                new Latitude(
                    source.Latitude + arc.LatitudeDifference));
            return result;
        }
    }
```

The +, -, *, /, %, &, |, ^, <<, and >> operators are implemented as binary static methods where at least one parameter is of the containing type. The method name is the operator prefixed by the word *operator* as a keyword. As shown in Listing 9.8, given the definition of the - and + binary operators, you can add and subtract an Arc to and from the coordinate.

Note that Longitude and Latitude will also require implementations of the + operator because they are called by source.Longitude + arc. LongitudeDifference and source.Latitude + arc.LatitudeDifference.

LISTING 9.8: Calling the – and + Binary Operators

```
public class Program
{
    public static void Main()
    {
        Coordinate coordinate1,coordinate2;
        coordinate1 = new Coordinate(
            new Longitude(48, 52), new Latitude(-2, -20));
        Arc arc = new Arc(new Longitude(3), new Latitude(1));

        coordinate2 = coordinate1 + arc;
        Console.WriteLine(coordinate2);

        coordinate2 = coordinate2 - arc;
        Console.WriteLine(coordinate2);

        coordinate2 += arc;
        Console.WriteLine(coordinate2);
    }
}
```

The results of Listing 9.8 appear in Output 9.3.

OUTPUT 9.3

```
51° 52' 0 E   -1° -20' 0 N
48° 52' 0 E   -2° -20' 0 N
51° 52' 0 E   -1° -20' 0 N
```

For `Coordinate`, implement the – and + operators to return coordinate locations after adding/subtracting `Arc`. This allows you to string multiple operators and operands together, as in `result = ((coordinate1 + arc1) + arc2) + arc3`. And, by supporting the same operators (+/-) on `Arc` (see Listing 9.9), you could eliminate the parenthesis.

This works because the result of the first operand (`arc1 + arc2`) is another `Arc`, which you can then add to the next operand of type `Arc` or `Coordinate`.

In contrast, consider if you provided a – operator that had two `Coordinates` as parameters and returned a `double` corresponding to the distance between the two `coordinates`. Adding a `double` to a `Coordinate` is undefined, and therefore, you could not string operators and operands. Caution is in order when defining operators that return a different type, because doing so is counterintuitive.

Combining Assignment with Binary Operators (+=, -=, *=, /=, %=, &=…)

As previously mentioned, there is no support for overloading the assignment operator. However, assignment operators in combination with binary operators (+=, -=, *=, /=, %=, &=, |=, ^=, <<=, and >>=) are effectively overloaded when overloading the binary operator. Given the definition of a binary operator without the assignment, C# automatically allows for assignment in combination with the operator. Using the definition of `Coordinate` in Listing 9.7, therefore, you can have code such as:

```
coordinate += arc;
```

which is equivalent to the following:

```
coordinate = coordinate + arc;
```

Conditional Logical Operators (&&, ||)

Like assignment operators, conditional logical operators cannot be overloaded explicitly. However, since the logical operators & and | can be overloaded, and the conditional operators comprise the logical operators, effectively it is possible to overload conditional operators. x && y is processed as x & y, where y must evaluate to `true`. Similarly, x || y is processed as x | y only if x is `false`. To enable support for evaluating a type to `true` or `false`—in an `if` statement, for example—it is necessary to override the `true`/`false` unary operators.

Unary Operators (+, -, !, ~, ++, --, `true`, `false`)

Overloading unary operators is very similar to overloading binary operators, except that they take only one parameter, also of the containing type. Listing 9.9 overloads the + and – operators for `Longitude` and `Latitude` and then uses these operators when overloading the same operators in `Arc`.

LISTING 9.9: Overloading the – and + Unary Operators

```csharp
public struct Latitude
{
    // ...
    public static Latitude operator -(Latitude latitude)
    {
        return new Latitude(-latitude.DecimalDegrees);
    }
    public static Latitude operator +(Latitude latitude)
    {
        return latitude;
    }
}

public struct Longitude
{
    // ...
    public static Longitude operator -(Longitude longitude)
    {
        return new Longitude(-longitude.DecimalDegrees);
    }
    public static Longitude operator +(Longitude longitude)
    {
        return longitude;
    }
}

public struct Arc
{
    // ...
    public static Arc operator -(Arc arc)
    {
        // Uses unary - operator defined on
        // Longitude and Latitude
        return new Arc(-arc.LongitudeDifference,
            -arc.LatitudeDifference);
    }
    public static Arc operator +(Arc arc)
    {
        return arc;
    }
}
```

Just as with numeric types, the + operator in this listing doesn't have any effect and is provided for symmetry.

Overloading `true` and `false` has the additional requirement that they both be overloaded. The signatures are the same as other operator overloads; however, the return must be a `bool`, as demonstrated in Listing 9.10.

LISTING 9.10: Overloading the `true` and `false` Operators

```
public static bool operator false(IsValid item)
{
    // ...
}
public static bool operator true(IsValid item)
{
    // ...
}
```

You can use types with overloaded `true` and `false` operators in `if`, `do`, `while`, and `for` controlling expressions.

Conversion Operators

Currently, there is no support in `Longitude`, `Latitude`, and `Coordinate` for casting to an alternate type. For example, there is no way to cast a `double` into a `Longitude` or `Latitude` instance. Similarly, there is no support for assigning a `Coordinate` using a `string`. Fortunately, C# provides for the definition of methods specifically to handle the converting of one type to another. Furthermore, the method declaration allows for specifying whether the conversion is implicit or explicit.

■ ADVANCED TOPIC

Cast Operator (())

Implementing the explicit and implicit conversion operators is not technically overloading the cast operator (()). However, this is effectively what takes place, so *defining a cast operator* is common terminology for implementing explicit or implicit conversion.

Defining a conversion operator is similar in style to defining any other operator, except that the "operator" is the resultant type of the conversion. Additionally, the `operator` keyword follows a keyword that indicates whether the conversion is implicit or explicit (see Listing 9.11).

LISTING 9.11: **Providing an Implicit Conversion between** Latitude **and** double

```
public struct Latitude
{
    // ...

    public Latitude(double decimalDegrees)
    {
        _DecimalDegrees = Normalize(decimalDegrees);
    }

    public double DecimalDegrees
    {
        get { return _DecimalDegrees; }
    }
    private readonly double _DecimalDegrees;

    // ...

    public static implicit operator double(Latitude latitude)
    {
        return latitude.DecimalDegrees;
    }
    public static implicit operator Latitude(double degrees)
    {
        return new Latitude(degrees);
    }

    // ...
}
```

With these conversion operators, you now can convert doubles implicitly to and from Latitude objects. Assuming similar conversions exist for Longitude, you can simplify the creation of a Coordinate object by specifying the decimal degrees portion of each coordinate portion (for example, coordinate = new Coordinate(43, 172);).

■■ **NOTE**

When implementing a conversion operator, either the return or the parameter must be of the enclosing type—in support of encapsulation. C# does not allow you to specify conversions outside the scope of the converted type.

Guidelines for Conversion Operators

The difference between defining an implicit and an explicit conversion operator centers on preventing an unintentional implicit conversion that results in undesirable behavior. You should be aware of two possible consequences of using the explicit conversion operator. First, conversion operators that throw exceptions should always be explicit. For example, it is highly likely that a string will not conform to the appropriate format that a conversion from `string` to `Coordinate` requires. Given the chance of a failed conversion, you should define the particular conversion operator as explicit, thereby requiring that you be intentional about the conversion and that you ensure that the format is correct, or that you provide code to handle the possible exception. Frequently, the pattern for conversion is that one direction (`string` to `Coordinate`) is explicit and the reverse (`Coordinate` to `string`) is implicit.

A second consideration is the fact that some conversions will be lossy. Converting from a `float` (4.2) to an `int` is entirely valid, assuming an awareness of the fact that the decimal portion of the `float` will be lost. Any conversions that will lose data and will not successfully convert back to the original type should be defined as explicit. If an explicit cast is unexpectedly lossy or invalid, consider throwing a `System.InvalidCastException`.

Guidelines

DO NOT provide an implicit conversion operator if the conversion is lossy.

DO NOT throw exceptions from implicit conversions.

Referencing Other Assemblies

Instead of placing all code into one monolithic binary file, C# and the underlying CLI platform allow you to spread code across multiple assemblies. This enables you to reuse assemblies across multiple executables.

■ BEGINNER TOPIC

Class Libraries

The HelloWorld.exe program is one of the most trivial programs you can write. Real-world programs are more complex, and as complexity increases, it helps to organize the complexity by breaking programs into multiple parts. To do this, developers move portions of a program into separate compiled units called **class libraries** or, simply, **libraries.** Programs then reference and rely on class libraries to provide parts of their functionality. The power of this concept is that two programs can rely on the same class library, thereby sharing the functionality of that class library across the two programs and reducing the total amount of code needed.

In other words, it is possible to write features once, place them into a class library, and allow multiple programs to include those features by referencing the same class library. Later on, when developers fix a bug or add functionality to the class library, all the programs will have access to the increased functionality, just because they continue to reference the now improved class library.

To reuse the code within a different assembly, it is necessary to reference the assembly when running the C# compiler. Generally, the referenced assembly is a class library, and creating a class library requires a different assembly target from the default console executable targets you created thus far.

Changing the Assembly Target

The compiler allows you to create four different assembly types via the `/target` option.

- *Console executable:* This is the default type of assembly, and all compilation thus far has been to a console executable. (Leaving off the `/target` option or specifying `/target:exe` creates a console executable.)
- *Class library:* Classes that are shared across multiple executables are generally defined in a class library (`/target:library`).
- *Windows executable:* Windows executables are designed to run in the Microsoft Windows family of operating systems and outside the command console (`/target:winexe`).

- *Module:* In order to facilitate multiple languages within the same assembly, code can be compiled to a module and multiple modules can be combined to form an assembly (/target:module).

Assemblies to be shared across multiple applications are generally compiled as class libraries. Consider, for example, a library dedicated to functionality around longitude and latitude coordinates. To compile the Coordinate, Longitude, and Latitude classes into their own library, you use the command line shown in Output 9.4.

OUTPUT 9.4

```
>csc /target:library /out:Coordinates.dll Coordinate.cs IAngle.cs
Latitude.cs Longitude.cs Arc.cs
Microsoft (R) Visual C# 2010 Compiler version 4.0.20506.1
Copyright (C) Microsoft Corporation. All rights reserved.
```

Assuming you use .NET and the C# compiler is in the path, this builds an assembly library called Coordinates.dll.

Referencing an Assembly

To access code within a different assembly, the C# compiler allows the developer to reference the assembly on the command line. The option is /reference (/r is the abbreviation), followed by the list of references. The Program class listing from Listing 9.8 uses the Coordinate class, and if you place this into a separate executable, you reference Coordinates.dll using the .NET command line shown in Output 9.5.

OUTPUT 9.5

```
csc.exe /R:Coordinates.dll Program.cs
```

The Mono command line appears in Output 9.6.

OUTPUT 9.6

```
msc.exe /R:Coordinates.dll Program.cs
```

Encapsulation of Types

Just as classes serve as an encapsulation boundary for behavior and data, assemblies provide a similar boundary among groups of types. Developers can break a system into assemblies and then share those assemblies with multiple applications or integrate them with assemblies provided by third parties.

By default, a class without any access modifier is defined as `internal`.[1] The result is that the class is inaccessible from outside the assembly. Even though another assembly references the assembly containing the class, all internal classes within the referenced assemblies will be inaccessible.

Just as `private` and `protected` provide levels of encapsulation to members within a class C# supports the use of access modifiers at the class level for control over the encapsulation of the classes within an assembly. The access modifiers available are `public` and `internal`, and in order to expose a class outside the assembly, the assembly must be marked as `public`. Therefore, before compiling the `Coordinates.dll` assembly, it is necessary to modify the type declarations as `public` (see Listing 9.12).

LISTING 9.12: **Making Types Available outside an Assembly**

```
public struct Coordinate
{
  // ...
}
```

```
public struct Latitude
{
  // ...
}
```

```
public struct Longitude
{
  // ...
}
```

```
public struct Arc
{
  // ...
}
```

Similarly, declarations such as `class` and `enum` can also be either `public` or `internal`.

---

1. Excluding nested types, which are `private` by default.

■ ADVANCED TOPIC

Additional Class Access Modifiers

You can decorate nested classes with any access modifier available to other class members (`private`, for example). However, outside the class scope, the only available access modifiers are `public` and `internal`.

The internal access modifier is not limited to type declarations. It is also available on type members. Therefore, you can designate a type as `public` but mark specific methods within the type as `internal` so that the members are available only from within the assembly. It is not possible for the members to have a greater accessibility than the type. If the class is declared as `internal`, public members on the type will be accessible only from within the assembly.

`protected internal` is another type member access modifier. Members with an accessibility modifier of `protected internal` will be accessible from all locations within the containing assembly *and* from classes that derive from the type, even if the derived class is not in the same assembly. The default state is `private`, so when you add an access modifier (other than `public`), the member becomes slightly more visible. Similarly, adding two modifiers compounds the effect.

■ NOTE

Members with an accessibility modifier of `protected internal` will be accessible from all locations within the containing assembly *and* from classes that derive from the type, even if the derived class is not in the same assembly.

■ BEGINNER TOPIC

Type Member Accessibility Modifiers

The full list of access modifiers appears in Table 9.1.

TABLE 9.1: Accessibility Modifiers

Modifier	Description
`public`	Declares that the member is accessible anywhere the type is accessible. If the class is `internal`, the member will be internally visible. Public members will be accessible from outside the assembly if the containing type is public.
`internal`	The member is accessible from within the assembly only.
`private`	The member is accessible from within the containing type, but inaccessible otherwise.
`protected`	The member is accessible within the containing type and any subtypes derived from it, regardless of assembly.
`protected internal`	The member is accessible from anywhere within the containing assembly *and* from any types derived from the containing type, even if the derived types are within a different assembly.

Defining Namespaces

As mentioned in Chapter 2, all data types are identified by the combination of their namespace and their name. In fact, in the CLR there is no such thing as a "namespace." The type's name actually is the fully qualified type name. For the classes you defined earlier, there was no explicit namespace declaration. Classes such as these are automatically declared as members of the default global namespace. It is likely that such classes will experience a name collision, which occurs when you attempt to define two classes with the same name. Once you begin referencing other assemblies from third parties, the likelihood of a name collision increases even further.

More importantly, there are thousands of types in the .NET Framework and multiple orders of magnitude more outside the framework. Finding the right type for a particular problem, therefore, could potentially be a significant battle.

The resolution to both of these problems is to organize all the types, grouping them into logical related categories called namespaces. For example, classes outside the `System` namespace are generally placed into a namespace corresponding with the company, product name, or both. Classes from Addison-Wesley, for example, are placed into an `Awl` or `AddisonWesley` namespace, and classes from Microsoft (not `System` classes) are located in the `Microsoft` namespace. The second level of a namespace should be a stable product name that will not vary between versions. Stability, in fact, is key at all levels. Changing a namespace name is a version-incompatible change that should be avoided. For this reason, avoid using volatile names (organization hierarchy, fleeting brands, and so on) with a namespace name.

Namespaces should be PascalCased, but if your brand uses nontraditional casing, it is acceptable to use the brand casing. (Consistency is key, so if that will be problematic—with Pascal or brand-based casing—favor the use of whichever will produce the greater consistency.) You should use the `namespace` keyword to create a namespace and to assign a class to it, as shown in Listing 9.13.

LISTING 9.13: Defining a Namespace

```
// Define the namespace AddisonWesley
namespace AddisonWesley
{
  class Program
  {
    // ...
  }
}
// End of AddisonWesley namespace declaration
```

All content between the namespace declaration's curly braces will then belong within the specified namespace. In Listing 9.13, `Program` is placed into the namespace `AddisonWesley`, making its full name `AddisonWesley.Program`.

■ NOTE

In the CLR there is no such thing as a "namespace." The type's name actually is the fully qualified type name.

Like classes, namespaces support nesting. This provides for a hierarchical organization of classes. All the `System` classes relating to network APIs are in the namespace `System.Net`, for example, and those relating to the Web are in `System.Web`.

There are two ways to nest namespaces. The first way is to nest them within one another (similar to classes), as demonstrated in Listing 9.14.

LISTING 9.14: **Nesting Namespaces within One Another**

```csharp
// Define the namespace AddisonWesley
namespace AddisonWesley
{
  // Define the namespace AddisonWesley.Michaelis
  namespace Michaelis
  {
    // Define the namespace
    // AddisonWesley.Michaelis.EssentialCSharp
    namespace EssentialCSharp
    {
      // Declare the class
      // AddisonWesley.Michaelis.EssentialCSharp.Program
      class Program
      {
        // ...
      }
    }
  }
}
// End of AddisonWesley namespace declaration
```

Such a nesting will assign the `Program` class to the `AddisonWesley .Michaelis.EssentialCSharp` namespace.

The second way is to use the full namespace in a single namespace declaration in which a period separates each identifier, as shown in Listing 9.15.

LISTING 9.15: **Nesting Namespaces Using a Period to Separate Each Identifier**

```csharp
// Define the namespace AddisonWesley.Michaelis.EssentialCSharp
namespace AddisonWesley.Michaelis.EssentialCSharp
{
  class Program
  {
    // ...
  }
}
// End of AddisonWesley namespace declaration
```

Regardless of whether a namespace declaration follows Listing 9.14, Listing 9.15, or a combination of the two, the resultant CIL code will be identical. The same namespace may occur multiple times, in multiple files, and even across assemblies. For example, with the convention of one-to-one correlation between files and classes, you can define each class in its own file and surround it with the same namespace declaration.

Given that namespaces are key for organizing types, it is frequently helpful to use the namespace for organizing all the class files. For this reason, it is helpful to create a folder for each namespace, placing a class such as `AddisonWesley.Fezzik.Services.Registration` into a folder hierarchy corresponding to the name.

When using Visual Studio projects, if the project name is `AddisonWesley.Fezzik`, create one subfolder called `Services` into which `RegistrationService.cs` is placed; then create another subfolder—`Data`, for example—into which you place classes relating to entities within the program—`RealestateProperty`, `Buyer`, and `Seller`, for example.

Guidelines

DO prefix namespace names with a company name to prevent namespaces from different companies having the same name.

DO use a stable, version-independent product name at the second level of a namespace name.

DO NOT define types without placing them into a namespace.

CONSIDER creating a folder structure that matches the namespace hierarchy.

Namespace Alias Qualifier

Namespaces on their own deal with the vast majority of naming conflicts that might arise. However, sometimes (albeit rarely) conflict can arise because of an overlap in the namespace and class names. To account for this, the C# 2.0 compiler includes an option for providing an alias with the `/reference` option. For example, if the assemblies `CoordinatesPlus.dll` and `Coordinates.dll` have an overlapping type of `Arc`, you can reference both assemblies on the command line by assigning one or both references with a **namespace alias qualifier** that further distinguishes one class from the other. The results of such a reference appear in Output 9.7.

OUTPUT 9.7

```
csc.exe /R:CoordPlus=CoordinatesPlus.dll /R:Coordinates.dll Program.cs
```

However, adding the alias during compilation is not sufficient on its own. In order to refer to classes in the aliased assembly, it is necessary to provide an `extern` directive that declares that the namespace alias qualifier is provided externally to the source code (see Listing 9.16).

LISTING 9.16: Using the `extern` Alias Directive

```
// extern must precede all other namespace elements
extern alias CoordPlus;

using System;
using CoordPlus::AddisonWesley.Michaelis.EssentialCSharp
// Equivalent also allowed
// using CoordPlus.AddisonWesley.Michaelis.EssentialCSharp

using global::AddisonWesley.Michaelis.EssentialCSharp
// Equivalent NOT allowed
// using global.AddisonWesley.Michaelis.EssentialCSharp

public class Program
{
  // ...
}
```

Once the `extern` alias for `CoordPlus` appears, you can reference the namespace using `CoordPlus`, followed by either two colons or a period.

To ensure that the lookup for the type occurs in the global namespace, C# 2.0 allows items to have the `global::` qualifier (but not `global.` because it could imaginably conflict with a real namespace of `global`).

XML Comments

Chapter 1 introduced comments. However, you can use XML comments for more than just notes to other developers reviewing the source code. XML-based comments follow a practice popularized with Java. Although the C# compiler ignores all comments as far as the resultant executable goes, the developer can use command-line options to instruct the compiler[2] to extract the XML comments into a separate XML file. By taking advantage of the XML file generation, the developer can generate documentation of the API from the XML comments. In addition, C# editors can parse the XML comments in the code and display them to developers

---

2. The C# standard does not specify whether the C# compiler or a separate utility takes care of extracting the XML data. However, all mainstream C# compilers include the functionality via a compile switch instead of within an additional utility.

as distinct regions (for example, as a different color from the rest of the code), or parse the XML comment data elements and display them to the developer.

Figure 9.2 demonstrates how an IDE can take advantage of XML comments to assist the developer with a tip about the code he is trying to write.

```
/// <summary>
/// Display the text specified
/// </summary>
/// <param name="text">The text to be displayed in the console.</param>
private static void Display(string text)
{
    Console.WriteLine(text);
}

static void Main()
{
    Display(|
        void Program.Display(string text)
        Display the text specified
        text: The text to be displayed in the console.
}
```

FIGURE 9.2: XML Comments As Tips in Visual Studio IDE

These coding tips offer significant assistance in large programs, especially when multiple developers share code. For this to work, however, the developer obviously must take the time to enter the XML comments within the code and then direct the compiler to create the XML file. The next section explains how to accomplish this.

Associating XML Comments with Programming Constructs

Consider the listing of the DataStorage class, as shown in Listing 9.17.

LISTING 9.17: Commenting Code with XML Comments

```
/// <summary>
/// DataStorage is used to persist and retrieve
/// employee data from the files.
/// </summary>
class DataStorage
```

```
{
    /// <summary>
    /// Save an employee object to a file
    /// named with the Employee name.
    /// </summary>
    /// <remarks>
    /// This method uses
    /// <seealso cref="System.IO.FileStream"/>
    /// in addition to
    /// <seealso cref="System.IO.StreamWriter"/>
    /// </remarks>
    /// <param name="employee">
    /// The employee to persist to a file</param>
    /// <date>January 1, 2000</date>
    public static void Store(Employee employee)
    {
        // ...
    }

    /**    <summary>
     *    Loads up an employee object
     *    </summary>
     *    <remarks>
     *    This method uses
     *    <seealso cref="System.IO.FileStream"/>
     *    in addition to
     *    <seealso cref="System.IO.StreamReader"/>
     *    </remarks>
     *    <param name="firstName">
     *    The first name of the employee</param>
     *    <param name="lastName">
     *    The last name of the employee</param>
     *    <returns>
     *    The employee object corresponding to the names
     *    </returns>
     *    <date>January 1, 2000</date>**/
    public static Employee Load(
        string firstName, string lastName)
    {
        // ...
    }
}

class Program
{
    // ...
}
```

Single-Line XML Comment

XML Delimited Comment (C# 2.0)

Listing 9.17 uses both XML delimited comments that span multiple lines, and single-line XML comments where each line requires a separate three-forward-slash delimiter (///).

Since XML comments are designed to document the API, they are intended for use only in association with C# declarations, such as the class or method shown in Listing 9.17. Any attempt to place an XML comment inline with the code, unassociated with a declaration, will result in a warning by the compiler. The compile makes the association simply because the XML comment appears immediately before the declaration.

Although C# allows any XML tag in comments, the C# standard explicitly defines a set of tags to be used. `<seealso cref="System.IO.StreamWriter"/>` is an example of using the `seealso` tag. This tag creates a link between the text and the `System.IO.StreamWriter` class.

Generating an XML Documentation File

The compiler will check that the XML comments are well formed, and will issue a warning if they are not. To generate the XML file, you need to use the /doc option when compiling, as shown in Output 9.8.

OUTPUT 9.8

```
>csc /doc:Comments.xml DataStorage.cs
```

The /doc option will create an XML file based on the name specified after the colon. Using the `CommentSamples` class listed earlier and the compiler options listed here, the resultant `CommentSamples.XML` file appears as shown in Listing 9.18.

LISTING 9.18: Comments.xml

```xml
<?xml version="1.0"?>
<doc>
    <assembly>
        <name>DataStorage</name>
    </assembly>
    <members>
        <member name="T:DataStorage">
            <summary>
            DataStorage is used to persist and retrieve
            employee data from the files.
            </summary>
```

```
        </member>
        <member name="M:DataStorage.Store(Employee)">
            <summary>
            Save an employee object to a file
            named with the Employee name.
            </summary>
            <remarks>
            This method uses
            <seealso cref="T:System.IO.FileStream"/>
            in addition to
            <seealso cref="T:System.IO.StreamWriter"/>
            </remarks>
            <param name="employee">
            The employee to persist to a file</param>
            <date>January 1, 2000</date>
        </member>
        <member name="M:DataStorage.Load(
                System.String,System.String)">
            <summary>
            Loads up an employee object
            </summary>
            <remarks>
            This method uses
            <seealso cref="T:System.IO.FileStream"/>
            in addition to
            <seealso cref="T:System.IO.StreamReader"/>
            </remarks>
            <param name="firstName">
            The first name of the employee</param>
            <param name="lastName">
            The last name of the employee</param>
            <returns>
            The employee object corresponding to the names
            </returns>
            <date>January 1, 2000</date>*
        </member>
    </members>
</doc>
```

The resultant file includes only the amount of metadata that is necessary to associate an element back to its corresponding C# declaration. This is important to note, because in general, it is necessary to use the XML output in combination with the generated assembly in order to produce any meaningful documentation. Fortunately, tools such as the free GhostDoc[3] and the open source project NDoc[4] can generate documentation.

---

3. See http://submain.com/ to learn more about GhostDoc.
4. See http://ndoc.sourceforge.net to learn more about NDoc.

> **Guidelines**
>
> **DO** provide XML comments on public APIs when they provide more context than the API signature alone. This includes member descriptions, parameter descriptions, and examples for calling the API.

Garbage Collection

Garbage collection is obviously a core function of the runtime. Its purpose is to restore memory consumed by objects that are no longer referenced. The emphasis in this statement lies with memory and references. The garbage collector is only responsible for restoring memory; it does not handle other resources such as database connections, handles (files, windows, and so on), network ports, and hardware devices such as serial ports. Also, the garbage collector determines what to clean up based on whether any references remain. Implicitly, this means that the garbage collector works with reference objects and restores memory on the heap only. Additionally, it means that maintaining a reference to an object will delay the garbage collector from reusing the memory consumed by the object.

■ ADVANCED TOPIC

Garbage Collection in .NET

Many details about the garbage collector pertain to the specific CLI implementation, and therefore, they could vary. This section discusses the .NET implementation, since it is the most prevalent.

In .NET, the garbage collector uses a mark-and-compact algorithm. At the beginning of an iteration, it identifies all **root references** to objects. Root references are any references from static variables, CPU registers, and local variables or parameter instances (and f-reachable objects as described later in this section). Given this list, the garbage collector is able to walk the tree identified by each root reference and determine recursively all the objects to which the root references point. In this manner, the garbage collector identifies a graph of all reachable objects.

Instead of enumerating all the inaccessible objects, the garbage collector performs garbage collection by compacting all reachable objects next to one another, thereby overwriting any memory consumed by objects that are inaccessible (and therefore are garbage).

Locating and moving all reachable objects requires that the system maintain a consistent state while the garbage collector runs. To achieve this, all managed threads within the process halt during garbage collection. This obviously can result in brief pauses in an application, which is generally insignificant unless a particularly large garbage collection cycle is necessary. In order to reduce the likelihood of a garbage collection cycle at an inopportune time, however, the System.GC object includes a Collect() method, which can be called immediately before the critical performing code. This will not prevent the garbage collector from running, but it will reduce the likelihood that it will run, assuming no intense memory utilization occurs during the critical performance code.

One perhaps surprising aspect of .NET garbage collection behavior is that not all garbage is necessarily cleaned up during an iteration. Studies of object lifetimes reveal that recently created objects are more likely to need garbage collection than long-standing objects. Capitalizing on this behavior, the .NET garbage collector is generational, attempting to clean up short-lived objects more frequently than objects that have already survived a garbage collection iteration. Specifically, there are three generations of objects. Each time an object survives a garbage collection cycle it is moved to the next generation, until it ends up in generation two (counting starts from zero). The garbage collector then runs more frequently for objects in generation zero than it does for objects in generation two.

Ultimately, in spite of the trepidation that .NET faced during its early beta releases when compared with unmanaged code, time has shown that .NET's garbage collection is extremely efficient. More importantly, the gains created in development productivity have far outweighed the costs in development for the few cases where managed code is dropped to optimize particular algorithms.

Weak References

All references discussed so far are **strong references** because they maintain an object's accessibility and they prevent the garbage collector from cleaning up the memory consumed by the object. The framework also supports the concept of **weak references,** however. Weak references will not prevent garbage collection on an object, but they will maintain a reference so that if the garbage collector does not clean up the object, it can be reused.

Weak references are designed for objects that are expensive to create and are too expensive to keep around. Consider, for example, a large list of objects loaded from a database and displayed to the user. The loading of this list is potentially expensive, and once the user closes the list, it should be available for garbage collection. However, if the user requests the list multiple times, a second expensive load call will always be required. However, with weak references, it is possible to use code to check whether the list has not yet been cleaned up, and if not, to rereference the same list. In this way, weak references serve as a memory cache for objects. Objects within the cache are retrieved quickly, but if the garbage collector has recovered the memory of these objects, they will need to be re-created.

Once an object (or collection of objects) is recognized for potential weak reference consideration, it needs to be assigned to System.WeakReference (see Listing 9.19).

LISTING 9.19: Using a Weak Reference

```csharp
// ...

private WeakReference Data;

public FileStream GetData()
{
    FileStream data = (FileStream)Data.Target;
    if (data != null)
    {
        return data;
    }
    else
    {
        // Load data
        // ...

        // Create a weak reference
        // to data for use later.
        Data.Target = data;
    }
    return data;
}

// ...
```

Given the assignment of `WeakReference` (Data), you can check for garbage collection by seeing if the weak reference is set to `null`. The key in doing this, however, is to first assign the weak reference to a strong reference (`FileStream data = Data`) to avoid the possibility that between checking for `null` and accessing the data, the garbage collector runs and cleans up the weak reference. The strong reference obviously prevents the garbage collector from cleaning up the object, so it must be assigned first (instead of checking `Target` for `null`).

Resource Cleanup

Garbage collection is a key responsibility of the runtime. It is important to note, however, that the garbage collection relates to memory utilization. It is not about the cleaning up of file handles, database connection strings, ports, or other limited resources.

Finalizers

Finalizers allow developers to write code that will clean up a class's resources. However, unlike constructors that are called explicitly using the `new` operator, finalizers cannot be called explicitly from within the code. There is no `new` equivalent such as a `delete` operator. Rather, the garbage collector is responsible for calling a finalizer on an object instance. Therefore, developers cannot determine at compile time exactly when the finalizer will execute. All they know is that the finalizer will run sometime between when an object was last used and before the application shuts down normally. (Finalizers might not execute if the process is terminated abnormally. For instance, events such as the computer being turned off or a forced termination of the process will prevent the finalizer from running.)

> **■ NOTE**
>
> It is nondeterministic at compile time exactly when the finalizer will execute.

The finalizer declaration is identical to the destructor syntax of C#'s predecessor—namely, C++. As shown in Listing 9.20, the finalizer declaration is prefixed with a tilde before the name of the class.

LISTING 9.20: Defining a Finalizer

```csharp
using System.IO;

class TemporaryFileStream
{
  public TemporaryFileStream()
  {
      _File = new FileInfo(Path.GetTempFileName());
      _Stream = new FileStream(
          File.FullName, FileMode.OpenOrCreate,
          FileAccess.ReadWrite);
  }

  // Finalizer
  ~TemporaryFileStream()
  {
      Close();
  }

  public FileStream Stream
  {
      get { return _Stream; }
  }
  readonly private FileStream _Stream;

  public FileInfo File
  {
      get { return _File; }
  }
  readonly private FileInfo _File =
      new FileInfo(Path.GetTempFileName());

  public void Close()
  {
      if(Stream != null)
      {
        Stream.Close();
      }
      if(File != null)
      {
        File.Delete();
      }
  }
}
```

Finalizers do not allow any parameters to be passed, and as a result, finalizers cannot be overloaded. Furthermore, finalizers cannot be called explicitly. Only the garbage collector can invoke a finalizer. Therefore, access modifiers on finalizers are meaningless, and as such, they are not supported.

Finalizers in base classes will be invoked automatically as part of an object finalization call.

■ NOTE

Finalizers cannot be called explicitly; only the garbage collector can invoke a finalizer.

Because the garbage collector handles all memory management, finalizers are not responsible for de-allocating memory. Rather, they are responsible for freeing up resources such as database connections and file handles, resources that require an explicit activity that the garbage collector doesn't know about.

Note that finalizers will execute on their own thread, making their execution even less deterministic. This indeterminacy makes an unhandled exception within a finalizer (outside of the debugger) difficult to diagnose because the circumstances that led to the exception are not clear. From the user's perspective, the unhandled exception will be thrown relatively randomly and with little regard for any action the user was performing. For this reason, take care to avoid exceptions within finalizers. Use defensive programming techniques such as checking for nulls (refer to Listing 9.20).

Deterministic Finalization with the `using` Statement

The problem with finalizers on their own is that they don't support **deterministic finalization** (the ability to know when a finalizer will run). Rather, finalizers serve the important role of a backup mechanism for cleaning up resources if a developer using a class neglects to call the requisite cleanup code explicitly.

For example, consider the `TemporaryFileStream` that includes not only a finalizer but also a `Close()` method. The class uses a file resource that could potentially consume a significant amount of disk space. The developer using `TemporaryFileStream` can explicitly call `Close()` in order to restore the disk space.

Providing a method for deterministic finalization is important because it eliminates a dependency on the indeterminate timing behavior of the finalizer. Even if the developer fails to call `Close()` explicitly, the finalizer will take care of the call. However, the finalizer will run later than if it was called explicitly—but it will be called.

Because of the importance of deterministic finalization, the Base Class Library includes a specific interface for the pattern and C# integrates the pattern into the language. The IDisposable interface defines the details of the pattern with a single method called Dispose(), which developers call on a resource class to "dispose" of the consumed resources. Listing 9.21 demonstrates the IDisposable interface and some code for calling it.

LISTING 9.21: Resource Cleanup with IDisposable

```csharp
using System;
using System.IO;

class Program
{
  // ...
  static void Search()
  {
      TemporaryFileStream fileStream =
          new TemporaryFileStream();

      // Use temporary file stream;
      // ...

      fileStream.Dispose();

      // ...
  }
}
```

```csharp
class TemporaryFileStream : IDisposable
{
  public TemporaryFileStream()
  {
      _File = new FileInfo(Path.GetTempFileName());
      _Stream = new FileStream(
          File.FullName, FileMode.OpenOrCreate,
          FileAccess.ReadWrite);
  }

  ~TemporaryFileStream()
  {
      Dispose(false);
  }

  public FileStream Stream
  {
      get { return _Stream; }
```

```
    }
    readonly private FileStream _Stream;

    public FileInfo File
    {
        get { return _File; }
    }
    readonly private FileInfo _File;

    public void Close()
    {
        Dispose();
    }
```

```
    #region IDisposable Members
    public void Dispose()
    {
        Dispose(true);

        // Turn off calling the finalizer
        System.GC.SuppressFinalize(this);
    }
    #endregion
    public void Dispose(bool disposing)
    {
        // Do not dispose of an owned managed object (one with a
        // finalizer) if called by member finalize
        // as the owned managed objects finalize method
        // will be (or has been) called by finalization queue
        // processing already
        if (disposing)
        {
            if (Stream != null)
            {
                Stream.Close();
            }
        }
        if(File != null)
        {
            File.Delete();
        }
    }
}
```

```
}
```

From `Program.Search()` there is an explicit call to `Dispose()` after using the `TemporaryFileStream`. `Dispose()` is the method responsible for cleaning up the resources (in this case, a file) that are not related to memory, and therefore are subject to cleanup implicitly by the garbage collector. However, there is still a hole in the execution here that would prevent `Dispose()` from being executed. The issue is that there is a chance that an exception will occur between the time `TemporaryFileStream` is instantiated and when `Dispose()` is called. If this happens, `Dispose()` will not be invoked and the resource cleanup will have to rely on the finalizer. To avoid this, callers need to implement a try/finally block. Instead of coding such a block explicitly, C# provides a `using` statement expressly for the purpose. The resultant code appears in Listing 9.22.

LISTING 9.22: Invoking the `using` Statement

```csharp
class Program
{
  // ...

  static void Search()
  {
      using (TemporaryFileStream fileStream1 =
          new TemporaryFileStream(),
          fileStream2 = new TemporaryFileStream())
      {
          // Use temporary file stream;
      }
  }
}
```

The resultant CIL code is identical to the code that would be created if there was an explicit try/finally block, where `fileStream.Dispose()` is called in the finally block. The `using` statement, however, provides a syntax shortcut for the try/finally block.

Within a `using` statement, you can instantiate more than one variable by separating each variable with a comma. The key is that all variables are of the same type and that they implement `IDisposable`. To enforce the use of the same type, the data type is specified only once rather than before each variable declaration.

Garbage Collection, Finalization, and `IDisposable`

There are several additional noteworthy items to point out in Listing 9.21. First, the `IDisposable.Dispose()` method contains an important call to `System.GC.SuppressFinalize()`. Its purpose is to remove the `TemporaryFileStream` class instance from the **finalization (f-reachable) queue.** This is possible because all cleanup was done in the `Dispose()` method rather than waiting for the finalizer to execute.

Without the call to SuppressFinalize(), the instance of the object will be included in the f-reachable queue—a list of all the objects that are mostly ready for garbage collection except they also have finalization implementations. The runtime cannot garbage-collect objects with finalizers until after their finalization methods have been called. However, garbage collection itself does not call the finalization method. Rather, references to finalization objects are added to the f-reachable queue, and are processed by an additional thread at a time deemed appropriate based on the execution context. Ironically, this delays garbage collection for the managed resources—when it is mostly likely that these very resources should likely be cleaned up earlier. The reason for the delay is because the f-reachable queue is a list of "references," and as such, the objects are not garbage until after their finalization methods are called and the object references are removed from the f-reachable queue.

> ■■ **NOTE**
>
> Objects with finalizers that are not explicitly disposed will end up with an extended object lifetime because even after all explicit references have gone out of scope, the f-reachable queue will have references, keeping the object alive until the f-reachable queue processing is complete.

It is for this reason that Dispose() invokes System.GC.SuppressFinalize. Invoking this method informs the runtime not to add this object to the finalization queue, but instead to allow the garbage collector to de-allocate the object when it no longer has any references (including any f-reachable references).

Second, Dispose() calls Dispose(bool disposing) with an argument of true. The result is that the Dispose() method on Stream is invoked (cleaning up its resources and suppressing its finalization). Next, the temporary file itself is deleted immediately upon calling Dispose(). This important call eliminates the need to wait for the finalization queue to be processed before cleaning up potentially expensive resources.

Third, rather than calling Close(), the finalizer now calls Dispose(bool disposing) with an argument of false. The result is that Stream is not closed (disposed) even though the file is deleted. The reason for the condition around closing Stream is that if Dispose(bool disposing) is called from the finalizer, the Stream instance itself will also be up for finalization processing (or possibly it would have already run depending on the order). Therefore, when executing the finalizer, objects owned by the managed resource should not be cleaned up as this will be the responsibility of the finalization queue.

Fourth, use caution when creating both a Close() type and a Dispose() method. It is not clear by looking at only the API that Close() calls Dispose(), so developers will be left wondering whether they need to explicitly call Close() and Dispose().

Guidelines

DO implement a finalizer method only on objects with resources that are scarce or expensive even though finalization delays garbage collection.

DO implement IDisposable to support deterministic finalization on classes with finalizers.

DO implement a finalizer method on classes that implement IDisposable in case Dispose() is not invoked explicitly.

DO refactor a finalization method to call the same code as IDisposable, perhaps simply calling the Dispose() method.

DO NOT throw exceptions from finalizer methods.

DO call System.GC.SuppressFinalize() from Dispose() to avoid repeating resource cleanup and delaying garbage collection on an object.

DO ensure that Dispose() is reentrant (it should be possible to call Dispose() multiple times).

DO keep Dispose() simple, focusing on resource cleanup required by finalization.

AVOID calling Dispose () on owned objects that have a finalizer. Instead, rely on the finalization queue to clean up the instance.

AVOID referencing other objects that are not being finalized during finalization.

DO invoke a base class's dispose method when overriding Dispose().

CONSIDER setting object state to unusable after Dispose() is called. After an object has been disposed, methods other than Dispose() (which could potentially be called multiple times) should throw an ObjectDisposedException.

DO implement IDisposable on types that own disposable fields (or properties) and dispose said fields.

Language Contrast: C++—Deterministic Destruction

Although finalizers are similar to destructors in C++, the fact that their execution cannot be determined at compile time makes them distinctly different. The garbage collector calls C# finalizers sometime after they were last used, but before the program shuts down; C++ destructors are automatically called when the object (not a pointer) goes out of scope.

Although running the garbage collector can be a relatively expensive process, the fact that garbage collection is intelligent enough to delay running until process utilization is somewhat reduced offers an advantage over deterministic destructors, which will run at compile-time-defined locations, even when a processor is in high demand.

■ **ADVANCED TOPIC**

Exception Propagating from Constructors

Even when an exception propagates out of a constructor, the object is still instantiated, although no new instance is returned by the new operator. If the type defines a finalizer, the method will run when the object becomes eligible for garbage collection (providing additional motivation to ensure the finalize method can run on partially constructed objects). Also note that if a constructor prematurely shares its this reference, it will still be accessible even if the constructor throws an exception. Do not allow this scenario to occur.

■ **ADVANCED TOPIC**

Resurrecting Objects

By the time an object's finalization method is called, all references to the object have disappeared and the only step before garbage collection is running the finalization code. However, it is possible to add a reference inadvertently for a finalization object back into the root reference's graph. In so doing, the rereferenced object is no longer inaccessible, and therefore, it is not ready for garbage collection. However, if the finalization method for the object has already run, it will not necessarily be run again unless it is explicitly marked for finalization (using the `GC.ReRegisterFinalize()` method).

Obviously, resurrecting objects like this is peculiar behavior and you should generally avoid it. Finalization code should be simple and should focus on cleaning up only the resources that it references.

Lazy Initialization

In this preceding section, we discussed how to deterministically dispose of an object with a `using` statement and how the finalization queue will dispose of resources in the event that no deterministic approach is used.

A related pattern is **lazy initialization** or **lazy loading**. Using lazy initialization, you can create (or obtain) objects when you need them rather than beforehand—especially when they were never used. Consider the `FileStream` property of Listing 9.23.

LISTING 9.23: Lazy Loading a Property

```
using System.IO;

class DataCache
{
  // ...

  public TemporaryFileStream FileStream
  {
    get
    {
      if (_FileStream == null)
      {
        _FileStream = new TemporaryFileStream();
      }
      return _FileStream;
    }
  }
  private TemporaryFileStream _FileStream = null;

  // ...
}
```

In the `FileStream` property, we instantiate the `TemporaryFileStream` object only when the getter on the property is called. If the getter is never invoked, the TemporaryFileStream object would not get instantiated and we would save whatever execution time such an instantiation would cost. Obviously, if the instantiation is negligible or inevitable (and postponing the inevitable is less desirable), simply assigning it during declaration or in the constructor makes sense. Deferring the initialization of an object until it is required is called **lazy initialization.**

■ **ADVANCED TOPIC**

Lazy Loading with Generics and Lambda Expressions

Starting with .NET Framework 4.0, a new class was added to the CLR to assist with lazy initialization: System.Lazy<T>. Listing 9.24 demonstrates how to use it.

LISTING 9.24: Lazy Loading a Property with System.Lazy<T>

```
using System.IO;

class DataCache
{
  // ...

  public string FileStreamName { get; set; }

  public DataCache()
  {
      _FileStream = new Lazy<TemporaryFileStream>(
          () => new TemporaryFileStream(FileStreamName));
  }

  public TemporaryFileStream FileStream
  {
      get
      {
          return _FileStream.Value;
      }
  }
  private Lazy<TemporaryFileStream> _FileStream;

  // ...
}
```

The System.Lazy<T> class takes a type parameter (T) that identifies what type the Value property on System.Lazy<T> will return. Instead of assigning a fully constructed TemporaryFileStream to the _FileStream field, an instance of `Lazy<TemporaryFileStream>` is assigned (a lightweight call), delaying the instantiation of the `TemporaryFileStream` itself, until the `Value` property (and therefore the `FileStream` property) is accessed.

If in addition to type parameters (generics) you use delegates, you can even provide a function for how to initialize an object when the `Value` property is accessed. Listing 9.24 demonstrates passing the delegate, a lambda expression in this case, into the constructor for `System.Lazy<T>`.

It is important to note that the lambda expression itself, `() => new TemporaryFileStream(FileStreamName)`, does not execute until `Value` is called. Rather, the lambda expression provides a means of passing the instructions for what will happen, but not actually performing those instructions until explicitly requested.

SUMMARY

This chapter provided a whirlwind tour of many topics related to building solid class libraries. All the topics pertain to internal development as well, but they are much more critical to building robust classes. Ultimately, the topic is about forming more robust and programmable APIs. In the category of robustness fit namespaces and garbage collection. Both of these items fit in the programmability category, along with the other items covered: overriding `object`'s virtual members, operator overloading, and XML comments for documentation.

Exception handling uses inheritance heavily by defining an exception hierarchy and enforcing custom exceptions to fit within this hierarchy. Furthermore, the C# compiler uses inheritance to verify catch block order. In the next chapter, you will see why inheritance is such a core part of exception handling.

■ 10 ■
Exception Handling

CHAPTER 4 DISCUSSED USING the try/catch/finally blocks for standard exception handling. In that chapter, the catch block always caught exceptions of type System.Exception. This chapter defines some additional details of exception handling—specifically, details surrounding additional exception types, defining custom exceptions, and multiple catch blocks for handling each type. This chapter also details exceptions because of their reliance on inheritance.

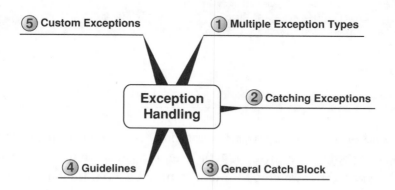

Multiple Exception Types

Listing 10.1 throws a `System.ArgumentException`, not the `System.Exception` type demonstrated in Chapter 4. C# allows code to throw any type that derives (perhaps indirectly) from `System.Exception`.

The code for throwing any exception is simply to prefix the exception instance with the keyword `throw`. The type of exception used is obviously the type that best describes the circumstances surrounding the error that caused the exception.

For example, consider the `TextNumberParser.Parse()` method in Listing 10.1.

LISTING 10.1: Throwing an Exception

```
public sealed class TextNumberParser
{
  public static int Parse(string textDigit)
  {
    string[] digitTexts =
        { "zero", "one", "two", "three", "four",
          "five", "six", "seven", "eight", "nine" };

    int result = Array.IndexOf(
        digitTexts, textDigit.ToLower());

    if (result < 0)
    {
        throw new ArgumentException(
            "The argument did not represent a digit",
            "textDigit");
    }

    return result;
  }
}
```

Instead of throwing `System.Exception`, it is more appropriate to throw `ArgumentException` because the type itself indicates what went wrong and includes special parameters for identifying which parameter was at fault.

Two similar exceptions are `ArgumentNullException` and `NullReference Exception`. `ArgumentNullException` should be thrown for the inappropriate passing of null arguments. This is a special case of an invalid parameter exception that would more generally (when it wasn't null) be thrown as an `ArgumentException` or an `ArgumentOutOfRange Exception`. `NullReferenceException` is generally something that only the

underlying runtime will throw with an attempt to dereference a null value—
to call a member on an object whose value is null. Instead of causing a
`NullReferenceException`, programmers should check parameters for `null`
before accessing them and then throw an `ArgumentNullException`, which
can provide more contextual information such as the parameter name.

There are several other exceptions that are only intended for the runtime
and that derive (sometimes indirectly) from `System.SystemException`. They
include `System.StackOverflowException`, `System.OutOfMemoryException`,
`System.Runtime.InteropServices.COMException`, `System.ExecutionEngineException`,
and `System.Runtime.InteropServices.SEHException`. Do not throw exceptions of these types. Similarly, avoid throwing a `System.Exception` or
`System.ApplicationException`, as these are so general that they provide
little indication of the cause of or resolution to the problem. Instead, throw
the most derived exception that fits the scenario. Obviously, developers
should avoid creating APIs that could potentially result in a system failure.
However, if the executing code reaches a certain state such that continuing
to execute is unsafe or unrecoverable, call `System.Environemnt.FailFast()`.
This will immediately terminate the process after writing a message to the
Windows Application event log, and will even include the message as part
of Windows Error Reporting if the user so chooses.

Guidelines

DO throw `ArgumentException` or one of its subtypes if bad arguments
are passed to a member. Prefer the most derived exception type
(`ArgumentNullException`, for example), if applicable.

DO set the `ParamName` property when throwing an `ArgumentException`
or one of the subclasses.

DO throw the most specific (most derived) exception that makes sense.

DO NOT throw a `NullReferenceException`. Instead, throw
`ArgumentNullException` when a value is unexpectedly null.

DO NOT throw a `System.SystemException` or an exception type that
derives from it.

DO NOT throw a `System.Exception` or
`System.ApplicationException`.

CONSIDER terminating the process by calling
`System.Environment.FailFast()` if the program encounters a
scenario where it is unsafe for further execution.

Catching Exceptions

Throwing a particular exception type enables the catcher to use the exception's type itself to identify the problem. It is not necessary, in other words, to catch the exception and use a `switch` statement on the exception message to determine what action to take in light of the exception. Instead, C# allows for multiple catch blocks, each targeting a specific exception type, as Listing 10.2 shows.

LISTING 10.2: **Catching Different Exception Types**

```csharp
using System;

public sealed class Program
{
  public static void Main(string[] args)
  {
    try
    {
        // ...
        throw new InvalidOperationException(
            "Arbitrary exception");
        // ...
    }
    catch (NullReferenceException exception)
    {
        // Handle NullReferenceException
    }
    catch (ArgumentException exception)
    {
        // Handle ArgumentException
    }
    catch (InvalidOperationException exception)
    {
      bool exceptionHandled=false;
      // Handle InvalidOperationException
      // ...
      if(!exceptionHandled)
      {
          throw;
      }
     }
    catch (SystemException)
    {
        // Handle SystemException
    }
    catch (Exception exception)
    {
        // Handle Exception
    }
```

```
        finally
        {
            // Handle any cleanup code here as it runs
            // regardless of an exception or not.
        }
    }
}
```

Listing 10.2 has five catch blocks, each handling a different type of exception. When an exception occurs, the execution will jump to the catch block with the exception type that most closely matches. The closeness of a match is determined by the inheritance chain. For example, even though the exception thrown is of type `System.Exception`, this "is a" relationship occurs through inheritance because `System.InvalidOperationException` ultimately derives from `System.Exception`. Since `InvalidOperationException` most closely matches the exception thrown, `catch(InvalidOperationException ...)` will catch the exception instead of the `catch(Exception...)` block.

Catch blocks must appear in order, from most specific to most general, to avoid a compile error. For example, moving the `catch(Exception ...)` block before any of the other exceptions will result in a compile error, since all prior exceptions derive from `System.Exception` at some point in their inheritance chain.

As shown with the catch (`SystemException`){ }) block, a named parameter for the catch block is not required. In fact, a final catch without even the type parameter is allowable, as you will see in the next section.

Language Contrast: Java—Exception Specifiers

C# has no equivalent for Java's exception specifiers. With exception specifiers, the Java compiler is able to verify that all possible exceptions thrown within a function (or a function's call hierarchy) are either caught or declared as possibly rethrown. The C# team considered this option and concluded that the maintenance burden that it imposed was not worth the perceived benefit. Therefore, it is not necessary to maintain a list of all possible exceptions throughout a particular call stack, but neither is it feasible to easily determine the possible exceptions. (As it turns out, this wasn't possible for Java either. Calling virtual methods or using late binding, such as reflection, made it impossible to fully resolve at compile time what exceptions a method could possibly throw.)

Notice that in the `InvalidOperationException` catch block there appears a throw statement without identifying the exception to throw (`throw` is on its own) even though there is the exception instance (`exception`) in the catch block scope that could be re-thrown. Throwing a specific exception would update all the stack information to match the new throw location. As a result, all the stack information indicating the call site the exception originally occurred would be lost making it significantly more difficult to diagnose the problem. For this reason, C# supports a throw statement without the explicit exception reference as long as it occurs within a catch block. This way, code can examine the exception to determine if it is possible to fully handle it, and if not, re-throw the exception (even though not specified explicitly) as though it was never caught and without replacing any stack information.

■ **ADVANCED TOPIC**

Throwing Existing Exceptions without Replacing Stack Information

In C# 5.0, a mechanism was added that enables the throwing of a previously thrown exception without losing the stack trace information in the original exception. This allows you to re-throw exceptions, for example, even from outside a catch block and, therefore, without using `throw;`. Although it is fairly rare to need to do this, there are occasions when exceptions are wrapped or saved until outside the catch block. For example, multithreaded code might wrap an exception with an `AggregateException`. The .NET 4.5 Framework provides a `System.Runtime.ExceptionServices.ExceptionDispatchInfo` class specifically to handle this scenario through the use of its static `Catch()` and instance `Throw()` methods. Listing 10.3 demonstrates re-throwing the exception without resetting the stack trace information or using an empty throw statement.

LISTING 10.3: Using `ExceptionDispatchInfo` to Re-throw an Exception

```
using System
using System.Runtime.ExceptionServices;

using System.Threading.Tasks;
Task task = WriteWebRequestSizeAsync(url);
```

```
try
{
  while (!task.Wait(100))
  {
      Console.Write(".");
  }
}
catch(AggregateException exception)
{
    exception = exception.Flatten();
    ExceptionDispatchInfo.Capture(
        exception.InnerException).Throw();
}
```

One thing worth noting about the `ExeptionDispatchInfo.Throw()` method is that the compile doesn't treat it as a return statement in the same way that it might a normal throw statement. For example, if the method signature returned a value but no value was returned from the code path with the `ExceptionDispatchInfo.Throw()`, the compile would issue an error indicating no value was returned. On occasion, therefore, developers will be forced to follow the `ExceptionDispatchInfo.Throw()` with a return statement even though such a statement would never execute at runtime—the exception would be thrown instead.

Language Contrast: Java—Exception Specifiers

C# has no equivalent for Java's exception specifiers. With exception specifiers, the Java compiler is able to verify that all possible exceptions thrown within a function (or a function's call hierarchy) are either caught or declared as possibly rethrown. The C# team considered this option and concluded that the maintenance burden that it imposed was not worth the perceived benefit. Therefore, it is not necessary to maintain a list of all possible exceptions throughout a particular call stack, but neither is it feasible to easily determine the possible exceptions. (As it turns out, this wasn't possible for Java either. Calling virtual methods or using late binding, such as reflection, made it impossible to fully resolve at compile time what exceptions a method could possibly throw.)

General Catch Block

C# requires that any object that code throws must derive from System .Exception. However, this requirement is not universal to all languages. C/C++, for example, allows any object type to be thrown, including managed exceptions that don't derive from System.Exception. Starting with C# 2.0, all exceptions, whether deriving from System.Exception or not, will propagate into C# assemblies as derived from System.Exception. The result is that System.Exception catch blocks will catch all exceptions not caught by earlier blocks.

C# also supports a **general catch block** (catch{ }) that behaves identically to the catch(System.Exception exception) block except that there is no type or variable name. Also, the general catch block must appear last within the list of catch blocks. Since the general catch block is identical to the catch(System.Exception exception) block and the general catch block must appear last, the compiler issues a warning if both exist within the same try/catch statement because the general catch block will never be invoked (see the Advanced Topic, General Catch Blocks in C# 1.0, for more information on general catch blocks).

■ **ADVANCED TOPIC**

General Catch Blocks in C# 1.0

In C# 1.0, if a non-System.Exception-derived exception was thrown from a method call (residing in an assembly not written in C#), the exception would not be caught by a catch(System.Exception) block. If a different language throws a string, for example, the exception could go unhandled. To avoid this, C# includes a catch block that takes no parameters. The term for such a catch block is *general catch block*, and Listing 10.4 includes one.

LISTING 10.4: **Catching Any Exception**

```
using System

public sealed class Program
{
  public static void Main()
  {
    try
```

```
        {
            // ...
            throw new InvalidOperationException (
                "Arbitrary exception");
            // ...
        }
        catch (NullReferenceException exception)
        {
            // Handle NullReferenceException
        }
        catch (ArgumentException exception)
        {
            // Handle ArgumentException
        }
        catch (InvalidOperationException exception)
        {
            // Handle ApplicationException
        }
        catch (SystemException exception)
        {
            // Handle SystemException
        }
        catch (Exception exception)
        {
            // Handle Exception
        }
        catch
        {
            // Any unhandled exception
        }
        finally
        {
            // Handle any cleanup code here as it runs
            // regardless of an exception or not.
        }
    }
}
```

The general catch block will catch all exceptions, regardless of whether they derive from `System.Exception`, assuming an earlier catch block does not catch them. The disadvantage of such a block is simply that there is no exception instance to access, and therefore no way to know the appropriate course of action. It wouldn't even be possible to recognize the unlikely case where such an exception is innocuous. The best course of action is to handle the exception with some cleanup code before shutting down the application. The catch block could save any volatile data, for example, before shutting down the application or rethrowing the exception.

■**ADVANCED TOPIC**

Empty Catch Block Internals

The CIL code corresponding to an empty catch block is, in fact, a `catch(object)` block. This means that regardless of the type thrown, the empty catch block will catch it. Interestingly, it is not possible to explicitly declare a `catch(object)` exception block within C# code. Therefore, there is no means of catching a non-`System.Exception`-derived exception and having an exception instance to scrutinize.

Ironically, unmanaged exceptions from languages such as C++ generally result in `System.Runtime.InteropServices.SEHException` type exceptions, which derive from the `System.Exception` type. Therefore, not only can the unmanaged type exceptions be caught using a general catch block, but the non-`System.Exception`-managed types that are thrown can be caught as well—for instance, types such as `string`.

Guidelines for Exception Handling

Exception handling provides much-needed structure to the error-handling mechanisms that preceded it. However, it can still make for some unwieldy results if used haphazardly. The following guidelines offer some best practices for exception handling.

- *Catch only the exceptions that you can handle.*

  Generally it is possible to handle some types of exceptions but not others. For example, opening a file for exclusive read-write access may throw a `System.IO.IOException` because the file is already in use. In catching this type of exception, the code can report to the user that the file is in use and allow the user the option of canceling the operation or retrying it. Only exceptions for which there is a known action should be caught. Other exception types should be left for callers higher in the stack.

- *Don't hide (bury) exceptions you don't fully handle.*

  New programmers are often tempted to catch all exceptions and then continue executing instead of reporting an unhandled exception to the user. However, this may result in a critical system problem going undetected. Unless code takes explicit action to handle an exception or explicitly determines certain exceptions to be innocuous, catch blocks should rethrow exceptions instead of catching them and hiding them from the caller. Predominantly, `catch(System.Exception)` and general catch blocks should occur higher in the call stack, unless the block ends by rethrowing the exception.

- *Use* `System.Exception` *and general catch blocks rarely.*

  Virtually all exceptions derive from `System.Exception`. However, the best way to handle some `System.Exceptions` is to allow them to go unhandled or to gracefully shut down the application sooner rather than later. These exceptions include things such as `System.OutOfMemoryException` and `System.StackOverflowException`. In CLR 4, such exceptions were defaulted to nonrecoverable such that catching them without rethrowing them will cause the CLR to rethrow them anyway. These exceptions are runtime exceptions that the developer cannot write code to recover from. Therefore, the best course of action is to shut down the application—something the runtime will force in CLR 4 and later. Code prior to CLR 4 should catch such exceptions only to run cleanup or emergency code (such as saving any volatile data) before shutting down the application or rethrowing the exception with `throw;`.

- *Avoid exception reporting or logging lower in the call stack.*

  Often, programmers are tempted to log exceptions or report exceptions to the user at the soonest possible location in the call stack. However, these locations are seldom able to handle the exception fully and they resort to rethrowing the exception. Such catch blocks should not log the exception or report it to a user while in the bowels of the call stack. If the exception is logged and rethrown, the callers higher in the call stack may do the same, resulting in duplicate log entries of the exception. Worse, displaying the exception to the user may not be appropriate for the type of application. (Using `System.Console.WriteLine()` in a Windows application will never be seen by the user, for example, and displaying a dialog in an unattended command-line process may go unnoticed and freeze the application.) Logging- and exception-related user interfaces should be reserved for high up in the call stack.

- *Use* `throw;` *rather than* `throw <exception object>` *inside a catch block.*

  It is possible to rethrow an exception inside a catch block. For example, the implementation of `catch(ArgumentNullException exception)` could include a call to `throw exception`. However, rethrowing the exception like this will reset the stack trace to the location of the rethrown call, instead of reusing the original throw point location. Therefore, unless you are rethrowing with a different exception type or intentionally hiding the original call stack, use `throw;` to allow the same exception to propagate up the call stack.

- *Use caution when rethrowing different exceptions.*

  From inside a catch block, rethrowing a different exception will not only reset the throw point, it will also hide the original exception. To preserve the original exception set the new exception's `InnerException` property, generally assignable via the constructor. Rethrowing a different exception should be reserved for the following situations.

  1. Changing the exception type clarifies the problem.

     For example, in a call to `Logon(User user)`, rethrowing a different exception type is perhaps more appropriate than propagating `System.IO.IOException` when the file with the user list is inaccessible.

  2. Private data is part of the original exception.

     In the preceding scenario, if the file path is included in the original `System.IO.IOException`, thereby exposing private security information about the system, the exception should be wrapped. This assumes, of course, that `InnerException` is not set with the original exception. (Funnily enough, a very early version of CLR v1 [pre-alpha even] had an exception that said something like "Security exception: You do not have permission to determine the path of `c:\temp\foo.txt`".)

  3. The exception type is too specific for the caller to handle appropriately.

     For example, instead of throwing an exception specific to a particular database system, a more generic exception is used so that database-specific code higher in the call stack can be avoided.

Defining Custom Exceptions

Once throwing an exception becomes the best course of action, it is preferable to use framework exceptions because they are well established and understood. Instead of throwing a custom invalid argument exception, for example, it is preferable to use the `System.ArgumentException` type. However, if the developers using a particular API will take special action—the exception-handling logic will vary to handle a custom exception type, for instance—it is appropriate to define a custom exception. For example, if a mapping API receives an address for which the ZIP Code is invalid, instead of throwing `System.ArgumentException`, it may be better to throw a custom `InvalidAddressException`. The key is whether the caller is likely to write a specific `InvalidAddressException` catch block with special handling rather than just a generic `System.ArgumentException` catch block.

Defining a custom exception simply involves deriving from `System .Exception` or some other exception type. Listing 10.5 provides an example.

LISTING 10.5: **Creating a Custom Exception**

```
class DatabaseException : System.Exception
{
  public DatabaseException(
      System.Data.SqlClient.SQLException exception)
  {
      InnerException = exception;
      // ...
  }

  public DatabaseException(
      System.Data.OracleClient.OracleException exception)
  {
      InnerException = exception;
      // ...
  }

  public DatabaseException()
  {
      // ...
  }

  public DatabaseException(string message)
  {
      // ...
  }

  public DatabaseException(
      string message, Exception innerException)
  {
      InnerException = innerException;
      // ...
  }
}
```

This custom exception might be created to wrap proprietary database exceptions. Since Oracle and SQL Server (for example) each throw different exceptions for similar errors, an application could define a custom exception that standardizes the database-specific exceptions into a common exception wrapper that the application can handle in a standard manner. That way, whether the application was using an Oracle or a SQL Server backend database, the same catch block could be used to handle the error higher up the stack.

The only requirement for a custom exception is that it derives from `System.Exception` or one of its descendants. However, there are several more good practices for custom exceptions.

- All exceptions should use the "Exception" suffix. This way, their purpose is easily established from the name.
- Generally, all exceptions should include constructors that take no parameters, a string parameter, and a parameter set of a string and an inner exception. Furthermore, since exceptions are usually constructed within the same statement in which they are thrown, any additional exception data should also be allowed as part of the constructor. (The obvious exception to creating all these constructors is if certain data is required and a constructor circumvents the requirements.)
- The inheritance chain should be kept relatively shallow (with fewer than approximately five levels).

The inner exception serves an important purpose when rethrowing an exception that is different from the one that was caught. For example, if a `System.Data.SqlClient.SqlException` is thrown by a database call but is caught within the data access layer to be rethrown as a `DatabaseException`, the `DatabaseException` constructor that takes the `SqlException` (or inner exception) will save the original `SqlException` in the `InnerException` property. That way, when requiring additional details about the original exception, developers can retrieve the exception from the `InnerException` property (for example, `exception.InnerException`).

Guidelines

DO NOT create a new exception type if the exception would not be handled differently than an existing CLR exception. Throw the existing framework exception instead.

DO create a new exception type to communicate a unique program error that cannot be communicated using an existing CLR exception and can be programmatically handled in a different way than any other existing CLR exception type.

DO provide a parameterless constructor on all custom exception types. Also provide constructors that take a message and an inner exception.

DO end exception class names with the "Exception" suffix.

DO make exceptions runtime-serializable.

CONSIDER providing exception properties for programmatic access to extra information relevant to the exception.

AVOID deep exception hierarchies.

Serializable Exceptions

Serializable objects are objects that the runtime can persist into a stream—a file stream, for example—and then reinstantiate out of the stream. In the case of exceptions, this may be necessary for certain distributed communication technologies. To support serialization, exception declarations should include the `System.SerializableAttribute` attribute or they should implement `ISerializable`. Furthermore, they must include a constructor that takes `System.Runtime.Serialization.SerializationInfo` and `System.Runtime.Serialization.StreamingContext`. Listing 10.6 shows an example of using `System.SerializableAttribute`.

LISTING 10.6: Defining a Serializable Exception

```
// Supporting serialization via an attribute
[Serializable]
class DatabaseException : System.Exception
{
  // ...

  // Used for deserialization of exceptions
  public DatabaseException(
      SerializationInfo serializationInfo,
      StreamingContext context)
  {
      //...
  }

}
```

The preceding `DatabaseException` example demonstrates both the attribute and the constructor requirement for making an exception serializable.

Wrapping an Exception and Rethrowing

On occasion, an exception thrown at a lower level in the stack will no longer make sense when caught at a higher level. For example, consider a `System.IO.IOException` that occurs because a system is out of disk space on the server. A client catching such an exception would not necessarily be able to understand the context of why there was even I/O activity. Similarly, consider a geographic coordinate request API that throws a `System.UnauthorizedAccessException` (an exception totally unrelated to the API called). In this second example, the caller has no context or understanding of what the API call has to do with security. From the perspective of the code that invokes the API, these exceptions cause more confusion than they help diagnose. Instead of exposing such exceptions to the client, it might make sense to catch the exception, and throw a different exception such as `InvalidOperationException` (or even perhaps a custom exception) as a means of communicating that the system is in an invalid state. In such scenarios, be sure to set the `InnerException` property of the wrapping exception (generally via the constructor call such as `new InvalidOperationException(String, Exception)`) so that there is additional context that can be used for diagnostics by someone closer to the framework that was invoked.

An important detail to remember when considering to wrap and rethrow an exception is the fact that the original stack trace—which provides the context of where the exception was thrown—will be replaced with the new stack trace of where the wrapping exception is thrown. Fortunately, by embedding the original exception into the wrapping exception, the original stack trace is still available.

Ultimately, remember that the intended recipient of the exception is the programmer writing code that calls your API—possibly incorrectly. Therefore, provide as much information to her that indicates both what she did wrong and (perhaps more importantly) how to fix it. The exception type is a critical piece of the communication mechanism. Therefore, choose the type carefully.

Guidelines

CONSIDER wrapping specific exceptions thrown from the lower layer in a more appropriate exception if the lower-layer exception does not make sense in the context of the higher-layer operation.

DO specify the inner exception when wrapping exceptions.

DO target developers as the audience for exceptions, identifying both the problem as well as the mechanism to resolve it, where possible.

DO use an empty throw statement (`throw;`) when rethrowing the same exception rather than passing the exception as an argument to `throw`.

■ BEGINNER TOPIC

Checked and Unchecked Conversions

As we first discussed in a Chapter 2 Advanced Topic, C# provides special keywords for marking a code block with instructions to the runtime of what should happen if the target data type is too small to contain the assigned data. By default, if the target data type cannot contain the assigned data, the data will truncate during assignment. For an example, see Listing 10.7.

LISTING 10.7: **Overflowing an Integer Value**

```csharp
using System;

public class Program
{
  public static void Main()
  {
      // int.MaxValue equals 2147483647
      int n = int.MaxValue;
      n = n + 1 ;
      System.Console.WriteLine(n);
  }
}
```

The results of Listing 10.7 appear in Output 10.1.

OUTPUT 10.1

```
-2147483648
```

The code in Listing 10.7 writes the value -2147483648 to the console. However, placing the code within a checked block or using the checked option when running the compiler will cause the runtime to throw an exception of type System.OverflowException. The syntax for a checked block uses the checked keyword, as shown in Listing 10.8.

LISTING 10.8: **A Checked Block Example**

```csharp
using System;

public class Program
{
  public static void Main()
```

```
    {
        checked
        {
            // int.MaxValue equals 2147483647
            int n = int.MaxValue;
            n = n + 1 ;
            System.Console.WriteLine(n);
        }
    }
}
```

If the calculation involves only constants, the calculation will be checked by default. The results of Listing 10.8 appear in Output 10.2.

OUTPUT 10.2

```
Unhandled Exception: System.OverflowException: Arithmetic operation
resulted in an overflow. at Program.Main() in ...Program.cs:line 12
```

In addition, depending on the version of Windows and whether a debugger is installed, a dialog may appear prompting the user to send an error message to Microsoft, check for a solution, or debug the application. Also, the location information (`Program.cs:line X`) will appear only in debug compilations—compilations using the `/Debug` option of the Microsoft `csc.exe` compiler.

The result is that an exception is thrown if, within the checked block, an overflow assignment occurs at runtime.

The C# compiler provides a command-line option for changing the default checked behavior from unchecked to checked. C# also supports an unchecked block that truncates the data instead of throwing an exception for assignments within the block (see Listing 10.9).

LISTING 10.9: An Unchecked Block Example

```
using System;

public class Program
{
    public static void Main()
    {
        unchecked
        {
            // int.MaxValue equals 2147483647
            int n = int.MaxValue;
```

```
                 n = n + 1 ;
                 System.Console.WriteLine(n);
            }
        }
    }
```

The results of Listing 10.8 appear in Output 10.3.

OUTPUT 10.3

```
-2147483648
```

Even if the checked option is on during compilation, the unchecked keyword in the code in Listing 10.8 will prevent the runtime from throwing an exception during execution.

There are equivalent checked and unchecked expressions for cases where statements are not allowed. For example, a field initializer may only be an expression, not a statement:

```
int _Number = unchecked(int.MaxValue + 1);
```

SUMMARY

Throwing an exception causes a significant performance hit. A single exception causes lots of runtime stack information to be loaded and processed, data that would not otherwise be loaded, and it takes a considerable amount of time. As pointed out in Chapter 4, use exceptions only to handle exceptional circumstances; APIs should provide mechanisms to check whether an exception will be thrown instead of forcing a particular API to be called in order to determine whether an exception will be thrown.

The next chapter introduces generics, a C# 2.0 feature that significantly enhances the code written in C# 1.0. In fact, it essentially deprecates any use of the System.Collections namespace, which was formerly used in nearly every project.

■ 11 ■
Generics

A S YOUR PROJECTS BECOME MORE sophisticated, you will need a better way to reuse and customize existing software. To facilitate code reuse, especially the reuse of algorithms, C# includes a feature called **generics.** Just as methods are powerful because they can take arguments, types and methods that take type arguments have significantly more functionality.

Generics are lexically similar to generic types in Java and templates in C++. In all three languages, these features enable the implementation of algorithms and patterns once, rather than requiring separate implementations for each type the algorithm or pattern operates upon. However, C# generics are very different from both Java generics and C++ templates in the details of their implementation and impact upon the type system of their respective languages.

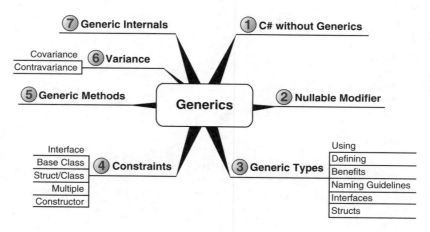

Generics were added to the runtime and C# in version 2.0.

C# without Generics

We begin the discussion of generics by examining a class that does not use generics. The class is `System.Collections.Stack`, and its purpose is to represent a collection of objects such that the last item to be added to the collection is the first item retrieved from the collection (called last in, first out, or LIFO). `Push()` and `Pop()`, the two main methods of the `Stack` class, add items to the stack and remove them from the stack, respectively. The declarations for the methods on the stack class appear in Listing 11.1.

LISTING 11.1: The `System.Collections.Stack` **Method Signatures**

```
public class Stack
{
   public virtual object Pop() { ... }
   public virtual void Push(object obj) { ... }
   // ...
}
```

Programs frequently use stack type collections to facilitate multiple undo operations. For example, Listing 11.2 uses the `System.Collections.Stack` class for undo operations within a program which simulates the Etch A Sketch® game.

LISTING 11.2: **Supporting Undo in a Program Similar to the Etch A Sketch Game**

```
using System;
using System.Collections;

class Program
{
  // ...

  public void Sketch()
  {
     Stack path = new Stack();
     Cell currentPosition;
     ConsoleKeyInfo key;  // Added in C# 2.0

     do
     {
        // Etch in the direction indicated by the
        // arrow keys that the user enters.
        key = Move();
```

```csharp
            switch (key.Key)
            {
                case ConsoleKey.Z:
                    // Undo the previous Move.
                    if (path.Count >= 1)
                    {
                        currentPosition = (Cell)path.Pop();
                        Console.SetCursorPosition(
                            currentPosition.X, currentPosition.Y);
                        Undo();
                    }
                    break;

                case ConsoleKey.DownArrow:
                case ConsoleKey.UpArrow:
                case ConsoleKey.LeftArrow:
                case ConsoleKey.RightArrow:
                    // SaveState()
                    currentPosition = new Cell(
                        Console.CursorLeft, Console.CursorTop);
                    path.Push(currentPosition);
                    break;

                default:
                    Console.Beep();  // Added in C# 2.0
                    break;
            }

        }
        while (key.Key != ConsoleKey.X);  // Use X to quit.

    }
}

public struct Cell
{
    readonly public int X;
    readonly public int Y;
    public Cell(int x, int y)
    {
        X = x;
        Y = y;
    }
}
```

The results of Listing 11.2 appear in Output 11.1.

OUTPUT 11.1

Using the variable path, which is declared as a System.Collections.Stack, you save the previous move by passing a custom type, Cell, into the Stack.Push() method using path.Push(currentPosition). If the user enters a Z (or Ctrl+Z), you undo the previous move by retrieving it from the stack using a Pop() method, setting the cursor position to be the previous position, and calling Undo(). Although the code is functional, there is a fundamental shortcoming in the System.Collections.Stack class. As shown in Listing 11.1, the Stack class collects values of type object. Because every object in the CLR derives from object, Stack provides no validation that the elements you place into it are homogenous or are of the intended type. For example, instead of passing currentPosition, you can pass a string in which X and Y are concatenated with a decimal point between them. However, the compiler must allow the inconsistent data types because the stack class is written to take any object, regardless of its more specific type.

Furthermore, when retrieving the data from the stack using the Pop() method, you must cast the return value to a Cell. But if the type of the value returned from the Pop() method is not Cell, an exception is thrown. By deferring type checking until runtime by using a cast, you make the program more brittle. The fundamental problem with creating classes that can work with multiple data types without generics is that they must work with a common base class (or interface), usually object.

Using value types, such as a struct or an integer, with classes that use object exacerbates the problem. If you pass a value type to the Stack.Push() method, for example, the runtime automatically boxes it. Similarly, when you retrieve a value type, you need to explicitly unbox the data and cast the object reference you obtain from the Pop() method into a value type. Casting a reference type to a base class or interface has a negligible performance impact, but the box operation for a value type introduces more overhead, because it must allocate memory, copy the value, and then later garbage-collect that memory.

C# is a language that encourages "type safety": The language is designed so that many type errors, such as assigning an integer to a variable of type string, can be caught at compile time. The fundamental problem is that the stack class is not as type-safe as one expects a C# program to be. To change the stack class to enforce type safety to restrict the contents of the stack to be a particular data type (without using generic types) you must create a specialized stack class, as in Listing 11.3.

LISTING 11.3: Defining a Specialized Stack Class

```
public class CellStack
{
  public virtual Cell Pop();
  public virtual void Push(Cell cell);
  // ...
}
```

Because CellStack can store only objects of type Cell, this solution requires a custom implementation of the stack methods, which is less than ideal. Implementing a type-safe stack of integers would require yet another custom implementation; each implementation would look remarkably like every other one. There would be lots of duplicated, redundant code.

■ BEGINNER TOPIC

Another Example: Nullable Value Types
Chapter 2 introduced the capability of declaring variables that could contain null by using the nullable modifier, ?, when declaring a value type variable. C# only began supporting this in version 2.0 because the right

implementation required generics. Prior to the introduction of generics, programmers faced essentially two options.

The first option was to declare a nullable data type for each value type that needs to handle null values, as shown in Listing 11.4.

LISTING 11.4: Declaring Versions of Various Value Types That Store null

```csharp
struct NullableInt
{
    /// <summary>
    /// Provides the value when HasValue returns true.
    /// </summary>
    public int Value{ get; private set; }

    /// <summary>
    /// Indicates whether there is a value or whether
    /// the value is "null"
    /// </summary>
    public bool HasValue{ get; private set; }

    // ...
}

struct NullableGuid
{
    /// <summary>
    /// Provides the value when HasValue returns true.
    /// </summary>
    public Guid Value{ get; private set; }

    /// <summary>
    /// Indicates whether there is a value or whether
    /// the value is "null"
    /// </summary>
    public bool HasValue{ get; private set; }

    ...
}
...
```

Listing 11.4 shows possible implementations of NullableInt and NullableGuid. If a program required additional nullable value types, you would have to create yet another struct with the properties modified to use the desired value type. Any improvement of the implementation (adding a user-defined implicit conversion from the underlying type to the nullable type, for example) would require modifying all of the nullable type declarations.

An alternative strategy for implementing a nullable type without generics is to make a single type with a `Value` property of type `object`, as shown in Listing 11.5.

LISTING 11.5: Declaring a Nullable Type That Contains a `Value` Property of Type `object`

```csharp
struct Nullable
{
    /// <summary>
    /// Provides the value when HasValue returns true.
    /// </summary>
    public object Value{ get; private set; }

    /// <summary>
    /// Indicates whether there is a value or whether
    /// the value is "null"
    /// </summary>
    public bool HasValue{ get; private set; }

    ...
}
```

Although this option requires only one implementation of a nullable type, the runtime always boxes value types when setting the `Value` property. Furthermore, retrieving the underlying value from the `Value` property will require a cast operation, which is potentially invalid at runtime.

Neither option is particularly attractive. To eliminate this problem, C# 2.0 introduced generics to C#. (And in fact, nullable types are actually implemented as the generic type `Nullable<T>`.)

Introducing Generic Types

Generics provide a facility for creating data structures that can be specialized to handle specific types. Programmers define these **parameterized types** so that each variable of a particular generic type has the same internal algorithm, but the types of data and method signatures can vary based on the type arguments provided for the type parameters.

To minimize the learning curve for developers, C# designers chose syntax that superficially resembles C++ templates. In C# the syntax for generic classes and structures uses angle brackets to both declare the generic type parameters in the type declaration, and specify the generic type arguments when the type is used.

Using a Generic Class

Listing 11.6 shows how you can specify the actual type argument used by the generic class. You instruct the `path` variable to be the "Stack of Cell" type by specifying `Cell` within angle bracket notation in both the object creation expression and the declaration statement. In other words, when declaring a variable (`path` in this case) using a generic data type, C# requires the developer to identify the actual type arguments used by the generic type. An example showing the new generic `Stack` class appears in Listing 11.6.

LISTING 11.6: **Implementing Undo with a Generic** Stack **Class**

```csharp
using System;
using System.Collections.Generic;

class Program
{
  // ...

  public void Sketch()
  {
      Stack<Cell> path;            // Generic variable declaration
      path = new Stack<Cell>();    // Generic object instantiation
      Cell currentPosition;
      ConsoleKeyInfo key;

      do
      {
          // Etch in the direction indicated by the
          // arrow keys entered by the user.
          key = Move();

          switch (key.Key)
          {
              case ConsoleKey.Z:
                  // Undo the previous Move.
                  if (path.Count >= 1)
                  {
                      // No cast required.
                      currentPosition = path.Pop();
                      Console.SetCursorPosition(
                          currentPosition.X, currentPosition.Y);
                      Undo();
                  }
                  break;

              case ConsoleKey.DownArrow:
              case ConsoleKey.UpArrow:
```

```
            case ConsoleKey.LeftArrow:
            case ConsoleKey.RightArrow:
                // SaveState()
                currentPosition = new Cell(
                    Console.CursorLeft, Console.CursorTop);
                // Only type Cell allowed in call to Push().
                path.Push(currentPosition);
                break;

            default:
                Console.Beep();   // Added in C# 2.0
                break;
        }

    } while (key.Key != ConsoleKey.X);   // Use X to quit.
  }
}
```

The results of Listing 11.6 appear in Output 11.2.

OUTPUT 11.2

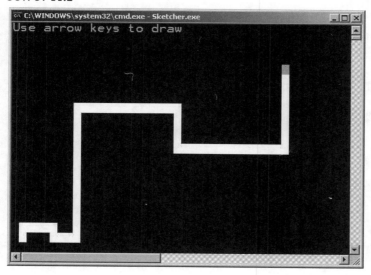

In the path declaration shown in Listing 11.6, you declare a variable and initialize it with a new instance of the System.Collections.Generic .Stack<Cell> class. You specify in angle brackets that the data type of the stack's elements is Cell. As a result, every object added to and retrieved from path is of type Cell. And, therefore, you no longer need to cast the return of path.Pop() or ensure that only Cell type objects are added to path in the Push() method.

Defining a Simple Generic Class

Generics allow you to author algorithms and patterns, and reuse the code for different data types. Listing 11.7 creates a generic Stack<T> class similar to the System.Collections.Generic.Stack<T> class used in the code in Listing 11.6. You specify a **type parameter** (in this case, T) within angle brackets after the class name. The generic Stack<T> can then be supplied with a single type argument that is "substituted" everywhere T appears in the class. Thus the stack can store items of any stated type, without duplicating code or converting the item to type object. The type parameter T is a placeholder that must be supplied with a type argument. In Listing 11.7, you can see that the type parameter will be used for the internal Items array, the type for the parameter to the Push() method, and the return type for the Pop() method.

LISTING 11.7: Declaring a Generic Class, Stack<T>

```
public class Stack<T>
{
    private T[] _Items;

    public void Push(T data)
    {
        ...
    }

    public T Pop()
    {
        ...
    }
}
```

Benefits of Generics

There are several advantages to using a generic class over a nongeneric version (such as the System.Collections.Generic.Stack<T> class used earlier instead of the original System.Collections.Stack type).

1. Generics facilitate increased type safety, preventing data types other than those explicitly intended by the members within the

parameterized class. In Listing 11.7, the parameterized stack class restricts you to the `Cell` data type when using `Stack<Cell>`. (For example, the statement `path.Push("garbage")` produces a compile-time error indicating that there is no overloaded method for `System.Collections.Generic.Stack<T>.Push(T)` that can work with the string, because it cannot be converted to a `Cell`.)

2. Compile-time type checking reduces the likelihood of `InvalidCast Exception` type errors at runtime.

3. Using value types with generic class members no longer causes a boxing conversion to `object`. (For example, `path.Pop()` and `path.Push()` do not require an item to be boxed when added or unboxed when removed.)

4. Generics in C# reduce code bloat. Generic types retain the benefits of specific class versions, without the overhead. (For example, it is no longer necessary to define a class such as `CellStack`.)

5. Performance improves because casting from an object is no longer required, thus eliminating a type check operation. Also, performance improves because boxing is no longer necessary for value types.

6. Generics reduce memory consumption by avoiding boxing and thus consuming less memory on the heap.

7. Code becomes more readable because of fewer casting checks and because of the need for fewer type-specific implementations.

8. Editors that assist coding via some type of IntelliSense® work directly with return parameters from generic classes. There is no need to cast the return data for IntelliSense to work.

At their core, generics offer the ability to code pattern implementations and then reuse those implementations wherever the patterns appear. Patterns describe problems that occur repeatedly within code, and templates provide a single implementation for these repeating patterns.

Type Parameter Naming Guidelines

Just as when you name a method's formal parameter, you should be as descriptive as possible when naming a type parameter. Furthermore, to distinguish the parameter as being a type parameter, its name should include a *T* prefix. For example, in defining a class such as Entity Collection<TEntity> you use the type parameter name "TEntity."

The only time you would not use a descriptive type parameter name is when the description would not add any value. For example, using "T" in the Stack<T> class is appropriate, since the indication that "T" is a type parameter is sufficiently descriptive; the stack works for any type.

In the next section, you will learn about constraints. It is a good practice to use constraint-descriptive type names. For example, if a type parameter must implement IComponent, consider a type name of "TComponent."

Guidelines

DO choose meaningful names for type parameters and prefix the name with "T".
CONSIDER indicating a constraint in the name of a type parameter.

Generic Interfaces and Structs

C# supports the use of generics throughout the language, including interfaces and structs. The syntax is identical to that used by classes. To declare an interface with a type parameter, place the type parameter in angle brackets immediately after the interface name, as shown in the example of IPair<T> in Listing 11.8.

LISTING 11.8: Declaring a Generic Interface

```
interface IPair<T>
{
    T First { get; set; }
    T Second { get; set; }
}
```

This interface represents pairs of like objects, such as the coordinates of a point, a person's genetic parents, or nodes of a binary tree. The type contained in the pair is the same for both items.

To implement the interface, you use the same syntax as you would for a nongeneric class. Note that it is legal, and indeed common, for the type argument for one generic type to be a type parameter of another, as shown in Listing 11.9. The type argument of the interface is the type parameter declared by the class. In addition, this example uses a struct rather than a class, demonstrating that C# supports custom generic value types.

LISTING 11.9: Implementing a Generic Interface

```csharp
public struct Pair<T>: IPair<T>
{
    public T First
    {
        get
        {
            return _First;
        }
        set
        {
            _First = value;
        }
    }
    private T _First;

    public T Second
    {
        get
        {
            return _Second;
        }
        set
        {
            _Second = value;
        }
    }
    private T _Second;
}
```

Support for generic interfaces is especially important for collection classes, where generics are most prevalent. Before generics, developers relied on a series of interfaces within the System.Collections namespace. Like their implementing classes, these interfaces worked only with type object, and as a result, the interface forced all access to and from these collection classes to require a cast. By using type-safe generic interfaces, you can avoid cast operations.

■ **ADVANCED TOPIC**

Implementing the Same Interface
Multiple Times on a Single Class

Two different constructions of the same generic interface are considered to be different types, and therefore, "the same" generic interface can be implemented multiple times by a class or struct. Consider the example in Listing 11.10.

LISTING 11.10: Duplicating an Interface Implementation on a Single Class

```csharp
public interface IContainer<T>
{
    ICollection<T> Items
    {
        get;
        set;
    }
}

public class Person: IContainer<Address>,
    IContainer<Phone>, IContainer<Email>
{
    ICollection<Address> IContainer<Address>.Items
    {
        get{...}
        set{...}
    }
    ICollection<Phone> IContainer<Phone>.Items
    {
        get{...}
        set{...}
    }
    ICollection<Email> IContainer<Email>.Items
    {
        get{...}
        set{...}
    }
}
```

In this example, the Items property appears multiple times using an explicit interface implementation with a varying type parameter. Without generics, this is not possible, and instead, the compiler would allow only one explicit IContainer.Items property.

However, this technique of implementing multiple versions of "the same" interface is considered by many to be a "bad code smell" because it is potentially confusing (particularly if the interface permits covariant or contravariant conversions). Moreover, the `Person` class here seems potentially badly designed; one does not normally think of a person as being "a thing that can provide a set of email addresses." When you feel tempted to make a class implement three versions of the same interface, consider whether it might be better to make it instead implement three properties: `EmailAddresses`, `PhoneNumbers`, and `MailingAddresses`, which each return the appropriate construction of the generic interface.

> ### Guidelines
>
> **AVOID** implementing multiple constructions of the same generic interface in one type.

Defining a Constructor and a Finalizer

Perhaps surprisingly, the constructors (and finalizer) of a generic class or struct do not require type parameters (in other words, they do not require `Pair<T>(){...}`). In the pair example in Listing 11.11, the constructor is declared using `public Pair(T first, T second)`.

LISTING 11.11: Declaring a Generic Type's Constructor

```
public struct Pair<T>: IPair<T>
{
    public Pair(T first, T second)
    {
        _First = first;
        _Second = second;
    }

    public T First
    {
        get{ return _First; }
        set{ _First = value; }
    }
    private T _First;

    public T Second
    {
        get{ return _Second; }
        set{ _Second = value; }
    }
    private T _Second;
}
```

Specifying a Default Value

Listing 11.11 included a constructor that takes the initial values for both First and Second, and assigns them to _First and _Second. Since Pair<T> is a struct, any constructor you provide must initialize all fields. This presents a problem, however. Consider a constructor for Pair<T> that initializes only half of the pair at instantiation time.

Defining such a constructor, as shown in Listing 11.12, causes a compile error because the field _Second is still uninitialized at the end of the constructor. Providing initialization for _Second presents a problem since you don't know the data type of T. If it is a reference type, null would work, but this would not work if T were a non-nullable value type.

LISTING 11.12: Not Initializing All Fields, Causing a Compile Error

```
public struct Pair<T>: IPair<T>
{
  // ERROR:  Field 'Pair<T>._second' must be fully assigned
  //         before control leaves the constructor
  // public Pair(T first)
  // {
  //     _First = first;
  // }

  // ...
}
```

To deal with this scenario, C# provides the default operator, first discussed in Chapter 8. In Chapter 8, we showed how the default value of int could be specified with default(int). In the case of T, which _Second requires, you can use default(T) as shown in Listing 11.13.

LISTING 11.13: Initializing a Field with the default Operator

```
public struct Pair<T>: IPair<T>
{
  public Pair(T first)
  {
      _First = first;
      _Second = default(T);
  }

  // ...
}
```

The `default` operator can provide the default value for any type, including type parameters.

Multiple Type Parameters

Generic types may declare any number of type parameters. The initial `Pair<T>` example contains only one type parameter. To enable support for storing a dichotomous pair of objects, such as a name/value pair, you could create a new version of the type that declares two type parameters, as shown in Listing 11.14.

LISTING 11.14: Declaring a Generic with Multiple Type Parameters

```csharp
interface IPair<TFirst, TSecond>
{
    TFirst First { get; set; }
    TSecond Second { get; set; }
}

public struct Pair<TFirst, TSecond>: IPair<TFirst, TSecond>
{
    public Pair(TFirst first, TSecond second)
    {
        _First = first;
        _Second = second;
    }

    public TFirst First
    {
        get{ return _First; }
        set{ _First = value; }
    }
    private TFirst _First;

    public TSecond Second
    {
        get{ return _Second; }
        set{ _Second = value; }
    }
    private TSecond _Second;
}
```

When you use the `Pair<TFirst, TSecond>` class, you supply multiple type parameters within the angle brackets of the declaration and instantiation statements, and then you supply matching types to the parameters of the methods when you call them, as shown in Listing 11.15.

LISTING 11.15: **Using a Type with Multiple Type Parameters**

```
Pair<int, string> historicalEvent =
    new Pair<int, string>(1914,
        "Shackleton leaves for South Pole on ship Endurance");
Console.WriteLine("{0}: {1}",
    historicalEvent.First, historicalEvent.Second);
```

The number of type parameters, the **arity,** uniquely distinguishes the class from others of the same name. Therefore, it is possible to define both `Pair<T>` and `Pair<TFirst, TSecond>` within the same namespace because of the arity variation. Furthermore, because of their close semantic relationship, generics that differ only by arity should be placed into the same C# file.

Guidelines

DO place multiple generic classes into a single file if they only differ by the number of generic parameters.

Arity in Abundance

In C# 4.0 the CLR team defined nine new generic types all called `Tuple`. As with `Pair<...>`, it was possible to reuse the same name because of the variation in arity (each class had a different number of type parameters) as shown in Listing 11.16.

LISTING 11.16: **Using Arity to Overload a Type Definition**

```
public class Tuple { ... }
public class Tuple<T1>:
  IStructuralEquatable, IStructuralComparable, IComparable {...}
public class Tuple<T1, T2>: ... {...}
public class Tuple<T1, T2, T3>: ... {...}
public class Tuple<T1, T2, T3, T4>: ... {...}
public class Tuple<T1, T2, T3, T4, T5>: ... {...}
public class Tuple<T1, T2, T3, T4, T5, T6>: ... {...}
public class Tuple<T1, T2, T3, T4, T5, T6, T7>: ... {...}
public class Tuple<T1, T2, T3, T4, T5, T6, T7, TRest>: ... {...}
```

The `Tuple<...>` set of classes was designed for the same purpose as the `Pair<T>` and `Pair<TFirst, TSecond>` classes, except together they can handle seven type arguments. In fact, using the last `Tuple` shown in Listing 11.16, `TRest` can be used to store another `Tuple`, making the number of elements of the tuple practically unlimited.

Another interesting member of the tuple family of classes is the nongeneric `Tuple` class. This class has eight static "factory" methods for instantiating the various generic tuple types. Although each generic type could be instantiated directly using its constructor, the `Tuple` type's factory methods allow for inference of the type arguments. Listing 11.17 shows the difference.

LISTING 11.17: Using a Tuple's `Create()` **Factory Methods**

```
Tuple<string, Contact> keyValuePair;
keyValuePair =
    Tuple.Create(
        "555-55-5555", new Contact("Inigo Montoya"));
keyValuePair =
    new Tuple<string, Contact>(
        "555-55-5555", new Contact("Inigo Montoya"));
```

Obviously, when the `Tuple` gets large, the number of type parameters to specify could be cumbersome without the `Create()` factory methods.

As you might have deduced from the fact that the framework libraries declare eight different generic tuple types, there is no support in the CLR type system for what are called "variadic" generic types. Methods can take an arbitrary number of arguments by using "parameter arrays," but there is no corresponding technique for generic types; every generic type must be of a specific arity.

Nested Generic Types

Type parameters on a containing generic type will "cascade" down to any nested types automatically. If the containing type declares a type parameter T, for example, all nested types will also be generic and type parameter T will be available on the nested type as well. If the nested type includes its own type parameter named T, this will hide the type parameter within the containing type and any reference to T in the nested type will refer to the nested T type parameter. Fortunately, reuse of the same type parameter name within the nested type will cause a compiler warning to prevent accidental overlap (see Listing 11.18).

LISTING 11.18: **Nested Generic Types**

```
class Container<T, U>
{
  // Nested classes inherit type parameters.
  // Reusing a type parameter name will cause
  // a warning.
  class Nested<U>
  {
      void Method(T param0, U param1)
      {
      }
  }
}
```

The containing type's type parameters are accessible in the nested type the same way that members of the containing type are also accessible from the nested type. The rule is simply that a type parameter is available anywhere within the body of the type that declares it.

> **Guidelines**
>
> **AVOID** shadowing a type parameter of an outer type with an identically named type parameter of a nested type.

Constraints

Generics support the ability to define constraints on type parameters. These constraints ensure that the types provided as type arguments conform to various rules. Take, for example, the BinaryTree<T> class shown in Listing 11.19.

LISTING 11.19: **Declaring a** BinaryTree<T> **Class with No Constraints**

```
public class BinaryTree<T>
{
    public BinaryTree ( T item)
    {
        Item = item;
    }

    public T Item
    {
        get{ return _Item;    }
        set{ _Item = value; }
    }
```

```
        private T _Item;

        public Pair<BinaryTree<T>> SubItems
        {
            get{ return _SubItems; }
            set{ _SubItems = value; }
        }
        private Pair<BinaryTree<T>> _SubItems;
}
```

(An interesting side note is that BinaryTree<T> uses Pair<T> internally, which is possible because Pair<T> is simply another type.)

Suppose you want the tree to sort the values within the Pair<T> value as it is assigned to the SubItems property. In order to achieve the sorting, the SubItems set accessor uses the CompareTo() method of the supplied key, as shown in Listing 11.20.

LISTING 11.20: Needing the Type Parameter to Support an Interface

```
public class BinaryTree<T>
{
    // ...
    public Pair<BinaryTree<T>> SubItems
    {
        get{ return _SubItems; }
        set
        {
            IComparable<T> first;
            // ERROR: Cannot implicitly convert type...
            first = value.First;  // Explicit cast required

            if (first.CompareTo(value.Second) < 0)
            {
                // first is less than second.
                // ...
            }
            else
            {
                // first and second are the same or
                // second is less than first.
                // ...
            }
            _SubItems = value;
        }
    }
    private Pair<BinaryTree<T>> _SubItems;
}
```

At compile time, the type parameter T is an unconstrained generic. When the code is written as shown, the compiler assumes that the only members available on T are those inherited from the base type object, since every type has object as a base class. Only methods such as ToString(), therefore, are available to call on an instance of the type parameter T. As a result, the compiler displays a compilation error because the CompareTo() method is not defined on type object.

You can cast the T parameter to the IComparable<T> interface in order to access the CompareTo() method, as shown in Listing 11.21.

LISTING 11.21: Needing the Type Parameter to Support an Interface or Exception Thrown

```
public class BinaryTree<T>
{
    ...
    public Pair<BinaryTree<T>> SubItems
    {
        get{ return _SubItems; }
        set
        {
            IComparable<T> first;
            first = (IComparable<T>)value.First.Item;

            if (first.CompareTo(value.Second.Item) < 0)
            {
                // first is less than second.
                ...
            }
            else
            {
                // second is less than or equal to first.
                ...
            }
            _SubItems = value;
        }
    }
    private Pair<BinaryTree<T>> _SubItems;
}
```

Unfortunately, however, if you now declare a BinaryTree<SomeType> class variable but the type argument does not implement the IComparable<SomeType> interface, you encounter an execution-time error—specifically, an InvalidCastException. This defeats a key reason for having generics in the first place: to improve type safety.

To avoid this exception and instead provide a compile-time error if the type argument does not implement the interface, C# enables you to supply an optional list of **constraints** for each type parameter declared in the generic type. A constraint declares the characteristics that the generic type requires of the type argument supplied for each type parameter. You declare a constraint using the `where` keyword, followed by a "parameter-requirements" pair, where the parameter must be one of those declared in the generic type and the requirements describe the class or interfaces to which the type argument must be convertible, the presence of a default constructor, or a reference/value type restriction.

Interface Constraints

In order to ensure that the binary tree has its nodes correctly ordered, you need to use the `CompareTo()` method in the `BinaryTree` class. To do this most effectively, you impose a constraint on the `T` type parameter. You need the `T` type parameter to implement the `IComparable<T>` interface. The syntax for this appears in Listing 11.22.

LISTING 11.22: **Declaring an Interface Constraint**

```
public class BinaryTree<T>
    where T: System.IComparable<T>
{
    ...
    public Pair<BinaryTree<T>> SubItems
    {
        get{ return _SubItems; }
        set
        {
            IComparable<T> first;
            // Notice that the cast can now be eliminated.
            first = value.First.Item;

            if (first.CompareTo(value.Second.Item) < 0)
            {
                // first is less than second
                ...
            }
            else
            {
                // second is less than or equal to first.
                ...
            }
            _SubItems = value;
        }
    }
    private Pair<BinaryTree<T>> _SubItems;
}
```

Language Contrast: C++—Templates

It is interesting to note that Microsoft's CLI support in C++ includes both generics and C++ templates because of the distinct characteristics of each.

Generics in C# and the CLR differ from similar constructs in other languages. Although other languages provide similar functionality, C# is significantly more type-safe. Generics in C# are a language feature and a platform feature—the underlying 2.0 runtime contains deep support for generics in its engine.

C++ templates differ significantly from C# generics; the fundamental difference is that C++ templates are compiled anew once for every type argument provided. The analysis of templatized code is almost exactly as though you had done a "search and replace," replacing the type parameter with the type argument, and compiled the resultant code. C# generics, on the other hand, compile the generic class to CIL once. C# takes advantage of the fact that generic types are a part of the CIL language. At runtime, the CLR's "just in time" compiler generates specialized code anew when a generic type has a value type for a type argument, though it cleverly reuses the generated code every time a type argument is a reference type.

Because C++ templates are reanalyzed anew at compile time for each type argument, there is no need for generic constraints; there is no requirement to prove to the compiler that the templatized code will work correctly for any type argument, only for the type arguments that are actually used.

An advantage of the C++ template strategy is that operators (+, -, and so on) may be used on the type argument. When type arguments are substituted in, the code will be analyzed anew to ensure that the type supplied is one that supports the operator, or will produce an error if it does not. (And unfortunately, typically the error is reported where the error would be in the substituted code, not where the bad type argument is used.) C# does not support the calling of operators on the type parameter because operators are static—they can't be identified by interfaces or base class constraints.

In short, C++ template errors are discovered and reported only when *using* the template with a particular bad type argument, not when defining it. Because C# generics can declare constraints, the compiler can prevent such errors when defining the generic, thereby identifying invalid assumptions sooner. Furthermore, when using a generic type with a type argument that does not meet the constraints, the error will point to the type usage, not to some location in the generic implementation.

It is interesting to note that Microsoft's CLI support in C++ includes both generics and C++ templates because of the distinct characteristics of each.

When given the interface constraint addition in Listing 11.22, the compiler ensures that each time you use the `BinaryTree<T>` class you specify a type parameter that implements the corresponding construction of the `IComparable<T>` interface. Furthermore, you no longer need to explicitly cast the variable to an `IComparable<T>` interface before calling the `CompareTo()` method. Casting is not even required to access members that use explicit interface implementation, which in other contexts would hide the member without a cast. When calling a method on a value typed as a generic type parameter, the compiler checks to see if the method matches any method on any of the interfaces declared as constraints.

If you tried to create a `BinaryTree<T>` variable using `System.Text.StringBuilder` as the type parameter, you would receive a compiler error because `StringBuilder` does not implement `IComparable<StringBuilder>`. The error is similar to the one shown in Output 11.3.

OUTPUT 11.3

```
error CS0311: The type 'System.Text.StringBuilder' cannot be used as type
parameter 'T' in the generic type or method 'BinaryTree<T>'. There is no
implicit reference conversion from 'System.Text.StringBuilder' to
'System.IComparable<System.Text.StringBuilder>'.
```

To specify an interface for the constraint you declare an **interface type constraint.** This constraint even circumvents the need to cast in order to call an explicit interface member implementation.

Class Type Constraints

Sometimes you might want to constrain a type argument to be convertible to a particular class type. You do this using a **class type constraint,** as shown in Listing 11.23.

LISTING 11.23: Declaring a Class Type Constraint

```
public class EntityDictionary<TKey, TValue>
    : System.Collections.Generic.Dictionary<TKey, TValue>
    where TValue : EntityBase
{
    ...
}
```

`EntityDictionary<TKey, TValue>` requires that all type arguments provided for the type parameter `TValue` be implicitly convertible to the `EntityBase` class. By requiring the conversion, it is possible to use the members of `EntityBase` on values of type `TValue` within the generic implementation, because the constraint will ensure that all type arguments can be implicitly converted to the `EntityBase` class.

The syntax for the class type constraint is the same as that for the interface type constraint, except that class type constraints must appear before any interface type constraints (just as the base class must appear before implemented interfaces in a class declaration). However, unlike interface constraints, multiple base class constraints are not allowed since it is not possible to derive from multiple unrelated classes. Similarly, base class constraints cannot specify sealed classes or nonclass types. For example, C# does not allow a type parameter to be constrained to `string` or `System.Nullable<T>` because there would then be only one possible type argument for that type parameter; that's hardly "generic." If the type parameter is constrained to a single type, there is no need for the type parameter in the first place; just use that type directly.

Certain "special" types are not legal as class type constraints: See the Advanced Topic Constraint Limitations, later in this chapter, for details.

struct/class **Constraints**

Another valuable generic constraint is the ability to restrict type arguments to be any non-nullable value type or any reference type. Instead, C# provides special syntax that works for reference types as well. Rather than specifying a class from which `T` must derive, you simply use the keyword `struct` or `class`, as shown in Listing 11.24.

LISTING 11.24: **Specifying the Type Parameter As a Value Type**

```csharp
public struct Nullable<T> :
    IFormattable, IComparable,
    IComparable<Nullable<T>>, INullable
    where T : struct
{
    // ...
}
```

Note that the `class` constraint somewhat confusingly does not restrict the type argument to class types; it restricts it to reference types. A type argument supplied for a type parameter constrained with the `class` constraint may be any class, interface, delegate, or array type.

Because a class type constraint requires a particular class, using a `struct` or `class` constraint with a class type constraint would be pointless and confusing. Therefore, you cannot combine `struct` and `class` constraints.

There is one special characteristic for the `struct` constraint: Nullable value types do not satisfy the constraint. Why? Nullable value types are implemented as the generic type `Nullable<T>`, which itself applies the `struct` constraint to T. If nullable value types satisfied that constraint, it would be possible to define the nonsense type `Nullable<Nullable<int>>`. A doubly nullable integer is confusing to the point of being meaningless. (As expected, the shorthand syntax `int??` is also disallowed.)

Multiple Constraints

For any given type parameter, you may specify any number of interface type constraints, but no more than one class type constraint (just as a class may implement any number of interfaces but inherit from only one other class). Each new constraint is declared in a comma-delimited list following the generic type parameter and a colon. If there is more than one type parameter, each must be preceded by the `where` keyword. In Listing 11.25, the generic `EntityDictionary` class declares two type parameters: `TKey` and `TValue`. The `TKey` type parameter has two interface type constraints, and the `TValue` type parameter has one class type constraint.

LISTING 11.25: Specifying Multiple Constraints

```
public class EntityDictionary<TKey, TValue>
    : Dictionary<TKey, TValue>
    where TKey : IComparable<TKey>, IFormattable
    where TValue : EntityBase
{
    ...
}
```

In this case, there are multiple constraints on `TKey` itself and an additional constraint on `TValue`. When specifying multiple constraints on one type parameter, an AND relationship is assumed. If a type C is supplied as the type argument for `TKey`, C must implement `IComparable<C>` and `IFormattable`, for example.

Notice there is no comma between each where clause.

Constructor Constraints

In some cases, it is desirable to create an instance of the type argument's type inside the generic class. In Listing 11.26, the MakeValue() method for the EntityDictionary<TKey, TValue> class must create an instance of the type argument corresponding to type parameter TValue.

LISTING 11.26: Requiring a Default Constructor Constraint

```csharp
public class EntityBase<TKey>
{
    public TKey Key
    {
        get{ return _Key;  }
        set{ _Key = value; }
    }
    private TKey _Key;
}

public class EntityDictionary<TKey, TValue> :
    Dictionary<TKey, TValue>
    where TKey: IComparable<TKey>, IFormattable
    where TValue : EntityBase<TKey>, new()
{
    // ...

    public TValue MakeValue(TKey key)
    {
        TValue newEntity = new TValue();
        newEntity.Key = key;
        Add(newEntity.Key, newEntity);
        return newEntity;
    }

    // ...
}
```

Because not all objects are guaranteed to have public default constructors, the compiler does not allow you to call the default constructor on an unconstrained type parameter. To override this compiler restriction, you add the text new() after all other constraints are specified. This text is a **constructor constraint,** and it requires the type argument corresponding to the constrained type parameter to have a public default constructor. Only the default constructor constraint is available. You cannot specify a constraint that ensures that the type argument supplied provides a constructor that takes formal parameters.

Constraint Inheritance

Neither generic type parameters nor their constraints are inherited by a derived class, because generic type parameters are not members. (Remember, class inheritance is the property that the derived class has all of the members of the base class.) It is a common practice to make new generic types that inherit from other generic types. Since the type parameters of the derived generic type are now the type arguments of the generic base class, the type parameters must have equal (or stronger) constraints as those on the base class. Confused? Consider Listing 11.27.

LISTING 11.27: Inherited Constraints Specified Explicitly

```
class EntityBase<T> where T : IComparable<T>
{
  // ...
}
```

```
// ERROR:
// The type 'U' must be convertible to
// 'System.IComparable<U>' in order to use it as parameter
// 'T' in the generic type or method.
// class Entity<U> : EntityBase<U>
// {
//     ...
// }
```

`EntityBase<T>` requires that the type argument U supplied for T by the base class specifier `EntityBase<U>` implement `IComparable<U>`. Therefore, the `Entity<U>` class needs to require the same constraint on U. Failure to do so will result in a compile error. This increases a programmer's awareness of the base class's type constraint in the derived class, avoiding confusion when using the derived class and discovering the constraint but not understanding where it comes from.

We have not covered generic methods yet; we'll get to them later in this chapter. But briefly, methods may also be generic and may also place constraints on the type arguments supplied for their type parameters. How, then, are constraints handled when a virtual generic method is inherited and overridden? In contrast to the situation with type parameters declared on a generic class, constraints on overriding virtual generic methods (or explicit interface) methods are inherited implicitly and may not be restated (see Listing 11.28).

LISTING 11.28: Repeating Inherited Constraints on Virtual Members Is Prohibited

```csharp
class EntityBase
{
  public virtual void Method<T>(T t)
      where T : IComparable<T>
  {
      // ...
  }

}

class Order : EntityBase
{
  public override void Method<T>(T t)
  //    Constraints may not be repeated on overriding
  //    members
  //    where T : IComparable<T>
  {
      // ...
  }
}
```

In the generic class inheritance case, the type parameter on the derived class can be additionally constrained by adding not only the constraints on the base class (required), but also additional constraints as well. However, overriding virtual generic methods need to conform exactly to the constraints defined by the base class method. Additional constraints could break polymorphism, so they are not allowed and the type parameter constraints on the overriding method are implied.

■ ADVANCED TOPIC

Constraint Limitations

Constraints are appropriately limited to avoid nonsensical code. For example, you cannot combine a class type constraint with a struct or class constraint. Also, you cannot specify constraints to restrict inheritance to special types such as object, arrays, System.ValueType, System.Enum (enum), System.Delegate, and System.MulticastDelegate.

In some cases, constraint limitations are perhaps more desirable, but they still are not supported. The following subsections provide some additional examples of constraints that are not allowed.

Operator Constraints Are Not Allowed

You cannot constrain a type parameter to a type that implements a particular method or operator, except via interface type constraints (for methods) or class type constraints (for methods and operators). Because of this, the generic Add() in Listing 11.29 does not work.

LISTING 11.29: Constraint Expressions Cannot Require Operators

```csharp
public abstract class MathEx<T>
{
    public static T Add(T first, T second)
    {
        // Error: Operator '+' cannot be applied to
        // operands of type 'T' and 'T'.
        // return first + second;
    }
}
```

In this case, the method assumes that the + operator is available on all types that could be supplied as type arguments for T. But there is no constraint that prevents you from supplying a type argument that does not have an associated addition operator, so an error occurs. Unfortunately, there is no way to specify that an addition operator is required within a constraint, aside from using a class type constraint where the class type implements an addition operator.

More generally, there is no way to constrain a type to have a static method.

OR Criteria Are Not Supported

If you supply multiple interfaces or class constraints for a type parameter, the compiler always assumes an AND relationship between constraints. For example, where T : IComparable<T>, IFormattable requires that both IComparable<T> and IFormattable are supported. There is no way to specify an OR relationship between constraints. Hence, an equivalent of Listing 11.30 is not supported.

LISTING 11.30: Combining Constraints Using an OR Relationship Is Not Allowed

```csharp
public class BinaryTree<T>
    // Error: OR is not supported.
```

```
      // where T: System.IComparable<T> || System.IFormattable
   {
      ...
   }
```

Supporting this would prevent the compiler from resolving which method to call at compile time.

Constraints of Type Delegate and Enum Are Not Valid

Delegate types, array types, and enumerated types may not be used as class type constraints, because they are all effectively "sealed" types. (If you are not familiar with delegate types, see Chapter 12.) Their base types, System.Delegate, System.MultiCastDelegate, System.Array, and System.Enum, may also not be used as constraints. For example, the compiler will output an error for the class declaration in Listing 11.31.

LISTING 11.31: Inheritance Constraints Cannot Be of Type System.Delegate

```
// Error:  Constraint cannot be special class 'System.Delegate'
public class Publisher<T>
    where T : System.Delegate
{
    public event T Event;
    public void Publish()
    {
        if (Event != null)
        {
            Event(this, new EventArgs());
        }
    }
}
```

All delegate types are considered special classes that cannot be specified as type parameters. Doing so would prevent compile-time validation on the call to Event() because the signature of the event firing is unknown with the data types System.Delegate and System.MulticastDelegate. The same restriction occurs for any enum type.

Constructor Constraints Are Allowed Only for Default Constructors

Listing 11.26 includes a constructor constraint that forces the type argument supplied for TValue to provide a public parameterless constructor. There is no constraint to force the type argument to provide a constructor that takes other formal parameters. For example, you might want to constrain TValue so that the type argument provided for TValue must provide a constructor that takes the type argument provided for TKey, but this is not possible. Listing 11.32 demonstrates the invalid code.

LISTING 11.32: **Constructor Constraints Can Be Specified Only for Default Constructors**

```
public TValue New(TKey key)
{
    // Error: 'TValue': Cannot provide arguments
    // when creating an instance of a variable type.
    TValue newEntity = null;
    // newEntity = new TValue(key);
    Add(newEntity.Key, newEntity);
    return newEntity;
}
```

One way to circumvent this restriction is to supply a factory interface that includes a method for instantiating the type. The factory implementing the interface takes responsibility for instantiating the entity rather than the EntityDictionary itself (see Listing 11.33).

LISTING 11.33: **Using a Factory Interface in Place of a Constructor Constraint**

```
public class EntityBase<TKey>
{
    public EntityBase(TKey key)
    {
        Key = key;
    }
    public TKey Key
    {
        get { return _key; }
        set { _key = value; }
    }
    private TKey _key;
}

public class EntityDictionary<TKey, TValue, TFactory> :
        Dictionary<TKey, TValue>
    where TKey : IComparable<TKey>, IFormattable
    where TValue : EntityBase<TKey>
    where TFactory : IEntityFactory<TKey, TValue>, new()
{
    ...
    public TValue New(TKey key)
    {
        TFactory factory = new TFactory();
        TValue newEntity = factory.CreateNew(key);
        Add(newEntity.Key, newEntity);
        return newEntity;
```

```
        }
        ...
    }

    public interface IEntityFactory<TKey, TValue>
    {
        TValue CreateNew(TKey key);
    }
    ...
```

A declaration such as this allows you to pass the new key to a TValue factory method that takes parameters, rather than relying on the default constructor. It no longer uses the constructor constraint on TValue because TFactory is responsible for instantiating value. (One modification to the code in Listing 11.33 would be to save a reference to the factory. This would enable you to reuse the factory instead of reinstantiating it every time.)

A declaration for a variable of type EntityDictionary<TKey, TValue, TFactory> would result in an entity declaration similar to the Order entity in Listing 11.34.

LISTING 11.34: Declaring an Entity to Be Used in EntityDictionary<...>

```
    public class Order : EntityBase<Guid>
    {
      public Order(Guid key) :
          base(key)
      {
          // ...
      }
    }

    public class OrderFactory : IEntityFactory<Guid, Order>
    {
      public Order CreateNew(Guid key)
      {
          return new Order(key);
      }
    }
```

Generic Methods

You already learned that it is relatively simple to add a method to a type when the type is generic, and that method can use the generic type parameters declared by the type. You did this in the generic class examples so far.

Generic methods are methods that use generic type parameters much as generic types do. They can be declared in generic or nongeneric types, and if declared in a generic type, their type parameters are distinct from those of their containing generic type. To declare a generic method, you specify the generic type parameters the same way you do for generic types: Add the type parameter declaration syntax immediately following the method name, as shown in the MathEx.Max<T> and MathEx.Min<T> examples in Listing 11.35.

LISTING 11.35: Defining Generic Methods

```csharp
public static class MathEx
{
  public static T Max<T>(T first, params T[] values)
      where T : IComparable<T>
  {
      T maximum = first;
      foreach (T item in values)
      {
          if (item.CompareTo(maximum) > 0)
          {
              maximum = item;
          }
      }
      return maximum;
  }

  public static T Min<T>(T first, params T[] values)
      where T : IComparable<T>
  {
      T minimum = first;

      foreach (T item in values)
      {
          if (item.CompareTo(minimum) < 0)
          {
              minimum = item;
          }
      }
      return minimum;
  }
}
```

In this example, the method is static but C# does not require this.

Note that generic methods, like generic types, can include more than one type parameter. The arity (the number of type parameters) is an additional distinguishing characteristic of a method signature. That is to say, it is legal to have two methods that are identical in their names and formal parameter types, as long as they differ in method type parameter arity.

Generic Method Type Inference

Just as type arguments are provided after the type name when using a generic type, the method type arguments are provided after the method type name. The code used to call the Min<T> and Max<T> methods looks like that shown in Listing 11.36.

LISTING 11.36: **Specifying the Type Parameter Explicitly**

```
Console.WriteLine(
    MathEx.Max<int>(7, 490));
Console.WriteLine(
    MathEx.Min<string>("R.O.U.S.", "Fireswamp"));
```

The output to Listing 11.36 appears in Output 11.4.

OUTPUT 11.4

```
490
Fireswamp
```

Not surprisingly, the type arguments, int and string, correspond to the actual types used in the generic method calls. However, specifying the type arguments is redundant because the compiler can infer the type parameters from the formal parameters passed to the method. Clearly, the caller of Max in Listing 11.36 intends the type argument to be int because both of the method arguments are of type int. To avoid redundancy, you can exclude the type parameters from the call in all cases when the compiler is able to logically infer what type arguments you must have intended. This is known as **method type inference,** and an example appears in Listing 11.37. The output appears in Output 11.5.

LISTING 11.37: **Inferring the Type Argument from the Arguments**

```
Console.WriteLine(
    MathEx.Max(7, 490)); // No type arguments!
Console.WriteLine(
    MathEx.Min("R.O.U.S'", "Fireswamp"));
```

OUTPUT 11.5

```
490
Fireswamp
```

For method type inference to succeed, the types of the arguments must be "matched" with the formal parameters of the generic method in such a way that the desired type arguments can be inferred. An interesting question to consider is what happens when contradictory inferences are made. For example, calling the Max<T> method using MathEx.Max(7.0, 490) could deduce from the first argument that the type argument should be double, and deduce from the second argument that the type argument is int, a contradiction. In C# 2.0, this would have produced an error. A more sophisticated analysis would notice that the contradiction can be resolved because every int can be converted to double, so double is the best choice for the type argument. C# 3.0 and C# 4.0 both included improvements to the method type inferencing algorithm that permit the compiler to make these more sophisticated analyses.

In cases where method type inference is still not sophisticated enough to deduce the type arguments, you can resolve the error by either inserting casts on the arguments that clarify to the compiler the argument types that should be used in the inferences, or giving up on type inferencing and including the type arguments explicitly.

Also note that when making its inferences, the method type inference algorithm considers only the arguments, the arguments' types, and the formal parameter types of the generic method. Other factors that could in practice be used in the analysis—such as the return type of the generic method, the type of the variable that the method's returned value is being assigned to, or the constraints on the method's generic type parameters—are not considered at all by the method type inference algorithm.

Specifying Constraints

Type parameters of generic methods may be constrained in exactly the same way that type parameters of generic types are constrained. For example, you can restrict a method's type parameter to implement an interface, or be convertible to a class type. The constraints are specified between the argument list and the method body, as shown in Listing 11.38.

LISTING 11.38: **Specifying Constraints on Generic Methods**

```
public class ConsoleTreeControl
{
    // Generic method Show<T>
    public static void Show<T>(BinaryTree<T> tree, int indent)
```

```
      where T :  IComparable<T>
  {
      Console.WriteLine("\n{0}{1}",
          "+ --".PadLeft(5*indent, ' '),
          tree.Item.ToString());
      if (tree.SubItems.First != null)
          Show(tree.SubItems.First, indent+1);
      if (tree.SubItems.Second != null)
          Show(tree.SubItems.Second, indent+1);
  }
}
```

Notice that the Show<T> implementation itself does not directly use any member of the IComparable<T> interface, so you might wonder why the constraint is required. Recall, however, that the BinaryTree<T> class did require this (see Listing 11.39).

LISTING 11.39: BinaryTree<T> **Requiring** IComparable<T> **Type Parameters**

```
  public class BinaryTree<T>
      where T: System.IComparable<T>
  {
      ...
  }
```

Because the BinaryTree<T> class requires this constraint on its T, and because Show<T> uses its T as a type argument corresponding to a constrained type parameter, Show<T> needs to ensure that the class's type parameter's constraint is met on its method type argument.

■ **ADVANCED TOPIC**

Casting inside a Generic Method

Sometimes you should be wary of using generics—for instance, when using them specifically to bury a cast operation. Consider the following method, which converts a stream into an object of a given type:

```
  public static T Deserialize<T>(
      Stream stream, IFormatter formatter)
  {
      return (T)formatter.Deserialize(stream);
  }
```

The `formatter` is responsible for removing data from the stream and converting it to an object. The `Deserialize()` call on the formatter returns data of type `object`. A call to use the generic version of `Deserialize()` looks something like this:

```
string greeting =
    Deserialization.Deserialize<string>(stream, formatter);
```

The problem with this code is that to the caller of the method, `Deserialize<T>()` appears to be type-safe. However, a cast operation is still performed on behalf of the caller, as in the case of the nongeneric equivalent shown here:

```
string greeting =
    (string)Deserialization.Deserialize(stream, formatter);
```

The cast could fail at runtime; the method might not be as type-safe as it appears. The `Deserialize<T>` method is generic solely so that it can hide the existence of the cast from the caller, which seems dangerously deceptive. It might be better for the method to be nongeneric and return `object`, making the caller aware that it is not type-safe. Developers should use care when casting in generic methods if there are no constraints to verify cast validity.

Guidelines

AVOID misleading the caller with generic methods that are not as type-safe as they appear.

Covariance and Contravariance

A common question asked by new users of generic types is why an expression of type `List<string>` may not be assigned to a variable of type `List<object>`—if a `string` may be converted to type `object`, surely a list of strings is similarly compatible with a list of objects. But this is not, generally speaking, either type-safe or legal. If you declare two variables with different type parameters using the same generic class, the variables are not type-compatible even if they are assigning from a more specific type to a more generic type—in other words, they are not **covariant.**

Covariant is a technical term from category theory, but the idea is straight-forward: Suppose two types X and Y have a special relationship, namely that every value of the type X may be converted to the type Y. If the types I<X> and I<Y> always also have that same special relationship, we say, "I<T> is covariant in T." When dealing with simple generic types with only one type parameter, the type parameter can be understood and we simply say, "I<T> is covariant." The conversion from I<X> to I<Y> is called a **covariant conversion.**

For example, instances of a generic class, Pair<Contact> and Pair <PdaItem>, are not type-compatible even when the type arguments are themselves compatible. In other words, the compiler prevents converting (implicitly or explicitly) Pair<Contact> to Pair<PdaItem>, even though Contact derives from PdaItem. Similarly, converting Pair<Contact> to the interface type IPair<PdaItem> will also fail. See Listing 11.40 for an example.

LISTING 11.40: Conversion between Generics with Different Type Parameters

```
// ...
// Error: Cannot convert type ...
Pair<PdaItem> pair = (Pair<PdaItem>) new Pair<Contact>();
IPair<PdaItem> duple = (IPair<PdaItem>) new Pair<Contact>();
```

But why is this not legal? Why are List<T> and Pair<T> not covariant? Listing 11.41 shows what would happen if the C# language allowed unrestricted generic covariance.

LISTING 11.41: Preventing Covariance Maintains Homogeneity

```
//...
Contact contact1 = new Contact("Princess Buttercup"),
Contact contact2 = new Contact("Inigo Montoya");
Pair<Contact> contacts = new Pair<Contact>(contact1, contact2);

// This gives an error: Cannot convert type ...
// But suppose it did not.
// IPair<PdaItem> pdaPair = (IPair<PdaItem>) contacts;
// This is perfectly legal, but not type safe.
// pdaPair.First = new Address("123 Sesame Street");
...
```

An IPair<PdaItem> can contain an address, but the object is really a Pair<Contact> that can only contain contacts, not addresses. Type safety is completely violated if unrestricted generic covariance is allowed

Now it should also be clear why a list of strings may not be used as a list of objects; you cannot insert an integer into a list of strings, but you can insert an integer into a list of objects, so it must be illegal to cast a list of strings to a list of objects so that this error can be prevented by the compiler.

Enabling Covariance with the out Type Parameter Modifier in C# 4.0

You might have noticed that both of the problems described above as consequences of unrestricted covariance arise because the generic pair and the generic list allow their contents to be written. Suppose we eliminated this possibility by making a read-only IReadOnlyPair<T> interface that only exposes T as coming "out" of the interface (that is, used as the return type of a method or read-only property) and never "into" it (that is, used as a formal parameter or writeable property type). If we restricted ourselves to an "out only" interface with respect to T, the covariance problem just described would not occur (see Listing 11.42).

LISTING 11.42: **Potentially Possible Covariance**

```
interface IReadOnlyPair<T>
{
  T First { get; }
  T Second { get; }
}


interface IPair<T>
{
  T First { get; set; }
  T Second { get; set; }
}


public struct Pair<T> : IPair<T>, IReadOnlyPair<T>
{
  // ...
}


class Program
{
  static void Main()
  {
      // Error: Only theoretically possible without
      // the out type parameter modifier
      Pair<Contact> contacts =
          new Pair<Contact>(
```

```
                new Contact("Princess Buttercupt"),
                new Contact("Inigo Montoya") );
       IReadOnlyPair<PdaItem> pair = contacts;
       PdaItem pdaItem1 = pair.First;
       PdaItem pdaItem2 = pair.Second;
    }
  }
```

By restricting the generic type declaration to only expose data out of the interface, there is no reason for the compiler to prevent covariance. All operations on an IReadOnlyPair<PdaItem> instance would convert Contacts (from the original Pair<Contact> object) up to the base class PdaItem—a perfectly valid conversion. There is no way to "write" an address into the object that is really a pair of contacts, because the interface does not expose any writeable properties.

The code above still does not compile. However, support for safe covariance was added to C# 4. To indicate that a generic interface is intended to be covariant in one of its type parameters, declare the type parameter with the out type parameter modifier. Listing 11.43 shows how to modify the interface declaration to indicate that it should be allowed to be covariant.

LISTING 11.43: Covariance Using the out Type Parameter Modifier

```
  ...
  interface IReadOnlyPair<out T>
  {
    T First { get; }
    T Second { get; }
  }
```

Modifying the type parameter on the IReadOnlyPair<out T> interface with out will cause the compiler to verify that indeed T is used only for "outputs"—method return types and read-only property return types—and never for formal parameters or property setters. From then on, the compiler will allow any covariant conversions involving the interface to succeed. With this modification made to the code in Listing 11.42, the code will now compile and execute successfully.

There are a number of important restrictions on covariant conversions.

- Only generic interfaces and generic delegates (described in Chapter 12) may be covariant. Generic classes and structs are never covariant.

- The varying type arguments of both the "source" and "target" generic types must be reference types, not value types. That is, an IReadOnlyPair <string> may be converted covariantly to IReadOnlyPair<object> because both string and IReadOnlyPair<object> are reference types. An IReadOnlyPair<int> may not be converted to IReadOnlyPair<object> because int is not a reference type.

- The interface or delegate must be declared as supporting covariance, and the compiler must be able to verify that the annotated type parameters are in fact used in only "output" positions.

Enabling Contravariance with the in Type Parameter Modifier in C# 4.0

Covariance that "goes backward" is called **contravariance.** Again, suppose two types X and Y are related such that every value of the type X may be converted to the type Y. If the types I<X> and I<Y> always have that same special relationship "backward"—that is, every value of the type I<Y> can be converted to the type I<X>—we say "I<T> is contravariant in T."

Most people find that contravariance is much harder to comprehend than covariance is. The canonical example of contravariance is a comparer. Suppose you have a derived type, Apple, and a base type, Fruit. Clearly, they have the special relationship: Every value of type Apple may be converted to Fruit.

Now suppose you have an interface ICompareThings<T> that has a method bool FirstIsBetter(T t1, T t2) that takes two Ts, and returns a bool saying whether the first one is better than the second one.

What happens when we provide type arguments? An ICompareThings <Apple> has a method that takes two Apples and compares them. An ICompareThings<Fruit> has a method that takes two Fruits and compares them. But since every Apple is a Fruit, clearly a value of type ICompareThings<Fruit> can be safely used anywhere that an ICompareThings<Apple> is needed. The "direction" of the convertibility has been "reversed"; hence the name "contra-variance."

Perhaps unsurprisingly, the opposite of the restrictions on a covariant interface are necessary to ensure safe contravariance. An interface that is contravariant in one of its type parameters must use that type parameter only in "input" positions such as formal parameters. (Or in the types of write-only properties, which are extremely rare.) You can mark an interface as being contravariant by declaring the type parameter with the in modifier, as shown in listing 11.44.

LISTING 11.44: Contravariance Using the in Type Parameter Modifier

```
class Fruit {}
class Apple : Fruit {}
class Orange : Fruit {}
```

```
interface ICompareThings<in T>
{
  bool FirstIsBetter(T t1, T t2);

}
```

```
class Program
{
  class FruitComparer : ICompareThings<Fruit>
  { ... }
  static void Main()
  {
      // Allowed in C# 4.0
      ICompareThings<Fruit> fc = new FruitComparer();
      Apple apple1 = new Apple();
      Apple apple2 = new Apple();
      Orange orange = new Orange();
      // A fruit comparer can compare apples and oranges:
      bool b1 = fc.FirstIsBetter(apple1, orange);
      // or apples and apples:
      bool b2 = fc.FirstIsBetter(apple1, apple2);
      // This is legal because the interface is
      // contravariant:
      ICompareThings<Apple> ac = fc;
      // This is really a fruit comparer, so it can
      // compare two apples still.
      bool b3 = ac.FirstIsBetter(apple1, apple2);
  }
}
```

Notice that similar to covariance support, contravariance uses a type parameter modifier: in, on the interface's type parameter declaration. This instructs the compiler to check that T never appears on a property getter or as the return type of a method, thus enabling contravariant conversions for this interface.

Contravariant conversions have all the analogous restrictions as described above for covariant conversions: They are only valid on generic interface and delegate types, the varying type arguments must be reference types, and the compiler must be able to verify that the interface is safe for the contravariant conversions.

An interface can be covariant in one type parameter and contravariant in the other. Imagine, for example, a device that can transform one thing into another described by the ITransformer<in TSource, out TTarget> interface defined in Listing 11.45.

LISTING 11.45: **Combining Covariance and Contravariance in a Single Generic Type**

```csharp
class Food {}
class Pizza : Food {}
class Salad : Food {}
class Document {}
class ComputerProgram : Document {}
interface ITransformer<in TSource, out TTarget>
{
  TTarget Transform(TSource source);
}
// A computer programmer is a device which transforms
// food into computer programs:

class Programmer : ITransformer<Food, ComputerProgram>
{
  public ComputerProgram Transform(Food f) { ... }
}
class Program
{
  static void Main()
  {
    var programmer = new Programmer();
    ComputerProgram cp = programmer.Transform(new Salad());
    // A computer programmer may be converted with
    // both co- and contra-variant conversions. Because
    // a programmer can turn any food into a computer
    // program, it can be used as a device that turns pizza
    // into documents.
    ITransformer<Pizza, Document> transformer = programmer;
    Document d = transformer.Transform(new Pizza());
  }
}
```

Lastly, note that the compiler will check validity of the covariance and contravariance type parameter modifiers throughout the source. Consider the PairInitializer<in T> interface in Listing 11.46.

LISTING 11.46: **Compiler Validation of Variance**

```
// ERROR:  Invalid variance, the type parameter 'T' is not
//          invariantly valid
interface IPairInitializer<in T>
{
  void Initialize(IPair<T> pair);
}
```

```
// Suppose the code above were legal, and see what goes
// wrong:
class FruitPairInitializer : IPairInitializer<Fruit>
{
  // Let's initiaize our pair of fruit with an
  // apple and an orange.
  public void Initialize(IPair<Fruit> pair)
  {
    pair.First = new Orange();
    pair.Second = new Apple();
  }
}
```

```
// ... Later ...
var f = new FruitPairInitializer();
// This would be legal if contravariance were legal:
IPairInitializer<Apple> a = f;
// And now we write an orange into a pair of apples:
a.Initialize(new Pair<Apple>());
```

A casual observer may be tempted to think that since IPair<T> is used only as an "input" formal parameter, the contravariant in modifier on IPairInitializer is valid. However, the IPair<T> interface cannot safely vary, and therefore, it cannot be constructed with a type argument that can vary. As you can see, this would not be type-safe, and therefore, the compiler disallows the IPairInitializer<T> interface from being declared as contravariant in the first place.

Support for Unsafe Covariance in Arrays

So far we have described covariance and contravariance as being properties of generic types. Of all the nongeneric types, arrays are most like generics; just as we think of a generic "list of T" or a generic "pair of T" we can think of an "array of T" as being the same sort of pattern. Since arrays clearly support both reading and writing, given what you know about covariance and contravariance, you probably would suppose that arrays may be neither safely contravariant nor covariant; an array can only be safely covariant if it is never written to, and only safely contravariant if it is never read from; neither seems like a realistic restriction.

Unfortunately, C# does support array covariance, even though doing so is not type-safe. For example, `Fruit[] fruits = new Apple[10];` is perfectly legal in C#, and if you then say `fruits[0] = new Orange();`, the runtime will issue a type safety violation in the form of an exception. It is deeply disturbing that it is not always legal to assign an `Orange` into an array of `Fruit` because it might really be an array of `Apples`, but that is the situation in not just C#, but all CLR languages that use the runtime's implementation of arrays.

Try to avoid using unsafe array covariance. Every array is convertible to the read-only (and therefore safely covariant) interface `IEnumerable<T>`; that is to say, `IEnumerable<Fruit> fruits = new Apple[10]` is both safe and legal because there is no way to insert an `Orange` into the array if all you have is the read-only interface.

Guidelines

AVOID unsafe array covariance. Instead, **CONSIDER** converting the array to the read-only interface `IEnumerable<T>`, which can be safely converted via covariant conversions.

Generic Internals

Given the discussions in earlier chapters about the prevalence of objects within the CLI type system, it is no surprise that generics are also objects. In fact, the type parameter on a generic class becomes metadata that the runtime uses to build appropriate classes when needed. Generics, therefore, support inheritance, polymorphism, and encapsulation. With generics, you can define methods, properties, fields, classes, interfaces, and delegates.

To achieve this, generics require support from the underlying runtime. So, the addition of generics to the C# language is a feature of both the compiler and the platform. To avoid boxing, for example, the implementation of generics is different for value-based type parameters than for generics with reference type parameters.

CIL Representation of Generics

When a generic class is compiled, it is not significantly different from a nongeneric class. The result of the compilation is nothing but metadata and CIL. The CIL is parameterized to accept a user-supplied type somewhere in code. Suppose you had a simple `Stack` class declared as shown in Listing 11.47.

LISTING 11.47: `Stack<T>` **Declaration**

```
public class Stack<T> where T : IComparable
{
    T[] items;
    // rest of the class here

}
```

When you compile the class, the generated CIL is parameterized and looks something like Listing 11.48.

LISTING 11.48: **CIL Code for** `Stack<T>`

```
.class private auto ansi beforefieldinit
    Stack'1<([mscorlib]System.IComparable)T>
    extends [mscorlib]System.Object
{
  ...
}
```

The first notable item is the `'1` that appears following `Stack` on the second line. That number is the arity. It declares the number of type parameters that the generic class will require type arguments for. A declaration such as `EntityDictionary<TKey, TValue>` would have an arity of 2.

The second line of the generated CIL shows the constraints imposed upon the class. The `T` type parameter is decorated with an interface declaration for the `IComparable` constraint.

If you continue looking through the CIL, you will find that the item's array declaration of type `T` is altered to contain a type parameter using "exclamation point notation," used in the generics-capable version of the CIL. The exclamation point denotes the presence of the first type parameter specified for the class, as shown in Listing 11.49.

LISTING 11.49: CIL with "Exclamation Point Notation" to Support Generics

```
.class public auto ansi beforefieldinit
    'Stack'1'<([mscorlib]System.IComparable) T>
    extends [mscorlib]System.Object
{
    .field private !0[ ] items
    ...
}
```

Beyond the inclusion of the arity and type parameter in the class header and the type parameter denoted with exclamation points in code, there is little difference between the CIL generated for a generic class and the CIL generated for a nongeneric class.

Instantiating Generics Based on Value Types

When a generic type is first constructed with a value type as a type parameter, the runtime creates a specialized generic type with the supplied type parameter(s) placed appropriately in the CIL. Therefore, the runtime creates new specialized generic types for each new parameter value type.

For example, suppose some code declared a `Stack` constructed of integers, as shown in Listing 11.50.

LISTING 11.50: Stack<int> Definition

```
Stack<int> stack;
```

When using this type, `Stack<int>`, for the first time, the runtime generates a specialized version of the `Stack` class with the type argument `int` substituted for its type parameter. From then on, whenever the code uses a `Stack<int>`, the runtime reuses the generated specialized `Stack<int>` class. In Listing 11.51, you declare two instances of a `Stack<int>`, both using the code already generated by the runtime for a `Stack<int>`.

LISTING 11.51: Declaring Variables of Type Stack<T>

```
Stack<int> stackOne = new Stack<int>();
Stack<int> stackTwo = new Stack<int>();
```

If later in the code, you create another `Stack` with a different value type substituted for the type parameter (such as a `long` or a user-defined `struct`) the runtime generates another version of the generic type. The benefit of specialized value type classes is better performance. Furthermore, the code is able to avoid conversions and boxing because each specialized generic class "natively" contains the value type.

Instantiating Generics Based on Reference Types

Generics work slightly differently for reference types. The first time a generic type is constructed with a reference type, the runtime creates a specialized generic type with `object` references substituted for type parameters in the CIL, not a specialized generic type based on the type argument. Each subsequent time a constructed type is instantiated with a reference type parameter, the runtime reuses the previously generated version of the generic type, even if the reference type is different from the first reference type.

For example, suppose you have two reference types, a `Customer` class and an `Order` class, and you create an `EntityDictionary` of `Customer` types, like so:

```
EntityDictionary<Guid, Customer> customers;
```

Prior to accessing this class, the runtime generates a specialized version of the `EntityDictionary` class that, instead of storing `Customer` as the specified data type, stores `object` references. Suppose the next line of code creates an `EntityDictionary` of another reference type, called `Order`:

```
EntityDictionary<Guid, Order> orders =
    new EntityDictionary<Guid, Order>();
```

Unlike value types, no new specialized version of the `EntityDictionary` class is created for the `EntityDictionary` that uses the `Order` type. Instead, an instance of the version of `EntityDictionary` that uses `object` references is instantiated and the `orders` variable is set to reference it. To still gain the advantage of type safety, for each object reference substituted in place of the type parameter, an area of memory for an `Order` type is specifically allocated and the pointer is set to that memory reference.

Suppose you then encountered a line of code to instantiate an `EntityDictionary` of a `Customer` type as follows:

```
customers = new EntityDictionary<Guid, Customer>();
```

As with the previous use of the `EntityDictionary` class created with the `Order` type, another instance of the specialized `EntityDictionary` class (the one based on `object` references) is instantiated and the pointers contained therein are set to reference a `Customer` type specifically. This implementation of generics greatly reduces code bloat by reducing to one the number of specialized classes created by the compiler for generic classes of reference types.

Even though the runtime uses the same internal generic type definition when the type parameter on a generic reference type varies, this behavior is superseded if the type parameter is a value type. `Dictionary<int, Customer>`, `Dictionary<Guid, Order>`, and `Dictionary<long, Order>` will require new internal type definitions, for example.

Language Contrast: Java—Generics

The implementation of generics for Java occurs within the compiler entirely, not within the Java Virtual Machine. Sun did this to ensure that no updated Java Virtual Machine would need to be distributed because generics were used.

The Java implementation uses syntax similar to the templates in C++ and the generics in C#, including type parameters and constraints. But because it does not treat value types differently from reference types, the unmodified Java Virtual Machine cannot support generics for value types. As such, generics in Java do not gain the execution efficiency of C#. Indeed, whenever the Java compiler needs to return data, it injects automatic downcasts from the specified constraint, if one is declared, or the base `Object` type if it is not declared. Further, the Java compiler generates a single specialized type at compile time, which it then uses to instantiate any constructed type. Finally, because the Java Virtual Machine does not support generics natively, there is no way to ascertain the type parameter for an instance of a generic type at execution time, and other uses of reflection are severely limited.

SUMMARY

The addition of generic types and methods to C# 2.0 fundamentally transformed the coding style of C# developers. In virtually all cases in which programmers used `object` within C# 1.0 code, generics became a better choice in C# 2.0. In modern C# programs, using `object` (particularly in the context of any collection type) should make you consider whether or not the problem would be better solved with generics. The increased type safety cause by elimination of casts, the elimination of the boxing performance penalty, and reduction of repeated code are all significant improvements.

Chapter 16 looks at one of the most pervasive generic namespaces, `System.Collections.Generic`. As the name implies, this namespace is composed almost exclusively of generic types. It provides clear examples of how some types that originally used objects were then converted to use generics. However, before we tackle these topics, we will investigate expressions, which provide a significant C# 3.0 (and later) improvement for working with collections.

12
Delegates and Lambda Expressions

PREVIOUS CHAPTERS DISCUSSED EXTENSIVELY HOW to create classes to encapsulate data and operations on data. As you create more and more classes, you see common patterns in the relationships among them. One common pattern is to pass an object to a method solely so that the method can in turn call a method on the object. For example, if you pass to a method a reference to IComparer<int>, odds are good that the called method will itself call the Compare() method on the object you provided. In this case, the interface is nothing more than a way to pass a reference to a single method that can be invoked. It seems unnecessary to have to define a new interface every time you want to pass a method around. In this chapter we describe how to create and use a special kind of class called a **delegate** that enables you to treat references to methods as you would any other data. We then show how to create custom delegates quickly and easily with **lambda expressions.**

Lambda expressions were added to the language in C# 3.0; the previous version, C# 2.0, supported a less elegant syntax for custom delegate creation, called **anonymous methods.** Every version of C# after C# 2.0 supports anonymous methods for backward compatibility, but in new code they should be deprecated in favor of using lambda expressions. This chapter includes Advanced Topic blocks that describe how to use anonymous methods should you need to work with legacy C# 2.0 code; you can largely ignore these if you are working only with newer code.

We conclude the chapter with a discussion of **expression trees,** which enable you to use the compiler's analysis of a lambda expression at execution time.

Introducing Delegates

Veteran C and C++ programmers have long used "function pointers" as a mechanism for passing a reference to one method as an argument to another method. C# achieves similar functionality by using **delegates.** Delegates allow you to capture a reference to a method and pass it around like any other object, and to call the captured method like any other method. Let's consider an example illustrating how this technique might be useful.

Defining the Scenario

Although it is not very efficient, one of the simplest sort routines is the bubble sort. Listing 12.1 shows the `BubbleSort()` method.

LISTING 12.1: `BubbleSort()` **Method**

```
static class SimpleSort1
{
  public static void BubbleSort(int[] items)
  {
      int i;
      int j;
      int temp;

      if(items==null)
      {
```

```
        return;
    }

    for (i = items.Length - 1; i >= 0; i--)
    {
        for (j = 1; j <= i; j++)
        {
            if (items[j - 1] > items[j])
            {
                temp = items[j - 1];
                items[j - 1] = items[j];
                items[j] = temp;
            }
        }
    }
}
// ...
}
```

This method will sort an array of integers in ascending order.

Suppose you need to sort the integers in Listing 12.1 in either ascending or descending order. You could duplicate the code and replace the greater-than operator with a less-than operator, but it seems like a bad idea to replicate several dozen lines of code merely to change a single operator. As a less verbose alternative, you could pass in an additional parameter indicating how to perform the sort, as shown in Listing 12.2.

LISTING 12.2: BubbleSort() **Method, Ascending or Descending**

```
class SimpleSort2
{
  public enum SortType
  {
      Ascending,
      Descending
  }

    public static void BubbleSort(int[] items, SortType sortOrder)
    {
        int i;
        int j;
        int temp;

        if(items==null)
        {
          return;
        }

        for (i = items.Length - 1; i >= 0; i--)
        {
```

```
        for (j = 1; j <= i; j++)
        {
            bool swap = false;
            switch (sortOrder)
            {
                case SortType.Ascending :
                    swap = items[j - 1] > items[j];
                    break;

                case SortType.Descending :
                    swap = items[j - 1] < items[j];
                    break;
            }
            if (swap)
            {
                temp = items[j - 1];
                items[j - 1] = items[j];
                items[j] = temp;
            }
        }
    }
    // ...
}
```

However, this handles only two of the possible sort orders. If you wanted to sort them lexicographically (that is, 1, 10, 11, 12, 2, 20,…), or order them via some other criterion, it would not take long before the number of SortType values and the corresponding switch cases would become cumbersome.

Delegate Data Types

To increase flexibility and reduce code duplication in the previous code listings, you can make the comparison method a parameter to the BubbleSort() method. In order to pass a method as an argument, a data type is required that can represent that method; that data type is called a **delegate,** because it "delegates" the call to the method referred to by the object. Listing 12.3 includes a modification to the BubbleSort() method that takes a delegate parameter. In this case, the delegate data type is ComparisonHandler.

LISTING 12.3: BubbleSort() **with Delegate Parameter**

```
class DelegateSample
{
```

```
      // ...

      public static void BubbleSort(
          int[] items, ComparisonHandler comparisonMethod)
      {
          int i;
          int j;
          int temp;

          if(comparisonMethod == null)
          {
              throw new ArgumentNullException("comparisonMethod");
          }

          if(items==null)
          {
            return;
          }

          for (i = items.Length - 1; i >= 0; i--)
          {
              for (j = 1; j <= i; j++)
              {
                  if (comparisonMethod(items[j - 1], items[j]))
                  {
                    temp = items[j - 1];
                    items[j - 1] = items[j];
                    items[j] = temp;
                  }
              }
          }
      }
      // ...
  }
```

ComparisonHandler is a delegate type that represents a method that compares two integers. Within the BubbleSort() method you then use the instance of the ComparisonHandler, referred to by the comparisonMethod parameter, to determine which integer is greater. Since comparisonMethod represents a method, the syntax to invoke the method is identical to calling any other method. In this case, the ComparisonHandler delegate takes two integer parameters and returns a Boolean value that indicates whether the first integer is greater than the second one.

Note that the ComparisonHandler delegate is strongly typed to represent a method that returns a bool and accepts exactly two integer parameters. Just as with any other method call, the call to a delegate is strongly typed, and if the data types for the arguments are not compatible with the parameters, the C# compiler reports an error.

Declaring a Delegate Type

You saw how to define a method that uses a delegate, and you learned how to invoke a call to the delegate simply by treating the delegate variable as a method. However, you have yet to learn how to declare a delegate type. To declare a delegate type you use the `delegate` keyword and follow it with what looks like a method declaration. The signature of that method is the signature of the method that the delegate can refer to, and the name of the delegate type appears where the name of the method would appear in a method declaration. Listing 12.4 shows how to declare the `ComparisonHandler` delegate type to require two integers and return a Boolean.

LISTING 12.4: Declaring a Delegate Type

```
public delegate bool ComparisonHandler (
  int first, int second);
```

Just as classes can be nested in other classes, delegates can also be nested in classes. If the delegate declaration appeared within another class, the delegate type would be a nested type, as shown in Listing 12.5.

LISTING 12.5: Declaring a Nested Delegate Type

```
class DelegateSample
{
  public delegate bool ComparisonHandler (
    int first, int second);
}
```

In this case, the data type would be `DelegateSample.ComparisonHandler` because it is defined as a nested type within `DelegateSample`.

Instantiating a Delegate

In this final step of implementing the `BubbleSort()` method with a delegate, you will learn how to call the method and pass a delegate instance—specifically, an instance of type `ComparisonHandler`. To instantiate a delegate, you need a method with parameters and a return type that matches the signature of the delegate type itself. In the case of `ComparisonHandler`, that method takes two integers and returns a `bool`. The name of the method need not match the name of the delegate, but the rest of the method signature has to be compatible with the delegate signature. Listing 12.6 shows the code for a greater-than method compatible with the delegate type.

LISTING 12.6: Declaring a ComparisonHandler-Compatible Method

```csharp
public delegate bool ComparisonHandler (
  int first, int second);

class DelegateSample
{
  public static void BubbleSort(
    int[] items, ComparisonHandler comparisonMethod)
  {
    // ...
  }

  public static bool GreaterThan(int first, int second)
  {
    return first > second;
  }
  // ...
}
```

With this method defined, you can call **BubbleSort()** and supply as the argument the name of the method that is to be captured by the delegate, as shown in Listing 12.7.

LISTING 12.7: Using a Method Name As an Argument

```csharp
public delegate bool ComparisonHandler (
    int first, int second);

class DelegateSample
{
  public static void BubbleSort(
      int[] items, ComparisonHandler comparisonMethod)
  {
      // ...
  }

  public static bool GreaterThan(int first, int second)
  {
      return first > second;
  }

  static void Main()
  {
      int i;
      int[] items = new int[5];
```

```
        for (i=0; i < items.Length; i++)
        {
            Console.Write("Enter an integer: ");
            items[i] = int.Parse(Console.ReadLine());
        }

        BubbleSort(items, GreaterThan);

        for (int i = 0; i < items.Length; i++)
        {
            Console.WriteLine(items[i]);
        }
    }

}
```

Note that the ComparisonHandler delegate is a reference type, but you do not necessarily use new to instantiate it. The conversion from the **method group**—the expression that names the method—to the delegate type automatically creates a new delegate object in C# 2.0 and later.

■ ADVANCED TOPIC

Delegate Instantiation in C# 1.0

In Listing 12.7, the delegate was instantiated by simply passing the name of the desired method, GreaterThan, as an argument to the call to the BubbleSort() method. The first version of C# required instantiation of the delegate, using the more verbose syntax shown in Listing 12.8.

LISTING 12.8: Passing a Delegate As a Parameter in C# 1.0

```
        BubbleSort(items,
            new ComparisonHandler(GreaterThan));
```

Later versions support both syntaxes; throughout the remainder of the book we will show only the modern, concise syntax.

Delegate Internals

A delegate is actually a special kind of class. Though the C# standard does not specify exactly what the class hierarchy is, a delegate must always derive directly or indirectly from `System.Delegate`. In fact, in .NET delegate types always derive from `System.MulticastDelegate`, which in turn derives from `System.Delegate`, as shown in Figure 12.1.

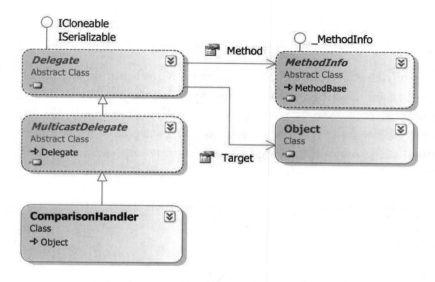

FIGURE 12.1: **Delegate Types Object Model**

The first property is of type `System.Reflection.MethodInfo`, which we cover in Chapter 17. `MethodInfo` describes the signature of a particular method, including its name, parameters, and return type. In addition to `MethodInfo`, a delegate also needs the instance of the object containing the method to invoke. This is the purpose of the second property, `Target`. In the case of a static method, `Target` corresponds to the type itself. The purpose of the `MulticastDelegate` class is the topic of the next chapter.

Note that all delegates are immutable; there is no way to change a delegate once you've created it. If you have a variable that contains a reference to a delegate and you want it to refer to a different method, you'll have to create a new delegate and assign it to the variable.

Although all delegate data types derive indirectly from `System.Delegate`, the C# compiler does not allow you to declare a class that derives directly or indirectly from `System.Delegate` or `System.MulticastDelegate`. The code shown in Listing 12.9 is not valid.

LISTING 12.9: `System.Delegate` **Cannot Explicitly Be a Base Class**

```
// ERROR: 'ComparisonHandler' cannot
// inherit from special class 'System.Delegate'
// public class ComparisonHandler: System.Delegate
{
  // ...
}
```

Passing the delegate to specify the sort order is significantly more flexible than the approach described at the beginning of this chapter. By passing a delegate you can change the sort order to be alphabetical simply by adding an alternative delegate to convert integers to strings as part of the comparison. Listing 12.10 shows a full listing that demonstrates alphabetical sorting, and Output 12.1 shows the results.

LISTING 12.10: Using a Different `ComparisonHandler`-**Compatible Method**

```
using System;
class DelegateSample
{

    public delegate bool ComparisonHandler(int first, int second);

    public static void BubbleSort(
        int[] items, ComparisonHandler comparisonMethod)
    {
        int i;
        int j;
        int temp;

        for (i = items.Length - 1; i >= 0; i--)
        {
            for (j = 1; j <= i; j++)
            {
                if (comparisonMethod(items[j - 1], items[j]))
                {
                    temp = items[j - 1];
                    items[j - 1] = items[j];
                    items[j] = temp;
                }
            }
        }
```

```csharp
        }
    }

    public static bool GreaterThan(int first, int second)
    {
        return first > second;
    }

    public static bool AlphabeticalGreaterThan(
        int first, int second)
    {
        int comparison;
        comparison = (first.ToString().CompareTo(
            second.ToString()));

        return comparison > 0;
    }

    static void Main(string[] args)
    {
        int i;
        int[] items = new int[5];

        for (i=0; i<items.Length; i++)
        {
            Console.Write("Enter an integer: ");
            items[i] = int.Parse(Console.ReadLine());
        }

        BubbleSort(items, AlphabeticalGreaterThan);

        for (i = 0; i < items.Length; i++)
        {
            Console.WriteLine(items[i]);
        }
    }
}
```

OUTPUT 12.1

```
Enter an integer: 1
Enter an integer: 12
Enter an integer: 13
Enter an integer: 5
Enter an integer: 4
1
12
13
4
5
```

The alphabetic order is different from the numeric order. Note how simple it was to add this additional sort mechanism, however, compared to the process used at the beginning of the chapter.

The only changes to create the alphabetical sort order were the addition of the `AlphabeticalGreaterThan` method and then passing that method into the call to `BubbleSort()`.

Lambda Expressions

In Listings 12.7 and 12.10 we saw that you can convert the expressions `GreaterThan` and `AlphabeticalGreaterThan` to a delegate type that is compatible with the parameter types and the return type of the named method. You might have noticed that the declaration of the `GreaterThan` method— the code that says it is a public, static, `bool`-returning method with two parameters of type `int` named `first` and `second`—was considerably larger than the body of the method, which simply compared its two parameters and returned the result. It is unfortunate that so much "ceremony" has to surround such a simple method merely so that it can be converted to a delegate type.

To address this concern, C# 2.0 introduced a far more compact syntax for creating a delegate, and C# 3.0 introduced several even more compact syntaxes than C# 2.0's syntax. The C# 2.0 feature is called **anonymous methods** and the C# 3.0 feature is called **lambda expressions.** When referring generally to either syntax, we'll refer to them as **anonymous functions.** Both syntaxes are still legal, but for new code the lambda expression syntax is preferred over the anonymous method syntax. Throughout this book we will generally use the lambda expression syntax except when specifically describing C# 2.0 anonymous methods.

Lambda expressions are themselves divided into two types: **statement lambdas** and **expression lambdas.** Figure 12.2 shows the hierarchical relationship between the terms.

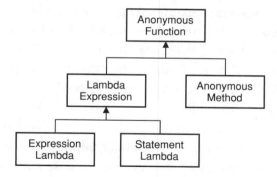

FIGURE 12.2: Anonymous Function Terminology

Statement Lambdas

The purpose of a lambda expression is to eliminate the hassle of declaring an entirely new member when you need to make a delegate from a very simple method. There are several different forms of lambda expression; a **statement lambda** consists of a formal parameter list, followed by the lambda operator =>, followed by a code block. Listing 12.11 shows equivalent functionality to the call to BubbleSort from Listing 12.7, except that Listing 12.11 uses a statement lambda to represent the comparison method, rather than creating a GreaterThan method. As you can see, much of the information that was in the GreaterThan method declaration is in the statement lambda; the formal parameter declarations and the block are the same, but the method name and its modifiers are missing.

LISTING 12.11: Creating a Delegate with a Statement Lambda

```
// ...

    BubbleSort(items,
        (int first, int second) =>
        {
            return first < second;
        }
    );

// ...
```

When reading code that includes a lambda operator, you would replace the lambda operator with the words *go/goes to*. For example, in Listing 12.11, you would read the second `BubbleSort()` parameter as "integers `first` and `second` go to returning the result of `first` less than `second`."

As readers will observe, the syntax in Listing 12.11 is virtually identical to that in Listing 12.7, apart from the fact that the comparison method is now found lexically where it is converted to the delegate type, rather than being found elsewhere and looked up by name. The name of the method is missing, which explains why such methods are called "anonymous functions." The return type is missing, but the compiler can see that the lambda expression is being converted to a delegate whose signature requires the return type `bool`. The compiler verifies that the expressions of every `return` statement in the statement lambda's block would be legal in a `bool`-returning method. The `public` modifier is missing; as the method is no longer an accessible member of the containing class, there is no need to describe its accessibility. Similarly, the `static` modifier is no longer necessary. The amount of "ceremony" around the method is already greatly reduced.

The syntax is still needlessly verbose, however. We have deduced from the delegate type that the lambda expression must be `bool`-returning; we can similarly deduce that both parameters must be of type `int`, as shown in Listing 12.12.

LISTING 12.12: Omitting Parameter Types from Statement Lambdas

```
// ...

    BubbleSort(items,
        (first, second) =>
        {
            return first < second;
        }
    );

// ...
```

In general, explicitly declared parameter types are optional in all lambda expressions if the compiler can infer the types from the delegate that the lambda expression is being converted to. For situations when specifying the type makes code more readable, however, C# enables doing so. In cases where inference is not possible, the C# language requires that the lambda parameter types be stated explicitly. If one lambda parameter type is specified explicitly, they must all be specified, and they must all match the delegate parameter types exactly.

Guidelines

CONSIDER omitting the types from lambda formal parameter lists when the types are obvious to the reader, or when they are an insignificant detail.

There is one additional possible reduction of syntax, shown in Listing 12.13: A lambda expression that has exactly one parameter whose type is inferred may omit the parentheses around the parameter list. If there are zero parameters or more than one parameter, or if the single parameter is explicitly typed, the lambda must have parentheses around the parameter list.

LISTING 12.13: Statement Lambdas with a Single Input Parameter

```
using System.Collections.Generic;
using System.Diagnostics;
using System.Linq;
 // ...
  IEnumerable<Process> processes = Process.GetProcesses().Where(
      process => { return process.WorkingSet64 > 1000000000; });
 // ...
```

In Listing 12.13, the `Where()` method returns a query for processes that have a physical memory utilization greater than 1 billion bytes.

Contrast this with Listing 12.14, which has a parameterless statement lambda. The empty parameter list requires parentheses. Note also that in Listing 12.14, the body of the statement lambda includes multiple statements inside the statement block (via curly braces). Although a statement lambda can have any number of statements, typically a statement lambda uses only two or three statements in its statement block. (The use of the generic Func delegate type is described in the section General-Purpose Delegates: `System.Func` and `System.Action`, later in this chapter.)

LISTING 12.14: Parameterless Statement Lambdas

```
using System;
 // ...
  Func<string> getUserInput =
      () =>
      {
          string input;
          do
          {
              input = Console.ReadLine();
          }
```

```
        while(input.Trim().Length == 0);
        return input;
    };
// ...
```

Expression Lambdas

The statement lambda syntax is already much less verbose than the corresponding method declaration; as we've seen it need not declare the method's name, accessibility, return type, or parameter types. But we can get even less verbose than that with an expression lambda. In Listings 12.12, 12.13, and 12.14 we saw statement lambdas whose blocks consisted of a single return statement. What if we eliminated the "ceremony" around that? The only relevant information in such a lambda block is the expression that is returned. An expression lambda has only that returned expression, with no statement block at all. Listing 12.15 is the same as Listing 12.11, except that it uses an expression lambda rather than a statement lambda.

LISTING 12.15: **Passing a Delegate with an Expression Lambda**

```
// ...
BubbleSort(items, (first, second) => first < second );
// ...
```

Generally, you would read the lambda operator => in an expression lambda the same way you would a statement lambda: as *goes to,* or *becomes.* When a lambda is used to return a bool, as it is in our BubbleSort() example, the lambda is called a **predicate.** In those cases it is common to read the lambda operator as *such that* or *where.* You might read the lambda in Listing 12.15 as "first and second such that first is less than second."

Like the null literal, an anonymous function does not have any type associated with it; rather, its type is determined by the type it is being converted to. In other words, the lambda expressions we've seen so far are not intrinsically of the ComparisonHandler type, but they are compatible with that type and may be converted to it. As a result, you cannot use the typeof() operator (see Chapter 17) on an anonymous method, and calling GetType() is possible only after converting the anonymous method to a particular type.

Table 12.1 contains additional lambda expression characteristics.

TABLE 12.1: Lambda Expression Notes and Examples

Statement	Example
Lambda expressions themselves do not have a type. Therefore, there are no members that can be accessed directly from a lambda expression, not even the methods of object.	```// ERROR: Operator '.' cannot be applied to
// operand of type 'lambda expression'
string s = ((int x) => x).ToString();```
Lambda expressions do not have a type and so cannot appear to the left of an is operator.	```// ERROR: The first operand of an 'is' or 'as'
// operator may not be a lambda expression or
// anonymous method
bool b = ((int x) => x) is Func<int, int>;```
A lambda expression can only be converted to a compatible delegate type; here an int-returning lambda may not be converted to a delegate type that represents a bool-returning method.	```// ERROR: Lambda expression is not compatible
// with Func<int, bool> type.
Func<int, bool> f = (int x) => x;```
A lambda expression does not have a type, so it cannot be used to infer the type of a local variable.	```// ERROR: Cannot assign lambda expression to
// an implicitly typed local variable
var v = x => x;```
Jump statements (break, goto, continue) inside lambda expressions cannot be used to jump to locations outside the lambda expression, and vice versa. Here the break statement inside the lambda would jump to the end of the switch statement outside the lambda.	```// ERROR: Control cannot leave the body of an
// anonymous method or lambda expression
string[] args;
Func<string> f;
switch(args[0])
{
case "/File":
f = () =>
{
if (!File.Exists(args[1]))
break;
return args[1];
};
// ...
}```
Parameters and locals introduced by a lambda expression are in scope only within the lambda body.	```// ERROR: The name 'first' does not
//   exist in the current context
Func<int, int, bool> expression =
(first, second) => first > second;
first++;```

Continues

TABLE 12.1: Lambda Expression Notes and Examples, *Continued*

Statement	Example
The compiler's definite assignment analysis is unable to detect initialization of "outer" local variables in lambda expressions.	```\nint number;\nFunc<string, bool> f =\n text => int.TryParse(text, out number);\nif (f("1"))\n{\n // ERROR: Use of unassigned local variable\n System.Console.Write(number);\n}\n```
	```\nint number;\nFunc<int, bool> isFortyTwo =\n x => 42 == (number = x);\nif (isFortyTwo(42))\n{\n // ERROR: Use of unassigned local variable\n System.Console.Write(number);\n}\n```

Anonymous Methods

Lambda expressions are not supported in C# 2.0. Instead, C# 2.0 uses a syntax called **anonymous methods.** An anonymous method is like a statement lambda, but without many of the features that make lambdas so compact. An anonymous method must explicitly type every parameter, and must have a statement block. Rather than using the lambda operator => between the parameter list and the code block, an anonymous method puts the keyword `delegate` before the parameter list, emphasizing that the anonymous method must be converted to a delegate type. Listing 12.16 shows the code from Listings 12.7, 12.12, and 12.15 rewritten to use an anonymous method.

LISTING 12.16: Passing an Anonymous Method in C# 2.0

```
// ...
BubbleSort(items,
    delegate(int first, int second)
    {
        return first < second;
    }
);
// ...
```

It is unfortunate that there are two very similar ways to define an anonymous function in C# 3.0 and later.

> ### Guidelines
>
> **AVOID** the anonymous method syntax in new code; prefer the more compact lambda expression syntax.

There is, however, one small feature that is supported in anonymous methods that is not supported in lambda expressions: Anonymous methods may omit their parameter list entirely in some circumstances.

■ **ADVANCED TOPIC**

Parameterless Anonymous Methods

Unlike lambda expressions, anonymous methods may omit the parameter list entirely provided that the anonymous method body does not use any parameter and the delegate type requires only "value" parameters. (That is, it does not require the parameters to be marked as `out` or `ref`.) For example, the anonymous method expression `delegate { return Console.ReadLine() != ""; }` is convertible to any delegate type that requires a return type of `bool` regardless of the number of parameters the delegate requires. This feature is not used frequently, but you might encounter it when reading legacy code.

■ **ADVANCED TOPIC**

Why "Lambda" Expressions?

It is fairly obvious why anonymous methods are called "anonymous methods"; they look very similar to method declarations but do not have a declared name associated with them. But where did the "lambda" in "lambda expressions" come from?

The idea of lambda expressions comes from the work of the logician Alonzo Church, who in the 1930s invented a technique for studying functions called the "lambda calculus." In Church's notation, a function which takes a parameter *x* and results in an expression *y* is notated by prefixing the entire expression with a small Greek letter lambda, and separating the parameter from the value with a dot. The C# lambda expression x=>y would be notated λx.y in Church's notation. Because it is inconvenient to use Greek letters in C# programs and because the dot already has many meanings in C#, the designers of C# chose to use the "fat arrow" notation rather than the original notation. The name "lambda expression" indicates that the theoretical underpinnings of the idea of anonymous functions are based on the lambda calculus, even though no letter lambda actually appears in the text.

General-Purpose Delegates: `System.Func` **and** `System.Action`

To reduce the need to define your own custom delegate types, the .NET 3.5 runtime library (which corresponds to C# 3.0) included a set of general-purpose delegates, most of them generic. The `System.Func` family of delegates is for referring to methods that return a value; the `System.Action` family of delegates is for referring to void-returning methods. The signatures for these delegates are shown in Listing 12.17 (although the in/out type modifiers were not added until C# 4.0, as discussed shortly).

LISTING 12.17: Func **and** Action **Delegate Declarations**

```
public delegate void Action ();
public delegate void Action<in T>(T arg)
public delegate void Action<in T1, in T2>(
    in T1 arg1, in T2 arg2)
public delegate void Action<in T1, in T2, in T3>(
    T1 arg1, T2 arg2, T3 arg3)
public delegate void Action<in T1, in T2, in T3, in T4(
    T1 arg1, T2 arg2, T3 arg3, T4 arg4)
...
public delegate void Action<
    in T1, in T2, in T3, in T4, in T5, in T6, in T7, in T8,
    in T9, in T10, in T11, in T12, in T13, in T14, in T16(
        T1 arg1, T2 arg2, T3 arg3, T4 arg4,
        T5 arg5, T6 arg6, T7 arg7, T8 arg8,
        T9 arg9, T10 arg10, T11 arg11, T12 arg12,
        T13 arg13, T14 arg14, T15 arg15, T16 arg16)

public delegate TResult Func<out TResult>();
public delegate TResult Func<in T, out TResult>(T arg)
public delegate TResult Func<in T1, in T2, out TResult>(
```

```
        in T1 arg1, in T2 arg2)
public delegate TResult Func<in T1, in T2, in T3, out TResult>(
        T1 arg1, T2 arg2, T3 arg3)
public delegate TResult Func<in T1, in T2, in T3, in T4,
        out TResult>(T1 arg1, T2 arg2, T3 arg3, T4 arg4)
...
public delegate TResult Func<
        in T1, in T2, in T3, in T4, in T5, in T6, in T7, in T8,
        in T9, in T10, in T11, in T12, in T13, in T14, in T16,
        out TResult>(
            T1 arg1, T2 arg2, T3 arg3, T4 arg4,
            T5 arg5, T6 arg6, T7 arg7, T8 arg8,
            T9 arg9, T10 arg10, T11 arg11, T12 arg12,
            T13 arg13, T14 arg14, T15 arg15, T16 arg16)
```

Since the delegate definitions in Listing 12.17 are generic, it is possible to use them instead of defining a custom delegate. The last type parameter of a Func delegate is always the return type of the delegate. The other type parameters correspond in sequence to the types of the delegate parameters. The BubbleSort method in Listing 12.3 requires a delegate that returns bool and takes two int parameters. Thus, rather than declaring the ComparisonHandler delegate type and using it, we could have declared the BubbleSort method as follows:

```
void BubbleSort(int[] items,
        Func<int, int, bool> comparisonMethod) { ... }
```

In many cases, the inclusion of Func and Action delegates in the .NET 3.5 Framework entirely eliminates the need to define your own delegate types. However, you should consider declaring your own delegate types when doing so significantly increases the readability of the code. A delegate named ComparisonHandler provides an explicit indication of what the delegate is used for, whereas using Func<int, int, bool> provides a more explicit indication of the delegate's formal parameters and return type.

Guidelines

CONSIDER whether the readability benefit of defining your own delegate type outweighs the convenience of using a predefined generic delegate type.

Delegates Do Not Have Structural Equality

Delegate types in .NET do not exhibit **structural equality.** That is, you cannot convert a reference to an object of one delegate type to an unrelated delegate type, even if the formal parameters and return types of both delegates are identical. For example, you cannot assign a reference to a `ComparisonHandler` to a variable of type `Func<int, int, bool>` even though both delegate types represent methods that take two `int` parameters and return a `bool`. Unfortunately, the only way to use a delegate of a given type when a delegate of a structurally identical but unrelated delegate type is needed is to create a new delegate that refers to the `Invoke` method of the old delegate. For example, if you have a variable c of type `ComparisonHandler`, and you need to assign its value to a variable f of type `Func<int, int, bool>`, you can say `f = c.Invoke;`.

However, thanks to the variance support added in C# 4.0, it is possible to make reference conversions between some delegate types. Consider the following contravariant example: Because `void Action<in T>(T arg)` has the `in` type parameter modifier, it is possible to assign a reference to a delegate of type `Action<object>` to a variable of type `Action<string>`.

Many people find delegate contravariance confusing; just remember that an action that can act on every object can be used as an action that acts on any string. But the opposite is not true; an action that can only act on strings cannot act on every object. Similarly, every type in the `Func` family of delegates is covariant in its return type, as indicated by the `out` type parameter modifier on `TResult`. Therefore it is possible to assign a reference to a delegate of type `Func<string>` to a variable of type `Func<object>`. Listing 12.18 shows examples of delegate covariance and contravariance.

LISTING 12.18: Using Variance for Delegates

```
// Contravariance
Action<object> broadAction =
  (object data) =>
  {
      Console.WriteLine(data);
  };
Action<string> narrowAction = broadAction;

// Covariance
Func<string> narrowFunction =
  () =>Console.ReadLine();
Func<object> broadFunction = narrowFunction;
```

```
// Contravariance & Covariance Combined
Func<object, string> func1 =
  (object data) => data.ToString();
Func<string, object> func2 = func1;
```

The last part of the listing combines both variance concepts into a single example, demonstrating how they can occur simultaneously if both in and out type parameters are involved.

Allowing reference conversions on generic delegate types was a key motivating scenario for adding covariant and contravariant conversions to C# 4.0. (The other was support for covariance to IEnumerable<out T>.)

■ ADVANCED TOPIC

Lambda Expression and Anonymous Method Internals

Lambda expressions (and anonymous methods) are not intrinsically "built in" to the CLR. Rather, when the compiler encounters an anonymous function, it translates it into special hidden classes, fields, and methods that implement the desired semantics. The C# compiler generates the implementation code for this pattern so that developers do not have to do it themselves. When given the code in Listing 12.11, 12.12, 12.15, or 12.16, the C# compiler generates CIL code that is similar to the code shown in Listing 12.19.

LISTING 12.19: C# Equivalent of CIL Generated by the Compiler for Lambda Expressions

```
class DelegateSample
{
  // ...
  static void Main(string[] args)
  {
      int i;
      int[] items = new int[5];

      for (i=0; i<items.Length; i++)
      {
          Console.Write("Enter an integer:");
          items[i] = int.Parse(Console.ReadLine());
      }

      BubbleSort(items,
          DelegateSample.__AnonymousMethod_00000000);
```

```
        for (i = 0; i < items.Length; i++)
        {
            Console.WriteLine(items[i]);
        }

    }

    private static bool __AnonymousMethod_00000000(
        int first, int second)
    {
        return first < second;
    }

}
```

In this example, the compiler transforms an anonymous function into a separately declared static method that is then instantiated as a delegate and passed as a parameter. Unsurprisingly, the compiler generates code that looks remarkably like the original code in Listing 12.7 that the anonymous function syntax was intended to streamline. However, the code transformation performed by the compiler can be considerably more complex than merely rewriting the anonymous function as a static method if "outer variables" are involved.

Outer Variables

Local variables declared outside a lambda expression (including parameters of the containing method) are called the **outer variables** of that lambda. (The `this` reference, though technically not a variable, is also considered to be an outer variable.) When a lambda body uses an outer variable, the variable is said to be **captured** (or, equivalently, **closed over**) by the lambda. In Listing 12.20 we use an outer variable to count how many times `BubbleSort()` performs a comparison. Output 12.2 shows the results of this listing.

LISTING 12.20: Using an Outer Variable in a Lambda Expression

```
class DelegateSample
{

    // ...

    static void Main(string[] args)
    {

        int i;
```

```
        int[] items = new int[5];
        int comparisonCount=0;

        for (i=0; i<items.Length; i++)
        {
            Console.Write("Enter an integer:");
            items[i] = int.Parse(Console.ReadLine());
        }

        BubbleSort(items,
            (int first, int second) =>
            {
                comparisonCount++;
                return first < second;
            }
        );

        for (i = 0; i < items.Length; i++)
        {
            Console.WriteLine(items[i]);
        }

        Console.WriteLine("Items were compared {0} times.",
                    comparisonCount);
    }
}
```

OUTPUT 12.2

```
Enter an integer:5
Enter an integer:1
Enter an integer:4
Enter an integer:2
Enter an integer:3
5
4
3
2
1
Items were compared 10 times.
```

Note that `comparisonCount` appears outside the lambda expression and is incremented inside it. After calling the `BubbleSort()` method, `comparisonCount` is printed out to the console.

Normally the lifetime of a local variable is tied to its scope; when control leaves the scope the storage location associated with the variable is no longer valid. But a delegate created from a lambda that captures an outer variable might have a longer (or shorter) lifetime than the local variable normally would, and the delegate must be able to safely access the outer variable every time the delegate is invoked. Therefore, the lifetime of a captured variable is extended; it is guaranteed to live at least as long as the longest-lived delegate object capturing it. (And it may live even longer than that; precisely how the compiler generates code that ensures outer variable lifetimes are extended is an implementation detail and subject to change.)

The C# compiler takes care of generating CIL code that shares `comparisonCount` between the anonymous method and the method that declares it.

ADVANCED TOPIC

Outer Variable CIL Implementation

The CIL code generated by the C# compiler for anonymous functions that capture outer variables is more complex than the code for a simple anonymous function that captures nothing. Listing 12.21 shows the C# equivalent of the CIL code used to implement outer variables for the code in Listing 12.20.

LISTING 12.21: C# Equivalent of CIL Code Generated by Compiler for Outer Variables

```csharp
class DelegateSample
{
    // ...
    private sealed class __LocalsDisplayClass_00000001
    {
        public int comparisonCount;
        public bool __AnonymousMethod_00000000(
            int first, int second)
        {
            comparisonCount++;
            return first < second;
        }
    }
    // ...
    static void Main(string[] args)
    {
        int i;
        __LocalsDisplayClass_00000001 locals =
            new __LocalsDisplayClass_00000001();
        locals.comparisonCount=0;
        int[] items = new int[5];

        for (i=0; i<items.Length; i++)
        {
            Console.Write("Enter an integer:");
```

```
                items[i] = int.Parse(Console.ReadLine());
        }

        BubbleSort(items, locals.__AnonymousMethod_00000000);
        for (i = 0; i < items.Length; i++)
        {
            Console.WriteLine(items[i]);
        }

        Console.WriteLine("Items were compared {0} times.",
                    locals.comparisonCount);
    }
}
```

Notice that the captured local variable is never "passed" anywhere and is never "copied" anywhere. Rather, the captured local variable (comparisonCount) is a single variable whose lifetime the compiler has extended by implementing it as an instance field rather than as a local variable. All usages of the local variable are rewritten to be usages of the field.

The generated class, __LocalsDisplayClass, is a **closure**—a data structure (class in C#) that contains an expression and the variables (public fields in C#) necessary to evaluate the expression.

■ ADVANCED TOPIC

Accidentally Capturing Loop Variables

What do you think the output of Listing 12.22 should be?

LISTING 12.22: Capturing Loop Variables in C# 5.0

```
class CaptureLoop
{
    static void Main()
    {
        var items = new string[] { "Moe", "Larry", "Curly" };
        var actions = new List<Action>();
        foreach (string item in items)
        {
            actions.Add( ()=> { Console.WriteLine(item); } );
        }
        foreach (Action action in actions)
        {
            action();
        }
    }
}
```

Most people expect that the output will be as shown in Output 12.3, and in C# 5.0 it is. In previous versions of C#, however, the output is as shown in Output 12.4.

OUTPUT 12.3—C# 5.0 OUTPUT

```
Moe
Larry
Curly
```

OUTPUT 12.4—C# 4.0 OUTPUT

```
Curly
Curly
Curly
```

A lambda captures a variable and always uses the latest value of the variable; it does not capture and preserve the value that the variable had when the delegate was created. This is normally what you want; the whole point of capturing `comparisonCount` in Listing 12.20 was to ensure that its latest value would be used when it was incremented. Loop variables are no different; when you capture a loop variable, every delegate captures the same loop variable. When the loop variable changes, every delegate that captured that loop variable sees the change. The C# 4.0 behavior is therefore justified, but is almost never what the author of the code wants.

In C# 5.0, the C# language was changed so that the loop variable of a `foreach` loop is now considered to be a "fresh" variable every time the loop iterates; therefore, each delegate creation captures a different variable, rather than all sharing the same variable. However, note that this change was not also applied to the `for` loop; if you write similar code using a `for` loop, any loop variable declared in the header of the `for` statement will be considered a single outer variable when captured. If you need to write code that works the same in both C# 5.0 and previous versions, use the pattern shown in Listing 12.23.

LISTING 12.23: Loop Variable Capture Workaround Before C#5.0

```csharp
class DoNotCaptureLoop
{
  static void Main()
```

```
    {
        var items = new string[] { "Moe", "Larry", "Curly" };
        var actions = new List<Action>();
        foreach (string item in items)
        {
            string _item = item;
            actions.Add(
                ()=> { Console.WriteLine(_item); } );
        }
        foreach (Action action in actions)
        {
            action();
        }
    }
}
```

Now there is clearly one fresh variable per loop iteration; each delegate
is therefore closed over a different variable.

> ## Guidelines
>
> **AVOID** capturing loop variables in anonymous functions.

Expression Trees

Thus far we've seen that lambda expressions are a succinct syntax for declaring an "inline" method that can be converted to a delegate type. Expression lambdas (but not statement lambdas or anonymous methods) can
also be converted to **expression trees.** A delegate is an object that enables
you to pass around a method like any other object and invoke it at any
time. An expression tree is an object that enables you to pass around the
compiler's analysis of the lambda body. But why would you ever need
that? Obviously, the compiler's analysis is useful to the compiler when
generating the CIL, but why is it useful to the developer to have an object representing that analysis at execution time? Let's take a look at an
example.

Using Lambda Expressions As Data

Consider the lambda expression in the following code:

```
persons.Where(
    person => person.Name.ToUpper() == "INIGO MONTOYA");
```

Suppose that persons is an array of Persons, and the formal parameter of the Where method that corresponds to the lambda expression argument is of delegate type Func<Person, bool>. The compiler emits a method that contains the code in the body of the lambda. It generates code that creates a delegate to the emitted method and passes the delegate to the Where method. The Where method returns a query object that, when executed, applies the delegate to each member of the array to determine the query results.

Now suppose that persons is not of type Person[], but rather is an object that represents a remote database table containing data on millions of people. Information about each row in the table can be streamed from the server to the client, and the client can then create a Person object corresponding to that row. The call to Where returns an object that represents the query. When the results of that query are requested on the client, how are the results determined?

One technique would be to transmit several million rows of data from the server to the client. You could create a Person object from each row, create a delegate from the lambda, and execute the delegate on every Person. This is conceptually no different from the array scenario, but it is far, far more expensive.

A second, far better technique is to somehow send the meaning of the lambda (filter out every row that names a person other than Inigo Montoya) to the server. Database servers are optimized to rapidly perform this sort of filtering. The server can then choose to stream only the tiny number of matching rows to the client; instead of creating millions of Person objects and rejecting almost all of them, the client only creates the objects that already match the query, as determined by the server. But how does the meaning of the lambda get sent to the server?

This scenario is the motivation for adding **expression trees** to the language. Lambda expressions converted to expression trees become objects that represent data that describes the lambda expression, rather than compiled code that implements an anonymous function. Since the expression tree represents data rather than compiled code, it is possible to analyze the lambda at execution time and use that information to construct a query that executes on a database, for example. The expression tree received by Where() might be converted into a SQL query that is passed to a database, as shown in Listing 12.24.

LISTING 12.24: **Converting an Expression Tree to a SQL** where **Clause**

```
persons.Where( person => person.Name.ToUpper() == "INIGO MONTOYA");




select * from Person where upper(Name) = 'INIGO MONTOYA';
```

The expression tree passed to the `Where()` call says that the lambda argument consists of the following:

- A read of the `Name` property of a `Person` object
- A call to a `string` method called `ToUpper()`
- A constant value, `"INIGO MONTOYA"`
- And an equality operator, `==`

The `Where()` method takes this data and converts it to the SQL `where` clause by examining the data and building a SQL query string. However, SQL is just one example; you can build an expression tree evaluator that converts expressions to any query language.

Expression Trees Are Object Graphs

At execution time, a lambda converted to an expression tree becomes an object graph containing objects from the `System.Linq.Expressions` namespace. The "root" object in the graph represents the lambda itself. This object refers to objects representing the parameters, a return type, and body expression, as shown in Figure 12.3. The object graph contains all the information that the compiler deduced about the lambda. That information can then be used at execution time to create a query; alternatively, the root lambda expression has a method, `Compile`, which generates CIL "on the fly" and creates a delegate that implements the described lambda.

Figure 12.4 shows the types found in object graphs for a unary and binary expression in the body of a lambda.

A `UnaryExpression` represents an expression such as `-count`. It has a single child `Operand` of type `Expression`. A `BinaryExpression` has two child expressions, `Left` and `Right`. Both types have a `NodeType` property that identifies the specific operator. Both inherit from the base class `Expression`. There are another thirty or so expression types, such as `NewExpression`,

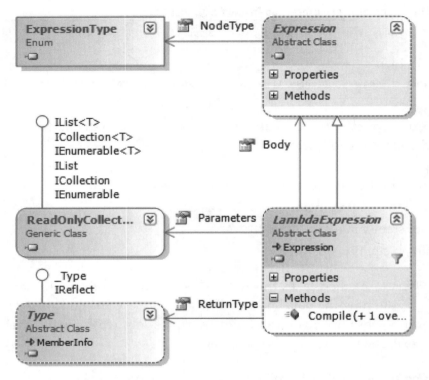

FIGURE 12.3: The Lambda Expression Tree Type

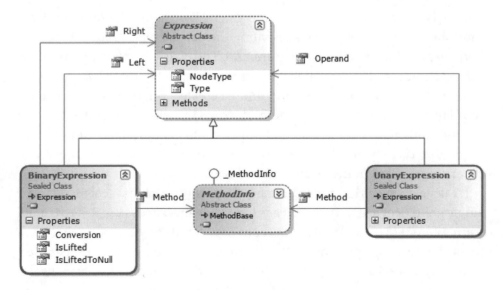

FIGURE 12.4: Unary and Binary Expression Tree Types

ParameterExpression, MethodCallExpression, LoopExpression, and so forth, to represent (almost) every possible expression in C# and Visual Basic.

Delegates versus Expression Trees

The validity of a lambda expression is verified at compile time with a full semantic analysis whether it is converted to a delegate or an expression tree. A lambda that is converted to a delegate causes the compiler to emit the lambda as a method, and generates code that creates a delegate to that method at execution time. A lambda that is converted to an expression tree causes the compiler to generate code that creates an instance of LambdaExpression at execution time. But when using LINQ, how does the compiler know whether to generate a delegate, to execute a query locally, or to generate an expression tree so that information about the query can be sent to the remote database server?

The methods used to build LINQ queries, such as Where(), are extension methods. The versions of those methods that extend the IEnumerable<T> interface take delegate parameters; the methods that extend the IQueryable<T> interface take expression tree parameters. The compiler can therefore use the type of the collection that is being queried to determine whether to create delegates or expression trees from lambdas supplied as arguments. Consider, for example, the Where() method in the following code:

```
persons.Where( person => person.Name.ToUpper() ==
    "INIGO MONTOYA");
```

The extension method signature declared in the System.Linq.Enumerable class is:

```
public IEnumerable<TSource> Where<TSource>(
    this IEnumerable<TSource> collection,
    Func<TSource, bool> predicate);
```

The extension method signature declared in the System.Linq.Queryable class is:

```
public IQueryable<TSource> Where<TSource>(
    this IQueryable<TSource> collection,
    Expression<Func<TSource, bool>> predicate);
```

The compiler decides which extension method to use based on the compile-time type of persons; if it is a type convertible to IQueryable<Person> the method from System.Linq.Queryable is chosen. It converts the lambda to an expression tree. At execution time the object referred to by persons receives the expression tree data and might use that data to build a SQL query that is passed to the database when the results of the query are requested. The result of the call to Where is an object that, when asked for query results, sends the query to the database and produces the results.

If persons cannot be converted implicitly to IQueryable<Person> but can be converted implicitly to IEnumerable<Person> the method from System.Linq.Enumerable is chosen, and the lambda is converted to a delegate. The result of the call to Where is an object that, when asked for query results, applies the generated delegate as a predicate to every member of the collection and produces the results which match the predicate.

Examining an Expression Tree

As we've seen, converting a lambda expression to an Expression <TDelegate> creates an expression tree rather than a delegate. We have seen previously in this chapter how to convert a lambda such as (x,y)=>x>y to a delegate type such as Func<int, int, bool>. To turn this same lambda into an expression tree, we simply convert it to Expression<Func<int, int, bool>>, as shown in Listing 12.25. We can then examine the generated object and display information about its structure, as well as that of a more complex expression tree.

Note that passing an instance of expression tree to Console.WriteLine() automatically converts the expression tree to a descriptive string form; the objects generated for expression trees all override ToString() so that you can see at a glance what the contents of an expression tree are when debugging.

LISTING 12.25: Examining an Expression Tree

```
using System;
using System.Linq.Expressions;

class Program
{
    static void Main()
    {
        Expression<Func<int, int, bool>> expression;
        expression = (x, y) => x > y;
        Console.WriteLine("-------------{0}-------------",
            expression);
        PrintNode(expression.Body, 0);
        Console.WriteLine();
        Console.WriteLine();
        expression = (x, y) => x * y > x + y;
```

```
        Console.WriteLine("-------------{0}-------------",
            expression);
        PrintNode(expression.Body, 0);
        Console.WriteLine();
        Console.WriteLine();
    }
    public static void PrintNode(Expression expression,
        int indent)
    {
        if (expression is BinaryExpression)
            PrintNode(expression as BinaryExpression, indent);
        else
            PrintSingle(expression, indent);
    }
    private static void PrintNode(BinaryExpression expression,
      int indent)
    {
        PrintNode(expression.Left, indent + 1);
        PrintSingle(expression, indent);
        PrintNode(expression.Right, indent + 1);
    }
    private static void PrintSingle(
        Expression expression, int indent)
    {
        Console.WriteLine("{0," + indent * 5 + "}{1}",
          "", NodeToString(expression));
    }
    private static string NodeToString(Expression expression)
    {
        switch (expression.NodeType)
        {
            case ExpressionType.Multiply:
                return "*";
            case ExpressionType.Add:
                return "+";
            case ExpressionType.Divide:
                return "/";
            case ExpressionType.Subtract:
                return "-";
            case ExpressionType.GreaterThan:
                return ">";
            case ExpressionType.LessThan:
                return "<";
            default:
                return expression.ToString() +
                    " (" + expression.NodeType.ToString() + ")";
        }
    }
}
```

In Output 12.5, we see that the Console.WriteLine() statements within Main() print out the body of the expression trees as text.

OUTPUT 12.5

```
------------- (x, y) => x > y -------------
    x (Parameter)
>
    y (Parameter)


------------- (x, y) => (x * y) > (x + y) -------------
        x (Parameter)
    *
        y (Parameter)
>
        x (Parameter)
    +
        y (Parameter)
```

The important point to note is that an expression tree is a collection of data, and by iterating over the data, it is possible to convert the data to another format; in this case we convert the expression tree to descriptive strings, but it could also be converted to expressions in another query language.

Using recursion, the `PrintNode()` function demonstrates that nodes in an expression tree are themselves trees containing zero or more child expression trees. The "root" tree that represents the lambda refers to the expression that is the body of the lambda with its `Body` property. Every expression tree node includes a `NodeType` property of enumerated type `ExpressionType` that describes what kind of expression it is. There are numerous types of expressions: `BinaryExpression`, `ConditionalExpression`, `LambdaExpression`, `MethodCallExpression`, `ParameterExpression`, and `ConstantExpression` are examples. Each type derives from `Expression`.

Note that, though the expression tree library now contains objects to represent most of the statements of C# and Visual Basic, neither language supports the conversion of statement lambdas to expression trees. Only expression lambdas can be converted to expression trees.

SUMMARY

This chapter began with a discussion of delegates and their use as references to methods or callbacks. It introduced a powerful concept for passing a set of instructions to call in a different location, rather than immediately, when the instructions are coded.

The chapter introduced the C# 3.0 concept of lambda expressions, a syntax that supersedes (although does not eliminate) the C# 2.0 anonymous method syntax. These constructs allow programmers to assign a set of instructions to a variable directly, without defining an explicit method that contains the instructions. This provides significant flexibility for programming instructions dynamically within the method—a powerful concept that greatly simplifies the programming of collections through an API known as LINQ, which stands for Language Integrated Query.

The chapter ended with a discussion of the concept of expression trees, and how they compile into objects that represent the semantic analysis of a lambda expression, rather than the delegate implementation itself. This is a key feature that enables such libraries as LINQ to SQL and LINQ to XML, libraries that interpret the expression tree and use it within contexts other than CIL.

The term *lambda expression* encompasses both *statement lambda* and *expression lambda*. In other words, both statement lambdas and expression lambdas are types of lambda expressions.

One thing that the chapter mentioned but did not elaborate on was multicast delegates. The next chapter investigates multicast delegates in detail and explains how they enable the publish-subscribe pattern with events.

■ 13 ■
Events

I N THE PRECEDING CHAPTER, YOU saw how to reference a method with an instance of a delegate type and invoke that method via the delegate. Delegates are the building blocks of a larger pattern called publish-subscribe. The use of delegates for the publish-subscribe pattern is the focus of this chapter. Virtually everything described within this chapter is possible to do using delegates alone. However, the event constructs that this chapter focuses on provide additional encapsulation, making the publish-subscribe pattern easier to implement and less error-prone.

In the preceding chapter, all delegates referenced a single method. However, a single delegate value can reference a whole collection of methods to be called in sequence; such a delegate is called a **multicast delegate.** This enables scenarios where notifications of single events, such as a change in object state, are published to multiple subscribers.

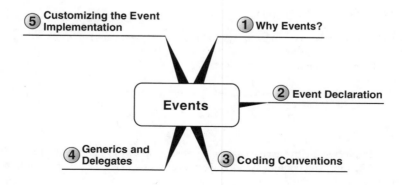

Although events existed in C# 1.0, the introduction of generics in C# 2.0 significantly changed the coding conventions because using a generic delegate data type meant that it was no longer necessary to declare a delegate for every possible event signature. For this reason, the chapter assumes a minimum of C# 2.0 throughout. Readers still living in the world of C# 1.0 can still use events; however, they will have to declare their own delegate data types (as discussed in Chapter 12).

Coding the Observer Pattern with Multicast Delegates

Consider a temperature control example, where a heater and a cooler are hooked up to the same thermostat. In order for a unit to turn on and off appropriately, you notify the unit of changes in temperature. One thermostat publishes temperature changes to multiple subscribers—the heating and cooling units. The next section investigates the code.[1]

Defining Subscriber Methods

Begin by defining the Heater and Cooler objects (see Listing 13.1).

LISTING 13.1: Heater and Cooler Event Subscriber Implementations

```
class Cooler
{
    public Cooler(float temperature)
    {
        Temperature = temperature;
    }

    public float Temperature
    {
        get{return _Temperature;}
        set{_Temperature = value;}
    }
    private float _Temperature;

    public void OnTemperatureChanged(float newTemperature)
    {
        if (newTemperature > Temperature)
        {
            System.Console.WriteLine("Cooler: On");
        }
        else
```

1. In this example, we use the term *thermostat* because people more commonly think of it in the context of heating and cooling systems. Technically, however, *thermometer* would be more appropriate.

```csharp
            {
                System.Console.WriteLine("Cooler: Off");
            }
        }
    }

    class Heater
    {
        public Heater(float temperature)
        {
            Temperature = temperature;
        }

        public float Temperature
        {
            get{return _Temperature;}
            set{_Temperature = value;}
        }
        private float _Temperature;

        public void OnTemperatureChanged(float newTemperature)
        {
            if (newTemperature < Temperature)
            {
                System.Console.WriteLine("Heater: On");
            }
            else
            {
                System.Console.WriteLine("Heater: Off");
            }
        }
    }
}
```

The two classes are essentially identical, with the exception of the temperature comparison. (In fact, you could eliminate one of the classes if you used a delegate to a comparison method within the OnTemperatureChanged method.) Each class stores the temperature for when to turn on the unit. In addition, both classes provide an OnTemperatureChanged() method. Calling the OnTemperatureChanged() method is the means to indicate to the Heater and Cooler classes that the temperature has changed. The method implementation uses newTemperature to compare against the stored trigger temperature to determine whether to turn on the device.

The OnTemperatureChanged() methods are the subscriber methods. It is important that they have the parameters and a return type that matches the delegate from the Thermostat class, which we discuss next.

Defining the Publisher

The `Thermostat` class is responsible for reporting temperature changes to the heater and cooler object instances. The `Thermostat` class code appears in Listing 13.2.

LISTING 13.2: **Defining the Event Publisher,** Thermostat

```
public class Thermostat
{
  // Define the event publisher
  public Action<float> OnTemperatureChange { get; set; }

  public float CurrentTemperature
  {
      get{return _CurrentTemperature;}
      set
      {
          if (value != CurrentTemperature)
          {
              _CurrentTemperature = value;
          }
      }
  }
  private float _CurrentTemperature;
}
```

The `Thermostat` includes a property called `OnTemperatureChange` that is of the `Action<float>` delegate type. `OnTemperatureChange` stores a list of subscribers. Notice that only one delegate field is required to store all the subscribers. In other words, both the `Cooler` and the `Heater` classes will receive notifications of a change in the temperature from this single publisher.

The last member of `Thermostat` is the `CurrentTemperature` property. This sets and retrieves the value of the current temperature reported by the `Thermostat` class.

Hooking Up the Publisher and Subscribers

Finally, put all these pieces together in a `Main()` method. Listing 13.3 shows a sample of what `Main()` could look like.

LISTING 13.3: **Connecting the Publisher and Subscribers**

```
class Program
{
  public static void Main()
  {
      Thermostat thermostat = new Thermostat();
```

```
        Heater heater = new Heater(60);
        Cooler cooler = new Cooler(80);
        string temperature;

        thermostat.OnTemperatureChange +=
            heater.OnTemperatureChanged;
        thermostat.OnTemperatureChange +=
            cooler.OnTemperatureChanged;

        Console.Write("Enter temperature: ");
        temperature = Console.ReadLine();
        thermostat.CurrentTemperature = int.Parse(temperature);
    }
  }
```

The code in this listing has registered two subscribers (heater.OnTemperatureChanged and cooler.OnTemperatureChanged) to the OnTemperatureChange delegate by directly assigning them using the += operator.

By taking the temperature value the user has entered, you can set the CurrentTemperature of thermostat. However, you have not yet written any code to publish the change temperature event to subscribers.

Invoking a Delegate

Every time the CurrentTemperature property on the Thermostat class changes, you want to **invoke the delegate** to notify the subscribers (heater and cooler) of the change in temperature. To do this, modify the CurrentTemperature property to save the new value and publish a notification to each subscriber. The code modification appears in Listing 13.4.

LISTING 13.4: Invoking a Delegate without Checking for null

```
  public class Thermostat
  {
    ...
    public float CurrentTemperature
    {
      get{return _CurrentTemperature;}
      set
      {
        if (value != CurrentTemperature)
        {
          _CurrentTemperature = value;

          // INCOMPLETE: Check for null needed
          // Call subscribers
```

```
                OnTemperatureChange(value);
            }
        }
    }
    private float _CurrentTemperature;
}
```

Now the assignment of `CurrentTemperature` includes some special logic to notify subscribers of changes in `CurrentTemperature`. The call to notify all subscribers is simply the single C# statement, `OnTemperatureChange(value)`. This single statement publishes the temperature change to the `cooler` and `heater` objects. Here, you see in practice that the ability to notify multiple subscribers using a single call is why delegates are more specifically known as multicast delegates.

Check for `null`

One important part of event publishing code is missing from Listing 13.4. If no subscriber registered to receive the notification, `OnTemperatureChange` would be `null` and executing the `OnTemperatureChange(value)` statement would throw a `NullReferenceException`. To avoid this, it is necessary to check for `null` before firing the event. Listing 13.5 demonstrates how to do this.

LISTING 13.5: **Invoking a Delegate**

```
public class Thermostat
{
  ...
  public float CurrentTemperature
  {
      get{return _CurrentTemperature;}
      set
      {
          if (value != CurrentTemperature)
          {
              _CurrentTemperature = value;
              // If there are any subscribers
              // then notify them of changes in
              // temperature
              Action<float> localOnChange =
                  OnTemperatureChange;
              if(localOnChange != null)
              {
                  // Call subscribers
                  localOnChange(value);
              }
          }
```

```
        }
    }
    private float _CurrentTemperature;
}
```

Instead of checking for `null` directly, first assign `OnTemperatureChange` to a second delegate variable, `localOnChange`. This simple modification ensures that if all `OnTemperatureChange` subscribers are removed (by a different thread) between checking for `null` and sending the notification, you will not raise a `NullReferenceException`.

> ### Guidelines
>
> **DO** check that the value of a delegate is not `null` before invoking it.

■ ADVANCED TOPIC

-= Operator for a Delegate Returns a New Instance

Given that a delegate is a reference type, it is perhaps somewhat surprising that assigning a local variable and then using that local variable is sufficient for making the null check thread-safe. Since `localOnChange` points at the same location that `OnTemperatureChange` points, one would think that any changes in `OnTemperatureChange` would be reflected in `localOnChange` as well.

This is not the case, because effectively, any calls to `OnTemperatureChange -= <listener>` will not simply remove a delegate from `OnTemperatureChange` so that it contains one less delegate than before. Rather, it will assign an entirely new multicast delegate without having any effect on the original multicast delegate to which `localOnChange` also points.

■ ADVANCED TOPIC

Thread-Safe Delegate Invocation

If subscribers can be added and removed from the delegate on different threads, it is wise (as noted above) to copy the delegate reference into a local variable before checking it for `null`. Though this prevents invoking a null delegate, it does not avoid all possible race conditions. For example, one thread could make the copy, and then another thread could reset the delegate to null, and then the original thread could invoke the previous value of the delegate, thereby notifying a subscriber that is no longer on the list of subscribers. Subscribers in multithreaded programs should ensure that they are robust in this scenario; it is always possible that a "stale" subscriber will be invoked.

Delegate Operators

To combine the two subscribers in the Thermostat example, you used the += operator. This takes the first delegate and adds the second delegate to the chain. Now, after the first delegate's method returns, the second delegate is called. To remove delegates from a delegate chain, use the -= operator, as shown in Listing 13.6.

LISTING 13.6: Using the += and -= Delegate Operators

```
// ...
Thermostat thermostat = new Thermostat();
Heater heater = new Heater(60);
Cooler cooler = new Cooler(80);

Action<float> delegate1;
Action<float> delegate2;
Action<float> delegate3;

delegate1 = heater.OnTemperatureChanged;
delegate2 = cooler.OnTemperatureChanged;

Console.WriteLine("Invoke both delegates:");
delegate3 = delegate1;
delegate3 += delegate2;
delegate3(90);

Console.WriteLine("Invoke only delegate2");
delegate3 -= delegate1;
delegate3(30);
// ...
```

The results of Listing 13.6 appear in Output 13.1.

OUTPUT 13.1

```
Invoke both delegates:
Heater: Off
Cooler: On
Invoke only delegate2
Cooler: Off
```

Furthermore, you can also use the + and – operators to combine delegates, as Listing 13.7 shows.

LISTING 13.7: Using the + and - Delegate Operators

```
// ...
Thermostat thermostat = new Thermostat();
Heater heater = new Heater(60);
Cooler cooler = new Cooler(80);

Action<float> delegate1;
Action<float> delegate2;
Action<float> delegate3;

// Note: Use new Action(
//       cooler.OnTemperatureChanged) for C# 1.0 syntax.
delegate1 = heater.OnTemperatureChanged;
delegate2 = cooler.OnTemperatureChanged;

Console.WriteLine("Combine delegates using + operator:");
delegate3 = delegate1 + delegate2;
delegate3(60);

Console.WriteLine("Uncombine delegates using - operator:");
delegate3 = delegate3 - delegate2;
delegate3(60);
// ...
```

Use of the assignment operator clears out all previous subscribers and allows you to replace them with new subscribers. This is an unfortunate characteristic of a delegate. It is simply too easy to mistakenly code an assignment when, in fact, the += operator is intended. The solution, called events, appears in the Events section, later in this chapter.

It should be noted that both the + and - operators and their assignment equivalents, += and -=, are implemented internally using the static methods System.Delegate.Combine() and System.Delegate.Remove(). Both methods take two parameters of type delegate. The first method, Combine(), joins the two parameters so that the first parameter points to the second within the list of delegates. The second, Remove(), searches through the chain of delegates specified in the first parameter and then removes the delegate specified by the second parameter.

One interesting thing to note about the Combine() method is that either or both of the parameters can be null. If one of them is null, Combine() returns the non-null parameter. If both are null, Combine() returns null. This explains why you can call thermostat.OnTemperatureChange += heater. OnTemperatureChanged; and not throw an exception, even if the value of thermostat.OnTemperatureChange is still null.

Sequential Invocation

Figure 13.1 highlights the sequential notification of both heater and cooler.

Although you coded only a single call to OnTemperatureChange(), the call is broadcast to both subscribers so that from that one call, both cooler and heater are notified of the change in temperature. If you added more subscribers, they too would be notified by OnTemperatureChange().

Although a single call, OnTemperatureChange(), caused the notification of each subscriber, the subscribers are still called sequentially, not simultaneously, because they are all called on the same thread of execution.

■ **ADVANCED TOPIC**

Multicast Delegate Internals

To understand how events work, you need to revisit the first examination of the System.Delegate type internals. Recall that the delegate keyword is an alias for a type derived from System.MulticastDelegate. In turn, System.MulticastDelegate is derived from System.Delegate, which, for its part, is composed of an object reference (needed for no-static methods) and a method reference. When you create a delegate, the compiler automatically employs the System.MulticastDelegate type rather than the System.Delegate type. The MulticastDelegate class includes an object reference and method reference, just like its Delegate base class, but it also contains a reference to another System.MulticastDelegate object.

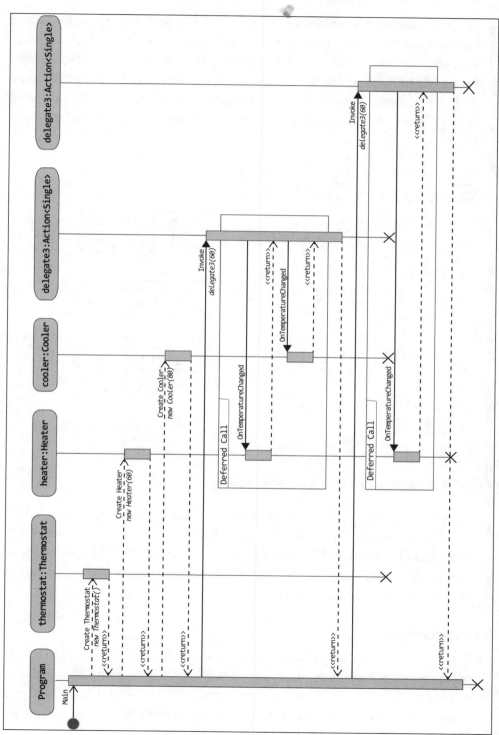

FIGURE 13.1: Delegate Invocation Sequence Diagram

When you add a method to a multicast delegate, the `MulticastDelegate` class creates a new instance of the delegate type, stores the object reference and the method reference for the added method into the new instance, and adds the new delegate instance as the next item in a list of delegate instances. In effect, the `MulticastDelegate` class maintains a linked list of `Delegate` objects. Conceptually, you can represent the thermostat example as shown in Figure 13.2.

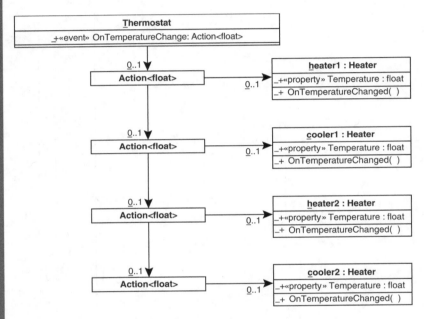

FIGURE 13.2: Multicast Delegates Chained Together

When invoking a multicast delegate, each delegate instance in the linked list is called sequentially. Generally, delegates are called in the order they were added, but this behavior is not specified within the CLI specification, and furthermore, it can be overridden. Therefore, programmers should not depend on an invocation order.

Error Handling

Error handling makes awareness of the sequential notification critical. If one subscriber throws an exception, later subscribers in the chain do not receive the notification. Consider, for example, what would happen if you changed the `Heater`'s `OnTemperatureChanged()` method so that it threw an exception, as shown in Listing 13.8.

LISTING 13.8: OnTemperatureChanged() **Throwing an Exception**

```csharp
class Program
{
  public static void Main()
  {
    Thermostat thermostat = new Thermostat();
    Heater heater = new Heater(60);
    Cooler cooler = new Cooler(80);
    string temperature;

    thermostat.OnTemperatureChange +=
        heater.OnTemperatureChanged;
    // Using C# 3.0.  Change to anonymous method
    // if using C# 2.0
    thermostat.OnTemperatureChange +=
        (newTemperature) =>
            {
                throw new InvalidOperationException();
            };
    thermostat.OnTemperatureChange +=
        cooler.OnTemperatureChanged;

    Console.Write("Enter temperature: ");
    temperature = Console.ReadLine();
    thermostat.CurrentTemperature = int.Parse(temperature);
  }
}
```

Figure 13.3 shows an updated sequence diagram.

FIGURE 13.3: **Delegate Invocation with Exception Sequence Diagram**

Even though `cooler` and `heater` subscribed to receive messages, the lambda expression exception terminates the chain and prevents the `cooler` object from receiving notification.

To avoid this problem so that all subscribers receive notification, regardless of the behavior of earlier subscribers, you must manually enumerate through the list of subscribers and call them individually. Listing 13.9 shows the updates required in the `CurrentTemperature` property. The results appear in Output 13.2.

LISTING 13.9: Handling Exceptions from Subscribers

```csharp
public class Thermostat
{
  // Define the event publisher
  public Action<float> OnTemperatureChange;

  public float CurrentTemperature
  {
      get{return _CurrentTemperature;}
      set
      {
          if (value != CurrentTemperature)
          {
              _CurrentTemperature = value;
              if(OnTemperatureChange != null)
              {
                  List<Exception> exceptionCollection =
                      new List<Exception>();
                  foreach (
                      Action<float> handler in
                      OnTemperatureChange.GetInvocationList())
                  {
                      try
                      {
                          handler(value);
                      }
                      catch (Exception exception)
                      {
                          exceptionCollection.Add(exception);
                      }
                  }
                  if (exceptionCollection.Count > 0)
                  {
                      throw new AggregateException(
                          "There were exceptions thrown by
OnTemperatureChange Event subscribers.",
                          exceptionCollection);
                  }
              }
          }
      }
```

```
        }
    }
    private float _CurrentTemperature;
}
```

OUTPUT 13.2

```
Enter temperature: 45
Heater: On
Error in the application
Cooler: Off
```

This listing demonstrates that you can retrieve a list of subscribers from a delegate's `GetInvocationList()` method. Enumerating over each item in this list returns the individual subscribers. If you then place each invocation of a subscriber within a try/catch block, you can handle any error conditions before continuing with the enumeration loop. In this sample, even though the delegate listener throws an exception, `cooler` still receives notification of the temperature change. After all notifications have been sent, Listing 13.9 reports any exceptions by throwing an `AggregateException`, which wraps a collection of exceptions that are accessible by the `InnerExceptions` property. In this way, all exceptions are still reported while at the same time, all subscribers are notified.

Method Returns and Pass-by-Reference

There is another scenario where it is useful to iterate over the delegate invocation list instead of simply activating a notification directly. This scenario relates to delegates that either do not return `void` or have `ref` or `out` parameters. In the thermostat example so far, the `OnTemperatureChange` delegate is of type `Action<float>`, which returns `void` and has no `out` or `ref` parameters. The result is that there is no data returned back to the publisher. This is important because an invocation of a delegate potentially triggers notification to multiple subscribers. If the subscribers return a value, it is ambiguous which subscriber's return value would be used.

If you changed `OnTemperatureChange` to return an enumeration value, indicating whether the device was on because of the temperature change, the new delegate would be of type `Func<float, Status>` where `Status` was an enum with elements `On` and `Off`. All subscriber methods would have to use the same method signature as the delegate, and therefore, each would be required to return a status value. And since `OnTemperatureChange` potentially corresponds to a chain of delegates, it is necessary to follow the same pattern that you used for error handling. In other words, you must iterate through each delegate invocation list, using the `GetInvocationList()` method, to retrieve each individual return value. Similarly, delegate types that use `ref` and `out` parameters need special consideration. However, although possible in exceptional circumstances, the guideline is to avoid this scenario entirely by returning `void`.

Events

There are two key problems with the delegates as you have used them so far in this chapter. To overcome these issues, C# uses the keyword `event`. In this section, you will see why you would use events, and how they work.

Why Events?

This chapter and the preceding one covered all you need to know about how delegates work. However, weaknesses in the delegate structure may inadvertently allow the programmer to introduce a bug. The issues relate to encapsulation that neither the subscription nor the publication of events can sufficiently control.

Encapsulating the Subscription

As demonstrated earlier, it is possible to assign one delegate to another using the assignment operator. Unfortunately, this capability introduces a common source for bugs. Consider Listing 13.10.

LISTING 13.10: Using the Assignment Operator = Rather Than +=

```
class Program
{
  public static void Main()
  {
      Thermostat thermostat = new Thermostat();
      Heater heater = new Heater(60);
      Cooler cooler = new Cooler(80);
      string temperature;

      // Note: Use new Action(
      //       cooler.OnTemperatureChanged) if C# 1.0
      thermostat.OnTemperatureChange =
          heater.OnTemperatureChanged;
```

```
      // Bug:  assignment operator overrides
      // previous assignment.
      thermostat.OnTemperatureChange =
         cooler.OnTemperatureChanged;

      Console.Write("Enter temperature: ");
      temperature = Console.ReadLine();
      thermostat.CurrentTemperature = int.Parse(temperature);
   }
 }
```

Listing 13.10 is almost identical to Listing 13.6, except that instead of using the += operator, you use a simple assignment operator. As a result, when code assigns cooler.OnTemperatureChanged to OnTemperatureChange, heater.OnTemperatureChanged is cleared out because an entirely new chain is assigned to replace the previous one. The potential for mistakenly using an assignment operator, when in fact the += assignment was intended, is so high that it would be preferable if the assignment operator were not even supported for objects except within the containing class. It is the purpose of the event keyword to provide additional encapsulation such that you cannot inadvertently cancel other subscribers.

Encapsulating the Publication

The second important difference between delegates and events is that events ensure that only the containing class can trigger an event notification. Consider Listing 13.11.

LISTING 13.11: **Firing the Event from Outside the Events Container**

```
class Program
{
   public static void Main()
   {
      Thermostat thermostat = new Thermostat();
      Heater heater = new Heater(60);
      Cooler cooler = new Cooler(80);
      string temperature;

      // Note: Use new Action(
      //       cooler.OnTemperatureChanged) if C# 1.0.
      thermostat.OnTemperatureChange +=
         heater.OnTemperatureChanged;

      thermostat.OnTemperatureChange +=
         cooler.OnTemperatureChanged;
```

```
                    thermostat.OnTemperatureChange(42);
            }
    }
```

In Listing 13.11, `Program` is able to invoke the `OnTemperatureChange` delegate even though the `CurrentTemperature` on `thermostat` did not change. `Program`, therefore, triggers a notification to all `thermostat` subscribers that the temperature changed, but in reality, there was no change in the thermostat temperature. As before, the problem with the delegate is that there is insufficient encapsulation. `Thermostat` should prevent any other class from being able to invoke the `OnTemperatureChange` delegate.

Declaring an Event

C# provides the event keyword to deal with both of these problems. Although seemingly like a field modifier, event defines a new type of member (see Listing 13.12).

LISTING 13.12: Using the event Keyword with the Event-Coding Pattern

```
public class Thermostat
{
    public class TemperatureArgs: System.EventArgs
    {
        public TemperatureArgs( float newTemperature )
        {
            NewTemperature = newTemperature;
        }

        public float NewTemperature
        {
            get{return _newTemperature;}
            set{_newTemperature = value;}
        }
        private float _newTemperature;
    }

    // Define the event publisher
    public event EventHandler<TemperatureArgs> OnTemperatureChange =
        delegate { };

    public float CurrentTemperature
    {
        ...
    }
```

```
    private float _CurrentTemperature;
}
```

The new `Thermostat` class has four changes from the original class. First, the `OnTemperatureChange` property has been removed, and instead, `OnTemperatureChange` has been declared as a public field. This seems contrary to solving the earlier encapsulation problem. It would make more sense to increase the encapsulation, not decrease it by making a field public. However, the second change was to add the `event` keyword immediately before the field declaration. This simple change provides all the encapsulation needed. By adding the `event` keyword, you prevent use of the assignment operator on a public delegate field (for example, `thermostat.OnTemperatureChange = cooler.OnTemperatureChanged`). In addition, only the containing class is able to invoke the delegate that triggers the publication to all subscribers (for example, disallowing `thermostat.OnTemperatureChange(42)` from outside the class). In other words, the `event` keyword provides the needed encapsulation that prevents any external class from publishing an event or unsubscribing previous subscribers they did not add. This resolves the two issues with plain delegates and is one of the key reasons for the `event` keyword in C#.

Another potential pitfall with plain delegates was the fact that it was easy to forget to check for `null` before invoking the delegate. This resulted in an unexpected `NullReferenceException`. Fortunately, the encapsulation that the `event` keyword provides enables an alternative possibility during declaration (or within the constructor), as shown in Listing 13.12. Notice that when declaring the event we assign `delegate { }`—an empty delegate representing a collection of zero listeners. By assigning the empty delegate we can raise the event without checking whether there are any listeners. (The behavior is similar to assigning a variable with an array of zero items. Doing so allows the invocation of an array member without first checking whether the variable is `null`.) Of course, if there is any chance that the delegate could be reassigned with `null`, a check will still be required. However, because the `event` keyword restricts assignment to occur only within the class, any reassignment of the delegate could occur only from within the class. Assuming `null` is never assigned, there will be no need to check for `null` whenever the code invokes the delegate.

Coding Conventions

All you need to do to gain the desired functionality is to change the original delegate variable declaration to a field, and add the `event` keyword. With these two changes, you provide the necessary encapsulation and all other functionality remains the same. However, an additional change occurs in the delegate declaration in the code in Listing 13.12. To follow standard C# coding conventions, you replaced `Action<float>` with a new delegate type: `EventHandler<TemperatureArgs>`, a CLR type whose declaration is shown in Listing 13.13 (new in .NET Framework 2.0).

LISTING 13.13: **Declaring a Generic Delegate Type**

```
public delegate void EventHandler<TEventArgs>(object sender, TEventArgs e)
    where TEventArgs : EventArgs;
```

The result was that the single temperature parameter in the `Action<TEventArgs>` delegate type was replaced with two new parameters, one for the sender and a second for the event data. This change is not something that the C# compiler will enforce, but passing two parameters of these types is the norm for a delegate intended for an event.

The first parameter, `sender`, should contain an instance of the class that invoked the delegate. This is especially helpful if the same subscriber method registers with multiple events—for example, if the `heater.OnTemperatureChanged` event subscribes to two different `Thermostat` instances. In such a scenario, either `Thermostat` instance can trigger a call to `heater.OnTemperatureChanged`. In order to determine which instance of `Thermostat` triggered the event, you use the `sender` parameter from inside `Heater.OnTemperatureChanged()`. If the event is static this will not be available, so pass `null` for the `sender` argument value.

The second parameter, `TEventArgs e`, is specified as type `Thermostat.TemperatureArgs`. The important part about `TemperatureArgs`, at least as far as the coding convention goes, is that it derives from `System.EventArgs`. (In fact, derivation from `System.EventArgs` is something that the framework forced with a generic constraint until .NET Framework 4.5.) The only significant property on `System.EventArgs` is `Empty` and it is used to indicate that there is no event data. When you derive `TemperatureArgs` from `System.EventArgs`, however, you add an additional property,

NewTemperature, as a means to pass the temperature from the thermostat to the subscribers.

To summarize the coding convention for events: The first argument, sender, is of type object and it contains a reference to the object that invoked the delegate or null if the event is static. The second argument is of type System.EventArgs or something that derives from System.EventArgs but contains additional data about the event. You invoke the delegate exactly as before, except for the additional parameters. Listing 13.14 shows an example.

LISTING 13.14: **Firing the Event Notification**

```
public class Thermostat
{
    ...
    public float CurrentTemperature
    {
        get{return _CurrentTemperature;}
        set
        {
            if (value != CurrentTemperature)
            {
                _CurrentTemperature = value;
                // If there are any subscribers
                // then notify them of changes in
                // temperature
                if(OnTemperatureChange != null)
                {
                    // Call subscribers
                    OnTemperatureChange(
                        this, new TemperatureArgs(value) );
                }
            }
        }
    }
    private float _CurrentTemperature;
}
```

You usually specify the sender using the container class (this) because that is the only class that can invoke the delegate for events.

In this example, the subscriber could cast the sender parameter to Thermostat and access the current temperature that way, as well as via the TemperatureArgs instance. However, the current temperature on the Thermostat instance may change via a different thread. In the case of events that occur due to state changes, passing the previous value along with the new value is a frequent pattern used to control what state transitions are allowable.

Guidelines

DO check that the value of a delegate is not `null` before invoking it.

DO NOT pass `null` as the value of the sender on nonstatic events, but **DO** pass null for the same value on static events.

DO NOT pass `null` as the value of eventArgs argument.

DO use a delegate type of `EventHandler<TEventArgs>` for the events.

DO use `System.EventArgs` or a type that derives from `System.EventArgs` for a TEventArgs.

CONSIDER using a subclass of `System.EventArgs` as the event argument type (TEventArgs), unless you are absolutely sure the event will never need to carry any data.

Generics and Delegates

The preceding section discussed that the guideline for defining a type for an event is to use a delegate type of `EventHandler<TEventArgs>`. In theory, any delegate type could be used, but by convention, the first parameter, `sender`, is of type `object` and the second parameter, `e`, should be a type deriving from `System.EventArgs`. One of the more cumbersome aspects of delegates in C# 1.0 was that you had to declare a new delegate type whenever the parameters on the handler change. Every creation of a new derivation from `System.EventArgs` (a relatively common occurrence) required the declaration of a new delegate data type that uses the new `EventArgs` derived type. For example, in order to use `TemperatureArgs` within the event notification code in Listing 13.14, it is necessary to declare the delegate type `TemperatureChangeHandler` that has `TemperatureArgs` as a parameter (see Listing 13.15).

LISTING 13.15: **Using a Custom Delegate Type**

```
public class Thermostat
{
  public class TemperatureArgs: System.EventArgs
  {
      public TemperatureArgs( float newTemperature )
      {
```

```
            NewTemperature = newTemperature;
        }

        public float NewTemperature
        {
            get{return _newTemperature;}
            set{_newTemperature = value;}
        }
        private float _newTemperature;
    }

    public delegate void TemperatureChangeHandler(
        object sender, TemperatureArgs newTemperature);

    public event TemperatureChangeHandler
        OnTemperatureChange;

    public float CurrentTemperature
    {
        ...
    }
    private float _CurrentTemperature;
}
```

Although generally `EventHandler<TEventArgs>` is preferred over creating a custom delegate type such as `TemperatureChangeHandler`, there is one advantage of such a type. Specifically, if a custom type is used, the parameter names can be specific to the event. In Listing 13.15, for example, when invoking the delegate to raise the event, the second parameter name will appear as `newTemperature` rather than simply e.

Another reason why a custom delegate type might be used concerns parts of the CLR API that were defined prior to C# 2.0. Since this is a pretty significant percentage of the more common types within the framework, it is therefore not uncommon to encounter specific delegate types rather than the generic form on events coming from the CLR API. Regardless, in the majority of circumstances when using events in C# 2.0 and later, it is not necessary to declare a custom delegate data type.

Guidelines

DO use `System.EventHandler<T>` instead of manually creating new delegate types for event handlers, unless the parameter names of a custom type offer significant clarification.

■ ADVANCED TOPIC

Event Internals

Events restrict external classes from doing anything other than adding subscribing methods to the publisher via the += operator and then unsubscribing using the -= operator. In addition, they restrict classes, other than the containing class, from invoking the event. To do this the C# compiler takes the public delegate variable with its event keyword modifier and declares the delegate as private. In addition, it adds a couple of methods and two special event blocks. Essentially, the event keyword is a C# shortcut for generating the appropriate encapsulation logic. Consider the example in the event declaration shown in Listing 13.16.

LISTING 13.16: **Declaring the** OnTemperatureChange **Event**

```
public class Thermostat
{
  public event EventHandler<TemperatureArgs> OnTemperatureChange

  ...
}
```

When the C# compiler encounters the event keyword, it generates CIL code equivalent to the C# code shown in Listing 13.17.

LISTING 13.17: **C# Conceptual Equivalent of the Event CIL Code Generated by the Compiler**

```
public class Thermostat
{
  // ...
  // Declaring the delegate field to save the
  // list of subscribers.
  private EventHandler<TemperatureArgs> _OnTemperatureChange;

  public void add_OnTemperatureChange(
      EventHandler<TemperatureArgs> handler)
  {
      System.Delegate.Combine(_OnTemperatureChange, handler);
  }

  public void remove_OnTemperatureChange(
      EventHandler<TemperatureArgs> handler)
  {
      System.Delegate.Remove(_OnTemperatureChange, handler);
  }

  public event EventHandler<TemperatureArgs> OnTemperatureChange
```

```
    {
        add
        {
            add_OnTemperatureChange(value)
        }
        remove
        {
            remove_OnTemperatureChange(value)
        }
    }
}
```

In other words, the code shown in Listing 13.16 is (conceptually) the C# shorthand that the compiler uses to trigger the code expansion shown in Listing 13.17. (The "conceptually" qualifier is needed because some details regarding thread synchronization have been eliminated for the purpose of elucidation.)

The C# compiler first takes the original event definition and defines a private delegate variable in its place. As a result, the delegate becomes unavailable to any external class, even to classes derived from it.

Next, the C# compiler defines two methods, add_OnTemperatureChange() and remove_OnTemperatureChange(), where the OnTemperatureChange suffix is taken from the original name of the event. These methods are responsible for implementing the += and -= assignment operators, respectively. As Listing 13.17 shows, these methods are implemented using the static System.Delegate.Combine() and System.Delegate.Remove() methods, discussed earlier in the chapter. The first parameter passed to each of these methods is the private EventHandler<TemperatureArgs> delegate instance, OnTemperatureChange.

Perhaps the most curious part of the code generated from the event keyword is the last part. The syntax is very similar to that of a property's getter and setter methods except that the methods are add and remove. The add block takes care of handling the += operator on the event by passing the call to add_OnTemperatureChange(). In a similar manner, the remove block operator handles the -= operator by passing the call on to remove_OnTemperatureChange.

It is important to notice the similarities between this code and the code generated for a property. Readers will recall that the C# implementation of a property is to create get_<propertyname> and set_<propertyname>, and then to pass calls to the get and set blocks on to these methods. Clearly, the event syntax is very similar.

Another important characteristic to note about the generated CIL code is that the CIL equivalent of the event keyword remains in the CIL. In other words, an event is something that the CIL code recognizes explicitly; it is not just a C# construct. By keeping an equivalent event keyword in the CIL code, all languages and editors are able to provide special functionality because they can recognize the event as a special class member.

Customizing the Event Implementation

You can customize the code for += and -= that the compiler generates. Consider, for example, changing the scope of the OnTemperatureChange delegate so that it is protected rather than private. This, of course, would allow classes derived from Thermostat to access the delegate directly instead of being limited to the same restrictions as external classes. To enable this, C# allows the same property as the syntax shown in Listing 13.15. In other words, C# allows you to define custom add and remove blocks to provide implementation for each aspect of the event encapsulation. Listing 13.18 provides an example.

LISTING 13.18: **Custom** add and remove **Handlers**

```csharp
public class Thermostat
{
    public class TemperatureArgs: System.EventArgs
    {
        ...
    }

    // Define the event publisher
    public event EventHandler<TemperatureArgs> OnTemperatureChange
    {
        add
        {
            System.Delegate.Combine(value, _OnTemperatureChange);
        }
        remove
        {
            System.Delegate.Remove(_OnTemperatureChange, value);
        }
    }
    protected EventHandler<TemperatureArgs> _OnTemperatureChange;

    public float CurrentTemperature
```

```
    {
        ...
    }
    private float _CurrentTemperature;
}
```

In this case, the delegate that stores each subscriber, _OnTemperature Change, was changed to protected. In addition, implementation of the add block switches around the delegate storage so that the last delegate added to the chain is the first delegate to receive a notification.

SUMMARY

Now that we have described events, it is worth mentioning that in general, method references are the only cases where it is advisable to work with a delegate variable outside the context of an event. In other words, given the additional encapsulation features of an event and the ability to custom-ize the implementation when necessary, the best practice is always to use events for the observer pattern.

It may take a little practice to be able to code events from scratch without sample code. However, they are a critical foundation to the asynchronous, multithreaded coding of later chapters.

▉14▉
Collection Interfaces with Standard Query Operators

The most significant features added in C# 3.0 were in the area of collections. Extension methods and lambda expressions enabled a far superior API for working with collections. In fact, in earlier editions of this book, the chapter on collections came immediately after the chapter on generics and just before the one on delegates. However, lambda expressions make such a significant impact on collection APIs that it is no longer possible to cover collections without first covering delegates (the basis of lambda expressions). Now that you have a solid foundation on lambda expressions from the preceding chapter, we can delve into the details of collections, a topic that spans three chapters.

To begin, this chapter introduces anonymous types and collection initializers, topics that we covered only briefly in a few Advanced Topic sections in Chapter 5. Next, this chapter covers the various collection interfaces and how they relate to one another. This is the basis for understanding collections, so readers should cover the material with diligence. The section on collection interfaces includes coverage of the `IEnumerable<T>` extension methods that were added in C# 3.0 to implement the standard query operators.

There are two categories of collection-related classes and interfaces: those that support generics and those that don't. This chapter primarily discusses the generic collection interfaces. You should use collection classes that don't support generics only when you are writing components that need to interoperate with earlier versions of the runtime. This is because everything that was available in the nongeneric form has a generic replacement that is strongly typed. Although the concepts still apply to both forms, we will not explicitly discuss the nongeneric versions.[1]

Anonymous Types and Implicitly Typed Local Variables

C# 3.0 significantly improved support for handling collections of items. What is amazing is that to support this advanced API, fewer than nine new language enhancements were made. However, these enhancements are critical to why C# 3.0 was such a marvelous improvement to the language. Two such enhancements were anonymous types and implicit local variables.

Anonymous Types

Anonymous types are data types that are declared by the compiler, rather than through the explicit class definitions of Chapter 5. Like anonymous functions, when the compiler sees an anonymous type, it does the work to make that class for you and then lets you use it as though you had declared it explicitly. Listing 14.1 shows such a declaration.

LISTING 14.1: **Implicit Local Variables with Anonymous Types**

```
using System;

class Program
```

---

1. In fact, in both Silverlight and WinRT, the nongeneric collections have been removed.

```
{
  static void Main()
  {
    var patent1 =
        new
        {
            Title = "Bifocals",
            YearOfPublication = "1784"
        };
    var patent2 =
        new
        {
            Title = "Phonograph",
            YearOfPublication = "1877"
        };
    var patent3 =
        new
        {
            patent1.Title,
            // Renamed to show property naming.
            Year = patent1.YearOfPublication
        };

    Console.WriteLine("{0} ({1})",
        patent1.Title, patent1.YearOfPublication);
    Console.WriteLine("{0} ({1})",
        patent2.Title, patent2.YearOfPublication);

    Console.WriteLine();
    Console.WriteLine(patent1);
    Console.WriteLine(patent2);

    Console.WriteLine();
    Console.WriteLine(patent3);
  }
}
```

The corresponding output is shown in Output 14.1.

OUTPUT 14.1

```
Bifocals (1784)
Phonograph (1784)

{ Title = Bifocals, YearOfPublication = 1784 }
{ Title = Phonograph, YearOfPublication = 1877 }

{ Title = Bifocals, Year = 1784 }
```

Anonymous types are purely a C# feature, not a new kind of type in the runtime. When the compiler encounters the anonymous type syntax, it generates a CIL class with properties corresponding to the named values and data types in the anonymous type declaration.

Implicitly Typed Local Variables (var)

Since an anonymous type by definition has no name, it is not possible to declare a local variable as explicitly being of an anonymous type. Rather, the local variable's type is replaced with var. However, by no means does this indicate that implicitly typed variables are untyped. On the contrary, they are fully typed to the data type of the value they are assigned. If an implicitly typed variable is assigned an anonymous type, the underlying CIL code for the local variable declaration will be of the type generated by the compiler. Similarly, if the implicitly typed variable is assigned a string, its data type in the underlying CIL will be a string. In fact, there is no difference in the resultant CIL code for implicitly typed variables whose assignment is not an anonymous type (such as string) and those that are declared as type string. If the declaration statement is `string text = "This is a test of the..."`, the resultant CIL code will be identical to an implicitly typed declaration, `var text = "This is a test of the..."`. The compiler determines the data type of the implicitly typed variable from the expression assigned. In an explicitly typed local variable with an initializer (`string s = "hello";`), the compiler first determines the type of s from the declared type on the left-hand side, then analyzes the right-hand side and verifies that the expression on the right-hand side is assignable to that type. In an implicitly typed local variable, the process is in some sense reversed. First the right-hand side is analyzed to determine its type, and then the "var" is logically replaced with that type.

Although there is no available name in C# for the anonymous type, it is still strongly typed as well. For example, the properties of the type are fully accessible. In Listing 14.1, `patent1.Title` and `patent2.YearOfPublication` are called within the `Console.WriteLine` statement. Any attempts to call nonexistent members will result in compile errors. Even IntelliSense in IDEs such as Visual Studio 2012 works with the anonymous type.

You should use implicitly typed variable declarations sparingly. Obviously, for anonymous types, it is not possible to specify the data type, and the use of var is required. However, for cases where the data type is not an anonymous type, it is frequently preferable to use the explicit data type. As is the case generally, you should focus on making the semantics of the code more readable while at the same time using the compiler to verify that the resultant variable is of the type you expect. To accomplish this with implicitly typed local variables, use them only when the type assigned to the implicitly typed variable is entirely obvious. For example, in var items = new Dictionary<string, List<Account>>();, the resultant code is more succinct and readable. In contrast, when the type is not obvious, such as when a method return is assigned, developers should favor an explicit variable type declaration such as the following:

```
Dictionary<string, List<Account>> dictionary = GetAccounts();
```

■ **NOTE**

Implicitly typed variables should generally be reserved for anonymous type declaration rather than used indiscriminately when the data type is known at compile time, unless the type assigned to the variable is entirely obvious.

Language Contrast: C++/Visual Basic/JavaScript—void*, Variant, and var

It is important to understand that an implicitly typed variable is not the equivalent of void* in C++, a Variant in Visual Basic, or var in JavaScript. In each of these cases, the variable declaration is not very restrictive since the variable may be assigned a value of any type, just as you could in C# with a variable declaration of type object. In contrast, var is definitively typed by the compiler, and once established at declaration, the type may not change, and type checks and member calls are verified at compile time.

More about Anonymous Types and Implicit Local Variables

In Listing 14.1, member names on the anonymous types are explicitly identified using the assignment of the value to the name for patent1 and patent2 (for example, `Title` = `"Phonograph"`). However, if the value assigned is a property or field call, the name may default to the name of the field or property rather than explicitly specifying the value. `patent3`, for example, is defined using a property named "Title" rather than an assignment to an explicit name. As Output 14.1 shows, the resultant property name is determined, by the compiler, to match the property from where the value was retrieved.

`patent1` and `patent2` both have the same property names with the same data types. Therefore, the C# compiler generates only one data type for these two anonymous declarations. `patent3`, however, forces the compiler to create a second anonymous type because the property name for the patent year is different from what it was in `patent1` and `patent2`. Furthermore, if the order of the properties were switched between `patent1` and `patent2`, these two anonymous types would also not be type-compatible. In other words, the requirements for two anonymous types to be type-compatible within the same assembly are a match in property names, data types, and order of properties. If these criteria are met, the types are compatible even if they appear in different methods or classes. Listing 14.2 demonstrates the type incompatibilities.

LISTING 14.2: **Type Safety and Immutability of Anonymous Types**

```
class Program
{
  static void Main()
  {
      var patent1 =
          new
          {
              Title = "Bifocals",
              YearOfPublication = "1784"
          };

      var patent2 =
          new
          {
              YearOfPublication = "1877",
              Title = "Phonograph"
          };

      var patent3 =
          new
          {
```

```
            patent1.Title,
            Year = patent1.YearOfPublication
        };

        // ERROR: Cannot implicitly convert type
        //        'AnonymousType#1' to 'AnonymousType#2'
        patent1 = patent2;
        // ERROR: Cannot implicitly convert type
        //        'AnonymousType#3' to 'AnonymousType#2'
        patent1 = patent3;

        // ERROR: Property or indexer 'AnonymousType#1.Title'
        //        cannot be assigned to -- it is read only'
        patent1.Title = "Swiss Cheese";
    }
}
```

The resultant two compile errors assert the fact that the types are not compatible, so they will not successfully convert from one to the other.

The third compile error is caused by the reassignment of the Title property. Anonymous types are immutable, so it is a compile error to change a property on an anonymous type once it has been instantiated.

Although not shown in Listing 14.2, it is not possible to declare a method with an implicit data type parameter (var). Therefore, instances of anonymous types can only be passed outside the method in which they are created in only two ways. First, if the method parameter is of type object, the anonymous type instance may pass outside the method because the anonymous type will convert implicitly. A second way is to use method type inference, whereby the anonymous type instance is passed as a method type parameter that the compiler can successfully infer. Calling void Method<T>(T parameter) using Function(patent1), therefore, would succeed, although the available operations on parameter within Function() are limited to those supported by object.

In spite of the fact that C# allows anonymous types such as the ones shown in Listing 14.1, it is generally not recommended that you define them in this way. Anonymous types provide critical functionality with C# 3.0 support for projections, such as joining/associating collections, as we discuss later in the chapter. However, generally you should reserve anonymous type definitions for circumstances where they are required, such as aggregation of data from multiple types.

■ **ADVANCED TOPIC**

Anonymous Type Generation

Even though `Console.WriteLine()`'s implementation is to call `ToString()`, notice in Listing 14.1 that the output from `Console.WriteLine()` is not the default `ToString()`, which writes out the fully qualified data type name. Rather, the output is a list of `PropertyName = value` pairs, one for each property on the anonymous type. This occurs because the compiler overrides `ToString()` in the anonymous type code generation, and instead formats the `ToString()` output as shown. Similarly, the generated type includes overriding implementations for `Equals()` and `GetHashCode()`.

The implementation of `ToString()` on its own is an important reason that variation in the order of properties causes a new data type to be generated. If two separate anonymous types, possibly in entirely separate types and even namespaces, were unified and then the order of properties changed, changes in the order of properties on one implementation would have noticeable and possibly unacceptable effects on the other's `ToString()` results. Furthermore, at execution time it is possible to reflect back on a type and examine the members on a type—even to call one of these members dynamically (determining at runtime which member to call). A variation in the order of members on two seemingly identical types could trigger unexpected results, and to avoid this, the C# designers decided to generate two different types.

Collection Initializers

Another feature added to C# in version 3.0 was **collection initializers.** A collection initializer allows programmers to construct a collection with an initial set of members at instantiation time in a manner similar to array declaration. Without collection initialization, elements had to be explicitly added to a collection after the collection was instantiated—using something like `System.Collections.Generic.ICollection<T>`'s `Add()` method. With collection initialization, the `Add()` calls are generated by the C# complier rather than explicitly coded by the developer. Listing 14.3 shows how to initialize the collection using a collection initializer instead.

LISTING 14.3: **Filtering with** `System.Linq.Enumerable.Where()`

```
using System;
using System.Collections.Generic;
```

```
class Program
{
  static void Main()
  {
      List<string> sevenWorldBlunders;
      sevenWorldBlunders = new List<string>()
      {
          // Quotes from Ghandi
          "Wealth without work",
          "Pleasure without conscience",
          "Knowledge without character",
          "Commerce without morality",
          "Science without humanity",
          "Worship without sacrifice",
          "Politics without principle"
      };

      Print(sevenWorldBlunders);

  }

  private static void Print<T>(IEnumerable<T> items)
  {
      foreach (T item in items)
      {
          Console.WriteLine(item);
      }
  }
}
```

The syntax is similar not only to the array initialization, but also to an object initializer with the curly braces following the constructor. If no parameters are passed in the constructor, the parentheses following the data type are optional (as they are with object initializers).

A few basic requirements are needed in order for a collection initializer to compile successfully. Ideally, the collection type to which a collection initializer is applied would be of a type that implements `System.Collections.Generic.ICollection<T>`. This ensures that the collection includes an `Add()` that the compiler-generated code can invoke. However, a relaxed version of the requirement also exists and simply demands that one or more `Add()` methods exist on a type that implements `IEnumerable<T>`—even if the collection doesn't implement `ICollection<T>`. The `Add()` methods need to take parameters that are compatible with the values specified in the collection initializer.

Allowing initializers on collections that don't support `ICollection<T>` was important for two reasons. First, it turns out that the majority of collections (types that implement `IEnumerable<T>`) do not also implement `ICollection<T>`, thus significantly reducing the usefulness of collection initializers.

Second, matching on the method name and signature compatibility with the collection initializer items enables greater diversity in the items initialized into the collection. For example, the initializer now can support `new DataStore(){ a, {b, c}}` as long as there is one `Add()` method whose signature is compatible with `a` and a second `Add()` method compatible with `b, c`.

Note that you cannot have a collection initializer for an anonymous type since the collection initializer requires a constructor call, and it is impossible to name the constructor. The workaround is to define a method such as `static List<T> CreateList<T>(T t) { return new List<T>(); }`. Method type inference allows the type parameter to be implied rather than specified explicitly, and so this workaround successfully allows for the creation of a collection of anonymous types.

Another approach to initializing a collection of anonymous types is to use an array initializer. Since it is not possible to specify the data type in the constructor, array initialization syntax allows for anonymous array initializers using `new[]` (see Listing 14.4).

LISTING 14.4: **Initializing Anonymous Type Arrays**

```
using System;
using System.Collections.Generic;
using System.Linq;

class Program
{
  static void Main()
  {
    var worldCup2006Finalists = new[]
    {
        new
        {
            TeamName = "France",
            Players = new string[]
            {
                "Fabien Barthez", "Gregory Coupet",
                "Mickael Landreau", "Eric Abidal",
                // ...
            }
        },
        new
```

```csharp
            {
                TeamName = "Italy",
                Players = new string[]
                {
                    "Gianluigi Buffon", "Angelo Peruzzi",
                    "Marco Amelia", "Cristian Zaccardo",
                    // ...
                }
            }
        };


        Print(worldCup2006Finalists);
    }

    private static void Print<T>(IEnumerable<T> items)
    {
        foreach (T item in items)
        {
            Console.WriteLine(item);
        }
    }
}
```

The resultant variable is an array of the anonymous type items, which must be homogeneous since it is an array.

What Makes a Class a Collection: IEnumerable<T>

By definition, a collection within .NET is a class that, at a minimum, implements IEnumerable<T> (or the nongeneric type IEnumerable). This interface is a key because implementing the methods of IEnumerable<T> is the minimum implementation requirement needed to support iterating over the collection.

Chapter 3 showed how to use a foreach statement to iterate over an array of elements. The syntax is simple and avoids the complication of having to know how many elements there are. The runtime does not directly support the foreach statement, however. Instead, the C# compiler transforms the code as described in this section.

foreach with Arrays

Listing 14.5 demonstrates a simple foreach loop iterating over an array of integers and then printing out each integer to the console.

LISTING 14.5: foreach **with Arrays**

```
int[] array = new int[]{1, 2, 3, 4, 5, 6};

foreach (int item in array)
{
    Console.WriteLine(item);
}
```

From this code, the C# compiler creates a CIL equivalent of the for loop, as shown in Listing 14.6.

LISTING 14.6: **Compiled Implementation of** foreach **with Arrays**

```
int number;
int[] tempArray;
int[] array = new int[]{1, 2, 3, 4, 5, 6};

tempArray = array;
for (int counter = 0; (counter < tempArray.Length); counter++)
{
  int item = tempArray[counter];

  Console.WriteLine(item);
}
```

In this example, note that foreach relies on support for the Length property and the index operator ([ ]). With the Length property, the C# compiler can use the for statement to iterate through each element in the array.

foreach **with** IEnumerable<T>

Although the code shown in Listing 14.6 works well on arrays where the length is fixed and the index operator is always supported, not all types of collections have a known number of elements. Furthermore, many of the collection classes, including the Stack<T>, Queue<T>, and Dictionary<Tkey, Tvalue> classes, do not support retrieving elements by index. Therefore, a more general approach of iterating over collections of elements is needed. The iterator pattern provides this capability. Assuming you can determine the first, next, and last elements, knowing the count and supporting retrieval of elements by index is unnecessary.

The System.Collections.Generic.IEnumerator<T> and nongeneric System.Collections.IEnumerator interfaces (see Listing 14.8) are designed to enable the iterator pattern for iterating over collections of elements, rather

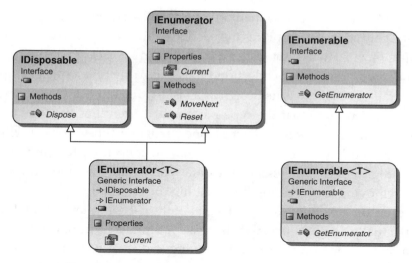

FIGURE 14.1: A Class Diagram of IEnumerator<T> and IEnumerator Interfaces

than the length-index pattern shown in Listing 14.6. A class diagram of their relationships appears in Figure 14.1.

IEnumerator, which IEnumerator<T> derives from, includes three members. The first is bool MoveNext(). Using this method, you can move from one element within the collection to the next while at the same time detecting when you have enumerated through every item. The second member, a read-only property called Current, returns the element currently in process. Current is overloaded in IEnumerator<T>, providing a type-specific implementation of it. With these two members on the collection class, it is possible to iterate over the collection simply using a while loop, as demonstrated in Listing 14.7. (The Reset() method usually throws a NotImplementedException, and therefore should never be called. If you need to restart an enumeration, just create a fresh enumerator.)

LISTING 14.7: Iterating over a Collection Using while

```csharp
System.Collections.Generic.Stack<int> stack =
  new System.Collections.Generic.Stack<int>();
int number;
// ...

// This code is conceptual, not the actual code.
while (stack.MoveNext())
{
  number = stack.Current;
  Console.WriteLine(number);
}
```

In Listing 14.7, the `MoveNext()` method returns `false` when it moves past the end of the collection. This replaces the need to count elements while looping.

Listing 14.7 uses a `System.Collections.Generic.Stack<T>` as the collection type. Numerous other collection types exist; this is just one example. The key trait of `Stack<T>` is its design as a last in, first out (LIFO) collection. It is important to note that the type parameter `T` identifies the type of all items within the collection. Collecting one particular type of object within a collection is a key characteristic of a generic collection. It is important that the programmer understands the data type within the collection when adding, removing, or accessing items within the collection.

The preceding example shows the gist of the C# compiler output, but it doesn't actually compile that way because it omits two important details concerning the implementation: interleaving and error handling.

State Is Shared

The problem with an implementation such as Listing 14.7 is that if two such loops interleaved each other—one `foreach` inside another, both using the same collection—the collection must maintain a state indicator of the current element so that when `MoveNext()` is called, the next element can be determined. The problem is that one interleaving loop can affect the other. (The same is true of loops executed by multiple threads.)

To overcome this problem, the collection classes do not support `IEnumerator<T>` and `IEnumerator` interfaces directly. As shown in Figure 14.1, there is a second interface, called `IEnumerable<T>`, whose only method is `GetEnumerator()`. The purpose of this method is to return an object that supports `IEnumerator<T>`. Instead of the collection class maintaining the state, a different class, usually a nested class so that it has access to the internals of the collection, will support the `IEnumerator<T>` interface and will keep the state of the iteration loop. The enumerator is like a "cursor" or a "bookmark" in the sequence. You can have multiple bookmarks, and moving each of them enumerates over the collection independently of the other. Using this pattern, the C# equivalent of a `foreach` loop will look like the code shown in Listing 14.8.

LISTING 14.8: A Separate Enumerator Maintaining State during an Iteration

```
System.Collections.Generic.Stack<int> stack =
  new System.Collections.Generic.Stack<int>();
int number;
```

```
System.Collections.Generic.Stack<int>.Enumerator
  enumerator;

// ...

// If IEnumerable<T> is implemented explicitly,
// then a cast is required.
// ((IEnumerable<int>)stack).GetEnumerator();
enumerator = stack.GetEnumerator();
while (enumerator.MoveNext())
{
  number = enumerator.Current;
  Console.WriteLine(number);
}
```

Cleaning Up Following Iteration

Since the classes that implement the `IEnumerator<T>` interface maintain the state, sometimes you need to clean up the state after it exits the loop (because either all iterations have completed or an exception is thrown). To achieve this, the `IEnumerator<T>` interface derives from `IDisposable`. Enumerators that implement `IEnumerator` do not necessarily implement `IDisposable`, but if they do, `Dispose()` will be called as well. This enables the calling of `Dispose()` after the `foreach` loop exits. The C# equivalent of the final CIL code, therefore, looks like Listing 14.9.

LISTING 14.9: Compiled Result of foreach on Collections

```
System.Collections.Generic.Stack<int> stack =
  new System.Collections.Generic.Stack<int>();
System.Collections.Generic.Stack<int>.Enumerator
  enumerator;
IDisposable disposable;

enumerator = stack.GetEnumerator();
try
{
  int number;
  while (enumerator.MoveNext())
  {
      number = enumerator.Current;
      Console.WriteLine(number);
  }
}
finally
{
  // Explicit cast used for IEnumerator<T>.
  disposable = (IDisposable) enumerator;
  disposable.Dispose();
```

```
    // IEnumerator will use the as operator unless IDisposable
    // support is known at compile time.
    // disposable = (enumerator as IDisposable);
    // if (disposable != null)
    // {
    //     disposable.Dispose();
    // }
}
```

Notice that because the `IDisposable` interface is supported by `IEnumerator<T>`, the `using` statement can simplify the code in Listing 14.9 to that shown in Listing 14.10.

LISTING 14.10: Error Handling and Resource Cleanup with using

```
System.Collections.Generic.Stack<int> stack =
  new System.Collections.Generic.Stack<int>();
int number;

using(
    System.Collections.Generic.Stack<int>.Enumerator
        enumerator = stack.GetEnumerator())
{
  while (enumerator.MoveNext())
  {
      number = enumerator.Current;
      Console.WriteLine(number);
  }
}
```

However, recall that the CIL also does not directly support the `using` keyword, so in reality, the code in Listing 14.9 is a more accurate C# representation of the `foreach` CIL code.

▪ ADVANCED TOPIC

foreach **without** IEnumerable

C# doesn't require that `IEnumerable`/`IEnumerable<T>` be implemented in order to iterate over a data type using `foreach`. Rather, the compiler uses a concept known as **duck typing;** it looks for a `GetEnumerator()` method that returns a type with a `Current` property and `MoveNext()` method. Duck typing involves searching by name rather than relying on an interface or explicit method call to the method. (The name "duck typing" comes from the whimsical idea that in order to be treated as a duck, the object must merely implement a `Quack()` method; it need not implement an `IDuck` interface.) If duck typing fails to find a suitable implementation of the enumerable pattern, the compiler checks to see if the collection implements the interfaces.

Do Not Modify Collections during foreach Iteration

Chapter 3 showed that the compiler prevents assignment of the `foreach` variable (`number`). As is demonstrated in Listing 14.10, an assignment to `number` would not be a change to the collection element itself, so the C# compiler prevents such an assignment altogether.

In addition, neither the element count within a collection nor the items themselves can generally be modified during the execution of a `foreach` loop. If, for example, you called `stack.Push(42)` inside the `foreach` loop, it would be ambiguous whether the `iterator` should ignore or incorporate the change to `stack`—in other words, whether `iterator` should iterate over the newly added item or ignore it and assume the same state as when it was instantiated.

Because of this ambiguity, an exception of type `System.Invalid OperationException` is generally thrown upon accessing the enumerator if the collection is modified within a `foreach` loop, reporting that the collection was modified after the enumerator was instantiated.

Standard Query Operators

Besides the methods on `System.Object`, any type that implements `IEnumerable<T>` is only required to implement one method, `GetEnumerator()`. And yet, it makes more than 50 methods available to all types implementing `IEnumerable<T>`, not including any overloading—and this happens without needing to explicitly implement any method except the `GetEnumerator()` method. The additional functionality is provided using C# 3.0's extension methods and it all resides in the class `System.Linq.Enumerable`. Therefore, including the `using` declarative for `System.Linq` is all it takes to make these methods available.

Each method on `IEnumerable<T>` is a **standard query operator;** it provides querying capability over the collection on which it operates. In the following sections, we will examine some of the most prominent of these standard query operators.

Many of the examples will depend on an Inventor and/or Patent class, both defined in Listing 14.11.

LISTING 14.11: Sample Classes for Use with Standard Query Operators

```csharp
using System;
using System.Collections.Generic;
using System.Linq;

public class Patent
{
  // Title of the published application
  public string Title { get; set; }

  // The date the application was officially published
  public string YearOfPublication { get; set; }

  // A unique number assigned to published applications
  public string ApplicationNumber { get; set; }

  public long[] InventorIds { get; set; }

  public override string ToString()
  {
      return string.Format("{0}({1})",
          Title, YearOfPublication);
  }
}

public class Inventor
{
  public long Id { get; set; }
  public string Name { get; set; }
  public string City { get; set; }
  public string State { get; set; }
  public string Country { get; set; }

  public override string ToString()
  {
      return string.Format("{0}({1}, {2})",
          Name, City, State);
  }
}

class Program
{
  static void Main()
  {
    IEnumerable<Patent> patents = PatentData.Patents;
    Print(patents);

    Console.WriteLine();
```

```csharp
        IEnumerable<Inventor> inventors = PatentData.Inventors;
        Print(inventors);
    }

    private static void Print<T>(IEnumerable<T> items)
    {
        foreach (T item in items)
        {
            Console.WriteLine(item);
        }
    }
}

public static class PatentData
{
    public static readonly Inventor[] Inventors = new Inventor[]
        {
            new Inventor(){
                Name="Benjamin Franklin", City="Philadelphia",
                State="PA", Country="USA", Id=1 },
            new Inventor(){
                Name="Orville Wright", City="Kitty Hawk",
                State="NC", Country="USA", Id=2},
            new Inventor(){
                Name="Wilbur Wright", City="Kitty Hawk",
                State="NC", Country="USA", Id=3},
            new Inventor(){
                Name="Samuel Morse", City="New York",
                State="NY", Country="USA", Id=4},
            new Inventor(){
                Name="George Stephenson", City="Wylam",
                State="Northumberland", Country="UK", Id=5},
            new Inventor(){
                Name="John Michaelis", City="Chicago",
                State="IL", Country="USA", Id=6},
            new Inventor(){
                Name="Mary Phelps Jacob", City="New York",
                State="NY", Country="USA", Id=7},
        };

    public static readonly Patent[] Patents = new Patent[]
        {
            new Patent(){
                Title="Bifocals", YearOfPublication="1784",
                InventorIds=new long[] {1}},
            new Patent(){
                Title="Phonograph", YearOfPublication="1877",
                InventorIds=new long[] {1}},
            new Patent(){
                Title="Kinetoscope", YearOfPublication="1888",
                InventorIds=new long[] {1}},
            new Patent(){
                Title="Electrical Telegraph",
```

```
                        YearOfPublication="1837",
                        InventorIds=new long[] {4}},
                new Patent(){
                        Title="Flying machine", YearOfPublication="1903",
                        InventorIds=new long[] {2,3}},
                new Patent(){
                        Title="Steam Locomotive",
                        YearOfPublication="1815",
                        InventorIds=new long[] {5}},
                new Patent(){
                        Title="Droplet deposition apparatus",
                        YearOfPublication="1989",
                        InventorIds=new long[] {6}},
                new Patent(){
                        Title="Backless Brassiere",
                        YearOfPublication="1914",
                        InventorIds=new long[] {7}},
        };
    }
```

Listing 14.11 also provides a selection of sample data. Output 14.2 displays the results.

OUTPUT 14.2

```
Bifocals(1784)
Phonograph(1877)
Kinetoscope(1888)
Electrical Telegraph(1837)
Flying machine(1903)
Steam Locomotive(1815)
Droplet deposition apparatus(1989)
Backless Brassiere(1914)

Benjamin Franklin(Philadelphia, PA)
Orville Wright(Kitty Hawk, NC)
Wilbur Wright(Kitty Hawk, NC)
Samuel Morse(New York, NY)
George Stephenson(Wylam, Northumberland)
John Michaelis(Chicago, IL)
Mary Phelps Jacob(New York, NY)
```

Filtering with Where()

In order to filter out data from a collection, we need to provide a filter method that returns true or false, indicating whether a particular element should be included or not. A delegate expression that takes an argument and returns a Boolean is called a **predicate,** and a collection's Where() method depends on predicates for identifying filter criteria, as

shown in Listing 14.12. (Technically, the result of the `Where()` method is
a **monad** which encapsulates the operation of filtering a given sequence
with a given predicate.) The output appears in Output 14.3.

LISTING 14.12: **Filtering with** `System.Linq.Enumerable.Where()`

```csharp
using System;
using System.Collections.Generic;
using System.Linq;

class Program
{
  static void Main()
  {
      IEnumerable<Patent> patents = PatentData.Patents;
      patents = patents.Where(
          patent => patent.YearOfPublication.StartsWith("18"));
      Print(patents);
  }

  // ...
}
```

OUTPUT 14.3

```
Phonograph(1877)
Kinetoscope(1888)
Electrical Telegraph(1837)
Steam Locomotive(1815)
```

Notice that the code assigns the output of the `Where()` call back to
`IEnumerable<T>`. In other words, the output of `IEnumerable<T>.Where()` is a
new `IEnumerable<T>` collection. In Listing 14.12, it is `IEnumerable<Patent>`.

Less obvious is that the `Where()` expression argument has not necessarily
executed at assignment time. This is true for many of the standard query
operators. In the case of `Where()`, for example, the expression is passed
in to the collection and "saved" but not executed. Instead, execution of
the expression occurs only when it is necessary to begin iterating over the
items within the collection. A `foreach` loop, for example, such as the one in
`Print()` (in Listing 14.11), will trigger the expression to be evaluated for
each item within the collection. At least conceptually, the `Where()` method
should be understood as a means of specifying the query regarding what
appears in the collection, not the actual work involved with iterating over
to produce a new collection with potentially fewer items.

Projecting with `Select()`

Since the output from the `IEnumerable<T>.Where()` method is a new `IEnumerable<T>` collection, it is possible to again call a standard query operator on the same collection. For example, rather than just filtering the data from the original collection, we could transform the data (see Listing 14.13).

LISTING 14.13: **Projection with** `System.Linq.Enumerable.Select()`

```
using System;
using System.Collections.Generic;
using System.Linq;

class Program
{
  static void Main()
  {
      IEnumerable<Patent> patents = PatentData.Patents;
      IEnumerable<Patent> patentsOf1800 = patents.Where(
          patent => patent.YearOfPublication.StartsWith("18"));
      IEnumerable<string> items = patentsOf1800.Select(
          patent => patent.ToString());

      Print(items);
  }

  // ...
}
```

In Listing 14.13, we create a new `IEnumerable<string>` collection. In this case, it just so happens that adding the `Select()` call doesn't change the output; but this is only because `Print()`'s `Console.WriteLine()` call used `ToString()` anyway. Obviously, a transform still occurred on each item from the `Patent` type of the original collection to the string type of the `items` collection.

Consider the example using `System.IO.FileInfo` in Listing 14.14.

LISTING 14.14: **Projection with** `System.Linq.Enumerable.Select()` **and** new

```
      // ...
      IEnumerable<string> fileList = Directory.GetFiles(
          rootDirectory, searchPattern);
      IEnumerable<FileInfo> files = fileList.Select(
          file => new FileInfo(file));
      // ...
```

`fileList` is of type `IEnumerable<string>`. However, using the projection offered by `Select`, we can transform each item in the collection to a `System.IO.FileInfo` object.

Lastly, capitalizing on anonymous types, we could create an `IEnumerable<T>` collection where `T` is an anonymous type (see Listing 14.15 and Output 14.4).

LISTING 14.15: **Projection to an Anonymous Type**

```
// ...
IEnumerable<string> fileList = Directory.GetFiles(
    rootDirectory, searchPattern);
var items = fileList.Select(
    file =>
    {
        FileInfo fileInfo = new FileInfo(file);
        return new
        {
            FileName = fileInfo.Name,
            Size = fileInfo.Length
        };
    });
// ...
```

OUTPUT 14.4

```
{ FileName = AssemblyInfo.cs, Size = 1704 }
{ FileName = CodeAnalysisRules.xml, Size = 735 }
{ FileName = CustomDictionary.xml, Size = 199 }
{ FileName = EssentialCSharp.sln, Size = 40415 }
{ FileName = EssentialCSharp.suo, Size = 454656 }
{ FileName = EssentialCSharp.vsmdi, Size = 499 }
{ FileName = EssentialCSharp.vssscc, Size = 256 }
{ FileName = intelliTechture.ConsoleTester.dll, Size = 24576 }
{ FileName = intelliTechture.ConsoleTester.pdb, Size = 30208 }
{ FileName = LocalTestRun.testrunconfig, Size = 1388 }
```

The output of an anonymous type automatically shows the property names and their values as part of the generated `ToString()` method associated with the anonymous type.

Projection using the `Select()` method is very powerful. We already saw how to filter a collection vertically (reducing the number of items in the collection) using the `Where()` standard query operator. Now, via the `Select()` standard query operator, we can also reduce the collection horizontally (making fewer columns) or transform the data entirely. In combination, `Where()` and `Select()` provide a means for extracting only the pieces of the original collection that are desirable for the current algorithm. These two methods alone provide a powerful collection manipulation API that would otherwise result in significantly more code that is less readable.

■ ADVANCED TOPIC

Running LINQ Queries in Parallel

With the abundance of computers having multiple processors and multiple cores within those processors, the ability to easily take advantage of the additional processing power becomes far more important. To do this, programs need to be changed to support multiple threads so that work can happen simultaneously on different CPUs within the computer. Listing 14.16 demonstrates one way to do this using Parallel LINQ (PLINQ).

LISTING 14.16: **Executing LINQ Queries in Parallel**

```
// ...
IEnumerable<string> fileList = Directory.GetFiles(
    rootDirectory, searchPattern);
var items = fileList.AsParallel().Select(
    file =>
    {
        FileInfo fileInfo = new FileInfo(file);
        return new
        {
            FileName = fileInfo.Name,
            Size = fileInfo.Length
        };
    });
// ...
```

As Listing 14.16 shows, the change in code to enable parallel support is minimal. All that it uses is a .NET Framework 4–introduced standard query operator, `AsParallel()`, on the static class `System.Linq.ParallelEnumerable`. Using this simple extension method, however, the runtime begins executing over the items within the `fileList` collection and returning the resultant objects in parallel. Each parallel operation in this case isn't particularly expensive (although it is relative to what other execution is taking place), but consider CPU-intensive operations such as encryption or compression. Running the query in parallel across multiple CPUs can decrease execution time by a factor corresponding to the number of CPUs.

An important caveat to be aware of (and the reason why `AsParallel()` appears as an Advanced Topic rather than in the standard text) is that parallel execution can introduce race conditions such that an operation on one thread can be intermingled with an operation on a different thread, causing data corruption. To avoid this, synchronization mechanisms are required on data with shared access from multiple threads in order to force the operations to be atomic where necessary. Synchronization itself, however, can introduce deadlocks that freeze the execution, further complicating the effective parallel programming.

More details on this and additional multithreading topics are covered in Chapter 18 and Chapter 19.

Counting Elements with `Count()`

Another common query performed on a collection of items is to retrieve the count. To support this LINQ includes the `Count()` extension method.

Listing 14.17 demonstrates that `Count()` is overloaded to simply count all elements (no parameters) or to take a predicate that only counts items identified by the predicate expression.

LISTING 14.17: Counting Items with `Count()`

```csharp
using System;
using System.Collections.Generic;
using System.Linq;

class Program
{
  static void Main()
  {
      IEnumerable<Patent> patents = PatentData.Patents;
      Console.WriteLine("Patent Count: {0}", patents.Count());
      Console.WriteLine("Patent Count in 1800s: {0}",
          patents.Count(patent =>
              patent.YearOfPublication.StartsWith("18")));
  }

  // ...
}
```

In spite of the simplicity of writing the `Count()` statement, `IEnumerable<T>` has not changed, so the executed code still involves iterating over all the items in the collection. Whenever a `Count` property is directly available on the collection, it is preferable to use that rather than LINQ's `Count()` method (a subtle difference). Fortunately, `ICollection<T>` includes the `Count` property, so code that calls the `Count()` method on a collection that supports `ICollection<T>` will cast the collection and call `Count` directly. However, if `ICollection<T>` is not supported, `Enumerable.Count()` will proceed to enumerate all the items in the collection rather than call the built-in `Count` mechanism. If the purpose of checking the count is only to see whether it is greater than zero (`if(patents.Count() > 0){...}`), a preferable approach would be to use the `Any()` operator (`if(patents.Any()){...}`). `Any()` attempts to iterate over only one of the items in the collection to return a true result, rather than the entire sequence.

> ## Guidelines
> **DO** use `System.Linq.Enumerable.Any()` rather than calling `patents.Count()` when checking if there are more than zero items.
>
> **DO** use a collection's `Count` property (if available) in favor of calling the `System.Linq.Enumerable.Count()` method.

Deferred Execution

One of the most important concepts to remember when using LINQ is deferred execution. Consider the code in Listing 14.18 and the corresponding output in Output 14.5.

LISTING 14.18: Filtering with `System.Linq.Enumerable.Where()`

```
using System;
using System.Collections.Generic;
using System.Linq;

// ...

    IEnumerable<Patent> patents = PatentData.Patents;
    bool result;
    patents = patents.Where(
        patent =>
        {
            if (result =
                patent.YearOfPublication.StartsWith("18"))
            {
```

```
            // Side effects like this in a predicate
            // are used here to demonstrate a
            // principle and should generally be
            // avoided.
            Console.WriteLine("\t" + patent);
        }
        return result;
    });

    Console.WriteLine("1. Patents prior to the 1900s are:");
    foreach (Patent patent in patents)
    {
    }

    Console.WriteLine();
    Console.WriteLine(
        "2. A second listing of patents prior to the 1900s:");
    Console.WriteLine(
        "   There are {0} patents prior to 1900.",
        patents.Count());

    Console.WriteLine();
    Console.WriteLine(
        "3. A third listing of patents prior to the 1900s:");
    patents = patents.ToArray();
    Console.Write("   There are ");
    Console.WriteLine("{0} patents prior to 1900.",
        patents.Count());

// ...
```

OUTPUT 14.5

```
1. Patents prior to the 1900s are:
        Phonograph(1877)
        Kinetoscope(1888)
        Electrical Telegraph(1837)
        Steam Locomotive(1815)

2. A second listing of patents prior to the 1900s:
        Phonograph(1877)
        Kinetoscope(1888)
        Electrical Telegraph(1837)
        Steam Locomotive(1815)
   There are 4 patents prior to 1900.

3. A third listing of patents prior to the 1900s:
        Phonograph(1877)
        Kinetoscope(1888)
        Electrical Telegraph(1837)
        Steam Locomotive(1815)
   There are 4 patents prior to 1900.
```

Notice that `Console.WriteLine("1. Patents prior...)` executes before the lambda expression. This is a very important characteristic to pay attention to because it is not obvious to those who are unaware of its importance. In general, predicates should do exactly one thing—evaluate a condition—and they should not have any side effects (even printing to the console, as in this example).

To understand what is happening, recall that lambda expressions are delegates—references to methods—that can be passed around. In the context of LINQ and standard query operators, each lambda expression forms part of the overall query to be executed.

At the time of declaration, lambda expressions do not execute. It isn't until the lambda expressions are invoked that the code within them begins to execute. Figure 14.2 shows the sequence of operations.

As Figure 14.2 shows, three calls in Listing 14.16 trigger the lambda expression, and each time it is fairly implicit. If the lambda expression were expensive (such as a call to a database) it would be important to minimize the lambda expression's execution.

First, the execution is triggered within the `foreach` loop. As we described earlier in the chapter, the `foreach` loop breaks down into a `MoveNext()` call and each call results in the lambda expression's execution for each item in the original collection. While iterating, the runtime invokes the lambda expression for each item to determine whether the item satisfies the predicate.

Second, a call to `Enumerable`'s `Count()` (the function) triggers the lambda expression for each item once more. Again, this is very subtle since `Count` (the property) is very common on collections that have not been queried with a standard query operator.

Third, the call to `ToArray()` (or `ToList()`, `ToDictionary()`, or `ToLookup()`) triggers the lambda expression for each item. However, converting the collection with one of these "To" methods is extremely helpful. Doing so returns a collection on which the standard query operator has already executed. In Listing 14.16, the conversion to an array means that when `Length` is called in the final `Console.WriteLine()`, the underlying object pointed to by `patents` is in fact an array (which obviously implements `IEnumerable<T>`), and therefore, `System.Array`'s implementation of `Length` is called and not `System.Linq.Enumerable`'s implementation. Consequently, following a conversion to one of the collection types returned by a "To" method, it is

FIGURE 14.2: **Sequence of Operations Invoking Lambda Expressions**

generally safe to work with the collection (until another standard query operator is called). However, be aware that this will bring the entire result set into memory (it may have been backed by a database or file before this). Furthermore, the "To" method will snapshot the underlying data so that no fresh results will be returned upon requerying the "To" method result.

We strongly encourage readers to review the sequence diagram in Figure 14.2 along with the corresponding code and understand the fact that the deferred execution of standard query operators can result in extremely subtle triggering of the standard query operators; therefore, developers should use caution to avoid unexpected calls. The query object represents the query, not the results. When you ask the query for the results, the whole query executes (perhaps even again) because the query object doesn't know that the results will be the same as they were during a previous execution (if one existed).

> **■ NOTE**
>
> To avoid such repeated execution, it is necessary to cache the data that the executed query retrieves. To do this, you assign the data to a local collection using one of the "To" method's collection methods. During the assignment call of a "To" method, the query obviously executes. However, iterating over the assigned collection after that will not involve the query expression any further. In general, if you want the behavior of an in-memory collection snapshot, it is a best practice to assign a query expression to a cached collection to avoid unnecessary iterations.

Sorting with `OrderBy()` and `ThenBy()`

Another common operation on a collection is to sort it. This involves a call to `System.Linq.Enumerable`'s `OrderBy()`, as shown in Listing 14.19 and Output 14.6.

LISTING 14.19: Ordering with `System.Linq.Enumerable.OrderBy()/ThenBy()`

```
using System;
using System.Collections.Generic;
using System.Linq;
```

```
// ...

        IEnumerable<Patent> items;
        Patent[] patents = PatentData.Patents;
        items = patents.OrderBy(
            patent => patent.YearOfPublication).ThenBy(
            patent => patent.Title);
        Print(items);
        Console.WriteLine();

        items = patents.OrderByDescending(
            patent => patent.YearOfPublication).ThenByDescending(
            patent => patent.Title);
        Print(items);

// ...
```

OUTPUT 14.6

```
Bifocals  (1784)
Steam Locomotive(1815)
Electrical Telegraph(1837)
Phonograph(1877)
Kinetoscope(1888)
Flying machine  (1903)
Backless Brassiere(1914)
Droplet deposition apparatus(1989)

Droplet deposition apparatus(1989)
Backless Brassiere(1914)
Flying machine  (1903)
Kinetoscope(1888)
Phonograph(1877)
Electrical Telegraph(1837)
Steam Locomotive(1815)
Bifocals  (1784)
```

The OrderBy() call takes a lambda expression that identifies the key on which to sort. In Listing 14.19, the initial sort uses the year that the patent was published.

However, notice that the OrderBy() call takes only a single parameter, which uses the name keySelector, to sort on. To sort on a second column, it is necessary to use a different method: ThenBy(). Similarly, code would use ThenBy() for any additional sorting.

OrderBy() returns an IOrderedEnumerable<T> interface, not an IEnumerable<T>. Furthermore, IOrderedEnumerable<T> derives from IEnumerable<T>, so all the standard query operators (including OrderBy()) are available on the OrderBy() return. However, repeated calls to OrderBy()

would undo the work of the previous call such that the end result would sort by only the keySelector in the final OrderBy() call. As a result, be careful not to call OrderBy() on a previous OrderBy() call.

Instead, you should specify additional sorting criteria using ThenBy(). Although ThenBy() is an extension method, it is not an extension of IEnumerable<T>, but rather IOrderedEnumerable<T>. The method, also defined on System.Linq.Extensions.Enumerable, is declared as follows:

```
public static IOrderedEnumerable<TSource>
    ThenBy<TSource, TKey>(
        this IOrderedEnumerable<TSource> source,
        Func<TSource, TKey> keySelector)
```

In summary, use OrderBy() first, followed by zero or more calls to ThenBy() to provide additional sorting "columns." The methods OrderByDescending() and ThenByDescending() provide the same function-ality except with descending order. Mixing and matching ascending and descending methods is not a problem, but if sorting further, use a ThenBy() call (either ascending or descending).

Two more important notes about sorting: First, the actual sort doesn't occur until you begin to access the members in the collection, at which point the entire query is processed. This occurs because you can't sort un-less you have all the items to sort; otherwise, you can't determine whether you have the first item. The fact that sorting is delayed until you begin to access the members is due to deferred execution, as we describe earlier in this chapter. Second, each subsequent call to sort the data (Orderby() followed by ThenBy() followed by ThenByDescending(), for example) does involve additional calls to the keySelector lambda expression of the earlier sorting calls. In other words, a call to OrderBy() will call its corresponding keySelector lambda expression once you iterate over the collection. Fur-thermore, a subsequent call to ThenBy() will again make calls to OrderBy()'s keySelector.

Guidelines

DO not call an OrderBy() following a prior OrderBy() method call. Use ThenBy() to sequence items by more than one value.

■ **BEGINNER TOPIC**

Join Operations

Consider two collections of objects as shown in the Venn diagram in Figure 14.3.

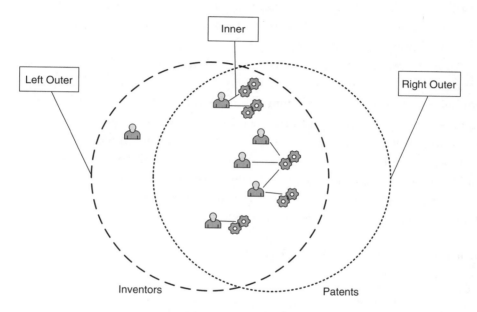

FIGURE 14.3: Venn Diagram of Inventor and Patent Collections

The left circle in the diagram includes all inventors, and the right circle contains all patents. Within the intersection, we have both inventors and patents and a line is formed for each case where there is a match of inventors to patents. As the diagram shows, each inventor may have multiple patents and each patent can have one or more inventors. Each patent has an inventor, but in some cases inventors do not yet have patents.

Matching up inventors within the intersection to patents is an **inner join.** The result is a collection of inventor-patent pairs in which both patents and inventions exist for a pair. A **left outer join** includes all the items within the left circle regardless of whether they have a corresponding patent. In this particular example, a **right outer join** would be the same as an inner join since there are no patents without inventors. Furthermore, the designation of left versus right is arbitrary, so there is really no distinction between left and outer joins. A **full outer join,** however, would include records from both outer sides; it is relatively rare to perform a full outer join.

Another important characteristic in the relationship between inventors and patents is that it is a **many-to-many** relationship. Each individual patent can have one or more inventors (the flying machine's invention by both Orville and Wilbur Wright, for example). Furthermore, each inventor can have one or more patents (Benjamin Franklin's invention of both bifocals and the phonograph, for example).

Another common relationship is a **one-to-many** relationship. For example, a company department may have many employees. However, each employee can belong to only one department at a time. (However, as is common with one-to-many relationships, adding the factor of time can transform them into many-to-many relationships. A particular employee may move from one department to another so that over time, she could potentially be associated with multiple departments, making another many-to-many relationship.)

Listing 14.20 provides a sample listing of Employee and Department data, and Output 14.7 shows the results.

LISTING 14.20: **Sample Employee and Department Data**

```csharp
public class Department
{
    public long Id { get; set; }
    public string Name { get; set; }
    public override string ToString()
    {
        return string.Format("{0}", Name);
    }
}
```

```csharp
public class Employee
{
    public int Id { get; set; }
    public string Name { get; set; }
    public string Title { get; set; }
    public int DepartmentId { get; set; }
    public override string ToString()
    {
        return string.Format("{0} ({1})", Name, Title);
    }
}
```

```csharp
public static class CorporateData
{
```

```csharp
public static readonly Department[] Departments =
    new Department[]
{
    new Department(){
        Name="Corporate", Id=0},
    new Department(){
        Name="Finance", Id=1},
    new Department(){
        Name="Engineering", Id=2},
    new Department(){
        Name="Information Technology",
        Id=3},
    new Department(){
        Name="Research",
        Id=4},
    new Department(){
        Name="Marketing",
        Id=5},
};

public static readonly Employee[] Employees = new Employee[]
{
    new Employee(){
        Name="Mark Michaelis",
        Title="Chief Computer Nerd",
        DepartmentId = 0},
    new Employee(){
        Name="Michael Stokesbary",
        Title="Senior Computer Wizard",
        DepartmentId=2},
    new Employee(){
        Name="Brian Jones",
        Title="Enterprise Integration Guru",
        DepartmentId=2},
    new Employee(){
        Name="Jewel Floch",
        Title="Bookkeeper Extraordinaire",
        DepartmentId=1},
    new Employee(){
        Name="Robert Stokesbary",
        Title="Expert Mainframe Engineer",
        DepartmentId = 3},
    new Employee(){
        Name="Paul R. Bramsman",
        Title="Programmer Extraordinaire",
        DepartmentId = 2},
    new Employee(){
        Name="Thomas Heavey",
        Title="Software Architect",
        DepartmentId = 2},
```

```
            new Employee(){
                Name="John Michaelis",
                Title="Inventor",
                DepartmentId = 4}
        };
    }

class Program
{

    static void Main()
    {
        IEnumerable<Department> departments =
            CorporateData.Departments;
        Print(departments);

        Console.WriteLine();

        IEnumerable<Employee> employees =
            CorporateData.Employees;
        Print(employees);
    }

    private static void Print<T>(IEnumerable<T> items)
    {
        foreach (T item in items)
        {
            Console.WriteLine(item);
        }
    }
}
```

OUTPUT 14.7

```
Corporate
Finance
Engineering
Information Technology
Research
Marketing

Mark Michaelis (Chief Computer Nerd)
Michael Stokesbary (Senior Computer Wizard)
Brian Jones (Enterprise Integration Guru)
Jewel Floch (Bookkeeper Extraordinaire)
Robert Stokesbary (Expert Mainframe Engineer)
Paul R. Bramsman (Programmer Extraordinaire)
Thomas Heavey (Software Architect)
John Michaelis (Inventor)
```

We will use the same data within the following section on joining data.

Performing an Inner Join with `Join()`

In the world of objects on the client side, relationships between objects are generally already set up. For example, the relationship between files and the directories in which they lie are preestablished with the `DirectoryInfo.GetFiles()` method and the `FileInfo.Directory` method. Frequently, however, this is not the case with data being loaded from non-object stores. Instead, the data needs to be joined together so that you can navigate from one type of object to the next in a way that makes sense for the data.

Consider the example of employees and company departments. In Listing 14.21, we join each employee to his or her department and then list each employee with his or her corresponding department. Since each employee belongs to only one (and exactly one) department, the total number of items in the list is equal to the total number of employees—each employee appears only once (each employee is said to be **normalized**). Output 14.8 follows.

LISTING 14.21: **An Inner Join Using** `System.Linq.Enumerable.Join()`

```csharp
using System;
using System.Linq;

// ...

    Department[] departments = CorporateData.Departments;
    Employee[] employees = CorporateData.Employees;

    var items = employees.Join(
        departments,
        employee => employee.DepartmentId,
        department => department.Id,
        (employee, department) => new
        {
            employee.Id,
            employee.Name,
            employee.Title,
            Department = department
        });

    foreach (var item in items)
    {
        Console.WriteLine("{0} ({1})",
            item.Name, item.Title);
        Console.WriteLine("\t" + item.Department);
    }

// ...
```

OUTPUT 14.8

```
Mark Michaelis (Chief Computer Nerd)
        Corporate
Michael Stokesbary (Senior Computer Wizard)
        Engineering
Brian Jones (Enterprise Integration Guru)
        Engineering
Jewel Floch (Bookkeeper Extraordinaire)
        Finance
Robert Stokesbary (Expert Mainframe Engineer)
        Information Technology
Paul R. Bramsman (Programmer Extraordinaire)
        Engineering
Thomas Heavey (Software Architect)
        Engineering
John Michaelis (Inventor)
        Research
```

The first parameter for Join() has the name inner. It specifies the collection, departments, that employees joins to. The next two parameters are lambda expressions that specify how the two collections will connect. employee => employee.DepartmentId (with a parameter name of outerKeySelector) identifies that on each employee the key will be DepartmentId. The next lambda expression (department => department.Id) specifies the Department's Id property as the key. In other words, for each employee, join a department where employee.DepartmentId equals department.Id. The last parameter, the anonymous type, is the resultant item that is selected. In this case, it is a class with Employee's Id, Name, and Title as well as a Department property with the joined department object.

Notice in the output that *Engineering* appears multiple times—once for each employee in CorporateData. In this case, the Join() call produces a **Cartesian product** between all the departments and all the employees such that a new record is created for every case where a record exists in both collections and the specified department IDs are the same. This type of join is an **inner join.**

The data could also be joined in reverse such that department joins to each employee so as to list each department-to-employee match. Notice that the output includes more records than there are departments because there are multiple employees for each department and the output is a record for each match. As we saw before, the Engineering department appears multiple times, once for each employee.

The code in Listing 14.22 and Output 14.9 is similar to that in Listing 14.21, except that the objects, Departments and Employees, are reversed. The first parameter to Join() is employees, indicating what departments joins to. The next two parameters are lambda expressions that specify how the two collections will connect: department => department.Id for departments and employee => employee.DepartmentId for employees. Just like before, a join occurs whenever department.Id equals employee.EmployeeId. The final anonymous type parameter specifies a class with int Id, string Name, and Employee Employee properties.

LISTING 14.22: Another Inner Join with System.Linq.Enumerable.Join()

```
using System;
using System.Linq;

// ...

        Department[] departments = CorporateData.Departments;
        Employee[] employees = CorporateData.Employees;

        var items = departments.Join(
            employees,
            department => department.Id,
            employee => employee.DepartmentId,
            (department, employee) => new
            {
                department.Id,
                department.Name,
                Employee = employee
            });

        foreach (var item in items)
        {
            Console.WriteLine("{0}",
                item.Name);
            Console.WriteLine("\t" + item.Employee);
        }

// ...
```

OUTPUT 14.9

```
Corporate
        Mark Michaelis (Chief Computer Nerd)
Finance
        Jewel Floch (Bookkeeper Extraordinaire)
Engineering
        Michael Stokesbary (Senior Computer Wizard)
Engineering
        Brian Jones (Enterprise Integration Guru)
Engineering
        Paul R. Bramsman (Programmer Extraordinaire)
Engineering
        Thomas Heavey (Software Architect)
Information Technology
        Robert Stokesbary (Expert Mainframe Engineer)
Research
        John Michaelis (Inventor)
```

Grouping Results with GroupBy()

In addition to ordering and joining a collection of objects, frequently you might want to group objects with like characteristics together. For the employee data, you might want to group employees by department, region, job title, and so forth. Listing 14.23 shows an example of how to do this using the GroupBy() standard query operator (see Output 14.10 to view the output).

LISTING 14.23: **Grouping Items Together Using** System.Linq.Enumerable.GroupBy()

```csharp
using System;
using System.Linq;

// ...

    IEnumerable<Employee> employees = CorporateData.Employees;

    IEnumerable<IGrouping<int, Employee>> groupedEmployees =
      employees.GroupBy((employee) => employee.DepartmentId);

    foreach(IGrouping<int, Employee> employeeGroup in
        groupedEmployees)
    {
        Console.WriteLine();
        foreach(Employee employee in employeeGroup)
        {
            Console.WriteLine("\t" + employee);
        }
```

```
            Console.WriteLine(
                "\tCount: " + employeeGroup.Count());
        }
    // ...
```

```
Mark Michaelis (Chief Computer Nerd)
    Count: 1

Michael Stokesbary (Senior Computer Wizard)
Brian Jones (Enterprise Integration Guru)
Paul R. Bramsman (Programmer Extraordinaire)
Thomas Heavey (Software Architect)
    Count: 4

Jewel Floch (Bookkeeper Extraordinaire)
    Count: 1

Robert Stokesbary (Expert Mainframe Engineer)
    Count: 1

John Michaelis (Inventor)
    Count: 1
```

Note that the items output from a `GroupBy()` call are of type
`IGrouping<TKey, TElement>` which has a property for the key that the query
is grouping on (`employee.DepartmentId`). However, it does not have a property for the items within the group. Rather, `IGrouping<TKey, TElement>`
derives from `IEnumerable<T>`, allowing for enumeration of the items
within the group using a `foreach` statement or for aggregating the data
into something such as a count of items (`employeeGroup.Count()`).

Implementing a One-to-Many Relationship with `GroupJoin()`

Listing 14.21 and Listing 14.22 are virtually identical. Either `Join()` call
could have produced the same output just by changing the anonymous
type definition. When trying to create a list of employees, Listing 14.21
provides the correct result. `department` ends up as a property of each anonymous type representing the joined employee. However, Listing 14.22 is
not optimal. Given support for collections, a preferable representation of
a department would have a collection of employees rather than a single
anonymous type record for each department-employee relationship. Listing 14.24 demonstrates; Output 14.11 shows the preferred output.

LISTING 14.24: **Creating a Child Collection with** System.Linq.Enumerable.GroupJoin()

```csharp
using System;
using System.Linq;

// ...

    Department[] departments = CorporateData.Departments;
    Employee[] employees = CorporateData.Employees;

    var items = departments.GroupJoin(
        employees,
        department => department.Id,
        employee => employee.DepartmentId,
        (department, departmentEmployees) => new
        {
            department.Id,
            department.Name,
            Employees = departmentEmployees
        });

    foreach (var item in items)
    {
        Console.WriteLine("{0}",
            item.Name);
        foreach (Employee employee in item.Employees)
        {
            Console.WriteLine("\t" + employee);
        }
    }

// ...
```

OUTPUT 14.11

```
Corporate
        Mark Michaelis (Chief Computer Nerd)
Finance
        Jewel Floch (Bookkeeper Extraordinaire)
Engineering
        Michael Stokesbary (Senior Computer Wizard)
        Brian Jones (Enterprise Integration Guru)
        Paul R. Bramsman (Programmer Extraordinaire)
        Thomas Heavey (Software Architect)
Information Technology
        Robert Stokesbary (Expert Mainframe Engineer)
Research
        John Michaelis (Inventor)
```

To achieve the preferred result we use System.Linq.Enumerable's GroupJoin() method. The parameters are the same as those in Listing 14.21, except for the final anonymous type selected. In Listing 14.21, the lambda expression is of type `Func<Department, IEnumerable<Employee>, TResult>` where `TResult` is the selected anonymous type. Notice that we use the second type argument (`IEnumerable<Employee>`) to project the collection of employees for each department onto the resultant department anonymous type.

(Readers familiar with SQL will notice that, unlike `Join()`, `GroupJoin()` doesn't have a SQL equivalent since data returned by SQL is record-based, and not hierarchical.)

■ ADVANCED TOPIC

Implementing an Outer Join with `GroupJoin()`

The earlier inner joins are *equi-joins* because they are based on an equivalent evaluation of the keys. Records appear in the resultant collection only if there are objects in both collections. On occasion, however, it is desirable to create a record even if the corresponding object doesn't exist. For example, rather than leaving the Marketing department out from the final department list simply because it doesn't have any employees, it would be preferable if we included it with an empty employee list. To accomplish this we perform a left outer join using a combination of both `GroupJoin()` and `SelectMany()` along with `DefaultIfEmpty()`. This is demonstrated in Listing 14.25 and Output 14.12.

LISTING 14.25: Implementing an Outer Join Using `GroupJoin()` with `SelectMany()`

```
using System;
using System.Linq;

// ...

    Department[] departments = CorporateData.Departments;
    Employee[] employees = CorporateData.Employees;

    var items = departments.GroupJoin(
        employees,
        department => department.Id,
        employee => employee.DepartmentId,
        (department, departmentEmployees) => new
        {
            department.Id,
            department.Name,
            Employees = departmentEmployees
        }).SelectMany(
```

```
            departmentRecord =>
                departmentRecord.Employees.DefaultIfEmpty(),
            (departmentRecord, employee) => new
                {
                    departmentRecord.Id,
                    departmentRecord.Name,
                    Employees =
                        departmentRecord.Employees
                }).Distinct();

        foreach (var item in items)
        {
            Console.WriteLine("{0}",
                item.Name);
            foreach (Employee employee in item.Employees)
            {
                Console.WriteLine("\t" + employee);
            }
        }

// ...
```

OUTPUT 14.12

```
Corporate
        Mark Michaelis (Chief Computer Nerd)
Finance
        Jewel Floch (Bookkeeper Extraordinaire)
Engineering
        Michael Stokesbary (Senior Computer Wizard)
        Brian Jones (Enterprise Integration Guru)
        Paul R. Bramsman (Programmer Extraordinaire)
        Thomas Heavey (Software Architect)
Information Technology
        Robert Stokesbary (Expert Mainframe Engineer)
Research
        John Michaelis (Inventor)
Marketing
```

Calling SelectMany()

On occasion, you may have collections of collections. Listing 14.26 provides an example of such a scenario. The teams array contains two teams, each with a string array of players.

LISTING 14.26: **Calling** SelectMany()

```
using System;
using System.Collections.Generic;
using System.Linq;
```

```csharp
// ...

var worldCup2006Finalists = new[]
{
    new
    {
        TeamName = "France",
        Players = new string[]
        {
            "Fabien Barthez", "Gregory Coupet",
            "Mickael Landreau", "Eric Abidal",
            "Jean-Alain Boumsong", "Pascal Chimbonda",
            "William Gallas", "Gael Givet",
            "Willy Sagnol", "Mikael Silvestre",
            "Lilian Thuram", "Vikash Dhorasoo",
            "Alou Diarra", "Claude Makelele",
            "Florent Malouda", "Patrick Vieira",
            "Zinedine Zidane", "Djibril Cisse",
            "Thierry Henry", "Franck Ribery",
            "Louis Saha", "David Trezeguet",
            "Sylvain Wiltord",
        }
    },
    new
    {
        TeamName = "Italy",
        Players = new string[]
        {
            "Gianluigi Buffon", "Angelo Peruzzi",
            "Marco Amelia", "Cristian Zaccardo",
            "Alessandro Nesta", "Gianluca Zambrotta",
            "Fabio Cannavaro", "Marco Materazzi",
            "Fabio Grosso", "Massimo Oddo",
            "Andrea Barzagli", "Andrea Pirlo",
            "Gennaro Gattuso", "Daniele De Rossi",
            "Mauro Camoranesi", "Simone Perrotta",
            "Simone Barone", "Luca Toni",
            "Alessandro Del Piero", "Francesco Totti",
            "Alberto Gilardino", "Filippo Inzaghi",
            "Vincenzo Iaquinta",
        }
    }
};

IEnumerable<string> players =
    worldCup2006Finalists.SelectMany(
        team => team.Players);

Print(players);

// ...
```

The output from this listing has each player's name displayed on its own line in the order in which it appears in the code. The difference between `Select()` and `SelectMany()` is the fact that `Select()` would return two items, one corresponding to each item in the original collection. `Select()` may project out a transform from the original type, but the number of items would not change. For example, `teams.Select(team => team.Players)` will return an `IEnumerable<string[]>`.

In contrast, `SelectMany()` iterates across each item identified by the lambda expression (the array selected by `Select()` earlier) and hoists out each item into a new collection that includes a union of all items within the child collection. Instead of two arrays of players, `SelectMany()` combines each array selected and produces a single collection of all items.

More Standard Query Operators

Listing 14.27 shows code that uses some of the simpler APIs enabled by Enumerable; Output 14.13 shows the results.

LISTING 14.27: More `System.Linq.Enumerable` **Method Calls**

```
using System;
using System.Collections.Generic;
using System.Linq;
using System.Text;

class Program
{
  static void Main()
  {
      IEnumerable<object> stuff =
        new object[] { new object(), 1, 3, 5, 7, 9,
            "\"thing\"", Guid.NewGuid() };
      Print("Stuff: {0}", stuff);
      IEnumerable<int> even = new int[] { 0, 2, 4, 6, 8 };
      Print("Even integers: {0}", even);

      IEnumerable<int> odd = stuff.OfType<int>();
      Print("Odd integers: {0}", odd);

      IEnumerable<int> numbers = even.Union(odd);
      Print("Union of odd and even: {0}", numbers);

      Print("Union with even: {0}", numbers.Union(even));
      Print("Concat with odd: {0}", numbers.Concat(odd));
      Print("Intersection with even: {0}",
          numbers.Intersect(even));
      Print("Distinct: {0}", numbers.Concat(odd).Distinct());
```

```csharp
        if (!numbers.SequenceEqual(
            numbers.Concat(odd).Distinct()))
        {
            throw new Exception("Unexpectedly unequal");
        }
        else
        {
            Console.WriteLine(
                @"Collection ""SequenceEquals""" +
                " collection.Concat(odd).Distinct())");
            Print("Reverse: {0}", numbers.Reverse());

            Print("Average: {0}", numbers.Average());
            Print("Sum: {0}", numbers.Sum());
            Print("Max: {0}", numbers.Max());
            Print("Min: {0}", numbers.Min());
        }
    }

    private static void Print<T>(
        string format, IEnumerable<T> items)
    {
        StringBuilder text = new StringBuilder();
        foreach (T item in items.Take(items.Count()-1))
        {
            text.Append(item + ", ");
        }
        text.Append(items.Last());

        Console.WriteLine(format, text);
    }

    private static void Print<T>(string format, T item)
    {
        Console.WriteLine(format, item);
    }
}
```

OUTPUT 14.13

```
Stuff: System.Object, 1, 3, 5, 7, 9, "thing"
24c24a41-ee05-41b9-958e-50dd12e3981e
Even integers: 0, 2, 4, 6, 8
Odd integers: 1, 3, 5, 7, 9
Union of odd and even: 0, 2, 4, 6, 8, 1, 3, 5, 7, 9
Union with even: 0, 2, 4, 6, 8, 1, 3, 5, 7, 9
Concat with odd: 0, 2, 4, 6, 8, 1, 3, 5, 7, 9, 1, 3, 5, 7, 9
Intersection with even: 0, 2, 4, 6, 8
Distinct: 0, 2, 4, 6, 8, 1, 3, 5, 7, 9
Collection "SequenceEquals"collection.Concat(odd).Distinct()
Reverse: 9, 7, 5, 3, 1, 8, 6, 4, 2, 0
Average: 4.5
Sum: 45
Max: 9
Min: 0
```

None of the API calls in Listing 14.20 requires a lambda expression. Table 14.1 and Table 14.2 describe each method and provide an example.

TABLE 14.1: Simpler Standard Query Operators

Comment Type	Description
OfType<T>()	Forms a query over a collection that returns only the items of a particular type, where the type is identified in the type parameter of the OfType<T>() method call.
Union()	Combines two collections to form a superset of all the items in both collections. The final collection does not include duplicate items even if the same item existed in both collections to start.
Concat()	Combines two collections together to form a superset of both collections. Duplicate items are not removed from the resultant collection. Concat()will preserve the ordering. That is, concatting {A, B} with {C, D} will produce {A, B, C, D}.
Intersect()	Extracts the collection of items that exist in both original collections.
Distinct()	Filters out duplicate items from a collection so that each item within the resultant collection is unique.
SequenceEquals()	Compares two collections and returns a Boolean indicating whether the collections are identical, including the order of items within the collection. (This is a very helpful message when testing expected results.)
Reverse()	Reverses the items within a collection so that they occur in reverse order when iterating over the collection.

Included on System.Linq.Enumerable is a collection of aggregate functions that enumerate the collection and calculate a result. Count is one example of an aggregate function already shown within the chapter.

TABLE 14.2: Aggregate Functions on `System.Linq.Enumerable`

Comment Type	Description
`Count()`	Provides a total count of the number of items within the collection
`Average()`	Calculates the average value for a numeric key selector
`Sum()`	Computes the sum values within a numeric collection
`Max()`	Determines the maximum value among a collection of numeric values
`Min()`	Determines the minimum value among a collection of numeric values

Note that each method listed in Tables 14.1 and 14.2 will trigger deferred execution.

■ **ADVANCED TOPIC**

Queryable **Extensions for** IQueryable<T>

One virtually identical interface to `IEnumerable<T>` is `IQueryable<T>`. Because `IQueryable<T>` derives from `IEnumerable<T>`, it has all the members of `IEnumerable<T>` but only those declared directly (`GetEnumerator()`, for example). Extension methods are not inherited, so `IQueryable<T>` doesn't have any of the `Enumerable` extension methods. However, it has a similar extending class called `System.Linq.Queryable` that adds to `IQueryable<T>` virtually all of the same methods that `Enumerable` added to `IEnumerable<T>`. Therefore, it provides a very similar programming interface.

What makes `IQueryable<T>` unique is the fact that it enables custom LINQ providers. A LINQ provider subdivides expressions into their constituent parts. Once divided, the expression can be translated into another language, serialized for remote execution, injected with an asynchronous execution pattern, and much more. Essentially, LINQ providers allow for an interception mechanism into a standard collection API, and via this seemingly limitless functionality, behavior relating to the queries and collection can be injected.

For example, LINQ providers allow for the translation of a query expression from C# into SQL that is then executed on a remote database. In so doing, the C# programmer can remain in her primary object-oriented language and leave the translation to SQL to the underlying LINQ provider. Through this type of expression, programming languages are able to span the impedance mismatch between the object-oriented world and the relational database.

In the case of `IQueryable<T>`, vigilance regarding deferred execution is even more critical. Imagine, for example, a LINQ provider that returns data from a database. Rather than retrieving the data from a database regardless of the selection criteria, the lambda expression would provide an implementation of `IQueryable<T>` that possibly includes context information such as the connection string, but not the data itself. The data retrieval wouldn't occur until the call to `GetEnumerator()` or even `MoveNext()`. However, the `GetEnumerator()` call is generally implicit, such as when iterating over the collection with `foreach` or calling an `Enumerable` method such as `Count<T>()` or `Cast<T>()`. Obviously, cases such as this require developers to be wary of the subtle and repeated calls to any expensive operation that deferred execution might involve. For example, if calling `GetEnumerator()` involves a distributed call over the network to a database, avoid unintentional duplicate calls to iterations with `Count()` or `foreach`.

SUMMARY

After introducing anonymous types, implicit variables, and collection initializers, this chapter described the internals of how the `foreach` loop works and what interfaces are required for its execution. In addition, developers frequently filter a collection so that there are fewer items and project the collection so that the items take a different form. Toward that end, this chapter discussed the details of how to use the standard query operators, common collection APIs on the `System.Linq.Enumerable` class, to perform collection manipulation.

In the introduction to standard query operators, we spent a few pages detailing deferred execution and how developers should take care to avoid unintentionally reexecuting an expression via a subtle call that enumerates over the collection contents. The deferred execution and resultant implicit execution of standard query operators is a significant quality, especially when the query execution is expensive. Programmers should treat the query object as the query object, not the results, and expect the query to execute fully even if it executed already. The query object doesn't know that the results will be the same as they were during a previous execution.

Listing 14.25 appeared within an Advanced Topic section because of the complexity of calling multiple standard query operators one after the other. Although requirements for similar execution may be common, it is not necessary to rely on standard query operators directly. C# 3.0 includes query expressions, a SQL-like syntax for manipulating collections in a way that is frequently easier to code and read, as we show in the next chapter.

■ 15 ■
LINQ with Query Expressions

THE END OF CHAPTER 14 SHOWED a query using standard query operators for GroupJoin(), SelectMany(), and Distinct(), in addition to the
creation of two anonymous types. The result was a statement that spanned
multiple lines and was rather more complex and difficult to comprehend
than statements typically written using only features of C# 2.0. Modern
programs that manipulate rich data sets often require such complex queries; it would therefore be nice if the language made them easier to read.
Domain-specific query languages such as SQL make it much easier to read
and understand a query, but lack the full power of the C# language. That
is why the C# language designers added **query expressions** syntax to C#
3.0. With query expressions, many standard query operator expressions
are transformed into more readable code, much like SQL.

In this chapter, we introduce query expressions and use them to express many of the queries from the preceding chapter.

Introducing Query Expressions

Two of the most frequent operations developers perform are **filtering** the collection to eliminate unwanted items and **projecting** the collection so that the items take a different form. For example, given a collection of files, we could filter it to create a new collection of only the files with a ".cs" extension, or only files larger than 1 million bytes. We could also project the file collection to create a new collection of paths to the directories the files are located in and the corresponding directory size. Query expressions provide straightforward syntaxes for both of these common operations. Listing 15.1 shows a query expression that filters a collection of strings; Output 15.1 shows the results.

LISTING 15.1: **Simple Query Expression**

```csharp
using System;
using System.Collections.Generic;
using System.Linq;

// ...

    static string[] Keywords = {
        "abstract", "add*", "alias*", "as", "ascending*",
        "async*", "await*", "base","bool", "break",
        "by*", "byte", "case", "catch", "char", "checked",
        "class", "const", "continue", "decimal", "default",
        "delegate", "descending*", "do", "double",
        "dynamic*", "else", "enum", "event", "equals*",
        "explicit", "extern", "false", "finally", "fixed",
        "from*", "float", "for", "foreach", "get*", "global*",
        "group*", "goto", "if", "implicit", "in", "int",
        "into*", "interface", "internal", "is", "lock", "long",
        "join*", "let*", "namespace", "new", "null", "object",
        "on*", "operator", "orderby*", "out", "override",
        "params", "partial*", "private", "protected", "public",
        "readonly", "ref", "remove*", "return", "sbyte", "sealed",
        "select*", "set*", "short", "sizeof", "stackalloc",
        "static", "string", "struct", "switch", "this", "throw",
        "true", "try", "typeof", "uint", "ulong", "unchecked",
        "unsafe", "ushort", "using", "value*", "var*", "virtual",
        "void", "volatile", "where*", "while", "yield*"};

    private static void ShowContextualKeywords1()
    {
        IEnumerable<string> selection =
```

```
            from word in Keywords
                where !word.Contains('*')
                select word;

        foreach (string keyword in selection)
        {
            Console.Write(keyword + " ");
        }
    }

// ...
```

OUTPUT 15.1

```
abstract as base bool break byte case catch char checked class const
continue decimal default delegate do double else enum event explicit
extern false finally fixed float for foreach goto if implicit in int
interface internal is lock long namespace new null object operator out
override params private protected public readonly ref return sbyte
sealed short sizeof stackalloc static string struct switch this throw
true try typeof uint ulong unchecked unsafe ushort using virtual void
volatile while
```

In this query expression, `selection` is assigned the collection of C# re-served keywords. The query expression in this example includes a `where` clause that filters out the noncontextual keywords.

Query expressions always begin with a "from clause" and end with a "select clause" or a "group clause," identified by the `from`, `select`, or group contextual keyword, respectively. The identifier `word` in the `from` clause is called a **range variable;** it represents each item in the collection, much as the loop variable in a `foreach` loop represents each item in a collection.

Developers familiar with SQL will notice that query expressions have a syntax that is similar to that of SQL. This design was deliberate so that LINQ would be easy to learn for programmers who already know SQL. However, there are some obvious differences. The first difference most developers familiar with SQL notice is that the C# query expression shown here has the clauses in the order `from`, then `where`, then `select`. The equivalent SQL query has the SELECT clause first, then the FROM clause, and ends with the WHERE clause.

One reason for this is to enable IntelliSense, the feature of the IDE whereby the editor produces helpful user interface elements such as drop-down lists that describe the members of a given object. Because `from` ap-pears first and identifies the string array `Keywords` as the data source, the code editor can deduce that the range variable word is of type string. When you are typing the code into the editor and reach the dot following word, the editor will display only the members of string.

If the from clause appeared after the select, as it does in SQL, as you were typing in the query the editor would not know what the data type of word was, and therefore would not be able to display a list of word's members. In Listing 15.1, for example, it wouldn't be possible to predict that Contains() was a possible member of word.

The C# query expression order also more closely matches the order in which operations are logically performed. When evaluating the query, you begin by identifying the collection (described by the from clause), then filter out the unwanted items (with the where clause), and finally describe the desired result (with the select clause).

Finally, the C# query expression order ensures that the rules about where (range) variables are in scope are mostly consistent with the scoping rules for local variables; for example, a (range) variable must be declared by a clause (typically a from clause) before the variable can be used, much as a local variable must always be declared before it can be used.

Projection

The result of a query expression is a collection of type IEnumerable<T> or IQueryable<T>.[1] The actual type T is inferred from the select or group by clause. In Listing 15.1, for example, the compiler knows that Keywords is of type string[], which is convertible to IEnumerable<string> and deduces that word is therefore of type string. The query ends with select word, and therefore, the result of the query expression must be a collection of strings, so the type of the query expression is IEnumerable<string>.

In this case the "input" and "output" of the query are both a collection of strings. However, the "output" type can be quite different from the "input" type if the expression in the select clause is of an entirely different type. Consider the query expression in Listing 15.2, and its corresponding output in Output 15.2.

---

1. The result of a query expression is, as a practical matter, almost always IEnumerable<T> or a type derived from it. It is legal, though somewhat perverse, to create an implementation of the query methods that return other types; there is no *requirement* in the language that the result of a query expression be convertible to IEnumerable<T>.

LISTING 15.2: Projection Using Query Expressions

```csharp
using System;
using System.Collections.Generic;
using System.Linq;
using System.IO;

// ...

    static void List1(string rootDirectory, string searchPattern)
    {
        IEnumerable<string> fileNames = Directory.GetFiles(
            rootDirectory, searchPattern);
        IEnumerable<FileInfo> fileInfos =
            from fileName in fileNames
            select new FileInfo(fileName);

        foreach (FileInfo fileInfo in fileInfos)
        {
            Console.WriteLine(".{0}({1})",
                fileInfo.Name, fileInfo.LastWriteTime);
        }
    }

// ...
```

OUTPUT 15.2

```
Account.cs(11/22/2011 11:56:11 AM)
Bill.cs(8/10/2011 9:33:55 PM)
Contact.cs(8/19/2011 11:40:30 PM)
Customer.cs(11/17/2011 2:02:52 AM)
Employee.cs(8/17/2011 1:33:22 AM)
Person.cs(10/22/2011 10:00:03 PM)
```

This query expression results in an `IEnumerable<FileInfo>` rather than the `IEnumerable<string>` data type returned by `Directory.GetFiles()`. The `select` clause of the query expression can potentially project out a data type that is different from what was collected by the `from` clause expression.

Notice that in this example, the type `FileInfo` was chosen because it has the two relevant fields needed for the desired output: the filename and the last write time. There might not be such a convenient type if you needed other information not captured in the `FileInfo` object. Anonymous types provide a convenient and concise way to project the exact data you need without having to find or create an explicit type. (In fact, this scenario was the key motivator for adding anonymous types to the language.) Listing 15.3 provides output similar to that in Listing 15.2, but via anonymous types rather than `FileInfo`.

LISTING 15.3: **Anonymous Types within Query Expressions**

```
using System;
using System.Collections.Generic;
using System.Linq;
using System.IO;

// ...

  static void List2(string rootDirectory, string searchPattern)
  {
      var fileNames =Directory.GetFiles(
          rootDirectory, searchPattern)
      var fileResults =
          from fileName in fileNames
          select new
          {
              Name = fileName,
              LastWriteTime = File.GetLastWriteTime(fileName)
          };

      foreach (var fileResult in fileResults)
      {
          Console.WriteLine("{0}({1})",
              fileResult.Name, fileResult.LastWriteTime);
      }
  }

// ...
```

In this example, the query projects out only the filename and its last file write time. A projection such as the one in Listing 15.3 makes little difference when working with something small such as `FileInfo`. However, "horizontal" projection that filters down the amount of data associated with each item in the collection is extremely powerful when the amount of data is significant and retrieving it (perhaps from a different computer over the Internet) is expensive. Rather than retrieving all the data when a query executes, the use of anonymous types enables the capability of storing and retrieving only the required data into the collection.

Imagine, for example, a large database that has tables with 30 or more columns. If there were no anonymous types, developers would be required to either use objects containing unnecessary information or define small, specialized classes useful only for storing the specific data required. Instead, anonymous types enable support for types to be defined by the compiler—types that contain only the data needed for their immediate scenario. Other scenarios can have a different projection of only the properties needed for that scenario.

■ BEGINNER TOPIC

Deferred Execution with Query Expressions

Queries written using query expression notation exhibit deferred execution, just as the queries written in the preceding chapter do. Consider again the assignment of a query object to variable `selection` in Listing 15.1. The creation of the query and the assignment to the variable do not execute the query; rather, they just build an object that represents the query. The method `word.Contains("*")` is not called when the query object is created. Rather, the query expression saves the selection criteria to be used when iterating over the collection identified by the `selection` variable.

To demonstrate this point, consider Listing 15.4 and the corresponding output (Output 15.3).

LISTING 15.4: **Deferred Execution and Query Expressions (Example 1)**

```
using System;
using System.Collections.Generic;
using System.Linq;

// ...

  private static void ShowContextualKeywords2()
  {
      IEnumerable<string> selection = from word in Keywords
                                      where IsKeyword(word)
                                      select word;
      Console.WriteLine("Query created.");
      foreach (string keyword in selection)
      {
          // No space output here.
          Console.Write(keyword);
      }
  }

// The side effect of console output is included
// in the predicate to demonstrate deferred execution;
// predicates with side effects are a poor practice in
```

```csharp
    // production code.
    private static bool IsKeyword(string word)
    {
        if (word.Contains('*'))
        {
            Console.Write(" ");
            return true;
        }
        else
        {
            return false;
        }
    }
    // ...
```

OUTPUT 15.3

```
Query created.
 add* alias* ascending* by* descending* dynamic* equals* from* get*
global* group* into* join* let* on* orderby* partial* remove* select*
set* value* var* where* yield*
```

Notice that in Listing 15.4, no space is output within the foreach loop. The side effect of printing a space when the predicate IsKeyword() is executed happens when the query is iterated over, not when the query is created.

The point is that although selection is a collection (it is of type IEnumerable<T> after all), at the time of assignment everything following the from clause comprises the selection criteria. Not until we begin to iterate over selection are the criteria applied.

Consider a second example (see Listing 15.5 and Output 15.4).

LISTING 15.5: Deferred Execution and Query Expressions (Example 2)

```csharp
using System;
using System.Collections.Generic;
using System.Linq;

// ...

  private static void CountContextualKeywords()
  {
      int delegateInvocations = 0;
      Func<string, string> func =
          text=>
          {
```

```csharp
            delegateInvocations++;
            return text;
        };

    IEnumerable<string> selection =
        from keyword in Keywords
        where keyword.Contains('*')
        select func(keyword);


    Console.WriteLine(
        "1. delegateInvocations={0}", delegateInvocations);

    // Executing count should invoke func once for
    // each item selected.
    Console.WriteLine(
        "2. Contextual keyword count={0}", selection.Count());

    Console.WriteLine(
        "3. delegateInvocations={0}", delegateInvocations);

    // Executing count should invoke func once for
    // each item selected.
    Console.WriteLine(
        "4. Contextual keyword count={0}", selection.Count());

    Console.WriteLine(
        "5. delegateInvocations={0}", delegateInvocations);

    // Cache the value so future counts will not trigger
    // another invocation of the query.
    List<string> selectionCache = selection.ToList();

    Console.WriteLine(
        "6. delegateInvocations={0}", delegateInvocations);

    // Retrieve the count from the cached collection.
    Console.WriteLine(
        "7. selectionCache count={0}",selectionCache.Count());

    Console.WriteLine(
        "8. delegateInvocations={0}", delegateInvocations);

}

// ...
```

OUTPUT 15.4

```
1. delegateInvocations=0
2. Contextual keyword count=15
3. delegateInvocations=15
4. Contextual keyword count=15
5. delegateInvocations=30
6. delegateInvocations=45
7. selectionCache count=15
8. delegateInvocations=45
```

Rather than defining a separate method, Listing 15.5 uses a statement lambda that counts the number of times the method is called.

Three things in the output are remarkable. First, notice that after `selection` is assigned, `DelegateInvocations` remains at zero. At the time of assignment to `selection`, no iteration over `Keywords` is performed. If `Keywords` were a property, the property call would run—in other words, the `from` clause executes at the time of assignment. However, neither the projection, nor the filtering, nor anything after the `from` clause will execute until the code iterates over the values within `selection`. It is as though at the time of assignment, `selection` would more appropriately be called "query."

However, once we call `Count()`, a term such as *selection* or *items* that indicates a container or collection is appropriate because we begin to count the items within the collection. In other words, the variable selection serves a dual purpose of saving the query information as well as acting like a container from which the data is retrieved.

A second important characteristic to notice is that calling `Count()` twice causes `func` to again be invoked once on each item selected. Since `selection` behaves both as a query and as a collection, requesting the count requires that the query be executed again by iterating over the `IEnumerable<string>` collection `selection` refers to and counting the items. The C# compiler does not know whether anyone has modified the strings in the array such that the count would now be different, so the counting has to happen fresh every time to ensure that the answer is correct and up-to-date. Similarly, a `foreach` loop over `selection` would trigger `func` to be called again for each item. The same is true of all the other extension methods provided via `System.Linq.Enumerable`.

Implementing Deferred Execution

Deferred execution is implemented by using delegates and expression trees. A delegate provides the ability to create and manipulate a reference to a method that contains an expression that can be invoked later. An expression tree similarly provides the ability to create and manipulate information about an expression that can be examined and manipulated later.

In Listing 15.5, the predicate expressions of the `where` clauses and the projection expressions of the `select` clauses are transformed by the compiler into expression lambdas, and then the lambdas are transformed into delegate creations. The result of the query expression is an object that holds onto references to these delegates. Only when the query results are iterated over does the query object actually execute the delegates.

Filtering

In Listing 15.1, we include a `where` clause that filters out reserved keywords but not contextual keywords. The `where` clause filters the collection "vertically"; if you think of the collection as a vertical list of items, the `where` clause makes that vertical list shorter so that there are fewer items within the collection. The filter criteria are expressed with a **predicate**—a lambda expression that returns a `bool` such as `word.Contains()` (as in Listing 15.1) or `File.GetLastWriteTime(file) < DateTime.Now.AddMonths(-1)`. The latter is shown in Listing 15.6, the output of which appears in Output 15.5.

LISTING 15.6: **Query Expression Filtering Using** where

```csharp
using System;
using System.Collections.Generic;
using System.Linq;
using System.IO;

// ...

    static void FindMonthOldFiles(
        string rootDirectory, string searchPattern)
    {
        IEnumerable<FileInfo> files =
            from fileName in Directory.GetFiles(
                rootDirectory, searchPattern)
            where File.GetLastWriteTime(fileName) <
                DateTime.Now.AddMonths(-1)
            select new FileInfo(fileName);
```

```
        foreach (FileInfo file in files)
        {
            //  As simplification, current directory is
            //  assumed to be a subdirectory of
            //  rootDirectory
            string relativePath = file.FullName.Substring(
                    Environment.CurrentDirectory.Length);
            Console.WriteLine(".{0}({1})",
                relativePath, file.LastWriteTime);
        }
    }

  // ...
```

OUTPUT 15.5

```
.\TestData\Bill.cs(8/10/2011 9:33:55 PM)
.\TestData\Contact.cs(8/19/2011 11:40:30 PM)
.\TestData\Employee.cs(8/17/2011 1:33:22 AM)
.\TestData\Person.cs(10/22/2011 10:00:03 PM)
```

Sorting

To order the items using a query expression you can use the orderby clause, as shown in Listing 15.7.

LISTING 15.7: **Sorting Using a Query Expression with an** orderby **Clause**

```
using System;
using System.Collections.Generic;
using System.Linq;
using System.IO;

// ...
  static void ListByFileSize1(
      string rootDirectory, string searchPattern)
  {
      IEnumerable<string> fileNames =
          from fileName in Directory.GetFiles(
              rootDirectory, searchPattern)
          orderby (new FileInfo(fileName)).Length descending,
              fileName
          select fileName;

      foreach (string fileName in fileNames)
      {
          Console.WriteLine("{0}", fileName);
      }
```

```
        }
    // ...
```

Listing 15.7 uses the `orderby` clause to sort the files returned by `Directory.GetFiles()` first by file size in descending order and then by filename in ascending order. Multiple sort criteria are separated by a comma such that first the items are ordered by size, and if the size is the same they are ordered by filename. `ascending` and `descending` are contextual keywords indicating the sort order direction. Specifying the order as ascending or descending is optional; if the direction is omitted (as it is here on `filename`) the default is `ascending`.

The `let` Clause

In Listing 15.8 we have a query that is very similar to that in Listing 15.7 except that the type argument of `IEnumerable<T>` is `FileInfo`. Notice that there is a problem with this query: We have to redundantly create a `FileInfo` twice, in both the `orderby` clause and the `select` clause.

LISTING 15.8: Projecting a `FileInfo` Collection and Sorting by File Size

```csharp
using System;
using System.Collections.Generic;
using System.Linq;
using System.IO;

// ...
    static void ListByFileSize2(
        string rootDirectory, string searchPattern)
    {
        IEnumerable<FileInfo> files =
            from fileName in Directory.GetFiles(
                rootDirectory, searchPattern)
            orderby new FileInfo(fileName).Length, fileName
            select new FileInfo(fileName);

        foreach (FileInfo file in files)
        {
            // As simplification, current directory is
            // assumed to be a subdirectory of
            // rootDirectory
            string relativePath = file.FullName.Substring(
                Environment.CurrentDirectory.Length);
            Console.WriteLine(".{0}({1})",
                relativePath, file.Length);
        }
```

```
    }
// ...
```

Unfortunately, although the end result is correct, Listing 15.8 ends up instantiating a `FileInfo` object twice for each item in the source collection, which seems wasteful and unnecessary. To avoid unnecessary and potentially expensive overhead like this, you can use a `let` clause, as demonstrated in Listing 15.9.

LISTING 15.9: Ordering the Results in a Query Expression

```
    // ...
    IEnumerable<FileInfo> files =
        from fileName in Directory.GetFiles(
            rootDirectory, searchPattern)
        let file = new FileInfo(fileName)
        orderby file.Length, fileName
        select file;
    // ...
```

The `let` clause introduces a new range variable that can hold the value of an expression that is used throughout the remainder of the query expression. You can add as many `let` clauses as you like; simply add each as an additional clause to the query after the first `from` clause but before the final `select`/`group by` clause.

Grouping

A common data manipulation scenario is the grouping of related items. In SQL, this generally involves aggregating the items to produce a summary or total or other aggregate value. LINQ, however, is more expressive than this. LINQ expressions allow for individual items to be grouped into a series of subcollections, and for those groups to be associated with items in the collection being queried. For example, Listing 15.10 and Output 15.6 demonstrate how to group together the contextual keywords and the regular keywords.

LISTING 15.10: Grouping Together Query Results

```
using System;
using System.Collections.Generic;
using System.Linq;

// ...
```

```csharp
private static void GroupKeywords1()
{
    IEnumerable<IGrouping<bool, string>> selection =
        from word in Keywords
        group word by word.Contains('*');

    foreach (IGrouping<bool, string> wordGroup
        in selection)
    {
        Console.WriteLine(Environment.NewLine + "{0}:",
            wordGroup.Key ?
                "Contextual Keywords" : "Keywords");
        foreach (string keyword in wordGroup)
        {
            Console.Write(" " +
                (wordGroup.Key ?
                    keyword.Replace("*", null) : keyword));
        }
    }
}

// ...
```

OUTPUT 15.6

```
Keywords:
 abstract as base bool break byte case catch char checked class const
continue decimal default delegate do double else enum event explicit
extern false finally fixed float for foreach goto if implicit in int
interface internal is lock long namespace new null object operator out
override params private protected public readonly ref return sbyte
sealed short sizeof stackalloc static string struct switch this throw
true try typeof uint ulong unchecked unsafe ushort using virtual void
volatile while
Contextual Keywords:
 add alias ascending async await by descending dynamic equals from
get global group into join let on orderby partial remove select
set value var where yield
```

There are several things to note in this listing. First, the query result is a sequence of elements of type IGrouping<bool, string>. The first type argument indicates that the "group key" expression following by was of type bool, and the second type argument indicates that the "group element" expression following group was of type string. That is, the query produces a sequence of groups where the Boolean key is the same for each string in the group.

Because a query with a groupby clause produces a sequence of collections, the common pattern for iterating over the results is to create nested foreach loops. In Listing 15.10, the outer loop iterates over the groupings and prints out the type of keyword as a header. The nested foreach loop prints each keyword in the group as an item below the header.

Since the result of this query expression is itself a sequence, you can query the resultant sequence like any other. Listing 15.11 and Output 15.7 show how to create an additional query that adds a projection onto a query that produces a sequence of groups. (The next section, on query continuations, shows a more pleasant syntax for adding additional query clauses to a complete query.)

LISTING 15.11: **Selecting an Anonymous Type Following the** group **Clause**

```csharp
using System;
using System.Collections.Generic;
using System.Linq;

// ...

    private static void GroupKeywords1()
    {
        IEnumerable<IGrouping<bool, string>> keywordGroups =
            from word in Keywords
            group word by word.Contains('*');

        var selection =
            from groups in keywordGroups
            select new
            {
                IsContextualKeyword = groups.Key,
                Items = groups
            };

        foreach (var wordGroup in selection)
        {
            Console.WriteLine(Environment.NewLine + "{0}:",
                wordGroup.IsContextualKeyword ?
                    "Contextual Keywords" : "Keywords");
            foreach (var keyword in wordGroup.Items)
            {
                Console.Write(" " +
                    keyword.Replace("*", null));
            }
        }
    }

// ...
```

OUTPUT 15.7

```
Keywords:
 abstract as base bool break byte case catch char checked class const
continue decimal default delegate do double else enum event explicit
extern false finally fixed float for foreach goto if implicit in int
interface internal is lock long namespace new null object operator out
override params private protected public readonly ref return sbyte
sealed short sizeof stackalloc static string struct switch this throw
true try typeof uint ulong unchecked unsafe ushort using virtual void
volatile while
Contextual Keywords:
 add alias ascending async await by descending dynamic equals from
get global group into join let on orderby partial remove select
set value var where yield
```

The group clause results in a query that produces a collection of `IGrouping<TKey, TElement>` objects—just as the `GroupBy()` standard query operator did (see Chapter 14). The `select` clause in the subsequent query uses an anonymous type to effectively rename `IGrouping<TKey, TElement>.Key` to `IsContextualKeyword` and naming the subcollection property `Items`. With this change, the nested `foreach` uses `wordGroup.Items` rather than `wordGroup` directly, as shown in Listing 15.10. Another potential property to add to the anonymous type would be the count of items within the subcollection. However, this is available on `wordGroup.Items.Count()`, so the benefit of adding it to the anonymous type directly is questionable.

Query Continuation with `into`

As we saw in Listing 15.11, you can use an existing query as the input to a second query. However, it is not necessary to write an entirely new query expression when you want to use the results of one query as the input to another. You can extend any query with a **query continuation clause** using the contextual keyword `into`. A query continuation is nothing more than syntactic sugar for creating two queries and using the first as the input to the second. The range variable introduced by the `into` clause (`groups` in Listing 15.11) becomes the range variable for the remainder of the query; any previous range variables are logically a part of the earlier query and cannot be used in the query continuation. Listing 15.12 shows how to rewrite the code of Listing 15.11 to use a query continuation instead of two queries.

LISTING 15.12: **Selecting without the Query Continuation**

```csharp
using System;
using System.Collections.Generic;
using System.Linq;

// ...

  private static void GroupKeywords1()
  {
      var selection =
          from word in Keywords
          group word by word.Contains('*')
          into groups
              select new
              {
                  IsContextualKeyword = groups.Key,
                  Items = groups
              };

      // ...

  }

// ...
```

The ability to run additional queries on the results of an existing query using into is not specific to queries ending with group clauses, but rather can be used on all query expressions. Query continuation is simply a shorthand for writing query expressions that consume the results of other query expressions. You can think of into as a "pipeline operator," because it "pipes" the results of the first query into the second query. You can arbitrarily chain together many queries in this way.

"Flattening" Sequences of Sequences with Multiple from Clauses

It is often desirable to "flatten" a sequence of sequences into a single sequence. For example, a sequence of customers might each have an associated sequence of orders, or a sequence of directories might each have an associated sequence of files. The SelectMany sequence operator (discussed in Chapter 14) concatenates together all the subsequences; to do the same thing with query expression syntax you can use multiple from clauses, as shown in Listing 15.13.

LISTING 15.13: **Multiple Selection**

```
var selection =
    from word in Keywords
    from character in word
    select character;
```

The preceding query will produce the sequence of characters a, b, s, t, r, a, c, t, a, s, b, a, s, e, ...

Multiple `from` clauses can also be used to produce the **Cartesian product**—the set of all possible combinations of several sequences—as shown in Listing 15.14.

LISTING 15.14: **Cartesian Product**

```
var numbers = new[] { 1, 2, 3 };
var product =
    from word in Keywords
    from number in numbers
    select new {word, number};
```

This would produce a sequence of pairs (abstract, 1), (abstract, 2), (abstract, 3), (as, 1), (as, 2), ...

■ BEGINNER TOPIC

Distinct Members

Often, it is desirable to return only distinct items from within a collection, discarding any duplicates. Query expressions do not have explicit syntax for distinct members, but the functionality is available via the query operator `Distinct()`, which was introduced in the preceding chapter. To apply a query operator to a query expression, the expression must be enclosed in parentheses so that the compiler does not think that the call to `Distinct()` is a part of the `select` clause. Listing 15.15 gives an example; Output 15.8 shows the results.

LISTING 15.15: **Obtaining Distinct Members from a Query Expression**

```
using System;
using System.Collections.Generic;
using System.Linq;

// ...
```

```
public static void ListMemberNames()
{
    IEnumerable<string> enumerableMethodNames = (
        from method in typeof(Enumerable).GetMembers(
            System.Reflection.BindingFlags.Static |
            System.Reflection.BindingFlags.Public)
        select method.Name).Distinct();
    foreach(string method in enumerableMethodNames)
    {
        Console.Write(" {0},", method);
    }
}
```

// ...

OUTPUT 15.8

```
Enumerable methods are: First, FirstOrDefault, Last, LastOrDefault,
Single, SingleOrDefault, ElementAt, ElementAtOrDefault, Repeat,
Empty, Any, All, Count, LongCount, Contains, Aggregate, Sum, Min, Max,
Average, Where, Select, SelectMany, Take, TakeWhile, Skip, SkipWhile,
Join, GroupJoin, OrderBy, OrderByDescending, ThenBy, ThenByDescending,
GroupBy, Concat, Distinct, Union, Intersect, Except, Reverse,
SequenceEqual, AsEnumerable, ToArray, ToList, ToDictionary, ToLookup,
DefaultIfEmpty, OfType, Cast, Range
```

In this example, `typeof(Enumerable).GetMembers()` returns a list of all the members (methods, properties, and so on) on `System.Linq.Enumerable`. However, many of these members are overloaded, sometimes more than once. Rather than displaying the same member multiple times, `Distinct()` is called from the query expression. This eliminates the duplicate names from the list. (We cover the details of `typeof()` and reflection [where methods like `GetMembers()` are available] in Chapter 17.)

Query Expressions Are Just Method Invocations

Somewhat surprisingly, adding query expressions to C# 3 required no changes to the CLR or to the CIL language. Rather, the C# compiler simply translates query expressions into a series of method calls. Consider, for example, the query expression from Listing 15.1, a portion of which appears in Listing 15.16.

LISTING 15.16: Simple Query Expression

```
private static void ShowContextualKeywords1()
{
```

```
        IEnumerable<string> selection =
            from word in Keywords
                where word.Contains('*')
                select word;
        // ...
    }

    // ...
```

After compilation, the expression from Listing 15.16 is converted to an
IEnumerable<T> extension method call from System.Linq.Enumerable, as
shown in Listing 15.17.

<u>LISTING 15.17:</u> **Query Expression Translated to Standard Query Operator Syntax**

```
    private static void ShowContextualKeywords3()
    {
        IEnumerable<string> selection =
            Keywords.Where(word => word.Contains('*'));

        // ...
    }

    // ...
```

As discussed in Chapter 14, the lambda expression is then itself translated
by the compiler to emit a method with the body of the lambda, and the
usage of it becomes allocation of a delegate to that method.

Every query expression can (and must) be translated to method calls,
but not every sequence of method calls has a corresponding query expression. For example, there is no query expression equivalent for the extension method TakeWhile<T>(Func<T, bool> predicate), which repeatedly
returns items from the collection as long as the predicate returns true.

For those queries that do have both a method call form and a query
expression form, which is better? This is a judgment call; some queries are
better suited for query expressions whereas others are more readable as
method invocations.

> ## Guidelines
>
> **DO** use query expression syntax to make queries easier to read, particularly if they involve complex `from`, `let`, `join`, or group clauses.
>
> **CONSIDER** using the standard query operators (method call form) if the query involves operations that do not have a query expression syntax, such as `Count()`, `TakeWhile()`, or `Distinct()`.

SUMMARY

This chapter introduced a new syntax, that of query expressions. Readers familiar with SQL will immediately see the similarities between query expressions and SQL. However, query expressions also introduce additional functionality, such as grouping into a hierarchical set of new objects, which was unavailable with SQL. All of the functionality of query expressions was already available via standard query operators, but query expressions frequently provide a simpler syntax for expressing such a query. Whether through standard query operators or query expression syntax, however, the end result is a significant improvement in the way developers are able to code against collection APIs, an improvement that ultimately provides a paradigm shift in the way object-oriented languages are able to interface with relational databases.

In the next chapter, we continue our discussion of collections: investigating some of the .NET Framework collection types as well as how to define custom collections.

■ 16 ■
Building Custom Collections

CHAPTER 14 COVERED THE STANDARD QUERY operators, the extension methods on `IEnumerable<T>` that provide methods common to all collections. However, these operators do not make all collections equally suited for all tasks; there is still a need for different collection types. Some collections are better suited to searching by key, whereas others are better suited to accessing items by position. Some collections act like queues: The first element in is the first out. Others are more like stacks: The first in is the last out. Others are not ordered at all.

The .NET Framework provides a plethora of collection types suited for many of the scenarios in which collections are needed. This chapter provides an introduction to some of these collection types and the interfaces they implement. The chapter also describes how to create custom-built collections that support standard functionality, such as indexing. It also includes a discussion of how to use the `yield return` statement to create classes and methods that implement IEnumerable<T>. This C# 2.0 feature greatly simplifies implementation of collections that can be enumerated with the `foreach` statement.

There are many nongeneric collection classes and interfaces in the .NET Framework, but in general these exist today only for backward compatibility with code written before generics. The generic collection types are both faster, because they avoid boxing costs, and more type-safe than the nongeneric collections. Thus, new code should almost always use the generic collection types exclusively. Throughout this book we are assuming that you are primarily using generic collection types.

More Collection Interfaces

We've already seen how collections implement IEnumerable<T>, the primary interface that enables iteration over the elements of a collection. There are many additional interfaces implemented by more complex collections. Figure 16.1 shows the hierarchy of interfaces implemented by collection classes.

These interfaces provide a standard way to perform common tasks such as iterating, indexing, and counting elements in a collection. This section examines these interfaces (at least all the generic ones), starting at the bottom of Figure 16.1 and moving upward.

IList<T> versus IDictionary<TKey, TValue>

An English-language dictionary can be thought of as a collection of definitions; a definition can be rapidly accessed by looking up its associated "key": the word being defined. A dictionary collection class is similarly a collection of values; each value can be rapidly accessed by using its associated unique key. Note, however, that a language dictionary typically stores the definitions sorted alphabetically by key; a dictionary class might choose to do so but typically does not. Dictionary collections are best thought of as an unordered list of keys and associated values unless specifically documented as being ordered. Similarly, one does not normally think of looking up "the sixth definition in the dictionary"; dictionary classes usually provide indexing only by key, not by position.

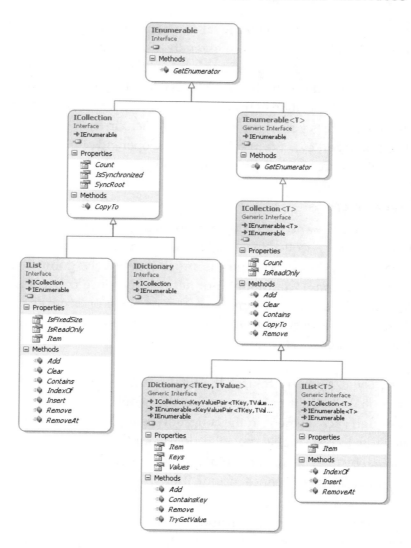

FIGURE 16.1: Generic Collection Interface Hierarchy

A list, by contrast, stores values in a specific order, and accesses them by their position. In a sense, lists are just the special case of dictionaries where the "key" is always an integer and the "key set" is always a contiguous set of non-negative integers starting with zero. But that is a strong enough difference that it is worth having an entirely different type to represent it.

Thus, when selecting a collection class to solve some data storage or retrieval problem, the first two interfaces to look for are IList<T> and IDictionary<TKey, TValue>. These interfaces indicate whether the collection type is focused on retrieval of a value when given its positional index or retrieval of a value when given its associated key.

Note that both of these interfaces require that a class that implements them provide an indexer. In the case of IList<T>, the operand of the indexer corresponds to the position of the element being retrieved: The indexer takes an integer and gives you access to the *n*th element in the list. In the case of the IDictionary<TKey, TValue> interface, the operand of the indexer corresponds to the key associated with a value, and gives you access to that value.

ICollection<T>

Both IList<T> and IDictionary<TKey, TValue> implement ICollection<T>. A collection that does not implement either IList<T> or IDictionary<TKey, TValue> is more than likely going to implement ICollection<T> (although not necessarily, since collections could implement the lesser requirement of IEnumerable or IEnumerable<T>). ICollection<T> is derived from IEnumerable<T> and includes two members: Count and CopyTo().

- The Count property returns the total number of elements in the collection. Initially, it may appear that this would be sufficient to iterate through each element in the collection using a for loop, but in order for this to be possible the collection would also need to support retrieval by index, which the ICollection<T> interface does not include (although IList<T> does include it).
- The CopyTo() method provides the ability to convert the collection into an array. The method includes an index parameter so that you can specify where to insert elements in the target array. Note that to use the method you must initialize the array target with sufficient capacity, starting at the index, to contain all the elements in ICollection<T>.

Primary Collection Classes

There are five key categories of collection classes, and they differ from one another in terms of how data is inserted, stored, and retrieved. Each generic class is located in the System.Collections.Generic namespace, and their nongeneric equivalents are in the System.Collections namespace.

List Collections: List<T>

The List<T> class has properties similar to an array. The key difference is that these classes automatically expand as the number of elements increases. (In contrast, an array size is constant.) Furthermore, lists can shrink via explicit calls to TrimToSize() or Capacity (see Figure 16.2).

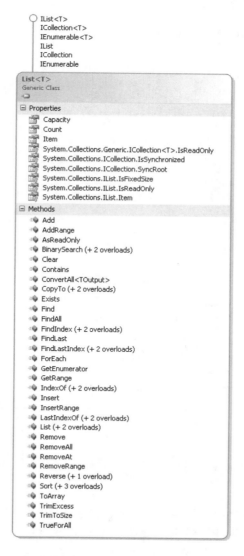

FIGURE 16.2: List<> Class Diagrams

These classes are categorized as **list collections** whose distinguishing functionality is that each element can be individually accessed by index, just like an array. Therefore, you can set and access elements in the list collection classes using the index operator, where the index parameter value corresponds to the position of an element in the collection. Listing 16.1 shows an example, and Output 16.1 shows the results.

LISTING 16.1: **Using** List<T>

```csharp
using System;
using System.Collections.Generic;

class Program
{
  static void Main()
  {
      List<string> list = new List<string>();

      // Lists automatically expand as elements
      // are added.
      list.Add("Sneezy");
      list.Add("Happy");
      list.Add("Dopey");
      list.Add("Doc");
      list.Add("Sleepy");
      list.Add("Bashful");
      list.Add("Grumpy");

      list.Sort();

      Console.WriteLine(
          "In alphabetical order {0} is the "
          + "first dwarf while {1} is the last.",
          list[0], list[6]);

      list.Remove("Grumpy");
  }
}
```

OUTPUT 16.1

```
In alphabetical order Bashful is the first dwarf while Sneezy is the last.
```

C# is zero-index-based; therefore, index 0 in Listing 16.1 corresponds to the first element and index 6 indicates the seventh element. Retrieving elements by index does not involve a search. It involves a quick and simple "jump" operation to a location in memory.

A List<T> is an ordered collection; the Add() method appends the given item to the end of the list. Before the call to Sort() in Listing 16.1, "Sneezy" was first and "Grumpy" was last; after the call, the list is sorted into alphabetical order, rather than the order in which items were added. Some collections automatically sort elements as they are added, but List<T> is not one of them; an explicit call to Sort() is required for the elements to be sorted.

To remove an element, you use the Remove() or RemoveAt() method, to either remove a given element or remove whatever element is at a particular index.

■ **ADVANCED TOPIC**

Customizing Collection Sorting

You might have wondered how it was that the List<T>.Sort() method in Listing 16.1 knew how to sort the elements of the list into alphabetical order. The string type implements the IComparable<string> interface, which has one method, CompareTo(). It returns an integer indicating whether the element passed is greater than, less than, or equal to the current element. If the element type implements the generic IComparable<T> interface (or the nongeneric IComparable interface) the sorting algorithm will, by default, use it to determine the sorted order.

But what if either the element type does not implement IComparable<T> or the default logic for comparing two things does not meet your needs? To specify a nondefault sort order you can call the overload of List<T>.Sort() which takes as an argument an IComparer<T>.

The difference between IComparable<T> and IComparer<T> is subtle but important: The first interface means, "I know how to compare *myself* to another instance of my type." The latter means, "I know how to compare *two things* of a given type."

The IComparer<T> interface is typically used when there are many different possible ways of sorting a data type and none is obviously the best. For example, you might have a collection of Contact objects that you sometimes want to sort by name, by location, by birthday, by geographic region, or by any number of other possibilities. Rather than choosing one and making the Contact class implement IComparable<Contact>, it might be wiser to create several different classes that implement IComparer<Contact>. Listing 16.2 shows a sample implementation of a LastName, FirstName comparison.

LISTING 16.2: **Implementing** IComparer<T>

```csharp
class Contact
{
  public string FirstName { get; private set; }
  public string LastName { get; private set; }
  public Contact(string firstName, string lastName)
  {
    this.FirstName = firstName;
    this.LastName = lastName;
  }
}
```

```csharp
using System;
using System.Collections.Generic;

class NameComparison : IComparer<Contact>
{
  public int Compare(Contact x, Contact y)
  {
      if (Object.ReferenceEquals(x, y))
          return 0;
      if (x == null)
          return 1;
      if (y == null)
          return -1;
      int result = StringCompare(x.LastName, y.LastName);
      if (result == 0)
          result = StringCompare(x.FirstName, y.FirstName);
      return result;
  }

  private static int StringCompare(string x, string y)
  {
      if (Object.ReferenceEquals(x, y))
          return 0;
      if (x == null)
          return 1;
      if (y == null)
          return -1;
      return x.CompareTo(y);
  }
}
```

To sort a List<Contact> by last name and then first name, you can call
contactList.Sort(new NameComparer()).

Total Ordering

You are required to produce a **total order** when implementing
IComparable<T> or IComparer<T>. Your implementation of CompareTo must

provide a fully consistent ordering for any possible pair of items. The ordering is required to have a number of basic characteristics: For example, every element is required to be considered equal to itself. If an element X is considered to be equal to element Y, and element Y is considered to be equal to element Z, all three elements X, Y, and Z must be considered equal to one another. If an element X is considered to be greater than Y, Y must be considered to be less than X. And there must be no "transitivity paradoxes"; you cannot have X greater than Y, Y greater than Z, and Z greater than X. If you fail to provide a total ordering, the action of the sort algorithm is undefined; it may produce a crazy ordering, it may crash, it may go into an infinite loop, and so on.

Notice, for example, how the comparer in Listing 16.2 ensures a total order, even if the arguments are null references. It would not be legal to say "if either element is null then return zero," for example, because then two non-null things could be equal to null but not equal to each other.

> ## Guidelines
>
> **DO** ensure that custom comparison logic produces a consistent "total order."

Searching a `List<T>`

To search `List<T>` for a particular element, you use the `Contains()`, `IndexOf()`, `LastIndexOf()`, and `BinarySearch()` methods. The first three methods search through the array, starting at the first element (or the last element for `LastIndexOf()`), and examine each element until the desired one is found. The execution time for these algorithms is proportional to the number of elements searched before a hit occurs. (Be aware that the collection classes do not require that all the elements within the collection are unique. If two or more elements in the collection are the same, `IndexOf()` returns the first index and `LastIndexOf()` returns the last index.)

`BinarySearch()` uses a much faster binary search algorithm but it requires that the elements be sorted. A useful feature of the `BinarySearch()` method is that if the element is not found, a negative integer is returned. The bitwise complement (~) of this value is the index of the next element larger than the element being sought, or the total element count if there is no greater value. This provides a convenient means to insert new values into the list at the specific location so as to maintain sorting. See Listing 16.3 for an example.

LISTING 16.3: **Using the Bit Complement of the** BinarySearch() **Result**

```csharp
using System;
using System.Collections.Generic;

class Program
{
  static void Main()
  {
      List<string> list = new List<string>();
      int search;

      list.Add("public");
      list.Add("protected");
      list.Add("private");

      list.Sort();

      search = list.BinarySearch("protected internal");
      if (search < 0)
      {
        list.Insert(~search, "protected internal");
      }

      foreach (string accessModifier in list)
      {
          Console.WriteLine(accessModifier);
      }
    }
}
```

Beware that if the list is not first sorted, an element will not necessarily be found, even if it is in the list. The results of Listing 16.3 appear in Output 16.2.

OUTPUT 16.2

```
private
protected
protected internal
public
```

■ ADVANCED TOPIC

Finding Multiple Items with FindAll()

Sometimes you must find multiple items within a list and your search criteria are more complex than merely looking for specific values. To support this, System.Collections.Generic.List<T> includes a FindAll() method. FindAll() takes a parameter of type Predicate<T>, which is a reference to a method called a delegate. Listing 16.4 demonstrates how to use the FindAll() method.

LISTING 16.4: Demonstrating FindAll() and Its Predicate Parameter

```csharp
using System;
using System.Collections.Generic;

class Program
{
  static void Main()
  {
      List<int> list = new List<int>();
      list.Add(1);
      list.Add(2);
      list.Add(3);
      list.Add(2);

      List<int> results = list.FindAll(Even);

      foreach(int number in results)
      {
          Console.WriteLine(number);
      }
  }

  public static bool Even(int value)
  {
      return (value % 2) == 0;
  }
}
```

In Listing 16.4's call to FindAll(), you pass a delegate instance, Even(). This method returns true when the integer argument value is even. FindAll() takes the delegate instance and calls into Even() for each item within the list (this listing uses C# 2.0's delegate type inferencing). Each time the return is true, it adds it to a new List<T> instance and then returns this instance once it has checked each item within list. A complete discussion of delegates occurs in Chapter 12.

Dictionary Collections: `Dictionary<TKey, TValue>`

Another category of collection classes is the dictionary classes—specifically, `Dictionary<TKey, TValue>` (see Figure 16.3). Unlike the list collections, dictionary classes store name/value pairs. The name functions as a unique key that can be used to look up the corresponding element in a manner similar to that of using a primary key to access a record in a database. This adds some complexity to the access of dictionary elements, but because lookups by key are efficient operations, this is a useful collection. Note that the key may be any data type, not just a string or a numeric value.

One option for inserting elements into a dictionary is to use the `Add()` method, passing both the key and the value, as shown in Listing 16.5.

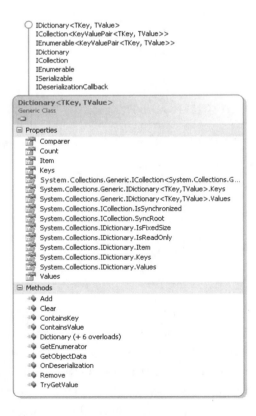

FIGURE 16.3: Dictionary Class Diagrams

LISTING 16.5: Adding Items to a `Dictionary<TKey, TValue>`

```csharp
using System;
using System.Collections.Generic;

class Program
{
  static void Main()
  {
      Dictionary<Guid,string> dictionary =
          new Dictionary<Guid, string>();
      Guid key = Guid.NewGuid();

      dictionary.Add(key, "hello");
  }
}
```

Listing 16.5 inserts the string `"hello"` using a `Guid` as its key. If an element with the same key has already been added, an exception is thrown.

An alternative is to use the indexer, as shown in Listing 16.6.

LISTING 16.6: Inserting Items in a `Dictionary<TKey, TValue>` **Using the Index Operator**

```csharp
using System;
using System.Collections.Generic;

class Program
{
  static void Main()
  {
      Dictionary<Guid, string> dictionary =
          new Dictionary<Guid, string>();
      Guid key = Guid.NewGuid();

      dictionary[key] = "hello";
      dictionary[key] = "goodbye";
  }
}
```

The first thing to observe in Listing 16.6 is that the index operator does not require an integer. Instead, the index operand type is specified by the first type argument (`Guid`), and the type of the value that is set or retrieved by the indexer is specified by the second type argument (`string`).

The second thing to notice in Listing 16.6 is that the same key is used twice. In the first assignment, no dictionary value corresponds to the given key. When this happens, the dictionary collection classes insert a new value with the supplied key. In the second assignment, an element with the specified key already exists. Instead of inserting an additional element, the value `"hello"` is removed and the value `"goodbye"` is associated with the key.

Attempting to read a value from a dictionary with a nonexistent key throws a KeyNotFoundException. The ContainsKey() method allows you to check whether a particular key is used before accessing its value, thereby avoiding the exception.

The Dictionary<TKey, TValue> is implemented as a "hash table"; this data structure provides extremely fast access when searching by key, regardless of the number of values stored in the dictionary. By contrast, checking whether there is a particular value in the dictionary collections is a time-consuming operation with linear performance characteristics, much like searching an unsorted list. To do this you use the ContainsValue() method, which searches sequentially through each element in the collection.

You remove a dictionary element using the Remove() method, passing the key, not the element value.

Because both the key and the value are required to add a value to the dictionary, the loop variable of a foreach loop that enumerates elements of a dictionary must be KeyValuePair<TKey, TValue>. Listing 16.7 shows a snippet of code demonstrating the use of a foreach loop to enumerate the keys and values in a dictionary. The output appears in Output 16.3.

LISTING 16.7: **Iterating over** Dictionary<TKey, TValue> **with** foreach

```
using System;
using System.Collections.Generic;

class Program
{
  static void Main()
  {
      var dictionary = newDictionary<string,string>();
      dictionary.Add("do", "a deer");
      dictionary.Add("re", "a drop");
      dictionary.Add("mi", "a name");
      dictionary.Add("fa", "a long way");
      dictionary.Add("so", "a needle");
      dictionary.Add("la", "a note");
      dictionary.Add("ti", "a drink");
      Console.WriteLine("Key   Value    ");
      Console.WriteLine("---   ------- ");
      foreach (KeyValuePair<string, string> i in dictionary)
      {
          Console.WriteLine("{0}   {1}", i.Key, i.Value);
      }
  }
}
```

OUTPUT 16.3

```
Key  Value
---  -------
do   a deer
re   a drop
mi   a name
fa   a long way
so   a needle
la   a note
ti   a drink
```

Note that the order of the items shown here is the order in which the items were added to the dictionary, just as if they had been added to a list. Implementations of dictionaries will often enumerate the keys and values in the order that they were added to the dictionary, but this feature is neither required nor documented, and therefore, you should not rely on it.

Guidelines

DO NOT make any unwarranted assumptions about the order in which elements of a collection will be enumerated; if the collection is not documented as enumerating its elements in a particular order, it is not guaranteed to produce elements in any particular order.

If you want to deal only with keys or only with elements within a dictionary class, they are available via the `Keys` and `Values` properties. The data type returned from these properties is of type `ICollection<T>`. The data returned by these properties is a reference to the data within the original dictionary collection, rather than a copy; changes within the dictionary are automatically reflected in the collection returned by the `Keys` and `Values` properties.

■ ADVANCED TOPIC

Customizing Dictionary Equality

In order to determine whether a given key matches any existing key in the dictionary, the dictionary must be able to compare two keys for equality. This is analogous to the way that lists must be able to compare two items to determine their order. (For an example, see the Advanced Topic,

Customizing Collection Sorting, earlier in this chapter.) By default, two instances of a value type are compared by checking to see if they contain exactly the same data, and two instances of a reference type are compared to see if they both reference the same object. However, it is occasionally necessary to be able to compare two instances as equal even if they are not exactly the same value or exactly the same reference.

For example, suppose you wish to create a `Dictionary<Contact, string>` using the `Contact` type from Listing 16.2. However, you want any two `Contact` objects to compare as equal if they have the same first and last names, regardless of whether the two objects are reference equal or not. Much as you can provide an implementation of `IComparer<T>` to sort a list, you can similarly provide an implementation of `IEqualityComparer<T>` to determine if two keys are to be considered equal. This interface requires two methods: one that returns whether or not two items are equal, and one that returns a "hash code" that the dictionary can use to facilitate fast indexing. Listing 16.8 shows an example.

LISTING 16.8: **Implementing** IEqualityComparer<T>

```csharp
using System;
using System.Collections.Generic;

class ContactEquality : IEqualityComparer<Contact>
{
  public bool Equals(Contact x, Contact y)
  {
      if (Object.ReferenceEquals(x, y))
         return true;
      if (x == null || y == null)
         return false;
      return x.LastName == y.LastName &&
         x.FirstName == y.FirstName;
  }

  public int GetHashCode(Contact x)
  {
      if (Object.ReferenceEquals(x, null))
         return 0;
      int h1 = x.FirstName == null ? 0 : x.FirstName.GetHashCode();
      int h2 = x.LastName == null ? 0 : x.LastName.GetHashCode();
      return h1 * 23 + h2;
  }
}
```

To create a dictionary that uses this equality comparer you can use the constructor new `Dictionary<Contact, string>(new ContactEquality)`.

■ **BEGINNER TOPIC**

Requirements of Equality Comparisons

As discussed in Chapter 9, Well-Formed Types, there are several important rules for the equality and hash code algorithms. Conformance to these rules is critical in the context of collections. Just as correctly sorting a list requires a custom ordering comparison to provide a total order, so too does a hash table require certain guarantees to be met by a custom equality comparison. The most important requirement is that if `Equals()` returns `true` for two objects, `GetHashCode()` must return the same value for those two objects. Note that the converse is not true: Two unequal items may have the same hash code. (And indeed, there *must* be two unequal items that have the same hash code because there are only 232 possible hash codes, but more than that many unequal objects!)

The second most important requirement is that two calls to `GetHashCode()` on the same item must produce the same result for at least as long as the item is in the hash table. Note, however, that two objects that "look equal" are not required to give the same hash code in two separate runs of a program. For example, it is perfectly legal for a given contact to be assigned one hash code today, and two weeks later when you run the program a second time for "the same" contact to be given a different hash code. Do not persist hash codes into a database and expect them to remain stable across different runs of a program.

Ideally, the result of `GetHashCode()` should appear to be "random." That is, small changes to the input should cause large changes to the output, and the result should be distributed roughly evenly across all possible integer values. It is difficult, however, to devise a hash algorithm that is extremely fast and produces extremely well-distributed output; try to find a good middle ground.

Finally, `GetHashCode()` and `Equals()` must not throw exceptions; notice how the code in Listing 16.8 is careful to never dereference a null reference, for example.

To summarize, here are the key principles:

- Equal objects must have equal hash codes.
- The Hash code of an object should not change for the life of the instance (at least while it is in a hash table).

- The hashing algorithm should quickly produces a well-distributed hash.
- The hashing algorithm should avoid throwing exceptions in all possible object states.

Sorted Collections: SortedDictionary<TKey, TValue> and SortedList<T>

The sorted collection classes (see Figure 16.4) store their elements sorted by key for SortedDictionary<TKey, TValue> and by value for SortedList<T>. (There is also a nongeneric SortedList class.) If we change the code in Listing 16.7 to use a SortedDictionary<string, string> instead of a Dictionary<string, string>, the output of the program is as appears in Output 16.4.

OUTPUT 16.4

```
Key  Value
---  -------
do   a deer
fa   a long way
la   a note
mi   a name
re   a drop
so   a needle
ti   a drink
```

Note that the elements are sorted into order by key, not by value.

Because sorted collections must do extra work to maintain the sorted order of their elements, insertion and removal is typically slightly slower than insertion and removal of values in an unordered dictionary.

Because sorted collections must store their items in a particular order, it is possible to access values both by key and by index. To access a key or value by its index in the sorted list, use the Keys and Values properties. These return IList<TKey> and IList<TValue> instances, respectively; the resultant collection can be indexed like any other list.

Stack Collections: Stack<T>

Chapter 11 discussed the stack collection classes (see Figure 16.5). The stack collection classes are designed as last in, first out (LIFO) collections. The two key methods are Push() and Pop().

FIGURE 16.4: SortedList<> and SortedDictionary<> Class Diagrams

- Push() inserts elements into the collection. The elements do not have to be unique.
- Pop() removes elements in the reverse order in which they were added.

To access the elements on the stack without modifying the stack, you use the Peek() and Contains() methods. The Peek() method returns the next element that Pop() will retrieve.

As with most collection classes, you use the Contains() method to determine whether an element exists anywhere in the stack. As with all collections, it is also possible to use a foreach loop to iterate over the elements in a stack. This allows you to access values from anywhere in the stack. Note, however, that accessing a value via the foreach loop does not remove it from the stack. Only Pop() provides this functionality.

FIGURE 16.5: `Stack<T>` Class Diagram

FIGURE 16.6: `Queue<T>` Class Diagram

Queue Collections: Queue<T>

Queue collection classes, shown in Figure 16.6, are identical to stack collection classes, except they follow the ordering pattern of first in, first out (FIFO). In place of the `Pop()` and `Push()` methods are the `Enqueue()` and `Dequeue()` methods. The queue collection behaves like a pipe: You place objects into the queue at one end using the `Enqueue()` method and remove them from the other end using the `Dequeue()` method. As with stack collection classes, the objects do not have to be unique, and queue collection classes automatically increase in size as required. As a queue shrinks it does not necessarily reclaim the storage space previously used, because that would make inserting a new element potentially more expensive; if you happen to know that a queue is going to remain the same size for a long time, you can hint to it that you would like to reclaim storage space using the `TrimToSize()` method.

Linked Lists: LinkedList<T>

In addition, `System.Collections.Generic` supports a linked list collection that enables both forward and reverse traversal. Figure 16.7 shows the class diagram. (There is no corresponding nongeneric type.)

FIGURE 16.7: `LinkedList<T>` and `LinkedListNode<T>` Class Diagrams

Providing an Indexer

Arrays, dictionaries, and lists all provide an **indexer** as a convenient way to get or set a member of a collection based on a key or index. As we've seen, to use the indexer you simply put the index (or indices) in square brackets after the collection. It is possible to define your own indexer; Listing 16.9 shows an example using `Pair<T>`.

LISTING 16.9: Defining an Indexer

```csharp
interface IPair<T>
{
  T First
  {
     get;
  }

  T Second
```

```
    {
        get;
    }

    T this[PairItem index]
    {
        get;
    }
}
```

```
public enum PairItem
{
    First,
    Second
}
```

```
public struct Pair<T> : IPair<T>
{
    public Pair(T first, T second)
    {
        _first = first;
        _second = second;
    }
    public T First
    {
        get{ return _first; }
        private set{ _first = value; }
    }
    private T _first;
    public T Second
    {
        get{ return _second; }
        private set{ _second = value; }
    }
    private T _second;

    public T this[PairItem index]
    {
        get
        {
            switch (index)
            {
                case PairItem.First:
                    return First;
                case PairItem.Second:
                    return Second;
                default :
                    throw new NotImplementedException(
                        string.Format(
                        "The enum {0} has not been implemented",
                        index.ToString()));
            }
        }
```

```
        set
        {
            switch (index)
            {
                case PairItem.First:
                    First = value;
                    break;
                case PairItem.Second:
                    Second = value;
                    break;
                default:
                    throw new NotImplementedException(
                        string.Format(
                        "The enum {0} has not been implemented",
                        index.ToString()));
            }
        }
    }
}
```

An indexer is declared much as a property is declared; instead of the name of the property, you use the keyword this followed by a parameter list in square brackets. The body is also like a property, with get and set blocks. As Listing 16.9 shows, the parameter does not have to be an int. In fact, the index can take multiple parameters and can even be overloaded. This example uses an enum to reduce the likelihood that callers will supply an index for a nonexistent item.

The resultant CIL code the C# compiler creates from an index operator is a special property called Item that takes an argument. Properties that accept arguments cannot be created explicitly in C#, so the Item property is unique in this aspect. This is because any additional member with the identifier Item, even if it has an entirely different signature, will conflict with the compiler-created member, and will therefore not be allowed.

■ ADVANCED TOPIC

Assigning the Indexer Property Name Using IndexerName

As indicated earlier, the CIL property name for an indexer defaults to Item. Using the IndexerNameAttribute you can specify a different name, however. Listing 16.10, for example, changes the name to "Entry".

LISTING 16.10: Changing the Indexer's Default Name

```
[System.Runtime.CompilerServices.IndexerName("Entry")]
public T this[params PairItem[] branches]
{
    // ...
}
```

This makes no difference to C# callers of the index, but it specifies the name for languages that do not support indexers directly.

This attribute is merely an instruction to the compiler to use a different name for the indexer; the attribute is not actually emitted into metadata by the compiler, and therefore, it is not available via reflection.

■ **ADVANCED TOPIC**

Defining an Index Operator with Variable Parameters

An index operator can also take a variable parameter list. For example, Listing 16.11 defines an index operator for BinaryTree<T>, discussed in Chapter 11 (and again in the next section).

LISTING 16.11: Defining an Index Operator with Variable Parameters

```
using System;
using System.Collections.Generic;

public class BinaryTree<T>:
    IEnumerable<T>
{

  // ...

    public T this[params PairItem[] branches]
    {
        get
        {
            BinaryTree<T> currentNode = this;
            int totalLevels =
                (branches == null) ? 0 : branches.Length;
            int currentLevel = 0;

            while (currentLevel < totalLevels)
            {
                currentNode = currentNode.SubItems[
                    branches[currentLevel]];
                if (currentNode == null)
```

```
        {
            // The binary tree at this location is null.
            throw new IndexOutOfRangeException();
        }
        currentLevel++;
    }

    return currentNode.Value;
}
set
{
    // ...
}
    }

}
```

Each item within branches is a PairItem and indicates which branch to navigate down in the binary tree.

Returning Null or an Empty Collection

When returning an array or collection, you must indicate that there are zero items by returning either null or a collection instance with no items. The better choice in general is to return a collection instance with no items. In so doing, you avoid forcing the caller to check for null before iterating over the items in the collection. For example, given a zero-size IEnumerable<T> collection, the caller can immediately and safely use a foreach loop over the collection without concern that the generated call to GetEnumerator() will throw a NullReferenceException. Consider using the Enumerable.Empty<T>() method to easily generate an empty collection of a given type.

One of the few times to deviate from this guideline is when null is intentionally indicating something different from zero items. For example, a collection of user names for a web site might be null to indicate that an up-to-date collection could not be obtained for some reason; that is semantically different from an empty collection.

> ### Guidelines
>
> **DO NOT** represent an empty collection with a null reference.
> **CONSIDER** using the `Enumerable.Empty<T>()` method instead.

Iterators

Chapter 14 went into detail on the internals of the `foreach` loop. This section discusses how to use **iterators** to create your own implementation of the `IEnumerator<T>`, `IEnumerable<T>`, and corresponding nongeneric interfaces for custom collections. Iterators provide clean syntax for specifying how to iterate on data in collection classes, especially using the `foreach` loop. The iterator allows end-users of a collection to navigate its internal structure without knowledge of that structure.

■ ADVANCED TOPIC

Origin of Iterators

In 1972, Barbara Liskov and a team of scientists at MIT began researching programming methodologies, focusing on user-defined data abstractions. To prove much of their work, they created a language called CLU that had a concept called "clusters" (CLU being the first three letters). Clusters were predecessors to the primary data abstraction that programmers use today: objects. As part of their research, the team realized that although they were able to use the CLU language to abstract some data representation away from end-users of their types, they consistently found themselves having to reveal the inner structure of their data in order to allow others to intelligently consume it. Through their consternation came the creation of a language construct called an iterator. (The CLU language offered many insights into what would eventually be popularized as object-oriented programming.)

If classes want to support iteration using the `foreach` loop construct, they must implement the enumerator pattern. As Chapter 14 describes, in C# the `foreach` loop construct is expanded by the compiler into the `while` loop construct based on the IEnumerator<T> interface that is retrieved from the IEnumerable<T> interface.

The problem with the enumeration pattern is that it can be cumbersome to implement manually, because it must maintain all the state necessary to describe the current position in the collection. This internal state may be simple for a list collection type class; the index of the current position suffices. But for data structures that require recursive traversal, such as binary trees, the state can be quite complicated. To mitigate the challenges associated with implementing this pattern, C# 2.0 included a construct that makes it easier for a class to dictate how the foreach loop iterates over its contents.

Defining an Iterator

Iterators are a means to implement methods of a class, and they are syntactic shortcuts for the more complex enumerator pattern. When the C# compiler encounters an iterator, it expands its contents into CIL code that implements the enumerator pattern. As such, there are no runtime dependencies for implementing iterators. Because the C# compiler handles implementation through CIL code generation, there is no real runtime performance benefit to using iterators. However, there is a substantial programmer productivity gain in choosing iterators over manual implementation of the enumerator pattern. To begin, the next section examines how an iterator is defined in code.

Iterator Syntax

An iterator provides shorthand implementation of iterator interfaces, the combination of the IEnumerable<T> and IEnumerator<T> interfaces. Listing 16.12 declares an iterator for the generic BinaryTree<T> type by creating a GetEnumerator() method. Next, you will add support for the iterator interfaces.

LISTING 16.12: Iterator Interfaces Pattern

```
using System;
using System.Collections.Generic;

public class BinaryTree<T>:
    IEnumerable<T>
{
    public BinaryTree ( T value)
    {
```

```
            Value = value;
        }

        #region IEnumerable<T>
        public IEnumerator<T> GetEnumerator()
        {
            //...
        }
        #endregion IEnumerable<T>

        public T Value
        { get; private set; }
        public Pair<BinaryTree<T>> SubItems
        { get; private set; }
    }

    public struct Pair<T>
    {
        public Pair(T first, T second) : this()
        {
            First = first;
            Second = second;
        }
        public T First { get; private set; }
        public T Second { get; private set; }
    }
```

As Listing 16.12 shows, we need to provide an implementation for the GetEnumerator() method.

Yielding Values from an Iterator

Iterators are like functions, but instead of returning a single value, they *yield* a sequence of values, one at a time. In the case of BinaryTree<T>, the iterator yields a sequence of values of the type argument provided for T. If the nongeneric version of IEnumerator is used, the yielded values will instead be of type object.

To correctly implement the iterator pattern, you need to maintain some internal state to keep track of where you are while enumerating the collection. In the BinaryTree<T> case, you track which elements within the tree have already been enumerated and which are still to come. Iterators are transformed by the compiler into a "state machine" that keeps track of the current position and knows how to "move itself" to the next position.

The yield return statement yields a value each time an iterator encounters it; control immediately returns to the caller that requested the item. When the caller requests the next item, the code begins to execute immediately following the previously executed `yield return` statement. In Listing 16.13, you return the C# built-in data type keywords sequentially.

LISTING 16.13: Yielding Some C# Keywords Sequentially

```csharp
using System;
using System.Collections.Generic;

public class CSharpBuiltInTypes: IEnumerable<string>
{
  public IEnumerator<string> GetEnumerator()
  {
      yield return "object";
      yield return "byte";
      yield return "uint";
      yield return "ulong";
      yield return "float";
      yield return "char";
      yield return "bool";
      yield return "ushort";
      yield return "decimal";
      yield return "int";
      yield return "sbyte";
      yield return "short";
      yield return "long";
      yield return "void";
      yield return "double";
      yield return "string";
  }

      // The IEnumerable.GetEnumerator method is also required
      // because IEnumerable<T> derives from IEnumerable.
  System.Collections.IEnumerator
      System.Collections.IEnumerable.GetEnumerator()
  {
      // Invoke IEnumerator<string> GetEnumerator() above
      return GetEnumerator();
  }
}

public class Program
{
  static void Main()
  {
      CSharpBuiltInTypes keywords =
          new CSharpBuiltInTypes();

      foreach (string keyword in keywords)
      {
          Console.WriteLine(keyword);
      }
  }
}
```

The results of Listing 16.13 appear in Output 16.5.

OUTPUT 16.5

```
object
byte
uint
ulong
float
char
bool
ushort
decimal
int
sbyte
short
long
void
double
string
```

The output from this listing is a listing of the C# built-in types.

Iterators and State

When `GetEnumerator()` is first called in a `foreach` statement (such as `foreach (string keyword in keywords)` in Listing 16.13), an iterator object is created and its state is initialized to a special "start" state that represents the fact that no code has executed in the iterator and thus no values have been yielded yet. The iterator maintains its state as long as the `foreach` statement at the call site continues to execute. Every time the loop requests the next value, control enters the iterator and continues where it left off the previous time around the loop; the state information stored in the iterator object is used to determine where control must resume. When the `foreach` statement at the call site terminates, the iterator's state is no longer saved.

It is always safe to call `GetEnumerator()` again; "fresh" enumerator objects will be created when necessary.

Figure 16.8 shows a high-level sequence diagram of what takes place. Remember that the `MoveNext()` method appears on the `IEnumerator<T>` interface.

In Listing 16.13, the `foreach` statement at the call site initiates a call to `GetEnumerator()` on the `CSharpBuiltInTypes` instance called `keywords`.

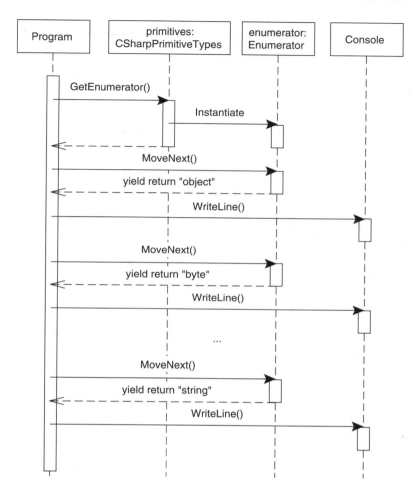

FIGURE 16.8: Sequence Diagram with yield return

Given the iterator instance (referenced by iterator), foreach begins each iteration with a call to MoveNext(). Within the iterator, you yield a value back to the foreach statement at the call site. After the yield return statement, the GetEnumerator() method seemingly pauses until the next MoveNext() request. Back at the loop body, the foreach statement displays the yielded value on the screen. It then loops back around and calls MoveNext() on the iterator again. Notice that the second time, control picks up at the second yield return statement. Once again, the foreach displays on the screen what CSharpBuiltInTypes yielded and starts the loop again. This process continues until there are no more yield return statements within the iterator. At that point, the foreach loop at the call site terminates because MoveNext() returns false.

More Iterator Examples

Before you modify BinaryTree<T>, you must modify Pair<T> to support the IEnumerable<T> interface using an iterator. Listing 16.14 is an example that yields each element in Pair<T>.

LISTING 16.14: **Using** yield **to Implement** BinaryTree<T>

```
public struct Pair<T>: IPair<T>,
    IEnumerable<T>
{
  public Pair(T first, T second) : this()
  {
     First = first;
     Second = second;
  }
  public T First { get; private set; }
  public T Second { get; private set; }

  #region IEnumerable<T>
  public IEnumerator<T> GetEnumerator()
  {
     yield return First;
     yield return Second;
  }
  #endregion IEnumerable<T>

  #region IEnumerable Members
  System.Collections.IEnumerator
     System.Collections.IEnumerable.GetEnumerator()
  {
     return GetEnumerator();
  }
  #endregion
}
```

In Listing 16.14, the iteration over the Pair<T> data type loops twice: first through yield return First, and then through yield return Second. Each time the yield return statement within GetEnumerator() is encountered, the state is saved and execution appears to "jump" out of the GetEnumerator() method context and into the loop body. When the second iteration starts, GetEnumerator() begins to execute again with the yield return Second statement.

System.Collections.Generic.IEnumerable<T> inherits from System.Collections .IEnumerable. Therefore, when implementing IEnumerable<T>, it is also necessary to implement IEnumerable. In Listing 16.14, you do so explicitly, and the implementation simply involves a call to IEnumerable<T>'s GetEnumerator() implementation. This call from IEnumerable.GetEnumerator() to IEnumerable<T>.GetEnumerator() will always work because of the type compatibility (via inheritance) between IEnumerable<T> and IEnumerable. Since the signatures for both GetEnumerator()s are identical (the return type does not distinguish a signature), one or both implementations must be explicit. Given the additional type safety offered by IEnumerable<T>'s version, you implement IEnumerable's implementation explicitly.

Listing 16.15 uses the Pair<T>.GetEnumerator() method and displays "Inigo" and "Montoya" on two consecutive lines.

LISTING 16.15: **Using** Pair<T>.GetEnumerator() **via** foreach

```
Pair<string> fullname = new Pair<string>("Inigo", "Montoya");
foreach (string name in fullname)
{
    Console.WriteLine(name);
}
```

Notice that the call to GetEnumerator() is implicit within the foreach loop.

Placing a yield return **within a Loop**

It is not necessary to hardcode each yield return statement, as you did in both CSharpPrimitiveTypes and Pair<T>. Using the yield return statement, you can return values from inside a loop construct. Listing 16.16 uses a foreach loop. Each time the foreach within GetEnumerator() executes, it returns the next value.

LISTING 16.16: **Placing** yield return **Statements within a Loop**

```
public class BinaryTree<T>: IEnumerable<T>
{
  // ...

  #region IEnumerable<T>
  public IEnumerator<T> GetEnumerator()
  {
      // Return the item at this node.
```

```
        yield return Value;

        // Iterate through each of the elements in the pair.
        foreach (BinaryTree<T> tree in SubItems)
        {
            if (tree != null)
            {
                // Since each element in the pair is a tree,
                // traverse the tree and yield each
                // element.
                foreach (T item in tree)
                {
                    yield return item;
                }
            }
        }
    }
    #endregion IEnumerable<T>

    #region IEnumerable Members
    System.Collections.IEnumerator
        System.Collections.IEnumerable.GetEnumerator()
    {
        return GetEnumerator();
    }
    #endregion
}
```

In Listing 16.16, the first iteration returns the root element within the binary tree. During the second iteration you traverse the pair of subelements. If the subelement pair contains a non-null value, you traverse into that child node and yield its elements. Note that foreach (T item in tree) is a recursive call to a child node.

As observed with CSharpBuiltInTypes and Pair<T>, you can now iterate over BinaryTree<T> using a foreach loop. Listing 16.17 demonstrates this, and Output 16.6 shows the results.

LISTING 16.17: Using foreach with BinaryTree<string>

```
// JFK
jfkFamilyTree = new BinaryTree<string>(
    "John Fitzgerald Kennedy");

jfkFamilyTree.SubItems = new Pair<BinaryTree<string>>(
    new BinaryTree<string>("Joseph Patrick Kennedy"),
    new BinaryTree<string>("Rose Elizabeth Fitzgerald"));

// Grandparents (Father's side)
jfkFamilyTree.SubItems.First.SubItems =
```

```
    new Pair<BinaryTree<string>>(
    new BinaryTree<string>("Patrick Joseph Kennedy"),
    new     BinaryTree<string>("Mary Augusta Hickey"));

// Grandparents (Mother's side)
jfkFamilyTree.SubItems.Second.SubItems =
    new Pair<BinaryTree<string>>(
    new BinaryTree<string>("John Francis Fitzgerald"),
    new BinaryTree<string>("Mary Josephine Hannon"));
```

```
foreach (string name in jfkFamilyTree)
{
    Console.WriteLine(name);
}
```

OUTPUT 16.6

```
John Fitzgerald Kennedy
Joseph Patrick Kennedy
Patrick Joseph Kennedy
Mary Augusta Hickey
Rose Elizabeth Fitzgerald
John Francis Fitzgerald
Mary Josephine Hannon
```

■ ADVANCED TOPIC

The Dangers of Recursive Iterators

The code in Listing 16.16 creates new "nested" iterators as it traverses the binary tree. This means that when the value is yielded by a node, the value is yielded by the node's iterator, and then yielded by its parent's iterator, and then yielded by its parent's iterator, and so on, until it is finally yielded to the original loop by the root's iterator. A value that is n levels deep must actually pass its value up a chain of n iterators. If the binary tree is relatively shallow, this is not typically a problem; however, an imbalanced binary tree can be extremely deep, and therefore expensive to iterate recursively.

Guidelines

CONSIDER using nonrecursive algorithms when iterating over potentially deep data structures.

■ **BEGINNER TOPIC**

struct **versus** class

An interesting side effect of defining `Pair<T>` as a `struct` rather than a `class` is that `SubItems.First` and `SubItems.Second` cannot be assigned directly, even if the setter were public. If you modify the setter to be public, the following will produce a compile error indicating that `SubItems` cannot be modified, "because it is not a variable":

```
jfkFamilyTree.SubItems.First =
    new BinaryTree<string>("Joseph Patrick Kennedy");
```

The issue is that `SubItems` is a property of type `Pair<T>`, a `struct`. Therefore, when the property returns the value, a copy of `SubItems` is made, and assigning `First` on a copy that is promptly lost at the end of the statement would be misleading. Fortunately, the C# compiler prevents this.

To overcome the issue, don't assign it (see the approach in Listing 16.17), use `class` rather than `struct` for `Pair<T>`, don't create a `SubItems` property and instead use a field, or provide properties in `BinaryTree<T>` that give direct access to `SubItems` members.

Canceling Further Iteration: `yield break`

Sometimes you might want to cancel further iteration. You can do this by including an `if` statement so that no further statements within the code are executed. However, you can also use `yield break` to cause `MoveNext()` to return `false` and control to return immediately to the caller and end the loop. Listing 16.18 shows an example of such a method.

LISTING 16.18: **Escaping Iteration via** `yield break`

```
public System.Collections.Generic.IEnumerable<T>
    GetNotNullEnumerator()
{
    if((First == null) || (Second == null))
    {
        yield break;
    }
    yield return Second;
    yield return First;
}
```

This method cancels the iteration if either of the elements in the `Pair<T>` class is `null`.

A yield break statement is similar to placing a return statement at the top of a function when it is determined that there is no work to do. It is a way to exit from further iterations without surrounding all remaining code with an if block. As such, it allows multiple exits, and therefore, you should use it with caution because casual reading of the code may miss the early exit.

■ ADVANCED TOPIC

How Iterators Work

When the C# compiler encounters an iterator, it expands the code into the appropriate CIL for the corresponding enumerator design pattern. In the generated code, the C# compiler first creates a nested private class to implement the IEnumerator<T> interface, along with its Current property and a MoveNext() method. The Current property returns a type corresponding to the return type of the iterator. Listing 16.14 of Pair<T> contains an iterator that returns a T type. The C# compiler examines the code contained within the iterator and creates the necessary code within the MoveNext method and the Current property to mimic its behavior. For the Pair<T> iterator, the C# compiler generates roughly equivalent code (see Listing 16.19).

LISTING 16.19: C# Equivalent of Compiler-Generated C# Code for Iterators

```csharp
using System;
using System.Collections.Generic;

public class Pair<T> : IPair<T>, IEnumerable<T>
{
  // ...

  // The iterator is expanded into the following
  // code by the compiler
  public virtual IEnumerator<T> GetEnumerator()
  {
      __ListEnumerator result = new __ListEnumerator(0);
      result._Pair = this;
      return result;
  }
  public virtual System.Collections.IEnumerator
      System.Collections.IEnumerable.GetEnumerator()
  {
      return new GetEnumerator();
  }

  private sealed class __ListEnumerator<T> : IEnumerator<T>
  {
      public __ListEnumerator(int itemCount)
```

```
        {
            _ItemCount = itemCount;
        }

        Pair<T> _Pair;
        T _Current;
        int _ItemCount;

        public object Current
        {
            get
            {
                return _Current;
            }
        }

        public bool MoveNext()
        {
            switch (_ItemCount)
            {
                case 0:
                    _Current = _Pair.First;
                    _ItemCount++;
                    return true;
                case 1:
                    _Current = _Pair.Second;
                    _ItemCount++;
                    return true;
                default:
                    return false;
            }
        }
    }
}
```

Because the compiler takes the `yield return` statement and generates classes that correspond to what you probably would have written manually, iterators in C# exhibit the same performance characteristics as classes that implement the enumerator design pattern manually. Although there is no performance improvement, the programmer productivity gained is significant.

▪ ADVANCED TOPIC

Contextual Keywords

Many C# keywords are "reserved" and cannot be used as identifiers unless preceded with an @ sign. The `yield` keyword is a contextual keyword, not a reserved keyword; it is legal (though confusing) to declare a local variable called `yield`. In fact, all the keywords added to C# after version 1.0 have been contextual keywords; this helps prevent accidental breakages when upgrading existing programs to use new versions of the language.

Had the C# designers chosen to use `yield value;` as the syntax for an iterator to yield instead of `yield return value;`, a possible ambiguity is introduced: `yield(1+2);` now might be yielding a value, or might be passing the value as an argument to a method called `yield`.

Since it was previously never legal to have the identifier `yield` appear immediately before `return` or `break`, the C# compiler knows that such a usage of `yield` must be as a keyword, not an identifier.

Creating Multiple Iterators in a Single Class

Previous iterator examples implemented `IEnumerable<T>.GetEnumerator()`. This is the method that `foreach` seeks implicitly. Sometimes you might want different iteration sequences, such as iterating in reverse, filtering the results, or iterating over an object projection other than the default. You can declare additional iterators in the class by encapsulating them within properties or methods that return `IEnumerable<T>` or `IEnumerable`. If you want to iterate over the elements of `Pair<T>` in reverse, for example, you provide a `GetReverseEnumerator()` method, as shown in Listing 16.20.

LISTING 16.20: Using `yield return` in a Method That Returns `IEnumerable<T>`

```csharp
public struct Pair<T>: IEnumerable<T>
{
    ...

    public IEnumerable<T> GetReverseEnumerator()
    {
        yield return Second;
        yield return First;
    }
    ...
}

public void Main()
{
    Pair<string> game = new Pair<string>("Redskins", "Eagles");
    foreach (string name in game.GetReverseEnumerator())
    {
        Console.WriteLine(name);
    }
}
```

Note that you return IEnumerable<T>, not IEnumerator<T>. This is different from IEnumerable<T>.GetEnumerator(), which returns IEnumerator<T>. The code in Main() demonstrates how to call GetReverseEnumerator() using a foreach loop.

yield **Statement Requirements**

You can use the yield return statement only in members that return an IEnumerator<T> or IEnumerable<T> type, or their nongeneric equivalents. Members whose bodies include a yield return statement may not have a simple return. If the member uses the yield return statement, the C# compiler generates the necessary code to maintain the state of the iterator. In contrast, if the member uses the return statement instead of yield return, the programmer is responsible for maintaining his own state machine and returning an instance of one of the iterator interfaces. Further, just as all code paths in a method with a return type must contain a return statement accompanied by a value (assuming they don't throw an exception), all code paths in an iterator must contain a yield return statement if they are to return any data.

Additional restrictions on the yield statement that result in compiler errors if violated are as follows.

- The yield statement may only appear inside a method, a user-defined operator, or the get accessor of an indexer or property. The member must not take any ref or out parameter.
- The yield statement may not appear anywhere inside an anonymous method or lambda expression (see Chapter 12).
- The yield statement may not appear inside the catch and finally clauses of the try statement. Furthermore, a yield statement may appear in a try block only if there is no catch block.

SUMMARY

The generic collection classes and interfaces made available in C# 2.0 are universally superior to their nongeneric counterparts; by avoiding boxing penalties and enforcing type rules at compile time, they are faster and safer. Unless you must maintain compatibility with legacy C# 1.0 code, you should consider the entire namespace of System.Collections as obsolete. (And in fact, it has been excluded from the Silverlight and WinRT CLR implementations entirely.) In other words, don't go back and necessarily remove all code that already uses this namespace. Instead, use `System.Collections.Generics` for any new code and, over time, consider migrating existing code to use the corresponding generic collections that contain both the interfaces and the classes for working with collections of objects.

Providing the `System.Collections.Generic` namespace is not the only change that C# 2.0 brought to collections. Another significant addition is the iterator. Iterators involve a new contextual keyword, `yield`, that C# uses to generate underlying CIL code that implements the iterator pattern used by the `foreach` loop.

In the next chapter we explore reflection, a topic briefly touched on before but with little to no explanation. Reflection allows one to examine the structure of a type within CIL code at runtime.

∎ 17 ∎
Reflection, Attributes, and Dynamic Programming

A TTRIBUTES ARE A MEANS OF inserting additional metadata into an assembly and associating the metadata with a programming construct such as a class, method, or property. This chapter investigates the details surrounding attributes that are built into the framework, as well as how to define custom attributes. In order to take advantage of custom attributes, it is necessary to identify them. This is handled through reflection. This chapter begins with a look at reflection, including how you can use it to dynamically bind at runtime and call a member using its name at compile time. This is frequently performed within tools such as a code generator. In addition, reflection is used at execution time when the call target is unknown.

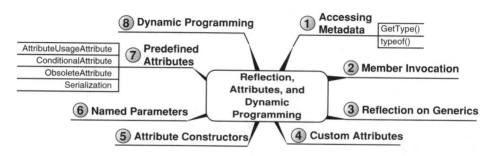

The chapter ends with a discussion of dynamic programming, a feature added in C# 4.0 that greatly simplifies working with data that is dynamic and requires execution-time rather than compile-time binding.

Reflection

Using reflection, it is possible to do the following.

- Access the metadata for types within an assembly. This includes constructs such as the full type name, member names, and any attributes decorating the construct.
- Dynamically invoke a type's members at runtime using the metadata, rather than a compile-time-defined binding.

Reflection is the process of examining the metadata within an assembly. Traditionally, when code compiles down to a machine language, all the metadata (such as type and method names) about the code is discarded. In contrast, when C# compiles into the CIL, it maintains most of the metadata about the code. Furthermore, using reflection, it is possible to enumerate through all the types within an assembly and search for those that match certain criteria. You access a type's metadata through instances of System.Type, and this object includes methods for enumerating the type instance's members. Additionally, it is possible to invoke those members on particular objects that are of the examined type.

The facility for reflection enables a host of new paradigms that otherwise are unavailable. For example, reflection enables you to enumerate over all the types within an assembly, along with their members, and in the process create stubs for documentation of the assembly API. You can then combine the metadata retrieved from reflection with the XML document created from XML comments (using the /doc switch) to create the API documentation. Similarly, programmers use reflection metadata to generate code for persisting (serializing) business objects into a database. It could also be used in a list control that displays a collection of objects. Given the collection, a list control could use reflection to iterate over all the properties of an object in the collection, defining a column within the list for each property. Furthermore, by invoking each property on each object, the list control could populate each row and column with the data contained in the object, even though the data type of the object is unknown at compile time.

XmlSerializer, ValueType, and DataBinder are a few of the classes in the framework that use reflection for portions of their implementation as well.

Accessing Metadata Using System.Type

The key to reading a type's metadata is to obtain an instance of System.Type that represents the target type instance. System.Type provides all the methods for retrieving the information about a type. You can use it to answer questions such as the following.

- What is the type's name (Type.Name)?
- Is the type public (Type.IsPublic)?
- What is the type's base type (Type.BaseType)?
- Does the type support any interfaces (Type.GetInterfaces())?
- Which assembly is the type defined in (Type.Assembly)?
- What are a type's properties, methods, fields, and so on (Type.Get Properties(), Type.GetMethods(), Type.GetFields(), and so on)?
- What attributes decorate a type (Type.GetCustomAttributes())?

There are more such members, but in summary, they all provide information about a particular type. The key is to obtain a reference to a type's Type object, and the two primary ways to do this are through object.GetType() and typeof().

Note that the GetMethods() call does not return extension methods. They are available only as static members on the implementing type.

GetType()

object includes a GetType() member, and therefore, all types include this function. You call GetType() to retrieve an instance of System.Type corresponding to the original object. Listing 17.1 demonstrates this, using a Type instance from DateTime. Output 17.1 shows the results.

LISTING 17.1: Using Type.GetProperties() to Obtain an Object's Public Properties

```
DateTime dateTime = new DateTime();

Type type = dateTime.GetType();
foreach (
    System.Reflection.PropertyInfo property in
        type.GetProperties())
{
```

```
        Console.WriteLine(property.Name);
    }
}
```

OUTPUT 17.1

```
Date
Day
DayOfWeek
DayOfYear
Hour
Kind
Millisecond
Minute
Month
Now
UtcNow
Second
Ticks
TimeOfDay
Today
Year
```

After calling `GetType()`, you iterate over each `System.Reflection.PropertyInfo` instance returned from `Type.GetProperties()` and display the property names. The key to calling `GetType()` is that you must have an object instance. However, sometimes no such instance is available. Static classes, for example, cannot be instantiated, so there is no way to call `GetType()`.

typeof()

Another way to retrieve a `Type` object is with the `typeof` expression. `typeof` binds at compile time to a particular `Type` instance, and it takes a type directly as a parameter. Listing 17.2 demonstrates the use of `typeof` with `Enum.Parse()`.

LISTING 17.2: **Using** typeof() **to Create a** System.Type **Instance**

```
using System.Diagnostics;
// ...
    ThreadPriorityLevel priority;
    priority = (ThreadPriorityLevel)Enum.Parse(
            typeof(ThreadPriorityLevel), "Idle");
// ...
```

`Enum.Parse()` takes a `Type` object identifying an enum and then converts a string to the specific enum value. In this case, it converts `"Idle"` to `System.Diagnostics.ThreadPriorityLevel.Idle`.

Member Invocation

The possibilities with reflection don't stop with retrieving the metadata. The next step is to take the metadata and dynamically invoke the members it references. Consider the possibility of defining a class to represent an application's command line. The difficulty with a `CommandLineInfo` class such as this has to do with populating the class with the actual command-line data that started the application. However, using reflection, you can map the command-line options to property names and then dynamically set the properties at runtime. Listing 17.3 demonstrates this example.

LISTING 17.3: **Dynamically Invoking a Member**

```
using System;
using System.Diagnostics;

public partial class Program
{
  public static void Main(string[] args)
  {
      string errorMessage;
      CommandLineInfo commandLine = new CommandLineInfo();
      if (!CommandLineHandler.TryParse(
          args, commandLine, out errorMessage))
      {
          Console.WriteLine(errorMessage);
          DisplayHelp();
      }

      if (commandLine.Help)
      {
          DisplayHelp();
      }
      else
      {
          if (commandLine.Priority !=
              ProcessPriorityClass.Normal)
          {
              // Change thread priority
          }

      }
      // ...

  }

  private static void DisplayHelp()
  {
      // Display the command-line help.
```

```
      }
    }
```

```csharp
using System;
using System.Diagnostics;

public partial class Program
{
  private class CommandLineInfo
  {
      public bool Help { get; set; }

      public string Out { get; set; }

      public ProcessPriorityClass Priority
      {
          get { return _Priority; }
          set { _Priority = value; }
      }
      private ProcessPriorityClass _Priority =
          ProcessPriorityClass.Normal;
  }
}
```

```csharp
using System;
using System.Diagnostics;
using System.Reflection;

public class CommandLineHandler
{
  public static void Parse(string[] args, object commandLine)
  {
      string errorMessage;
      if (!TryParse(args, commandLine, out errorMessage))
      {
          throw new ApplicationException(errorMessage);
      }
  }

  public static bool TryParse(string[] args, object commandLine,
      out string errorMessage)
  {
      bool success = false;
      errorMessage = null;
      foreach (string arg in args)
      {
          string option;
          if (arg[0] == '/' || arg[0] == '-')
          {
              string[] optionParts = arg.Split(
                  new char[] { ':' }, 2);

              // Remove the slash/dash
```

```csharp
            option = optionParts[0].Remove(0, 1);
            PropertyInfo property =
                commandLine.GetType().GetProperty(option,
                    BindingFlags.IgnoreCase |
                    BindingFlags.Instance |
                    BindingFlags.Public);
            if (property != null)
            {
                if (property.PropertyType == typeof(bool))
                {
                    // Last parameters for handling indexers
                    property.SetValue(
                        commandLine, true, null);
                    success = true;
                }
                else if (
                    property.PropertyType == typeof(string))
                {
                    property.SetValue(
                        commandLine, optionParts[1], null);
                    success = true;
                }
                else if (property.PropertyType.IsEnum)
                {
                    try
                    {
                        property.SetValue(commandLine,
                            Enum.Parse(
                                typeof(ProcessPriorityClass),
                                optionParts[1], true),
                            null);
                        success = true;
                    }
                    catch (ArgumentException )
                    {
                        success = false;
                        errorMessage =
                            string.Format(
                                "The option '{0}' is " +
                                "invalid for '{1}'",
                            optionParts[1], option);
                    }
                }
                else
                {
                    success = false;
                    errorMessage = string.Format(
                        "Data type '{0}' on {1} is not"
                        + " supported.",
                        property.PropertyType.ToString(),
                        commandLine.GetType().ToString());
                }
            }
```

```
            else
            {
                success = false;
                errorMessage = string.Format(
                    "Option '{0}' is not supported.",
                    option);
            }
        }
    }
    return success;
    }
}
```

Although Listing 17.3 is long, the code is relatively simple. `Main()` begins by instantiating a `CommandLineInfo` class. This type is defined specifically to contain the command-line data for this program. Each property corresponds to a command-line option for the program where the command line is as shown in Output 17.2.

OUTPUT 17.2

```
Compress.exe /Out:<file name> /Help
    /Priority:RealTime|High|AboveNormal|Normal|BelowNormal|Idle
```

The `CommandLineInfo` object is passed to the `CommandLineHandler`'s `TryParse()` method. This method begins by enumerating through each option and separating out the option name (`Help` or `Out`, for example). Once the name is determined, the code reflects on the `CommandLineInfo` object, looking for an instance property with the same name. If the property is found, it assigns the property using a call to `SetValue()` and specifies the data corresponding to the property type. (For arguments, this call accepts the object on which to set the value, the new value, and an additional `index` parameter that is `null` unless the property is an indexer.) This listing handles three property types: Boolean, string, and enum. In the case of enums, you parse the option value and assign the property the text's enum equivalent. Assuming the `TryParse()` call was successful, the method exits and the `CommandLineInfo` object is initialized with the data from the command line.

Interestingly, in spite of the fact that `CommandLineInfo` is a private class nested within `Program`, `CommandLineHandler` has no trouble reflecting over it and even invoking its members. In other words, reflection is able to circumvent accessibility rules as long as appropriate code access security (CAS; see

Chapter 21) permissions are established. If, for example, Out was private, it would still be possible for the TryParse() method to assign it a value. Because of this, it would be possible to move CommandLineHandler into a separate assembly and share it across multiple programs, each with their own CommandLineInfo class.

In this particular example, you invoke a member on CommandLineInfo using PropertyInfo.SetValue(). Not surprisingly, PropertyInfo also includes a GetValue() method for retrieving data from the property. For a method, however, there is a MethodInfo class with an Invoke() member. Both MethodInfo and PropertyInfo derive from MemberInfo (although indirectly), as shown in Figure 17.1.

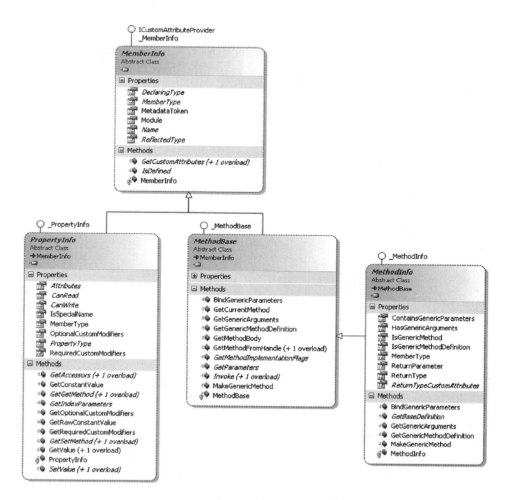

FIGURE 17.1: **MemberInfo** Derived Classes

The CAS permissions are set up to allow private member invocation in this case because the program runs from the local computer, and by default, locally installed programs are part of the trusted zone and have appropriate permissions granted. Programs run from a remote location will need to be explicitly granted such a right.

Reflection on Generic Types

The introduction of generic types in version 2.0 of the CLR necessitated additional reflection features. Runtime reflection on generics determines whether a class or method contains a generic type, and any type parameters or arguments it may include.

Determining the Type of Type Parameters

In the same way that you can use a typeof operator with nongeneric types to retrieve an instance of System.Type, you can use the typeof operator on type parameters in a generic type or generic method. Listing 17.4 applies the typeof operator to the type parameter in the Add method of a Stack class.

LISTING 17.4: **Declaring the** Stack<T> **Class**

```
public class Stack<T>
{
    // ...
    public void Add(T i)
    {
        // ...
        Type t = typeof(T);
        // ...
    }
    // ...
}
```

Once you have an instance of the Type object for the type parameter, you may then use reflection on the type parameter itself to determine its behavior and tailor the Add method to the specific type more effectively.

Determining Whether a Class or Method Supports Generics

In the System.Type class for the version 2.0 release of the CLR, a handful of methods were added to determine whether a given type supports generic parameters and arguments. A generic argument is a type parameter supplied when a generic class is instantiated. You can determine whether a class or method contains generic parameters that have not yet been set by querying the `Type.ContainsGenericParameters` property, as demonstrated in Listing 17.5.

LISTING 17.5: Reflection with Generics

```
using System;

public class Program
{
  static void Main()
  {
      Type type;
      type = typeof(System.Nullable<>);
      Console.WriteLine(type.ContainsGenericParameters);
      Console.WriteLine(type.IsGenericType);

      type = typeof(System.Nullable<DateTime>);
      Console.WriteLine(!type.ContainsGenericParameters);
      Console.WriteLine(type.IsGenericType);
  }
}
```

Output 17.3 shows the results of Listing 17.5.

OUTPUT 17.3

```
True
True
True
True
```

`Type.IsGenericType` is a Boolean property that evaluates whether a type is generic.

Obtaining Type Parameters for a Generic Class or Method

You can obtain a list of generic arguments, or type parameters, from a generic class by calling the `GetGenericArguments()` method. The result is an array of `System.Type` instances that corresponds to the order in which they are declared as type parameters of the generic class. Listing 17.6 reflects into a generic type and obtains each type parameter. Output 17.4 shows the results.

LISTING 17.6: **Using Reflection with Generic Types**

```csharp
using System;
using System.Collections.Generic;

public partial class Program
{
  public static void Main()
  {

      Stack<int> s = new Stack<int>();

      Type t = s.GetType();

      foreach(Type type in t.GetGenericArguments())
      {
          System.Console.WriteLine(
              "Type parameter: " + type.FullName);
      }
      // ...
  }
}
```

OUTPUT 17.4

```
Type parameter: System.Int32
```

Attributes

Before delving into details on how to program attributes, we should consider a use case that demonstrates their utility. In the `CommandLineHandler` example in Listing 17.3, you dynamically set a class's properties based on the command-line option matching the property name. This approach is insufficient, however, when the command-line option is an invalid property name. /?, for example, cannot be supported. Furthermore, this mechanism doesn't provide any way of identifying which options are required versus which are optional.

Instead of relying on an exact match between the option name and the property name, attributes provide a way of identifying additional metadata about the decorated construct—in this case, the option that the attribute decorates. With attributes, you can decorate a property as `Required` and provide a /? option alias. In other words, attributes are a means of associating additional data with a property (and other constructs).

Attributes appear within square brackets preceding the construct they decorate. For example, you can modify the CommandLineInfo class to include attributes, as shown in Listing 17.7.

LISTING 17.7: Decorating a Property with an Attribute

```csharp
class CommandLineInfo
{
  [CommandLineSwitchAlias("?")]
  public bool Help
  {
      get { return _Help; }
      set { _Help = value; }
  }
  private bool _Help;

  [CommandLineSwitchRequired]
  public string Out
  {
      get { return _Out; }
      set { _Out = value; }
  }
  private string _Out;

  public System.Diagnostics.ProcessPriorityClass Priority
  {
      get { return _Priority; }
      set { _Priority = value; }
  }
  private System.Diagnostics.ProcessPriorityClass _Priority =
      System.Diagnostics.ProcessPriorityClass.Normal;
}
```

In Listing 17.7, the Help and Out properties are decorated with attributes. The purpose of these attributes is to allow an alias of /? for /Help, and to indicate that /Out is a required parameter. The idea is that from within the CommandLineHandler.TryParse() method, you enable support for option aliases and, assuming the parsing was successful, you can check that all the required switches were specified.

There are two ways to combine attributes on the same construct. You can either separate the attributes with commas within the same square brackets, or place each attribute within its own square brackets, as shown in Listing 17.8.

LISTING 17.8: **Decorating a Property with Multiple Attributes**

```
[CommandLineSwitchRequired]
[CommandLineSwitchAlias("FileName")]
public string Out
{
    get { return _Out; }
    set { _Out = value; }
}
```

```
[CommandLineSwitchRequired,
CommandLineSwitchAlias("FileName")]
public string Out
{
    get { return _Out; }
    set { _Out = value; }
}
```

In addition to decorating properties, developers can use attributes to decorate classes, interfaces, structs, enums, delegates, events, methods, constructors, fields, parameters, return values, assemblies, type parameters, and modules. For the majority of these, applying an attribute involves the same square bracket syntax shown in Listing 17.8. However, this syntax doesn't work for return values, assemblies, and modules.

Assembly attributes are used to add additional metadata about the assembly. Visual Studio's Project Wizard, for example, generates an AssemblyInfo.cs file that includes numerous attributes about the assembly. Listing 17.9 is an example of such a file.

LISTING 17.9: **Assembly Attributes within** AssemblyInfo.cs

```
using System.Reflection;
using System.Runtime.CompilerServices;
using System.Runtime.InteropServices;

// General information about an assembly is controlled
// through the following set of attributes. Change these
// attribute values to modify the information
// associated with an assembly.
[assembly: AssemblyTitle("CompressionLibrary")]
[assembly: AssemblyDescription("")]
[assembly: AssemblyConfiguration("")]
[assembly: AssemblyCompany("Michaelis.net")]
[assembly: AssemblyProduct("CompressionLibrary")]
[assembly: AssemblyCopyright("Copyright© Michaelis.net 2006-2012")]
[assembly: AssemblyTrademark("")]
[assembly: AssemblyCulture("")]
```

```
// Setting ComVisible to false makes the types in this
// assembly not visible to COM components. If you need to
// access a type in this assembly from COM, set the ComVisible
// attribute to true on that type.
[assembly: ComVisible(false)]

// The following GUID is for the ID of the typelib if this project is
exposed to COM
[assembly: Guid("417a9609-24ae-4323-b1d6-cef0f87a42c3")]

// Version information for an assembly consists
// of the following four values:
//
//      Major Version
//      Minor Version
//      Build Number
//      Revision
//
// You can specify all the values or you can
// default the Revision and Build Numbers
// by using the '*' as shown below:
// [assembly: AssemblyVersion("1.0.*")]
[assembly: AssemblyVersion("1.0.0.0")]
[assembly: AssemblyFileVersion("1.0.0.0")]
```

The `assembly` attributes define things such as company, product, and assembly version number. Similar to `assembly`, identifying an attribute usage as `module` requires prefixing it with `module:`. The restriction on `assembly` and `module` attributes is that they appear after the `using` directive but before any namespace or class declarations. The attributes listed above are generated by the Visual Studio Project Wizard and should be included in all projects to mark the resultant binaries with information about the contents of the executable or DLL.

Return attributes, such as the one shown in Listing 17.10, appear before a method declaration but use the same type of syntax structure.

LISTING 17.10: Specifying a Return Attribute

```
[return: Description(
    "Returns true if the object is in a valid state.")]
public bool IsValid()
{
  // ...
  return true;
}
```

In addition to `assembly:` and `return:`, C# allows for explicit target identifications of `module:`, `class:`, and `method:`, corresponding to attributes that decorate the module, class, and method. `class:` and `method:`, however, are optional, as demonstrated earlier.

One of the conveniences of using attributes is that the language takes into consideration the attribute naming convention, which is to place `Attribute` at the end of the name. However, in all the attribute *uses* in the preceding listings, no such suffix appears, despite the fact that each attribute used follows the naming convention. This is because although the full name (`DescriptionAttribute`, `AssemblyVersionAttribute`, and so on) is allowed when applying an attribute, C# makes the suffix optional. Generally, no such suffix appears when *applying* an attribute; it appears only when defining one or using the attribute inline (such as `typeof(DescriptionAttribute)`).

Guidelines

DO apply `AssemblyVersionAttribute` to assemblies with public types.

CONSIDER applying the `AssemblyFileVersionAttribute` and `AssemblyCopyrightAttribute` in order to provide additional information about the assembly.

DO apply the following information assembly attributes:
`System.Reflection.AssemblyTitleAttribute`,
`System.Reflection.AssemblyCompanyAttribute`,
`System.Reflection.AssemblyProductAttribute`,
`System.Reflection.AssemblyDescriptionAttribute`,
`System.Reflection.AssemblyFileVersionAttribute`, and
`System.Reflection.AssemblyCopyrightAttribute`.

Custom Attributes

Defining a custom attribute is relatively trivial. Attributes are objects; therefore, to define an attribute, you need to define a class. The characteristic that turns a general class into an attribute is that it derives from `System.Attribute`. Consequently, you can create a `CommandLineSwitchRequiredAttribute` class, as shown in Listing 17.11.

LISTING 17.11: Defining a Custom Attribute

```
public class CommandLineSwitchRequiredAttribute : Attribute
{
}
```

With that simple definition, you now can use the attribute as demonstrated in Listing 17.7. So far, no code responds to the attribute; therefore, the Out property that includes the attribute will have no effect on command-line parsing.

Guidelines

DO name custom attribute classes with the suffix "Attribute".

Looking for Attributes

In addition to providing properties for reflecting on a type's members, Type includes methods to retrieve the Attributes decorating that type. Similarly, all the reflection types (PropertyInfo and MethodInfo, for example) include members for retrieving a list of attributes that decorate a type. Listing 17.12 defines a method to return a list of required switches that are missing from the command line.

LISTING 17.12: Retrieving a Custom Attribute

```
using System;
using System.Collections.Specialized;
using System.Reflection;

public class CommandLineSwitchRequiredAttribute : Attribute
{
    public static string[] GetMissingRequiredOptions(
        object commandLine)
    {
        StringCollection missingOptions = new StringCollection();
        PropertyInfo[] properties =
            commandLine.GetType().GetProperties();

        foreach (PropertyInfo property in properties)
        {
            Attribute[] attributes =
                (Attribute[])property.GetCustomAttributes(
                    typeof(CommandLineSwitchRequiredAttribute),
                    false);
            if ((attributes.Length > 0) &&
```

```
                (property.GetValue(commandLine, null) == null))
        {
            missingOptions.Add(property.Name);
        }
    }
    return missingOptions.ToArray();
  }
}
```

The code that checks for an attribute is relatively simple. Given a `PropertyInfo` object (obtained via reflection), you call `GetCustom Attributes()` and specify the attribute sought, followed by whether to check any overloaded methods. (Alternatively, you can call the `GetCustomAttributes()` method without the attribute type to return all of the attributes.)

Although it is possible to place code for finding the `CommandLine SwitchRequiredAttribute` attribute within the `CommandLineHandler`'s code directly, it makes for better object encapsulation to place the code within the `CommandLineSwitchRequiredAttribute` class itself. This is frequently the pattern for custom attributes. What better location to place code for finding an attribute than in a static method on the attribute class?

Initializing an Attribute through a Constructor

The call to `GetCustomAttributes()` returns an array of objects that will successfully cast to an `Attribute` array. But since the attribute in this example didn't have any instance members, the only metadata information that it provided in the returned attribute was whether it appeared. Attributes can also encapsulate data, however. Listing 17.13 defines a `CommandLineAliasAttribute` attribute. This is another custom attribute, and it provides alias command-line options. For example, you can provide command-line support for `/Help` or `/?` as an abbreviation. Similarly, `/S` could provide an alias to `/Subfolders` that indicates that the command should traverse all the subdirectories.

To support this, you need to provide a constructor on the attribute. Specifically, for the alias you need a constructor that takes a string argument. (Similarly, if you want to allow multiple aliases, you need to define an attribute that has a `params string` array for a parameter.)

LISTING 17.13: Providing an Attribute Constructor

```csharp
public class CommandLineSwitchAliasAttribute : Attribute
{
    public CommandLineSwitchAliasAttribute(string alias)
    {
        Alias = alias;
    }

    public string Alias
    {
        get { return _Alias; }
        private set { _Alias = value; }
    }
    private string _Alias;
}

class CommandLineInfo
{
    [CommandLineSwitchAlias("?")]
    public bool Help
    {
        get { return _Help; }
        set { _Help = value; }
    }
    private bool _Help;

    // ...
}
```

The only restriction on the constructor is that when applying an attribute to a construct, only literal values and types (such as typeof(int)) are allowed as arguments. This is to enable their serialization into the resultant CIL. Therefore, it is not possible to call a static method when applying an attribute. In addition, providing a constructor that takes arguments of type System.DateTime would be of little value, since there is no System.DateTime literal.

Given the constructor call, the objects returned from PropertyInfo .GetCustomAttributes() will be initialized with the specified constructor arguments, as demonstrated in Listing 17.14.

LISTING 17.14: Retrieving a Specific Attribute and Checking Its Initialization

```csharp
PropertyInfo property =
    typeof(CommandLineInfo).GetProperty("Help");
CommandLineSwitchAliasAttribute attribute =
    (CommandLineSwitchAliasAttribute)
```

```
          property.GetCustomAttributes(
            typeof(CommandLineSwitchAliasAttribute), false)[0];
  if(attribute.Alias == "?")
  {
    Console.WriteLine("Help(?)");
  };
```

Furthermore, as Listing 17.15 and Listing 17.16 demonstrate, you can use similar code in a GetSwitches() method on CommandLineAliasAttribute that returns a dictionary collection of all the switches, including those from the property names, and associate each name with the corresponding attribute on the command-line object.

LISTING 17.15: Retrieving Custom Attribute Instances

```
using System;
using System.Reflection;
using System.Collections.Generic;

public class CommandLineSwitchAliasAttribute : Attribute
{
  public CommandLineSwitchAliasAttribute(string alias)
  {
      Alias = alias;
  }

  public string Alias
  {
      get { return _Alias; }
      private set { _Alias = value; }
  }
  private string _Alias;

  public static Dictionary<string, PropertyInfo> GetSwitches(
      object commandLine)
  {
      PropertyInfo[] properties = null;
      Dictionary<string, PropertyInfo> options =
          new Dictionary<string, PropertyInfo>();

      properties = commandLine.GetType().GetProperties(
          BindingFlags.Public | BindingFlags.NonPublic |
          BindingFlags.Instance);
      foreach (PropertyInfo property in properties)
      {
          options.Add(property.Name.ToLower(), property);
          foreach (CommandLineSwitchAliasAttribute attribute in
              property.GetCustomAttributes(
              typeof(CommandLineSwitchAliasAttribute), false))
          {
```

```
                options.Add(attribute.Alias.ToLower(), property);
            }
        }
        return options;
    }
}
```

LISTING 17.16: **Updating** CommandLineHandler.TryParse() **to Handle Aliases**

```
using System;
using System.Reflection;
using System.Collections.Generic;

public class CommandLineHandler
{
    // ...

    public static bool TryParse(
        string[] args, object commandLine,
        out string errorMessage)
    {
        bool success = false;
        errorMessage = null;

        Dictionary<string, PropertyInfo> options =
            CommandLineSwitchAliasAttribute.GetSwitches(
                commandLine);

        foreach (string arg in args)
        {
            PropertyInfo property;
            string option;
            if (arg[0] == '/' || arg[0] == '-')
            {
                string[] optionParts = arg.Split(
                    new char[] { ':' }, 2);
                option = optionParts[0].Remove(0, 1).ToLower();

                if (options.TryGetValue(option, out property))
                {
                    success = SetOption(
                        commandLine, property,
                        optionParts, ref errorMessage);
                }
                else
                {
                    success = false;
                    errorMessage = string.Format(
                        "Option '{0}' is not supported.",
                        option);
```

```csharp
                }
            }
        }

        return success;
    }

    private static bool SetOption(
        object commandLine, PropertyInfo property,
        string[] optionParts, ref string errorMessage)
    {
        bool success;

        if (property.PropertyType == typeof(bool))
        {
            // Last parameters for handling indexers
            property.SetValue(
                commandLine, true, null);
            success = true;
        }
        else
        {

            if ((optionParts.Length < 2)
                || optionParts[1] == ""
                || optionParts[1] == ":")
            {
                // No setting was provided for the switch.
                success = false;
                errorMessage = string.Format(
                    "You must specify the value for the {0} option.",
                    property.Name);
            }
            else if (
                property.PropertyType == typeof(string))
            {
                property.SetValue(
                    commandLine, optionParts[1], null);
                success = true;
            }
            else if (property.PropertyType.IsEnum)
            {
                success = TryParseEnumSwitch(
                    commandLine, optionParts,
                    property, ref errorMessage);
            }
            else
            {
                success = false;
                errorMessage = string.Format(
                    "Data type '{0}' on {1} is not supported.",
                    property.PropertyType.ToString(),
                    commandLine.GetType().ToString());
```

```
        }
      }
      return success;
    }
  }
```

System.AttributeUsageAttribute

Most attributes are intended to decorate only particular constructs. For example, it makes no sense to allow `CommandLineOptionAttribute` to decorate a class or an assembly. The attribute in those contexts would be meaningless. To avoid inappropriate use of an attribute, custom attributes can be decorated with `System.AttributeUsageAttribute`. Listing 17.17 (for `CommandLineOptionAttribute`) demonstrates how to do this.

LISTING 17.17: Restricting the Constructs an Attribute Can Decorate

```
[AttributeUsage(AttributeTargets.Property)]
public class CommandLineSwitchAliasAttribute : Attribute
{
  // ...
}
```

If the attribute is used inappropriately, as it is in Listing 17.18, it will cause a compile-time error, as Output 17.5 demonstrates.

LISTING 17.18: `AttributeUsageAttribute` **Restricting Where to Apply an Attribute**

```
// ERROR: The attribute usage is restricted to properties
[CommandLineSwitchAlias("?")]
class CommandLineInfo
{
}
```

OUTPUT 17.5

```
...Program+CommandLineInfo.cs(24,17): error CS0592: Attribute
'CommandLineSwitchAlias' is not valid on this declaration type. It is
valid on 'property, indexer' declarations only.
```

AttributeUsageAttribute's constructor takes an AttributesTargets flag. This enum provides a list of all the possible targets that the runtime allows an attribute to decorate. For example, if you also allowed CommandLineSwitchAliasAttribute on a field, you would update the AttributeUsageAttribute class as shown in Listing 17.19.

LISTING 17.19: Limiting an Attribute's Usage with AttributeUsageAttribute

```
// Restrict the attribute to properties and methods
[AttributeUsage(
    AttributeTargets.Field | AttributeTargets.Property)]
public class CommandLineSwitchAliasAttribute : Attribute
{
    // ...
}
```

Guidelines

DO apply the AttributeUsageAttribute class to custom attributes.

Named Parameters

In addition to restricting what an attribute can decorate, AttributeUsageAttribute provides a mechanism for allowing duplicates of the same attribute on a single construct. The syntax appears in Listing 17.20.

LISTING 17.20: Using a Named Parameter

```
[AttributeUsage(AttributeTargets.Property, AllowMultiple=true)]
public class CommandLineSwitchAliasAttribute : Attribute
{
    // ...
}
```

The syntax is different from the constructor initialization syntax discussed earlier. The AllowMultiple parameter is a **named parameter,** similar to the named parameter syntax used for optional method parameters (added in C# 4.0). Named parameters provide a mechanism for setting specific public properties and fields within the attribute constructor call, even though the constructor includes no corresponding parameters. The named attributes are optional designations, but they provide a means of setting additional instance data on the attribute without providing a constructor parameter for the purpose. In this case, `AttributeUsageAttribute` includes a public member called `AllowMultiple`. Therefore, you can set this member using a named parameter assignment when you use the attribute. Assigning named parameters must occur as the last portion of a constructor, following any explicitly declared constructor parameters. ·

Named parameters allow for assigning attribute data without providing constructors for every conceivable combination of which attribute properties are specified and which are not. Since many of an attribute's properties may be optional, this is a useful construct in many cases.

■ BEGINNER TOPIC

FlagsAttribute

Chapter 8 introduced enums and included an Advanced Topic in regard to `FlagsAttribute`. This is a framework-defined attribute that targets enums that represent flag type values. Here is similar text as a Beginner Topic, starting with the sample code shown in Listing 17.21.

LISTING 17.21: **Using** FlagsAttribute

```csharp
// FileAttributes defined in System.IO.

[Flags]  // Decorating an enum with FlagsAttribute.
public enum FileAttributes
{
  ReadOnly =          1<<0,     // 000000000000001
  Hidden =            1<<1,     // 000000000000010
  // ...
}


using System;
using System.Diagnostics;
using System.IO;

class Program
{
```

```
public static void Main()
{
    // ...

    string fileName = @"enumtest.txt";
    FileInfo file = new FileInfo(fileName);

    file.Attributes = FileAttributes.Hidden |
        FileAttributes.ReadOnly;

    Console.WriteLine("\"{0}\" outputs as \"{1}\"",
        file.Attributes.ToString().Replace(",", " |"),
        file.Attributes);

    FileAttributes attributes =
        (FileAttributes)Enum.Parse(typeof(FileAttributes),
        file.Attributes.ToString());

    Console.WriteLine(attributes);

    // ...
    }
}
```

Output 17.6 shows the results of Listing 17.21.

OUTPUT 17.6

```
"ReadOnly | Hidden" outputs as "ReadOnly, Hidden"
```

The flag documents that the enumeration values can be combined. Furthermore, it changes the behavior of the ToString() and Parse() methods. For example, calling ToString() on an enumeration that is decorated with FlagsAttribute writes out the strings for each enumeration flag that is set. In Listing 17.21, file.Attributes.ToString() returns "ReadOnly, Hidden" rather than the 3 it would have returned without the FlagsAttribute flag. If two enumeration values are the same, the ToString() call would return the first one. As mentioned earlier, however, you should use this with caution because it is not localizable.

Parsing a value from a string to the enumeration also works, provided each enumeration value identifier is separated by a comma.

It is important to note that FlagsAttribute does not automatically assign the unique flag values or check that they have unique values. The values of each enumeration item still must be assigned explicitly.

Predefined Attributes

The `AttributeUsageAttribute` attribute has a special characteristic that you didn't see in the custom attributes you have created thus far in this book. This attribute affects the behavior of the compiler, causing the compiler to sometimes report an error. Unlike the reflection code you wrote earlier for retrieving `CommandLineRequiredAttribute` and `CommandLineSwitchAliasAttribute`, `AttributeUsageAttribute` has no runtime code; instead, it has built-in compiler support.

`AttributeUsageAttribute` is a predefined attribute. Not only do such attributes provide additional metadata about the constructs they decorate, but also the runtime and compiler behave differently in order to facilitate these attributes' functionality. Attributes such as `AttributeUsageAttribute`, `FlagsAttribute`, `ObsoleteAttribute`, and `ConditionalAttribute` are examples of predefined attributes. They include special behavior that only the CLI provider or compiler can offer because there are no extension points for additional noncustom attributes. In contrast, custom attributes are entirely passive. Listing 17.21 includes a couple of predefined attributes; Chapter 18 includes a few more.

System. ConditionalAttribute

Within a single assembly, the `System.Diagnostics.ConditionalAttribute` attribute behaves a little like the `#if/#endif` preprocessor identifier. However, instead of eliminating the CIL code from the assembly, `System.Diagnostics.ConditionalAttribute` will optionally cause the call to behave like a **no-op,** an instruction that does nothing. Listing 17.22 demonstrates the concept, and Output 17.7 shows the results.

LISTING 17.22: **Using** ConditionalAttribute **to Eliminate a Call**

```
#define CONDITION_A

using System;
using System.Diagnostics;

public class Program
{
  public static void Main()
  {
      Console.WriteLine("Begin...");
      MethodA();
      MethodB();
      Console.WriteLine("End...");
```

```
    }

    [Conditional("CONDITION_A")]
    static void MethodA()
    {
        Console.WriteLine("MethodA() executing...");
    }

    [Conditional("CONDITION_B")]
    static void MethodB()
    {
        Console.WriteLine("MethodB() executing...");
    }
}
```

OUTPUT 17.7

```
Begin...
MethodA() executing...
End...
```

This example defined CONDITION_A, so MethodA() executed normally. CONDITION_B, however, was not defined either through #define or by using the csc.exe /Define option. As a result, all calls to Program.MethodB() from within this assembly will do nothing.

Functionally, ConditionalAttribute is similar to placing an #if/#endif around the method invocation. The syntax is cleaner, however, because developers create the effect by adding the ConditionalAttribute attribute to the target method without making any changes to the caller itself.

Note that the C# compiler notices the attribute on a called method during compilation, and assuming the preprocessor identifier exists, it eliminates any calls to the method. Note also that ConditionalAttribute does not affect the compiled CIL code on the target method itself (besides the addition of the attribute metadata). Instead, it affects the call site during compilation by removing the calls. This further distinguishes ConditionalAttribute from #if/#endif when calling across assemblies. Because the decorated method is still compiled and included in the target assembly, the determination of whether to call a method is based not on the preprocessor identifier in the callee's assembly, but rather on the caller's assembly. In other words, if you create a second assembly that defines CONDITION_B, any calls to Program.MethodB() from the second assembly will execute. This is a useful characteristic in many tracing and testing scenarios. In fact, calls to System.Diagnostics.Trace and System.Diagnostics.Debug use this trait with ConditionalAttributes on TRACE and DEBUG preprocessor identifiers.

Because methods don't execute whenever the preprocessor identifier is not defined, ConditionalAttribute may not be used on methods that include an out parameter or specify a return other than void. Doing so causes a compile-time error. This makes sense because possibly none of the code within the decorated method will execute, so it is unknown what to return to the caller. Similarly, properties cannot be decorated with ConditionalAttribute. The AttributeUsage (see the section titled System.AttributeUsageAttribute, earlier in this chapter) for ConditionalAttribute is AttributeTargets.Class (starting in .NET 2.0) and AttributeTargets.Method. This allows the attribute to be used on either a method or a class. However, the class usage is special because ConditionalAttribute is allowed only on System.Attribute-derived classes.

When ConditionalAttribute decorates a custom attribute, a feature started in .NET 2.0, the latter can be retrieved via reflection only if the conditional string is defined in the calling assembly. Without such a conditional string, reflection that looks for the custom attribute will fail to find it.

System.ObsoleteAttribute

As mentioned earlier, predefined attributes affect the compiler's and/or the runtime's behavior. ObsoleteAttribute provides another example of attributes affecting the compiler's behavior. The purpose of ObsoleteAttribute is to help with the versioning of code, providing a means of indicating to callers that a particular member or type is no longer current. Listing 17.23 is an example of ObsoleteAttribute usage. As Output 17.8 shows, any callers that compile code that invokes a member marked with ObsoleteAttribute will cause a compile-time warning, optionally an error.

LISTING 17.23: **Using** ObsoleteAttribute

```
class Program
{
  public static void Main()
  {
      ObsoleteMethod();
  }
```

```
    [Obsolete]
    public static void ObsoleteMethod()
    {
    }
}
```

OUTPUT 17.8

```
c:\SampleCode\ObsoleteAttributeTest.cs(24,17): warning CS0612:
Program.ObsoleteMethod()' is obsolete
```

In this case, `ObsoleteAttribute` simply displays a warning. However, there are two additional constructors on the attribute. One of them, `ObsoleteAttribute(string message)`, appends the additional message argument to the compiler's obsolete message. The best practice for this message is to provide direction on what replaces the obsolete code. The second, however, is a `bool error` parameter that forces the warning to be recorded as an error instead.

`ObsoleteAttribute` allows third parties to notify developers of deprecated APIs. The warning (not an error) allows the original API to work until the developer is able to update the calling code.

Serialization-Related Attributes

Using predefined attributes, the framework supports the capacity to serialize objects onto a stream so that they can be deserialized back into objects at a later time. This provides a means of easily saving a document type object to disk before shutting down an application. Later on, the document may be deserialized so that the user can continue to work on it.

In spite of the fact that an object can be relatively complex and can include links to many other types of objects that also need to be serialized, the serialization framework is easy to use. In order for an object to be serializable, the only requirement is that it includes a `System.SerializableAttribute`. Given the attribute, a formatter class reflects over the serializable object and copies it into a stream (see Listing 17.24).

LISTING 17.24: Saving a Document Using `System.SerializableAttribute`

```
using System;
using System.IO;
using System.Runtime.Serialization.Formatters.Binary;
```

```csharp
class Program
{
  public static void Main()
  {
      Stream stream;
      Document documentBefore = new Document();
      documentBefore.Title =
          "A cacophony of ramblings from my potpourri of notes";
      Document documentAfter;

      using (stream = File.Open(
          documentBefore.Title + ".bin", FileMode.Create))
      {
          BinaryFormatter formatter =
              new BinaryFormatter();
          formatter.Serialize(stream, documentBefore);
      }

      using (stream = File.Open(
          documentBefore.Title + ".bin", FileMode.Open))
      {
          BinaryFormatter formatter =
              new BinaryFormatter();
          documentAfter = (Document)formatter.Deserialize(
              stream);
      }

      Console.WriteLine(documentAfter.Title);
  }
}

// Serializable classes use SerializableAttribute.
[Serializable]
class Document
{

  public string Title = null;
  public string Data = null;

  [NonSerialized]
  public long _WindowHandle = 0;

  class Image
  {
  }
  [NonSerialized]
  private Image Picture = new Image();
}
```

Output 17.9 shows the results of Listing 17.24.

OUTPUT 17.9

A cacophony of ramblings from my potpourri of notes

Listing 17.24 serializes and deserializes a Document object. Serialization involves instantiating a formatter (this example uses System.Runtime.Serialization.Formatters.Binary.BinaryFormatter) and calling Serialization() with the appropriate stream object. Deserializing the object simply involves a call to the formatter's Deserialize() method, specifying the stream that contains the serialized object as an argument. However, since the return from Deserialize() is of type object, you also need to cast it specifically to the type that was serialized.

Notice that serialization occurs for the entire object graph (all the items associated with the serialized object [Document] via a field). Therefore, all fields in the object graph also must be serializable.

System.NonSerializable

Fields that are not serializable should be decorated with the System.NonSerializable attribute. This tells the serialization framework to ignore them. The same attribute should appear on fields that should not be persisted for use case reasons. Passwords and Windows handles are good examples of fields that should not be serialized: Windows handles because they change each time a window is re-created, and passwords because data serialized into a stream is not encrypted and can easily be accessed. Consider the Notepad view of the serialized document in Figure 17.2.

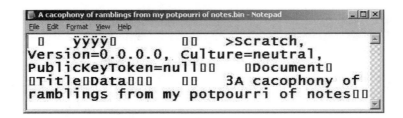

FIGURE 17.2: BinaryFormatter Does Not Encrypt Data

Listing 17.24 set the Title field, and the resultant *.BIN file includes the text in plain view.

Providing Custom Serialization

One way to add encryption is to provide custom serialization. Ignoring the complexities of encrypting and decrypting, this requires implementing the ISerializable interface in addition to using SerializableAttribute. The interface requires only the GetObjectData() method to be implemented. However, this is sufficient only for serialization. In order to also support deserialization, it is necessary to provide a constructor that takes parameters of type System.Runtime.Serialization.SerializationInfo and System.Runtime.Serialization.StreamingContext (see Listing 17.25).

LISTING 17.25: Implementing System.Runtime.Serialization.ISerializable

```csharp
using System;
using System.Runtime.Serialization;

[Serializable]
class EncryptableDocument :
    ISerializable
{
  public EncryptableDocument(){ }

  enum Field
  {
      Title,
      Data
  }
  public string Title;
  public string Data;

  public static string Encrypt(string data)
  {
      string encryptedData = data;
      // Key-based encryption ...
      return encryptedData;
  }

  public static string Decrypt(string encryptedData)
  {
      string data = encryptedData;
    // Key-based decryption...
      return data;
  }

 #region ISerializable Members
      public void GetObjectData(
      SerializationInfo info, StreamingContext context)
  {
      info.AddValue(
          Field.Title.ToString(), Title);
```

```
    info.AddValue(
        Field.Data.ToString(), Encrypt(Data));
}

public EncryptableDocument(
    SerializationInfo info, StreamingContext context)
{
    Title = info.GetString(
        Field.Title.ToString());
    Data = Decrypt(info.GetString(
        Field.Data.ToString()));
}
#endregion
}
```

Essentially, the `System.Runtime.Serialization.SerializationInfo` object is a collection of name/value pairs. When serializing, the `GetObject()` implementation calls `AddValue()`. To reverse the process, you call one of the `Get*()` members. In this case, you encrypt and decrypt prior to serialization and deserialization, respectively.

Versioning the Serialization

One more serialization point deserves mention: versioning. Objects such as documents may be serialized using one version of an assembly and deserialized using a newer version, sometimes the reverse. Without paying attention, however, version incompatibilities can easily be introduced, sometimes unexpectedly. Consider the scenario shown in Table 17.1.

Surprisingly, even though all you did was to add a new field, deserializing the original file throws a `System.Runtime.Serialization.SerializationException`. This is because the formatter looks for data corresponding to the new field within the stream. Failure to locate such data throws an exception.

To avoid this, the 2.0 framework and later includes a `System.Runtime.Serialization.OptionalFieldAttribute`. When you require backward compatibility, you must decorate serialized fields—even private ones—with `OptionalFieldAttribute` (unless, of course, a latter version begins to require it).

TABLE 17.1: Deserialization of a New Version Throws an Exception

Step	Description	Code
1.	Define a class decorated with System.SerializableAttribute.	```[Serializable]``` ```class Document```

2.	Add a field or two (public or private) of any serializable type.	```{```
		 ``` public string Title;```
		 ``` public string Data;```
		 ```}```

3.	Serialize the object to a file called *.v1.bin.	```Stream stream;```
		 ```Document documentBefore = new```
		 ```Document();```
		 ```documentBefore.Title =```
		 ``` "A cacophony of ramblings from my```
		 ```potpourri of notes";```
		 ```Document documentAfter;```
		
		 ```using (stream = File.Open(```
		 ``` documentBefore.Title + ".bin",```
		 ``` FileMode.Create))```
		 ```{```
		 ``` BinaryFormatter formatter =```
		 ``` new BinaryFormatter();```
		 ``` formatter.Serialize(```
		 ``` stream, documentBefore);```
		 ```}```

4.	Add an additional field to the serializable class.	```[Serializable]```
		 ```class Document```
		 ```{```
		 ``` public string Title;```
		 ``` public string Author;```
		 ``` public string Data;```
		 ```}```

5.	Deserialize the *v1.bin file into the new object (Document) version.	```using (stream = File.Open(```
		 ``` documentBefore.Title + ".bin",```
		 ``` FileMode.Open))```
		 ```{```
		 ``` BinaryFormatter formatter =```
		 ``` new BinaryFormatter();```
		 ``` documentAfter =```
		 ``` (Document)formatter.```
		 ```Deserialize(```
		 ``` stream);```
		 ```}```

Unfortunately, System.Runtime.Serialization.OptionalFieldAttribute is not supported in the earlier framework version. Instead, it is necessary to implement ISerializable, just as you did for encryption, saving and retrieving only the fields that are available. Assuming the addition of the Author field, for example, the implementation shown in Listing 17.26 is required for backward-compatibility support prior to the 2.0 framework.

LISTING 17.26: Backward Compatibility Prior to the 2.0 Framework

```
[Serializable]
public class VersionableDocument : ISerializable
{
  enum Field
  {
      Title,
      Author,
      Data,
  }

  public VersionableDocument()
  {
  }

  public string Title;
  public string Author;
  public string Data;

  #region ISerializable Members
  public void GetObjectData(
      SerializationInfo info, StreamingContext context)
  {
      info.AddValue(Field.Title.ToString(), Title);
      info.AddValue(Field.Author.ToString(), Author);
      info.AddValue(Field.Data.ToString(), Data);
  }
  public VersionableDocument(
      SerializationInfo info, StreamingContext context)
  {
      foreach(SerializationEntry entry in info)
      {
          switch ((Field)Enum.Parse(typeof(Field), entry.Name))
          {
              case Field.Title:
                  Title = info.GetString(
                      Field.Title.ToString());
                  break;
              case Field.Author:
                  Author = info.GetString(
                      Field.Author.ToString());
                  break;
              case Field.Data:
                  Data = info.GetString(
                      Field.Data.ToString());
                  break;
          }
```

```
    }
  }
  #endregion
}
```

Serializing in `GetObjectData()` simply involves serializing all fields (assume here that version 1 does not need to open documents from version 2). On deserialization, however, you can't simply call `GetString("Author")` because if no such entry exists, it will throw an exception. Instead, iterate through all the entries that are in `info` and retrieve them individually.

■ **ADVANCED TOPIC**

System.SerializableAttribute and the CIL

In many ways, the serialization attributes behave just like custom attributes. At runtime, the formatter class searches for these attributes, and if the attributes exist, the classes are formatted appropriately. One of the characteristics that make `System.SerializableAttribute` not just a custom attribute, however, is the fact that the CIL has a special header notation for serializable classes. Listing 17.27 shows the class header for the `Person` class in the CIL.

LISTING 17.27: The CIL for `SerializableAttribute`

```
class auto ansi serializable nested private
  beforefieldinit Person
  extends [mscorlib]System.Object
{
} // end of class Person
```

In contrast, attributes (including most predefined attributes) generally appear within a class definition (see Listing 17.28).

LISTING 17.28: The CIL for Attributes in General

```
.class private auto ansi beforefieldinit Person
      extends [mscorlib]System.Object
{
  .custom instance void CustomAttribute::.ctor() =
    ( 01 00 00 00 )
} // end of class Person
```

In Listing 17.28, `CustomAttribute` is the full name of the decorating attribute.

`SerializableAttribute` translates to a set bit within the metadata tables. This makes `SerializableAttribute` a **pseudoattribute:** an attribute that sets bits or fields in the metadata tables.

Programming with Dynamic Objects

The introduction of dynamic objects in C# 4.0 simplifies a host of programming scenarios and enables several new ones previously not available. At its core, programming with dynamic objects enables developers to code operations using a dynamic dispatch mechanism that the runtime will resolve at execution time, rather than the compiler verifying and binding to it at compile time.

Why? Because there are many times when objects are inherently not statically typed. Examples include loading data from an XML/CSV file, a database table, the Internet Explorer DOM, or COM's `IDispatch` interface, or calling code in a dynamic language such as an IronPython object. C# 4.0's Dynamic object support provides a common solution for talking to runtime environments that don't necessarily have a compile-time-defined structure. In the initial implementation of dynamic objects in C# 4.0, four binding methods are available:

1. Using reflection against an underlying CLR type
2. Invoking a custom `IDynamicMetaObjectProvider` which makes available a `DynamicMetaObject`
3. Calling through the `IUnknown` and `IDispatch` interfaces of COM
4. Calling type defined by dynamic languages such as IronPython

Of these, we are going to delve into the first two. The principles found there translate seamlessly to the remaining cases—COM interoperability and dynamic language interoperability.

Invoking Reflection Using `dynamic`

One of the key features of reflection is the ability to dynamically find and invoke a member on a particular type based on an execution time identification of the member name or some other quality, such as an attribute (see Listing 17.3). However, C# 4.0's addition of dynamic objects provides a simpler way of invoking a member by reflection, assuming compile-time knowledge of the member signature. Again: The restriction is that at compile time we need to know the member name along with the signature (number of parameters and whether the specified parameters will be type-compatible with the signature). Listing 17.29 (with Output 17.10) provides an example.

LISTING 17.29: Dynamic Programming Using "Reflection"

```
using System;

// ...
dynamic data =
  "Hello!  My name is Inigo Montoya";
Console.WriteLine(data);
data = (double)data.Length;
data = data*3.5 + 28.6;
if(data == 2.4 + 112 + 26.2)
{
  Console.WriteLine(
      "{0} makes for a long triathlon.", data);
}
else
{
  data.NonExistentMethodCallStillCompiles();
}
// ...
```

OUTPUT 17.10

```
Hello!  My name is Inigo Montoya
140.6 makes for a long triathlon.
```

In this example, there is no explicit code for determining the object type, finding a particular `MemberInfo` instance, and then invoking it. Instead, `data` is declared as type `dynamic` and methods are called against it directly. At compile time, there is no check as to whether the members specified are available, or even a check regarding what type underlies the `dynamic` object. Hence, it is possible at compile time to make any call so long as the syntax is valid. At compile time, it is irrelevant whether there is a corresponding member or not.

However, type safety is not abandoned altogether. For standard CLR types (such as those used in Listing 17.29), the same type checker normally used at compile time for non-dynamic types is instead invoked at execution time for the `dynamic` type. Therefore, at execution time, if in fact no such member is available, the call will result in a `Microsoft.CSharp.RuntimeBinder.RuntimeBinderException`.

Note again that this is not nearly as flexible as the reflection earlier in the chapter, although the API is undoubtedly simpler. The key difference when using a dynamic object is that it is necessary to identify the signature at compile time, rather than determine things such as the member name at runtime (like we did when parsing the command-line arguments).

dynamic **Principles and Behaviors**

Listing 17.29 and the accompanying text reveal several characteristics of the `dynamic` data type.

- `dynamic` *is a directive to the compiler to generate code.*

  `dynamic` involves an interception mechanism so that when a dynamic call is encountered by the runtime, it can compile the request to CIL and then invoke the newly compiled call. (See the Advanced Block titled `dynamic` Uncovered, later in this chapter, for more details.)

  The principle at work when a type is assigned to `dynamic` is to conceptually "wrap" the original type so that no compile-time validation occurs. Additionally, when a member is invoked at runtime, the "wrapper" intercepts the call and dispatches it appropriately (or rejects it). Calling `GetType()` on the `dynamic` object reveals the type underlying the dynamic instance—it does not return `dynamic` as a type.

- *Any type that converts to* `object` *will convert to* `dynamic`.

  In Listing 17.29, we successfully cast both a value type (`double`) and a reference type (`string`) to `dynamic`. In fact, all types can successfully be converted into a `dynamic` object. There is an implicit conversion from any reference type to `dynamic`. Similarly, there is an implicit conversion (a boxing conversion) from a value type to `dynamic`. In addition, there is an implicit conversion from `dynamic` to `dynamic`. This is perhaps obvious, but with `dynamic` this is more complicated than simply copying the "pointer" (address) from one location to the next.

- *Successful conversion from* `dynamic` *to an alternate type depends on support in the underlying type.*

  Conversion from a `dynamic` object to a standard CLR type is an explicit cast (for example, `(double)data.Length`). Not surprisingly, if the target type is a value type, an unboxing conversion is required. If the underlying type supports the conversion to the target type, the conversion from `dynamic` will also succeed.

- *The type underlying the dynamic type can change from one assignment to the next.*

  Unlike the implicitly typed variable (`var`) which cannot be reassigned to a different type, `dynamic` involves an interception mechanism for compilation before the underlying type's code is executed. Therefore, it is possible to successfully swap out the underlying type instance to an entirely different type. This will result in another interception call site that will need to be compiled before invocation.

- *Verification that the specified signature exists on the underlying type doesn't occur until runtime—but it does occur.*

  As the method call to `person.NonExistentMethodCallStillCompiles()` demonstrates, the compiler makes almost no verification of operations on a `dynamic` type. This is left entirely to the work of the runtime when the code executes. And if the code never executes, even though surrounding code does (as in the case with `person.NonExistent-MethodCallStillCompiles()`), no verification and binding to the member will ever occur.

- *The result of any* `dynamic` *member invocation is of compile-time type* `dynamic`.

  A call to any member on a `dynamic` object will return a `dynamic` object. Therefore, calls such as `data.ToString()` will return a `dynamic` object rather than the underlying `string` type. However, at execution time, when `GetType()` is called on the `dynamic` object, an object representing the runtime type is returned.

- *If the member specified does not exist at runtime, the runtime will throw a* `Microsoft.CSharp.RuntimeBinder.RuntimeBinderException` *exception.*

  If an attempt to invoke a member at execution time does occur, the runtime will verify that in fact the member call is valid (that the

signatures are type-compatible in the case of reflection, for example).
If the method signatures are not compatible, the runtime will throw
a `Microsoft.CSharp.RuntimeBinder.RuntimeBinderException`.

- `dynamic` *with reflection does not support extension methods.*

  Just like with reflection using `System.Type`, reflection using `dy-`
  `namic` does not support extension methods. Invocation of extension
  methods is still available on the implementing type (`System.Linq.`
  `Enumerable`, for example), just not on the extended type directly.

- *At its core,* `dynamic` *is a* `System.Object`.

  Given that any object will successfully convert to `dynamic` and
  `dynamic` may be explicitly converted to a different object type,
  `dynamic` behaves like `System.Object`. Like `System.Object`, it even
  returns `null` for its default value (`default(dynamic)`), indicating it is
  a reference type. The special dynamic behavior of `dynamic` that distinguishes it from a `System.Object` appears only at compile time.

■ ADVANCED TOPIC

`dynamic` **Uncovered**

ILDASM reveals that within the CIL, the `dynamic` type is actually a `Sys-`
`tem.Object`. In fact, without any invocations, declaration of the `dynamic`
type is indistinguishable from `System.Object`. However, the difference is
apparent when invoking a member. In order to invoke the member, the
compiler declares a variable of type `System.Runtime.CompilerServices.`
`CallSite<T>`. T varies based on the member signature, but something
simple such as the invocation of `ToString()` would require instantiation of the following type: `CallSite<Func<CallSite, object, string>>`,
and a method call with parameters of `CallSite site, object dynamic-`
`Target`, and `string result`. `site` is the call site itself, `dynamicTarget` is
the `object` on which the method call is invoked, and `result` is the underlying return value from the `ToString()` method call. Rather than
instantiate `CallSite<Func<CallSite _site, object dynamicTarget,`
`string result>>` directly, there is a `Create()` factory method for instantiating
it. (`Create()` takes a parameter of type `Microsoft.CSharp.RuntimeBinder`
`.CSharpConvertBinder`.) Given an instance of the `CallSite<T>`, the final
step involves a call to `CallSite<T>.Target()` to invoke the actual member.

Under the covers at execution time, the framework uses reflection to look up members and to verify that the signatures match. Next, the runtime builds an expression tree that represents the dynamic expression as defined by the call site. Once the expression tree is compiled we have a CIL method body that is similar to what the compiler would have generated had the call not been dynamic. This CIL code is then cached in the call site and the invocation occurs using a delegate invoke. Since the CIL is now cached at the call site, the next invocation doesn't require all the reflection and compilation overhead again.

Why Dynamic Binding?

In addition to reflection, we can define custom types to invoke dynamically. Consider using dynamic invocation to retrieve the values of an XML element, for example. Rather than using the strongly typed syntax of Listing 17.30, using dynamic invocation we could call person.FirstName and person.LastName.

LISTING 17.30: Runtime Binding to XML Elements without dynamic

```
using System;
using System.Xml.Linq;

// ...
XElement person = XElement.Parse(
    @"<Person>
        <FirstName>Inigo</FirstName>
        <LastName>Montoya</LastName>
</Person>");

Console.WriteLine("{0} {1}",
    person.Descendants("FirstName").FirstOrDefault().Value,
    person.Descendants("LastName").FirstOrDefault().Value);
    // ...
```

Although the code in Listing 17.30 is not overly complex, compare it to Listing 17.31—an alternative approach that uses a dynamically typed object.

LISTING 17.31: Runtime Binding to XML Elements with dynamic

```
using System;

// ...
dynamic person = DynamicXml.Parse(
```

```
@"<Person>
    <FirstName>Inigo</FirstName>
    <LastName>Montoya</LastName>
</Person>");

Console.WriteLine("{0} {1}",
    person.FirstName, person.LastName);
// ...
```

The advantages are clear, but does that mean dynamic programming is preferable to static compilation?

Static Compilation versus Dynamic Programming

In Listing 17.31, we have the same functionality as in Listing 17.30, but there is one very important difference. Listing 17.30 is entirely statically typed. This means that at compile time, all types and their member signatures are verified. Method names are required to match, and all parameters are checked for type compatibility. This is a key feature of C# and something we have highlighted throughout the book.

In contrast, Listing 17.31 has virtually no statically typed code; the variable person is instead dynamic. As a result, there is no compile-time verification that person has a FirstName or LastName property, or any other members, for that matter. Furthermore, when coding within an IDE, there is no IntelliSense identifying any members on person.

The loss of typing would seem to result in a significant decrease in functionality. Why is such a possibility even available in C#—a functionality that was added in C# 4.0, in fact? Let's examine Listing 17.31 again. Notice the call to retrieve the "FirstName" element: Element.Descendants("LastName").FirstOrDefault().Value. The listing uses a string ("LastName") to identify the element name. However, there is no compile-time verification that the string is correct. If the casing was inconsistent with the element name or if there was a space, the compile would still succeed, even though a NullReferenceException would occur with the call to the Value property. Furthermore, the compiler makes no verification that the "FirstName" element even exists, and if it doesn't, we would also get the NullReferenceException. In other words, in spite of all the type-safety advantages, type safety doesn't offer much advantage to accessing the dynamic data stored within the XML element.

Listing 17.31 is no better than Listing 17.30 when it comes to compile-time verification of the element retrieval. If there is a case mismatch or if the FirstName element didn't exist, there would still be an exception.[1] However, compare the call to access the first name in Listing 17.31 (person.FirstName) with the call in Listing 17.30. The call in the latter listing is undoubtedly significantly simpler. In summary, there are situations where type safety doesn't—and likely can't—make certain checks. And in such cases, being able to make a dynamic call that is only runtime-verified rather than also compile-time-verified is significantly more readable and succinct. Obviously, if compile-time verification is possible, statically typed programming is preferred because readable and succinct APIs can accompany it. However, in the cases where it isn't effective, C# 4.0 enables simpler code rather than the purity of type safety.

Implementing a Custom Dynamic Object

Listing 17.31 included a method call to DynamicXml.Parse(...) that was essentially a factory method call for DynamicXml—a custom type rather than one built into the CLR Framework. However, DynamicXml doesn't implement a FirstName or LastName property. To do so would break the dynamic support for retrieving data from the XML file at execution time, rather than compile-time-based implementation of the XML elements. In other words, DynamicXml does not use reflection for accessing its members, but rather it dynamically binds to the values based on the XML content.

The key to defining a custom dynamic type is implementation of the System.Dynamic.IDynamicMetaObjectProvider interface. Rather than implementing the interface from scratch, however, the preferred approach is to derive the custom dynamic type from System.Dynamic.DynamicObject. This provides default implementation for a host of members and allows you to override the ones that don't fit. Listing 17.32 shows the full implementation.

LISTING 17.32: Implementing a Custom Dynamic Object

```
using System;
using System.Dynamic;
using System.Xml.Linq;


public class DynamicXml : DynamicObject
```

---

1. You cannot use a space in the FirstName property call, but if XML supported spaces in element names, this would be a potential disadvantage, so let's ignore this fact.

```csharp
{
    private XElement Element { get; set; }

    public DynamicXml(System.Xml.Linq.XElement element)
    {
        Element = element;
    }

    public static DynamicXml Parse(string text)
    {
        return new DynamicXml(XElement.Parse(text));
    }

    public override bool TryGetMember(
        GetMemberBinder binder, out object result)
    {
        bool success = false;
        result = null;
        XElement firstDescendant =
            Element.Descendants(binder.Name).FirstOrDefault();
        if (firstDescendant != null)
        {
            if (firstDescendant.Descendants().Count() > 0)
            {
                result = new DynamicXml(firstDescendant);
            }
            else
            {
                result = firstDescendant.Value;
            }
            success = true;
        }
        return success;
    }

    public override bool TrySetMember(
        SetMemberBinder binder, object value)
    {
        bool success = false;
        XElement firstDescendant =
            Element.Descendants(binder.Name).FirstOrDefault();
        if (firstDescendant != null)
        {
            if (value.GetType() == typeof(XElement))
            {
                firstDescendant.ReplaceWith(value);
            }
            else
            {
                firstDescendant.Value = value.ToString();
            }
            success = true;
        }
```

```
        return success;
    }
}
```

The key dynamic implementation methods for this use case are TryGetMember() and TrySetMember() (assuming you also want to assign the elements as well). Only these two method implementations are necessary to support the invocation of the dynamic getter and setter properties. Furthermore, the implementations are straightforward. First, they examine the contained XElement, looking for an element with the same name as the binder.Name—the name of the member invoked. If a corresponding XML element exists, the value is retrieved (or set). The return value is set to true if the element exists and false if it doesn't. Automatically, a return value of false will cause the runtime to throw a Microsoft.CSharp.RuntimeBinder.RuntimeBinderException at the call site of the dynamic member invocation.

System.Dynamic.DynamicObject supports additional virtual methods if additional dynamic invocations are required. Listing 17.33 shows the list of all the overridable members.

LISTING 17.33: Overridable Members on System.Dynamic.DynamicObject

```csharp
using System.Dynamic;

public class DynamicObject : IDynamicMetaObjectProvider
{
    protected DynamicObject();

    public virtual IEnumerable<string> GetDynamicMemberNames();
    public virtual DynamicMetaObject GetMetaObject(
        Expression parameter);
    public virtual bool TryBinaryOperation(
        BinaryOperationBinder binder, object arg,
            out object result);
    public virtual bool TryConvert(
        ConvertBinder binder, out object result);
    public virtual bool TryCreateInstance(
        CreateInstanceBinder binder, object[] args,
            out object result);
    public virtual bool TryDeleteIndex(
        DeleteIndexBinder binder, object[] indexes);
    public virtual bool TryDeleteMember(
        DeleteMemberBinder binder);
    public virtual bool TryGetIndex(
        GetIndexBinder binder, object[] indexes,
            out object result);
```

```
public virtual bool TryGetMember(
    GetMemberBinder binder, out object result);
public virtual bool TryInvoke(
    InvokeBinder binder, object[] args, out object result);
public virtual bool TryInvokeMember(
    InvokeMemberBinder binder, object[] args,
        out object result);
public virtual bool TrySetIndex(
    SetIndexBinder binder, object[] indexes, object value);
public virtual bool TrySetMember(
    SetMemberBinder binder, object value);
public virtual bool TryUnaryOperation(
    UnaryOperationBinder binder, out object result);
}
```

As Listing 17.33 shows, there are member implementations for every-thing—from casts and various operations, through to index invocations. In addition, there is a method for retrieving all the possible member names: GetDynamicMemberNames().

SUMMARY

This chapter discussed how to use reflection to read the metadata that is compiled into the CIL. Using reflection, you saw how to provide a late binding in which the code to call is defined at execution time rather than at compile time. Although reflection is entirely feasible for deploying a dynamic system, it is considerably slower than statically linked (compile-time), defined code. This tends to make it more prevalent and useful in development tools.

Reflection also enables the retrieval of additional metadata decorating various constructs in the form of attributes. Typically, custom attributes are sought using reflection. It is possible to define your own custom at-tributes that insert additional metadata of your own choosing into the CIL. At runtime, it is then possible to retrieve this metadata and use it within the programming logic.

Many view attributes as a precursor to a concept known as aspect-oriented programming, in which you add functionality through constructs such as attributes instead of manually implementing the functionality wher-ever it is needed. It will take some time before you see true aspects within C# (if ever); however, attributes provide a clear steppingstone in that direction, without forcing a significant risk to the stability of the language.

Finally, the chapter included a C# 4.0 introduced feature—dynamic programming using the new type `dynamic`. This section included a discussion of why static binding, although preferred when the API is strongly typed, has limitations when working with dynamic data.

The next chapter looks at multithreading, where attributes are used for synchronization.

■ 18 ■
Multithreading

TWO SIGNIFICANT TRENDS OF THE past decade have had an enormous effect on the field of software development. First, the continued decrease in the cost of performing computations is no longer driven by increases in clock speed and transistor density, as illustrated by Figure 18.1. Rather, the cost of computation is now falling because it is economical to make hardware that has multiple CPUs.

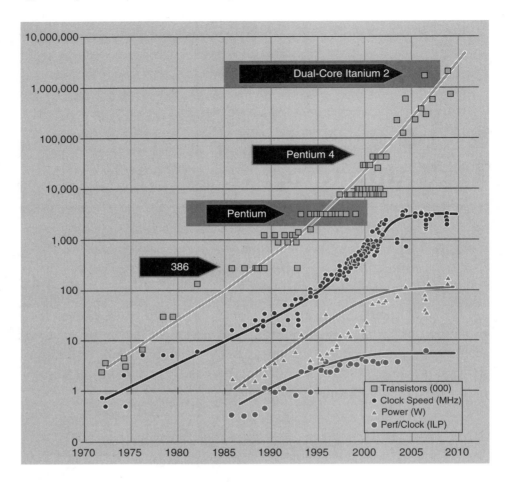

FIGURE 18.1: Clock Speeds over Time (Graph compiled by Herb Sutter. Used with permission. Original at www.gotw.ca.)

Second, computations now routinely involve enormous **latency.** Latency is, simply put, the amount of time required to obtain a desired result. There are two principal causes of latency. **Processor-bound latency** occurs when the computational task is complex; if a computation requires performing 12 billion arithmetic operations and the total processing power available is only 6 billion operations per second, at least two seconds of processor-bound latency will be incurred between asking for the result and obtaining it. **I/O-bound latency,** by contrast, is latency incurred by the need to obtain data from an external source such as a disk drive, Web server, and so on. Any computation that requires fetching data from a Web server physically located far from the client machine will incur latency equivalent to millions of processor cycles.

These two trends together create an enormous challenge for modern software developers. Given that machines have more computing power than ever, how are we to make effective use of that power to deliver results to the user quickly, and without compromising on the user experience? How do we avoid creating frustrating user interfaces that freeze up when a high-latency operation is triggered? Moreover, how do we go about splitting CPU-bound work among multiple processors to decrease the time required for the computation?

The standard technique for engineering software that keeps the user interface responsive and CPU utilization high is to write **multithreaded** programs that do multiple computations "in parallel." Unfortunately, multithreading logic is notoriously difficult to get right; we'll spend the next two chapters exploring what makes multithreading difficult, and how to use higher-level abstractions and new language features to ease that burden.

The higher-level abstractions we'll discuss are, first, the two principal components of the Parallel Extensions library that was released with .NET 4.0[1] —the **Task Parallel Library (TPL)** and **Parallel LINQ (PLINQ)**—and second, the **Task-based Asynchronous Pattern (TAP)** and its accompanying language support in C# 5.0. Though we strongly encourage you to use these higher-level abstractions, we will also cover some of the lower-level threading APIs from previous versions of the .NET runtime in this chapter, and in Appendixes C and D. In addition, the multithreading chapters from preceding editions of this book (*Essential C# 3.0* and *Essential C# 4.0*) are available for download at http://IntelliTect.com/EssentialCSharp. This is so that if you want to fully understand the resources from multithreaded programming without the later features, you still have access to that material.

We'll start this chapter with a few beginner topics in case you are new to multithreading. Then we'll briefly discuss "traditional" thread manipulation without using the Parallel Extensions libraries to ensure that you have a basic understanding of thread manipulation; the following chapter goes into more details on that topic. We'll then spend most of this chapter covering the TPL, TAP, and PLINQ, in that order.

---

1. These libraries are available in .NET 3.5 by downloading the Reactive Extensions library for .NET 3.5, but this is not officially supported.

Multithreading Basics

▪■ BEGINNER TOPIC

Multithreading Jargon

There is a lot of confusing jargon associated with multithreading, so let's define a few terms.

A **CPU** (central processing unit) or **core**[2] is the unit of hardware that actually executes a given program. Every machine has at least one CPU, though today multiple CPU machines are common. Many modern CPUs support **simultaneous multithreading** (which Intel trademarks as **Hyper-Threading**), a mode where a single CPU can appear as multiple "virtual" CPUs.

A **process** is a currently executing instance of a given program; the fundamental purpose of the operating system is to manage processes. Each process contains one or more threads. A process is represented by an instance of the `Process` class in the `System.Diagnostics` namespace.

C# programming at the level of statements and expressions is fundamentally about describing **flow of control**, and thus far in this book we've made the implicit assumption that a given program only has a single "point of control." You can imagine the point of control as being a cursor that enters the text of your program at the Main method when you start it up, and then moves around the program as the various conditions, loops, method calls, and so on, are executed. A **thread** is this point of control. A thread is represented by an instance of the `System.Threading.Thread` class and the API for manipulating a `Thread` is in the same `System.Threading` namespace.

A **single-threaded** program is one in which there is only one thread in the process. A **multithreaded** program has two or more threads in the process.

A piece of code is said to be **thread safe** if it behaves correctly when used in a multithreaded program. The **threading model** of a piece of code is the set of requirements that the code places upon its caller in exchange for guaranteeing thread safety. (For example, the threading model of many classes

---

2. Technically we ought to say that "CPU" always refers to the physical chip and "core" may refer to a physical or virtual CPU. This distinction is unimportant for the purposes of this book and we will therefore use the terms interchangeably.

is "static methods may be called from any thread but instance methods may only be called from the thread that allocated the instance.")

A **task** is a unit of potentially high-latency work that produces a resultant value or desired side effect. The distinction between tasks and threads is as follows: A task represents a job that needs to be performed, whereas a thread represents the worker that does the job. A task is useful only for its side effects and is represented by an instance of the Task class. A task used to produce a value of a given type is represented by the Task<T> class, which derives from the nongeneric Task type. These can be found in the System.Threading.Tasks namespace.

A **thread pool** is a collection of threads, and logic for determining how to assign work to those threads. When your program has a task to perform, it can delegate a worker thread from the pool, assign the thread to perform the task, and then de-allocate it when the work completes, thereby making it available the next time additional work is requested.

■ **BEGINNER TOPIC**

The Why and How of Multithreading

There are two principal scenarios for multithreading: enabling multitasking and dealing with latency.

Users think nothing of running dozens of processes at the same time. They might have presentations and spreadsheets open for editing while at the same time they are browsing documents on the Internet, listening to music, receiving instant messages and email arrival notifications, and watching the little clock in the corner. Each of these processes has to continue to do its job even though it is not the only task the machine has to attend to. This kind of multitasking is usually implemented at the process level, but there are situations in which you want to do this sort of multitasking within a single process.

For the purposes of this book, however, we will mostly be considering multithreading as a technique for dealing with latency. For example, in order to import a large file while simultaneously allowing a user to click Cancel, a developer creates an additional thread to perform the import. By performing the import on a different thread, the user can request cancellation instead of freezing the user interface until the import completes.

If there are enough cores that each thread can be assigned a core, each thread essentially gets its own little machine. However, more often than not there are more threads than cores as even the relatively common multicore machines of today still have only a handful of cores while each process could quite possibly run dozens of threads.

To overcome the discrepancy of numerous threads to only a handful of cores, an operating system simulates multiple threads running concurrently by **time slicing.** The operating system switches execution from one thread to the next so quickly that it appears the threads are executing simultaneously. The period of time that the processor executes a particular thread before switching to another is the **time slice** or **quantum.** The act of changing which thread is executing in a given core is called a **context switch.**

The effect is similar to that of a fiber optic telephone line in which the fiber optic line represents the processor and each conversation represents a thread. A (single-mode) fiber optic telephone line can send only one signal at a time, but many people can hold simultaneous conversations over the line. The fiber optic channel is fast enough to switch between conversations so quickly that each conversation appears uninterrupted. Similarly, each thread of a multithreaded process appears to run continuously with other threads.

If two operations are running "in parallel," via either true multicore parallelism or simulated parallelism using time slicing, they are said to be **concurrent.** To implement such concurrency you invoke it **asynchronously,** such that both the execution and completion of the invoked operation are separate from the control flow that invoked it. Concurrency, therefore, occurs when work dispatched asynchronously executes in parallel with the current control flow. **Parallel programming** is the act of taking a single problem and splitting it into pieces, whereby you **asynchronously** initiate the process of each piece such that the pieces can all be processed concurrently.

■ BEGINNER TOPIC

Performance Considerations

A thread that is servicing an I/O bound operation can essentially be ignored by the operating system until the result is available from the I/O subsystem; switching away from an I/O bound thread to a processor-bound thread results in more efficient processor utilization because the CPU is not idle while waiting for the I/O operation to complete.

However, context switching is not free; the current internal state of the CPU must be saved to memory, and the state associated with the new thread must be loaded. If there are too many threads, the switching overhead can begin to noticeably affect performance. Adding more threads will likely decrease performance further, to the point where the processor spends more time switching from one thread to another than it does accomplishing the work of each thread.

Even if we ignore the cost of context switching, time slicing itself can have a huge impact on performance. Suppose, for example, that you have two processor-bound high-latency tasks, each working out the average of two lists of 1 billion numbers each. Suppose the processor can perform 1 billion operations per second. If the two tasks are each associated with a thread, and the two threads each have their own core, obviously we can get both results in one second.

If, however, we have a single processor that the two threads share, time slicing will perform a few hundred thousand operations on one thread, then switch to the other thread, then switch back, and so on. Each task will consume a total of one second of processor time, and the results of both will therefore be available after two seconds, leading to an average completion time of two seconds. (Again, we are ignoring the cost of context switching.)

If we assigned those two tasks to a single thread that performed the first task and did not even start the second until after the first was completed, the result of the first task would be obtained in one second and the result of the subsequent task would be obtained one second after that, leading to an average time of 1.5 seconds (a task completes in either 1 or 2 seconds and, therefore, on average completes in 1.5 seconds).

Guidelines

DO NOT fall into the common error of believing that more threads always makes code faster.

DO carefully measure performance when attempting to speed up processor-bound problems through multithreading.

■ BEGINNER TOPIC

Threading Problems

We've said several times that writing multithreaded programs is complex and difficult, but we have not said why. In a nutshell, the problem is that many of our reasonable assumptions that are true of single-threaded programs are violated in multithreaded programs. The issues include a lack of atomicity, race conditions, complex memory models, and deadlocks.

Most Operations Are Not Atomic

An atomic operation is one that always is observed to be either not started or already completed. Its state is never externally visible as "in progress." Consider, for example, this code fragment:

```
if (bankAccounts.Checking.Balance >= 1000.00m)
{
  bankAccounts.Checking.Balance -= 1000.00m;
  bankAccounts.Savings.Balance += 1000.00m;
}
```

This operation—checking for available funds, and then conditionally debiting one account and crediting another—needs to be atomic. In other words, in order for it to be correctly executed, we must ensure that there is never a moment when the operation can be observed to be partially completed. Imagine, for example, that two threads are running in this code concurrently. It is possible that both threads verify that there are sufficient funds in the account, and then both threads do a transfer of funds, even if there are only sufficient funds in the account to do the transfer once. And, in fact, the situation is considerably worse as there are *no* operations in this code fragment that are atomic! Even operations like compound addition/subtraction or reading and writing a property of decimal type are non-atomic operations in C#. As such, they can all be observed to be "partially complete" in multithreaded scenarios—only partially incremented or decremented. The observation of inconsistent state due to partially completed nonatomic operations is a special case of a more general problem, called a race condition.

Uncertainty Caused by Race Conditions

As we discussed above, concurrency is often simulated by time slicing. In the absence of special control flow structures that we will discuss in the next chapter in detail, the operating system can switch contexts between any two threads at any time of its choosing. This means that when two threads are accessing the same object, which thread "wins the race" and gets to run first is unpredictable. If there are two threads running in the code fragment above, for example, it is possible that one thread wins the race and gets all the way to the end before the second thread gets a chance to run. It is also possible that the context switch happens after the first thread does the balance check, and the second thread then wins the race to get all the way to the end first.

The behavior of code that contains race conditions depends on the timing of context switches. This dependency introduces uncertainty concerning program execution. The order in which one instruction will execute relative to an instruction in a different thread is unknown. The worst of it is that often code containing race conditions will behave correctly 99.9 percent of the time, and then one time in a thousand a different thread wins the race due to an accident of timing. This unpredictability is what makes multithreaded programming so difficult.

Because such race conditions are difficult to replicate in the laboratory, much of the quality assurance of multithreaded code depends on long-running stress tests, specially designed code analysis tools, and a significant investment in code analysis and code review by experts.

The following chapter is about techniques for dealing with race conditions.

Memory Models Are Complex

The existence of race conditions, where two points of control can "race" through a piece of code at unpredictable and inconsistent speeds, is bad enough, but it gets worse. Consider two threads that are running on two different processors, but are accessing the same fields of some object. Modern processors do not actually access main memory every time you use a variable. Rather, they make a local copy in special "cache" memory on the processor; these caches are then periodically synchronized with main memory. This means that two threads that read and write the same location on two different processors can in fact be failing to observe each other's updates to that memory, or observing inconsistent results. Essentially what we have here is a race condition that depends upon when processors choose to synchronize their caches.

Locking Leads to Deadlocks

Clearly there must exist mechanisms to make nonatomic operations into atomic operations, to instruct the operating system to schedule threads so as to avoid races, and to ensure that processor caches are synchronized when necessary. The primary mechanism used to solve all these problems in C# programs is the `lock` statement. This statement allows the developer to identify a section of code as "critical" code that only one thread may be in at one time; if multiple threads try to enter the critical section, the operating system will suspend all but one. The operating system also ensures that processor caches are synchronized properly upon encountering a lock.

However, locks introduce problems of their own. Most notably, if the order of lock acquisition between threads varies, a **deadlock** could occur such that threads freeze, each waiting for the other to release its lock.

For example:

Time

THREAD A	THREAD B
Acquires a lock on a	Acquires a lock on b
Requests a lock on b	Requests a lock on a
Deadlocks, waiting for b	Deadlocks, waiting for a

At this point, each thread is waiting on the other thread before proceeding, so each thread is blocked, leading to an overall deadlock in the execution of that code.

We discuss various locking techniques in detail in Chapter 19.

Guidelines

DO NOT make an unwarranted assumption that any operation that is atomic in regular code will be atomic in multithreaded code.

DO NOT assume that all threads will observe all side effects of operations on shared memory in a consistent order.

DO ensure that code that concurrently holds multiple locks always acquires them in the same order.

AVOID all "race conditions," that is, conditions where program behavior depends on how the operating system chooses to schedule threads.

Working with System.Threading

The Parallel Extensions library is extraordinarily useful because it allows you to manipulate a higher-level abstraction, the task, rather than working directly with threads. However, you might need to work with code written before the TPL and PLINQ were available (prior to .NET 4.0), or you might have a programming problem not directly addressed by them. In this section, we briefly cover some of the basic underlying APIs for directly manipulating threads.

Asynchronous Operations with System.Threading.Thread

The operating system implements threads and provides various unmanaged APIs to create and manage those threads. The CLR wraps these unmanaged threads and exposes them in managed code via the System.Threading.Thread class, an instance of which represents a "point of control" in the program. As mentioned above, you can think of a thread as a "worker" that independently follows the instructions that make up your program.

Listing 18.1 provides an example. The independent point of control is represented by an instance of Thread that runs concurrently. A thread needs to know what code to run when it starts up, so its constructor takes a delegate that refers to the code that is to be executed. In this case we convert a method group, DoWork, to the appropriate delegate type, ThreadStart. We then start the thread running by calling Start(). While the new thread is running, the main thread attempts to print 10,000 hyphens to the console. We instruct the main thread to then wait for the worker thread to complete its work by calling Join(). The result is shown in Output 18.1.

LISTING 18.1: **Starting a Method Using** System.Threading.Thread

```csharp
using System;
using System.Threading;

public class RunningASeparateThread
{
  public const int Repetitions = 1000;

  public static void Main()
  {
    ThreadStart threadStart = DoWork;
    Thread thread = new Thread(threadStart);
    thread.Start();
```

```
    for(int count = 0; count < Repetitions; count++)
    {
        Console.Write('-');
    }
    thread.Join();
}

public static void DoWork()
{
    for(int count = 0; count < Repetitions; count++)
    {
        Console.Write('+');
    }
}
}
}
```

OUTPUT 18.1

As you can see, the threads appear to be taking turns executing, each printing out a few hundred characters before the context switches. The two loops are running "in parallel," rather than the first one running to completion before the second one begins, as it would if the delegate had been executed synchronously.

In order for code to run under the context of a different thread, you need a delegate of type ThreadStart or ParameterizedThreadStart to identify the code to execute. (The latter allows for a single parameter of type object; both are found in the System.Threading namespace.) Given a Thread instance created using the thread-start delegate constructor, you can start the thread executing with a call to thread.Start(). (Listing 18.1 creates a variable of type ThreadStart explicitly to show the delegate type in the source code. The method group DoWork could have been passed directly to the thread constructor.) The call to Thread.Start() tells the operating system to begin concurrent execution of the new thread; control on the main thread immediately returns from the call and executes the for loop in the Main() method. The threads are now independent and neither waits for the other until the call to Join().

Thread Management

Threads include a number of methods and properties for managing their execution. Here are some of the basic ones.

- As we saw in Listing 18.1, you can cause one thread to wait for another with Join(). This tells the operating system to suspend execution of the current thread until the other thread is terminated. The Join() method is overloaded to take either an int or a TimeSpan to support a maximum time to wait for thread completion before continuing execution.

- By default, a new thread is a "foreground" thread; the operating system will terminate a process when all its foreground threads are complete. You can mark a thread as a "background" thread by setting the IsBackground property to true. The operating system will then allow the process to be terminated even if the background thread is still running. However, it is still a good idea to ensure that all threads are not aborted and instead to exit cleanly before the process exits; see the section on thread aborting below for more details.

- Every thread has an associated priority, which you can change by setting the Priority property to a new ThreadPriority enum value. The possible values are Lowest, BelowNormal, Normal, AboveNormal, and Highest. The operating system prefers to schedule time slices to higher-priority threads. Be careful; by setting priorities incorrectly you can end up with "starvation" situations where one high-priority thread prevents many low-priority threads from ever running.

- If you want to simply know whether a thread is still "alive" or has finished all of its work, you can use the Boolean IsAlive property. A more informative picture of a thread's state is accessible through the ThreadState property. The ThreadState enum values are Aborted, AbortRequested, Background, Running, Stopped, StopRequested, Suspended, SuspendRequested, Unstarted, and WaitSleepJoin. These are flags; some of these values can be combined.

There are two commonly used, and commonly abused, methods for controlling threads that deserve to be called out in their own sections: Sleep() and Abort().

Do Not Put Threads to Sleep in Production Code

The static Thread.Sleep() method puts the current thread to sleep, essentially telling the operating system to not schedule any time slices to this thread until the given amount of time has passed. A single parameter, either a number of milliseconds or a TimeSpan, specifies how long the operating system will wait before continuing execution. While it is waiting, the operating system will of course schedule time slices for any other threads that might be waiting their turn to execute. This might sound like a sensible thing to do, but it is a "bad code smell" that indicates that the design of the program could probably be better thought through.

Threads are often put to sleep to try to synchronize a thread with some event in time. However, the operating system does not guarantee any level of precision in its timing. That is, if you say "put me to sleep for 123 milliseconds," the operating system will put the thread to sleep for *at least* 123 milliseconds, and possibly much longer. The actual amount of time between the thread going to sleep and it waking up again is not deterministic and can be arbitrarily long. Do not attempt to use Thread.Sleep() as a high-precision timer, because it is not.

Worse, Thread.Sleep() is often used as a "poor man's synchronization system." That is, if you have some unit of asynchronous work, and the current thread cannot proceed until that work is done, you might be tempted to put the thread to sleep for much longer than you think the asynchronous work will take, in the hopes that it will be finished when the current thread wakes up. This is a bad idea; asynchronous work by its nature can take longer than you think. Use proper thread synchronization mechanisms, described in the next chapter, to synchronize threads. (We'll give an example of this sort of abuse in Listing 18.2, below.)

Putting a thread to sleep is also a bad programming practice because it means that the sleeping thread is, obviously, unresponsive to attempts to run code on it. If you put the main thread of a Windows application to sleep, that thread will no longer be processing messages from the user interface, and will therefore appear to be hung.

More generally, putting a thread to sleep is a bad programming practice because the whole point of allocating an expensive resource like a thread is to get work out of that resource. You wouldn't pay an employee to sleep, so do not pay the price of allocating an expensive thread only to put it to sleep for millions or billions of processor cycles.

That said, there are some valid uses of `Thread.Sleep()`. First, putting a thread to sleep with a time delay of zero tells the operating system "the current thread is politely giving up the rest of its quantum to another thread if there is one that can use it." The polite thread will then be scheduled normally, without any further delay. Second, `Thread.Sleep()` is commonly used in test code to simulate a thread that is working on some high-latency operation without actually having to burn a processor doing some pointless arithmetic. Other uses in production code should be reviewed carefully to ensure that there is not a better way to obtain the desired effect.

In task-based asynchronous programming in C# 5 you can use the `await` operator on the result of the `Task.Delay()` method to introduce an asynchronous delay without blocking the current thread. See the Timers section in the next chapter for further detail.

Guidelines

AVOID calling `Thread.Sleep()` in production code.

Do Not Abort Threads in Production Code

The `Thread` object has an `Abort()` method which, when executed, attempts to destroy the thread. It does so by causing the runtime to throw a `ThreadAbortException` in the thread; this exception can be caught, but even if it is caught and ignored, it is automatically rethrown to try to ensure that the thread is in fact destroyed. There are many reasons why it is a very bad idea to attempt to abort a thread. Here are some of them.

- The method only promises to *try* to abort the thread; there is no guarantee that it will succeed. For example, the runtime will not attempt to cause a `ThreadAbortException` if the point of control of the thread is currently inside a `finally` block (because critical cleanup code could be running right now and should not be interrupted) or is in unmanaged code (because doing so could corrupt the CLR itself). Rather, the CLR defers throwing the exception until control leaves the `finally` block or returns to managed code. But there is no guarantee that this ever happens. The thread being aborted might contain an infinite loop inside a `finally` block. (Ironically, the fact that the thread has an infinite loop might be the reason you are attempting to abort it in the first place.)

- The aborted thread might be in critical code protected by a `lock` statement. (See the next chapter for details.) Unlike a `finally`, a `lock` will not prevent the exception. The critical code will be interrupted halfway through by the exception, and the `lock` object will be automatically released, allowing other code that is waiting on the `lock` object to enter the critical section and observe the state of the halfway-executed code. The whole point of locking is to prevent that scenario, and therefore, aborting a thread can transform what looks like thread-safe code into dangerously incorrect code.

- The CLR guarantees that its internal data structures will never be corrupted if a thread is aborted, but the BCL does not make this guarantee. Aborting a thread can leave any of your data structures or the BCL's data structures in an arbitrarily bad state if the exception is thrown at the wrong time. Code running on other threads, or in the `finally` blocks of the aborted thread, can see this corrupted state and crash or behave badly.

In short, you should never abort a thread unless you are doing so as a last resort; ideally you should only abort a thread as part of a larger emergency shutdown whereby the entire AppDomain or the entire process is being destroyed. Fortunately, task-based asynchrony uses a more robust and safe cooperative cancellation pattern to terminate a "thread" whose results are no longer needed, as discussed in the next major section, Asynchronous Tasks.

> ### Guidelines
>
> **AVOID** aborting a thread in production code; doing so has unpredictable results and can destabilize a program.

Thread Pooling

As we discussed earlier, in the Beginner Topic titled Performance Considerations, it is possible for an excess of threads to negatively impact performance. Threads are expensive resources, thread context switching is not free, and running two jobs in simulated parallelism via time slicing can be hugely slower than running them one after the other.

To mitigate these problems, the BCL provides a thread pool. Instead of allocating threads directly, you can tell the thread pool what work you want to perform. When the work is finished, rather than the thread terminating and being destroyed, it is returned to the pool, saving on the cost of allocating a new thread when more work comes along. Listing 18.2 shows how to do the same thing as Listing 18.1, but this time with a pooled thread.

LISTING 18.2: Using `ThreadPool` Instead of Instantiating Threads Explicitly

```csharp
using System;
using System.Threading;

public class Program
{
  public const int Repetitions = 1000;
  public static void Main()
  {
      ThreadPool.QueueUserWorkItem(DoWork, '+');

      for(int count = 0; count < Repetitions; count++)
      {
          Console.Write('-');
      }

      // Pause until the thread completes
      // This is for illustrative purposes; do not
      // use Thread.Sleep for synchronization in
      // production code.
      Thread.Sleep(1000);
```

```
    }
    public static void DoWork(object state)
    {
        for(int count = 0; count < Repetitions; count++)
        {
            Console.Write(state);
        }
    }
}
```

The output is similar to Output 18.1, an intermingling of periods and hyphens. If we had a lot of different jobs to perform asynchronously, this pooling technique would provide more efficient execution on single- and multiprocessor computers. The efficiency is achieved by reusing threads over and over, rather than reconstructing them for every asynchronous call. Unfortunately, thread pool use is not without its pitfalls: There are still performance and synchronization problems to consider when using a thread pool.

In order to make efficient use of processors, the thread pool assumes that all the work you schedule on the thread pool will finish in a timely manner so that the thread can be returned to the thread pool and reused by another task. The thread pool also assumes that all the work will be relatively short-running (that is, consuming milliseconds or seconds of processor time, not hours or days). By making this assumption, it can ensure that each processor is working full out on a task, and not inefficiently time slicing multiple tasks, as described in the Beginner Topic on performance. The thread pool attempts to prevent excessive time slicing by ensuring that thread creation is "throttled" so that no one processor is "oversubscribed" with too many threads. But that then means that consuming all threads within the pool can delay execution of queued-up work. If all the threads in the pool are consumed by long-running or I/O bound work, the queued-up work will be delayed.

Unlike Thread and Task, which are objects that you can manipulate directly, the thread pool does not provide a reference to the thread used to execute a given piece of work. This prevents the calling thread from synchronizing with, or controlling, the worker thread via the thread management functions described earlier in the chapter. In Listing 18.2 we use the "poor man's synchronization" that we earlier discouraged; this would be a bad idea in production code because we do not actually know how long the work will take to complete.

In short, the thread pool does its job well, but that job does not include providing services to deal with long-running jobs or jobs that need to be synchronized with the main thread or with one another. What we really need to do is build a higher-level abstraction that can use threads and thread pools as an implementation detail; that abstraction is implemented by the Task Parallel Library, which is the topic of most of the rest of this chapter.

For more details on other techniques for managing worker threads that were commonly used prior to .NET 4, see Appendix D.

Guidelines

DO use the thread pool to efficiently assign processor time to processor-bound tasks.

AVOID allocating a pooled worker thread to a task that is I/O bound or long-running; use TPL instead.

Asynchronous Tasks

Multithreaded programming includes the following complexities.

1. *Monitoring an asynchronous operation state for completion:* This includes determining when an asynchronous operation has completed, preferably not by polling the thread's state or by blocking and waiting.

2. *Thread pooling:* This avoids the significant cost of starting and tearing down threads. In addition, thread pooling avoids the creation of too many threads, such that the system spends more time switching threads than running them.

3. *Avoiding deadlocks:* This involves preventing the occurrence of deadlocks while attempting to protect the data from simultaneous access by two different threads.

4. *Providing atomicity across operations and synchronizing data access:* Adding synchronization around groups of operations ensures that operations execute as a single unit and that they are appropriately interrupted by another thread. Locking is provided so that two different threads do not access the data simultaneously.

Furthermore, anytime a method is long-running, it is probable that multithreaded programming is going to be required—invoking the long-running method asynchronously. As developers write more multithreaded code, a common set of scenarios and programming patterns for handling those scenarios emerges.

C# 5.0 enhanced the programmability of one such pattern—TAP—by leveraging the TPL from .NET 4.0 and enhancing the C# language with new constructs to support it. This and the following section delve into the details of the TPL on its own and then the TPL with the async/await contextual keywords that simplify TAP programming. In the second half of Chapter 19 we consider several additional multithreading patterns that are important to be familiar with if the TPL and C# 5.0 are not available or you are programming against a non-TPL-based API.

From Thread to Task

Creating a thread is a relatively expensive operation, and each thread consumes a large amount (one megabyte, by default) of virtual memory. We saw earlier in this chapter that it is potentially more efficient to use a thread pool to allocate threads when needed, assign asynchronous work to the thread, run the work to completion, and then reuse the thread for subsequent asynchronous work, rather than destroying the thread when the work is complete and creating a new one later.

In .NET Framework 4, instead of creating an operating system thread each time asynchronous work is started, the TPL creates a Task and tells the **task scheduler** that there is asynchronous work to perform. There are many different strategies that a task scheduler might use, but by default the task scheduler requests a worker thread from the **thread pool.** The thread pool, as we've seen already, might decide that it is more efficient to run the task later, after some currently executing tasks have completed, or might decide to schedule the task's worker thread to a particular processor. The thread pool determines whether it is more efficient to create an entirely new thread or to reuse an existing thread that previously finished executing.

By abstracting the concept of asynchronous work into the Task object, the TPL provides an object that represents asynchronous work and provides an object-oriented API for interacting with that work. And by providing an object that represents the unit of work, the TPL enables programmatically building up workflows by composing small tasks into larger ones, as we'll see.

A task is an object that encapsulates work that executes asynchronously. This should sound familiar; a *delegate* is also an object that represents code. The difference between a task and a delegate is that delegates are **synchronous** and tasks are **asynchronous.** Executing a delegate, say, an Action, immediately transfers the point of control of the current thread to the delegate's code; control does not return to the caller until the delegate is finished. By contrast, starting a task almost immediately returns control to the caller, no matter how much work the task has to perform. The task executes asynchronously, typically on another thread (though, as we will see later in this chapter, it is in fact possible and even beneficial to execute tasks asynchronously with only one thread). A task essentially transforms a delegate from a synchronous to an asynchronous execution pattern.

Introducing Asynchronous Tasks

You know when a delegate is done executing on the current thread because the caller cannot do anything until the delegate is done. But how do you know when a task is done, and how do you get the result, if there is one? Consider the example of turning a synchronous delegate into an asynchronous task. We'll do the same thing we did with threads in Listing 18.1 and thread pools in Listing 18.2, but this time with tasks: The worker thread will write periods to the console while the main thread writes hyphens.

Starting the task obtains a new thread from the thread pool, creating a second "point of control," and executes the delegate on that thread. The point of control on the main thread continues normally after the call to start the task (Task.Run()). The results of Listing 18.3 will be almost identical to Output 18.1.

LISTING 18.3: Invoking an Asynchronous Task

```
using System;
using System.Threading.Tasks;

public class Program
{
  public static void Main()
  {
      const int Repetitions = 10000;
      // Use Task.Factory.StartNew<string>() for
      // TPL prior to .NET 4.5
      Task task = Task.Run(() =>
          {
              for(int count = 0;
                  count < Repetitions; count++)
```

```
        {
            Console.Write('-');
        }
    });
    for(int count = 0; count < Repetitions; count++)
    {
        Console.Write('+');
    }

    // Wait until the Task completes
    task.Wait();
    }
}
```

The code that is to run in a new thread is defined in the delegate (of type `Action` in this case) passed to the `Task.Run()` method. This delegate (in the form of a lambda expression) prints out dashes to the console repeatedly. The loop that follows the starting of the task is virtually identical, except that it displays periods.

Notice that following the call to `Task.Run()` the `Action` passed as the argument immediately starts executing. The `Task` is said to be "hot," meaning that it has already been triggered to start executing—as opposed to a "cold" task that needs to be explicitly started before the asynchronous work begins.

Although a `Task` can also be instantiated in a "cold" state via the `Task` constructor, doing so is generally only appropriate as an implementation detail internal to an API that returns an already running ("hot") `Task`, one triggered by a call to `Task.Start()`.

Notice that the exact state of a "hot" task is indeterminate immediately following the call to `Run()`. The state is instead determined by the operating system and whether it chooses to run the task's worker thread immediately or delay it until additional resources are available. In fact, it is possible that the hot task is already finished by the time the code on the calling thread gets its turn to execute again. The call to `Wait()` forces the main thread to wait until all the work assigned to the task has completed executing. This is analogous to calling `Join()` on the worker thread as we did in Listing 18.1.

In this scenario we have a single task, but of course it is possible for many tasks to be running asynchronously. It is common to have a set of tasks where you want to wait for all of them to complete, or for any one of them to complete, before continuing execution of the current thread. The `Task.WaitAll()` and `Task.WaitAny()` methods do so.

So far we've seen how a task can take an `Action` and run it asynchronously. What if the work executed in the task returns a result? We can use the `Task<T>` type to run a `Func<T>` asynchronously. When executing a delegate synchronously we know that control will not return until the result is available. When executing a `Task<T>` asynchronously we can poll it from one thread to see if it is done, and fetch the result when it is.[3] Listing 18.4 demonstrates how to do so in a console application. Note that this sample uses a `PiCalculator.Calculate()` method that we will delve into further in the section Executing Loop Iterations in Parallel.

LISTING 18.4: Polling a `Task<T>`

```csharp
using System;
using System.Threading.Tasks;
using AddisonWesley.Michaelis.EssentialCSharp.Shared;

public class Program
{
  public static void Main()
  {
      // Use Task.Factory.StartNew<string>() for
      // TPL prior to .NET 4.5
      Task<string> task =
          Task.Run<string>(
              () => PiCalculator.Calculate(100));

      foreach(
          char busySymbol in Utility.BusySymbols())
      {
          if(task.IsCompleted)
          {
              Console.Write('\b');
              break;
          }
          Console.Write(busySymbol);
      }

      Console.WriteLine();

      Console.WriteLine(task.Result);
```

---

3. Exercise caution when using this polling technique. When creating a task from a delegate, as we have here, the task will be scheduled to run on a worker thread from the thread pool. This means that the current thread will loop until the work is complete on the worker thread. This technique works, but it might consume CPU resources unnecessarily. This polling technique is dangerously broken if, instead of scheduling the task to run on a worker thread, you schedule the task to execute in the future on the current thread. Since the current thread is in a loop polling the task, it will loop forever because the task will not complete until the current thread exits the loop.

```
        System.Diagnostics.Trace.Assert(
            task.IsCompleted);
    }
}
```

```
public class PiCalculator
{
    public static string Calculate(int digits = 100)
    {
        \\ ...
    }
}
```

```
public class Utility
{
    public static IEnumerable<char> BusySymbols()
    {
        string busySymbols = @"-\|/-\|/";
        int next = 0;
        while(true)
        {
            yield return busySymbols[next];
            next = (next + 1) % busySymbols.Length;
            yield return '\b';
        }
    }
}
```

This listing shows that the data type of the task is Task<string>. The generic type includes a Result property from which to retrieve the value returned by the Func<string> that the Task<string> executes.

Note that in Listing 18.4 there is no call to Wait(). Instead, reading from the Result property automatically causes the current thread to wait until the result is available, if it isn't already; in this case we know that it will already be complete when the result is fetched.

In addition to the IsCompleted and Result properties on Task<T>, there are several others worth noting.

- The IsCompleted property is set to true when a task completes whether it completed normally or faulted (that is, ended because it threw an exception). More detailed information on the status of a task can be determined by reading the Status property, which returns a value of type TaskStatus. Possible values are Created, WaitingForActivation, WaitingToRun, Running, WaitingForChildrenToComplete, RanToCompletion, Canceled, and Faulted. IsCompleted is true whenever the Status is

RanToCompletion, Canceled, or Faulted. Note that, of course, if the task is running on another thread and you read the status as "Running," the status could change to "Completed" at any time, including immediately after you read the value of the property. The same is true of many other states—even Created could potentially change if a different thread starts it. Only RanToCompletion, Canceled, and Faulted can be considered final states that can no longer be transitioned.

- A task can be uniquely identified by the value of the Id property. The static Task.CurrentId property provides the identifier for the currently executing Task (that is, the task that is executing the Task.CurrentId call). These properties are especially useful when debugging.

- You can use the AsyncState to associate additional data with a task. For example, imagine a List<T> whose values will be computed by various tasks. Each task could contain the index of the value in the AsyncState property. This way, when the task completes, the code can index into the list using the AsyncState (first casting it to an int).[4]

There are other useful properties that we will discuss later in this chapter, in the section on task cancellation.

Task Continuation

We've talked several times about the "control flow" of a program without ever saying what the most fundamental nature of control flow is: **Control flow determines what happens next.** When you have a simple control flow like Console.WriteLine(x.ToString()); the control flow tells you that when ToString completes normally, the next thing that is going to happen is a call to WriteLine with the value returned as the argument. The concept of "what happens next" is called **continuation;** each point in a control flow has a continuation. In our example, the continuation of ToString is WriteLine (and the continuation of WriteLine is whatever code runs in the next statement). The idea of continuation is so elementary to C# programming that most programmers don't even think about it; it's part of the invisible air that they breathe. The act of C# programming is the

---

4. Be careful when using tasks to asynchronously mutate collections. The tasks might be running on worker threads, and the collection might not be thread-safe. It is safer to fill in the collection from the main thread after the tasks are completed.

act of constructing continuation upon continuation until the control flow of the entire program is complete.

Notice that the continuation of a given piece of code in a normal C# program will be executed *immediately* upon the completion of that code. When ToString() returns, the point of control on the current thread immediately does a synchronous call to WriteLine. Notice also that there are actually two possible continuations of a given piece of code: the "normal" continuation and the "exceptional" continuation that will be executed if the current piece of code throws an exception.

Asynchronous method calls, such as starting a Task, add an additional dimension to the control flow. With an asynchronous Task invocation, the control flow goes immediately to the statement after the Task.Start() while at the same time, it begins executing within the body of the Task delegate. In other words, "what happens next" when asynchrony is involved is multidimensional. Unlike with exceptions where the continuation is just a different path, with asynchrony continuation is an additional, parallel path.

Asynchronous tasks also allow composition of larger tasks out of smaller tasks by describing asynchronous continuations. Just as with regular control flow, a task can have different continuations to handle error situations, and tasks can be composed together by manipulating their continuations. There are several techniques for doing so, the most explicit of which is the ContinueWith() method (see Listing 18.5 and its corresponding output, Output 18.2).

LISTING 18.5: **Calling** Task.ContinueWith()

```
using System;
using System.Threading.Tasks;

public class Program
{
  public static void Main()
  {
      Console.WriteLine("Before");
      // Use Task.Factory.StartNew<string>() for
      // TPL prior to .NET 4.5
      Task taskA =
          Task.Run( () =>
              Console.WriteLine("Starting..."))
          .ContinueWith(antecedent =>
              Console.WriteLine("Continuing A..."));
      Task taskB = taskA.ContinueWith( antecedent =>
          Console.WriteLine("Continuing B..."));
      Task taskC = taskA.ContinueWith( antecedent =>
```

```
            Console.WriteLine("Continuing C..."));
        Task.WaitAll(taskB, taskC);
        Console.WriteLine("Finished!");
    }
}
```

OUTPUT 18.2

```
Before
Starting...
Continuing A...
Continuing C...
Continuing B...
Finished!
```

The `ContinueWith()` method enables "chaining" two tasks together, such that when the predecessor task—the **antecedent task**—completes, the second task—the **continuation task**—is automatically started asynchronously. In Listing 18.5, for example, `Console.WriteLine("Starting...")` is the antecedent task body and `Console.WriteLine("Continuing A...")` is its continuation task body. The continuation task takes a `Task` as its argument (antecedent), thus allowing the continuation task's code to access the antecedent task's completion state. When the antecedent task is completed, the continuation task will start automatically, asynchronously executing the second delegate, and passing the just-completed antecedent task as an argument to that delegate. Furthermore, since the `ContinueWith()` method returns a `Task` as well, that `Task` can of course be used as the antecedent of yet another `Task`, and so on, thus forming a continuation chain of `Tasks` that can be arbitrarily long.

If you call `ContinueWith()` twice on the same antecedent task (as Listing 18.5 shows with `taskB` and `taskC` comprising continuation tasks for `TaskA`), the antecedent task (`taskA`) has two continuation tasks and when the antecedent task completes, both continuation tasks will be executed asynchronously. Notice that the order of execution of the continuation tasks from a single antecedent is indeterminate at compile time. Output 18.2 happens to show `taskC` executing before `taskB`, but in a second execution of the program, the order may be reversed. However, `taskA` will always execute before `taskB` and `taskC` since the latter are continuation tasks of `taskA`, and therefore, they can't start before `taskA` completes. Similarly, the `Console.WriteLine("Starting...")` delegate will always execute to completion before `taskA` (`Console.WriteLine("Continuing A...")`) since the latter is a continuation task of the former. Furthermore, "Finished!" will always appear last because of the call to `Task.WaitAll(taskB, taskC)` that blocks the control flow from continuing until both `taskB` and `taskC` complete.

There are many different overloads of `ContinueWith()`, and some of them take a `TaskContinuationOptions` value to tweak the behavior of the continuation chain. The values are flags, so they can be combined using the logical OR operator (`|`). A brief description of some of the possible flag values appears in Table 18.1; see the online MSDN documentation[5] for more details.

TABLE 18.1: List of Available `TaskContinuationOptions` Enums

Enum	Description
`None`	This is the default behavior. The continuation task will be executed when the antecedent task completes, regardless of its task status.
`PreferFairness`	If two tasks were both asynchronously started, one before the other, there is no guarantee that the one that was started first actually gets to run first. This flag asks the task scheduler to try to increase the likelihood that the first task started is the first task to execute—something that is particularly relevant when the two tasks you describe are created from different thread pool threads.
`LongRunning`	This tells the task scheduler that the task is likely to be an I/O bound high-latency task. This is so that the scheduler can allow other queued work to be processed rather than starved because of the long-running task. This option should be used sparingly.
`AttachedToParent`	This specifies that a task should attempt to attach to a parent task within the task hierarchy.
`DenyChildAttach` (.NET 4.5)	This throws an exception if creation of a child task is attempted. If code within the continuation tries to use `AttachedToParent`, it'll behave as if there was no parent.
`NotOnRanToCompletion*`	This specifies that the continuation task should not be scheduled if its antecedent ran to completion. This option is not valid for multitask continuations.

---

5. MSDN .NET Framework Developer Center, http://msdn.microsoft.com/en-us/library/system.threading.tasks.taskcontinuationoptions(v=vs.110).aspx.

TABLE 18.1: List of Available `TaskContinuationOptions` Enums, *Continued*

Enum	Description
NotOnFaulted*	This specifies that the continuation task should not be scheduled if its antecedent threw an unhandled exception. This option is not valid for multitask continuations.
OnlyOnCanceled*	This specifies that the continuation task should be scheduled only if its antecedent was canceled. This option is not valid for multitask continuations.
NotOnCanceled*	This specifies that the continuation task should not be scheduled if its antecedent was canceled. This option is not valid for multitask continuations.
OnlyOnFaulted*	This specifies that the continuation task should be scheduled only if its antecedent threw an unhandled exception. This option is not valid for multitask continuations.
OnlyOnRanToCompletion*	This specifies that the continuation task should be scheduled only if its antecedent ran to completion. This option is not valid for multitask continuations.
ExecuteSynchronously	This specifies that the continuation task should be executed synchronously. With this option specified, the continuation the schedule will attempt to execute the work on is the same thread that causes the antecedent task to transition into its final state. If the antecedent is already complete when the continuation is created, the continuation will run on the thread creating the continuation.
HideScheduler (.NET 4.5)	This prevents the ambient scheduler from being seen as the current scheduler in the created task. This means that operations like `Run`/`StartNew` and `ContinueWith` that are performed in the created task will see `TaskScheduler.Default` (null) as the current scheduler. This is useful when continuation should run on a particular scheduler, but the continuation is calling out to additional code that should not schedule work on the same scheduler.
LazyCancellation (.NET 4.5)	This causes the continuation to delay monitoring the supplied cancellation token for a cancellation request until the antecedent has completed. Consider tasks t1, t2, and t3 where the latter is a continuation of the former. If t2 is canceled before t1 completes, it is possible that t3 could start before t1 completes. Setting `LazyCancellation` avoids this.

The items decorated with a star (*) indicate under what conditions the continuation task will be executed, and are therefore particularly useful for creating continuations that act like event handlers for the antecedent task's behavior. Listing 18.6 demonstrates how an antecedent task can be given multiple continuations that execute conditionally, depending on how the antecedent task completed.

LISTING 18.6: **Registering for Notifications of Task Behavior with** ContinueWith()

```csharp
using System;
using System.Threading.Tasks;
using AddisonWesley.Michaelis.EssentialCSharp.Shared;

public class Program
{
  public static void Main()
  {
      // Use Task.Factory.StartNew<string>() for
      // TPL prior to .NET 4.5
      Task<string> task =
          Task.Run<string>(
              () => PiCalculator.Calculate(10));

      Task faultedTask = task.ContinueWith(
          (antecedentTask) =>
          {
              Trace.Assert(task.IsFaulted);
              Console.WriteLine(
                  "Task State: Faulted");
          },
          TaskContinuationOptions.OnlyOnFaulted);

      Task canceledTask = task.ContinueWith(
          (antecedentTask) =>
          {
              Trace.Assert(task.IsCanceled);
              Console.WriteLine(
                  "Task State: Canceled");
          },
          TaskContinuationOptions.OnlyOnCanceled);

      Task completedTask = task.ContinueWith(
          (antecedentTask) =>
          {
              Trace.Assert(task.IsCompleted);
              Console.WriteLine(
                  "Task State: Completed");
          }, TaskContinuationOptions.
              OnlyOnRanToCompletion);
```

```
        completedTask.Wait();
    }
  }
```

In this listing, we effectively register "listeners" for "events" on the antecedent's task so that when the task completes normally or abnormally, the particular "listening" task will begin executing. This is a powerful capability, particularly if the original task is a "fire and forget" task; that is, a task that we start, hook up to continuation tasks, and then never refer to again. You'll notice that in Listing 18.6, we do not wait for the original antecedent task; we wait for the continuation task that handles the completion event to finish. We can discard the reference to the original task; the task will begin executing asynchronously without any need for follow-up code that checks the status. In this case, we instead call `completedTask.Wait()` so that the main thread does not exit the program before the completed output appears (see Output 18.3).

OUTPUT 18.3

```
Task State: Completed.
```

Note that in Listing 18.6, we must not call `Wait()` on `canceledTask` or `faultedTask`. Those continuation tasks only run if the antecedent task is canceled or throws an exception, and since that is not going to happen in this program, those tasks will never be scheduled to run, and waiting for them to complete would throw an exception. The continuation options in Listing 18.3 happen to be mutually exclusive, so when the antecedent task runs to completion and the task associated with `completedTask` executes, the task scheduler automatically cancels the tasks associated with `canceledTask` and `faultedTask`. The canceled tasks end with their state set to `Canceled`. Therefore, calling `Wait()` (or any other invocation that would cause the current thread to wait for a task completion) on either of these tasks will throw an exception indicating that they are canceled.

Unhandled Exception Handling on Task with `AggregateException`

When calling a method synchronously we can wrap it in a `try` block with a `catch` clause to identify to the compiler what code we want to execute when an exception occurs. This does not work with an asynchronous call, however. We cannot simply wrap a `try` around a call to `Start()` in order to catch an exception because control immediately returns from the call, and control will then leave the `try` block, possibly long before the exception occurs on the worker thread. One solution is to wrap the body of the task delegate with a try/catch block. Exceptions thrown on and subsequently caught by the worker thread will consequently not present problems as a try block will work normally on the worker thread. This is not the case, however, for unhandled exceptions—those that the worker thread does not catch.

Generally (starting with version 2.0[6] of the CLR), unhandled exceptions on any thread are treated as fatal, trigger the Windows Error Reporting dialog, and cause the application to terminate abnormally. All exceptions on all threads must be caught, and if they are not, the application is not allowed to continue to run. (For some advanced techniques for dealing with unhandled exceptions, see the upcoming Advanced Topic titled Dealing with Unhandled Exceptions.) Fortunately, this is not the case, however, for unhandled exceptions in an asynchronously running task. Rather, the task scheduler inserts a "catchall" exception handler around the delegate so that if the task throws an otherwise unhandled exception, the catchall handler will catch it and record the details of the exception in the task, avoiding any trigger of the CLR automatically terminating the process.

As we saw in Listing 18.6, one technique for dealing with a faulted task is to explicitly create a continuation task that is the "fault handler" for that task; the task scheduler will automatically schedule the continuation when it detects that the antecedent task threw an unhandled exception. If no such handler is present, however, and `Wait()` (or an attempt to get the `Result`) executes on a faulted task, an `AggregateException` will be thrown (see Listing 18.7 and Output 18.4).

LISTING 18.7: Handling a Task's Unhandled Exception

```
using System;
using System.Threading.Tasks;

public class Program
```

---

6. In version 1.0 of the CLR, an unhandled exception on a worker thread terminated the thread but not the application. As a result, it was possible for a buggy program to have all its worker threads die, but the main thread would continue to run, even though the program was no longer doing any work. This is a confusing situation for users to be in; it is better to signal to the user that the application is in a bad state and terminate it before it can do any more harm.

```
{
  public static void Main()
  {
      // Use Task.Factory.StartNew<string>() for
      // TPL prior to .NET 4.5
      Task task = Task.Run(() =>
      {
          throw new InvalidOperationException();
      });

      try
      {
          task.Wait();
      }
      catch(AggregateException exception)
      {
          exception.Handle(eachException =>
            {
                Console.WriteLine(
                    "ERROR: {0}",
                    eachException.Message);
                return true;
            });
      }
  }
}
```

OUTPUT 18.4

```
ERROR: Operation is not valid due to the current state of the object.
```

The aggregate exception is so-called because it may contain many exceptions collected from one or more faulted tasks. Imagine, for example, asynchronously executing ten tasks in parallel and five of them throwing exceptions. In order to report all five exceptions and have them handled in a single catch block, the framework uses the AggregateException as a means of collecting the exceptions and reporting them as a single exception. Furthermore, since it is unknown at compile time whether a worker task will throw one or more exceptions, an unhandled faulted task will always throw an AggregateException. Listing 18.7 and Output 18.4 demonstrate this. Even though the unhandled exception thrown on the worker thread was of type InvalidOperationException, the type of the exception caught on the main thread is still an AggregateException. And, as expected, to catch the exception requires an AggregateException catch block.

A list of the exceptions contained within an `AggregateException` is available from the `InnerExceptions` property. As a result, you can iterate over this property to examine each exception and determine the appropriate course of action. Alternatively, and shown in Listing 18.7, you can use the `AggregateException.Handle()` method, specifying an expression to execute against each individual exception contained within the `AggregateException`. One important characteristic of the `Handle()` method to consider, however, is that it is a predicate. As such, the predicate should return `true` for any exceptions that the `Handle()` delegate successfully addresses. If any exception handling invocation returns `false` for an exception, the `Handle()` method will throw a new `AggregateException` that contains the composite list of such corresponding exceptions.

You can also observe the state of a faulted task without causing the exception to be rethrown on the current thread by simply looking at the `Exception` property of the task. Listing 18.8 demonstrates this by waiting for the completion of a fault continuation of a task[7] that we know will throw an exception.

LISTING 18.8: Observing Unhandled Exceptions on a Task Using `ContinueWith()`

```
using System;
using System.Diagnostics;
using System.Threading.Tasks;

public class Program
{
  public static void Main()
  {
      bool parentTaskFaulted = false;
      Task task = new Task(() =>
          {
              throw new InvalidOperationException();
          });
      Task continuationTask = task.ContinueWith(
          (antecedentTask) =>
          {
              antecedentTaskIsFaulted =
                  antecedentTask.IsFaulted;
          }, TaskContinuationOptions.OnlyOnFaulted);
      task.Start();
      continuationTask.Wait();
      Trace.Assert(antecedentTaskIsFaulted);
      if (!task.IsFaulted)
```

---

7. As we discussed earlier, waiting for a fault continuation to complete is a strange thing to do because most of the time it will never be scheduled to run in the first place. This code is for illustrative purposes.

```
    {
        task.Wait();
    }
    else
    {
        task.Exception.Handle(eachException =>
        {
            Console.WriteLine(
                "ERROR: {0}",
                eachException.Message);
            return true;
        });
    }
}
}
```

Notice that to retrieve the unhandled exception on the original task we use the `Exception` property. The result is output identical to Output 18.4.

If an exception that occurs within a task goes entirely unobserved—a) it isn't caught from within the task; b) the completion of the task is never observed, via `Wait()`, `Result`, or accessing the `Exception` property, for example; and c) the faulted `ContinueWith()` is never observed—then the exception is likely to go unhandled entirely, resulting in a process-wide unhandled exception. In .NET 4.0 such a faulted task would get rethrown by the finalizer thread and likely crash the process. In contrast, in .NET 4.5 the crashing has been suppressed (although the CLR can be configured for the crashing behavior if preferred).

In either case, you can register for an unhandled task exception via the `TaskScheduler.UnobservedTaskException` event.

■ **ADVANCED TOPIC**

Dealing with Unhandled Exceptions on a Thread

As we discussed above, an unhandled exception on any thread by default causes the application to shut down. An unhandled exception is a fatal, unexpected bug, and the exception may have occurred because a crucial data structure is corrupt. You therefore have no idea what the program could possibly be doing, so the safest thing to do is to shut down the whole thing immediately.

Ideally, no programs would ever throw unhandled exceptions on any thread; programs that do so have bugs, and the best course of action is to find and fix the bug before the software is shipped to customers. However, there is a school of thought that says that instead of shutting down an application as soon as possible when an unhandled exception occurs, it is often desirable to save any working data, and/or log the exception for error reporting and future debugging. This requires a mechanism to register for notifications of unhandled exceptions.

Every AppDomain provides such a mechanism, and to observe the unhandled exceptions that occur in an AppDomain, you must add a handler to the `UnhandledException` event. The `UnhandledException` event will fire for all unhandled exceptions on threads within the application domain, whether it is the main thread or a worker thread. Note that the purpose of this mechanism is notification; it does not permit the application to recover from the unhandled exception and continue executing. After the event handlers run, the application will display the Window Error Reporting dialog and then the application will exit. (For console applications, the exception details will also appear on the console.)

In Listing 18.9 we show how to create a second thread which throws an exception that is then handled by the application domain's unhandled exception event handler. For demonstration purposes, to ensure that thread timing issues do not come into play, we insert some artificial delays using `Thread.Sleep`. Output 18.5 shows the results.

LISTING 18.9: **Registering for Unhandled Exceptions**

```csharp
using System;
using System.Diagnostics;
using System.Threading;

public class Program
{
  public static Stopwatch clock = new Stopwatch();
  public static void Main()
  {
    try
    {
      clock.Start();
      // Register a callback to receive notifications
      // of any unhandled exception.
      AppDomain.CurrentDomain.UnhandledException +=
        (s, e) =>
          {
            Message("Event handler starting");
            Delay(4000);
          };
```

```
    Thread thread = new Thread(() =>
    {
      Message("Throwing exception.");
      throw new Exception();
    });
    thread.Start();

    Delay(2000);
  }
  finally
  {
    Message("Finally block running.");
  }
}

static void Delay(int i)
{
  Message(string.Format("Sleeping for {0} ms", i));
  Thread.Sleep(i);
  Message("Awake");
}

static void Message(string text)
{
  Console.WriteLine("{0}:{1:0000}:{2}",
    Thread.CurrentThread.ManagedThreadId,
    clock.ElapsedMilliseconds,
    text);
}
}
```

OUTPUT 18.5

```
3:0047:Throwing exception.
3:0052:Unhandled exception handler starting.
3:0055:Sleeping for 4000 ms
1:0058:Sleeping for 2000 ms
1:2059:Awake
1:2060:finally block running.
3:4059:Awake
Unhandled Exception: System.Exception: Exception of type 'System.
Exception' was thrown.
```

As you can see in Output 18.5, the new thread is assigned thread ID 3 and the main thread is assigned thread ID 1. The operating system schedules thread 3 to run for a while; it throws an unhandled exception, the event handler is invoked, and it goes to sleep. Soon thereafter, the operating system realizes that thread 1 can be scheduled, but its code immediately puts it to sleep. Thread 1 wakes up first and runs the finally block, and then two seconds later thread 3 wakes up, and the unhandled exception finally crashes the process.

This sequence of events—the event handler executing, and the process crashing after it is finished—is typical, but not guaranteed. The moment there is an unhandled exception in your program, all bets are off; the program is now in an unknown and potentially very unstable state, and therefore, its behavior can be unexpected. In this case, as you can see, the CLR allows the main thread to continue running and executes its finally block, even though it knows by the time that control gets to the finally block, another thread is in the AppDomain's unhanded exception event handler.

To emphasize this fact, try changing the delays so that the main thread sleeps longer than the event handler. In that scenario, the finally block will not be run! The process will be destroyed by the unhandled exception before thread 1 wakes up. You can also get different results depending on whether the exception-throwing thread is created by the thread pool or not. The best practice is therefore to avoid all possible unhandled exceptions, whether they occur in worker threads or in the main thread.

How does this pertain to tasks? What if there are unfinished tasks hanging around the system when you want to shut it down? We'll look at task cancellation in the next section.

Guidelines

AVOID writing programs that produce unhandled exceptions on any thread.

CONSIDER registering an unhandled exception event handler for debugging, logging, and emergency shutdown purposes.

DO cancel unfinished tasks, rather than allowing them to run during application shutdown.

Canceling a Task

Earlier in this chapter we described why it's a bad idea to rudely abort a thread in order to cancel a task being performed by that thread. The TPL uses **cooperative cancellation,** a far more polite, robust, and reliable technique for safely canceling a task that is no longer needed. A task that supports cancellation monitors a `CancellationToken` object (found in the `System.Threading` namespace) by periodically polling it to see if a cancellation request has been issued. Listing 18.10 demonstrates both the cancellation request and the response to the request. Output 18.6 shows the results.

LISTING 18.10: **Canceling a Task Using** `CancellationToken`

```csharp
using System;
using System.Threading;
using System.Threading.Tasks;
using AddisonWesley.Michaelis.EssentialCSharp.Shared;

public class Program
{
  public static void Main()
  {
      string stars =
          "*".PadRight(Console.WindowWidth-1, '*');
      Console.WriteLine("Push ENTER to exit.");

      CancellationTokenSource cancellationTokenSource=
          new CancellationTokenSource();
      // Use Task.Factory.StartNew<string>() for
      // TPL prior to .NET 4.5
      Task task = Task.Run(
          () =>
              WritePi(cancellationTokenSource.Token),
                  cancellationTokenSource.Token);

      // Wait for the user's input
      Console.ReadLine();

      cancellationTokenSource.Cancel();
      Console.WriteLine(stars);
      task.Wait();
      Console.WriteLine();
  }

  private static void WritePi(
      CancellationToken cancellationToken)
  {
      const int batchSize = 1;
      string piSection = string.Empty;
      int i = 0;

      while(!cancellationToken.IsCancellationRequested
          || i == int.MaxValue)
      {
          piSection = PiCalculator.Calculate(
              batchSize, (i++) * batchSize);
          Console.Write(piSection);
```

```
            }
        }
    }
```

OUTPUT 18.6

```
Push ENTER to exit.
3.14159265358979323846264338327950288419716939937510582097494459230781b
40b28b208998b280348253421170b79821480865132823066470938446095505822317e
5359408128481117450
**************************************************************************
2
```

After starting the task, a `Console.Read()` blocks the main thread. At the same time, the task continues to execute, calculating the next digit of pi and printing it out. Once the user presses Enter, the execution encounters a call to `CancellationTokenSource.Cancel()`. In Listing 18.10, we split the call to `task.Cancel()` from the call to `task.Wait()` and print out a line of asterisks in between. The purpose of this is to show that quite possibly an additional iteration will occur before the cancellation token is observed— hence the additional 2 in Output 18.6 following the stars. The 2 appears because the `CancellationTokenSource.Cancel()` doesn't rudely stop the task from executing. The task keeps on running until it checks the token, and politely shuts down when it sees that the owner of the token is requesting cancellation of the task.

The `Cancel()` call effectively sets the `IsCancellationRequested` property on all cancellation tokens copied from `CancellationTokenSource.Token`. There are a few things to note, however.

- A `CancellationToken`, not a `CancellationTokenSource`, is given to the asynchronous task. A `CancellationToken` enables polling for a cancellation request; the `CancellationTokenSource` provides the token and signals it when it is canceled (see Figure 18.2).
- A `CancellationToken` is a struct, and therefore is copied by value. The value returned by `CancellationTokenSource.Token` produces a copy of the token.

FIGURE 18.2: CancellationTokenSource and CancellationToken Class Diagrams

To monitor the IsCancellationRequested property, a copy of the CancellationToken (retrieved from CancellationTokenSource.Token) is passed to the task. In Listing 18.9, we then occasionally check the IsCancellationRequested property on the CancellationToken parameter; in this case, we check after each digit calculation. If IsCancellationRequested returns true, the while loop exits. Unlike a thread abort, which would throw an exception at essentially a random point, we exit the loop using normal control flow. We guarantee that the code is responsive to cancellation requests by polling frequently.

One other point to note about the CancellationToken is the overloaded Register() method. Via this method, you can register an action that will be invoked whenever the token is canceled. In other words, calling the Register() method subscribes to a listener delegate on the corresponding CancellationTokenSource's Cancel().

Since canceling before completing is expected behavior in this program, the code in Listing 18.9 does not throw a System.Threading .Tasks.TaskCanceledException. Because of this, task.Status will return TaskStatus.RanToCompletion—providing no indication that the work of the task was in fact canceled. In this example, there is no need for such an indication; however, the TPL does include the capability to do this. If the cancel call were disruptive in some way—preventing a valid result from returning, for example—throwing a `TaskCanceledException` (which derives from `System.OperationCanceledException`) would be the TPL pattern for reporting it. Instead of throwing the exception explicitly, `CancellationToken` includes a `ThrowIfCancellationRequested()` method to report the exception more easily, assuming an instance of `CancellationToken` is available.

If you attempt to call `Wait()` (or obtain the `Result`) on a task that threw `TaskCanceledException`, the behavior is the same as if any other exception had been thrown in the task: The call will throw an `AggregateException`. The exception is a means of communicating that the state of execution following the task is potentially incomplete. Unlike a successfully completed task in which all expected work executed successfully, a canceled task potentially has partially completed work—the state of the work is untrusted.

This example demonstrates how a long-running processor-bound operation (calculating pi almost indefinitely) can monitor for a cancellation request and respond if one occurs. There are some cases, however, when cancellation can occur without explicitly coding for it within the target task. For example, the `Parallel` class discussed later in the chapter offers such a behavior by default.

`Task.Run()`: A Shortcut and Simplification to `Task.Factory.StartNew()`

In .NET 4.0 the general practice for obtaining a task was to call `Task.Factory.StartNew()`. In .NET 4.5, a simpler calling structure was provided in `Task.Run()`.

Like `Task.Run()`, `Task.Factory.StartNew()` could be used in C# 4.0 scenarios to invoke CPU-intensive methods that require an additional thread to be created.

Given .NET 4.5, `Task.Run()` should be used by default unless it proves insufficient. For example, if you need to control the task with `TaskCreationOptions`, if you need to specify an alternative scheduler, or if, for performance reasons, you want to pass in object state, `Task.Factory.StartNew()` should be considered. Only in rare cases, where you need to separate creation from scheduling, should constructor instantiation followed by a call to `Start()` be considered.

Listing 18.11 provide an example using `Task.Factory.StartNew()`.

LISTING 18.11: **Using** `Task.Factory.StartNew()`

```csharp
public Task<string> CalculatePiAsync(int digits)
{
  return Task.Factory.StartNew<string>(
      () => CalculatePi(digits));
}

private string CalculatePi(int digits)
{
    // ...
}
```

Long-Running Tasks

As we discussed earlier in the commentary on Listing 18.2, the thread pool assumes that work items will be processor-bound and relatively short-lived; it makes these assumptions in order to effectively throttle the number of threads created. This prevents both overallocation of expensive thread resources and oversubscription of processors that would lead to excessive context switching and time slicing.

But if the developer knows that a `Task` is going to be long-running and therefore holding on to an underlying thread resource for a long time, the developer can notify the scheduler that it is unlikely to complete its work anytime soon. This has two effects. First, it hints to the scheduler that perhaps a dedicated thread ought to be created specifically for this task, rather than attempting to use a thread from the thread pool. Second, it hints to the scheduler that perhaps this would be a good time to allow more tasks to be scheduled than there are processors to handle them. This will cause more time slicing to happen, which is a good thing. We do not want one long-running task to hog an entire processor and prevent shorter-running tasks from using it. The short-running tasks will be able to use their time slice to finish a large percentage of their work, and the long-running task is unlikely to notice the relatively slight delays caused by sharing a processor with other tasks. To accomplish this, use the `TaskCreationOptions.LongRunning` option when calling `StartNew()` (`Task.Run()` does not support a `TaskCreationOptions` parameter), as shown in Listing 18.12.

LISTING 18.12: **Cooperatively Executing Long-Running Tasks**

```csharp
using System.Threading.Tasks;

// ...
```

```
Task task = Task.Factory.StartNew(
    () =>
        WritePi(cancellationTokenSource.Token),
            TaskCreationOptions.LongRunning);
// ...
```

Guidelines

DO inform the task factory that a newly created task is likely to be long-running so that it can manage it appropriately.

DO use `TaskCreationOptions.LongRunning` sparingly.

Tasks Are Disposable

Note that `Task` also supports `IDisposable`. This is necessary because `Task` may allocate a `WaitHandle` when waiting for it to complete, and since `WaitHandle` supports `IDisposable`, `Task` also supports `IDisposable` in accordance with best practices. However, readers will note that the preceding code samples do not include a `Dispose()` call nor do they rely on such a call implicitly via the `using` statement. The listings are instead relying on an automatic `WaitHandle` finalizer invocation when the program exits.

The result is that first the handles live longer and hence consume more resources than they ought to, and second, the garbage collector is slightly less efficient because finalized objects survive into the next generation. However, both of these concerns are inconsequential in the `Task` case unless there are an extraordinarily large number of tasks being finalized. Therefore, even though technically speaking all code should be disposing of tasks, don't bother unless performance metrics require it and it's easy—namely, you're certain that `Task`s have completed and no other code is using them.

The Task-Based Asynchronous Pattern in C# 5.0

As we've seen so far, tasks provide a better abstraction for the manipulation of asynchronous work than threads do. Tasks are automatically scheduled to the right number of threads and large tasks can be composed out of small tasks, just as large programs can be composed out of small methods.

However, there are some drawbacks to tasks as we've seen them thus far. The principal difficulty with tasks is that they turn your program logic "inside out." To illustrate this, we first consider a synchronous method that is blocked on an I/O-bound, high-latency operation—a Web request. Next, we compare it to an asynchronous version prior to C# 5.0 and the **Task-based Asynchronous Pattern (TAP).** Lastly, we review the same example except using C# 5.0 and the async/await contextual keywords.

Synchronously Invoking a High-Latency Operation

In Listing 18.13 the code uses a WebRequest to download a Web page and display its size. If the operation fails an exception is thrown.

LISTING 18.13: A Synchronous Web Request

```csharp
using System;
using System.IO;
using System.Net;
using System.Linq;

public class Program
{
  public static void Main(string[] args)
  {
      string url = "http://www.IntelliTect.com";
      if(args.Length > 0)
      {
          url = args[0];
      }

      try
      {
          Console.Write(url);
          WebRequest webRequest =
              WebRequest.Create(url);

          WebResponse response =
              webRequest.GetResponse();

          Console.Write(".....");

          using(StreamReader reader =
              new StreamReader(
                  response.GetResponseStream()))
          {
              string text =
                  reader.ReadToEnd();
              Console.WriteLine(
                  FormatBytes(text.Length));
          }
      }
      catch(WebException)
```

```
            {
                // ...
            }
            catch(IOException )
            {
                // ...
            }
            catch(NotSupportedException )
            {
                // ...
            }
        }

        static public string FormatBytes(long bytes)
        {
            string[] magnitudes =
                new string[] { "GB", "MB", "KB", "Bytes" };
            long max =
                (long)Math.Pow(1024, magnitudes.Length);

            return string.Format("{1:##.##} {0}",
                magnitudes.FirstOrDefault(
                    magnitude =>
                        bytes > (max /= 1024)) ?? "0 Bytes",
                    (decimal)bytes / (decimal)max).Trim();
        }
    }
```

The logic in Listing 18.13 is relatively straightforward—using common C# idioms like try/catch blocks and `return` statements to describe the control flow. Given a `WebRequest` it calls `GetResponse()` to download the page. To gain stream access to the page it calls `GetResponseStream()` and assigns the result to a `StreamReader`. Finally, it reads to the end of the stream with `ReadToEnd()` in order to determine the size of the page and then print that out to the screen.

The problem with this approach is, of course, that the calling thread is blocked until the I/O operation completes; this is wasting a thread that could be doing useful work while the asynchronous operation executes. For this reason, we can't, for example, execute any other code, such as code that indicates progress.

Asynchronously Invoking a High-Latency Operation Using the TPL

To address this problem, Listing 18.14 takes a similar approach but instead uses task-based asynchrony with the TPL.

LISTING 18.14: An Asynchronous Web Request

```csharp
using System;
using System.IO;
using System.Net;
using System.Linq;
using System.Threading.Tasks;

public class Program
{
  public static void Main(string[] args)
  {
      string url = "http://www.IntelliTect.com";
      if(args.Length > 0)
      {
          url = args[0];
      }

      Console.Write(url);

      Task task = WriteWebRequestSizeAsync(url);

      try
      {
          while(!task.Wait(100))
          {
              Console.Write(".");
          }
      }
      catch(AggregateException exception)
      {
          exception = exception.Flatten();
          try
          {
              exception.Handle(innerException =>
              {
                  // Rethrowing rather than using
                  // if condition on the type.
                  ExceptionDispatchInfo.Capture(
                      exception.InnerException)
                      .Throw();
                  return true;
              });
          }
          catch(WebException)
          {
              // ...
          }
          catch(IOException )
          {
              // ...
          }
          catch(NotSupportedException )
```

```
        {
            // ...
        }
    }
}


private static Task WriteWebRequestSizeAsync(
    string url)
{
    StreamReader reader = null;
    WebRequest webRequest =
        WebRequest.Create(url);

    Task task =
        webRequest.GetResponseAsync()
    .ContinueWith( antecedent =>
    {
        WebResponse response =
            antecedent.Result;

        reader =
            new StreamReader(
                response.GetResponseStream());
        return reader.ReadToEndAsync();
    })
    .Unwrap()
    .ContinueWith(antecedent =>
    {
        if(reader != null) reader.Dispose();
        string text = antecedent.Result;
        Console.WriteLine(
            ·   FormatBytes(text.Length));
    });

    return task;
}

    // ...
}
```

Unlike Listing 18.13, when Listing 18.14 executes it prints periods to the console while the page is downloading. The result is that instead of simply printing four periods ("....") to the console, Listing 18.14 is able to continuously print periods for as long as it takes to download the file, read it from the stream, and determine its size.

Unfortunately, the asynchrony comes at the cost of complexity. Interspersed throughout the code we have TPL-related code that interrupts the flow. Rather than simply following on the WebRequest.GetResponseAsync()

call with retrieving the StreamReader and calling ReadToEndAsync(), the asynchronous version of the code requires ContinueWith() statements. The first ContinueWith() statement identifies what to execute after the WebRequest.GetResponseAsync(). Notice that the return statement in the first ContinueWith() expression returns StreamReader.ReadToEndAsync() which returns another Task.

Without the Unwrap() call, therefore, the antecedent in the second ContinueWith() statement is a Task<Task<string>>, which alone indicates the complexity. As a result, it is necessary to call Result twice—once on the antecedent directly and a second time on the Task<string>.Result property antecedent.Result returned, the latter of which will block until the ReadToEnd() operation completes. To avoid the Task<Task<TResult>> structure, however, we preface the call to ContinueWith() with a call to Unwrap(), thereby shedding the outer Task and appropriately handling any errors or cancellation requests.

The complexity doesn't stop with Tasks and ContinueWith(), however, as the exception handling adds an entirely new dimension to the complexity. As discussed earlier in the chapter, the TPL generally throws an AggregateException exception because of the possibility that an asynchronous operation could encounter multiple exceptions. However, because we are calling the Result property from within ContinueWith() blocks, it is possible that inside the worker thread we might also throw an AggregateException.

As you have learned earlier in the chapter, there are multiple ways to handle these exceptions.

1. Add continuation tasks to all *Async methods that return a task along with each ContinueWith() method call. However, doing so would prevent us from using the fluid API in which ContinueWith()'s chain together one after the other. Furthermore, this would force us to deeply embed error handling logic into the control flow rather than simply relying on exception handling.

2. Surround each delegate body with a try/catch so that no exceptions go unhandled from the task. Unfortunately, this approach is less than ideal as well. First of all, some exceptions (like those triggered when calling antecedent.Result) will throw an AggregateException from which we will need to unwrap the InnerException(s) in order

to handle them individually. In unwrapping them we either rethrow them so as to catch a specific type or conditionally check for the type of the exception separately from any other catch blocks (even catch blocks for the same type). Second, each delegate body will require its own separate try/catch handler even if some of the exception types between blocks are the same. Third, Main's call to task.Wait() could still throw an exception because WebRequest.GetRespon-seAsync() could potentially throw an exception and there is no way to surround it with a try/catch block. Therefore, there is no way to eliminate the try/catch block in Main that surrounds task.Wait().

3. Ignore all exception handling from within WriteWebRequesSizeAsync() and instead rely solely on the try/catch block that surrounds Main's task.Wait(). And given that we know the exception will be an AggregateException, we only have a catch for that exception. Within the catch block we handle the exception by calling AggregateException. Handle() and throwing each exception using the ExceptionDispatch-Info object so as not to lose the original stack trace. These exceptions are then caught by the expected exception handles and addressed accordingly. Notice, however, that before handling the AggregateException's InnerExceptions we first call AggregateException.Flatten(). This is to address the issue of an AggregateException wrapping inner exceptions that are also of type AggregateException (and so on). By calling Flatten(), all exceptions are moved to the first level and all contained AggregateExceptions removed.

And, as shown in Listing 18.14, Option 3 is probably the preferred approach because it keeps the exception handling outside the control flow for the most part. This doesn't eliminate the error handling complexity entirely; it simply minimizes interspersing it within the regular control flow.

Although the asynchronous version in Listing 18.14 has virtually the same logical control flow as the synchronous version in Listing 18.13, both versions attempt to download a resource from a server and, if the download succeeds, the result is returned. (If the download fails, the exception's type is interrogated to determine the right course of action.) However, it is clear that the asynchronous version of Listing 18.14 is significantly harder to read, understand, and change than the corresponding synchronous version in Listing 18.13. Unlike the synchronous version that uses standard control flow statements, the asynchronous version is forced to create multiple lambda expressions to express the continuation logic in the form of delegates.

Unfortunately, this is a fairly simple example! Imagine what the asynchronous code would look like if, for example, the synchronous code had a loop in it to retry the operation three times if it failed, if it tried to contact multiple different servers, if it took a collection of resources rather than a single one, or all of these possible features together. Adding those features to the synchronous version would be straightforward, but it is not at all clear how to do so in the asynchronous version. Rewriting synchronous methods into asynchronous methods by explicitly specifying the continuation of each task gets very complicated very quickly even if the synchronous continuations are what appear to be very simple control flows.

The Task-Based Asynchronous Pattern with `async` and `await`

Fortunately, it turns out that it is actually not too difficult to write a computer program that does these complex code transformations for you. The designers of the C# language realized this, and have added such a capability to the C# 5.0 compiler. In C# 5.0, you can rewrite the synchronous program above into an asynchronous program much more easily using the **Task-based Asynchronous Pattern (TAP);** the C# compiler then does the tedious work of transforming your method into a series of task continuations. Listing 18.15 shows how to rewrite Listing 18.13 into an asynchronous method without the major structural changes of Listing 18.14.

LISTING 18.15: An Asynchronous Web Request Using the Task-Based Asynchronous Pattern

```csharp
using System;
using System.IO;
using System.Net;
using System.Linq;
using System.Threading.Tasks;

public class Program
{
  private static async Task WriteWebRequestSizeAsync(
      string url)
  {
    try
    {
      WebRequest webRequest =
          WebRequest.Create(url);
      WebResponse response =
          await webRequest.GetResponseAsync();
```

```
                using(StreamReader reader =
                    new StreamReader(
                        response.GetResponseStream()))
                {
                    string text =
                        await reader.ReadToEndAsync();
                    Console.WriteLine(
                        FormatBytes(text.Length));
                }
            }
            catch(WebException)
            {
                // ...
            }
            catch(IOException )
            {
                // ...
            }
            catch(NotSupportedException )
            {
                // ...
            }
        }

        public static void Main(string[] args)
        {
            string url = "http://www.IntelliTect.com";
            if(args.Length > 0)
            {
                url = args[0];
            }

            Console.Write(url);

            Task task = WriteWebRequestSizeAsync(url);

            while(!task.Wait(100))
            {
                Console.Write(".");
            }
        }

        // ...

    }
```

Notice the small differences between Listing 18.13 and Listing 18.15. First, we refactor the body of the Web request functionality into a new method (`WriteWebRequestSizeAsync()`) and add the new contextual keyword async to the method's declaration. A method decorated with this keyword must return `Task`, `Task<T>` or `void`. In this case, since there is no data returned by the body of the method but we still want the capability of returning information about the asynchronous activity back to the caller, `WriteWebRequestSizeAsync()` returns `Task`. Notice the method name suffix is `Async`; this is not necessary, but it is conventional to mark asynchronous methods this way in order to identify their asynchronous behavior. Finally, everywhere for which there is an asynchronous equivalent for the synchronous method, we insert the new contextual keyword `await` before invoking the asynchronous version.

Notice that nothing else changes between Listings 18.13 and 18.15. The asynchronous method versions seemingly still return the same data types as before—in spite of the fact that in actuality they each return a `Task<T>`. This is not via some magical implicit cast, either. `GetResponseAsync()` is declared as:

```
public virtual Task<WebResponse> GetResponseAsync() { ... }
```

while at the call site we assign the return value to `WebResponse`:

```
WebResponse response = await webRequest.GetResponseAsync()
```

The key is the `async` contextual keyword, which signals to the compiler to rewrite the expression into a state machine that represents all the control flow we saw in Listing 18.14 (and more).

Notice the try/catch logic improvements over Listing 18.14 that appear in Listing 18.15 as well. In all of Listing 18.15 there is no need to catch an `AggregateException`. The `catch` clause continues to catch the exact type of exception expected, no unwrapping the inner exceptions required. Rather, the compiler's rewrite seemingly ensures that the `AggregateException` in the task is processed as though it had been a normal, synchronously thrown exception. Whereas, in reality, the `AggregateException` (and its internal exception collection) still continue to operate as expected only when you await the task, the rewrite pulls the first exception from the collection and throws it. The aim is to make the asynchronous code look as much as possible like the synchronous code.

To better understand the control flow, Table 18.2 shows each task in a separate column along with the execution that occurs on each task.

TABLE 18.2: Control Flow within Each Task

Description	Main() Thread/	GetResponseAsync() Task	ReadToEndAsync() Task
1. Execution flows normally into Main and up through the first Console.Write(url) statement.	string url = "http://www.IntelliTect.com"; if(args.Length > 0) { url = args[0]; }		
2. A call is made to WriteWebRequestSizeAsync() and so control flows into that method as it would normally.	Console.Write(url);		
3. Instructions within WriteWebRequestSizeAsync() execute normally (still on the Main() thread) including the call to WebRequest.Create(url).	Task task = WriteWebRequestSizeAsync(url); WebRequest webRequest = WebRequest.Create(url);		
4. The first await modifier begins, generating a new Task on which the GetResponseAsync() can execute. And, assuming it didn't execute virtually instantaneously, the control flow returns to Main() and begins executing the while loop.	while(!task.Wait(100)) { Console.Write(". "); }	WebResponse response = await webRequest.GetResponseAsync(); StreamReader reader = new StreamReader(response.GetResponseStream()));	
5. Once the GetResponseAsync() task completes, execution within the same task continues with the implicit assignment of the said task's result to the response variable. Then the StreamReader is instantiated from the response.			
6. Upon the occurrence of another await, another task is created, this time to execute ReadToEndAsync(). (All the while Main's while loop continues executing.)			
7. Upon completion of the ReadToEndAsync() task, the result is assigned to text, whose Length is then displayed on the console.			string text = (await reader.ReadToEndAsync()); Console.WriteLine(FormatBytes(text.Length));
8. Finally, task.Wait() returns true and the process executes.			

There are a couple of important misconceptions that the table helps to dismiss.

- **Misconception #1: A method decorated with the** async **keyword is automatically executed on a worker thread when called.** This is absolutely not true; the method is executed normally, on the calling thread, and if the implementation doesn't await any incomplete awaitable tasks, it will complete synchronously on the same thread. It's the method's implementation that is responsible for starting any asynchronous work. Just using the async keyword does not change where the method's code executes. Also, there is nothing unusual about a call to an async method from the caller's perspective; it is a method typed as returning a Task, it is called normally, and it returns an object of its return type normally.

- **Misconception #2: The** await **keyword causes the current thread to block until the awaited task is completed.** That is also absolutely not true. If you want the current thread to block until the task completes, call the Wait() method, as we have already described, and, in fact, the Main thread does repeatedly while waiting for the other tasks to complete. However, the while(!task.Wait(100)) { } executes concurrently with the other tasks—not synchronously. The await keyword evaluates the expression which follows it, which is usually of type Task or Task<T>, adds a continuation to the resultant task, and then *immediately* returns control to the caller. The creation of the task has started asynchronous work; the await keyword means that the developer wishes the caller of this method to continue executing its work on this thread while the asynchronous work is processed. At some point after that asynchronous work is complete, execution will resume at the point of control following the await expression.

In fact, the principal reasons why the async keyword exists in the first place are first, to make it crystal clear to the reader of the code that the method which follows will be automatically rewritten by the compiler, and second, to inform the compiler that usages of the await contextual keyword in the method are to be treated as asynchronous control flow, and not as an ordinary identifier.

Asynchronous Lambdas

Just as a lambda expression converted to a delegate can be used as a concise syntax for declaring a normal method, C# 5.0 allows lambdas containing `await` expressions to be converted to delegates also. Just precede the lambda expression with the `async` keyword. In Listing 18.16 we rewrite the `GetResourceAsync()` method from Listing 18.15 from an async method to an async lambda.

LISTING 18.16: An Asynchronous Client-Server Interaction As a Lambda Expression

```csharp
using System;
using System.IO;
using System.Net;
using System.Linq;
using System.Threading.Tasks;

public class Program
{

  public static void Main(string[] args)
  {
      string url = "http://www.IntelliTect.com";
      if(args.Length > 0)
      {
          url = args[0];
      }

      Console.Write(url);

      Func<string, Task> writeWebRequestSizeAsync =
          async (string webRequestUrl) =>
          {
              // Error handling ommitted for
              // elucidation.
              WebRequest webRequest =
                WebRequest.Create(url);

              WebResponse response =
                  await webRequest.GetResponseAsync();
              using(StreamReader reader =
                new StreamReader(
                    response.GetResponseStream()))
              {
                  string text =
                      (await reader.ReadToEndAsync());
                  Console.WriteLine(
                      FormatBytes(text.Length));
              }
          };
```

```
Task task = writeWebRequestSizeAsync(url);

    while (!task.Wait(100))
    {
        Console.Write(".");
    }
}

// ...

}
```

Note that an `async` lambda expression has the exact same restrictions as the named `async` method.

- An `async` lambda expression must be converted to a delegate whose return type is `void`, `Task` or `Task<T>`.
- The lambda is rewritten so that `return` statements become signals that the task returned by the lambda has completed with the given result.
- Execution within the lambda expression occurs synchronously until the first await on an incomplete awaitable is executed.
- All instructions following the await will execute as continuations on the return from the invoked asynchronous method (or, if the awaitable is already complete, will be simply executed synchronously rather than as continuations).
- An `async` lambda expression can be invoked with an `await` (not shown in Listing 18.16).

■ ADVANCED TOPIC

Implementing a Custom Asynchronous Method

Implementing an asynchronous method by relying on other asynchronous methods (which in turn rely on more asynchronous methods) is relatively easy with the `await` keyword. However, at some point in the call hierarchy it becomes necessary to write a "leaf" asynchronous `Task`-returning method. Consider, for example, an asynchronous method for running a command-line program with the eventual goal that the output could be accessed. Such a method would be declared as follows:

```
static public Task<Process> RunProcessAsync(string filename)
```

The simplest implementation would, of course, be to rely on `Task.Run()` again and calling both `System.Diagnostics.Process`'s `Start()` and `WaitForExit()` methods. However, creating an additional thread in the current process is unnecessary when the invoked process itself will have its own collection of one or more threads. To implement the `RunProcessAsync()` method and return to the caller's synchronization context when the invoked process completes, we can rely on a `TaskCompletionSource<T>` object, as shown in Listing 18.17.

LISTING 18.17: Implementing a Custom Asynchronous Method

```csharp
using System.Diagnostics;
using System.Threading;
using System.Threading.Tasks;
class Program
{
  static public Task<Process> RunProcessAsync(
      string fileName,
      string arguments = null,
      CancellationToken cancellationToken =
          default(CancellationToken))
  {
      TaskCompletionSource<Process> taskCS =
          new TaskCompletionSource<Process>();

      Process process = new Process()
      {
          StartInfo = new ProcessStartInfo(fileName)
          {
              UseShellExecute = false,
              Arguments = arguments,
          },
          EnableRaisingEvents = true,
      };

      process.Exited += (sender, localEventArgs) =>
      {
          taskCS.SetResult(process);
      };

      cancellationToken
          .ThrowIfCancellationRequested();

      process.Start();

      cancellationToken.Register(() =>
      {
          process.CloseMainWindow();
      });
```

```
        return taskCS.Task;
    }

    // ...
}
```

Ignore the highlighting for the moment and instead focus on the pattern of using an event for notification when the process completes. Since `System.Diagnostics.Process` includes a notification upon exit, we register for this notification and use it as a callback from which we can invoke `TaskCompletionSource.SetResult()`. The code above provides a fairly common pattern with which to create an asynchronous method without having to resort to `Task.Run()`.

Another important characteristic that an `async` method might require is cancellation, and TAP relies on the same methods as the TPL—namely, a `System.Threading.CancellationToken`. The listing above highlights the code necessary to support cancellation. In this example we allow for canceling before the process ever starts, as well as an attempt to close the application's main window (if there is one). A more aggressive approach would be to call `Process.Kill()`, but this could potentially cause problems for the program that is executing.

Notice that we don't register for the cancellation event until after the process is started. This avoids any race conditions that might occur if cancellation is triggered before the process is actually started.

One last feature to consider supporting is a progress update. Listing 18.18 is the full `RunProcessAsync()` with just such an update.

LISTING 18.18: Implementing a Custom Asynchronous Method with Progress Support

```
using System;
using System.Diagnostics;
using System.Threading;
using System.Threading.Tasks;
class Program
{
    static public Task<Process> RunProcessAsync(
        string fileName,
        string arguments = null,
        CancellationToken cancellationToken =
            default(CancellationToken),
        IProgress<ProcessProgressEventArgs> progress =
            null,
        object objectState = null)
```

```csharp
    {
        TaskCompletionSource<Process> taskCS =
            new TaskCompletionSource<Process>();

        Process process = new Process()
        {
            StartInfo = new ProcessStartInfo(fileName)
            {
                UseShellExecute = false,
                Arguments = arguments,
                RedirectStandardOutput =
                    progress != null
            },
            EnableRaisingEvents = true,
        };

        process.Exited += (sender, localEventArgs) =>
        {
            taskCS.SetResult(process);
        };

        if(progress != null)
        {
            process.OutputDataReceived +=
                (sender, localEventArgs) =>
                {
                    progress.Report(
                        new ProcessProgressEventArgs(
                            localEventArgs.Data,
                            objectState));
                };
        }

        if(cancellationToken.IsCancellationRequested)
        {
            cancellationToken
                .ThrowIfCancellationRequested();
        }

        process.Start();

        if(progress != null)
        {
            process.BeginOutputReadLine();
        }

        cancellationToken.Register(() =>
        {
            process.CloseMainWindow();
            cancellationToken
                .ThrowIfCancellationRequested();
        });

        return taskCS.Task;
    }

    // ...
}
```

■ ADVANCED TOPIC

Awaiting Non-Task<T> Values

Generally, the expression that follows the await keyword is of type Task, or Task<T>. And in the examples of await shown so far, the expressions that follows the keyword all return Task<T>. From a syntax perspective, an await operating on type Task is essentially the equivalent of an expression that returns void. In fact, because the compiler does not even know whether the task has a result, much less what type it is, such an expression is classified the same as a call to a void-returning method; you can only use it in a statement context. Listing 18.19 shows some await expressions used as statement expressions.

LISTING 18.19: An Await Expression May Be a Statement Expression

```
async Task<int> DoStuffAsync()
{
  await DoSomethingAsync();
  await DoSomethingElseAsync();
  return await GetAnIntegerAsync() + 1;
}
```

Here we presume that the first methods return a Task, rather than a Task<T>. Since there is no result value associated with the first two tasks, awaiting them produces no value, and therefore, the expression must appear as a statement. The third task is presumably of type Task<int>, and its value can be used in the computation of the value of the task returned by DoStuffAsync().

This Advanced Topic begins with the word *Generally*. In fact, the exact rule regarding the return type that await requires is more generic than just Task, or Task<T>. Rather, it requires that the type support a GetAwaiter. This method produces an object that has certain properties and methods needed by the compiler's rewriting logic. This makes the system extensible by third parties;[8] if you want to design your own non-Task-based asynchrony system that uses some other type to represent asynchronous work, you can do so and still use the await syntax.

---

8. This technique of allowing third-party extension by looking for a particular method by its signature is used in two other C# features: LINQ looks for methods like Select() and Where() by name to implement the select and where contextual keywords, and the foreach loop does not require that the collection implement IEnumerable, just that it have an appropriate GetEnumerator() method.

Note, however, it is not possible to make `async` methods return something other than `void`, `Task`, or `Task<T>`, no matter what type is awaited inside the method.

Wrapping your head around precisely what is happening in an `async` method can be difficult, but it is far less difficult than trying to figure out what asynchronous code written with explicit continuations in lambdas is doing. The key points to remember are as follows.

- When control reaches an `await` keyword, the expression which follows it produces a task.[9] Control then returns to the caller so that it can continue to do work while the task completes asynchronously.
- Some time after the task completes, control resumes at the point following the `await`. If the awaited task produces a result, that result is then obtained. If it faulted, the exception is thrown.
- A `return` statement in an `async` method causes the task associated with the method invocation to become completed; if the `return` statement has a value, the value returned becomes the result of the task.

Task Schedulers and the Synchronization Context

On occasion this chapter mentions the task scheduler and its role in determining how to assign work to threads efficiently. Programmatically, the task scheduler is an instance of the `System.Threading.Tasks.TaskScheduler`. This class, by default, uses thread pool to schedule tasks appropriately, determining how to safely and efficiently execute them—when to reuse them, dispose them, or create additional ones.

It is possible to create your own task scheduler that makes different choices about how to schedule tasks by deriving a new type from the `TaskScheduler` class. You can obtain a `TaskScheduler` that will schedule a task to the current thread (or, more precisely, to the **synchronization context** associated with the current thread), rather than to a different worker thread, by using the static `FromCurrentSynchronizationContext()` method.[10]

---

9. Technically, it is an awaitable type as described in the Advanced Topic titled Awaiting Non-`Task<T>` Values.
10. For an example see Listing C.8 in Appendix C.

The **synchronization context** under which a task executes and, in turn, the continuation task(s) execute, is important because the awaiting task consults the synchronization context (assuming there is one) in order for a task to execute efficiently and safely. Listing 18.20 (along with Output 18.7) is similar to Listing 18.5 except that it also prints out the thread ID when it displays the message.

LISTING 18.20: **Calling** Task.ContinueWith()

```csharp
using System;
using System.Threading.Tasks;

public class Program
{
  public static void Main()
  {
      DisplayStatus("Before");
      Task taskA =
          Task.Run(() =>
                DisplayStatus("Starting..."))
          .ContinueWith( antecedent =>
                DisplayStatus("Continuing A..."));
      Task taskB = taskA.ContinueWith( antecedent =>
          DisplayStatus("Continuing B..."));
      Task taskC = taskA.ContinueWith( antecedent =>
          DisplayStatus("Continuing C..."));
      Task.WaitAll(taskB, taskC);
      DisplayStatus("Finished!");
  }

  private static void DisplayStatus(string message)
  {
      string text =
          string.Format("{0}: {1}",
                Thread.CurrentThread.ManagedThreadId,
                message);
      Console.WriteLine(text);
  }
}
```

OUTPUT 18.7

```
1: Before
3: Starting...
4: Continuing A...
3: Continuing C...
4: Continuing B...
1: Finished!
```

What is noteworthy about the output is the fact that the thread ID changes sometimes and gets repeated other times. In a plain console application like this, the synchronization context (accessible from `SynchronizationContext.Current`) is null—the default synchronization context causes the thread pool to handle thread allocation instead. This explains why the thread ID changes between tasks; sometimes the thread pool determines that it is more efficient to use a new thread and sometimes to reuse an existing thread.

Fortunately, the synchronization context gets set automatically for types of applications where that is critical. For example, if the code creating tasks is running in a thread created by ASP.NET, the thread will have a synchronization context of type `AspNetSynchronizationContext` associated with it, whereas if your code is running in a thread created in a WPF application, the thread will have an instance of `DispatcherSynchronizationContext` associated with it. (And for console applications, there is no synchronization context by default.) Since the TPL consults the synchronization context and the synchronization context varies depending on the circumstances of the execution, the TPL is able to schedule continuations executing in contexts that are both efficient and safe.

To modify the code so that the synchronization context is leveraged instead requires first setting the synchronization context, and second, using `async`/`await` so that the synchronization context gets consulted.[11]

It is possible to define custom synchronization contexts, and to work with existing synchronization contexts to improve their performance in some specific scenarios. However, describing how to do so is beyond the scope of this text.

`async`/`await` with the Windows UI

One place that synchronization is especially important is in the context of UI and Web programming. With the Windows UI, for example, there is a message pump that processes messages such as mouse click and move events. Furthermore, the UI is single-threaded and interaction with any UI components (a text box, for example) must always occur from the single UI thread. One of the key advantages of the `async`/`await` pattern is the fact that it leverages the synchronization context so that continuation

---

11. For a simple example of how to set the synchronization context of a thread, and how to use a task scheduler to schedule a task to that thread, see Listing C.8 in Appendix C.

work—work that appears after the `await` statement—will always execute on the same synchronization task that invoked the `await` statement. This is of significant value because it eliminates the need to explicitly switch back to the UI thread in order to update a control.

To appreciate this, consider the example of a UI event for a button click in WPF, as follows in Listing 18.21.

LISTING 18.21: **Synchronous High-Latency Invocation in WPF**

```
using System;

private void PingButton_Click(
  object sender, RoutedEventArgs e)
{
  StatusLabel.Content = "Pinging…";
  Ping ping = new Ping();
  PingReply pingReply =
      ping.Send("www.IntelliTect.com");
  StatusLabel.Content = pingReply.Status.ToString();
}
```

Given that `StatusLabel` is a WPF `System.Windows.Label` control and we have updated the `Content` property twice within the `PingButton_Click()` event subscriber, it would be a reasonable assumption that first "Pinging…" would be displayed until `Ping.Send()` returned, and then the label would be updated with the status of the `Send()` reply. As those experienced with WPF well know, this is not, in fact, what happens. Rather, a message is posted to the Windows message pump to update the content with "Pinging…" but, since the UI thread is busy executing the `PingButton_Click()` method, the Windows message pump is not processed. By the time the UI thread frees up to look at the Windows message pump, a second `Content` property update request has been queued and the only message that the user is able to observe is the final status.

To fix this problem using TAP, we change the code highlighted in Listing 18.22.

LISTING 18.22: **Synchronous High-Latency Invocation in WPF Using** `await`

```
using System;
async private void PingButton_Click(
  object sender, RoutedEventArgs e)
{
  StatusLabel.Content = "Pinging…";
  Ping ping = new Ping();
```

```
PingReply pingReply =
    await ping.SendPingAsync("www.IntelliTect.com");
StatusLabel.Content = pingReply.Status.ToString();
}
```

There are two advantages to this change. First, the asynchronous nature of the ping call frees up the caller thread to return to the Windows message pump caller's synchronization context, and processes the update to `StatusLabel.Content` so that "Pinging..." appears to the user. Second, when awaiting `ping.SendTaskAsync()` completes, it will always execute on the same synchronization context as the caller. And, since the synchronization context is specifically appropriate for WPF, it is single-threaded, and therefore, the return will always be to the same thread—the UI thread. In other words, rather than immediately executing the continuation task, the TPL consults the synchronization context, which instead posts a message regarding the continuation work to the message pump. Next, because the UI thread monitors the message pump, upon picking up the continuation work message, it invokes the code following the `await` call. (As a result, the invocation of the continuation code is on the same thread as the caller that processed the message pump.)

There is a key code readability feature built into the TAP language pattern. Notice in Listing 18.22 that the call to return `pingReply.Status` appears to flow naturally after the `await`, providing clear indication that it will execute immediately following the previous line. However, writing what really happens from scratch would be far less understandable for multiple reasons.

await **Operators**

There is no limitation on the number of times `await` can be placed into a single method. And in fact, they are not limited to appearing one after another. Rather, `await` can be placed into loops and processed consecutively one after the other, thereby following a natural control flow the way code appears. Consider the example in Listing 18.23.

LISTING 18.23: Iterating over an Await Operation

```
using System;
async private void PingButton_Click(
  object sender, RoutedEventArgs e)
{
  List<string> urls = new List<string>()
```

```
    {
        "www.habitat-spokane.org",
        "www.partnersintl.org",
        "www.iassist.org",
        "www.fh.org",
        "www.worldvision.org"
    };
IPStatus status;

Func<string, Task<IPStatus>> func =
    async (localUrl) =>
    {
        Ping ping = new Ping();
        PingReply pingReply =
            await ping.SendPingAsync(localUrl);
        return pingReply.Status;
    };

StatusLabel.Content = "Pinging…";

    foreach(string url in urls)
    {
        status = await func(url);
        StatusLabel.Content =
            string.Format("{0}: {1} ({2})",
                url, status.ToString(),
                Thread.CurrentThread.ManagedThreadId);
    }
}
```

Note that regardless of whether the `awaits` occur within an iteration or as separate entries they will execute serially, one after the other and in the same order they were invoked from the calling thread. The underlying implementation is to string them together in the semantic equivalent of `Task.ContinueWith()`, except the code between the `await` operators will all execute in the caller's synchronization context.

Support for TAP from the UI is one of the key scenarios that led to TAP's creation. A second scenario takes place on the server where a request comes in from a client to query an entire table's worth of data from the database. Since querying the data could be time-consuming, a new thread should be created rather than consuming one from the limited number allocated to the thread pool. The problem with this approach is that the work to query from the database is executing entirely on another machine. There is no reason to block an entire thread since the thread is generally not active anyway.

To summarize, TAP was created to address these key problems:

- There is a need to allow long-running activities to occur without blocking the UI thread.

- Creating a new thread (or `Task`) for non-CPU-intensive work is relatively expensive when you consider that all the thread is doing is waiting for the activity to complete.

- When the activity completes (by either using a new thread or via a callback) it is frequently necessary to make a thread synchronization context switch back to the original caller that initiated the activity.

- It provides a new pattern that works for both CPU- and non-CPU-intensive asynchronous invocations—one that all .NET languages support explicitly.

Executing Loop Iterations in Parallel

Consider the following `for` loop statement and associated code (see Listing 18.24 and the corresponding output, Output 18.8). The listing calls a method for calculating a section of the decimal expansion of pi where the parameters are the number of digits and the digit to start with. The actual calculation is not germane to the discussion. What is interesting about this calculation is that it is **embarrassingly parallelizable;** that is, it is almost embarrassing how easy it is to split up a large task—say, computing 1 million decimal digits of pi—into any desired number of smaller tasks that can all be run in parallel. These types of computations are the easiest ones to speed up by adding parallelism.

LISTING 18.24: For **Loop Synchronously Calculating Pi in Sections**

```
using System;
using AddisonWesley.Michaelis.EssentialCSharp.Shared;

class Program
{
  const int TotalDigits = 100;
  const int BatchSize = 10;

  static void Main()
  {
      string pi = null;
      int iterations = TotalDigits / BatchSize;
      for(int i = 0; i < iterations; i++)
      {
          pi += PiCalculator.Calculate(
```

```
            BatchSize, i * BatchSize);
        }

        Console.WriteLine(pi);
    }
}
```

```
using System;

class PiCalculator
{
  public static string Calculate(
      int digits, int startingAt)
  {
    // ...
  }

    // ...
}
```

OUTPUT 18.8

```
>3.1415926535897932384626433832795028841971693993751058209749445923078
1640628620899862803482534211706798214808651328230664709384460955058223
1725359408128481117450284102701938521105559644622948954930381964428810
9756659334461284756482337867831652712019091456485669234603486104543266
4821339360726024914127372458700660631558817488152092096282925409171536
4367892590360011330530548820466521384146951941511609433057270365759591
9530921861173819326117931051185480744623799627495673518857527248912279
3818301194912
```

The `for` loop executes each iteration synchronously and sequentially. However, since the pi calculation algorithm splits the pi calculation into independent pieces, it is not necessary to compute the pieces sequentially just as long as the results are appended in the right order. Therefore, imagine if you could have all the iterations of this loop run concurrently: Each processor could take a single iteration and execute it in parallel with other processors executing other iterations. Given the simultaneous execution of iterations, we could decrease the execution time more and more based on the number of processors.

The TPL provides a convenient method, `Parallel.For()`, that does precisely that. Listing 18.25 shows how to modify the sequential, single-threaded program in Listing 18.24 to use the helper method.

LISTING 18.25: For **Loop Calculating Pi in Sections in Parallel**

```csharp
using System;
using System.Threading.Tasks;
using AddisonWesley.Michaelis.EssentialCSharp.Shared;

// ...

class Program
{
  static void Main()
  {
      string pi = null;
      int iterations = TotalDigits / BatchSize;
      string[] sections = new string[iterations];
      Parallel.For(0, iterations, (i) =>
      {
          sections[i] = PiCalculator.Calculate(
              BatchSize, i * BatchSize);
      });
      pi = string.Join("", sections);
      Console.WriteLine(pi);
  }
}
```

The output for Listing 18.25 is identical to Output 18.8; however, the execution time is significantly faster if you have multiple CPUs (and possibly slower if you do not). The `Parallel.For()` API is designed to look similar to a standard `for` loop. The first parameter is the `fromInclusive` value, the second is the `toExclusive` value, and the last is the `Action<int>` to perform as the loop body. When using an expression lambda for the action, the code looks similar to a `for` loop statement except now each iteration may execute in parallel. As with the `for` loop, the call to `Parallel.For()` will not complete until all iterations are complete. In other words, by the time execution reaches the `string.Join()` statement, all sections of pi will have been calculated.

It is important to note that the code for combining the various sections of pi no longer occurs inside the iteration (`action`). Since sections of the pi calculation will very likely not complete sequentially, appending a section whenever an iteration completes will likely append them out of order. Even if sequence was not a problem, there is still a potential race condition because the `+=` operator is not atomic. To address both of these problems, each section of pi is stored into an array and no two or more iterations will access a single element within the array simultaneously. Only once all sections of pi are calculated does `string.Join()` combine them. In other words, we postpone concatenating the sections until after the `Parallel.For()` loop has completed. This avoids any race condition caused by sections not yet calculated or sections concatenating out of order.

The TPL uses the same sorts of thread pooling techniques that it uses for task scheduling to ensure good performance of the parallel loop: It will try to ensure that CPUs are not overscheduled, and so on.

Guidelines

DO use parallel loops when the computations performed can be easily split up into many mutually independent processor-bound computations that can be executed in any order on any thread.

The TPL also provides a similar parallel version of the `foreach` statement, as shown in Listing 18.26.

LISTING 18.26: **Parallel Execution of a** `foreach` **Loop**

```csharp
using System;
using System.Collections.Generic;
using System.IO;
using System.Threading.Tasks;

class Program
{
  // ...
  static void EncryptFiles(
      string directoryPath, string searchPattern)
  {
      IEnumerable<string> files = Directory.GetFiles(
          directoryPath, searchPattern,
          SearchOption.AllDirectories);

      Parallel.ForEach(files, (fileName) =>
      {
          Encrypt(fileName);
      });
  }
  // ...
}
```

In this example, we call a method that encrypts each file within the `files` collection and it does so in parallel, executing as many threads as the TPL determines is efficient.

■ **ADVANCED TOPIC**

How the TPL Tunes Its Own Performance

The default scheduler within the TPL targets the thread pool, resulting in a variety of heuristics to try to ensure that the right number of threads are executing at any one time. Two of the heuristics it uses are **hill climbing** and **work stealing.**

The hill climbing algorithm involves creating threads to run tasks, and then monitoring the performance of those tasks to try to experimentally determine the point at which adding more threads is making performance worse. Once that point is reached, the number of threads can then be decreased back to the number that produced the best performance.

The TPL associates "top-level" tasks that are waiting to be executed with no particular thread. If, however, a task running on a thread itself creates another task, the newly created task is associated with that thread automatically. When the new "child" task is eventually scheduled to run, it usually runs on the same thread as the task that created it. The work stealing algorithm identifies threads that have an unusually large or unusually small amount of pending work; a thread that has too few tasks associated with it will sometimes "steal" not-yet-executed tasks from threads that have too many tasks waiting to run.

The key feature of these algorithms is that they enable the TPL to dynamically tune its own performance to mitigate processor overscheduling and underscheduling, and to balance the work among the available processors.

The TPL generally does a good job of tuning its own performance, but you can help it do a good job. Specifying the TPL `TaskCreationOptions.LongRunning` option described earlier in the section Long-Running Tasks is an example of such a hint. You can also explicitly tell the task scheduler how many threads you think would be best to service a parallel loop; see the Advanced Topic titled Parallel Loop Options for more details.

■ **BEGINNER TOPIC**

Parallel Loop Exception Handling with `AggregateException`

We know already that the TPL catches and saves exceptions associated with tasks in an `AggregateException`, because a given task might have several exceptions obtained from its subtasks. This is also the case with parallel execution of loops: Each iteration could have produced an exception, and therefore, the exceptions need to be gathered up into one aggregating exception. Consider the example in Listing 18.27 and its output in Output 18.9.

LISTING 18.27: Unhandled Exception Handling for Parallel Iterations

```csharp
using System;
using System.Collections.Generic;
using System.IO;
using System.Threading;
using System.Threading.Tasks;

class Program
{
  // ...
  static void EncryptFiles(
      string directoryPath, string searchPattern)
  {
      IEnumerable<string> files = Directory.GetFiles(
          directoryPath, searchPattern,
          SearchOption.AllDirectories);
      try
      {
          Parallel.ForEach(files, (fileName) =>
          {
              Encrypt(fileName);
          });
      }
      catch(AggregateException exception)
      {
          Console.WriteLine(
              "ERROR: {0}:",
              exception.GetType().Name);
          foreach(Exception item in
              exception.InnerExceptions)
          {
              Console.WriteLine("  {0} - {1}",
                  item.GetType().Name, item.Message);
          }
      }
  }
  // ...
}
```

OUTPUT 18.9

```
ERROR: AggregateException:
  UnauthorizedAccessException - Attempted to perform an unauthorized
operation.
  UnauthorizedAccessException - Attempted to perform an unauthorized
operation.
  UnauthorizedAccessException - Attempted to perform an unauthorized
operation.
```

Output 18.9 shows that three exceptions occurred while executing the `Parallel.ForEach<T>(...)` loop. However, in the code, there is only one catch of type `System.AggregateException`. The `UnauthorizedAccessExceptions` were retrieved from the `InnerExceptions` property on the `AggregateException`. With a `Parallel.ForEach<T>()` loop, each iteration could potentially throw an exception and so the `System.AggregateException` thrown by the method call will contain each of those exceptions within its `InnerExceptions` property.

Canceling a Parallel Loop

Unlike a task which requires an explicit call in order to block until it completes, a parallel loop executes iterations in parallel but does not itself return until the entire parallel loop completes. Canceling a parallel loop, therefore, generally involves invocation of the cancellation request from a thread other than the one executing the parallel loop. In Listing 18.28, we invoke `Parallel.ForEach<T>()` using `Task.Run()`. In this manner, not only does the query execute in parallel, but it also executes asynchronously, allowing the code to prompt the user to "Push ENTER to exit."

LISTING 18.28: Canceling a Parallel Loop

```
using System;
using System.Collections.Generic;
using System.Diagnostics;
using System.IO;
using System.Threading;
using System.Threading.Tasks;

public class Program
{
    // ...

  static void EncryptFiles(
      string directoryPath, string searchPattern)
  {

      string stars =
          "*".PadRight(Console.WindowWidth-1, '*');

      IEnumerable<string> files = Directory.GetFiles(
          directoryPath, searchPattern,
          SearchOption.AllDirectories);

          CancellationTokenSource cts =
              new CancellationTokenSource();
```

```
        ParallelOptions parallelOptions =
            new ParallelOptions
                { CancellationToken = cts.Token };
    cts.Token.Register(
        () => Console.WriteLine("Cancelling..."));

    Console.WriteLine("Push ENTER to exit.");

    // Use Task.Factory.StartNew<string>() for
    // TPL prior to .NET 4.5
    Task task = Task.Run(() =>
        {
            try
            {
                Parallel.ForEach(
                    files, parallelOptions,
                    (fileName, loopState) =>
                        {
                            Encrypt(fileName);
                        });
            }
            catch(OperationCanceledException){}
        });

    // Wait for the user's input
    Console.Read();

    // Cancel the query
    cts.Cancel();
    Console.Write(stars);
    task.Wait();
    }
}
```

The parallel loops use the same cancellation token pattern that tasks use. The token obtained from a `CancellationTokenSource` is associated with the parallel loop by calling an overload of the `ForEach()` method that has a parameter of type `ParallelOptions`. This object contains the cancellation token.

Note that if you cancel a parallel loop operation, any iterations that have not started yet are prevented from starting by checking the `IsCancellationRequested` property. Existing executing iterations will run to their respective termination points. Furthermore, calling `Cancel()` even after all iterations have completed will still cause the registered cancel event (via `cts.Token.Register()`) to execute.

The only means by which the ForEach() method is able to acknowledge that the loop has been canceled is via the OperationCanceledException. Given that cancellation in this example is expected, the exception is caught and ignored, allowing the application to display "Canceling..." followed by a line of stars before exiting.

■ **ADVANCED TOPIC**

Parallel Loop Options

Although not generally necessary, it is possible to control the maximum degree of parallelism (that is, the number of threads that are scheduled to run at the same time) via the ParallelOptions parameter on overloads of both the Parallel.For() and Parallel.ForEach<T>() loops. There are specific cases where the developer knows more about the particular algorithm or circumstance such that changing the maximum degree of parallelism makes sense. These circumstances include the following.

- Scenarios where you want to disable parallelism to make debugging or analysis easier. Setting the maximum degree of parallelism to 1 ensures that the loop iterations do not run concurrently.
- Scenarios where you know ahead of time that the degree of parallelism will be gated on an external factor such as a hardware constraint. For example, if your parallel operation involves using multiple USB ports, it is possible that there is no point in creating more threads than there are available ports.
- Scenarios with really long-running loop iterations (for example, minutes or hours). The thread pool can't distinguish long-running iterations from blocked operations, and therefore could end up introducing many new threads, all of which will be consumed by the for loop. This can result in incremental thread growth over time, resulting in a huge number of threads in the process.

And so on. To control the maximum degree of parallelism, use the MaxDegreeOfParallelism property on the ParallelOptions object.

You can also use the ParallelOptions object's TaskScheduler property to specify a custom task scheduler to use to schedule the tasks associated with each iteration. For example, you might have an asynchronous event handler that responds to the user's clicks of a "Next" button. If the user clicks the button several times, you might want to use a custom task scheduler that prioritizes the most recently created task, rather than prioritizing the task that has waited the longest. The task scheduler provides a means of specifying how the tasks will execute in relation to one another.

The `ParallelOptions` object also has a `CancellationToken` property that provides a mechanism to communicate to the loop that no further iterations should start. Additionally, the body of an iteration can watch the cancellation token to determine if an early exit from the iteration is in order.

■ ADVANCED TOPIC

Breaking a Parallel Loop

Like a standard `for` loop, the `Parallel.For()` loop also supports the concept of "breaking" to exit the loop and canceling any further iterations. In the context of parallel `for` execution, however, a break signifies that no *new* iterations following the breaking iteration should start. All currently executing iterations will run to completion.

To break a parallel loop, you can provide a cancellation token and cancel it on another thread, as described in the preceding Advanced Topic. You can also use an overload of the `Parallel.For()` method whose body delegate takes two parameters: the index, and a `ParallelLoopState` object. An iteration that wishes to "break" the loop can call the `Break()` or `Stop()` method on the loop state object passed to the delegate. The `Break()` method indicates that no more iterations with index values higher than the current value need to execute; the `Stop()` method indicates that no more iterations need to run at all.

For example, suppose you have a `Parallel.For()` loop that is performing ten iterations in parallel. Some of those iterations might run faster than others, and the task scheduler does not guarantee that they run in any particular order. Suppose the first iteration has completed, iterations 3, 5, 7, and 9 are "in flight," scheduled to four different threads, and iterations 5 and 7 both call `Break()`. In this scenario, iterations 6 and 8 will never start, but iterations 2 and 4 will still be scheduled to run. Iterations 3 and 9 will run to completion because they were already started when the break happened.

The `Parallel.For()` and `Parallel.ForEach<T>()` methods return a reference to a `ParallelLoopResult` object that contains useful information about what happened during the loop. This result object has the following properties.

- `IsCompleted`: returns a Boolean indicating whether all iterations started.
- `LowestBreakIteration`: identifies the lowest iteration that executed a break. The value is of type `long?`, where a value of null indicates no break statement was encountered.

Returning to the ten-iteration example, the `IsCompleted` property will return `false` and the `LowestBreakIteration` will return a value of 5.

Running LINQ Queries in Parallel

Just as it is possible to execute a loop in parallel using `Parallel.For()`, it is also possible to execute LINQ queries in parallel using the Parallel LINQ API (PLINQ for short). An example of a simple nonparallel LINQ expression is shown in Listing 18.29; in Listing 18.30 we'll modify it to run in parallel.

LISTING 18.29: LINQ `Select()`

```
using System.Collections.Generic;
using System.Linq;

class Cryptographer
{
  // ...
  public List<string>
    Encrypt(IEnumerable<string> data)
  {
      return data.Select(
          item => Encrypt(item)).ToList();
  }
  // ...
}
```

In Listing 18.29, we have a LINQ query using the `Select()` standard query operator to encrypt each string within a sequence of strings, and convert the resultant sequence to a list. This seems like an "embarrassingly parallel" operation; each encryption is likely to be a high-latency

processor-bound operation that could be farmed out to a worker thread
on another CPU.

Listing 18.30 shows how to modify Listing 18.29 so that the code that
encrypts the strings is executed in parallel.

LISTING 18.30: Parallel LINQ Select()

```csharp
using System.Linq;

class Cryptographer
{
  // ...
  public List<string>
    Encrypt (IEnumerable<string> data)
  {
      return data.AsParallel().Select(
          item => Encrypt(item)).ToList();
  }
  // ...
}
```

As Listing 18.30 shows, the change to enable parallel support is extremely
small! All that it uses is a .NET Framework 4.0–introduced standard
query operator, AsParallel(), which can be found on the static class
System.Linq.ParallelEnumerable. This simple extension method tells
the runtime that it can execute the query in parallel. The result is that on
machines with multiple available CPUs, the total time taken to execute the
query can be significantly shorter.

System.Linq.ParallelEnumerable includes a superset of the query
operators available on System.Linq.Enumerable, resulting in possible performance improvements for all of the common query operators, including
those used for sorting, filtering (Where()), projecting (Select()), joining,
grouping, and aggregating. Listing 18.31 shows how to do a parallel sort.

LISTING 18.31: Parallel LINQ with Standard Query Operators

```csharp
// ...
    OrderedParallelQuery<string> parallelGroups =
        data.AsParallel().OrderBy(item => item);

    // Show the total count of items still
    // matches the original count
    System.Diagnostics.Trace.Assert(
        data.Count == parallelGroups.Sum(
            item => item.Count()));
// ...
```

As Listing 18.31 shows, invoking the parallel version simply involves a call to the `AsParallel()` extension method. Notice that the type of the result returned by the parallel standard query operators is `ParallelQuery<T>`, or `Ordered ParallelQuery<T>`, which informs the compiler that it should continue to use the parallel versions of the standard query operations that are available.

Since query expressions are simply a syntactic sugar for the method call form of the query used in the listings above, you can just as easily use `AsParallel()` with the expression form. Listing 18.32 shows an example of executing a grouping operation in parallel using query expression syntax.

LISTING 18.32: Parallel LINQ with Query Expressions

```
// ...
    ParallelQuery<IGrouping<char, string>> parallelGroups;
    parallelGroups =
        from text in data.AsParallel()
        orderby text
        group text by text[0];

    // Show the total count of items still
    // matches the original count
    System.Diagnostics.Trace.Assert(
        data.Count == parallelGroups.Sum(
            item => item.Count()));
// ...
```

As you saw in the previous examples, converting a query or iteration loop to execute in parallel is simple. There is one significant caveat, however. As we will discuss in depth in the next chapter, you must take care not to allow multiple threads to inappropriately access and modify the same memory simultaneously. Doing so will cause a race condition.

As we saw earlier in this chapter, the `Parallel.For()` and `Parallel .ForEach<T>` 4() methods will gather up any exceptions thrown during the parallel iterations and then throw one aggregating exception containing all of the original exceptions. PLINQ operations are no different; they also have the potential of returning multiple exceptions for the exact same reason: When the query logic is run on each element in parallel, the code executing on each element can independently throw an exception. Unsurprisingly, PLINQ deals with this situation in exactly the same way as do parallel loops and the TPL: Exceptions thrown during parallel queries are accessible via the `InnerExceptions` property of the `AggregateException`. Therefore, wrapping a PLINQ query in a try/catch block with the exception type of

`System.AggregateException` will successfully handle any exceptions within each iteration that were unhandled.

Canceling a PLINQ Query

As expected, the cancellation request pattern is also available on PLINQ queries. Listing 18.33 (with Output 18.10) provides an example. Like the parallel loops, canceled PLINQ queries will throw a `System.OperationCanceledException`. Like parallel loops, executing a PLINQ query is a synchronous operation on the invoking thread. Thus, a common technique is to wrap the parallel query in a task that runs on another thread so that the current thread can cancel it if necessary—the same solution that is used in Listing 18.28.

LISTING 18.33: Canceling a PLINQ Query

```
using System;
using System.Collections.Generic;
using System.Linq;
using System.Threading;
using System.Threading.Tasks;

public class Program
{

  public static List<string> ParallelEncrypt(
      List<string> data,
      CancellationToken cancellationToken)
  {
      return data.AsParallel().WithCancellation(
          cancellationToken).Select(
              (item) => Encrypt(item)).ToList();
  }

  public static void Main()
  {
      List<string> data = Utility.GetData(1000000).ToList();

      CancellationTokenSource cts =
          new CancellationTokenSource();

      Console.WriteLine("Push ENTER to exit.");

      // Use Task.Factory.StartNew<string>() for
      // TPL prior to .NET 4.5
      Task task = Task.Run(() =>
          {
              data = ParallelEncrypt(data, cts.Token);
          }, cts.Token);
```

```
        // Wait for the user's input
        Console.Read();

        cts.Cancel();
        Console.Write(stars);
        try{ task.Wait(); }
        catch(AggregateException){}
    }

    // ...
}
```

OUTPUT 18.10

```
ERROR: The operation was canceled.
```

As with a parallel loop or task, canceling a PLINQ query requires a `CancellationToken`, which is available from a `CancellationTokenSource`. However, rather than overloading every PLINQ query to support the cancellation token, the `ParallelQuery<T>` object returned by `IEnumerable`'s `AsParallel()` method includes a `WithCancellation()` extension method that simply takes a `CancellationToken`. As a result, calling `Cancel()` on the `CancellationTokenSource` object will request the parallel query to cancel—because it checks the `IsCancellationRequested` property on the `CancellationToken`.

As mentioned, canceling a PLINQ query will throw an exception in place of returning the complete result. One common technique for dealing with a possibly canceled PLINQ query is to wrap the query in a try block and catch the `OperationCanceledException`. A second common technique, used in Listing 18.33, is to pass the `CancellationToken` to both `ParallelEncrypt()` and as a second parameter on `Run()`. This will cause `task.Wait()` to throw an `AggregateException` whose `InnerException` property will be set to a `TaskCanceledException`. The aggregating exception can then be caught, as you would catch any other exception from a parallel operation.

SUMMARY

In this chapter, we started with a look at the basic parts of multithreaded programs: the `Thread` class, which represents an independent "point of control" in a program, and the `ThreadPool`, which encourages efficient allocation and scheduling of threads to multiple CPUs. However, these APIs are low-level and difficult to work with directly; version 4.0 of the .NET Framework provides the Parallel Extensions library, which includes the Task Parallel Library (TPL) and Parallel LINQ (PLINQ). Both provide new APIs for creating and scheduling units of work represented by `Task` objects, executing loops in parallel using `Parallel.For()` and `Parallel.ForEach()`, and automatically parallelizing LINQ queries with `AsParallel()`.

We also discussed how C# 5.0 makes programming complex workflows with `Task` objects much easier by automatically rewriting your programs to manage the continuation "wiring" that composes larger tasks out of smaller tasks.

At the beginning of this chapter, we briefly glossed over some of the difficult problems that developers often face when writing multithreaded programs: atomicity problems, deadlocks, and other "race conditions" that introduce uncertainty and bad behavior into multithreaded programs. We mentioned that the standard way to avoid these problems is to carefully write code that uses "locks" to synchronize access to shared resources; this is the topic of the next chapter.

■19■
Thread Synchronization

I N THE PRECEDING CHAPTER, we discussed the details of multithreaded programming using the Task Parallel Library (TPL) and Parallel LINQ (PLINQ). One topic we specifically avoided, however, was thread synchronization, which prevents race conditions while avoiding deadlocks. Thread synchronization is the topic of this chapter.

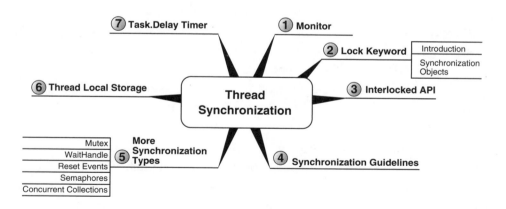

We begin with a multithreaded example with no thread synchronization around shared data—resulting in a race condition in which data integrity is lost. This serves as the introduction for why we need thread synchronization followed by myriad mechanisms and best practices for doing it.

Prior editions of this book also included a significant section on additional multithreading patterns and another on various timer callback mechanisms. With the introduction of the async/await pattern, however, those approaches have essentially been replaced unless programming with frameworks prior to C# 5.0/.NET 4.5. In order to make the pre-C# 5.0 material still available, it has been moved to Appendix C, Interfacing with Multithreading Patterns prior to C# 5.0, and Appendix D, Timers prior to the Async/Await Pattern of C# 5.0.

This entire chapter uses the TPL, so the samples cannot be compiled on frameworks prior to .NET Framework 4. However, unless specifically identified as a .NET Framework 4 API, the only reason for the .NET Framework 4 restriction is the use of the `System.Threading.Tasks.Task` class to execute the asynchronous operation. Modifying the code to instantiate a `System.Threading.Thread` and use a `Thread.Join()` to wait for the thread to execute will allow the vast majority of samples to compile on earlier frameworks.

That being said, the specific API for starting tasks throughout this chapter is the .NET 4.5-specific `System.Threading.Tasks.Task.Run()`. As we discussed in the preceding chapter, this method is preferred over `System.Threading.Tasks.Task.Factory.StartNew()` because it is simpler and sufficient for the majority of scenarios. Those readers limited to .NET 4 can replace `Task.Run()` with `Task.Factory.StartNew()` without any additional modifications. (For this reason the chapter does not explicitly highlight such code as .NET 4.5-specific code when only this method is used.)

Furthermore, Microsoft released the Reactive Extensions to .NET (Rx), a separate download that adds support for the TPL and PLINQ within the .NET 3.5 Framework.[1] This framework also includes the concurrent and synchronization types introduced in this chapter. For this reason, code listings that depend on `Task` or that introduce C# 4.0 synchronization classes are, in fact, available from .NET 3.5 using the functionality backported to the .NET 3.5 Framework via Rx and a reference to the `System.Threading.dll` assembly.

In summary, most of the samples in the chapter will require only minor modification to work with .NET prior to .NET 4.5 either by using `Task.Factory.StartNew()` or by relying on `Thread.Start()` if the TPL is not available.

---

1. See http://bit.ly/Rx3point5

Why Synchronization?

Running a new thread is a relatively simple programming task. What makes multithreaded programming difficult, however, is identifying which data multiple threads can safely access simultaneously. The program must synchronize such data to prevent simultaneous access, thereby creating the "safety." Consider Listing 19.1.

LISTING 19.1: Unsynchronized State

```
using System;
using System.Threading.Tasks;

public class Program
{
    const int _Total = int.MaxValue;
    static long _Count = 0;

    public static void Main()
    {
        // Use Task.Factory.StartNew for .NET 4.0
        Task task = Task.Run(()=>Decrement());

        // Increment
        for(int i = 0; i < _Total; i++)
        {
            _Count++;
        }

        task.Wait();
        Console.WriteLine("Count = {0}", _Count);
    }

    static void Decrement()
    {
        // Decrement
        for(int i = 0; i < _Total; i++)
        {
            _Count--;
        }
    }
}
```

One possible result of Listing 19.1 appears in Output 19.1.

OUTPUT 19.1

```
Count = 113449949
```

The important thing to note about Listing 19.1 is that the output is not 0. It would have been if `Decrement()` was called directly (sequentially). However, when calling `Decrement()` asynchronously, a race condition occurs because the individual steps within `_Count++` and `_Count--` statements intermingle. (As discussed in the Beginner Topic titled Multithreading Jargon early in Chapter 18, a single statement in C# will likely involve multiple steps.) Consider the sample execution in Table 19.1.

TABLE 19.1: Sample Pseudocode Execution

Main Thread	Decrement Thread	Count
...	...	...
Copy the value 0 out of _Count.		0
Increment the copied value (0), resulting in 1.		0
Copy the resultant value (1) into _Count.		1
Copy the value 1 out of _Count.		1
	Copy the value 1 out of _Count.	1
Increment the copied value (1), resulting in 2.		1
Copy the resultant value (2) into _Count.		2
	Decrement the copied value (1), resulting in 0.	2
	Copy the resultant value (0) into _Count.	0
...	...	...

Table 19.1 shows a parallel execution (or a thread context switch) by the transition of instructions appearing from one column to the other. The value of _Count after a particular line has completed appears in the last column. In this sample execution, `_Count++` executes twice and `_Count--` occurs once.

However, the resultant _Count value is 0, not 1. Copying a result back to _Count essentially wipes out any _Count value changes that occurred since the read of _Count on the same thread.

The problem in Listing 19.1 is a race condition, where multiple threads have simultaneous access to the same data elements. As this sample execution demonstrates, allowing multiple threads to access the same data elements likely undermines data integrity, even on a single-processor computer. To remedy this, the code needs synchronization around the data. Code or data synchronized for simultaneous access by multiple threads is **thread-safe.**

There is one important point to note about atomicity of reading and writing to variables. The runtime guarantees that a type whose size is no bigger than a native (pointer-size) integer will not be read or written partially. Assuming a 64-bit operating system, therefore, reads and writes to a long (64 bits) will be atomic. However, reads and writes to a 128-bit variable such as decimal may not be atomic. Therefore, write operations to change a decimal variable may be interrupted after copying only 32 bits, resulting in the reading of an incorrect value, known as a **torn read.**

■ BEGINNER TOPIC

Multiple Threads and Local Variables

Note that it is not necessary to synchronize local variables. Local variables are loaded onto the stack and each thread has its own logical stack. Therefore, each local variable has its own instance for each method call. By default, local variables are not shared across method calls; therefore, they are also not shared among multiple threads.

However, this does not mean local variables are entirely without concurrency issues since code could easily expose the local variable to multiple threads.[2] A parallel for loop that shares a local variable between iterations, for example, will expose the variable to concurrent access and a race condition (see Listing 19.2).

LISTING 19.2: Unsynchronized Local Variables

```
using System;
using System.Threading.Tasks;
```

---

2. While at the C# level it's a local, at the IL level it's a field, and fields can be accessed from multiple threads.

```
public class Program
{
  public static void Main()
  {
      int x = 0;
      Parallel.For(0, int.MaxValue, i =>
          {
              x++;
              x--;
          });
      Console.WriteLine("Count = {0}", x);
  }
}
```

In this example, x (a local variable) is accessed within a parallel for loop and so multiple threads will modify it simultaneously, creating a race condition very similar to Listing 19.1. The output is unlikely to yield the value 0 even though x is incremented and decremented the same number of times.

■■ **BEGINNER TOPIC**

Task **Return with No** await

Notice in Listing 19.1 that although Task.Run(()=>Decrement()) returns a Task, the await operator is not used. The reason for this is that await is only allowable in an async-decorated method and Main() doesn't support using async. Refactoring the code outside of Main() would allow it to easily leverage the await/async pattern as shown in Listing 19.3.

LISTING 19.3: **Unsynchronized Local Variables**

```
using System;
using System.Threading.Tasks;

public class Program
{
  // ...

  public static async void CountAsync()
  {
      // Use Task.Factory.StartNew for .NET 4.0
      Task task = Task.Run(()=>Decrement());
```

```
    // Increment
    for(int i = 0; i < _Total; i++)
    {
        _Count++;
    }

    await task;
    Console.WriteLine("Count = {0}", _Count);
  }
 }
```

Synchronization Using Monitor

To synchronize multiple threads so that they cannot execute particular sections of code simultaneously, use a **monitor** to block the second thread from entering a protected code section before the first thread has exited that section. The monitor functionality is part of a class called System.Threading.Monitor, and the beginning and end of protected code sections are marked with calls to the static methods Monitor.Enter() and Monitor.Exit(), respectively.

Listing 19.4 demonstrates synchronization using the Monitor class explicitly. As this listing shows, it is important that all code between calls to Monitor.Enter() and Monitor.Exit() be surrounded with a try/finally block. Without this, an exception could occur within the protected section and Monitor.Exit() may never be called, thereby blocking other threads indefinitely.

LISTING 19.4: **Synchronizing with a Monitor Explicitly**

```
using System;
using System.Threading;
using System.Threading.Tasks;

public class Program
{
    readonly static object _Sync = new object();
    const int _Total = int.MaxValue;
    static long _Count = 0;

    public static void Main()
    {
        // Use Task.Factory.StartNew for .NET 4.0
        Task task = Task.Run(()=>Decrement());
```

```csharp
            // Increment
            for(int i = 0; i < _Total; i++)
            {
                bool lockTaken = false;
                try
                {
                    Monitor.Enter(_Sync, ref lockTaken);
                    _Count++;
                }
                finally
                {
                    if (lockTaken)
                    {
                        Monitor.Exit(_Sync);
                    }
                }
            }

            task.Wait();
            Console.WriteLine("Count = {0}", _Count);
        }

        static void Decrement()
        {
            for(int i = 0; i < _Total; i++)
            {
                bool lockTaken = false;
                try
                {
                    Monitor.Enter(_Sync, ref lockTaken);
                    _Count--;
                }
                finally
                {
                    if(lockTaken)
                    {
                        Monitor.Exit(_Sync);
                    }
                }
            }
        }
    }
}
```

The results of Listing 19.4 appear in Output 19.2.

OUTPUT 19.2

```
Count = 0
```

Note that calls to `Monitor.Enter()` and `Monitor.Exit()` are associated with one another by sharing the same object reference passed as the parameter (in this case, `_Sync`).

The `Monitor.Enter()` overload method that takes the `lockTaken` parameter was only added to the framework in .NET 4.0. Before that, no such `lockTaken` parameter was available and there was no way to reliably catch an exception that occurred between the `Monitor.Enter()` and the try block. Placing the try block immediately following the `Monitor.Enter()` call was reliable in release code because the JIT prevented any such asynchronous exception from sneaking in. However, anything other than a try block immediately following the `Monitor.Enter()`, including any instructions that the compiler may have injected within debug code, could prevent the JIT from reliably returning execution within the try block. Therefore, if an exception did occur, it would leak the lock (the lock remains acquired) rather than executing the finally block and releasing it—likely causing a deadlock when another thread tries to acquire the lock. In summary, prior to .NET 4.0, always follow `Monitor.Enter()` with a try/finally{`Monitor.Exit(_Sync))`} block.

`Monitor` also supports a `Pulse()` method for allowing a thread to enter the "ready queue," indicating it is up next for execution. This is a common means of synchronizing producer-consumer patterns so that no "consume" occurs until there has been a "produce." The producer thread that owns the monitor (by calling `Monitor.Enter()`) calls `Monitor.Pulse()` to signal the consumer thread (which may already have called `Monitor.Enter()`) that an item is available for consumption, so "get ready." For a single `Pulse()` call, only one thread (consumer in this case) can enter the ready queue. When the producer thread calls `Monitor.Exit()`, the consumer thread takes the lock (`Monitor.Enter()` completes) and enters the critical section to begin "consuming" the item. Once the consumer processes the waiting item, it calls `Exit()`, thus allowing the producer (currently blocked with `Monitor.Enter()`) to produce again. In this example, only one thread can enter the ready queue at a time, ensuring that there is no "consumption" without "production" and vice versa.

Using the `lock` Keyword

Because of the frequent need for synchronization using `Monitor` in multi-threaded code, and the fact that the try/finally block could easily be forgotten, C# provides a special keyword to handle this locking synchronization pattern. Listing 19.5 demonstrates the use of the lock keyword, and Output 19.3 shows the results.

LISTING 19.5: Synchronization Using the lock Keyword

```csharp
using System;
using System.Threading;
using System.Threading.Tasks;

public class Program
{
    readonly static object _Sync = new object();
    const int _Total = int.MaxValue;
    static long _Count = 0;

    public static void Main()
    {
        // Use Task.Factory.StartNew for .NET 4.0
        Task task = Task.Run(()=>Decrement());

        // Increment
        for(int i = 0; i < _Total; i++)
        {
            lock(_Sync)
            {
                _Count++;
            }
        }

        task.Wait();
        Console.WriteLine("Count = {0}", _Count);
    }

    static void Decrement()
    {
        for(int i = 0; i < _Total; i++)
        {
            lock(_Sync)
            {
                _Count--;
            }
        }
    }
}
```

OUTPUT 19.3

```
Count = 0
```

By locking the section of code accessing _Count (using either lock or Monitor), you make the Main() and Decrement() methods thread-safe, meaning they can be safely called from multiple threads simultaneously. (Prior to C# 4.0 the concept was the same except the compiler-emitted code depended on the lockTaken-less Monitor.Enter() method and the Monitor.Enter() called was emitted before the try block.)

The price of synchronization is a reduction in performance. Listing 19.5, for example, takes an order of magnitude longer to execute than Listing 19.1 does, which demonstrates lock's relatively slow execution compared to the execution of incrementing and decrementing the count.

Even when lock is insignificant in comparison with the work it synchronizes, programmers should avoid indiscriminate synchronization in order to avoid the possibility of deadlocks and unnecessary synchronization on multiprocessor computers that could instead be executing code in parallel. The general best practice for object design is to synchronize *mutable static* state and not any instance data. (There is no need to synchronize something that never changes.) Programmers who allow multiple threads to access a particular object must provide synchronization for the object. Any class that explicitly deals with threads is likely to want to make instances thread-safe to some extent.

Choosing a lock Object

Whether or not the lock keyword or the Monitor class is explicitly used, it is crucial that programmers carefully select the lock object.

In the previous examples, the synchronization variable, _Sync, is declared as both private and read-only. It is declared read-only to ensure that the value is not changed between calls to Monitor.Enter() and Monitor.Exit(). This allows correlation between entering and exiting the synchronized block.

Similarly, the code declares _Sync as private so that no synchronization block outside the class can synchronize the same object instance, causing the code to block.

If the data is public, the synchronization object may be public so that other classes can synchronize using the same object instance. This makes it harder to avoid deadlock. Fortunately, the need for this pattern is rare. For public data, it is preferable to leave synchronization entirely outside the class, allowing the calling code to take locks with its own synchronization object.

It's important that the synchronization object not be a value type. If the `lock` keyword is used on a value type, the compiler will report an error. (In the case of accessing the `System.Threading.Monitor` class explicitly [not via `lock`], no such error will occur at compile time. Instead, the code will throw an exception with the call to `Monitor.Exit()`, indicating there was no corresponding `Monitor.Enter()` call.) The issue is that when using a value type, the runtime makes a copy of the value, places it in the heap (boxing occurs), and passes the boxed value to `Monitor.Enter()`. Similarly, `Monitor.Exit()` receives a boxed copy of the original variable. The result is that `Monitor.Enter()` and `Monitor.Exit()` receive different synchronization object instances so that no correlation between the two calls occurs.

Why to Avoid Locking on `this`, `typeof(type)`, and `string`

One common pattern is to lock on the `this` keyword for instance data in a class, and on the type instance obtained from `typeof(type)` (for example, `typeof(MyType)`) for static data. Such a pattern provides a synchronization target for all states associated with a particular object instance when `this` is used, and all static data for a type when `typeof(type)` is used. The problem is that the synchronization target that `this` (or `typeof(type)`) points to could participate in the synchronization target for an entirely different synchronization block created in an unrelated block of code. In other words, although only the code within the instance itself can block using the `this` keyword, the caller that created the instance can pass that instance to a synchronization lock.

The result is that two different synchronization blocks that synchronize two entirely different sets of data could block each other. Although perhaps unlikely, sharing the same synchronization target could have an unintended performance impact and, in extreme cases, even cause a deadlock. Instead of locking on `this` or even `typeof(type)`, it is better to define a private, read-only field on which no one will block except for the class that has access to it.

Another lock type to avoid is `string` due to string interning. If the same `string` constant appears within multiple locations it is likely that all locations will refer to the same instance, making the scope of the lock a lot greater than expected.

In summary, use a per-synchronization context instance of type `object` for the lock target.

■ ADVANCED TOPIC

Avoid Synchronizing with `MethodImplAttribute`

One synchronization mechanism that was introduced in .NET
1.0 was the `MethodImplAttribute`. Used in conjunction with the
`MethodImplOptions.Synchronized` method, this attribute marks a method
as synchronized so that only one thread can execute the method at a time.
To achieve this, the just-in-time compiler essentially treats the method as
though it was surrounded by `lock(this)` or locking on the type in the case
of a static method. Such an implementation means that, in fact, the method
and all other methods on the same class, decorated with the same attribute
and enum parameter, are synchronized, not just each method relative to
itself. In other words, given two or more methods on the same class decorated with the attribute, only one of them will be able to execute at a time
and the one executing will block all calls by other threads to itself or to any
other method in the class with the same decoration. Furthermore, since the
synchronization is on `this` (or even worse, on the type), it suffers the same
detriments as `lock(this)` (or worse, for the static) discussed in the preceding section. As a result, it is a best practice to avoid the attribute altogether.

Declaring Fields As `volatile`

On occasion, the compiler and/or CPU may optimize code in such a way
that the instructions do not occur in the exact order they are coded, or
some instructions are optimized out. Such optimizations are innocuous

when code executes on one thread. However, with multiple threads, such optimizations may have unintended consequences because the optimizations may change the order of execution of a field's read or write operations relative to an alternate thread's access to the same field.

One way to stabilize this is to declare fields using the volatile keyword. This keyword forces all reads and writes to the volatile field to occur at the exact location the code identifies instead of at some other location that the optimization produces. The volatile modifier identifies that the field is susceptible to modification by the hardware, operating system, or another thread. As such, the data is "volatile," and the keyword instructs the compilers and runtime to handle it more exactly.

In general, the use of the volatile modifier is rare and fraught with complications that will likely lead to incorrect usage. Using lock is preferred to the volatile modifier unless you are absolutely certain about the volatile usage.

Using the System.Threading.Interlocked Class

The mutual exclusion pattern described so far provides the minimum of tools for handling synchronization within a process (application domain). However, synchronization with System.Threading.Monitor is a relatively expensive operation, and an alternative solution that the processor supports directly targets specific synchronization patterns.

Listing 19.6 sets _Data to a new value as long as the preceding value was null. As indicated by the method name, this pattern is the compare/exchange pattern. Instead of manually placing a lock around behaviorally equivalent compare and exchange code, the Interlocked.CompareExchange() method provides a built-in method for a synchronous operation that does the same check for a value (null) and updates the first parameter if the value is equal to the second parameter. Table 19.2 shows other synchronization methods supported by Interlocked.

LISTING 19.6: **Synchronization Using** System.Threading.Interlocked

```
public class SynchronizationUsingInterlocked
{
    private static object _Data;

    // Initialize data if not yet assigned.
    static void Initialize(object newValue)
    {
        // If _Data is null then set it to newValue.
```

```
        Interlocked.CompareExchange(
            ref _Data, newValue, null);
    }

    // ...
}
```

TABLE 19.2: Interlocked's Synchronization-Related Methods

Method Signature	Description
```public static T CompareExchange<T>(` ` T location,` ` T value,` ` T comparand` `);```	Checks `location` for the value in comparand. If the values are equal, it sets `location` to `value` and returns the original data stored in `location`.
```public static T Exchange<T>(` ` T location,` ` T value` `);```	Assigns `location` with `value` and returns the previous value.
```public static int Decrement(` ` ref int location` `);```	Decrements `location` by one. It is equivalent to the `--` operator, except `Decrement()` is thread-safe.
```public static int Increment(` ` ref int location` `);```	Increments `location` by one. It is equivalent to the `++` operator, except `Increment()` is thread-safe.
```public static int Add(` ` ref int location,` ` int value` `);```	Adds `value` to `location` and assigns `location` the result. It is equivalent to the `+=` operator
```public static long Read(` ` ref long location` `);```	Returns a 64-bit value in a single atomic operation.

Most of these methods are overloaded with additional data type signatures, such as support for `long`. Table 19.2 provides the general signatures and descriptions.

Note that you can use `Increment()` and `Decrement()` in place of the synchronized `++` and `--` operators from Listing 19.6, and doing so will yield better performance. Also note that if a different thread accessed `location` using a non-interlocked method, the two accesses would not be synchronized correctly.

Event Notification with Multiple Threads

One area where developers often overlook synchronization is when firing events. The unsafe thread code for publishing an event is similar to Listing 19.7.

LISTING 19.7: Firing an Event Notification

```
// Not thread-safe
if(OnTemperatureChanged != null)
{
  // Call subscribers
  OnTemperatureChanged(
      this, new TemperatureEventArgs(value) );
}
```

This code is valid as long as there is no race condition between this method and modifying the event. However, the code is not atomic, so multiple threads could introduce a race condition. It is possible that between the time when OnTemperatureChange is checked for null and the event is actually fired, OnTemperatureChange could be set to null, thereby throwing a NullReferenceException. In other words, if multiple threads could possibly access a delegate simultaneously, it is necessary to synchronize the assignment and firing of the delegate.

Fortunately, the operators for adding and removing listeners are thread-safe and static (operator overloading is done with static methods). To correct Listing 19.7 and make it thread-safe, assign a copy, check the copy for null, and fire the copy (see Listing 19.8).

LISTING 19.8: Thread-Safe Event Notification

```
// ...
TemperatureChangedHandler localOnChange =
    OnTemperatureChanged;
if(localOnChanged != null)
{
  // Call subscribers
  localOnChanged(
      this, new TemperatureEventArgs(value) );
}
// ...
```

Given that a delegate is a reference type, it is perhaps surprising that assigning a local variable and then firing with the local variable is sufficient for making the null check thread-safe. Since `localOnChange` points to the same location that `OnTemperatureChange` points to, one would think that any changes in `OnTemperatureChange` would be reflected in `localOnChange` as well.

However, this is not the case because any calls to `OnTemperatureChange += <listener>` will not add a new delegate to `OnTemperatureChange`, but rather will assign it an entirely new multicast delegate without having any effect on the original multicast delegate to which `localOnChange` also points. This makes the code thread-safe because only one thread will access the `localOnChange` instance, and `OnTemperatureChange` will be an entirely new instance if listeners are added or removed.

Synchronization Design Best Practices

Along with the complexities of multithreaded programming come several best practices for handling those complexities.

Avoiding Deadlock

With the introduction of synchronization comes the potential for deadlock. Deadlock occurs when two or more threads wait for one another to release a synchronization lock. For example, Thread 1 requests a lock on `_Sync1`, and then later requests a lock on `_Sync2` before releasing the lock on `_Sync1`. At the same time, Thread 2 requests a lock on `_Sync2`, followed by a lock on `_Sync1`, before releasing the lock on `_Sync2`. This sets the stage for the deadlock. The deadlock actually occurs if both Thread 1 and Thread 2 successfully acquire their initial locks (`_Sync1` and `_Sync2`, respectively) before obtaining their second locks.

For a deadlock to occur, four fundamental conditions must be met:

1. *Mutual exclusion:* One thread (`ThreadA`) exclusively owns a resource such that no other thread (`ThreadB`) can acquire the same resource.

2. *Hold and wait:* One thread (`ThreadA`) with a mutual exclusion is waiting to acquire a resource held by another thread (`ThreadB`).

3. *No preemption:* The resource held by a thread (`ThreadA`) cannot be forcibly removed (`ThreadA` needs to release its own locked resource).

4. *Circular wait condition:* Two or more threads form a circular chain such that they lock on the same two or more resources and each waits on the resource held by the next thread in the chain.

Removing any one of these conditions will prevent the deadlock.

A scenario likely to cause a deadlock is when two or more threads request exclusive ownership on the same two or more synchronization targets (resources) and the locks are requested in different orders. This is avoided when developers are careful to ensure that multiple lock acquisitions are always in the same order. Another cause of a deadlock is locks that are not **reentrant.** When a lock from one thread can block the same thread—that is, it is re-requesting the same lock—the lock is not reentrant. For example, if ThreadA acquires a lock and then re-requests the same lock but is blocked because the lock is already owned (by itself), the lock is not reentrant and the additional request will deadlock. Therefore, locks that are not reentrant can occur only with a single thread.

The code generated by the lock keyword (with the underlying Monitor class) is reentrant. However, as we shall see in the More Synchronization Types section, there are lock types that are not reentrant.

When to Provide Synchronization

As we already discussed, all static data should be thread-safe. Therefore, synchronization needs to surround static data that is mutable. Generally, this means that programmers should declare private static variables and then provide public methods for modifying the data. Such methods should internally handle the synchronization.

In contrast, instance state is not expected to include synchronization. Synchronization may significantly decrease performance and increase the chance of a lock contention or deadlock. With the exception of classes that are explicitly designed for multithreaded access, programmers sharing objects across multiple threads are expected to handle their own synchronization of the data being shared.

Avoiding Unnecessary Locking

Without compromising data integrity, programmers should avoid unnecessary synchronization where possible. For example, use immutable types between threads so that no synchronization is necessary (this approach has proven invaluable in functional programming languages such as F#). Similarly, avoid locking on thread-safe operations such as simple reads and writes of values smaller than a native (pointer-size) integer as such operations are automatically atomic.

Guidelines

DO NOT request exclusive ownership on the same two or more synchronization targets in different orders.

DO ensure that code that concurrently holds multiple locks always acquires them in the same order.

DO encapsulate mutable static data in public APIs with synchronization logic.

AVOID synchronization on simple reading or writing of values no bigger than a native (pointer-size) integer as such operations are automatically atomic.

More Synchronization Types

In addition to `System.Threading.Monitor` and `System.Threading.Interlocked`, several more synchronization techniques are available.

Using *System.Threading.Mutex*

`System.Threading.Mutex` is similar in concept to the `System.Threading.Monitor` class (without the `Pulse()` method support), except that the `lock` keyword does not use it and `Mutex`es can be named so that they support synchronization across multiple processes. Using the `Mutex` class, you can synchronize access to a file or some other cross-process resource. Since `Mutex` is a cross-process resource, .NET 2.0 added support to allow for setting the access control via a `System.Security.AccessControl.MutexSecurity` object. One use for the `Mutex` class is to limit an application so that it cannot run multiple times simultaneously, as Listing 19.9 demonstrates.

LISTING 19.9: **Creating a Single Instance Application**

```
using System;
using System.Threading;
using System.Reflection;

public class Program
{
  public static void Main()
  {
    // Indicates whether this is the first
    // application instance
    bool firstApplicationInstance;
```

```
// Obtain the mutex name from the full
// assembly name.
string mutexName =
    Assembly.GetEntryAssembly().FullName;

using(Mutex mutex = new Mutex(false, mutexName,
    out firstApplicationInstance))
{

    if(!firstApplicationInstance)
    {
        Console.WriteLine(
            "This application is already running.");
    }
    else
    {
        Console.WriteLine("ENTER to shutdown");
        Console.ReadLine();
    }
}
}
}
```

The results from running the first instance of the application appear in Output 19.4.

OUTPUT 19.4

```
ENTER to shutdown
```

The results of the second instance of the application while the first instance is still running appear in Output 19.5.

OUTPUT 19.5

```
This application is already running.
```

In this case, the application can run only once on the machine, even if it is launched by different users. To restrict the instances to once per user, prefix `Assembly.GetEntryAssembly().FullName` with `System.Windows.Forms.Application.UserAppDataPath.Replace("\\", "+")` instead. This change requires a reference to the `System.Windows.Forms` assembly.

Mutex derives from System.Threading.WaitHandle, and therefore includes WaitAll(), WaitAny(), and SignalAndWait() methods, allowing it to acquire multiple locks automatically (something Monitor does not support).

WaitHandle

The base class for Mutex is a System.Threading.WaitHandle. This is a fundamental synchronization class used by the Mutex, EventWaitHandle, and Semaphore synchronization classes. The key methods on a WaitHandle are the WaitOne() methods. These methods block execution until the WaitHandle instance is signaled or set. The WaitOne() methods include several overloads allowing for an indefinite wait: void WaitOne(), a millisecond timed wait; bool WaitOne(int milliseconds); and bool WaitOne(TimeSpan timeout), a TimeSpan wait. The versions that return a Boolean will return a value of true whenever the WaitHandle is signaled before the timeout.

In addition to the WaitHandle instance methods, there are two key static members: WaitAll() and WaitAny(). Like their instance cousins, the static members also support timeouts. In addition, they take a collection of WaitHandles, in the form of an array, so that they can respond to signals coming from any within the collection.

One last point to note about WaitHandle is that it contains a handle (of type SafeWaitHandle) that implements IDisposable. As such, care is needed to ensure that WaitHandles are disposed when they are no longer needed.

Reset Events: *ManualResetEvent* and *ManualResetEventSlim*

One way to control uncertainty about when particular instructions in a thread will execute relative to instructions in another thread is with reset events. In spite of the term *events,* reset events have nothing to do with C# delegates and events. Instead, reset events are a way to force code to wait for the execution of another thread until the other thread signals. These are especially useful for testing multithreaded code because it is possible to wait for a particular state before verifying the results.

The reset event types are System.Threading.ManualResetEvent and the .NET Framework 4–added lightweight version, System.Threading .ManualResetEventSlim. (As discussed in the upcoming Advanced Topic, there is a third type, System.Threading.AutoResetEvent, but programmers should avoid it in favor of one of the first two—see the Advanced Topic, Favor ManualResetEvent and Semaphores over AutoResetEvent.) The key

methods on the reset events are Set() and Wait() (called WaitOne() on
ManualResetEvent). Calling the Wait() method will cause a thread to block
until a different thread calls Set(), or until the wait period times out. Listing 19.10 demonstrates how this works, and Output 19.6 shows the results.

LISTING 19.10: **Waiting for** ManualResetEventSlim

```csharp
using System;
using System.Threading;
using System.Threading.Tasks;

public class Program
{
  static ManualResetEventSlim MainSignaledResetEvent;
  static ManualResetEventSlim DoWorkSignaledResetEvent;

  public static void DoWork()
  {
      Console.WriteLine("DoWork() started....");
      DoWorkSignaledResetEvent.Set();
      MainSignaledResetEvent.Wait();
      Console.WriteLine("DoWork() ending....");
  }

  public static void Main()
  {
      using(MainSignaledResetEvent =
          new ManualResetEventSlim())
      using (DoWorkSignaledResetEvent =
          new ManualResetEventSlim())
      {
          Console.WriteLine(
              "Application started....");
          Console.WriteLine("Starting task....");

          // Use Task.Factory.StartNew for .NET 4.0
          Task task = Task.Run(()=>DoWork());

          // Block until DoWork() has started.
          DoWorkSignaledResetEvent.Wait();
          Console.WriteLine(
              " Waiting while thread executes...");
          MainSignaledResetEvent.Set();
          task.Wait();
          Console.WriteLine("Thread completed");
          Console.WriteLine(
              "Application shutting down....");
      }
  }
}
```

Output 19.6

```
Application started....
Starting thread....
DoWork() started....
Waiting while thread executes...
DoWork() ending.....
Thread completed
Application shutting down....
```

Listing 19.10 begins by instantiating and starting a new Task. Table 19.3 shows the execution path in which each column represents a thread. In cases where code appears on the same row, it is indeterminate which side executes first.

TABLE 19.3: Execution Path with ManualResetEvent Synchronization

Main()	DoWork()
...	
Console.WriteLine("Application started....");	
Task task = new Task(DoWork);	
Console.WriteLine("Starting thread....");	
task.Start();	
DoWorkSignaledResetEvent.Wait();	Console.WriteLine("DoWork() started....");
	DoWorkSignaledResetEvent.Set();
Console.WriteLine("Thread executing...");	MainSignaledResetEvent.Wait();
MainSignaledResetEvent.Set();	
task.Wait();	Console.WriteLine("DoWork() ending....");
Console.WriteLine("Thread completed");	
Console.WriteLine("Application exiting....");	

Calling a reset event's `Wait()` method (for a `ManualResetEvent` it is called `WaitOne()`) blocks the calling thread until another thread signals and allows the blocked thread to continue. Instead of blocking indefinitely, `Wait()`/`WaitOne()` overrides include a parameter, either in milliseconds or as a `TimeSpan` object, for the maximum amount of time to block. When specifying a timeout period, the return from `WaitOne()` will be `false` if the timeout occurs before the reset event is signaled. `ManualResetEvent.Wait()` also includes a version that takes a cancellation token, allowing cancellation requests as discussed in the preceding chapter.

The difference between `ManualResetEventSlim` and `ManualResetEvent` is the fact that the latter uses kernel synchronization by default whereas the former is optimized to avoid trips to the kernel except as a last resort. Thus, `ManualResetEventSlim` is more performant even though it could possibly use more CPU cycles. Therefore, use `ManualResetEventSlim` in general unless waiting on multiple events or across processes is required.

Notice that reset events implement `IDisposable`, so they should be disposed when they are no longer needed. In Listing 19.10, we do this via a `using` statement. (`CancellationTokenSource` contains a `ManualResetEvent`, which is why it too implements `IDisposable`.)

Although not exactly the same, `System.Threading.Monitor`'s `Wait()` and `Pulse()` methods provide similar functionality to reset events in some circumstances.

■ ADVANCED TOPIC

Favor `ManualResetEvent` and Semaphores over `AutoResetEvent`

There is a third reset event, `System.Threading.AutoResetEvent`, that, like `ManualResetEvent`, allows one thread to signal (with a call to `Set()`) another thread that this first thread has reached a certain location in the code. The difference is that the `AutoResetEvent` unblocks only one thread's `Wait()` call because after the first thread passes through the auto-reset gate, it goes back to locked. With the auto-reset event, however, it is too easy to mistakenly code the producer thread with more iterations than the consumer thread. Therefore, it is generally preferred to favor using `Monitor`'s `Wait()`/`Pulse()` pattern or to use a semaphore (if fewer than *n* threads can participate in a particular block).

In contrast to an `AutoResetEvent`, the `ManualResetEvent` won't return to the unsignaled state until `Reset()` is called explicitly.

Semaphore/SemaphoreSlim **and** *CountdownEvent*

Semaphore and SemaphoreSlim have the same performance differences as ManualResetEvent and ManualResetEventSlim. Unlike ManualResetEvent/ManualResetEventSlim, which provide a lock (like a gate) that is either open or closed, semaphores restrict only N calls to pass within a critical section simultaneously. The semaphore essentially keeps a count on a pool of resources. When the count reaches zero, it blocks any further access to the pool until one of the resources is returned, making it available for the next blocked request that is queued.

CountdownEvent is much like the semaphore except it achieves the opposite synchronization. Rather than protecting further access to a pool of resources that are all used up, the CountdownEvent allows access only once the count reaches zero. Consider, for example, a parallel operation that downloads a multitude of stock quotes. Only when all of the quotes are downloaded can a particular search algorithm execute. The CountdownEvent may be used for synchronizing the search algorithm, decrementing as each stock is downloading and then releasing the search to start once the count reaches zero.

Notice that SemaphoreSlim and CountdownEvent were introduced with .NET Framework 4. In .NET 4.5, the former includes a SemaphoreSlim.WaitAsync() method so that TAP can be used when waiting to enter the semaphore.

Concurrent Collection Classes

Another series of classes introduced with .NET Framework 4 is the concurrent collection classes. These classes are especially designed to include built-in synchronization code so that they can support simultaneous access by multiple threads without concern for race conditions. A list of the concurrent collection classes appears in Table 19.4.

A common pattern enabled by concurrent collections is support for thread-safe access by producers and consumers. Classes that implement IProducerConsumerCollection<T> (identified by * in Table 19.4) are specifically designed to support this. This enables one or more classes to be pumping data into the collection while a different set reads it out, removing it. The order in which data is added and removed is determined by the individual collection classes that implement the IProducerConsumerCollection<T> interface.

TABLE 19.4: Concurrent Collection Classes

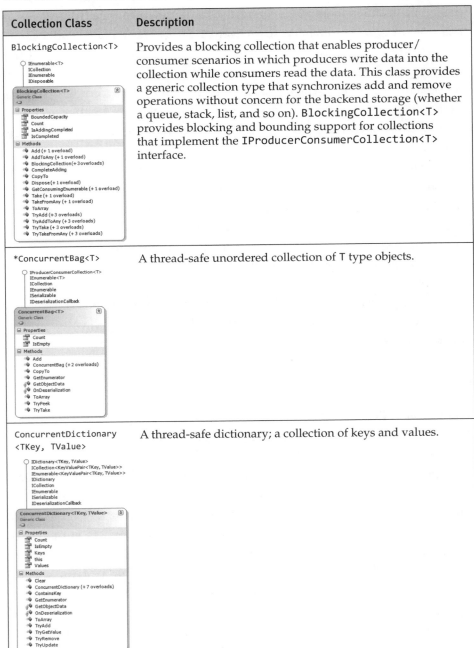

Collection Class	Description
BlockingCollection<T>	Provides a blocking collection that enables producer/ consumer scenarios in which producers write data into the collection while consumers read the data. This class provides a generic collection type that synchronizes add and remove operations without concern for the backend storage (whether a queue, stack, list, and so on). BlockingCollection<T> provides blocking and bounding support for collections that implement the IProducerConsumerCollection<T> interface.
*ConcurrentBag<T>	A thread-safe unordered collection of T type objects.
ConcurrentDictionary <TKey, TValue>	A thread-safe dictionary; a collection of keys and values.

TABLE 19.4: Concurrent Collection Classes, *Continued*

Collection Class	Description
*ConcurrentQueue<T>	A thread-safe queue supporting first in, first out (FIFO) semantics on objects of type T.
*ConcurrentStack<T>	A thread-safe stack supporting first in, last out (FILO) semantics on objects of type T.

* Collection classes that implement `IProducerConsumerCollection<T>`.

Thread Local Storage

In some cases, using synchronization locks can lead to unacceptable performance and scalability restrictions. In other instances, providing synchronization around a particular data element may be too complex, especially when it is added after the original coding.

One alternative solution to synchronization is isolation and one method for implementing isolation is **thread local storage.** With thread local storage, each thread has its own dedicated instance of a variable. As a result, there is no need for synchronization, as there is no point in synchronizing data that occurs within only a single thread's context. Two examples of thread local storage implementations are `ThreadLocal<T>` and `ThreadStaticAttribute`.

ThreadLocal<T>

Use of thread local storage with .NET Framework 4 involves declaring a field (or variable in the case of closure by the complier) of type ThreadLocal<T>. The result is a different instance of the field for each thread, as demonstrated in Listing 19.11 and Output 19.7. Note that a different instance exists even if the field is static.

LISTING 19.11: **Using** ThreadLocal<T> **for Thread Local Storage**

```csharp
using System;
using System.Threading;

public class Program
{
    static ThreadLocal<double> _Count =
        new ThreadLocal<double>(() => 0.01134);

    public static double Count
    {
        get { return _Count.Value; }
        set { _Count.Value = value; }
    }

    public static void Main()
    {
        Thread thread = new Thread(Decrement);
        thread.Start();

        // Increment
        for(double i = 0; i < short.MaxValue; i++)
        {
            Count++;
        }

        thread.Join();
        Console.WriteLine("Main Count = {0}", Count);
    }

    static void Decrement()
    {
        Count = -Count;
        for (double i = 0; i < short.MaxValue; i++)
        {
            Count--;
        }
        Console.WriteLine(
            "Decrement Count = {0}", Count);
    }
}
```

OUTPUT 19.7

```
Decrement Count = -32767.01134
Main Count = 32767.01134
```

As Output 19.7 demonstrates, the value of Count for the thread executing Main() is never decremented by the thread executing Decrement(). For Main()'s thread the initial value is 0.01134 and the final value is 32767.01134. Decrement() has similar values except they are negative. Since Count is based on the static field of type ThreadLocal<T>, the thread running Main() and the thread running Decrement() have independent values stored in _Count.Value.

Thread Local Storage with *ThreadStaticAttribute*

Decorating a static field with a ThreadStaticAttribute, as in Listing 19.12, is a second way to designate a static variable as an instance per thread. This technique has a few caveats over ThreadLocal<T> but it also has the advantage that it is available prior to .NET Framework 4. (Also, since ThreadLocal<T> is based on the ThreadStaticAttribute, it would consume less memory and give a slight performance advantage given frequently enough repeated small iterations.)

LISTING 19.12: Using ThreadStaticAttribute for Thread Local Storage

```csharp
using System;
using System.Threading;

public class Program
{
    [ThreadStatic]
    static double _Count = 0.01134;
    public static double Count
    {
        get { return Program._Count; }
        set { Program._Count = value; }
    }

    public static void Main()
    {
        Thread thread = new Thread(Decrement);
        thread.Start();

        // Increment
        for(int i = 0; i < short.MaxValue; i++)
```

```
        {
            Count++;
        }

        thread.Join();
        Console.WriteLine("Main Count = {0}", Count);
    }

    static void Decrement()
    {
        for(int i = 0; i < short.MaxValue; i++)
        {
            Count--;
        }
        Console.WriteLine("Decrement Count = {0}", Count);
    }
}
```

The results of Listing 19.12 appear in Output 19.8.

OUTPUT 19.8

```
Decrement Count = -32767
Main Count = 32767.01134
```

As in the preceding listing, the value of `Count` for the thread executing `Main()` is never decremented by the thread executing `Decrement()`. For `Main()`'s thread the initial value is a negative `_Total` and the final value is 0. In other words, with `ThreadStaticAttribute` the value of `Count` for each thread is specific to the thread and not accessible across threads.

Notice that unlike Listing 19.11, the value displayed for the "Decrement Count" does not have any decimal digits indicating it was never initialized to 0.01134. Although the value of `_Count` is assigned during declaration—`private double _Count = 0.01134` in this example—only the thread static instance associated with the thread running the static constructor will be initialized. In Listing 19.12, only the thread executing `Main()` will have a thread local storage variable initialized to 0.01134. The value of `_Count` that `Decrement()` decrements will always be initialized to 0 (`default(double)`) since `_Count` is an `int`). Similarly, if a constructor initializes a thread local storage field, only the constructor calling that thread will initialize the thread local storage instance. For this reason, it is a good practice to initialize a thread local storage field within the method that each thread initially calls. However, this is not always reasonable, especially in connection with `async`, in which different pieces of computation might run on different threads resulting in unexpectedly differing thread local storage values on each piece.

The decision to use thread local storage requires some degree of cost-benefit analysis. For example, consider using thread local storage for a database connection. Depending on the database management system, database connections are relatively expensive, so creating a connection for every thread could be costly. Similarly, locking a connection so that all database calls are synchronized places a significantly lower ceiling on scalability. Each pattern has its costs and benefits, and the correct choice depends largely on the individual implementation.

Another reason to use thread local storage is to make commonly needed context information available to other methods without explicitly passing the data via parameters. For example, if multiple methods in the call stack require user security information, you can pass the data using thread local storage fields instead of as parameters. This keeps APIs cleaner while still making the information available to methods in a thread-safe manner. This requires that you ensure that the thread local data is always set, and it is especially important on `Tasks` or other thread pool threads because the underlying threads are reused.

Timers

On occasion it is necessary to delay code execution for a specific period of time or to register for a notification after a specific period of time. Examples include refreshing the screen at a specific period rather than immediately when frequent data changes occur. One approach to implementing timers is to leverage the async/await pattern of C# 5.0 and the `Task.Delay()` method added in .NET 4.5. As we pointed out in the preceding chapter, one key feature of TAP is that the code executing after an async call will continue in a supported thread context, thereby avoiding any UI cross-threading issues. Listing 19.13 provides an example of how to use the `Task.Delay()` method.

LISTING 19.13: **Using** Task.Delay() **As a Timer**

```csharp
using System;
using System.Threading.Tasks;

public class Pomodoro
{
  // ...

  private static async Task TickAsync(
      System.Threading.CancellationToken token)
  {
      for(int minute = 0; minute < 25; minute++)
      {
          DisplayMinuteTicker(minute);
          for(int second = 0; second < 60; second++)
          {
              await Task.Delay(1000);
              if(token.IsCancellationRequested) break;
              DisplaySecondTicker();
          }
          if(token.IsCancellationRequested) break;
      }
  }
}
```

The call to `Task.Delay(1000)` will set a countdown timer that triggers after a second and executes the continuation code that appears after it.

Fortunately, in C# 5.0, TAP's use of the synchronization context specifically addressed this issue. Prior to that, it was necessary to use specific timer classes that were UI-thread-safe—or could be configured as such. Timers such as `System.Windows.Forms.Timer`, `System.Windows.Threading.DispatcherTimer`, and `System.Timers.Timer` (if configured appropriately) are UI-thread-friendly. Others, such as `System.Threading.Timer`, are optimized for performance.

Additional details and sample code regarding timers prior to the availability of C# 5.0's async/await are covered in Appendix D.

▪ ADVANCED TOPIC

Controlling the COM Threading Model with the STAThreadAttribute

With COM, four different apartment-threading models determine the threading rules relating to calls between COM objects. Fortunately, these rules—and the complexity that accompanied them—have disappeared from .NET as long as the program invokes no COM components. The general approach to handling COM Interop is to place all .NET components within the main, single-threaded apartment by decorating a process's `Main` method with the `System.STAThreadAttribute`. In so doing, it is not necessary to cross apartment boundaries to invoke the majority of COM components. Furthermore, apartment initialization does not occur, unless a COM Interop call is made. The caveat to this approach is that all other threads (including those of `Task`) will default to using a Multithreaded Apartment (MTA). The result is that care needs to be taken when invoking COM components from other threads besides the main one.

COM Interop is not necessarily an explicit action by the developer. Microsoft implemented many of the components within the .NET Framework by creating a runtime callable wrapper (RCW) rather than rewriting all the COM functionality within managed code. As a result, COM calls are often made unknowingly. To ensure that these calls are always made from a single-threaded apartment, it is generally a good practice to decorate the main method of all Windows Forms executables with the `System.STAThreadAttribute`.

SUMMARY

In this chapter, we looked at various synchronization mechanisms and how a variety of classes are available to protect against race conditions. Coverage included the `lock` keyword, which leverages `System.Threading.Monitor` under the covers. Other synchronization classes include `System.Threading.Interlocked`, `System.Threading.Mutext`, `System.Threading.WaitHandle`, reset events, semaphores, and the concurrent collection classes.

In spite of all the progress to improving multithreaded programming between early versions of .NET and today, synchronization of multithreaded programming still comes with numerous pitfalls. To avoid these, there are numerous best practices to follow. These include consistently acquiring synchronization targets in the same order and wrapping static members with synchronization logic.

Before closing the chapter, we considered the `Task.Delay()` method, a .NET 4.5 API for implementing a timer based on TAP.

The next chapter investigates another complex .NET technology: that of marshalling calls out of .NET and into unmanaged code using P/Invoke. In addition, it introduces a concept known as unsafe code, which C# uses to access memory pointers directly, as unmanaged code does (for example, C++).

■ 20 ■
Platform Interoperability and Unsafe Code

C# HAS GREAT CAPABILITIES, PARTICULARLY WHEN paired with the .NET libraries. Sometimes, however, you do need to escape out of all the safety that C# provides and step back into the world of memory addresses and pointers. C# supports this in four ways. The first is through the Windows Runtime (WinRT) API, which is exposing more and more of the operating system functions and making them directly available in C# 5.0. The second way is to go through Platform Invoke (P/Invoke) and calls into APIs exposed by unmanaged DLLs. The third approach is through **unsafe code,** which enables access to memory pointers and addresses. The last way, which is not covered in this text, is through COM interoperability.

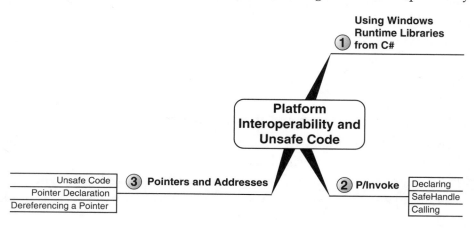

We begin this chapter by briefly discussing some of the quirks of WinRT that developers should be aware of before using it. The remainder of the chapter discusses interoperability with unmanaged code, and the use of unsafe code. This chapter culminates with a small program that determines whether the computer is a virtual computer. The code requires that you do the following.

1. Call into an operating system DLL and request allocation of a portion of memory for executing instructions.
2. Write some assembler instructions into the allocated area.
3. Inject an address location into the assembler instructions.
4. Execute the assembler code.

Aside from the P/Invoke and unsafe constructs covered here, the final listing demonstrates the full power of C# and the fact that the capabilities of unmanaged code are still accessible from C# and managed code.

Using the Windows Runtime Libraries from C#

Windows RT is the version of the Windows 8 operating system that supports only immersive "Metro-style" applications, not traditional "desktop" applications. The library of operating system APIs that support immersive applications is the **Windows Runtime,** or **WinRT** for short.

Though WinRT APIs are fundamentally unmanaged COM APIs, they are described using the same metadata format that the .NET runtime uses; thus WinRT supports development of immersive Windows applications written not only in unmanaged languages but also in managed languages such as C#, without using the P/Invoke tricks described in the remainder of this chapter.

The WinRT APIs have been carefully designed to seem natural to C# users. However, there are a few small "impedance mismatches" that you should be aware of when writing C# programs that target WinRT.

WinRT Events with Custom Add and Remove Handlers

There are many different ways to implement the "observer" pattern; in C#, as we have already discussed, events are typically implemented as a field of multicast delegate type. That is, there is a field of delegate type, and that delegate can refer to many different methods. When the event is fired, the delegate methods are invoked. To add an event handler to or remove an event handler from the event, you essentially create a new multicast delegate and replace the value of the field with the new delegate.

All those mechanisms are implemented for you automatically when you use the += and -= operators on an event. C# also allows you to run custom code when the user of your class adds or removes an event handler, via the add and remove event accessor methods.

From the consumer's perspective, WinRT events are no different. You can use += and -= as usual in a C# program when adding or removing event handlers from a WinRT object; the C# compiler will take care of ensuring that the right WinRT mechanisms are used when the code is generated. However, WinRT uses a slightly different mechanism than traditional C# programs for custom event accessors, and this affects how you write custom event accessors for WinRT types in C#.

In a regular C# event, when you remove a delegate from an event, the delegate gets passed as the hidden value argument of the remove accessor. Neither the add nor the remove accessor returns a value. WinRT events with custom accessors use a slightly different mechanism: When you add a delegate to an event, the add accessor returns a "token." To remove that delegate from the event you pass the token, not the delegate, to the remove accessor. Should you wish to write a custom accessor for a WinRT event you must follow the WinRT event pattern.

Fortunately, the WinRT library provides a special helper class to keep track of the tokens and their corresponding delegates for you. The pattern looks like the code shown in Listing 20.1.

LISTING 20.1: The WinRT Event Pattern

```
using System;
class WinRTEvent
{
  EventRegistrationTokenTable<EventHandler> table = null;
  public event EventHandler MyEvent
  {
    add
    {
      return EventRegistrationTokenTable<EventHandler>
        .GetOrCreateEventRegistrationTokenTable(ref table)
        .AddEventHandler(value);
    }
    remove
    {
      return EventRegistrationTokenTable<EventHandler>
        .GetOrCreateEventRegistrationTokenTable(ref table)
```

```
        .RemoveEventHandler(value);
    }
  }
  void OnMyEvent()
  {
    EventHandler handler =
      EventRegistrationTokenTable<EventHandler>
        .GetOrCreateEventRegistrationTokenTable(ref table)
        .InvocationList;
    if (handler != null)
      handler(this, new EventArgs());
  }
}
```

As you can see, every time a handler is added to the event, removed from the event, or invoked, a table is created if one does not exist already. (There should be one table variable per event.) The table manages the relationship between the token returned from the adder and the multicast delegate in the table. Just replace the `EventHandler` type with the appropriate delegate type for your event, and add whatever code you want to the add and remove accessors.

Automatically Shimmed Interfaces

Another difference between WinRT invocation and regular .NET invocation code is that certain frequently used interfaces have slightly different names and members in WinRT. The C# compiler and .NET runtime know about these, and automatically generate code behind the scenes that "shims" one interface to another in order to minimize the impact on the developer. The two most notable examples are `IEnumerable<T>`, which is called `IIterable<T>` in WinRT, and `IDisposable`, which is called `ICloseable` in WinRT.

Because these are automatically shimmed, you can use a method that returns `ICloseable` in any context that requires an `IDisposable`, such as a using statement. Similarly, sequences and collections behave the same regardless of whether they use the C# standard interface or the WinRT version.

Task-Based Asynchrony

The WinRT APIs do not use `Task<T>` to represent asynchronous work. (See Chapter 18 for a detailed explanation of how to use `Task<T>` and the C# 5 await operator.) Rather, they use the `IAsyncAction<T>` interface. This type has many of the same features as `Task<T>`; for example, it supports a cancellation mechanism, a progress-reporting mechanism, and so on.

The C# 5 `await` operator works just as well with an operand of type `IAsyncAction<T>` as it does with `Task<T>`. However, a C# 5 method decorated with the `async` keyword that contains an `await` operator still must return `Task` or `Task<T>`, or be `void`-returning; it is not legal for an `async` method to return `IAsyncAction<T>`. To convert an `IAsyncAction<T>` to an equivalent `Task<T>`, just call the `AsTask()` method on it.

The vast majority of other issues related to WinRT are essentially API changes, and a detailed discussion of these is beyond the scope of this book. It is important to note, however, that in WinRT all high-latency synchronous methods previously available in .NET 4.5 and earlier have been dropped, leaving only the *Async asynchronous equivalents.

Platform Invoke

Whether a developer is trying to call a library of existing unmanaged code, accessing unmanaged code in the operating system not exposed in any managed API, or trying to achieve maximum performance for a particular algorithm by avoiding the runtime overhead of type checking and garbage collection, at some point there must be a call into unmanaged code. The CLI provides this capability through P/Invoke. With P/Invoke, you can make API calls into exported functions of unmanaged DLLs.

All of the APIs invoked in this section are Windows APIs. Although the same APIs are not available on other platforms, developers can still use P/Invoke for APIs native to their platform, or for calls into their own DLLs. The guidelines and syntax are the same.

Declaring External Functions

Once the target function is identified, the next step of P/Invoke is to declare the function with managed code. Just like all regular methods that belong to a class, you need to declare the targeted API within the context of a class, but by using the `extern` modifier. Listing 20.2 demonstrates how to do this.

LISTING 20.2: **Declaring an External Method**

```csharp
using System;
using System.Runtime.InteropServices;
class VirtualMemoryManager
{
  [DllImport("kernel32.dll", EntryPoint="GetCurrentProcess")]
```

```
    internal static extern IntPtr GetCurrentProcessHandle();
}
```

In this case, the class is `VirtualMemoryManager`, because it will contain functions associated with managing memory. (This particular function is available directly off the `System.Diagnostics.Processor` class, so there is no need to declare it in real code.) Note that the method returns an `IntPtr`; this type is explained in the next section.

`extern` methods never include any body and are (almost) always static. Instead of a method body, the `DllImport` attribute, which accompanies the method declaration, points to the implementation. At a minimum, the attribute needs the name of the DLL that defines the function. The runtime determines the function name from the method name. However, it is possible to override this default using the `EntryPoint` named parameter to provide the function name. (The .NET platform will automatically attempt calls to the Unicode [...W] or ASCII [...A] API version.)

It this case, the external function, `GetCurrentProcess()`, retrieves a pseudohandle for the current process which you will use in the call for virtual memory allocation. Here's the unmanaged declaration:

```
    HANDLE GetCurrentProcess();
```

Parameter Data Types

Assuming the developer has identified the targeted DLL and exported function, the most difficult step is identifying or creating the managed data types that correspond to the unmanaged types in the external function.[1] Listing 20.3 shows a more difficult API.

LISTING 20.3: The `VirtualAllocEx()` API

```
    LPVOID VirtualAllocEx(
        HANDLE hProcess,      // The handle to a process. The
                              // function allocates memory within
                              // the virtual address space of this
                              // process.
        LPVOID lpAddress,     // The pointer that specifies a
                              // desired starting address for the
                              // region of pages that you want to
```

---

1. One particularly helpful resource for declaring Win32 APIs is www.pinvoke.net. This provides a great starting point for many APIs, helping to avoid some of the subtle problems that can arise when coding an external API call from scratch.

```
                          // allocate. If lpAddress is NULL,
                          // the function determines where to
                          // allocate the region.
        SIZE_T dwSize,    // The size of the region of memory to
                          // allocate, in bytes. If lpAddress
                          // is NULL, the function rounds dwSize
                          // up to the next page boundary.
    DWORD flAllocationType, // The type of memory allocation.
    DWORD flProtect);   // The type of memory. allocation.
```

VirtualAllocEx() allocates virtual memory that the operating system specifically designates for execution or data. To call it, you also need corresponding definitions in managed code for each data type; although common in Win32 programming, HANDLE, LPVOID, SIZE_T, and DWORD are undefined in the CLI managed code. The declaration in C# for VirtualAllocEx(), therefore, is shown in Listing 20.4.

LISTING 20.4: **Declaring the** VirtualAllocEx() **API in C#**

```csharp
using System;
using System.Runtime.InteropServices;
class VirtualMemoryManager
{
  [DllImport("kernel32.dll")]
  internal static extern IntPtr GetCurrentProcess();

  [DllImport("kernel32.dll", SetLastError = true)]
  private static extern IntPtr VirtualAllocEx(
      IntPtr hProcess,
      IntPtr lpAddress,
      IntPtr dwSize,
      AllocationType flAllocationType,
      uint flProtect);
}
```

One distinct characteristic of managed code is the fact that primitive data types such as int do not change size based on the processor. Whether the processor is 16, 32, or 64 bits, int is always 32 bits. In unmanaged code, however, memory pointers will vary depending on the processor. Therefore, instead of mapping types such as HANDLE and LPVOID simply to ints, you need to map to System.IntPtr, whose size will vary depending on the processor memory layout. This example also uses an AllocationType enum, which we discuss in the section Simplifying API Calls with Wrappers, later in this chapter.

An interesting point to note about Listing 20.4 is that `IntPtr` is not just useful for pointers; it is also useful for other things such as quantities. `IntPtr` does not just mean "pointer stored in an integer"; it also means "integer that is the size of a pointer." An `IntPtr` need not contain a pointer; it just needs to contain something the size of a pointer. Lots of things are the size of a pointer but are nevertheless not pointers.

Using ref Rather Than Pointers

Frequently, unmanaged code uses pointers for pass-by-reference parameters. In these cases, P/Invoke doesn't require that you map the data type to a pointer in managed code. Instead, you map the corresponding parameters to `ref` (or out), depending on whether the parameter is in-out or just out. In Listing 20.5, `lpflOldProtect`, whose data type is `PDWORD`, is an example that returns the "pointer to a variable that receives the previous access protection of the first page in the specified region of pages."[2]

LISTING 20.5: Using ref and out Rather Than Pointers

```
class VirtualMemoryManager
{
  // ...
  [DllImport("kernel32.dll", SetLastError = true)]
  static extern bool VirtualProtectEx(
      IntPtr hProcess, IntPtr lpAddress,
      IntPtr dwSize, uint flNewProtect,
      ref uint lpflOldProtect);
}
```

In spite of the fact that `lpflOldProtect` is documented as [out] (even though the signature doesn't enforce it), the description goes on to mention that the parameter must point to a valid variable and not `NULL`. The inconsistency is confusing, but common. The guideline is to use `ref` rather than out for P/Invoke type parameters since the callee can always ignore the data passed with `ref`, but the converse will not necessarily succeed.

The other parameters are virtually the same as `VirtualAllocEx()`, except that the `lpAddress` is the address returned from `VirtualAllocEx()`. In addition, `flNewProtect` specifies the exact type of memory protection: page execute, page read-only, and so on.

---

2.   MSDN documentation

Using StructLayoutAttribute for Sequential Layout

Some APIs involve types that have no corresponding managed type. To call these requires redeclaration of the type in managed code. You declare the unmanaged COLORREF struct, for example, in managed code (see Listing 20.6).

LISTING 20.6: Declaring Types from Unmanaged Structs

```csharp
[StructLayout(LayoutKind.Sequential)]
struct ColorRef
{
  public byte Red;
  public byte Green;
  public byte Blue;
  // Turn off warning about not accessing Unused.
  #pragma warning disable 414
  private byte Unused;
  #pragma warning restore 414

  public ColorRef(byte red, byte green, byte blue)
  {
      Blue = blue;
      Green = green;
      Red = red;
      Unused = 0;
  }
}
```

Various Microsoft Windows color APIs use COLORREF to represent RGB colors (levels of red, green, and blue).

The key in this declaration is StructLayoutAttribute. By default, managed code can optimize the memory layouts of types, so layouts may not be sequential from one field to the next. To force sequential layouts so that a type maps directly and can be copied bit for bit (blitted) from managed to unmanaged code and vice versa, you add the StructLayoutAttribute with the LayoutKind.Sequential enum value. (This is also useful when writing data to and from filestreams where a sequential layout may be expected.)

Since the unmanaged (C++) definition for struct does not map to the C# definition, there is not a direct mapping of unmanaged struct to managed struct. Instead, developers should follow the usual C# guidelines about whether the type should behave like a value or a reference type, and whether the size is small (approximately less than 16 bytes).

Error Handling

One inconvenient characteristic of Win32 API programming is the fact that it frequently reports errors in inconsistent ways. For example, some APIs return a value (0, 1, false, and so on) to indicate an error, and others set an out parameter in some way. Furthermore, the details of what went wrong require additional calls to the GetLastError() API and then an additional call to FormatMessage() to retrieve an error message corresponding to the error. In summary, Win32 error reporting in unmanaged code seldom occurs via exceptions.

Fortunately, the P/Invoke designers provided a mechanism for handling this. To enable this, given the SetLastError named parameter of the DllImport attribute is true, it is possible to instantiate a System.ComponentModel.Win32Exception() that is automatically initialized with the Win32 error data immediately following the P/Invoke call (see Listing 20.7).

LISTING 20.7: **Win32 Error Handling**

```csharp
class VirtualMemoryManager
{
  [DllImport("kernel32.dll", ", SetLastError = true)]
  private static extern IntPtr VirtualAllocEx(
      IntPtr hProcess,
      IntPtr lpAddress,
      IntPtr dwSize,
      AllocationType flAllocationType,
      uint flProtect);

  // ...
  [DllImport("kernel32.dll", SetLastError = true)]
  static extern bool VirtualProtectEx(
      IntPtr hProcess, IntPtr lpAddress,
      IntPtr dwSize, uint flNewProtect,
      ref uint lpflOldProtect);

  [Flags]
  private enum AllocationType : uint
  {
      // ...
  }

  [Flags]
  private enum ProtectionOptions
  {
      // ...
  }
```

```csharp
[Flags]
private enum MemoryFreeType
{
    // ...
}

public static IntPtr AllocExecutionBlock(
    int size, IntPtr hProcess)
{
    IntPtr codeBytesPtr;
    codeBytesPtr = VirtualAllocEx(
        hProcess, IntPtr.Zero,
        (IntPtr)size,
        AllocationType.Reserve | AllocationType.Commit,
        (uint)ProtectionOptions.PageExecuteReadWrite);

    if (codeBytesPtr == IntPtr.Zero)
    {
        throw new System.ComponentModel.Win32Exception();
    }

    uint lpflOldProtect = 0;
    if (!VirtualProtectEx(
        hProcess, codeBytesPtr,
        (IntPtr)size,
        (uint)ProtectionOptions.PageExecuteReadWrite,
        ref lpflOldProtect))
    {
        throw new System.ComponentModel.Win32Exception();
    }
    return codeBytesPtr;
}

public static IntPtr AllocExecutionBlock(int size)
{
    return AllocExecutionBlock(
        size, GetCurrentProcessHandle());
}
}
```

This enables developers to provide the custom error checking that each API uses while still reporting the error in a standard manner.

Listing 20.2 and Listing 20.4 declared the P/Invoke methods as internal or private. Except for the simplest of APIs, wrapping methods in public wrappers that reduce the complexity of the P/Invoke API calls is a good guideline that increases API usability and moves toward object-oriented type structure. The `AllocExecutionBlock()` declaration in Listing 20.7 provides a good example of this.

> ### Guidelines
>
> **DO** create public managed wrappers around unmanaged methods that use the conventions of managed code, such as structured exception handling.

Using SafeHandle

Frequently, P/Invoke involves a resource, such as a window handle, that code needs to clean up after using it. Instead of requiring developers to remember this and manually code it each time, it is helpful to provide a class that implements IDisposable and a finalizer. In Listing 20.8, for example, the address returned after VirtualAllocEx() and VirtualProtectEx() requires a follow-up call to VirtualFreeEx(). To provide built-in support for this, you define a VirtualMemoryPtr class that derives from System.Runtime.InteropServices.SafeHandle.

LISTING 20.8: **Managed Resources Using** SafeHandle

```
public class VirtualMemoryPtr :
  System.Runtime.InteropServices.SafeHandle
{
  public VirtualMemoryPtr(int memorySize) :
      base(IntPtr.Zero, true)
  {
      ProcessHandle =
          VirtualMemoryManager.GetCurrentProcessHandle();
      MemorySize = (IntPtr)memorySize;
      AllocatedPointer =
          VirtualMemoryManager.AllocExecutionBlock(
          memorySize, ProcessHandle);
      Disposed = false;
  }

  public readonly IntPtr AllocatedPointer;
  readonly IntPtr ProcessHandle;
  readonly IntPtr MemorySize;
  bool Disposed;

  public static implicit operator IntPtr(
      VirtualMemoryPtr virtualMemoryPointer)
  {
      return virtualMemoryPointer.AllocatedPointer;
  }

  // SafeHandle abstract member
```

```
    public override bool IsInvalid
    {
        get
        {
            return Disposed;
        }
    }


    // SafeHandle abstract member
    protected override bool ReleaseHandle()
    {
        if (!Disposed)
        {
            Disposed = true;
            GC.SuppressFinalize(this);
            VirtualMemoryManager.VirtualFreeEx(ProcessHandle,
                AllocatedPointer, MemorySize);
        }
        return true;
    }
}
```

System.Runtime.InteropServices.SafeHandle includes the abstract members IsInvalid and ReleaseHandle(). In the latter, you place your cleanup code; the former indicates whether the cleanup code has executed yet.

With VirtualMemoryPtr, you can allocate memory simply by instantiating the type and specifying the needed memory allocation.

■ ADVANCED TOPIC

Using IDisposable Explicitly in Place of SafeHandle

In C# 1.0, System.Runtime.InteropServices.SafeHandle is not available. Instead, a custom implementation of IDisposable, as shown in Listing 20.9, is necessary.

LISTING 20.9: **Managed Resources without** SafeHandle **but Using** IDisposable

```
public struct VirtualMemoryPtr : IDisposable
{
    public VirtualMemoryPtr(int memorySize)
    {
        ProcessHandle =
            VirtualMemoryManager.GetCurrentProcessHandle();
        MemorySize = (IntPtr)memorySize;
        AllocatedPointer =
```

```
            VirtualMemoryManager.AllocExecutionBlock(
            memorySize, ProcessHandle);
        Disposed = false;
    }

    public readonly IntPtr AllocatedPointer;
    readonly IntPtr ProcessHandle;
    readonly IntPtr MemorySize;
    bool Disposed;

    public static implicit operator IntPtr(
        VirtualMemoryPtr virtualMemoryPointer)
    {
        return virtualMemoryPointer.AllocatedPointer;
    }

    #region IDisposable Members
    public void Dispose()
    {
        if (!Disposed)
        {
            Disposed = true;
            GC.SuppressFinalize(this);
            VirtualMemoryManager.VirtualFreeEx(ProcessHandle,
                AllocatedPointer, MemorySize);
        }
    }
    #endregion
}
```

In order for `VirtualMemoryPtr` to behave with value type semantics, you need to implement it as a `struct`. However, the consequence of this is that there can be no finalizer, since the garbage collector does not manage value types. This means the developer using the type must remember to clean up the code. There is no fallback mechanism if he doesn't.

The second restriction is not to pass or copy the instance outside the method. This is a common guideline of `IDisposable` implementing types. Their scope should be left within a `using` statement and they should not be passed as parameters to other methods that could potentially save them beyond the life of the `using` scope.

Calling External Functions

Once you declare the P/Invoke functions, you invoke them just as you would any other class member. The key, however, is that the imported DLL must be in the path, including the executable directory, so that it can be successfully loaded. Listing 20.7 and Listing 20.8 provide demonstrations of this. However, they rely on some constants.

Since `flAllocationType` and `flProtect` are flags, it is a good practice to provide constants or enums for each. Instead of expecting the caller to define these, encapsulation suggests you provide them as part of the API declaration, as shown in Listing 20.10.

LISTING 20.10: Encapsulating the APIs Together

```csharp
class VirtualMemoryManager
{
  // ...

  /// <summary>
  /// The type of memory allocation. This parameter must
  /// contain one of the following values.
  /// </summary>
  [Flags]
  private enum AllocationType : uint
  {
      /// <summary>
      /// Allocates physical storage in memory or in the
      /// paging file on disk for the specified reserved
      /// memory pages. The function initializes the memory
      /// to zero.
      /// </summary>
      Commit = 0x1000,
      /// <summary>
      /// Reserves a range of the process's virtual address
      /// space without allocating any actual physical
      /// storage in memory or in the paging file on disk.
      /// </summary>
      Reserve = 0x2000,
      /// <summary>
      /// Indicates that data in the memory range specified by
      /// lpAddress and dwSize is no longer of interest. The
      /// pages should not be read from or written to the
      /// paging file. However, the memory block will be used
      /// again later, so it should not be decommitted. This
      /// value cannot be used with any other value.
      /// </summary>
      Reset = 0x80000,
      /// <summary>
      /// Allocates physical memory with read-write access.
      /// This value is solely for use with Address Windowing
      /// Extensions (AWE) memory.
      /// </summary>
      Physical = 0x400000,
      /// <summary>
      /// Allocates memory at the highest possible address.
```

```csharp
        /// </summary>
        TopDown = 0x100000,
    }


    /// <summary>
    /// The memory protection for the region of pages to be
    /// allocated.
    /// </summary>
    [Flags]
    private enum ProtectionOptions : uint
    {
        /// <summary>
        /// Enables execute access to the committed region of
        /// pages. An attempt to read or write to the committed
        /// region results in an access violation.
        /// </summary>
        Execute = 0x10,
        /// <summary>
        /// Enables execute and read access to the committed
        /// region of pages. An attempt to write to the
        /// committed region results in an access violation.
        /// </summary>
        PageExecuteRead = 0x20,
        /// <summary>
        /// Enables execute, read, and write access to the
        /// committed region of pages.
        /// </summary>
        PageExecuteReadWrite = 0x40,
        // ...
    }


    /// <summary>
    /// The type of free operation
    /// </summary>
    [Flags]
    private enum MemoryFreeType : uint
    {
        /// <summary>
        /// Decommits the specified region of committed pages.
        /// After the operation, the pages are in the reserved
        /// state.
        /// </summary>
        Decommit = 0x4000,
        /// <summary>
        /// Releases the specified region of pages. After this
        /// operation, the pages are in the free state.
        /// </summary>
        Release = 0x8000
    }

    // ...
}
```

The advantage of enums is that they group together each value. Furthermore, they can limit the scope to nothing else besides these values.

Simplifying API Calls with Wrappers

Whether it is error handling, structs, or constant values, one goal of good API developers is to provide a simplified managed API that wraps the underlying Win32 API. For example, Listing 20.11 overloads `VirtualFreeEx()` with public versions that simplify the call.

LISTING 20.11: **Wrapping the Underlying API**

```
class VirtualMemoryManager
{
  // ...

  [DllImport("kernel32.dll", SetLastError = true)]
  static extern bool VirtualFreeEx(
      IntPtr hProcess, IntPtr lpAddress,
      IntPtr dwSize, IntPtr dwFreeType);
  public static bool VirtualFreeEx(
      IntPtr hProcess, IntPtr lpAddress,
      IntPtr dwSize)
  {
      bool result = VirtualFreeEx(
          hProcess, lpAddress, dwSize,
          (IntPtr)MemoryFreeType.Decommit);
      if (!result)
      {
          throw new System.ComponentModel.Win32Exception();
      }
      return result;
  }
  public static bool VirtualFreeEx(
      IntPtr lpAddress, IntPtr dwSize)
  {
      return VirtualFreeEx(
          GetCurrentProcessHandle(), lpAddress, dwSize);
  }

  [DllImport("kernel32", SetLastError = true)]
  static extern IntPtr VirtualAllocEx(
      IntPtr hProcess,
      IntPtr lpAddress,
      IntPtr dwSize,
      AllocationType flAllocationType,
      uint flProtect);

  // ...
}
```

Function Pointers Map to Delegates

One last P/Invoke key is that function pointers in unmanaged code map to delegates in managed code. To set up a Microsoft Windows timer, for example, you would provide a function pointer that the timer could call back on, once it had expired. Specifically, you would pass a delegate instance that matched the signature of the callback.

Guidelines

Given the idiosyncrasies of P/Invoke, there are several guidelines to aid in the process of writing such code.

Guidelines

DO NOT unnecessarily replicate existing managed classes that already perform the function of the unmanaged API.

DO declare extern methods as private or internal.

DO provide public wrapper methods that use managed conventions such as structured exception handling, use of enums for special values, and so on.

DO simplify the wrapper methods by choosing default values for unnecessary parameters.

DO use the `SetLastErrorAttribute` to turn APIs that use `SetLastError` error codes into methods that throw `Win32Exception`.

DO extend `SafeHandle` or implement `IDisposable` and create a finalizer to ensure that unmanaged resources can be cleaned up effectively.

DO use delegate types that match the signature of the desired method when an unmanaged API requires a function pointer.

DO use `ref` parameters rather than pointer types when possible.

Pointers and Addresses

On occasion, developers will want to be able to access and work with memory, and with pointers to memory locations, directly. This is necessary for certain operating system interaction as well as with certain types of time-critical algorithms. To support this, C# requires use of the unsafe code construct.

Unsafe Code

One of C#'s great features is the fact that it is strongly typed and supports type checking throughout the runtime execution. What makes this feature especially great is that it is possible to circumvent this support and manipulate memory and addresses directly. You would do this when working with things such as memory-mapped devices, or if you wanted to implement time-critical algorithms. The key is to designate a portion of the code as unsafe.

Unsafe code is an explicit code block and compilation option, as shown in Listing 20.12. The unsafe modifier has no effect on the generated CIL code itself. It is only a directive to the compiler to permit pointer and address manipulation within the unsafe block. Furthermore, *unsafe* does not imply *unmanaged*.

LISTING 20.12: **Designating a Method for Unsafe Code**

```
class Program
{
  unsafe static int Main(string[] args)
  {
      // ...
  }
}
```

You can use unsafe as a modifier to the type or to specific members within the type.

In addition, C# allows unsafe as a statement that flags a code block to allow unsafe code (see Listing 20.13).

LISTING 20.13: **Designating a Code Block for Unsafe Code**

```
class Program
{
  static int Main(string[] args)
  {
      unsafe
      {
          // ...
      }
  }
}
```

Code within the unsafe block can include unsafe constructs such as pointers.

> **■. NOTE**
>
> It is important to note that it is necessary to explicitly indicate to the compiler that unsafe code is supported.

From the command line, this requires the /unsafe switch. For example, to compile the preceding code, you need to use the command shown in Output 20.1.

OUTPUT 20.1

```
csc.exe /unsafe Program.cs
```

With Visual Studio you can activate this by checking the Allow Unsafe Code checkbox from the Build tab of the Project Properties window.

You need to use the /unsafe switch because unsafe code opens up the possibility of buffer overflows and similar possibilities that expose the potential for security holes. The /unsafe switch includes the ability to directly manipulate memory and execute instructions that are unmanaged. Requiring /unsafe, therefore, makes the choice of potential exposure explicit.

Pointer Declaration

Now that you have marked a code block as unsafe, it is time to look at how to write unsafe code. First, unsafe code allows the declaration of a pointer. Consider the following example:

```
byte* pData;
```

Assuming pData is not null, its value points to a location that contains one or more sequential bytes; the value of pData represents the memory address of the bytes. The type specified before the * is the **referent** *type*, or the type located where the value of the pointer refers. In this example, pData is the pointer and byte is the referent type, as shown in Figure 20.1.

Because pointers are simply integers that happen to refer to a memory address, they are not subject to garbage collection. C# does not allow referent types other than **unmanaged types,** which are types that are not reference types, are not generics, and do not contain reference types. Therefore, the following is not valid:

```
string* pMessage;
```

Neither is this:

```
ServiceStatus* pStatus;
```

where `ServiceStatus` is defined as shown in Listing 20.14; the problem again is that `ServiceStatus` includes a `string` field.

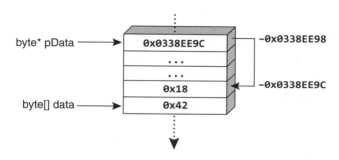

FIGURE 20.1: Pointers Contain the Address of the Data

Language Contrast: C/C++—Pointer Declaration

In C/C++, multiple pointers within the same declaration are declared as follows:

```
int *p1, *p2;
```

Notice the * on p2; this makes p2 an `int*` rather than an `int`. In contrast, C# always places the * with the data type:

```
int* p1, p2;
```

The result is two variables of type `int*`. The syntax matches that of declaring multiple arrays in a single statement:

```
int[] array1, array2;
```

Pointers are an entirely new category of type. Unlike structs, enums, and classes, pointers don't ultimately derive from `System.Object` and are not even convertible to `System.Object`. Instead, they are convertible (explicitly) to `System.IntPtr` (which does convert to `System.Object`).

LISTING 20.14: **Invalid Referent Type Example**

```
struct ServiceStatus
{
  int State;
  string Description;  // Description is a reference type
}
```

In addition to custom structs that contain only unmanaged types, valid referent types include enums, predefined value types (sbyte, byte, short, ushort, int, uint, long, ulong, char, float, double, decimal, and bool), and pointer types (such as byte**). Lastly, valid syntax includes void* pointers, which represent pointers to an unknown type.

Assigning a Pointer

Once code defines a pointer, it needs to assign a value before accessing it. Just like reference types, pointers can hold the value null; this is their default value. The value stored by the pointer is the address of a location. Therefore, in order to assign it, you must first retrieve the address of the data.

You could explicitly cast an integer or a long into a pointer, but this rarely occurs without a means of determining the address of a particular data value at execution time. Instead, you need to use the address operator (&) to retrieve the address of the value type:

```
byte* pData = &bytes[0];  // Compile error
```

The problem is that in a managed environment, data can move, thereby invalidating the address. The error message is "You can only take the address of [an] unfixed expression inside a fixed statement initializer." In this case, the byte referenced appears within an array and an array is a reference type (a movable type). Reference types appear on the heap and are subject to garbage collection or relocation. A similar problem occurs when referring to a value type field on a movable type:

```
int* a = &"message".Length;
```

Either way, to assign an address of some data requires the following.

- The data must be classified as a variable.
- The data must be an unmanaged type.
- The variable needs to be classified as fixed, not movable.

If the data is an unmanaged variable type but is not fixed, use the fixed statement to fix a movable variable.

Fixing Data

To retrieve the address of a movable data item, it is necessary to fix, or pin, the data, as demonstrated in Listing 20.15.

LISTING 20.15: Fixed Statement

```
byte[] bytes = new byte[24];
fixed (byte* pData = &bytes[0]) // pData = bytes also allowed
{
  // ...
}
```

Within the code block of a fixed statement, the assigned data will not move. In this example, `bytes` will remain at the same address, at least until the end of the fixed statement.

The fixed statement requires the declaration of the pointer variable within its scope. This avoids accessing the variable outside the fixed statement, when the data is no longer fixed. However, it is your responsibility to ensure that you do not assign the pointer to another variable that survives beyond the scope of the fixed statement—possibly in an API call, for example. Unsafe code is called "unsafe" for a reason; you are required to ensure that you use the pointers safely rather than relying on the runtime to enforce safety for you. Similarly, using `ref` or `out` parameters will be problematic for data that will not survive beyond the method call.

Since a string is an invalid referent type, it would appear invalid to define pointers to strings. However, as in C++, internally a string is a pointer to the first character of an array of characters, and it is possible to declare pointers to characters using `char*`. Therefore, C# allows declaring a pointer of type `char*` and assigning it to a string within a fixed statement. The fixed statement prevents the movement of the string during the life of the pointer. Similarly, it allows any movable type that supports an implicit conversion to a pointer of another type, given a fixed statement.

You can replace the verbose assignment of `&bytes[0]` with the abbreviated `bytes`, as shown in Listing 20.16.

LISTING 20.16: **Fixed Statement without Address or Array Indexer**

```
byte[] bytes = new byte[24];
fixed (byte* pData = bytes)
{
  // ...
}
```

Depending on the frequency and time to execute, fixed statements have the potential to cause fragmentation in the heap because the garbage collector cannot compact fixed objects. To reduce this problem, the best practice is to pin blocks early in the execution and to pin fewer large blocks rather than many small blocks. Unfortunately, this has to be tempered with pinning as little as possible for as short a time as possible, to minimize the chance that a collection will happen during the time that the data is pinned. To some extent, .NET 2.0 reduces the problem, due to some additional fragmentation-aware code.

It is possible that you might need to fix an object in place in one method body and have it remain fixed until another method is called; this is not possible with the `fixed` statement. If you are in this unfortunate situation, you can use methods on the GCHandle object to fix an object in place indefinitely. You should only do so if it is absolutely necessary, however; fixing an object for a long time makes it highly likely that the garbage collector will be unable to efficiently compact memory.

Allocating on the Stack

You should use the `fixed` statement on an array to prevent the garbage collector from moving the data. However, an alternative is to allocate the array on the call stack. Stack allocated data is not subject to garbage collection or to the finalizer patterns that accompany it. Like referent types, the requirement is that the `stackalloc` data is an array of unmanaged types. For example, instead of allocating an array of bytes on the heap, you can place it onto the call stack, as shown in Listing 20.17.

LISTING 20.17: **Allocating Data on the Call Stack**

```
byte* bytes = stackalloc byte[42];
```

Because the data type is an array of unmanaged types, it is possible for the runtime to allocate a fixed buffer size for the array and then to restore that buffer once the pointer goes out of scope. Specifically, it allocates `sizeof(T) * E`, where `E` is the array size and `T` is the referent type. Given the requirement of using `stackalloc` only on an array of unmanaged types, the runtime restores the buffer back to the system simply by unwinding the stack, eliminating the complexities of iterating over the f-reachable queue (see, in Chapter 9, the section titled Garbage Collection and the discussion of finalization) and compacting reachable data. Therefore, there is no way to explicitly free `stackalloc` data.

Note that the stack is a precious resource and, although small, running out of stack space will result in a program crashing; every effort should be taken to avoid running out. If a program does run out of stack space, the best thing that can happen is for the program to shut down/crash immediately. Generally, programs have less than 1MB of stack space (possibly a lot less). Therefore, take great care to avoid allocating arbitrarily sized buffers on the stack.

Dereferencing a Pointer

Accessing the data stored in a variable of a type referred to by a pointer requires that you dereference the pointer, placing the indirection operator prior to the expression. `byte data = *pData;`, for example, dereferences the location of the `byte` referred to by `pData` and produces a variable of type `byte`. The variable provides read/write access to the single `byte` at that location.

Using this principle in unsafe code allows the unorthodox behavior of modifying the "immutable" string, as shown in Listing 20.18. In no way is this recommended, but it does expose the potential of low-level memory manipulation.

LISTING 20.18: **Modifying an Immutable String**

```
string text = "S5280ft";
Console.Write("{0} = ", text);
unsafe  // Requires /unsafe switch.
{
  fixed (char* pText = text)
  {
      char* p = pText;
      *++p = 'm';
      *++p = 'i';
      *++p = 'l';
      *++p = 'e';
```

```
        *++p = ' ';
        *++p = ' ';
    }
}
Console.WriteLine(text);
```

The results of Listing 20.18 appear in Output 20.2.

OUTPUT 20.2

```
S5280ft = Smile
```

In this case, you take the original address and increment it by the size of the referent type (`sizeof(char)`), using the preincrement operator. Next, you dereference the address using the indirection operator and then assign the location with a different character. Similarly, using the + and – operators on a pointer changes the address by the * `sizeof(T)` operand, where T is the referent type.

Similarly, the comparison operators (==, !=, <, >, <=, and =>) work to compare pointers translating effectively to the comparison of address location values.

One restriction on the dereferencing operator is the inability to dereference a void*. The `void*` data type represents a pointer to an unknown type. Since the data type is unknown, it can't be dereferenced to produce a variable. Instead, to access the data referenced by a `void*`, you must convert it to any other pointer type and then dereference the later type.

You can achieve the same behavior as Listing 20.18 by using the index operator rather than the indirection operator (see Listing 20.19).

LISTING 20.19: Modifying an Immutable String with the Index Operator in Unsafe Code

```
string text;
text = "S5280ft";
Console.Write("{0} = ", text);

unsafe  // Requires /unsafe switch.
{
  fixed (char* pText = text)
  {
      pText[1] = 'm';
      pText[2] = 'i';
      pText[3] = 'l';
      pText[4] = 'e';
      pText[5] = ' ';
      pText[6] = ' ';
```

```
    }
  }
  Console.WriteLine(text);
```

The results of Listing 20.19 appear in Output 20.3.

OUTPUT 20.3

```
S5280ft = Smile
```

Modifications such as those in Listing 20.18 and Listing 20.19 lead to unexpected behavior. For example, if you reassigned text to "S5280ft" following the Console.WriteLine() statement and then redisplayed text, the output would still be Smile because the address of two equal string literals is optimized to one string literal referenced by both variables. In spite of the apparent assignment

```
    text = "S5280ft";
```

after the unsafe code in Listing 20.18, the internals of the string assignment are an address assignment of the modified "S5280ft" location, so text is never set to the intended value.

Accessing the Member of a Referent Type

Dereferencing a pointer produces a variable of the pointer's underlying type. You can then access the members of the underlying type using the member access "dot" operator normally. However, the rules of operator precedence require that *x.y means *(x.y) which is probably not what you intended. If x is a pointer, the correct code is (*x).y, which is an unpleasant syntax. To make it easier to access members of a dereferenced pointer, C# provides a special member access operator: x->y is a shorthand for (*x).y, as shown in Listing 20.20.

LISTING 20.20: Directly Accessing a Referent Type's Members

```
  unsafe
  {
    Angle angle = new Angle(30, 18, 0);
    Angle* pAngle = &angle;
    System.Console.WriteLine("{0}° {1}' {2}\"",
        pAngle->Hours, pAngle->Minutes, pAngle->Seconds);
  }
```

The results of Listing 20.20 appear in Output 20.4.

OUTPUT 20.4

```
30° 18' 0
```

Executing Unsafe Code via a Delegate

As promised at the beginning of this chapter, we finish up with a full working example of pretty much the most "unsafe" thing you can do in C#: Obtain a pointer to a block of memory, fill it with the bytes of machine code, make a delegate that refers to the new code, and execute it. This particular bit of assembly code determines if the machine that is executing the code is a virtual machine or a real machine. If the machine is virtual, it outputs "Inside Matrix!" Listing 20.21 shows how to do it.

■ **BEGINNER TOPIC**

What Is a Virtual Computer?

A **virtual computer** (or virtual machine), also called a **guest computer,** is virtualized or emulated through software running on the host operating system and interacting with the host computer's hardware. For example, virtual computer software (such as VMware Workstation and Microsoft Virtual PC) can be installed on a computer running a recent version of Windows. Once the software is installed, users can configure a guest computer within the software, boot it, and install an operating system as though it were a real computer, not just one virtualized with software.

LISTING 20.21: **Designating a Block for Unsafe Code**

```csharp
using System.Runtime.InteropServices;

class Program
{
  unsafe static int Main(string[] args)
  {
      // Assign redpill
```

```csharp
byte[] redpill = {
    0x0f, 0x01, 0x0d,        // asm SIDT instruction
    0x00, 0x00, 0x00, 0x00,  // placeholder for an address
    0xc3};                   // asm return instruction

unsafe
{
    fixed (byte* matrix = new byte[6],
        redpillPtr = redpill)
    {
        // Move the address of matrix immediately
        // following the SIDT instruction of memory.
        *(uint*)&redpillPtr[3] = (uint)&matrix[0];

        using (VirtualMemoryPtr codeBytesPtr =
            new VirtualMemoryPtr(redpill.Length))
        {
            Marshal.Copy(
                redpill, 0,
                codeBytesPtr, redpill.Length);

            MethodInvoker method =
                (MethodInvoker)Marshal.GetDelegateForFunctionPointer(
                codeBytesPtr, typeof(MethodInvoker));

            method();
        }
        if (matrix[5] > 0xd0)
        {
            Console.WriteLine("Inside Matrix!\n");
            return 1;
        }
        else
        {
            Console.WriteLine("Not in Matrix.\n");
            return 0;
        }
    } // fixed
} // unsafe
    }
}
```

The results of Listing 20.21 appear in Output 20.5.

OUTPUT 20.5

```
Inside Matrix!
```

SUMMARY

This book has demonstrated the power, flexibility, consistency, and fantastic structure of C#. This chapter demonstrated the ability of C# programs to perform very low-level machine-code operations.

Before we end the book, the next chapter briefly describes the underlying execution platform and shifts the focus from the C# language to the broader platform in which C# programs execute.

◼21◼
The Common Language Infrastructure

ONE OF THE FIRST ITEMS that C# programmers encounter beyond the syntax is the context under which a C# program executes. This chapter discusses the underpinnings of how C# handles memory allocation and de-allocation, type checking, interoperability with other languages, cross-platform execution, and support for programming metadata. In other words, this chapter investigates the Common Language Infrastructure

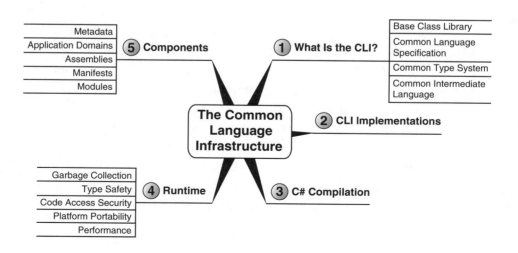

(CLI) on which C# relies both at compile time and during execution. It covers the execution engine that governs a C# program at runtime and how C# fits into a broader set of languages that are governed by the same execution engine. Because of C#'s close ties with this infrastructure, most of the features that come with the infrastructure are made available to C#.

Defining the Common Language Infrastructure (CLI)

Instead of generating instructions that a processor can interpret directly, the C# compiler generates instructions in an intermediate language, the **Common Intermediate Language (CIL).** A second compilation step occurs, generally at execution time, converting the CIL to **machine code** that the processor can understand. Conversion to machine code is still not sufficient for code execution, however. It is also necessary for a C# program to execute under the context of an agent. The agent responsible for managing the execution of a C# program is the **Virtual Execution System (VES),** generally more casually referred to as the **runtime.** (Note that the runtime in this context does not refer to a time, such as execution time; rather, the run-time—the Virtual Execution System—is an agent responsible for managing the execution of a C# program.) The runtime is responsible for loading and running programs and providing additional services (security, garbage collection, and so on) to the program as it executes.

The specification for the CIL and the runtime is contained within an international standard known as the **Common Language Infrastructure (CLI).** This is a key specification for understanding the context in which a C# program executes and how it can seamlessly interact with other programs and libraries, even when they are written in alternate languages. Note that the CLI does not prescribe the implementation for the standard, but rather identifies the requirements for how a CLI platform should behave once it conforms to the standard. This provides CLI implementers with the flexibility to innovate where necessary, while still providing enough structure that programs created by one platform can execute on a different CLI implementation, and even on a different operating system.

> **■ NOTE**
>
> Note the similarity between these two acronyms and the names they stand for. Take care to understand these upfront to avoid confusion later on.

Contained within the CLI standard are specifications for the following:

- The Virtual Execution System (VES, or runtime)
- The Common Intermediate Language (CIL)
- The Common Type System (CTS)
- The Common Language Specification (CLS)
- Metadata
- And the framework

This chapter broadens your view of C# to include the CLI, which is critical to how C# programs operate and interact with programs and with the operating system.

CLI Implementations

There are currently seven predominant implementations of the CLI (four of which are from Microsoft), each with an accompanying implementation of a C# compiler. Table 21.1 (on the next page) describes these implementations.

Although none of these platforms and compilers would have any problems with the source code shown in Chapter 1, note that each CLI and C# compiler implementation is at a different stage of compliance with the specifications. For example, some implementations will not compile all the newer syntax. All implementations, however, are intended to comply with the ECMA-334 specification for C# 1.0[1] and the ECMA-335 specification for the CLI 1.2.[2] Furthermore, many implementations include prototype features prior to the establishment of those features in standards.

---

1. This is available for free via mail, or via download at www.ecma-international.org/publications/standards/Ecma-334.htm.
2. This is available for free via mail, or via download at www.ecma-international.org/publications/standards/Ecma-335.htm.

TABLE 21.1: Primary C# Compilers

Compiler	Description
Microsoft Visual C# .NET Compiler	Microsoft's .NET C# compiler is dominant in the industry, but it is limited to running on the Windows family of operating systems. You can download it free as part of the Microsoft .NET Framework SDK from http://msdn.microsoft.com/en-us/netframework/default.aspx.
Microsoft Silverlight	This is a cross-platform implementation of the CLI that runs on both the Windows family of operating systems and the Macintosh. Resources for getting started with development on this platform are available at http://silverlight.net/getstarted.
Microsoft Compact Framework	This is a trimmed-down implementation of the .NET Framework designed to run on PDAs and phones.
Microsoft XNA	This is a CLI implementation for game developers targeting Xbox and Windows Vista. For more information, see http://create.msdn.com.
Mono Project	The Mono Project is an open source implementation sponsored by Ximian and designed to provide a Windows-, Linux-, and Unix-compatible version of the CLI specification and C# compiler. Source code and binaries are available at www.go-mono.com.
DotGNU	This is focused on creating platform-portable applications that will run under both the .NET and the DotGNU.Portable.NET implementations of the CLI. This implementation is available from www.dotgnu.org. Supported operating systems include GNU/Linux *BSD, Cygwin/Mingw32, Mac OS X, Solaris, AIX, and PARISC. DotGNU and Mono have used portions of each other's libraries at various times.
Rotor	The Rotor program, also known as the Shared Source CLI, is an implementation of the CLI that Microsoft developed to run on Windows, Mac OS X, and FreeBSD. Both the implementation and the source code are available free at http://msdn.microsoft.com/en-us/library/ms973880.aspx. Note that although the source code is available for download, Microsoft has not licensed Rotor for developing commercial applications, and instead has targeted it as a learning tool.

C# Compilation to Machine Code

The HelloWorld program listing in Chapter 1 is obviously C# code, and you compiled it for execution using the C# compiler. However, the processor still cannot directly interpret compiled C# code. An additional compilation step is required to convert the result of C# compilation into machine code. Furthermore, the execution requires the involvement of an agent that adds additional services to the C# program, services that it was not necessary to code for explicitly.

All computer languages define syntax and semantics for programming. Since languages such as C and C++ compile to machine code, the platform for these languages is the underlying operating system and machine instruction set, be it Microsoft Windows, Linux, Unix, or others. Languages such as C# are different; the underlying platform is the runtime (or VES).

CIL is what the C# compiler produces after compiling. It is termed a "common intermediate language" (CIL) because an additional step is required to transform the CIL into something that processors can understand. Figure 21.1 shows the process.

In other words, C# compilation requires two steps:

1. Conversion from C# to CIL by the C# compiler
2. Conversion from CIL to instructions that the processor can execute

The runtime is able to understand CIL statements and compile them to machine code. Generally, a **component** within the runtime performs this compilation from CIL to machine code. This component is the **just-in-time (JIT) compiler,** and **jitting** can occur when the program is installed or executed. Most CLI implementations favor execution-time compilation of the CIL, but the CLI does not specify when the compilation needs to occur. In fact, the CLI even allows the CIL to be interpreted rather than compiled, similar to the way many scripting languages work. In addition, .NET includes a tool called NGEN that enables compilation to machine code prior to actually running the program. This preexecution-time compilation needs to take place on the computer on which the program will be executing because it will evaluate the machine characteristics (processor, memory, and so on) in order to generate more efficient code. The advantage of using NGEN at installation (or at any time prior to execution) is that you can reduce the need for the jitter to run at startup, thereby decreasing startup time.

FIGURE 21.1: Compiling C# to Machine Code

Runtime

Even after the runtime converts the CIL code to machine code and starts to execute, it continues to maintain control of its execution. The code that executes under the context of an agent such as the runtime is **managed code,** and the process of executing under control of the runtime is **managed execution.** The control over execution transfers to the data; this makes it **managed data** because memory for the data is automatically allocated and de-allocated by the runtime.

Somewhat inconsistently, the term *Common Language Runtime (CLR)* is not technically a generic term that is part of the CLI. Rather, CLR is the Microsoft-specific implementation of the runtime for the .NET platform. Regardless, CLR is casually used as a generic term for *runtime,* and the technically accurate term, *Virtual Execution System,* is seldom used outside the context of the CLI specification.

Because an agent controls program execution, it is possible to inject additional services into a program, even though programmers did not explicitly code for them. Managed code, therefore, provides information to allow these services to be attached. Among other items, managed code enables the location of metadata about a type member, exception handling, access to security information, and the capability to walk the stack. The remainder of this section includes a description of some additional services made available via the runtime and managed execution. The CLI does not explicitly require all of them, but the established CLI platforms have an implementation of each.

Garbage Collection

Garbage collection is the process of automatically de-allocating memory based on the program's needs. This is a significant programming problem for languages that don't have an automated system for doing this. Without the garbage collector, programmers must remember to always free any memory allocations they make. Forgetting to do so, or doing so repeatedly for the same memory allocation, introduces memory leaks or corruption into the program, something exacerbated by long-running programs such as web servers. Because of the runtime's built-in support for garbage collection, programmers targeting runtime execution can focus on adding program features rather than "plumbing" related to memory management.

Language Contrast: C++—Deterministic Destruction

The exact mechanics for how the garbage collector works are not part of the CLI specification; therefore, each implementation can take a slightly different approach. (In fact, garbage collection is one item not explicitly required by the CLI.) One key concept that may take C++ programmers a little getting used to is that garbage-collected objects are not necessarily collected **deterministically** (at well-defined, compile-time-known locations). In fact, objects can be garbage-collected anytime between when they are last accessed and when the program shuts down. This includes collection prior to falling out of scope, or waiting until well after an object instance is accessible by the code.

It should be noted that the garbage collector only takes responsibility for handling memory management. It does not provide an automated system for managing resources unrelated to memory. Therefore, if an explicit action to free a resource (other than memory) is required, programmers using that resource should utilize special CLI-compatible programming patterns that will aid in the cleanup of those resources (see Chapter 9).

Garbage Collection on .NET

The .NET platform implementation of garbage collection uses a generational, compacting, mark-and-sweep-based algorithm. It is generational because objects that have lived for only a short period will be cleaned up sooner than objects that have already survived garbage collection sweeps because they were still in use. This conforms to the general pattern of memory allocation that objects that have been around longer will continue to outlive objects that have only recently been instantiated.

Additionally, the .NET garbage collector uses a mark-and-sweep algorithm. During each garbage collection execution, it marks objects that are to be de-allocated and compacts together the objects that remain so that there is no "dirty" space between them. The use of compression to fill in the space left by de-allocated objects often results in faster instantiation of new objects (than with unmanaged code), because it is not necessary to search through memory to locate space for a new allocation. This also decreases the chance of paging because more objects are located in the same page, which improves performance as well.

The garbage collector takes into consideration the resources on the machine and the demand on those resources at execution time. For example, if memory on the computer is still largely untapped, the garbage collector is less likely to run and take time to clean up those resources. This is an optimization rarely taken by platforms and languages that are not based on garbage collection.

Type Safety

One of the key advantages the runtime offers is checking conversions between types, or **type checking.** Via type checking, the runtime prevents programmers from unintentionally introducing invalid casts that can lead to buffer overrun vulnerabilities. Such vulnerabilities are one of the most common means of breaking into a computer system, and having the runtime automatically prevent these is a significant gain.[3] Type checking provided by the runtime ensures the following.

- Both the variables and the data that the variables refer to are typed, and the type of the variable is compatible with the data that it refers to.
- It is possible to locally analyze a type (without analyzing all of the code in which the type is used) to determine what permissions will be required to execute that type's members.
- Each type has a compile-time-defined set of methods and the data they contain. The runtime enforces rules about what classes can access those methods and data. Methods marked as "private," for example, are accessible only by the containing type.

∎ ADVANCED TOPIC

Circumventing Encapsulation and Access Modifiers
Given appropriate permissions, it is possible to circumvent encapsulation and access modifiers via a mechanism known as **reflection.** Reflection provides late binding by enabling support for browsing through a type's members, looking up the names of particular constructs within an object's metadata, and invoking the type's members.

---

3. Assuming you are not the unscrupulous type that is looking for such vulnerabilities.

Code Access Security

The runtime can make security checks as the program executes, allowing and disallowing the specific types of operations depending on permissions. Permission to execute a specific function is not restricted to authentication of the user running the program. The runtime also controls execution based on who created the program and whether she is a trusted provider. Similarly, you might want to note that code access security (CAS) also applies security policy based on the location of the code—by default, code installed on the local machine is more trusted than code from the LAN, which is much more trusted than code on the Internet. Permissions can be tuned such that partially trusted providers can read and write files from controlled locations on the disk, but they are prevented from accessing other locations (such as email addresses from an email program) for which the provider has not been granted permission. Identification of a provider is handled by certificates that are embedded into the program when the provider compiles the code.

Platform Portability

One theoretical feature of the runtime is the opportunity it provides for C# code and the resultant programs to be **platform-portable,** capable of running on multiple operating systems and executing on different CLI implementations. Portability in this context is not limited to the source code such that recompiling is necessary. A single CLI module compiled for one platform should run on any CLI-compatible platform without needing to be recompiled. This portability occurs because the work of porting the code lies in the hands of the runtime implementation rather than the application developer.

The restriction is, of course, that no platform-specific APIs are used. Because of this restriction, many developers forgo CLI platform-neutral code in favor of accessing the underlying platform functionality, rather than writing it all from scratch.

The platform portability offered by .NET, WinRT, DotGNU, Rotor, and Mono varies depending on the goals of the platform developers.

- .NET was originally targeted to run only on the Microsoft series of operating systems.

- Rotor, also produced by Microsoft, was primarily designed as a means for teaching and fostering research into future CLI development. Its inclusion of support for FreeBSD proves the portability characteristics of the CLI. Some of the libraries included in .NET (such as WinForms, ASP.NET, ADO.NET, and more) are considered proprietary, and therefore are not available in Rotor.

- DotGNU and Mono were initially targeted at Linux but have since been ported to many different operating systems (including iOS and Android). Furthermore, the goal of these CLIs was to provide a means for porting .NET applications to operating systems in addition to those controlled by Microsoft. In so doing, there is a large overlap between the APIs found in .NET and those available in Mono and DotGNU.

- WinRT was a reset for Microsoft in many ways, and as such, compatibility was intentionally dropped in favor of an improved API both for .NET and for access to the underlying operating system. For example, .NET/BCL APIs that previously might have taken longer than 50 milliseconds were dropped in favor of asynchronous equivalents. Win32 access was similarly abandoned and replaced with a much-improved WinRT API.

Unfortunately, the variance in the Based Class Library alone (even just within the Microsoft-developed CLI platforms) makes portability difficult at best. Even the APIs between WinRT, the Desktop .NET Framework, and Silverlight are not the same. To achieve portability, the best option is to use Visual Studio 2012 to create a Portable Class Library project (also available in Visual Studio 2010 using the Portable Library Tools; http://msdn.microsoft.com/en-us/library/gg597391.aspx). By no means is this solution perfect, however, as it is liable to disable the use of some more recent C# language features, including the `await` and `dynamic`, keywords, for example. This is to be expected, though, if backward compatibility prior to the availability of such features is to be supported.

Performance

Many programmers accustomed to writing unmanaged code will correctly point out that managed environments impose overhead on applications, no matter how simple. The trade-off is one of increased development productivity and reduced bugs in managed code versus runtime performance.

The same dichotomy emerged as programming went from assembler to higher-level languages such as C, and from structured programming to object-oriented development. In the vast majority of scenarios, development productivity wins out, especially as the speed and reduced price of hardware surpass the demands of applications. Time spent on architectural design is much more likely to yield big performance gains than the complexities of a low-level development platform. In the climate of security holes caused by buffer overruns, managed execution is even more compelling.

Undoubtedly, certain development scenarios (device drivers, for example) may not yet fit with managed execution. However, as managed execution increases in capability and sophistication, many of these performance considerations will likely vanish. Unmanaged execution will then be reserved for development where precise control or circumvention of the runtime is deemed necessary.[4]

Furthermore, the runtime introduces several factors that can contribute to improved performance over native compilation. For example, because translation to machine code takes place on the destination machine, the resultant compiled code matches the processor and memory layout of that machine, resulting in performance gains generally not leveraged by nonjitted languages. Also, the runtime is able to respond to execution conditions that direct compilation to machine code rarely takes into account. If, for example, there is more memory on the box than is required, unmanaged languages will still de-allocate their memory at deterministic, compile-time-defined execution points in the code. Alternatively, jit-compiled languages will need to de-allocate memory only when it is running low or when the program is shutting down. Even though jitting can add a compile step to the execution process, code efficiencies that a jitter can insert lead to performance rivaling that of programs compiled directly to machine code. Ultimately, CLI programs are not necessarily faster than non-CLI programs, but their performance is competitive.

---

4. Indeed, Microsoft has indicated that managed development will be the predominant means of writing applications for its Windows platform in the future, even those applications that integrate with the operating system.

Application Domains

By introducing a layer between the program and the operating system, it is possible to implement virtual processes or applications known as **application domains (app domains).** An application domain behaves like an operating system process in that it offers a level of isolation between other application domains. For example, an app domain has its own virtual memory allocation, and communication between application domains requires distributed communication paradigms, just as it would between two operating system processes. Similarly, static data is not shared between application domains, so static constructors run for each application domain, and assuming a single thread per application domain, there is no need to synchronize the static data because each application has its own instance of the data. Furthermore, each application domain has its own threads, and just like with an operating system process, threads cannot cross application domain boundaries.

The point of an application domain is that processes are considered relatively expensive. With application domains, you can avoid this additional expense by running multiple application domains within a single process. For example, you can use a single process to host a series of web sites. However, you can isolate the web sites from one another by placing them in their own application domain. In summary, application domains represent a virtual process on a layer between an operating system process and the threads.

Assemblies, Manifests, and Modules

Included in the CLI is the specification of the CIL output from a source language compiler, usually an assembly. In addition to the CIL instructions themselves, an assembly includes a **manifest** that is made up of the following:

- The types that an assembly defines and imports
- Version information about the assembly itself
- Additional files the assembly depends on
- And security permissions for the assembly

The manifest is essentially a header to the assembly, providing all the information about what an assembly is composed of, along with the information that uniquely identifies it.

Assemblies can be class libraries or the executables themselves, and one assembly can reference other assemblies (which, in turn, can reference more assemblies), thereby establishing an application composed of many components rather than one large, monolithic program. This is an important feature that modern programming platforms take for granted, because it significantly improves maintainability and allows a single component to be shared across multiple programs.

In addition to the manifest, an assembly contains the CIL code within one or more modules. Generally, the assembly and the manifest are combined into a single file, as was the case with `HelloWorld.exe` in Chapter 1. However, it is possible to place modules into their own separate files and then use an assembly linker (`al.exe`) to create an assembly file that includes a manifest that references each module.[5] This not only provides another means of breaking a program into components, but it also enables the development of one assembly using multiple source languages.

Casually, the terms *module* and *assembly* are somewhat interchangeable. However, the term *assembly* is predominant for those talking about CLI-compatible programs or libraries. Figure 21.2 depicts the various component terms.

Note that both assemblies and modules can also reference files such as resource files that have been localized to a particular language. Although it is rare, two different assemblies can reference the same module or file.

In spite of the fact that an assembly can include multiple modules and files, there is only one version number for the entire group of files and it is placed in the assembly manifest. Therefore, the smallest versionable component within an application is the assembly, even if that assembly is composed of multiple files. If you change any of the referenced files—even to release a patch—without updating the assembly manifest, you will violate the integrity of the manifest and the entire assembly itself. As a result, assemblies form the logical construct of a component or unit of deployment.

---

5. This is partly because one of the primary CLI IDEs, Visual Studio .NET, lacks functionality for working with assemblies composed of multiple modules. Current implementations of Visual Studio .NET do not have integrated tools for building multimodule assemblies, and when they use such assemblies, IntelliSense does not fully function.

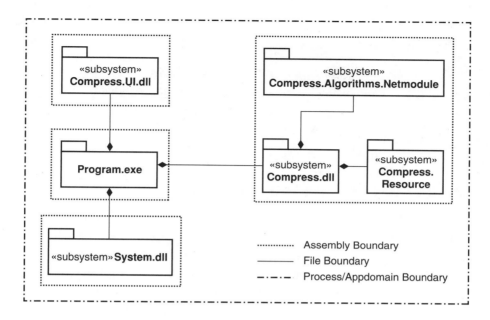

FIGURE 21.2: Assemblies with the Modules and Files They Reference

> **■ NOTE**
>
> Assemblies form the smallest unit that can be versioned and installed, not the individual modules that comprise them.

Even though an assembly (the logical construct) could consist of multiple modules, most assemblies contain only one. Furthermore, Microsoft now provides an ILMerge.exe utility for combining multiple modules and their manifests into a single file assembly.

Because the manifest includes a reference to all the files an assembly depends on, it is possible to use the manifest to determine an assembly's dependencies. Furthermore, at execution time, the runtime needs to examine only the manifest to determine what files it requires. Only tool vendors distributing libraries shared by multiple applications (Microsoft, for example) need to register those files at deployment time. This makes deployment significantly easier. Often, deployment of a CLI-based application is referred to as **xcopy deployment,** after the Windows xcopy command that simply copies files to a selected destination.

Language Contrast: COM DLL Registration

Unlike Microsoft's COM files of the past, CLI assemblies rarely require any type of registration. Instead, it is possible to deploy applications by copying all the files that comprise a program into a particular directory, and then executing the program.

Common Intermediate Language (CIL)

Considering the Common Language Infrastructure (CLI) name, another important feature of the CIL and the CLI is to support the interaction of multiple languages within the same application (instead of portability of source code across multiple operating systems). As a result, the CIL is the intermediate language not only for C#, but also for many other languages, including Visual Basic .NET, the Java-like language of J#, some incantations of Smalltalk, C++, and a host of others (more than 20 at the time of this writing, including versions of COBOL and FORTRAN). Languages that compile to the CIL are **source languages** and each has a custom compiler that converts the source language to the CIL. Once compiled to the CIL, the source language is insignificant. This powerful feature enables the development of libraries by different development groups across multiple organizations, without concern for the language choice of a particular group. Thus, the CIL enables programming language interoperability as well as platform portability.

> ■ **NOTE**
>
> A powerful feature of the CLI is support for multiple languages. This enables the creation of programs using multiple languages and the accessibility of libraries written in one language from code written in a different language.

Common Type System (CTS)

Regardless of the programming language, the resultant program operates internally on data types; therefore, the CLI includes the **Common Type System (CTS).** The CTS defines how types are structured and laid out in memory, as well as the concepts and behaviors that surround types. It includes type manipulation directives alongside the information about the data stored within the type. The CTS standard applies to how types appear and behave at the external boundary of a language because the purpose of the CTS is to achieve interoperability between languages. It is the responsibility of the runtime at execution time to enforce the contracts established by the CTS.

Within the CTS, types are broken down into two categories.

- **Values** are bit patterns used to represent basic types, such as integers and characters, as well as more complex data in the form of structures. Each value type corresponds to a separate type designation not stored within the bits themselves. The separate type designation refers to the type definition that provides the meaning of each bit within the value and the operations that the value supports.
- **Objects** contain within them the object's type designation. (This helps in enabling type checking.) Objects have identity that makes each instance unique. Furthermore, objects have slots that can store other types (either values or object references). Unlike values, changing the contents of a slot does not change the identity of the object.

These two categories of types translate directly to C# syntax that provide a means of declaring each type.

Common Language Specification (CLS)

Since the language integration advantages provided by the CTS generally outweigh the costs of implementing it, the majority of source languages support the CTS. However, there is also a subset of CTS language conformance called the **Common Language Specification (CLS).** Its focus is toward library implementations. It targets library developers, providing them with standards for writing libraries that are accessible from the majority of source languages, regardless of whether the source languages using the library are CTS-compliant. It is called the Common Language Specification because it is intended to also encourage CLI languages to provide a means of creating interoperable libraries, or libraries that are accessible from other languages.

For example, although it is perfectly reasonable for a language to provide support for an unsigned integer, such a type is not included as part of the CLS. Therefore, developers implementing a class library should not externally expose unsigned integers because doing so would cause the library to be less accessible from CLS-compliant source languages that do not support unsigned integers. Ideally, therefore, any development of libraries that is to be accessible from multiple languages should conform to the CLS. Note that the CLS is not concerned with types that are not exposed externally to the assembly.

Also note that it is possible to have the compiler issue a warning when you create an API that is not CLS-compliant. To accomplish this use the assembly attribute `System.CLSCompliant` and specify a value of `true` for the parameter.

Base Class Library (BCL)

In addition to providing a platform in which CIL code can execute, the CLI also defines a core set of class libraries that programs may employ, called the **Base Class Library (BCL).** These libraries provide foundational types and APIs, allowing the program to interact with the runtime and underlying operating system in a consistent manner. The BCL includes support for collections, simple file access, some security, fundamental data types (`string`, and so on), streams, and the like.

Similarly, there is a Microsoft-specific library called the **Framework Class Library (FCL)** that adds to this and includes support for rich client user interfaces, web user interfaces, database access, distributed communication, and more.

Metadata

In addition to execution instructions, CIL code includes **metadata** about the types and files included in a program. The metadata includes the following:

- Descriptions of each type within a program or class library

- The manifest information containing data about the program itself, along with the libraries it depends on
- And custom attributes embedded in the code, providing additional information about the constructs the attributes decorate

The metadata is not a cursory, nonessential add-on to the CIL. Instead, it forms a core part of the CLI implementation. It provides the representation and the behavior information about a type and includes location information about which assembly contains a particular type definition. It serves a key role in saving data from the compiler and making it accessible at execution time to debuggers and the runtime. This data not only is available in the CIL code, but also is accessible during machine code execution so that the runtime can continue to make any necessary type checks.

Metadata provides a mechanism for the runtime to handle a mixture of native and managed code execution. Also, it increases code and execution robustness because it smoothes the migration from one library version to the next, replacing compile-time-defined binding with a load-time implementation.

All header information about a library and its dependencies is in a portion of the metadata known as the manifest. As a result, the manifest portion of the metadata enables developers to determine a module's dependencies, including information about particular versions of the dependencies and signatures of who created the module. At execution time, the runtime uses the manifest to determine what dependent libraries to load, whether the libraries or the main program has been tampered with, and whether assemblies are missing.

The metadata also contains **custom attributes** that may decorate the code. Attributes provide additional metadata about CIL instructions that are accessible via the program at execution time.

Metadata is available at execution time by a mechanism known as **reflection.** With reflection, it is possible to look up a type or its member at execution time and then invoke that member or determine whether a construct is decorated with a particular attribute. This provides **late binding,** determining what code to execute at execution time rather than at compile time. Reflection can even be used for generating documentation by iterating through metadata and copying it into a help document of some kind (see Chapter 17).

SUMMARY

This chapter described many new terms and acronyms that are important to understanding the context under which C# programs run. The preponderance of three-letter acronyms can be confusing. Table 21.2 provides a summary list of the terms and acronyms that are part of the CLI.

TABLE 21.2: Common C#-Related Acronyms

Acronym	Definition	Description
.NET	None	Microsoft's implementation of the entire CLI stack. Includes the CLR, CIL, and various languages, all of which are CLS-compliant.
BCL	Base Class Library	The portion of the CLI specification that defines the collection, threading, console, and other base classes necessary to build virtually all programs.
C#	None	A programming language. Note that separate from the CLI standard there is a C# Language Specification, also ratified by the ECMA and ISO standards bodies.
CIL (IL)	Common Intermediate Language	The language of the CLI specification that defines the instructions for the code executable on implementations of the CLI. This is sometimes also referred to as IL or Microsoft IL (MSIL) to distinguish it from other intermediate languages. (To indicate that it is a standard broader than Microsoft, CIL is preferred over MSIL and even IL.)
CLI	Common Language Infrastructure	The specification that defines the intermediate language, base classes, and behavioral characteristics which enable implementers to create Virtual Execution Systems and compilers in which source languages are interoperable on top of a common execution environment.
CLR	Common Language Runtime	Microsoft's implementation of the runtime, as defined in the CLI specification.

TABLE 21.2: Common C#-Related Acronyms, *Continued*

Acronym	Definition	Description
CLS	Common Language Specification	The portion of the CLI specification that defines the core subset of features which source languages *must* support in order to be executable on runtimes implemented according to the CLI specification.
CTS	Common Type System	A standard generally implemented by CLI-compliant languages that defines the representation and behavior of types that the language exposes visibly outside a module. It includes concepts for how types can be combined to form new types.
FCL	.NET Framework Class Library	The class library that comprises Microsoft's .NET Framework. It includes Microsoft's implementation of the BCL as well as a large library of classes for such things as web development, distributed communication, database access, rich client user interface development, and a host of others.
WinRT	Windows Runtime	The Windows 8–based platform under which Metro style applications execute. WinRT includes the WinAPI, a new and improved Windows 8 operating system API that includes .NET-styled metadata, making it seamlessly accessible from C#.
VES (runtime)	Virtual Execution System	An agent that manages the execution of a program that is compiled for the CLI.

■ A ■
Downloading and Installing the C# Compiler and CLI Platform

TO COMPILE AND RUN C# programs, it is necessary to install a version of the compiler and the CLI platform.

Microsoft's .NET

The predominant CLI platform is Microsoft .NET and this is the platform of choice for development on Microsoft Windows.

- The minimum installation that includes the compiler and the .NET Framework with C# 2.0 syntax support is the redistributable package for the .NET Framework 2.0 or later. This is available at http://www.microsoft.com/net.

- For a rich IDE that includes IntelliSense and support for project files, install a version of the Visual Studio IDE, for which there are free and trial versions available at http://www.microsoft.com/visualstudio/eng/downloads.

For command-line compilation, regardless of a Visual Studio install or only the runtime, you must set the PATH environment variable to include the C# compiler, CSC.EXE.

Setting Up the Compiler Path with Microsoft .NET

If Visual Studio .NET is installed on your computer, open the command prompt from the Start menu by selecting All Programs, Microsoft Visual Studio 2012, Visual Studio Tools, Developer Command Prompt for VS2012. This command prompt places `CSC.EXE` in the path to be available for execution from any directory.

Without Visual Studio .NET installed, no special compiler command prompt item appears in the Start menu. Instead, you need to reference the full compiler pathname explicitly or add it to the path. The compiler is located at `%Windir%\Microsoft.NET\Framework\<version>`, where `<version>` is the version of the .NET Framework (v1.0.3705, v1.1.4322, v2.0.50727, and so on) and `%Windir%` is the environment variable that points to the location of the Windows directory. To add this location to the path use `Set PATH=%PATH%;%Windir%\Microsoft.NET\Framework\<version>`, again substituting the value of `<version>` appropriately. Output A.1 provides an example.

OUTPUT A.1

```
Set PATH=%PATH%;%Windir%\Microsoft.NET\Framework\v2.0.50727
```

Once the path includes the framework, it is possible to use the .NET C# compiler, `CSC.EXE`, without providing the full path to its location.

Mono

For CLI development on platforms other than Microsoft Windows, consider Mono, which is a platform you can download at www.mono-project.com. As with the .NET platform, Mono requires the full path to the C# compiler if it is not already in the search path. The default installation path on Linux is `/usr/lib/mono/<version>` and the compiler is `gmcs.exe` or `mcs.exe`, depending on the version. (If Mono is installed on Microsoft Windows, the default path is `%ProgramFiles%\Mono-<version>\lib\mono\<version>\`.)

One option for a Linux version that includes an installation of Mono is Monoppix. This builds on the CD-bootable Linux distribution known as Knoppix and is available for download at www.monoppix.com.

Instead of CSC.EXE, the Mono platform's compiler is MCS.EXE or GMCS.EXE, depending on the compiler version. Therefore, the command for compiling HelloWorld.cs is as shown in Output A.2.

OUTPUT A.2

```
C:\SAMPLES>msc.exe HelloWorld.cs
```

Unfortunately, the Linux environment cannot run the resultant binaries directly; instead, it requires explicit execution of the runtime using mono.exe, as shown in Output A.3.

OUTPUT A.3

```
C:\SAMPLES>mono.exe HelloWorld.exe
Hello. My name is Inigo Montoya.
```

B

Tic-Tac-Toe Source Code Listing

LISTING B.1: Tic-Tac-Toe

```csharp
#define CSHARP2

using System;

#pragma warning disable 1030 // Disable user-defined warnings

// The TicTacToe class enables two players to
// play tic-tac-toe.
class TicTacToeGame        // Declares the TicTacToeGame class
{
    static void Main()  // Declares the entry point to the program
    {
        // Stores locations each player has moved.
        int[] playerPositions = { 0, 0 };

        // Initially set the currentPlayer to Player 1;
        int currentPlayer = 1;

        // Winning player
        int winner = 0;

        string input = null;


        // Display the board and prompt the current player
        // for his next move.
```

```csharp
        for (int turn = 1; turn <= 10; ++turn)
        {
            DisplayBoard(playerPositions);

             #region Check for End Game
            if (EndGame(winner, turn, input))
            {
                break;
            }
             #endregion Check for End Game

            input = NextMove(playerPositions, currentPlayer);

            winner = DetermineWinner(playerPositions);

             // Switch players
            currentPlayer = (currentPlayer == 2) ? 1 : 2;
        }
    }

    private static string NextMove(int[] playerPositions,
                int currentPlayer)
{

        string input;

         // Repeatedly prompt the player for a move
         // until a valid move is entered.
        bool validMove;
        do
    {

            // Request a move from the current player.
            System.Console.Write("\nPlayer {0} - Enter move:",
                    currentPlayer);
            input = System.Console.ReadLine();
            validMove = ValidateAndMove(playerPositions,
                        currentPlayer, input);
        } while (!validMove);

        return input;
    }

    static bool EndGame(int winner, int turn, string input)
    {
        bool endGame = false;
        if (winner > 0)
        {
            System.Console.WriteLine("\nPlayer {0} has won!!!!",
                        winner);
            endGame = true;
        }
        else if (turn == 10)
```

```csharp
    {
        // After completing the 10th display of the
        // board, exit out rather than prompting the
        // user again.
        System.Console.WriteLine("\nThe game was a tie!");
        endGame = true;
    }
    else if (input == "" || input == "quit")
    {
        // Check if user quit by hitting Enter without
        // any characters or by typing "quit".
        System.Console.WriteLine("The last player quit");
        endGame = true;
    }
    return endGame;
}

static int DetermineWinner(int[] playerPositions)
{
    int winner = 0;

    // Determine if there is a winner
    int[] winningMasks = {
        7, 56, 448, 73, 146, 292, 84, 273};

    foreach (int mask in winningMasks)
    {
        if ((mask & playerPositions[0]) == mask)
        {
            winner = 1;
            break;
        }
        else if ((mask & playerPositions[1]) == mask)
        {
            winner = 2;
            break;
        }
    }
    return winner;
}

static bool ValidateAndMove(
  int[] playerPositions, int currentPlayer, string input)
{
    bool valid = false;

    // Check the current player's input.
    switch (input)
    {
        case "1":
        case "2":
        case "3":
        case "4":
        case "5":
```

```csharp
                case "6":
                case "7":
                case "8":
                case "9":
#warning  "Same move allowed multiple times."
                    int shifter;  // The number of places to shift
                      // over in order to set a bit.
                    int position;  // The bit which is to be set.

                    // int.Parse() converts "input" to an integer.
                    // "int.Parse(input) - 1" because arrays
                    // are zero-based.
                    shifter = int.Parse(input) - 1;

                    // Shift mask of 00000000000000000000000000000001
                    // over by cellLocations.
                    position = 1 << shifter;

                    // Take the current player cells and OR them
                    // to set the new position as well.
                    // Since currentPlayer is either 1 or 2 you
                    // subtract one to use currentPlayer as an
                    // index in a 0-based array.
                    playerPositions[currentPlayer - 1] |= position;

                    valid = true;
                    break;

                case "":
                case "quit":
                    valid = true;
                    break;

                default:
                    // If none of the other case statements
                    // is encountered, then the text is invalid.
                    System.Console.WriteLine(
                        "\nERROR:  Enter a value from 1-9. "
                        + "Push ENTER to quit");
                    break;
            }

        return valid;
    }

    static void DisplayBoard(int[] playerPositions)
    {
        // This represents the borders between each cell
        // for one row.
        string[] borders = {
"|", "|", "\n---+---+---\n", "|", "|",
"\n---+---+---\n", "|", "|", ""
};
```

```csharp
            // Display the current board;
        int border = 0;  // set the first border (border[0] = "|")

#if CSHARP2
        System.Console.Clear();
#endif

        for (int position = 1;
            position <= 256;
            position <<= 1, border++)
        {
            char token = CalculateToken(
                playerPositions, position);

            // Write out a cell value and the border that
            // comes after it.
            System.Console.Write(" {0} {1}",
                token, borders[border]);
        }
    }

    static char CalculateToken(
        int[] playerPositions, int position)
    {
        // Initialize the players to 'X' and 'O'
        char[] players = {'X', 'O'};

        char token;
        // If player has the position set,
        // then set the token to that player.
        if ((position & playerPositions[0]) == position)
        {
            // Player 1 has that position marked
            token = players[0];
        }
        else if ((position & playerPositions[1]) == position)
        {
            // Player 2 has that position marked
            token = players[1];
        }
        else
        {
            // The position is empty.
            token = ' ';
        }
        return token;
    }

    #line 113 "TicTacToe.cs"
    // Generated code goes here
    #line default
}
```

▪ C ▪

Interfacing with Mutithreading Patterns Prior to the TPL and C# 5.0

F ROM CHAPTER 18 READERS WILL RECALL that multithreading patterns are used to address the multithreading complexities of monitoring an asynchronous operation, thread pooling, avoiding deadlocks, and implementing atomicity and synchronization across operations and data access. In the ten years prior to .NET 4.5 and C# 5.0 there have been six versions of the .NET Framework and four versions of the C# language, and a similar number of corresponding multithreading patterns has emerged. During that time, however, there have been numerous improvements in multithreading and, as is frequently the case with frameworks and even languages, some patterns from those earlier versions are suboptimal. Suboptimal or not, however, as a C# developer you are likely to encounter these patterns either because you are developing for a .NET/C# version prior to .NET 4.5/C# 5.0 or because you are using an API from another framework that is still exposing one of the earlier patterns. The purpose of this appendix is to discuss these patterns. If you are lucky enough to be working with the most recent version of .NET and C# only, consider this appendix an Advanced Topic, only reading it so as to gain familiarity with the details of multithreading in the past. Alternatively, if you are still programming without the Task Programming Library (TPL) and the

Task-based Asynchronous Pattern (TAP) and its `async`/`await` keywords, treat the remaining topics as an important part of the multithreading API available to you. Perhaps most importantly, this content includes how to effectively interact with the earlier patterns using the TPL and C# 5.0.

Throughout these examples, exception handling has been eliminated for the purposes of elucidation.

Asynchronous Programming Model

One particularly prominent pattern established prior to the TPL is the Asynchronous Programming Model (APM) pattern. Given a long-running synchronous method `X()`, the APM pattern uses a `BeginX()` method to start `X()` equivalent work asynchronously and an `EndX()` method to conclude it. (Henceforth we will name these methods `X`, `BeginX`, and `EndX`.)

Using the APM Pattern

Listing C.1 demonstrates the pattern using the `System.Net.WebRequest` class to download a Web page. The functionality is the same as that found in the section titled The Task-Based Asynchrony Pattern in C# 5.0, in Chapter 18; however, this time we assume that the TPL and TAP are not available, and instead we use the APM pattern. To maintain backward compatibility prior to TPL-related asynchronous methods being added, `WebRequest` also supports the APM pattern with the methods `BeginGetResponse()` (`BeginX`) and `EndGetResponse()` (`EndX`)—asynchronous versions of the synchronous `GetResponse()` (`X`) method.

LISTING C.1: **Using the APM Pattern with** `WebRequest`

```
using System;
using System.IO;
using System.Net;
using System.Linq;

public class Program
{
  public static void Main(string[] args)
  {
      string url = "http://www.IntelliTect.com";
      if (args.Length > 0)
      {
          url = args[0];
      }

      Console.Write(url);
```

```csharp
        WebRequest webRequest =
            WebRequest.Create(url);

        IAsyncResult asyncResult =
            webRequest.BeginGetResponse(null, null);

        // Indicate busy using dots Ideally (at least in a non-Console
        // implementation) should use a callback rather than a wait.
        while (
            !asyncResult.AsyncWaitHandle.WaitOne(100))
        {
            Console.Write('.');
        }

        // Retrieve the results when finished downloading
        WebResponse response =
            webRequest.EndGetResponse(asyncResult);
        using (StreamReader reader =
            new StreamReader(response.GetResponseStream()))
        {
            // Note: ReadToEnd() is blocking. A production implementation
            //should offload this to another thread.
            int length = reader.ReadToEnd().Length;
            Console.WriteLine(FormatBytes(length));
        }
    }

    static public string FormatBytes(long bytes)
    {
        string[] magnitudes =
            new string[] { "GB", "MB", "KB", "Bytes" };
        long max =
            (long)Math.Pow(1024, magnitudes.Length);

        return string.Format("{1:##.##} {0}",
            magnitudes.FirstOrDefault(
                magnitude =>
                    bytes > (max /= 1024) )?? "0 Bytes",
                (decimal)bytes / (decimal)max).Trim();
    }
}
```

The results of Listing C.1 appear in Output C.1.

OUTPUT C.1

```
http://www.IntelliTect.com..........29.36 KB
```

As mentioned, the key aspect of the APM pattern is the pair of `BeginX` and `EndX` methods with well-established signatures. The `BeginX` method returns a `System.IAsyncResult` object providing access to the state of the asynchronous call in order to wait or poll for completion. The `EndX` method then takes this return as an input parameter. This pairs up the two methods so that it is clear which `BeginX` method call pairs with which `EndX` method call. The APM pattern requires that for all `BeginX` invocations there must be exactly one `EndX` invocation, so no two calls to `EndX` for the same `IAsyncResult` instance should occur.

In Listing C.1, we also use the `IAsyncResult`'s `WaitHandle` to determine when the asynchronous method completes. As we iteratively poll the `WaitHandle` we print out periods to the console indicating that the download is running. Following that, we call `EndGetResponse()`.

The `EndX` method serves four purposes. First, calling `EndX` will block further execution until the work requested completes successfully (or errors out with an exception). Second, if method `X` returns data, this data is accessible from the `EndX` method call. Third, if an exception occurs while performing the requested work, the exception will be rethrown on the call to `EndX`, ensuring that the exception is visible to the calling code as though it had occurred on a synchronous invocation. Finally, if any resource needs cleanup due to `X`'s invocation, `EndX` will be responsible for cleaning up these resources.

APM Signatures

Together, the combination of the `BeginX` and `EndX` APM methods should match the synchronous version of the signature. Therefore, the return parameter on `EndX` should match the return parameters on the `X` method (`GetReponse()` in this case). Furthermore, the input parameters on the `BeginX` method also need to match. In the case of `WebRequest.GetResponse()` there are no parameters, but let's consider a fictitious synchronous method, `bool TryDoSomething(string url, ref string data, out string[] links)`. The parameters map from the synchronous method to the APM methods as shown in Figure C.1.

```
System.IAsyncResult BeginTryDoSomething(
    String url, ref string data, out string[] links,
    System.AsyncCallback callback, object state)

bool TryDosomething(
    string url, ref string data, out string[] links)

bool EndTryDoSomething(ref string data, out string[] links,
    System.IAsyncResult result);
```

FIGURE C.1: APM Parameter Distribution

All input parameters map to the BeginX method. Similarly, the return parameter maps to the EndX return parameter. Also, notice that since ref and out parameters return results, these are included in the EndX method signature. In contrast, since url is only an input parameter, it is not included in the EndX method.

Continuation Passing Style (CPS) with *AsyncCallback*

There are two additional parameters on the BeginX method that were not included in the synchronous method. These are the callback parameter, a System.AsyncCallback delegate to be called when the method completes, and a state parameter of type object. Listing C.2 demonstrates how they are used. (The Output is the same as Output C.1.)

LISTING C.2: Invoking an APM Method with Callback and State

```csharp
using System;
using System.IO;
using System.Net;
using System.Linq;
using System.Threading;

public class Program
{
    public static void Main(string[] args)
    {
        string url = "http://www.intelliTechture.com";
        if (args.Length > 0)
        {
            url = args[0];
        }

        Console.Write(url);
        WebRequest webRequest = WebRequest.Create(url);
        WebRequestState state =
            new WebRequestState(webRequest);
        IAsyncResult asyncResult =
            webRequest.BeginGetResponse(
```

```
                    GetResponseAsyncCompleted, state);

        // Indicate busy using dots
        while (
            !asyncResult.AsyncWaitHandle.WaitOne(100))
        {
            Console.Write('.');
        }
        state.ResetEvent.Wait();
    }

    // Retrieve the results when finished downloading
    private static void GetResponseAsyncCompleted(
        IAsyncResult asyncResult)
    {
        WebRequestState completedState =
            (WebRequestState)asyncResult.AsyncState;
        HttpWebResponse response =
            (HttpWebResponse)completedState.WebRequest
                .EndGetResponse(asyncResult);
        Stream stream = response.GetResponseStream();
        StreamReader reader = new StreamReader(stream);
        // Note: ReadToEnd() is blocking. A production implementation
        //should offload this to another thread.
        int length = reader.ReadToEnd().Length;

        Console.WriteLine(FormatBytes(length));
        completedState.ResetEvent.Set();
        completedState.Dispose();
    }
    // ...
}
```

```
class WebRequestState : IDisposable
{
    public WebRequestState(WebRequest webRequest)
    {
        WebRequest = webRequest;
    }
    public WebRequest WebRequest { get; private set; }
    private ManualResetEventSlim _ResetEvent =
        new ManualResetEventSlim();
    public ManualResetEventSlim ResetEvent
        { get { return _ResetEvent; } }

    public void Dispose()
    {
        ResetEvent.Dispose();
        GC.SuppressFinalize(this);
    }
}
```

Notice that in Listing C.2, we pass data for both of the parameters on `BeginGetResponse()`. The first parameter is a delegate of type `System.AsyncCallback` that takes a single parameter of type `System.Async Result`. The `AsyncCallback` identifies the code that will execute once the asynchronous call completes. Registering a callback enables a fire-and-forget calling pattern called **continuation passing style (CPS)** rather than placing the `EndGetResponse()` and `Console.WriteLine()` code sequentially below `BeginGetResponse()`. With CPS we can "register" the code that will execute upon completion of the asynchronous method. Note that it is still necessary to call `EndGetResponse()`, but by placing it in the callback we ensure that it doesn't block the main thread while the asynchronous call completes.

Passing State between APM Methods

In addition to the `AsyncCallback` parameter, there is the `state` parameter, which is used to pass additional data to the callback when it executes. Listing C.2 includes a `WebRequestState` class for passing additional data into the callback, and it includes the `WebRequest` itself in this case so that we can use it to call `EndGetResponse()`. One alternative to the `WebRequestState` class itself would be to use an anonymous method (including a lambda expression) with closures for the additional data, as shown in Listing C.3.

LISTING C.3: Passing State Using Closure on an Anonymous Method

```csharp
using System;
using System.IO;
using System.Net;
using System.Linq;
using System.Threading;

public class Program
{
  public static void Main(string[] args)
  {
      string url = "http://www.intelliTechture.com";
      if (args.Length > 0)
      {
          url = args[0];
      }

      Console.Write(url);
      WebRequest webRequest = WebRequest.Create(url);
      ManualResetEventSlim resetEvent =
          new ManualResetEventSlim();
      IAsyncResult asyncResult =
```

```
                webRequest.BeginGetResponse(
                    (completedAsyncResult) =>
                    {
                        HttpWebResponse response =
                        (HttpWebResponse)webRequest.EndGetResponse(
                            completedAsyncResult);
                Stream stream =
                    response.GetResponseStream();
                StreamReader reader =
                    new StreamReader(stream);
                int length = reader.ReadToEnd().Length;

                Console.WriteLine(FormatBytes(length));
                        resetEvent.Set();
                        resetEvent.Dispose();
                    },
                null);

            // Indicate busy using dots
            while (
                !asyncResult.AsyncWaitHandle.WaitOne(100))
            {
                Console.Write('.');
            }
            resetEvent.Wait();
        }

    // ...
    }
```

Regardless of whether we pass the state via closures or not, notice that we are using a ManualResetEvent to signal when the AsyncCallback has completed. This is somewhat peculiar because IAsyncResult includes a WaitHandle already. The difference, however, is that the IAsyncResult's WaitHandle is set when the asynchronous method completes but before the AsyncCallback executes. If we only blocked on the IAsyncResult's WaitHandle we are likely to exit the program before the AsyncCallback has executed. For this reason we use a separate ManualResetEvent.

Resource Cleanup

Another important APM rule is that no resource leaks should occur, even if the EndX method is mistakenly not called. Since WebRequestState owns the ManualResetEvent, it specifically owns a resource that requires such cleanup. To handle this the state object uses the standard IDisposable pattern with the IDispose() method.

Calling APM Methods Using the TPL

Even though the TPL greatly simplifies making an asynchronous call on a long-running method, it is generally better to use the API-provided APM methods than to code the TPL against the synchronous version. The reason for this is that the API developer best understands the most efficient threading code to write, which data to synchronize, and what type of synchronization to use. Fortunately, there are special methods on the TPL's `TaskFactory` that are designed specifically for invoking the APM methods. As a result, if you have access to the TPL but you are using APM-related APIs, you can still use the TPL to invoke them.

APM with the TPL and CPS

The TPL includes a set of overloads on `FromAsync` for invoking APM methods. Listing C.4 provides an example. The same listing expands on the other APM examples to support downloading of multiple URLs; see Output C.2.

LISTING C.4: Using the TPL to Call the APM

```
using System;
using System.IO;
using System.Net;
using System.Linq;
using System.Threading.Tasks;

public class Program
{
    static private object ConsoleSyncObject =
        new object();

    public static void Main(string[] args)
    {
        string[] urls = args;
        if (args.Length == 0)
        {
            urls = new string[]
                {
                    "http://www.habitat-spokane.org",
                    "http://www.partnersintl.org",
                    "http://www.iassist.org",
                    "http://www.fh.org",
                    "http://www.worldvision.org"
                };
        }

        Task[] tasks = new Task[urls.Length];
        for (int line = 0; line < urls.Length; line++)
```

```csharp
        {
            tasks[line] = DisplayPageSizeAsync(
                urls[line], line);
        }

        while (!Task.WaitAll(tasks, 50))
        {
            DisplayProgress(tasks);
        }
        Console.SetCursorPosition(0, urls.Length);
    }

    private static Task<WebResponse>
        DisplayPageSizeAsync(string url, int line)
    {
        WebRequest webRequest = WebRequest.Create(url);
        WebRequestState state =
            new WebRequestState(webRequest, line);
        Write(state, url + " ");
        return Task<WebResponse>.Factory.FromAsync(
                webRequest.BeginGetResponse,
                GetResponseAsyncCompleted, state);
    }

    private static WebResponse GetResponseAsyncCompleted(
        IAsyncResult asyncResult)
    {
        WebRequestState completedState =
                (WebRequestState)asyncResult.AsyncState;
        HttpWebResponse response =
            (HttpWebResponse)completedState.WebRequest
                .EndGetResponse(asyncResult);
        Stream stream =
            response.GetResponseStream();
        using (StreamReader reader =
            new StreamReader(stream))
        {
            int length = reader.ReadToEnd().Length;
            Write(
                completedState, FormatBytes(length));
        }
        return response;
    }

    private static void Write(
        WebRequestState completedState, string text)
    {
        lock (ConsoleSyncObject)
        {
            Console.SetCursorPosition(
                completedState.ConsoleColumn,
                completedState.ConsoleLine);
            Console.Write(text);
```

```csharp
            completedState.ConsoleColumn +=
                text.Length;
        }
    }

    private static void DisplayProgress(
        Task[] tasks)
    {
        for (int i = 0; i < tasks.Length; i++)
        {
            if (!tasks[i].IsCompleted)
            {
                DisplayProgress(
                    (WebRequestState)tasks[i]
                    .AsyncState);
            }
        }
    }


    private static void DisplayProgress(
        WebRequestState state)
    {
        lock (ConsoleSyncObject)
        {
            int left = state.ConsoleColumn;
            int top = state.ConsoleLine;
            if (left >= Console.BufferWidth -
                int.MaxValue.ToString().Length)
            {
                left = state.Url.Length;

                Console.SetCursorPosition(left, top);
                Console.Write("".PadRight(
                    Console.BufferWidth -
                        state.Url.Length));

                state.ConsoleColumn = left;
            }

            Write(state, ".");
        }
    }

    static public string FormatBytes(long bytes)
    {
        string[] magnitudes =
            new string[] { "GB", "MB", "KB", "Bytes" };
        long max =
            (long)Math.Pow(1024, magnitudes.Length);

        return string.Format("{1:##.##} {0}",
            magnitudes.FirstOrDefault(
```

```
                magnitude =>
                    bytes > (max /= 1024) )?? "0 Bytes",
                (decimal)bytes / (decimal)max).Trim();
    }
}

class WebRequestState
{
    public WebRequestState(
        WebRequest webRequest, int line)
    {
        WebRequest = webRequest;
        ConsoleLine = line;
        ConsoleColumn = 0;
    }
    public WebRequestState(WebRequest webRequest)
    {
        WebRequest = webRequest;
    }
    public WebRequest WebRequest { get; private set; }
    public string Url
    {
        get
        {
            return WebRequest.RequestUri.ToString();
        }
    }
    public int ConsoleLine { get; set; }
    public int ConsoleColumn { get; set; }
}
```

OUTPUT C.2

```
http://www.habitat-spokane.org ..9.18 KB
http://www.partnersintl.org .........14.74 KB
http://www.iassist.org  .17.12 KB
http://www.fh.org ..................35.09 KB
http://www.worldvision.org ...........54.56 KB
```

Connecting a `Task` with the APM method pair is relatively easy. The overload used in Listing C.4 takes three parameters. First, there is the `BeginX` method delegate (`webRequest.BeginGetResponse`). Next is a delegate that matches the `EndX` method. Although the `EndX` method (`webRequest.EndGetResponse`) could be used directly, passing a delegate (`GetResponseAsyncCompleted`) and using the CPS allows additional completion activity to execute. The last parameter is the state parameter similar to what the `BeginX` method accepts.

One of the advantages of invoking a pair of APM methods using the TPL is that we don't have to worry about signaling the conclusion of the

AsyncCallback method. Instead, we monitor the Task for completion. As a result, WebRequestState no longer needs to contain a ManualResetEventSlim.

Using the TPL and *ContinueWith()* to Call an APM Method

Another option when calling TaskFactory.FromAsync() is to pass the EndX method directly and then to use ContinueWith() for any follow-up code. The result is that you have a single object to represent any kind of asynchronous operation, and therefore, you can start composing task-based operations together, even if the underlying implementation is APM-based. In addition, you can query the continue-with-Task parameter (see continueWithTask in Listing C.5) for the result (continueWithTask.Result) rather than storing a means to access the EndX method via an async-state object or using closure and an anonymous delegate (we store WebRequest in Listing C.4).

LISTING C.5: Using the TPL to Call an APM Method Using ContinueWith()

```
// ...

    private static Task
        DisplayPageSizeAsync(string url, int line)
    {
        WebRequest webRequest = WebRequest.Create(url);
        WebRequestState state =
            new WebRequestState(webRequest, line);
        Write(state, url + " ");
        return Task<WebResponse>.Factory.FromAsync(
                webRequest.BeginGetResponse,
                webRequest.EndGetResponse, state)
            .ContinueWith(
                (antecedent, antecedentState) =>
            {
                Stream stream =
                    antecedent.Result.
                        GetResponseStream();
                using (StreamReader reader =
                    new StreamReader(stream))
                {
                    int length =
                        reader.ReadToEnd().Length;
                    Write(state,
                        FormatBytes(length).ToString());
                }
            }, state);
    }

// ...
```

Notice that in order for the state to be passed into the Task returned from ContinueWith(), the ContinueWith() call explicitly includes antecedentState in the delegate in addition to having it as a parameter.

Using TAP to Call an APM Method

Given that TAP is essentially designed for handling the continuation tasks, an obvious enhancement (albeit depending on C# 5.0) is to use async/ await rather than ContinueWith(), as shown in Listing C.6.

LISTING C.6: Using TAP to Call the APM

```
// ...

    private async static Task
        DisplayPageSizeAsync(string url, int line)
    {
        WebRequestState state =
            new WebRequestState(url, line);
        Write(state, url + " ");
        WebRequest webRequest = WebRequest.Create(url);
        WebResponse webResponse =
            await Task<WebResponse>.Factory.FromAsync(
                webRequest.BeginGetResponse,
                webRequest.EndGetResponse, state);
        Stream stream =
            webResponse.GetResponseStream();
        using (StreamReader reader =
            new StreamReader(stream))
        {
            int length = reader.ReadToEnd().Length;
            Write(state,
                FormatBytes(length).ToString());
        }
    }

// ...
```

■ BEGINNER TOPIC

Synchronizing Console Using lock

In Listing C.4, we repeatedly change the location of the console's cursor and then proceed to write text to the console. Since multiple threads are executing that are also writing to the console, possibly changing the cursor location as well, we need to synchronize changes to the cursor location with write operations so that together they are atomic.

Listing C.4 includes a `ConsoleSyncObject` of type `object` as the synchronization lock identifier. Using this within a lock construct whenever we are moving the cursor or writing to the console prevents an interim update between move and write operations to the console. Notice that even one-line `Console.WriteLine()` statements are surrounded with `lock`. Although they will be atomic, we don't want them interrupting a different block that is not atomic. Therefore, all console changes require the synchronization as long as there are multiple threads of execution.

Asynchronous Delegate Invocation

One specific implementation of the APM pattern is the "asynchronous delegate invocation," which leverages special C# compiler-generated code on all delegate data types. Given a delegate instance of `Func<string, int>`, for example, there is an APM pair of methods available on the instance:

```
System.IAsyncResult BeginInvoke(
    string arg, AsyncCallback callback, object @object)
int EndInvoke(IAsyncResult result)
```

The result is that you can call any delegate (and therefore any method) synchronously just by using the C# compiler-generated methods.

Unfortunately, the underlying technology used by the asynchronous delegate invocation pattern is an end-of-further-development technology for distributed programming known as **remoting.** And although Microsoft still supports the use of asynchronous delegate invocation and for the foreseeable future it will continue to function as it does today, the performance characteristics are suboptimal given other approaches—namely `Thread`, `ThreadPool`, and the TPL. Therefore, developers should tend to favor one of these alternatives rather than implementing new development using the asynchronous delegate invocation API. Further discussion of the pattern is included in the Advanced Topic text that follows so that developers who encounter it will understand how it works.

■ ADVANCED TOPIC

Asynchronous Delegate Invocation in Detail

With asynchronous delegate invocation, you do not code using an explicit reference to Task or Thread. Instead, you use delegate instances and the compiler-generated BeginInvoke() and EndInvoke() methods—whose implementation requests threads from the ThreadPool. Consider the code in Listing C.7.

LISTING C.7: Asynchronous Delegate Invocation

```
using System;

public class Program
{
  public static void Main(string[] args)
  {
      Console.WriteLine("Application started....");

      Console.WriteLine("Starting thread....");
      Func<int,string> workerMethod =
          PiCalculator.Calculate;
      IAsyncResult asyncResult =
          workerMethod.BeginInvoke(500, null, null);

      // Display periods as progress bar.
      while(!asyncResult.AsyncWaitHandle.WaitOne(
          100, false))
      {
          Console.Write('.');
      }
      Console.WriteLine();

      Console.WriteLine("Thread ending....");
      Console.WriteLine(
          workerMethod.EndInvoke(asyncResult));

      Console.WriteLine(
          "Application shutting down....");
  }
}
```

The results of Listing C.7 appear in Output C.3.

OUTPUT C.3

```
Application started....
Starting thread....
......................
Thread ending....
3.141592653589793238462643383279502884197169399375105820974944592307816
406286208998628034825342117067982148086513282306647093844609550582231
725359408128481117450284102701938521105559644622948954930381964428810
975665933446128475648233786783165271201909145648566923460348610545432664
821339360726024914127372458700660631558817488152092096282925409171536436
78925903600113305305488204665213841469519415116094330572703657595919
53092186117381932611793105118548074462379962749567351885752724891227938
18301194912
Application shutting down....
```

Main() begins by assigning a delegate of type Func<int, string> that is pointing to PiCalculator.Calculate(int digits).

Next, the code calls BeginInvoke(). This method will start the PiCalculator.Calculate() method on a thread from the thread pool and then return immediately. This allows other code to run in parallel with the pi calculation. In this example, we print periods while waiting for the PiCalculator.Calculate() method to complete.

We poll the status of the delegate using IAsyncResult.AsyncWaitHandle .WaitOne() on asyncResult—the same mechanism available on APM. As a result, the code prints periods to the screen each second during which the PiCalculator.Calculate() method is executing.

Once the wait handle signals, the code calls EndInvoke(). As with all APM implementations, it is important to pass to EndInvoke() the same IAsyncResult reference returned when calling BeginInvoke(). In this example, EndInvoke() doesn't block because we poll the thread's state in the while loop and call EndInvoke() only after the thread has completed.

The example in Listing C.5 passed an integer and received a string—the signature of Func<int, string>. The key feature of the asynchronous delegate invocation is the fact that passing data in and out of the target invocation is trivial; it just lines up with the synchronous method signature as it did in the APM pattern. Consider a delegate type that includes out and ref parameters, as shown in Figure C.2. (Although more common, this example intentionally doesn't use Func or Action since generics don't allow ref and out modifiers on type parameters.)

```
System.IAsyncResult UpdateHandler.BeginInvoke(
    Object[] data, ref object value, out string text
        AsyncCallback callback, object @object);

delegate bool UpdateHandlerFunc
    object[] data, ref object value, out string text);

bool UpdateHandler.EndInvoke(
    ref object value, out text);
```

FIGURE C.2: Delegate Parameter Distribution to `BeginInvoke()` and `EndInvoke()`

The `BeginInvoke()` method matches the delegate signature except for the additional `AsyncCallback` and `object` parameters. Like the `IAsyncResult` return, the additional parameters correspond to the standard APM parameters specifying a callback and passing state object. Similarly, the `EndInvoke()` method matches the original signature except only outgoing parameters appear. Since `object[] data` is only incoming, it doesn't appear in the `EndInvoke()` method. Also, since the `EndInvoke()` method concludes the asynchronous call, its return matches the original delegate's return as well.

Since all delegates include the C# compiler-generated `BeginInvoke()` and `EndInvoke()` methods used by the asynchronous delegate invocation pattern, invoking any method synchronously—especially given `Func` and `Action` delegates—becomes relatively easy. Furthermore, it makes it simple for the caller to invoke a method asynchronously regardless of whether the API programmer explicitly implemented it.

And before the TPL, the asynchronous delegate invocation pattern was significantly easier than the alternatives, making it a common practice when an API didn't provide explicit asynchronous calling patterns. However, apart from support for .NET 3.5 and earlier frameworks, the advent of the TPL diminishes the need for using the asynchronous delegate invocation approach if it occurs at all.

The Event-based Asynchronous Pattern (EAP)[1]

Thus far we've made the assumption that an asynchronous method will return a task; the caller is notified that the asynchronous work is completed when the status and result of the task become set. Doing so may in turn

---

1. See *Concurrent Programming on Windows* by Joe Duffy (Addison-Wesley, 2009), pp. 421–426, for more information.

cause completions of the task to execute asynchronously as well. Though this pattern is common and powerful, it is not the only common pattern for dealing with asynchrony. Another common pattern is the **Event-based Asynchronous Pattern (EAP)**. This pattern is particularly common for long-running asynchronous work.

A method that uses the EAP typically has a name that ends in `Async`, returns `void`, and has no out parameters. It is common for EAP methods to also take an `object` or generic parameter that contains caller-determined state that is associated with the asynchronous work, and sometimes also to take a cancellation token if the asynchronous work is cancellable. For example, if we had an EAP method that computes a given number of digits of pi and returns them in a string, the signature of the method might be

```
void CalculateAsync(int digits)
```

or

```
void CalculateAsync(
    int digits, object state, CancellationToken ct)
```

What is clearly missing from these signatures is the result. The asynchronous methods we've seen so far would return a `Task<string>` that could be used to fetch the asynchronously computed value after the computation has finished. In contrast, the EAP methods have no return value at all.

We have not yet seen the "event" part of the Event-based Asynchronous Pattern. The method is associated with an event; the caller of the EAP method registers an event handler on the associated event and then calls the method. The method starts the asynchronous work and returns; when the asynchronous work completes the event is fired and the handler executes. The event arguments passed to the handler contain the computed string and any other information that the asynchronous method feels would be useful to the listener, such as the caller-provided state, information about any exceptions or cancellations that occurred during the asynchronous operation, and so on. (Unsurprisingly, the exact information that would be available on a task object is instead made available in the event handler arguments.)

In Listing C.8 we show one way to use task-based asynchrony as an implementation detail of an EAP method. The EAP method `Calculate Async<TState>()` has associated with it the `CalculateCompleted` event. The asynchronous method creates a task (which, by default, will run on a thread obtained from the thread pool) to do the calculation. The continuation of that task triggers the event when the task completes.

Like with `async`/`await`, we wish to ensure that the continuation that fires the event is always run on the same thread on which the original asynchronous method was run. To achieve this we request the synchronization context from the `TaskScheduler` class. Since this is a console application, the current thread has no synchronization (causing it to depend on the thread pool by default), so Listing C.8 shows creation of the default context first.

LISTING C.8: **Event-Based Asynchronous Pattern**

```csharp
using System;
using System.ComponentModel;
using System.Threading;
using System.Threading.Tasks;
using AddisonWesley.Michaelis.EssentialCSharp.Shared;

partial class PiCalculation
{

    public void CalculateAsync<TState>(
        int digits,
        CancellationToken cancelToken
          = default(CancellationToken),
        TState userState
          = default(TState))
    {
        SynchronizationContext.
            SetSynchronizationContext(
                AsyncOperationManager.
                    SynchronizationContext);

        // Ensure the continuation runs on the current thread, and that
        // therefore the event will be raised on the same thread that
        // called this method in the first place.
        TaskScheduler scheduler =
            TaskScheduler.
                FromCurrentSynchronizationContext();
        Task.Run(
            () =>
            {
                return PiCalculator.Calculate(digits);
            }, cancelToken)
            .ContinueWith(
                continueTask =>
                {
                    Exception exception =
                        continueTask.Exception == null ?
                        continueTask.Exception :
                        continueTask.Exception.
                            InnerException;
```

```
            CalculateCompleted(
                typeof(PiCalculator),
                new CalculateCompletedEventArgs(
                    continueTask.Result,
                    exception,
                    cancelToken.IsCancellationRequested,
                    userState));
        }, scheduler);
}
```

```
public event
    EventHandler<CalculateCompletedEventArgs>
        CalculateCompleted = delegate { };
```

```
public class CalculateCompletedEventArgs
    : AsyncCompletedEventArgs
{
    public CalculateCompletedEventArgs(
        string value,
        Exception error,
        bool cancelled,
        object userState) : base(
          error, cancelled, userState)
    {
        Result = value;
    }
    public string Result { get; private set; }
}
}
```

As we mentioned above, EAP methods are often used for long-running asynchronous operations. Long-running operations frequently provide not only notification when the task completes, fails, or is canceled, but also occasional progress updates. This is particularly useful if the user interface is displaying the progress of the long-running asynchronous operation with some sort of progress bar or other indicator. The standard way to do so in an EAP method is to associate the method with a second event named ProgressChanged of type ProgressChangedEventHandler.

Note that the EAP method and its associated event (or events, if the method produces progress updates) are typically instance members, not static members. This makes it easier to support multiple concurrent operations because each separate operation can be associated with a different instance.

Background Worker Pattern

Another pattern that provides operation status and the possibility of cancellation is the **background worker pattern,** a specific implementation of EAP. The .NET Framework 2.0 (or later) includes a BackgroundWorker class for programming this type of pattern.

Listing C.9 is an example of this pattern—again calculating pi to the number of digits specified.

LISTING C.9: Using the Background Worker API

```
using System;
using System.Threading;
using System.ComponentModel;
using System.Text;

public class PiCalculator
{
    public static BackgroundWorker calculationWorker =
        new BackgroundWorker();
    public static AutoResetEvent resetEvent =
        new AutoResetEvent(false);

    public static void Main()
    {
        int digitCount;

        Console.Write(
            "Enter the number of digits to calculate:");
        if (int.TryParse(
            Console.ReadLine(), out digitCount))
        {
            Console.WriteLine("ENTER to cancel");
            // C# 2.0 Syntax for registering delegates
            calculationWorker.DoWork += CalculatePi;
            // Register the ProgressChanged callback
            calculationWorker.ProgressChanged +=
                UpdateDisplayWithMoreDigits;
            calculationWorker.WorkerReportsProgress =
                true;
            // Register a callback for when the calculation completes
            calculationWorker.RunWorkerCompleted +=
                new RunWorkerCompletedEventHandler(
                    Complete);
            calculationWorker.
                WorkerSupportsCancellation = true;

            // Begin calculating pi for up to digitCount digits
            calculationWorker.RunWorkerAsync(
                digitCount);
```

```
        Console.ReadLine();
        // If cancel is called after the calculation
        // has completed it doesn't matter.
        calculationWorker.CancelAsync();
        // Wait for Complete() to run.
        resetEvent.WaitOne();
    }
    else
    {
        Console.WriteLine(
            "The value entered is an invalid integer.");
    }
}


private static void CalculatePi(
    object sender, DoWorkEventArgs eventArgs)
{
    int digits = (int)eventArgs.Argument;

    StringBuilder pi =
        new StringBuilder("3.", digits + 2);
    calculationWorker.ReportProgress(
        0, pi.ToString());

    // Calculate rest of pi, if required
    if (digits > 0)
    {
        for (int i = 0; i < digits; i += 9)
        {
            // Calculate next i decimal places
            int nextDigit =
                PiDigitCalculator.StartingAt(
                    i + 1);
            int digitCount =
                Math.Min(digits - i, 9);
            string ds =
                string.Format("{0:D9}", nextDigit);
            pi.Append(ds.Substring(0, digitCount));

            // Show current progress
            calculationWorker.ReportProgress(
                0, ds.Substring(0, digitCount));

            // Check for cancellation
            if (
              calculationWorker.CancellationPending)
            {
                // Need to set Cancel if you need to
                // distinguish how a worker thread completed
                // i.e., by checking
```

```
                //RunWorkerCompletedEventArgs.Cancelled
                eventArgs.Cancel = true;
                break;
            }
        }
    }

    eventArgs.Result = pi.ToString();
}

private static void UpdateDisplayWithMoreDigits(
    object sender,
    ProgressChangedEventArgs eventArgs)
{
    string digits = (string)eventArgs.UserState;

    Console.Write(digits);
}


static void Complete(
    object sender,
    RunWorkerCompletedEventArgs eventArgs)
{
    // ...
}
}

public class PiDigitCalculator
{
    // ...
}
```

Establishing the Pattern

The process of hooking up the background worker pattern is as follows.

1. Register the long-running method with the `BackgroundWorker.DoWork` event. In this example, the long-running task is the call to `CalculatePi()`.

2. To receive progress or status notifications, hook up a listener to `Background Worker.ProgressChanged` and set `BackgroundWorker.WorkerReports Progress` to true. In Listing C.9, the `UpdateDisplayWithMoreDigits()` method takes care of updating the display as more digits become available.

3. Register a method (`Complete()`) with the `BackgroundWorker.Run WorkerCompleted` event.

4. Assign the `WorkerSupportsCancellation` property to support cancellation. Once this property is assigned the value `true`, a call to `Background Worker.CancelAsync` will set the `DoWorkEventArgs.CancellationPending` flag.

5. Within the `DoWork`-provided method (`CalculatePi()`), check the `DoWorkEventArgs.CancellationPending` property and exit the method when it is `true`.

6. Once everything is set up, you can start the work by calling `BackgroundWorker.RunWorkerAsync()` and providing a state parameter that is passed to the specified `DoWork()` method.

When you break it into steps, the background worker pattern is relatively easy to follow and, true to EAP, it provides explicit support for progress notification. The drawback is that you cannot use it arbitrarily on any method. Instead, the `DoWork()` method has to conform to a `System.ComponentModel.DoWorkEventHandler` delegate, which takes arguments of type `object` and `DoWorkEventArgs`. If this isn't the case, a wrapper function is required—something fairly trivial using anonymous methods. The cancellation- and progress-related methods also require specific signatures, but these are in control of the programmer setting up the background worker pattern.

Exception Handling

If an unhandled exception occurs while the background worker thread is executing, the `RunWorkerCompletedEventArgs` parameter of the `RunWorkerCompleted` delegate (`Completed`'s `eventArgs`) will have an `Error` property set with the exception. As a result, checking the `Error` property within the `RunWorkerCompleted` callback in Listing C.10 provides a means of handling the exception.

LISTING C.10: **Handling Unhandled Exceptions from the Worker Thread**

```
// ...
static void Complete(
    object sender, RunWorkerCompletedEventArgs eventArgs)
{
    Console.WriteLine();
    if (eventArgs.Cancelled)
    {
        Console.WriteLine("Cancelled");
    }
```

```
        else if (eventArgs.Error != null)
        {
            // IMPORTANT: check error to retrieve any exceptions.
            Console.WriteLine(
                "ERROR: {0}", eventArgs.Error.Message);
        }
        else
        {
            Console.WriteLine("Finished");
        }
        resetEvent.Set();
    }
    // ...
```

It is important that the code check `eventArgs.Error` inside the `RunWorkerCompleted` callback. Otherwise, the exception will go undetected; it won't even be reported to `AppDomain`.

Dispatching to the Windows UI

One more important threading concept relates to user interface development using the `System.Windows.Forms` and `System.Windows` namespaces. As already discussed in the UI-related content of Chapter 18, the Microsoft Windows suite of operating systems uses a single-threaded, message-processing-based user interface. This means that only one thread at a time should access the user interface, and code should marshal any alternate thread interaction via the Windows message pump. Fortunately, thanks to the fact that TAP uses the synchronization context when executing the continuation task, calls following an `await` expression call can freely invoke the UI API without concern for dispatching invocations to the UI thread. Unfortunately, in prior versions of C# this was not the case. Instead, invoking a UI method on the UI thread required special invocation logic both for Windows Forms and the Windows Presentation Framework API, as we discuss in the following sections.

Windows Forms

When programming against Windows Forms, the process of checking whether UI invocation is allowable from a thread involves calling a component's `InvokeRequired` property to determine whether marshalling is necessary. If `InvokeRequired` returns `true`, marshalling is necessary and can be implemented via a call to `Invoke()`. Internally, `Invoke()` will check

InvokeRequired anyway, but it can be more efficient to do so beforehand explicitly. Listing C.11 demonstrates this pattern.

LISTING C.11: **Accessing the User Interface via** Invoke()

```csharp
using System;
using System.Drawing;
using System.Threading;
using System.Windows.Forms;

class Program : Form
{
    private System.Windows.Forms.ProgressBar _ProgressBar;

    [STAThread]
    static void Main()
    {
        Application.Run(new Program());
    }

    public Program()
    {
        InitializeComponent();
        // Use Task.Factory.StartNew for .NET 4.0
        Task task = Task.Run((Action)Increment);
    }

    void UpdateProgressBar()
    {
        if (_ProgressBar.InvokeRequired)
        {
            MethodInvoker updateProgressBar =
                UpdateProgressBar;
            _ProgressBar.BeginInvoke(updateProgressBar);
        }
        else
        {
            _ProgressBar.Increment(1);
        }
    }

    private void Increment()
    {
        for (int i = 0; i < 100; i++)
        {
            UpdateProgressBar();
            Thread.Sleep(100);
        }

        if (InvokeRequired)
        {
            // Close cannot be called directly from a non-UI thread.
            Invoke(new MethodInvoker(Close));
```

```
        }
        else
        {
            Close();
        }
    }

    private void InitializeComponent()
    {
        _ProgressBar = new ProgressBar();
        SuspendLayout();

        _ProgressBar.Location = new Point(13, 17);
        _ProgressBar.Size = new Size(267, 19);

        ClientSize = new Size(292, 53);
        Controls.Add(this._ProgressBar);
        Text = "Multithreading in Windows Forms";
        ResumeLayout(false);
    }
}
```

This program displays a window that contains a progress bar that automatically starts incrementing. Once the progress bar reaches 100 percent, the dialog box closes.

Notice from Listing C.11 that you have to check InvokeRequired twice, and then the marshal calls across to the user interface thread if it returns true. In both cases, the marshalling involves instantiating a MethodInvoker delegate that is then passed to Invoke(). Since marshalling across to another thread could be relatively slow, an asynchronous invocation of the call is also available via BeginInvoke() and EndInvoke().

Invoke(), BeginInvoke(), EndInvoke(), and InvokeRequired comprise the members of the System.ComponentModel.ISynchronizeInvoke interface which is implemented by System.Windows.Forms.Control, from which Windows Forms controls derive.

Windows Presentation Foundation (WPF)

Achieving the same marshalling check on the **Windows Presentation Foundation (WPF)** platform involves a slightly different approach. WPF includes a static member property called Current of type DispatcherObject on the System.Windows.Application class. Calling CheckAccess() on the dispatcher serves the same function as InvokeRequired on controls in Windows Forms.

Listing C.12 demonstrates the approach with a static UIAction object. Anytime a developer wants to call a method that might interact with the user interface she simply calls UIAction.Invoke() and passes a delegate for the UI code she wishes to call. This, in turn, checks the dispatcher to see if marshalling is necessary and then responds accordingly.

LISTING C.12: Safely Invoking User Interface Objects

```csharp
using System;
using System.Windows;
using System.Windows.Threading;

public static class UIAction
{
  public static void Invoke<T>(
      Action<T> action, T parameter)
  {
      Invoke(() => action(parameter));
  }
  public static void Invoke(Action action)
  {
      DispatcherObject dispatcher =
          Application.Current;
      if (dispatcher == null
          || dispatcher.CheckAccess()
          || dispatcher.Dispatcher == null
          )
      {
          action();
      }
      else
      {
          SafeInvoke(action);
      }
  }
}

// We want to catch all exceptions here so we can rethrow
private static void SafeInvoke(Action action)
{
    Exception exceptionThrown = null;
    Action target = () =>
    {
        try
        {
            action();
        }
        catch (Exception exception)
        {
            exceptionThrown = exception;
        }
```

```
        };
        Application.Current.Dispatcher.Invoke(target);
        if (exceptionThrown != null)
        {
            // Use ExceptionDispatchInfo.Throw() for .NET 4.5+
            throw exceptionThrown;
        }
    }
}
```

One additional feature in the UIAction of Listing C.12 is the "marshalling" of any exceptions on the UI thread that may have occurred. SafeInvoke() wraps all requested delegate calls in a try/catch block and, if an exception is thrown, it saves the exception off and then rethrows it once context returns back to the calling thread. In this way, UIAction avoids throwing unhandled exceptions on the UI thread.

D.
Timers Prior to the Async/Await Pattern of C# 5.0

CHAPTER 19 INTRODUCED THE USE of `Task.Delay()` when a timer was required. For scenarios prior to .NET 4.5, several timer classes are available, including `System.Windows.Forms.Timer`, `System.Timers.Timer`, and `System.Threading.Timer`.

The development team designed `System.Windows.Forms.Timer` specifically for use within a rich client user interface. Programmers can drag it onto a form as a nonvisual control and regulate the behavior from within the Properties window. Most importantly, it will always safely fire an event from a thread that can interact with the user interface.

The other two timers are very similar. `System.Timers.Timer` is a wrapper for `System.Threading.Timer`, abstracting and layering on functionality. Specifically, `System.Threading.Timer` does not derive from `System.ComponentModel.Component`, and therefore, you cannot use it as a component within a component container, something that implements `System.ComponentModel.IContainer`. Another difference is that `System.Threading.Timer` enables the passing of state, an object parameter, from the call to start the timer and then into the call that fires the timer notification. The remaining differences simply concern API usability, with `System.Timers.Timer` supporting a synchronization object and having calls that are slightly more intuitive. Both `System.Timers.Timer` and `System.Threading.Timer` are designed for use in server-type processes, but `System.Timers.Timer` includes a synchronization object to allow it to interact with the UI. Furthermore, both timers use the system thread pool. Table D.1 provides an overall comparison of the various timers.

TABLE D.1: Overview of the Various Timer Characteristics

Feature Description	System.Timers.Timer	System.Threading.Timer	System.Windows.Forms.Timer
Supports adding and removing listeners after the timer is instantiated	Yes	No	Yes
Supports callbacks on the user interface thread	Yes	No	Yes
Calls back from threads obtained from the thread pool	Yes	Yes	No
Supports drag-and-drop in the Windows Forms Designer	Yes	No	Yes
Suitable for running in a multithreaded server environment	Yes	Yes	No
Includes support for passing arbitrary state from the timer initialization to the callback	No	Yes	No
Implements `IDisposable`	Yes	Yes	Yes
Supports on-off callbacks as well as periodic repeating callbacks	Yes	Yes	Yes
Accessible across application domain boundaries	Yes	Yes	Yes
Supports `IComponent`; hostable in an `IContainer`	Yes	No	Yes

Using `System.Windows.Forms.Timer` is a relatively obvious choice for user interface programming with Windows Forms. The only caution is that a long-running operation on the user interface thread may delay the arrival of a timer's expiration.[1] Choosing between the other two options is less obvious, and generally, the difference between the two is insignificant. If hosting within an `IContainer` is necessary, `System.Timers.Timer` is the right choice. However, if no specific `System.Timers.Timer` feature is required, choose `System.Threading.Timer` by default, simply because it is a slightly lighter-weight implementation.

Listing D.1 and Listing D.2 provide sample code for using `System.Timers.Timer` and `System.Threading.Timer`, respectively. Their code is very similar, including the fact that both support instantiation within a `using` statement because both support `IDispose`. The output for both listings is identical, and it appears in Output D.1. The purpose of each is to display a timestamp in association with a counting value indicating the number of times the timer fired. Once complete, the output verifies that the timer thread is not the same as the Main thread along with the final value of the count.

LISTING D.1: Using System.Timers.Timer

```csharp
using System;
using System.Timers;
using System.Threading;
// Because Timer exists in both the System.Timers and
// System.Threading namespaces, you disambiguate "Timer"
// using an alias directive.
using Timer = System.Timers.Timer;

class UsingSystemTimersTimer
{
    private static int _Count=0;
    private static readonly ManualResetEvent _ResetEvent =
        new ManualResetEvent(false);
    private static int _AlarmThreadId;

    public static void Main()
    {
        using( Timer timer = new Timer() )
        {
            // Initialize Timer
            timer.AutoReset = true;
            timer.Interval = 1000;
            timer.Elapsed +=
                new ElapsedEventHandler(Alarm);

            timer.Start();
```

---

1. In theory, a similar delay is possible with timers that depend on a thread pool as well because the thread pool may already be busy.

```csharp
        // Wait for Alarm to fire for the 10th time.
            _ResetEvent.WaitOne();
    }


            // Verify that the thread executing the alarm
            // Is different from the thread executing Main
            if(_AlarmThreadId ==
                Thread.CurrentThread.ManagedThreadId)
            {
                throw new ApplicationException(
                    "Thread Ids are the same.");
            }
            if(_Count < 9)
            {
                throw new ApplicationException(
                    " _Count < 9");
            };

            Console.WriteLine(
                "(Alarm Thread Id) {0} != {1} (Main Thread Id)",
                _AlarmThreadId,
                Thread.CurrentThread.ManagedThreadId);
            Console.WriteLine(
                "Final Count = {0}", _Count);
    }

    static void Alarm(
        object sender, ElapsedEventArgs eventArgs)
    {
        _Count++;

        Console.WriteLine("{0}:- {1}",
            eventArgs.SignalTime.ToString("T"),
            _Count);

        if (_Count >= 9)
        {
            _AlarmThreadId =
                Thread.CurrentThread.ManagedThreadId;
            _ResetEvent.Set();
        }
    }
}
```

In Listing D.1, you have using directives for both System.Threading and System.Timers. This makes the Timer type ambiguous. Therefore, use an alias to explicitly associate Timer with System.Timers.Timer.

One noteworthy characteristic of `System.Threading.Timer` is that it takes the callback delegate and interval within the constructor.

LISTING D.2: **Using** `System.Threading.Timer`

```csharp
using System;
using System.Threading;

class UsingSystemThreadingTimer
{
    private static int _Count=0;
    private static readonly AutoResetEvent _ResetEvent =
        new AutoResetEvent(false);
    private static int _AlarmThreadId;

    public static void Main()
    {
        // Timer(callback, state, dueTime, period)
        using( Timer timer =
            new Timer(Alarm, null, 0, 1000) )
        {
            // Wait for Alarm to fire for the 10th time.
            _ResetEvent.WaitOne();
        }

        // Verify that the thread executing the alarm
        // Is different from the thread executing Main
        if(_AlarmThreadId ==
            Thread.CurrentThread.ManagedThreadId)
        {
            throw new ApplicationException(
                "Thread Ids are the same.");
        }
        if(_Count < 9)
        {
            throw new ApplicationException(
                " _Count < 9");
        };

        Console.WriteLine(
            "(Alarm Thread Id) {0} != {1} (Main Thread Id)",
            _AlarmThreadId,
            Thread.CurrentThread.ManagedThreadId);
        Console.WriteLine(
            "Final Count = {0}", _Count);
    }

    static void Alarm(object state)
    {
        _Count++;
```

```
        Console.WriteLine("{0}:- {1}",
            DateTime.Now.ToString("T"),
            _Count);

        if (_Count >= 9)
        {
            _AlarmThreadId =
                Thread.CurrentThread.ManagedThreadId;
            _ResetEvent.Set();
        }
    }
}
```

OUTPUT D.1

```
12:19:36 AM:- 1
12:19:37 AM:- 2
12:19:38 AM:- 3
12:19:39 AM:- 4
12:19:40 AM:- 5
12:19:41 AM:- 6
12:19:42 AM:- 7
12:19:43 AM:- 8
12:19:44 AM:- 9
(Alarm Thread Id) 4 != 1 (Main Thread Id)
Final Count = 9
```

You can change the interval or time due after instantiation on System.Threading.Timer via the Change() method. However, you cannot change the callback listeners after instantiation. Instead, you must create a new instance.

Index

Index of 5.0 Topics

Index of 4.0 Topics

Index of 3.0 Topics

IntelliTect

INTELLITECT CORPORATION IS A HIGH-END software architecture and development consulting firm based in Spokane, Washington. The company hires the best and brightest engineers and focuses on providing architecture consulting, software development, and training to enable their customers to solve the most challenging of problems. IntelliTect has principal and senior engineers specializing in the latest Microsoft technologies—including Microsoft .NET (WCF/WPF/WF), Visual Studio VSTS/TFS, SharePoint, and BizTalk Server.

IntelliTect uses best practice application life-cycle management (ALM) to deliver quality software solutions on time, on scope, and within budget. IntelliTect specializes in the following services:

- From concept phase to deployment, IntelliTect offers and delivers training, consulting and implementation using state of the art software—Visual Studio Team System (VSTS) and Team Foundation Server (TFS).

- IntelliTect enables companies to achieve efficient and effective collaboration, corporate publishing and enterprise content management (ECM) using Microsoft SharePoint. SharePoint services include consulting, training, deployment/upgrading, internet/intranet portals and application development.

- IntelliTect conducts software architecture workshops to design service oriented architectures (SOA), security solutions, solution scoping, solution architecture, and production deployment blueprints.

- For the integration and migration of large enterprise applications as well as business-to-business transactions, IntelliTect offerings include BizTalk and SQL Server Integration Services (SSIS) solutions. BizTalk integrations include the use of line-of-business adapters and the Enterprise Service Bus (ESB).

IntelliTect personnel serve on numerous software advisory boards at Microsoft, publish frequently, and present at conferences such as TechEd, DevConnections, and VSLive.

IntelliTect has extensive industry experience in Utilities, Manufacturing, Healthcare Integration, and Insurance Services. IntelliTect has the capability and experience to quickly identify and understand its customer's needs and then develop strategies to address the identified needs.

IntelliTect is committed to devoting a significant portion of its profits to the fight against extreme poverty around the world.

Addison Wesley

REGISTER

THIS PRODUCT

informit.com/register

Register the Addison-Wesley, Exam Cram, Prentice Hall, Que, and Sams products you own to unlock great benefits.

To begin the registration process, simply go to **informit.com/register** to sign in or create an account. You will then be prompted to enter the 10- or 13-digit ISBN that appears on the back cover of your product.

Registering your products can unlock the following benefits:

- Access to supplemental content, including bonus chapters, source code, or project files.
- A coupon to be used on your next purchase.

Registration benefits vary by product. Benefits will be listed on your Account page under Registered Products.

About InformIT — THE TRUSTED TECHNOLOGY LEARNING SOURCE

INFORMIT IS HOME TO THE LEADING TECHNOLOGY PUBLISHING IMPRINTS Addison-Wesley Professional, Cisco Press, Exam Cram, IBM Press, Prentice Hall Professional, Que, and Sams. Here you will gain access to quality and trusted content and resources from the authors, creators, innovators, and leaders of technology. Whether you're looking for a book on a new technology, a helpful article, timely newsletters, or access to the Safari Books Online digital library, InformIT has a solution for you.

informIT.com

THE TRUSTED TECHNOLOGY LEARNING SOURCE

Addison-Wesley | Cisco Press | Exam Cram
IBM Press | Que | Prentice Hall | Sams

SAFARI BOOKS ONLINE

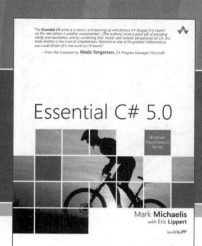

Safari

Books Online

FREE
Online Edition

Your purchase of **Essential C# 5.0** includes access to a free online edition for 45 days through the **Safari Books Online** subscription service. Nearly every Addison-Wesley Professional book is available online through **Safari Books Online**, along with thousands of books and videos from publishers such as Cisco Press, Exam Cram, IBM Press, O'Reilly Media, Prentice Hall, Que, Sams, and VMware Press.

Safari Books Online is a digital library providing searchable, on-demand access to thousands of technology, digital media, and professional development books and videos from leading publishers. With one monthly or yearly subscription price, you get unlimited access to learning tools and information on topics including mobile app and software development, tips and tricks on using your favorite gadgets, networking, project management, graphic design, and much more.

Activate your FREE Online Edition at
informit.com/safarifree

STEP 1: Enter the coupon code: HNMREAA.

STEP 2: New Safari users, complete the brief registration form. Safari subscribers, just log in.

If you have difficulty registering on Safari or accessing the online edition, please e-mail customer-service@safaribooksonline.com